ETHNIC CONFLICT

ETHNIC CONFLICT
A SYSTEMATIC APPROACH
TO CASES OF CONFLICT

Neal G. Jesse, Bowling Green State University

Kristen P. Williams, Clark University

CQ PRESS

A Division of SAGE

Washington, D.C.

CQ Press
2300 N Street, NW, Suite 800
Washington, DC 20037

Phone: 202-729-1900; toll-free, 1-866-4CQ-PRESS (1-866-427-7737)

Web: www.cqpress.com

Portions of chapters 1 and 3 were previously published by the authors in "Resolving Nationalist Conflicts: Promoting Overlapping Identities and Pooling Sovereignty—The 1998 Northern Irish Peace Agreement," *Political Psychology* 22, 3 (September 2001): 571–599. Reprinted with permission.

Portions of chapters 2 and 3 were previously published by the authors in *Identity and Institutions: Conflict Reduction in Divided Societies* (Albany, SUNY Press, 2005). Reprinted with permission.

Cover design: Jeffrey Everett/El Jefe Design
Cover photo: Gary S. Chapman, Getty Images
Maps: International Mapping Associates
Composition: C&M Digitals (P) Ltd.

∞ The paper used in this publication exceeds the requirements of the American National Standard for Information Sciences—Permanence of Paper for Printed Library Materials, ANSI Z39.48-1992.

Printed and bound in the United States of America

14 13 12 11 10   1 2 3 4 5

Library of Congress Cataloging-in-Publication Data

Jesse, Neal G.
Ethnic conflict : a systematic approach to cases of conflict / Neal G. Jesse, Kristen P. Williams.
    p. cm.
Includes bibliographical references and index.
ISBN 978-0-87289-492-1 (pbk. : alk. paper) 1. Ethnic conflict—Case studies.
2. Conflict management—Case studies. I. Williams, Kristen P. II. Title.

  HM1121.J49 2011
  305.8009′049—dc22

                                        2009050349

To our families

CONTENTS

MAPS AND TABLES

T wo decades after the Cold War ended, conflicts continue to plague the international community. Violence, both across and within states, continues to result in deaths and injuries. In particular, conflicts over ethnic and national identity underlie much of the violence witnessed in the contemporary period. Our interest in these conflicts led to our earlier work, *Identity and Institutions: Conflict Reduction in Divided Societies*, in which we examined the link between identity and institutions as a means to reduce ethnic/nationalist conflicts. In challenging consociational and federal models of conflict reduction, we argued that cross-border institutions that foster overlapping identities may be the key to reducing ethnic/nationalist conflicts. Building on this work, we sought to combine literature in the fields of comparative politics and international relations to explore the causes of and solutions to ethnic conflict. The study of international relations focuses on the structure of the international system and the role of powerful states as well as international institutions, international organizations, and international norms to account for state behavior. Comparative politics focuses on the domestic factors within states, such as elites, political parties, interest groups, and regime type, to understand conflict (ethnic or otherwise), thereby opening up the "black box" of the state. We contribute to these two literatures by applying the "levels of analysis" approach in the field of international relations to examine ethnic/nationalist conflicts. This book, therefore, bridges the divide between these two political science fields.

In utilizing the levels of analysis framework, at the individual level we look at the motivations and behavior of individual elites; at the domestic level we consider social identity, nationalism, gendered nationalism, political parties, and economic and political conditions; and at the international level we assess the impact of third-party intervention and mediation, as well as international institutions. We consider factors at all three levels in our examination of five case studies of ethnic/nationalist conflict, demonstrating how the various factors have manifested themselves in these conflicts. We do not claim that one level is a better explanation for the causes of and solutions to such conflicts and, as will be evident, no one level can explain all conflicts. Rather, an exploration of the factors at all three levels provides a more thorough approach to understanding these conflicts.

The book is organized into two parts. The first part (chapters 1 and 2) focuses on theories and concepts. Chapter 1 looks at nationalism and ethnic conflict and the theories used to explain these concepts. Chapter 2 introduces the levels of analysis framework to account for ethnic conflict. The second part of the book, chapters 3–7, examines five cases of ethnic conflict. These cases were chosen because they encompass various regions of the world: Africa, Europe, the Middle East, and South Asia. The cases are all contemporary, in that they occur in the post–Cold War period (although several predated the end of the Cold War). In each case we provide a brief historical overview, by way of introduction, and then apply the levels of analysis, examining factors at the individual, domestic, and international levels to account for the causes of and possible solutions to the conflicts. Chapter 8 concludes with an overview of the main themes of the book, looking at the similarities and differences found in these conflicts with the hopes of learning lessons for future research.

Portions of chapters 2 and 3 appeared in our book, *Identity and Institutions: Conflict Reduction in Divided Societies* (Albany: SUNY Press, 2005). We are appreciative of SUNY Press for permission to reproduce parts of those chapters. Parts of chapter 1 and chapter 3 are drawn from our article, "Resolving Nationalist Conflicts: Promoting Overlapping Identities and Pooling Sovereignty—The 1998 Northern Irish Peace Agreement," published in the journal *Political Psychology* (September 2001). We are grateful to Blackwell Publishing for permission to reproduce those parts of our article.

ACKNOWLEDGMENTS

We thank the five reviewers of the manuscript proposal for their helpful suggestions as we developed the book, including Stanley Clark (California State University Bakersfield), Terry D. Clark (Creighton University), Alfred Cuzan (University of West Florida), Shale Horowitz (University of Wisconsin–Milwaukee), and one anonymous reviewer. We also thank the three anonymous reviewers solicited by CQ Press, who reviewed four of the completed chapters, for their useful comments. A big thank you goes to Charlotte Tidy, Jesse's graduate assistant at BGSU, who provided immeasurable help tracking down sources, calling to our attention interesting articles and books, and compiling the bibliography.

We also express our thanks to the students in Williams's spring 2008 semester seminar, "Ethnicity, Nationalism, and International Conflict," at Clark University. The seminar is designed for students focusing on international relations and thus provided an opportunity to bring together IR theories and apply the levels of analysis to ethnic conflict and nationalism, which are the framework of this book.

Finally, we would like to express our thanks to a number of people at CQ Press for their role in developing this book and for their enthusiasm and support as the project moved through its various stages of production. Editorial Director Charisse Kiino encouraged us from the very beginning to pursue the idea for the project, bridging comparative politics and international relations by applying the levels of analysis to ethnic conflict. We couldn't have asked for a more supportive acquisitions editor in Elise Frasier. She was extremely patient when we needed extra time to complete the manuscript and also offered constructive advice as it developed. In the marketing division, Erin Snow was instrumental in providing guidance in promoting the book. Our production editor, Emily Bakely, provided timely responses to our queries involved with the copyediting and page proof stages as we neared the end of production. We also thank Kathryn Krug for her meticulous copyediting and Deborah Patton for her thorough indexing.

Last, but by no means least, we thank our families for their enduring support and patience from the project's inception to its conclusion.

CHAPTER 1

Ethnic Conflict and Approaches to Understanding It

The post–Cold War period is now nearly two decades old. A world characterized by increased economic, political, and social/cultural globalization is, at the same time, a world marked by ethnic conflict within states and between states, with implications for the international community of states. In analyzing conflicts since the end of the Cold War, scholars have found that there has been a noticeable decrease in major armed conflicts around the world. One contributing factor is that the number of democratic regimes increased. However, the picture is not all positive. The data also indicate that "the frequency of onsets of new armed conflicts in the world has not decreased substantially since the end of the Cold War in 1991."[1] Moreover, a distinction must be made between interstate and intrastate conflicts. Interstate conflicts have declined significantly since the Cold War ended.[2] Yet, intrastate conflicts still plague the international community: in 2008, twenty-one states were involved in major armed conflicts. Twenty of those conflicts were internal ones. From Afghanistan to Ethiopia, from Sri Lanka to Yemen, many states are afflicted by such conflicts.[3]

The question arises, if major armed conflict is in decline, why this book? Recent data show approximately fifteen cases of ongoing intrastate ethnic violence or war around the world. Some of these ethnic conflicts began during the Cold War, others after the Cold War ended.[4] In the twenty-first century, such conflicts continue as ethnic groups continue to fight over various issues, including territory, economic resources, cultural rights, and political rights. Moreover, ethnic groups within states look to their ethnic kin in other states for support. The international community sometimes attempts to stop the fighting and find solutions, in large part because ethnic conflicts can diffuse and escalate. Diffusion of intrastate ethnic conflict occurs when these conflicts expand beyond the existing territorial borders of a state into neighboring states. Escalation entails "the drawing or pulling in of other states, non-state actors, or outside ethnic groups into the internal conflict."[5]

Thus, to answer the question posed above, Why this book? Simply stated, we sought to write a book that integrated the literature in the fields of comparative

MAP 1.1
Ethnic Conflict in the World

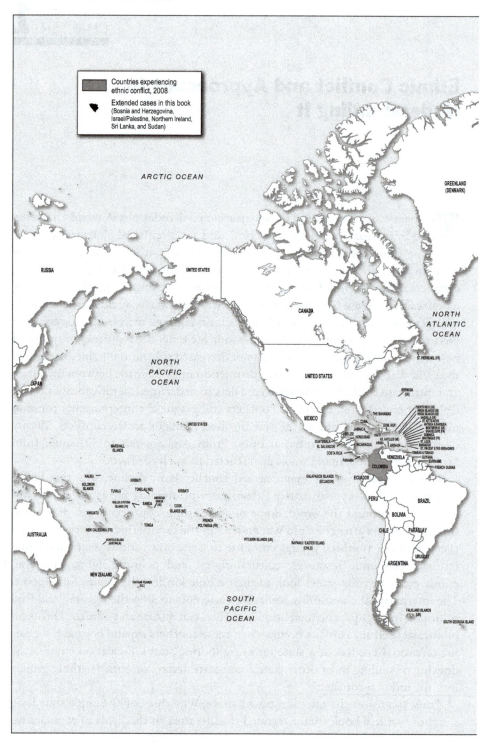

Countries experiencing ethnic conflict, 2008

Extended cases in this book (Bosnia and Herzegovina, Israel/Palestine, Northern Ireland, Sri Lanka, and Sudan)

Source: Data from Monty G. Marshall and Benjamin G. Cole, "Global Report on Conflict, Governance and State Fragility 2008," *Foreign Policy Bulletin* (Winter 2008): 3–21.

politics and international relations within political science, in order to understand and analyze the causes of and solutions to ethnic conflicts. Comparative politics focuses on the domestic factors within states that determine state and group behavior, looking at elites, political parties, bureaucracies, interest groups, and so forth. The study of international relations, however, traditionally tends to focus on the international system—the big picture, such as the distribution of power and international institutions. This is not to say that international relations scholars do not examine domestic factors—many do. The two dominant theories (realism and liberalism) in the field, however, claim that the state is the major actor in the international system, and tend not to look at factors within states to account for state behavior. Likewise, comparative politics scholars do not neglect the international system, but rather focus on domestic actors and effects. We contribute to these two literatures by applying the levels of analysis framework in international relations to understand ethnic conflict. Importantly, as will be shown in chapter 2, the levels of analysis approach, in essence, bridges the divide between international relations and comparative politics, and serves as the framework for the case study chapters that follow.

We begin this chapter with definitions of various concepts found in the study of ethnic conflict, including the definition of ethnic conflict itself. For example, what is a nation? What is nationalism? How is nationalism different from ethnicity? What are secessionism and irredentism? It is important to have a grasp of the terminology before we can begin to examine the causes of and solutions to ethnic conflict. The chapter then turns to the dominant theories of ethnicity and nationalism, and how these relate to ethnic conflict.

The next section focuses on the major theories and approaches in the study of international relations—namely, realism, liberalism, and constructivism. Importantly, international relations scholars have, in the last decade or so, begun to apply these major theories and approaches to the issues of ethnicity and nationalism, recognizing that they can contribute to our understanding of these issues. We then conclude with a discussion of the structure of the book, particularly the topics covered in the subsequent chapters.

DEFINING OUR TERMS

Scholars in many disciplines, including history, sociology, anthropology, and psychology, as well as political science, have been interested in the issues of ethnicity, nationalism, and ethnic conflict, seeking to provide definitions and categorize the causes of and solutions to these conflicts.[6]

Ethnicity is distinct from nation and nationalism, and yet is related. Often the terms nation and ethnicity are used interchangeably, but there are differences, nonetheless. These differences matter in terms of the goals of an ethnic group versus those of a nationalist group. In both cases, however, those goals can lead to conflict, and even violence, within and between states with territorially defined borders.

As defined by most scholars, ethnicity is "that part of a person's identity which is drawn from one or more 'markers' like race, religion, shared history, region, social symbols or language."[7] Anthony Smith, one of the most prominent scholars of nationalism, defines an *ethnie,* which forms the basis of an ethnic community, as having a proper name, common myths of ancestry, shared memories, shared culture, and a connection to a homeland.[8] An ethnic group, therefore, "is a group of people bound together by a belief of common kinship and group distinctiveness, often reinforced by religion, language, and history."[9] Ethnic groups then feel an ethnic sentiment, which, as noted by Milton Esman, entails "an expression of who I am, how I identify myself, to what group of people I belong. As a member of that group this becomes to me a collective identity."[10] The ethnic sentiment can lead to ethnic solidarity, in which people express an "in-group identity" based on ethnicity.[11] Importantly, ethnicity is a relational concept—in other words, having an in-group identity means there is an out-group—members of a different ethnic group.[12]

The emergence of the modern nation-state relates directly to the ideology of nationalism, in which groups of people made demands for self-determination over a particular territory. The modern nation-state as the key political unit of sovereignty, as it emerged with the Treaty of Westphalia that ended the Thirty Years' War in Europe in 1648, with its well-defined geographical boundaries, delineates the political boundaries of citizenship.[13] Such well-defined geographical boundaries and political boundaries of citizenship are features of how a nation (and thus national identity and nationalism) differs from ethnicity and ethnic groups. A nation has many of the same elements as an ethnic community, such as a proper name, common myths, shared history, unified economy, shared language, rights and duties of citizens, and a common public culture.[14] It also has an occupation of a historic homeland—or at least the desire for occupation of a historic homeland.[15] As Lowell W. Barrington states, "The importance of the belief in territorial self-determination for the group is a central part of most definitions of 'nation' in the nationalism literature and provides an important criterion for differentiating between nations and other social categories."[16] Barrington continues: "A nation is more than an ethnic group, differing from such a group because of a nation's belief in its right to territorial control."[17] If ethnic groups seek "equal representation and rights . . . within a given political system," this is considered "ethnic politics." Nationalism results from ethnic groups making "claims to jurisdiction, to some degree of self-government in a given territory."[18]

In essence, the connection between nation and ethnicity is one in which nations and nationalism stem from the "interactions of ethnicity-making and state-making processes."[19] As Ashutosh Varshney concludes: "Ethnic groups . . . can live without a state of their own, making do with some cultural rights (e.g., use of mother tongue in schools) or affirmative action, but a nation means bringing ethnicity and statehood together."[20]

Gender, Ethnicity, and Nationalism

The mainstream scholarship on nationalism and ethnicity does not address the gendered nature of these concepts. Feminist scholars have attempted to rectify this omission by pointing out how ethnicity and nationalism, as well as the nation-state, are very much tied to conceptions of gender.[21] Gender is defined as "socially learned behavior and expectations that distinguish between masculinity and femininity." Societies value masculine and feminine behaviors differently, and in general masculinity is deemed superior to femininity, with resulting inequality between men and women.[22] This differential valuation of men and women is part and parcel of nationalism and ethnicity. Gender is "a system of power that not only divides men and women as masculine and feminine but typically also places men and masculinity above women and femininity."[23]

Feminist scholars Floya Anthias and Nira Yuval-Davis have noted the different ways that women "participate in ethnic and national processes and in relation to state practices." Women are the "biological reproducers of members of ethnic collectivities" as well as the "reproducers of the boundaries of ethnic/national groups" in that they give birth to children, who are members of particular ethnic groups. Women also contribute "centrally in the ideological reproduction of the collectivity and as transmitters of its culture"; as mothers they communicate the ideology of the ethnic/national group. Women are the "signifiers of ethnic/national differences—as a focus and symbol in ideological discourses used in the construction, reproduction and transformation of ethnic/national categories." Ethnic and national leaders reinforce the important symbol that women, as mothers and wives, play in promoting a particular ethnic/national identity. Finally, they contend that women also participate "in national, economic, political and military struggles."[24] In addition to these points, V. Spike Peterson adds that states are concerned with heterosexist sex/gender identities as related to nationalism—that nationalism privileges heterosexual relationships in which men (husbands) are elevated over women (wives).[25]

As Deniz Kandiyoti explains, "The association of women with the private domain [home/domestic sphere] reinforces the merging of the nation/community with the selfless mother/devout wife; the obvious response of coming to her defense and even dying for her is automatically triggered."[26] In fact, in times of conflict and war, leaders will utilize feminine metaphors ("mothers of the nation," "motherland") in order to reinforce threats to the nation/ethnic group. Leaders advance the idea that women must be submissive to the goals of the ethnic or national group by accepting their "natural roles" as women and mothers.[27] Thus, ethnic violence is "strongly gendered"[28] as evidenced by rape in wartime in which women of the enemy ethnic group are targeted by virtue of their ethnic identity.

According to Joane Nagel, "correct heterosexual masculine and feminine behavior constitutes gender regimes that often lie at the core of ethnic cultures. . . . Because of the common importance of proper gender role and sexual behavior to ethnic community honor and respectability, a great deal of attention is paid to the sexual demeanor of group members (by outsiders and insiders) in inspection and enforcement of both formal and informal rules of sexual conduct." In other words, "ethnic boundaries are also sexual boundaries."[29] We will see this "gendered nationalism" and the ethnic boundaries as sexual boundaries evident in the case studies examined in the remaining chapters.

Ethnic and National Conflicts

How do ethnicity and nationalism lead to tension and conflict? This is, in essence, the central question of this book. Ethnic conflict differs from other types of conflict, such as ideological ones, because of the aspect of ascriptive identity that defines ethnicity. These identities are not easily changed because they are "based on an individual's descent," and thus this ascriptive aspect "can lead militant organizations to identify entire ethnic groups as loyal or disloyal within a country's population in a way that ideological conflicts cannot."[30] Groups may demand rights, status, territorial autonomy, representation in political institutions, and power.[31] These demands may turn violent, but that is not a given. In terms of ethnic conflict and national conflicts, the former can occur due to language policies, affirmative action laws, and so forth. The latter, national conflicts, result from disputes over territory.[32] Moreover, groups may demand to secede from an existing state (secessionism). Alternatively, in the case of irredentism, a state may seek territory and ethnic/national groups from another state with the goal of "incorporation within its boundaries."[33] What matters in defining an ethnic conflict is that ethnic difference is "integral rather than incidental to the violence."[34]

According to Daniel Byman, "An ethnic conflict is a violent conflict between ethnic groups or between an ethnic group and government forces that consist of one or more different ethnic groups. There are two main types of conflict: group versus group conflict, with the government acting as a third party of some kind . . . and group versus government conflict, where the government is an active party acting on behalf of one ethnic group."[35] Ilan Peleg provides a useful distinction to illustrate the different roles that governments can play in internal ethnic relations: neutral states and hegemonic states. Neutral states are those that act to regulate conflict between ethnic groups within the state, whereas hegemonic states are those that promote the interests of the dominant ethnic group.[36]

Ethnic conflicts can also diffuse and escalate, and are considered interstate ethnic conflicts if they cross state boundaries. As noted earlier, diffusion occurs when conflict in one state spreads to another state. Escalation occurs when other states, transnational ethnic kin, or non-state actors are pulled into the ethnic conflict.[37] The conflict between Hutus and Tutsis in Rwanda in 1994, which spread to neighboring Zaire (itself comprised of Tutsis and Hutus, as well as other ethnic groups), is an example of diffusion.[38] Following the collapse of the Soviet Union, the intervention of Armenia and Russia in Nagorno-Karabakh, the Armenian-dominated region of Azerbaijan, represents a case of escalation of an ethnic conflict.[39]

Scholars focus on several factors to understand the causes of and solutions to ethnic conflict such as weak states, political elites, economic sectors, and so forth (chapter 2 explores these factors in more detail, and we will see how these factors matter in particular cases of ethnic conflict in chapters 3–7). Before turning to the theories of nationalism, nation and ethnicity, and their relation to ethnic conflict, we present a brief overview of different ethnic groups found within states.

Typology of Ethnic Groups

Barbara Harff and Ted Robert Gurr provide a very useful typology of ethnic groups found within states. These include ethno-nationalists, indigenous peoples, ethnoclasses, communal contenders, and dominant minorities. Ethno-nationalists are large ethnic groups based on a historical tradition of political autonomy and/ or territory. For example, the Kurds in Iraq or the Scots in the United Kingdom are ethno-nationalists. Each represents a large community of individuals with a similar ethnicity, shared history, and common occupation of a recognized territory. These groups often have an organized, political leadership. Most commonly this is a political party. In democratic states these parties participate in routinized and institutionalized elections and legislative structures.[40] For example, the Scottish Nationalist Party represents the Scottish people and their demands. It nominates candidates for elections, helps govern the Scottish parliament, and encourages political participation in its constituent group. In a nondemocratic state, the political representation may still be a political party, but the party typically takes on more functions. For example, the Kurdistan Democratic Party has represented Kurdish interests in Iraq since 1946. It has at times run in elections, fought against the government, fought against other Kurdish political parties, and jointly administered northern Iraq, all the while representing the interests of the Kurdish minority.[41]

Indigenous people are descendents of inhabitants of lands that were colonized or conquered. They typically do not have a recognized national boundary nor do they have large-scale political organizations. They tend to live on the margins of the modern nation-states, surviving in small tribes or communities. Examples of indigenous people are the Aborigines in Australia or the Native Americans in many South American countries. Their collective interests usually include obtaining a right to the land, equal political rights, economic opportunity, and protection of resources from governmental actors and/or business.[42]

Ethnoclasses are distinct ethnic groups that represent a social class in a society. For example, the Turks in Germany are members of the "working class" in German society. But the ethnoclass does not need to be disadvantaged. The Chinese minority in Malaysia possesses great wealth and represents the middle class in that society. These ethnic groups, like social classes, tend to be dispersed throughout the society, although some community segregation is possible. They normally lack direct political party representation and pressure groups. Given such circumstances, they tend to make demands for greater inclusion in society, better treatment, and/or economic opportunity as a social movement. Because of their loose organization, collective action is difficult to achieve, leaving ethnoclasses particularly vulnerable to more centrally organized groups.[43]

Communal contenders are ethnic groups that wish to share governance with other ethnic groups in the same state. They typically have been the victims of discrimination or marginalization. Thus, they press for greater political participation and representation. Examples of these groups abound in Africa and the Middle East, where plural societies of many contending ethnic groups exist. Nigeria provides a clear illustration. A number of ethnic groups representing different communities have made claims for either a multiethnic coalition government or regional autonomy. The plural society of Lebanon, with its religious divisions between Christians and Muslims, provides another example.[44]

Finally, dominant minorities represent those ethnic groups that are minorities within their own state but have typically controlled and dominated the state. A historical example is the Afrikaaner rule in South Africa. The minority White population instituted the system of Apartheid to control and subdue the much larger majority group of Blacks.[45]

This typology is useful as a first step in understanding the link between ethnic groups, causes of ethnic conflict, and the means to resolve (or at least manage) those conflicts.

THEORIES OF ETHNICITY/NATIONALISM

Scholars have developed several theories in attempting to determine which factors best explain the origins of ethnicity, nation, and nationalism. In analyzing and evaluating the various factors necessary and sufficient for their origins, scholars have developed two main theoretical approaches often at the center of the debate on ethnicity, nations, and nationalism: primordialism and constructivism. Additionally, within constructivist approaches, scholars look at the role of modernization and instrumentalism. These theories are also used to explain the causes of ethnic conflict.

Primordialism

Primordialism argues that ethnic and national identity (and thus nationalism) are derived from human nature (either a result of biology or originally constructed by individuals) and are unchangeable—they are "fixed" or "given." Group consciousness develops from language, culture, traditions, and history. This group consciousness is reinforced over time through socialization as a result of shared cultural and historical memory, with the creation of myths and symbols.[46] For primordialists, ethnic identity is a particularly important identity relative to others such as ideology and class, as "[f]ew other attributes of individuals or communities are fixed in the same way as ethnicity or are as necessarily conflictual."[47] Supporters of primordialism point to the tribes in Sub-Saharan Africa and the nomadic tribes of the Middle East (for example, the Kurds) as examples of groups with "untraceable, but sociologically real kinship," in which identity as part of the community trumps other identities.[48]

How, then, do such primordial sentiments lead to ethnic conflict? Primordialists assert that "ethnic divisions and tensions are 'natural.'"[49] Ethnic differences lead to conflict when ethnic identity and ethnic consciousness produce political demands perceived as favorable for one's own group. In other words, the interests of the ethnic group are generated independently by the very nature of the group as different from others, and the ethnic group will make political demands for self-determination, self-governance, or benefits even without the existence and/or proof of discrimination or dominance. To the primordialist school, ethnic identity is an independent variable that explains ethnic conflict.[50]

While primordialism is found in many ethnic conflicts (such as the Serbs' use of primordialist sentiments in the breakup of Yugoslavia—the invocation of their 1389 defeat by the Ottomans in Kosovo as well as Croatian fascist behavior toward Serbs during World War II—which contributed to the belief among Serbs of the need for a separate Serbian state), other factors may act as catalysts for the emergence of ethnic conflict, such as economic competition and weak states (see chapter 2 for domestic factors). Critics of the primordialist approach, as Anthony Smith points out, argue that it cannot explain the considerable differentiation of human beings in terms of "ethnic origin and culture." The approach does not provide an adequate explanation of the advent of specific ethnic communities nor how such communities change or even disappear. Relatedly, the approach fails to elucidate "why people choose to emigrate and assimilate to other ethnies." Finally, primordialism cannot account for instances of "fierce xenophobic ethnic nationalism" and instances of "a more tolerant, multicultural identity."[51] The approach assumes identities are unchanging, thus cannot account for why the level of conflict varies "over time and place" or why different ethnic groups can live peacefully with each other.[52] One example of this problem with primordialism is in explaining the peaceful coexistence of Protestants and Catholics in Belgium versus the constant conflict between the two religious communities in Northern Ireland.

Constructivism

In opposition to primordialism, the social constructivist approach claims that identities are "molded, refabricated, and mobilized in accord with reigning cultural scripts and centers of power."[53] The various social categories to which people belong result from behaviors and speech. Because the "membership rules, content, and valuation" of social categories are the product of human behavior, these social categories "can and do change over time."[54] Constructivist approaches see ethnicity as "a social phenomenon"[55] that satisfies needs, whether political-psychological or social-psychological.[56] Importantly, the "collective consciousness" leads to the "politically salient identity."[57]

In terms of conflict and tensions, "constructivists do not see ethnicity as inherently conflictual." When violence is possible within the social system, ethnicity as a social construct can lead to conflict.[58] For example, as will be discussed in more detail in chapter 4, the simmering tensions between ethnic groups in Yugoslavia escalated as economic problems increased and challenges to the political structure emerged. These social processes provided the opening for armed militias and nationalist leaders to push for ethnically pure states, thereby accelerating the violent demise of the multiethnic country.

Instrumentalism

Ethnicity and nationalism can serve an instrumentalist purpose: political elites, intellectuals, and the intelligentsia draw on ethnicity and nationalism in order to acquire the support of the masses for some political ends.[59] As Anthony Marx asserts, elites construct group consciousness through the "selective evocations of history to project an image of prior legitimacy and purposefully forget inconvenient images or experiences of past or present internal division. The images of a common identity, unifying ethnicity, and shared language [are] gradually invented, constructed, and reinforced, often explicitly, to bolster social cohesion."[60]

Thus, the instrumentalist approach is a rational choice approach in which individuals, especially among the elites, can use ethnicity for political benefit. Leaders bent on engaging in conflict can mobilize ethnicity, tapping into ethnic differences and perceived threats to the ethnic group by other ethnic groups.[61] For example, in the late 1980s, Serb leader Slobodan Milosevic sought to expand Serb territory. He exploited the perceptions of threat to Serbs living in the Krajina area of Croatia in order to start a war with the Croats, which eventually led to the demise of Yugoslavia (see chapter 4).[62]

Critics of constructivism and its instrumentalist variant make several points. These two approaches are unable to elucidate how particular ethnic communities are able to endure. Further, why are people so willing to die for their nations?[63] Why would the masses follow the elites? What mechanism accounts for such following?[64] Constructivism and instrumentalism fail to appreciate the potency of emotion and ethnic sentiment that emerged prior to the development of the modern nation-state and yet persists today.[65] Moreover, the evidence shows that when mass literacy is achieved, ethnic identities harden and thus are less able to be changed (reconstructed). According to Stephen Van Evera, "mass literacy allows the identity to be stored in writing and purveyed in common form to a mass audience. . . . A more developed identity—one that includes more historical and cultural content—inspires more loyalty because it offers more substance to be loyal to."[66] He further argues that ethnic conflict hardens ethnic identity, making reconstruction nearly impossible. "Conflict enhances the hardening effect of mass literacy on identity by enhancing the emotional impact of recorded national memories."[67]

In a further critique of instrumentalism, Anthony Marx notes, "beliefs and collectivities often persist even when they become costly rather than profitable."[68] Elites, knowing they are constrained by these persistent beliefs, "then simplify, distort, and select to serve the purpose of unifying the core group. Primordial imagery is what gives power to this process. . . . [I]t is the image of prejudice coming out of the past that gives elites such a powerful tool."[69]

Modernization

On the one hand, the historical process of industrialization—modernization—can change states, or subgroups within them, in such a way as to make them more culturally homogenous societies. Ethnic and national identity, and the ideology of nationalism, emerges as a result of this modernization process in which societies become more homogenous. Societies are able to unify when various developments, including universal literacy, education, political centralization, and mobility, occur.[70] As Benedict Anderson asserts, capitalism and print technology led to the idea of an "imagined community." This "imagined community" promoted a sense of identity and belonging among people in a particular society.[71] Thus, the social construction of an "imagined community" results from the process of modernization.

On the other hand, the effects of the modernization processes can create social fragmentation and/or state transformation, and these factors lead to ethnic conflict. Once competing mobilization occurs, demands often escalate, and competition between groups becomes even fiercer than before. Karl Deutsch argues that the rate of mobilization in the political sphere during modernization outpaces assimilation. The gap between the two produces political fragmentation and the rise of ethnic nationalism.[72] Georg Simmel argues that modernization produces a more segmented society and identity polarization.[73] Samuel Huntington points to the gap between rising expectations produced by modernization and the uneven distribution of new wealth and resources. This gap creates rising frustrations on the part of ethnic groups.[74] Huntington cites modernization and inequality as marking the emergence of such various ethnic groups as the Muslim Brotherhood in Egypt and the Yoruba in Nigeria.[75] Peleg suggests that during the process of state-building and modernization, one ethnic group captures the state. The democratic state is no longer a neutral arena for political competition. The hegemonic national group uses the state to sustain its power and privilege.[76] As an example, Peleg cites the minority White domination of the majority Black population in South Africa.[77]

Critics of the modernization approach point to the fact that the modern nations that modernization theorists speak of are very much nations whose identities are the result of "pre-existing ethnies." Moreover, elements that define ethnic nationalism, yet are left out of modernization theories, such as shared symbols, memories, sentiments, and values, are in fact very much a part of countless ethnic nationalisms found today.[78] Thus, as Hearn notes, modernist approaches "fail to appreciate the historical depth of ethnicities."[79] Further, scholars note that "It is difficult to see how such a broad historical process as economic modernization could explain violence between particular ethnic groups."[80] In other words, why would these particular ethnic groups end up in conflict with each other?

In sum, all these theories and approaches can shed light on the development and continued existence of nationalism and ethnic identity. Many scholars argue for an approach that acknowledges primordial sentiments as the backdrop to ethnic and national identity, while also acknowledging that identities are constructed as a result of elite manipulation or modernization processes.[81] As Harff and Gurr argue, "We think ethnic groups are most likely to mobilize when all conditions—a strong sense of ethnic identity, based on 'primordial' attachments, in combination with imposed disadvantages—are present."[82]

A body of scholarship in the field of social psychology makes the link between enduring "primordial" attachments and the social construction of identity. Of particular importance is the link between a collective identity and modernity, which reinforces the sense of an "in-group" and the recognition that there is an "out-group." Social identity theory asserts that individuals and groups have a social psychological "need to belong" and express this need through their social identities (or categories such as ethnic group, nationality, or political identification).[83] These social identities enhance their self-esteem and cohesiveness through the comparison of their group with others, the out-group.[84]

Building on social identity theory, Marilynn B. Brewer's theory of "optimal distinctiveness" further explains the process of social identification. Individuals have two important, yet opposing, needs: (1) the need for assimilation and inclusion (which leads individuals to become members of groups), and (2) the need for differentiation from others (which acts in opposition to the need for assimilation in a group). These opposing individual needs are assuaged through membership in a social identity group (need for inclusion and belonging) that distinguishes itself from other groups (need for differentiation from out-groups).[85] In the case of nationalist or ethnic groups, individuals' need for inclusion leads to socialization into perceiving themselves as belonging to a particular nationalist or ethnic group, in contrast (differentiation) to another group or nationality.[86] For example, Catholics in Northern Ireland perceive themselves as Irish, in opposition to Protestants, who perceive themselves as British.

Social identity theory further posits that the need for a positive in-group evaluation and perception can lead to comparisons with the out-group as negative. This in-group favoritism can lead to conflict with other groups, particularly if there is a perception of threat to group identity. From the perception of threat to one's group identity, enemy images about the other group emerge based on exaggerated differences, historical antagonisms, past experience, and collective memories. According to Shannon Lindsey Blanton, the "adherence to rigid images reduces the likelihood that even genuine attempts to resolve issues will be successful."[87] As will be seen in the various cases explored throughout this book, the perception of threat and enemy images become entrenched, making solutions to ethnic conflict difficult, but not impossible. For now, we present an overview of international relations scholarship and its application to ethnic conflict.

INTERNATIONAL RELATIONS AND ETHNIC CONFLICT

There are three main theories and approaches in the field of international relations that are used to explain events in world politics: realism, liberalism, and constructivism. Realism and liberalism are the leading theories in the discipline, with constructivism a relatively recent entry into the study of international relations. Importantly, the study of international relations can tell us much about ethnic conflict. As will be demonstrated below, scholars have also applied these theories and approaches to explain ethnic conflict.

Realism

Realism is the dominant theory in international relations. In realist theory, states are the most important political actors in the international system, and the state is a rational unitary actor. The roots of realism go as far back as Thucydides in his writings on the Peloponnesian Wars in ancient Greece. Realist theory is divided between classical realists and structural (or neo-) realists. Classical realists "believed that states, like human beings, had an innate desire to dominate others, which led them to fight wars."[88] Rather than focusing on human nature, neorealists look at "the effects of the international system," namely the anarchic structure, in which there is no central authority above states, and the balance of power (bipolar or multipolar). The anarchic international system means that states cannot look to others for survival.[89] Given that states have no central authority to call upon in case of disputes, states engage in self-help policies and behavior to increase their survival and security (such as forming alliances or building up their military power). Other states assume that another's gain is their loss, and thus respond in kind by forming alliances or increasing arms, leading to a security dilemma, where all states become less secure.[90]

Further, realists do not put much faith in international institutions, viewing them as "basically a reflection of the distribution of power in the world." It is "the self-interested calculations of the great powers" that form the core of such institutions. Only when the great powers see institutions as mechanisms for increasing or enhancing their power, do the great powers support them. Importantly, international institutions do not have an "independent effect on state behavior."[91]

As Spiegel and others note, "At the core of the realist paradigm is an emphasis on the study of war and peace (high politics) over trade and domestic issues (low politics), combined with a belief that people are inherently and primarily motivated by self-interest and the quest for security from, if not power over, their peers."[92]

For realists, the change in the balance of power following the end of the Cold War afforded the possibility of nationalist and ethnic conflicts to emerge in full force, many of which had been minimized during the Cold War as the East-West conflict dominated the international system.[93] For example, the eruption of war in Bosnia in the early 1990s resulted in large part from the emergence of issues thought contained in the post-1945 period—the challenge by the various ethnic groups (Serbs, Croats, and Muslims) for control of the same territory.

Consequently, realists have applied realist theory to ethnic conflict. In looking at different cases of ethnic conflict with the end of the Cold War, Barry Posen seeks to "assess the factors that could produce an intense security dilemma when imperial order breaks down, thus producing an early resort to violence."[94] He raises the question of what happens when the sovereign state (for example, USSR, Yugoslavia) no longer exists and ethnic groups are then concerned about their security, security that had previously been provided by the state. In utilizing realist theory, he focuses on how anarchy, which makes security the most important issue for states, can affect security for ethnic groups within states. When the state breaks down, groups fear for their survival and security. As a result, they must figure out if other ethnic groups are a threat. To determine this, groups look at the military capabilities of the other groups, particularly their offensive capabilities. Can they mobilize soldiers to fight? What kinds of weapons do they have? Such groups then may pursue measures to increase their security for defensive reasons, which, in turn, reduces the security of others as they perceive the first group's actions as offensive, leading the second group to increase security in response. The security dilemma in the international system, therefore, plays out for ethnic groups as well.[95]

Posen examines relations between Serbs and Croats as Yugoslavia disintegrated and demonstrates how the security dilemma affected relations between these two groups. He argues that the groups remembered their experiences with each other during World War II, in which "they slaughtered one another with abandon." Moreover, men had been trained for war, and weapons, namely infantry armaments, had been dispensed around the country—weapons that became readily available for ethnic clashes. The groups also perceived that the offense had the advantage, thus the ethnic groups believed that they needed to act preemptively to protect their kin living in the other republics.[96] Another factor that affected the security dilemma was the inequality of power between the groups. Different republics within the former Yugoslavia possessed varying levels of economic resources, demographic resources, and external actors who could serve as allies. Each group also worried about potential external enemies. Finally, Posen notes the existence of "small bands of fanatics" with access to weapons. These militias would prove to be quite adept at fighting and engaging in ethnic cleansing.[97] In the end, he argues that "Croats and Serbs found each other's identity a threat because of the primitive military capabilities they could field and the terrible record of their historical relationship." Serbs living in Croatia found themselves "militarily vulnerable, and Serbs in Serbia had only one way to defend them—a speedy, powerful offensive." Further, Croats were in a better position to acquire allies both from the other republics within Yugoslavia and other states.[98] He concludes by asserting that realist theory in international relations and the security dilemma offers a useful explanation of ethnic conflict. Given that the international system, as realists argue, is one of self-help for states, external actors, whether other states or international institutions, will be hard pressed to intervene in ethnic conflicts.[99]

The need to take into account domestic and individual factors (which will be discussed in greater detail in chapter 2) demonstrates the limits of a realist approach to nationalism and ethnic conflict. As Jack Snyder notes, "A narrowly realist focus risks ignoring socioeconomic processes that foster aggressive nationalism, while neglecting policy tools that might prevent intense security fears from developing." Moreover, "the realists' starting point, the fear-ridden war of all against all, is sometimes not the root cause of nationalism, but rather a symptom of other social processes that spurred nationalist consciousness in the first place."[100] Snyder further comments that "realist approaches to the study of nationalism risk reifying the sometimes arbitrary distinction between international and domestic 'levels of analysis.'"[101] He notes that "Disputes on the causes of nationalism, mostly carried among sociologists who are happily ignorant of the levels-of-analysis question in international relations theory, divide 'primordialists' from 'modernists,' those stressing culture from those stressing economics and those stressing irrational myths from those stressing rational calculation. Both sides of these debates draw on international as well as domestic factors."[102]

Snyder cautions, though, that there is a benefit to separating out international and domestic causes. If we look at "the effects of the international factors, it draws attention to the effects of others states' policies on one state's nationalism. This allows those states to disentangle the consequences of their own actions from the other factors at work and thus facilitates policy evaluation and policy choice." As a result, he argues that "the most important interaction effects to assess include interactions between the indigenous sources of nationalism within a state and the policies of other states." There is thus all the more reason to preserve "the analytical distinction between domestic and international causes." At the same time, Snyder also notes that scholars should be aware of those theories and approaches that cross both levels.[103] It is because such an analytical distinction matters that we argue for the necessity to employ the levels of analysis framework in understanding ethnic conflict. As will be seen in the case studies we explore, the levels of analysis framework can inform our knowledge of the causes of and solutions to ethnic conflicts and help us to appreciate fully the complexity of these conflicts.

Liberalism/Liberal Institutionalism

Liberalism (and its variants: liberal institutionalism and neoliberal institutionalism) challenges realism by arguing that states are not inherently prone to conflict; rather, states can cooperate. As with realism, states are still the primary (but not the only) actors in international relations, but this does not mean the world is a zero-sum game, where one state's gain is another's loss. Instead, through cooperation states can live in a variable-sum game world, in which all states can gain. Liberalism's roots are in economics, and the notion of cooperating in the economic realm can lead to prosperity for all. While liberalism also focuses on the state as the dominant actor in the international system, liberalism stresses the important role that international institutions can play in helping states cooperate.[104] Institutions provide information, establish rules, safeguard expectations, and reduce uncertainty. Institutions also make commitments more credible. Institutions matter because they can change state preferences and, therefore, behavior.[105] The post–Cold War period has witnessed the continued significance of international institutions such as the European Union and NATO. Rather than being weakened as a result of the end of the Cold War and the conflict between the United States and the Soviet Union, as many realists predicted, these institutions have endured, much as neoliberal institutionalist theory argues.[106]

Liberalism also claims that democracy encourages cooperation.[107] Consequently, an aspect of liberalism that has received significant attention in the literature and policy world is the democratic peace theory. The argument is that democracies "rarely, if ever, fight one another." The democratic norms of compromise, rather than resorting to force, enabled democratic societies to be relatively peaceful.[108]

Critics of liberal theory argue, however, that the evidence that democracies did not fight each other in the post-1945 period could be explained by the need for these states to come together to contain the Soviet Union. Moreover, democracies may not fight with each other, but they have indeed engaged in behavior to undermine other democracies (such as the CIA's role in the overthrow of the democratically elected regime of Salvador Allende in Chile in the 1970s). Finally, the transition to democracy turns out to be a quite violent period of time for many states. Thus, it is only established democracies that may be relatively peaceful.[109] In fact, many of the states experiencing a transition to democracy in the post–Cold War period were states rife with ethnic tensions and even outright war as ethnic groups sought their own states at the expense of other groups.[110]

The ethnic conflicts in the post-communist states of Azerbaijan, Chechnya, Moldova, and Bosnia point to the prevalence of these ethnic tensions.[111]

Thus, the implications of liberal theory for ethnic and nationalist groups are significant: "institutions may promote cooperation if they are structured in such ways that they change the behavior of previously conflicting groups to one of cooperation." In cases where there are majority and minority ethnic groups within the state, both must have access to policy making. In addition, ethnic groups must be able to express their grievances and interests.[112] As will be discussed in chapter 2, two institutions within states, consociationalism and federalism, are often promoted as effective means to manage (if not resolve) ethnic conflict within states.

International institutions can also play a role in addressing nationalist and ethnic conflicts. Though in the past neoliberal institutionalism did not address nationalism[113] and ethnicity, the fact that states are members of international institutions provides for a mechanism for attending to issues of nationalism and ethnicity. The most obvious example is the European Union. In this case, the member states are part of an international institution with its own anthem, flag, currency, legislative body, and so forth, as a means to promote a European identity.[114] At the same time, the European Union has played a role in dealing with nationalist and ethnic conflict issues. The EU Programme for Peace and Reconciliation in Northern Ireland and the Border Region of Ireland provides funds "aimed at reinforcing progress towards a peaceful and stable society and promoting reconciliation." By funding economic development projects and employment programs, the Programme (now in PEACE III phase) endeavors to build peace and reconciliation between the two groups, Protestants and Catholics, in Northern Ireland, who, as will be seen in chapter 3, have had a long-standing ethnic/nationalist conflict.[115]

Constructivism

Constructivism is a fairly recent approach in the study of international relations, though not new in other disciplines (as evidenced by the discussion of constructivism and nationalism earlier in the chapter). As Stephen Walt asserts, "Instead of taking the state for granted and assuming that it simply seeks to survive, constructivists regard the interest and identities of states as a highly malleable product of specific historical processes."[116] Moreover, he observes that, for example, "From a constructivist perspective, in fact, the central issue in the post–Cold War is how different groups conceive their identities and interests."[117] Identities are, in many instances, the result of international interaction.[118] As Hopf points out, identities provide states with a mechanism to understand other states, including their actions, attitudes, interests, and motives. He notes that

"Understanding another state as one identity, rather than another, has consequences for the possible actions of both."[119]

In challenging the realist assumptions of anarchy and self-help, constructivists would argue that as the modern state system developed, had states chosen behavior that demonstrated benign intentions rather than aggressive intentions, anarchy "would have been irrelevant" as states would not have feared each other. States "are not driven by the system; the system does not predetermine their behaviors; they have choices and those choices will be reflected back at them as other states respond."[120] For constructivists, the international system is "a social structure."[121]

Consequently, constructivists focus on understanding "how preferences are formed and knowledge is generated" and "on the importance of social processes that generate changes in normative beliefs."[122] Empirical research applying a constructivist approach has looked at how beliefs and norms influence international behavior, such as human rights, decolonization, anti-apartheid, and the nuclear weapons taboo.[123] Additionally, Hopf intimates that constructivism brings domestic politics and culture into consideration for international relations theory (rather than the systemic focus of neorealism): "constructivism provides a promising approach for uncovering those features of domestic society, culture, and politics that should matter to state identity and state action in global politics."[124]

Scholars argue that because neorealism takes as given issues of threats and security dilemmas, it fails to understand how threats are constructed, what objectives states or groups seek, and how to minimize the security dilemma.[125] The constructivist focus on identity necessitates the examination of the "other." For identities to have meaning, they are usually constructed in contrast to the "other"—oppositional identities that are "denigrated, feared, or emulated."[126] Thus, the idea of the construction of threats by states or groups matters for determining the causes of ethnic conflict. In the case of Yugoslavia, Serbian leaders claimed threats to Serbian ethnic identity and survival that influenced the behavior and actions of the Serbian masses toward the other ethnic groups, culminating in atrocities such as ethnic cleansing of Croats and Muslims.[127]

Critics of constructivism argue that it is not a theory—one cannot test variables or factors that explain state cooperation or conflict.[128] As John Gerard Ruggie, himself a constructivist, readily acknowledges, constructivism "lacks rigor and specification."[129] There is no "causal theory of identity."[130] Moreover, as Theo Farrell points out, "Constructivist approaches to security studies face two methodological problems: proving the existence of norms, and showing the impact of norms on behavioral outcomes." Granted that constructivists contend that norms are important and the social "practices they yield" are observable, still one cannot observe "the shared beliefs they embody." Farrell asks, "So how do we know these shared beliefs exist?" Scholars must be able to discern from actors' statements their beliefs and whether these beliefs are shared,[131] and constructivists must be able to provide measures of norm strength as well as the impact of norms.[132] Additionally, Katzenstein and others note that while constructivists are interested in norms, knowledge, identities, and interests, their "arguments do not provide a way to analyze strategies," which rationalist arguments, such as realism and liberalism, do in order to account for political outcomes.[133]

Although each of these approaches faces challenges and criticisms, they also enable us to understand and interpret much of what happens in the world today between states and within them. As Walt notes, "Most realists recognize that nationalism, militarism, ethnicity, and other domestic factors are important; liberals acknowledge that power is central to international behavior, and some constructivists admit that ideas will have greater impact when backed by powerful states and reinforced by enduring material forces."[134]

CONCLUSION

We began this chapter introducing the important concepts found in the study of ethnic conflict, including the dominant theories of ethnicity and nationalism, and how these relate to ethnic conflict. We presented a discussion of the major theories and approaches in the study of international relations (realism, liberalism, and constructivism), and how these have been applied to ethnic conflict.

The book contributes to the literature on ethnic conflict as it bridges the gap between the fields of comparative politics and international relations within political science by utilizing the levels of analysis framework to categorize the relevant factors for understanding such conflicts. By examining international, domestic, and individual level factors, we are able to construct a more complete picture of an ethnic conflict. The case studies demonstrate the complexity of ethnic conflict, and that the causes for one conflict may not be the same as for another, and this holds for solutions to manage and resolve these conflicts. Thus, one of the major conclusions of the book is that in studying ethnic conflicts, one size does not fit all—no one theory or factors can account for all ethnic conflicts.

The remainder of the book is as follows. Chapter 2 introduces the levels of analysis framework utilized in the study of international relations to explore factors within states and between states that account for ethnic conflict. In the subsequent chapters (3–7), we apply the levels of analysis to understand the causes of and solutions to five cases of ethnic conflict (Northern Ireland, Bosnia, Sudan, Sri Lanka, and Israel/Palestine). We have chosen these cases because they encompass various regions of the world: Africa, Europe, the Middle East, and South Asia. The cases are all contemporary; in other words, they have occurred in the post–Cold War period, although several predate the demise of the East-West conflict that characterized the Cold War. Chapter 8 concludes with a recap of the approach and major themes of the book. We are particularly interested in the similarities and differences regarding the causes and solutions of these conflicts, and therefore what lessons we can learn. We end with suggestions for areas of future research.

NOTES

1. Monty G. Marshall and Benjamin R. Cole, "Global Report on Conflict, Governance and State Fragility 2008," *Foreign Policy Bulletin* (Winter 2008): 3.
2. Marshall and Cole, "Global Report," 7.
3. Marshall and Cole, "Global Report," 7.
4. Monty G. Marshall, "Major Episodes of Political Violence 1946–2009," Center for Systemic Peace (November 9, 2009), www.systemicpeace.org/warlist. htm. Ethnic-intrastate conflicts are those that involve "the state agent and a distinct ethnic group"; violence refers to "the use of instrumental violence without necessarily exclusive goals," while war refers to "violence between distinct, exclusive groups with the intent to impose a unilateral result to the contention."
5. Steven E. Lobell and Philip Mauceri, "Diffusion and Escalation of Ethnic Conflict," in *Ethnic Conflict and International Politics: Explaining Diffusion and Escalation,* ed. Steven E. Lobell and Philip Mauceri (New York: Palgrave, 2004), 3. See also chapters in David A. Lake and Donald Rothchild, eds., *The International Spread of Ethnic Conflict: Fear, Diffusion and Escalation* (Princeton: Princeton University Press, 1998).
6. Michael Brown et al., *Nationalism and Ethnic Conflict* (Cambridge, Mass.: MIT Press, 2001); Donald Horowitz, *Ethnic Groups in Conflict* (Berkeley: University of California Press, 1985); Lake and Rothchild, *The International Spread of Ethnic Conflict;* Lobell and Mauceri, *Ethnic Conflict and International Politics;* Anthony D. Smith, *National Identity* (Reno: University of Nevada Press, 1991).
7. Bruce Gilley, "Against the Concept of Ethnic Conflict," *Third World Quarterly* 25, no. 6 (2004): 1158.
8. Anthony D. Smith, *Nationalism: Theory, Ideology, History* (Cambridge: Polity, 2001), 13.
9. Daniel L. Byman, *Keeping the Peace: Lasting Solutions to Ethnic Conflict* (Baltimore: Johns Hopkins University Press, 2002), 5. See also Milton J. Esman, *An Introduction to Ethnic Conflict* (Cambridge: Polity, 2004), 28.

10. Esman, *An Introduction to Ethnic Conflict,* 27.
11. Esman, *An Introduction to Ethnic Conflict,* 27.
12. Esman, *An Introduction to Ethnic Conflict,* 29. See also Jonathan Hearn, *Rethinking Nationalism: A Critical Introduction* (New York: Palgrave Macmillan, 2006), 8.
13. Steven L. Spiegel, Elizabeth G. Matthews, Jennifer M. Taw, and Kristen P. Williams, *World Politics in a New Era,* 4th edition (New York: Oxford University Press, 2009), 58.
14. Smith, *Nationalism,* 12–13, 116.
15. Smith, *Nationalism,* 12–13.
16. Lowell W. Barrington, "'Nation' and 'Nationalism': The Misuse of Key Concepts in Political Science," *PS: Political Science and Politics* 30, no. 4 (December 1997): 712.
17. Barrington, "'Nation' and 'Nationalism,'" 713.
18. Hearn, *Rethinking Nationalism,* 8–9. The literature on nationalism has distinguished between civic and ethnic nationalism. Ethnic nationalism is exclusive—only members of the same ethnic group can be members of the state/nation. Civic nationalism, on the other hand, is inclusive—all individuals can become members of the state/nation. In both types there is a particular culture, regardless of whether it is civic or ethnic, that determines membership in the nation (Hearn, *Rethinking Nationalism,* 90).
19. Hearn, *Rethinking Nationalism,* 37.
20. Ashutosh Varshney, "Nationalism, Ethnic Conflict, and Rationality," *Perspectives on Politics* 1, no. 1 (March 2003): 86.
21. See Joyce P. Kaufman and Kristen P. Williams, *Women, the State, and War: A Comparative Perspective on Citizenship and Nationalism* (Lanham, Md.: Lexington, 2007).
22. Sex refers to the biological differences between men and women. V. Spike Peterson and Anne Sisson Runyan, *Global Gender Issues,* 2nd ed. (Boulder: Westview Press, 1999), 5.
23. Peterson and Runyan, *Global Gender Issues,* 31.
24. Floya Anthias and Nira Yuval-Davis, "Introduction," in *Woman-Nation-State,* ed. Nira Yuval-Davis and Floya Anthias (London: Macmillan, 1989), 7.
25. V. Spike Peterson, "Sexing Political Identities/Nationalism as Heterosexism," *International Feminist Journal of Politics* 1, no. 1 (June 1999): 34–65.
26. Deniz Kandiyoti, "Women, Ethnicity and Nationalism," in *Ethnicity,* ed. John Hutchinson and Anthony D. Smith (Oxford: Oxford University Press, 1996), 315.
27. Julie Mostov, "Sexing the Nation/Desexing the body: Politics of National Identity in the Former Yugoslavia," in *Gender Ironies of Nationalism: Sexing the Nation,* ed. Tamar Mayer (London: Routledge, 2000), 98–102.

28. Rogers Brubaker and David D. Laitin, "Ethnic and Nationalist Violence," *Annual Review of Sociology* 24 (1998): 444.

29. Joane Nagel, "Ethnicity and Sexuality," *Annual Review of Sociology* 26 (2000): 113.

30. Carter Johnson, "Partitioning to Peace: Sovereignty, Demography, and Ethnic Civil Wars," *International Security* 32, no. 4 (Spring 2008): 145.

31. Roland Axtmann, "The State of the State: The Model of the Modern State and Its Contemporary Transformation," *International Political Science Review* 25, no. 3 (2004): 264.

32. Barrington, "'Nation' and 'Nationalism,'" 715. See also Esman, *An Introduction to Ethnic Conflict,* 6–7.

33. David Carment and Patrick James, "Internal Constraints and Interstate Ethnic Conflict," *Journal of Conflict Resolution* 39, no. 1 (March 1995): 83.

34. Brubaker and Laitin, "Ethnic and Nationalist Violence," 428.

35. Byman, *Keeping the Peace,* 6.

36. Ilan Peleg, "Transforming Ethnic Orders to Pluralist Regimes: Theoretical, Comparative, and Historical Analysis," in *Democracy and Ethnic Conflict: Advancing Peace in Deeply Divided Societies,* ed. Adrian Guelke (New York: Palgrave, 2004), 7–25.

37. Lobell and Mauceri, "Diffusion and Escalation of Ethnic Conflict," 3; David A. Lake and Donald Rothchild, "Spreading Fear: The Genesis of Transnational Ethnic Conflict," in *The International Spread of Ethnic Conflict: Fear, Diffusion, and Escalation,* eds. David A. Lake and Donald Rothchild (Princeton: Princeton University Press, 1998), 4.

38. John James Quinn, "Diffusion and Escalation in the Great Lakes Region: The Rwandan Genocide, the Rebellion in Zaire, and Mobutu's Overthrow," in *Ethnic Conflict and International Politics: Explaining Diffusion and Escalation,* ed. Steven E. Lobell and Philip Mauceri (New York: Palgrave, 2004), 111–131.

39. Shale Horowitz, "Identities Unbound: Escalating Ethnic Conflict in Post-Soviet Azerbaijan, Georgia, Moldova, and Tajikistan," in *Ethnic Conflict and International Politics: Explaining Diffusion and Escalation,* ed. Steven E. Lobell and Philip Mauceri (New York: Palgrave, 2004), 51–74.

40. Barbara Harff and Ted Robert Gurr, *Ethnic Conflict in World Politics,* 2nd ed. (Boulder: Westview Press, 2004), 23–25.

41. David McDowell, *A Modern History of the Kurds,* rev. 3rd ed. (London/New York: I.B. Tauris, 2004).

42. Harff and Gurr, *Ethnic Conflict in World Politics,* 25–27.

43. Harff and Gurr, *Ethnic Conflict in World Politics,* 27–28.

44. Harff and Gurr, *Ethnic Conflict in World Politics,* 28–29.
45. Harff and Gurr, *Ethnic Conflicts in World Politics,* 29–30.
46. Esman, *An Introduction to Ethnic Conflict,* 30–31; Edward Shils, "Nation, Nationality, Nationalism and Civil Society," *Nations and Nationalism* 1, no. 1 (March 1995): 93–118; Paul C. Stern, "Why Do People Sacrifice for Their Nations?" *Political Psychology* 16, no. 2 (1995): 217–235; Kandhan Chandra, "Cumulative Findings in the Study of Ethnic Politics," *APSA-CP Newsletter* 12, no. 1 (Winter 2001): 7.
47. Lake and Rothchild, "Spreading Fear," 5.
48. Clifford Geertz, "Primordial Ties," in *Ethnicity,* ed. John Hutchinson and Anthony D. Smith (Oxford: Oxford University Press, 1996), 41.
49. Lake and Rothchild, "Spreading Fear," 5.
50. Horowitz, *Ethnic Groups in Conflict;* Walker Connor, *Ethno-Nationalism: The Quest for Understanding* (Princeton: Princeton University Press, 1994); Anthony D. Smith, *The Ethnic Revival* (Cambridge: Cambridge University Press, 1981).
51. Anthony D. Smith, "Culture, Community and Territory: The Politics of Ethnicity and Nationalism," *International Affairs* 72 (1996): 446.
52. Lake and Rothchild, "Spreading Fear," 5.
53. Karen A. Cerulo, "Identity Construction: New Issues, New Directions," *Annual Review of Sociology* 23 (1997), 387.
54. James D. Fearon and David D. Laitin, "Violence and the Social Construction of Ethnic Identity," *International Organization* 54, no. 4 (Autumn 2000): 848.
55. Lake and Rothchild, "Spreading Fear," 6.
56. Gilley, "Against the Concept of Ethnic Conflict," 1158.
57. John L. Comaroff and Paul C. Stern, "New Perspectives on Nationalism and War," *Theory and Society* 23 (1994): 38.
58. Lake and Rothchild, "Spreading Fear," 6.
59. Adeed Dawisha, "Nation and Nationalism: Historical Antecedents to Contemporary Debates," *International Studies Review* 4, no. 1 (Spring 2002): 5. See also Daniele Conversi, "Reassessing Current Theories of Nationalism: Nationalism as Boundary Maintenance and Creation," *Nationalism and Ethnic Politics* 1, no. 1 (Spring 1995): 74; Lake and Rothchild, "Spreading Fear," 5–6.
60. Anthony D. Marx, "The Nation-State and Its Exclusion," *Political Science Quarterly* 117, no. 1 (Spring 2002): 105.
61. Lake and Rothchild, "Spreading Fear," 6–7.
62. Kristen P. Williams, *Despite Nationalist Conflicts: Theory and Practice of Maintaining World Peace* (Westport, Conn.: Praeger, 2001), 93.
63. Smith, "Culture, Community and Territory," 446.

64. Fearon and Laitin, "Violence and the Social Construction of Ethnic Identity," 853–854; Esman, *An Introduction to Ethnic Conflict,* 33.

65. Smith, *Nationalism,* 57–61.

66. Stephen Van Evera, "Primordialism Lives!" *APSA-CP Newsletter* 12, no. 1 (Winter 2001): 20.

67. Van Evera, "Primordialism Lives!" 20–21.

68. Marx, "The Nation-State and Its Exclusion," 119.

69. Marx, "The Nation-State and Its Exclusion," 120–121.

70. Fearon and Laitin, "Violence and the Social Construction of Ethnic Identity," 851; Ernest Gellner, *Nations and Nationalism* (Ithaca: Cornell University Press, 1983); Eric J. Hobsbawm, *Nations and Nationalism since 1780: Programme, Myth, Reality* (Cambridge: Cambridge University Press, 1990); Byman, *Keeping the Peace.*

71. Benedict Anderson, *Imagined Communities: Reflections on the Origin and Spread of Nationalism* (London: Verso, 1991).

72. Karl Deutsch, *Political Community at the International Level: Problems of Definition and Measurement* (Princeton: Princeton University Press, 1953).

73. Georg Simmel, *Conflict and the Web of Group Affiliations* (New York: Free Press, 1955).

74. Samuel P. Huntington, *Political Order in Changing Societies* (New Haven: Yale University Press, 1968).

75. Huntington, *Political Order in Changing Societies,* 38.

76. Peleg, "Transforming Ethnic Orders to Pluralist Regimes."

77. Peleg, "Transforming Ethnic Orders to Pluralist Regimes," 12.

78. Smith, "Culture, Community and Territory," 446.

79. Hearn, *Rethinking Nationalism,* 95.

80. Fearon and Laitin, "Violence and the Social Construction of Ethnic Identity," 851.

81. Dawisha, "Nation and Nationalism," 21. Smith's ethno-symbolist approach is one such middle position between primordialism and constructivism, acknowledging that identities are constructed to some extent and manipulated by elites, but that these national identities are related to "prior ethnic ties," in which shared memories, myths, and culture continue to resonate with people. Smith, *Nationalism,* 60.

82. Harff and Gurr, *Ethnic Conflict in World Politics,* 97.

83. Michael A. Hogg, Deborah J. Terry, and Katherine M. White, "A Tale of Two Theories: A Critical Comparison of Identity Theory with Social Identity Theory," *Social Psychology Quarterly* 58 (1995): 255–269.

84. Henri Tajfel, *Human Groups and Social Categories: Studies in Social Psychology* (Cambridge: Cambridge University Press, 1981); see also Marilynn B. Brewer

and Wendi Gardner, "Who Is This 'We'? Levels of Collective Identity and Self-Representations," *Journal of Personality and Social Psychology* 71 (1996): 83–93.

85. Marilynn Brewer, "The Social Psychology of Intergroup Relations: Can Research Inform Practice?" *Journal of Social Issues* 53 (1997): 203–204; Brewer, "Ingroup Identification and Intergroup Conflict: When Does Ingroup Love Become Outgroup Hate?" in *Social Identity, Intergroup Conflict, and Conflict Reduction,* ed. Richard D. Ashmore, Lee Jussim, and David Wilder (Oxford: Oxford University Press, 2001), 21–22.

86. D. Katz, "Nationalism and Strategies of International Conflict Resolution," in *International Behavior: A Social-Psychological Analysis,* ed. Herbert C. Kelman (New York: Holt, 1964), 356–390.

87. Shannon Lindsey Blanton, "Images in Conflict: The Case of Ronald Reagan and El Salvador," *International Studies Quarterly* 40, no. 1 (March 1996): 41.

88. Stephen M. Walt, "International Relations: One World, Many Theories," *Foreign Policy* 110 (Spring 1998): 31. Recently, some scholars are considered "neoclassical realists," who look at "how systemic variables are filtered through the domestic and individual levels to produce outcomes." Jennifer Sterling-Folker, "Realism and the Constructivist Challenge: Rejecting, Reconstructing, or Rereading," *International Studies Review* 4, no. 1 (Spring 2002): 82, fn. 28.

89. Walt, "International Relations," 31. Realism is further divided between offensive and defensive realism. In offensive realism, the anarchic international system always "provides strong incentives for expansion," whereas in defensive realism, "the international system provides incentives for expansion under certain conditions." In defensive realism, the balance of power works as a constraint on state expansion. See Jeffrey W. Taliaferro, "Security Seeking under Anarchy: Defensive Realism Revisited," *International Security* 25, no. 3 (Winter 2000/2001): 128–129. The debate between offensive and defensive realists continues, but for our purposes, we seek only to provide a condensed overview of the realist paradigm.

90. Robert Jervis, *Perception and Misperception in International Relations* (Princeton: Princeton University Press, 1976), 66.

91. John J. Mearsheimer, "The False Promise of International Institutions," *International Security* 19, no. 3 (Winter 1994/1995): 7.

92. Spiegel et al., *World Politics in a New Era,* 35.

93. John J. Mearsheimer, "Back to the Future," in *The Cold War and After: Prospects for Peace,* ed. Sean M. Lynn-Jones (Cambridge, Mass.: MIT Press, 1991), 148, 151, 171.

94. Barry R. Posen, "The Security Dilemma and Ethnic Conflict," *Survival* 35, no. 1 (Spring 1993): 27.

95. Posen, "The Security Dilemma and Ethnic Conflict," 27–29.

96. Posen, "The Security Dilemma and Ethnic Conflict," 35.

97. Posen, "The Security Dilemma and Ethnic Conflict," 35–37.

98. Posen, "The Security Dilemma and Ethnic Conflict," 42.

99. Posen, "The Security Dilemma and Ethnic Conflict," 43–44.

100. Jack Snyder, "The New Nationalism: Realist Interpretations and Beyond," in *The Domestic Bases of Grand Strategy*, ed. Richard Rosecrance and Arthur A. Stein (Ithaca: Cornell University Press, 1993), 181.

101. Snyder, "The New Nationalism," 181.

102. Snyder, "The New Nationalism," 182.

103. Snyder, "The New Nationalism," 182.

104. Walt, "International Relations," 32; Spiegel et al., *World Politics in a New Era*, 39–40.

105. Robert O. Keohane and Lisa L. Martin, "The Promise of Institutionalist Theory," *International Security* 20 (1995): 39–51.

106. Peter J. Katzenstein, Robert O. Keohane, and Stephen D. Krasner, "*International Organization* and the Study of World Politics," *International Organization* 52, no. 4 (Autumn 1998): 673.

107. Spiegel et al., *World Politics in a New Era*, 39.

108. Walt, "International Relations," 39.

109. Walt, "International Relations," 39.

110. Jack Snyder, "One World, Rival Theories," *Foreign Policy* 145 (November/December 2004): 58.

111. Charles H. Fairbanks, "The Postcommunist Wars," *Armed Forces and Democracy* 6, no. 4 (1995): 18–34.

112. Neal G. Jesse and Kristen P. Williams, *Identity and Institutions: Conflict Reduction in Divided Societies* (Albany: SUNY Press, 2005), 10.

113. Katzenstein, et al., "*International Organization* and the Study of World Politics," 673–674.

114. Jesse and Williams, *Identity and Institutions*, 15–16.

115. Special EU Programmes Body, *PEACE III: EU Programme for Peace and Reconciliation 2007–2013* (November 2008).

116. Walt, "International Relations," 40.

117. Walt, "International Relations," 41.

118. John Gerard Ruggie, "What Makes the World Hang Together? Neo-utilitarianism and the Social Constructivist Challenge," *International Organization* 52, no. 4 (Autumn 1998): 879.

119. Ted Hopf, "The Promise of Constructivism in International Relations Theory," *International Security* 23, no. 1 (Summer 1998): 193.

120. Spiegel et al., *World Politics in a New Era,* 45.
121. Ruggie, "What Makes the World Hang Together?" 879.
122. Katzenstein et al., *"International Organization* and the Study of World Politics," 681–682. Scholars delineate three categories of constructivism: conventional, critical, and postmodern. We present the general arguments made for constructivism as a whole. See Katzenstein et al., *"International Organization* and the Study of World Politics," 675–678; Hopf, "The Promise of Constructivism in International Relations Theory," 181–185.
123. Ruggie, "What Makes the World Hang Together?" 867.
124. Hopf, "The Promise of Constructivism in International Relations Theory," 194–195.
125. Keith Krause and Michael C. Williams, "Broadening the Agenda of Security Studies: Politics and Methods," *Mershon International Studies Review* 40, no. 2 (October 1996): 248.
126. Ruggie, "What Makes the World Hang Together?" 873.
127. V. P. Gagnon, "Ethnic Nationalism and International Conflict: The Case of Serbia," *International Security* 19, no. 3 (Winter 1994–1995): 132.
128. Spiegel et al., *World Politics in a New Era,* 45; Hopf, "The Promise of Constructivism in International Relations Theory," 196.
129. Ruggie, "What Makes the World Hang Together?" 883.
130. Hopf, "The Promise of Constructivism in International Relations Theory," 197.
131. Theo Farrell, "Constructivist Security Studies: Portrait of a Research Program," *International Studies Review* 4, no. 1 (Spring 2002): 60.
132. Farrell, "Constructivist Security Studies," 61.
133. Katzenstein et al., *"International Organization* and the Study of World Politics," 678–679.
134. Walt, "International Relations," 43.

CHAPTER 2

Levels of Analysis and Ethnic Conflict

The theories and approaches discussed in chapter 1 inform our understanding of international relations, and state behavior specifically, and offer a means for understanding ethnic conflict. Yet, how can we capture all the relevant players in intrastate ethnic conflict? The levels of analysis framework that has been a mainstay in international relations scholarship[1] allows us to take into account those important players, or actors, that matter for understanding ethnic conflict, both its causes and possible solutions.

The levels of analysis approach usually considers three levels, or "images": international (balance of power, anarchic international system), domestic (factors within states such as legislatures, bureaucracies, interest groups, military, political parties), and individual (elites/leaders). In this chapter we examine the three levels of analysis, which are then applied to each of the case studies of ethnic conflict in chapters 3–7. As will become quite clear, though the levels are in many ways distinct, they also overlap in actual cases of ethnic conflict. In order for scholars and practitioners alike to discern the factors that matter in determining the causes of and solutions to ethnic conflict, however, the levels of analysis framework is useful as a means to categorize and identify relevant factors.

INDIVIDUAL LEVEL

At the end of the day, decisions about policies, whether domestic or international, are made by individuals, the elites in the government. Scholars have focused on decision-making theories to account for the decisions of elites, namely in the fields of social psychology and psychology.[2] As Jerel Rosati argues, "In reality, countries do not act; people act. States (and organizations) are made up of individuals who act on their behalf. Ultimately, human cognition matters—in politics, foreign policy, and world politics."[3] Leaders matter because they are able to get others to follow, whether in terms of domestic or foreign policy. As Michael Brown notes, the decision of whether disputes lead to war or peace rests with domestic elites.[4]

Yet, there are also limitations to the efficacy of action on the individual level. The question arises as to how much individuals really matter given the structure of the international system or domestic level factors. Individual leaders are constrained by domestic forces, such as interest groups, political parties, and political institutions. Whether elites can get the masses to follow depends on their ability to mobilize constituents (including ethnic constituents). Leaders are also constrained by the structure of the system. For example, during the Cold War, U.S. leaders were influenced by the bipolar structure in which the Soviet Union was the other major power in the system. The East-West conflict dominated the relationship between the two superpowers, affecting their foreign policy actions and decisions. U.S. leaders maintained a consistent containment policy toward the Soviet Union.

While these limitations are important to recognize, it is useful to look at the role of political elites/leaders in examining intrastate and interstate behavior. We begin this section with a brief discussion of the general theories and approaches to understanding individual elite behavior. The second section addresses the role elites play in ethnic conflict, particularly how ethnic elites are able to manipulate identity and convince the masses to follow, as well as how elites engage in ethnic outbidding in order to obtain and maintain power.

Political Leadership

In general, the study of political leadership concerns itself with each leader's individual style of decision making and the effect that it has on his or her society.[5] The literature on political leadership abounds. It runs the gamut from personal biographies and autobiographies, each detailing an individual's style, to classical political theories of leadership, to a more general analysis of political leadership.[6] Classifying leaders into different categories of style requires looking at their personal characteristics, the instruments that they use and have at their disposal, the obstacles that they face, the structure in which they operate, and the choices that they make given all of these other factors. The literature on successful and failed political leadership offers three different explanations, according to Lewis Edinger. Leadership is affected by contextual factors (such as organizational structures and domestic socioeconomic conditions), individual attributes (personal characteristics of leaders), and "qualities attributed to other persons involved" (such as "attitudinal dispositions and cognitions of others").[7]

In the study of political leadership, scholars have utilized several approaches, including a focus on the "formal-legal authority of individuals in key policymaking positions," which is the institutionalized executive authority within a country. Others have utilized the rational actor approach, focusing on the rational calculation (cost-benefit) of self-interested leaders.[8]

However, the rational actor model embraced by realism and liberalism may not be the best way to understand what states do, or do not do, both internally and externally. Instead of a rational actor model, which looks at an individual's preferences and outcomes, some scholars have utilized cognitive approaches, focusing on the ways in which individuals' beliefs, images, and attitudes influence their behavior.[9] Cognitive approaches can be used to help us understand foreign policy behavior,[10] though these approaches can also be applied to elites and leaders' behavior within states (including understanding ethnic conflict, as we will discuss later).

In brief, scholars have found that individuals tend to seek consistency and avoid "cognitive dissonance." When new information does not correspond with their preexisting beliefs, individuals will discount that new information. In addition, individuals are likely to use schemas—"mental constructs that represent different clumps of knowledge (or comprehension) about various facets of the environment." With an increasingly uncertain and complex environment, individuals will find themselves utilizing schemas and other cognitive devices that are "shortcuts in information processing" so as to be able "to make sense of the world and the situation at hand."[11] For example, President George W. Bush's January 2002 State of the Union speech labeled Iran, Iraq, and North Korea as the "Axis of Evil." He asserted that "[s]tates like these, and their terrorist allies, constitute an axis of evil, arming to threaten the peace of the world. By seeking weapons of mass destruction, these regimes pose a grave and growing danger. They could provide these arms to terrorists, giving them the means to match their hatred. They could attack our allies or attempt to blackmail the United States. In any of these cases, the price of indifference would be catastrophic." In linking the September 11, 2001, terrorist attacks to state-sponsored terrorism, he claimed that "[o]ur war on terror is well begun, but is only begun."[12] By categorizing perceived enemies as supporters of terrorism, his rhetoric of the Axis of Evil served as a device to understand and simplify a world filled with complexity and uncertainty.

Importantly, as Rosati observes, once such beliefs and images are obtained by an individual, "the mind tends to close; the closure is reinforced by the organizational, political, and social contexts in which the individuals operate."[13] In this way, leaders as well as other individuals are often constrained in their ability to learn when they obtain new information, and thus are often unable to "adjust to new situations and changes in their environment."[14]

In processing information about the world, individuals classify and categorize items. The classification and sorting can result in the emergence of stereotypes.[15] Stereotyping others can lead to what are called mirror images and enemy images: In a hostile relationship, individuals' image of themselves is positive, but the image of others is negative (enemy image).[16] In the study of foreign policy, scholars, such as Noel Kaplowitz, have noted that leaders' "perceptions of [enemies'] character, intent, power, strengths, weaknesses, trustworthiness, and that which the [enemy] actor admires and dislikes" matter. These perceptions of the enemy are the result of a leader's "experiences with the enemy" as well as "interpretations of enemy behavior," among other factors. Kaplowitz contends that though "self-images and perceptions of enemies" can change (due to "traumatic and catastrophic events" or after long periods of time have passed), they tend to be "relatively stable."[17] Such consistent self-images and perceptions of the enemy can lead to misperceptions. For example, when leaders exaggerate their country's strength relative to their enemy, they may engage in aggressive behavior, including war.[18] In the end, because images and beliefs are difficult to change, leaders are constrained in their ability to contend with possible conflict.[19]

This brief overview of the research on political leadership and cognitive approaches is meant to illustrate how individuals matter for the understanding and evaluation of the policy decisions that elites make. Yet, even though decisions are made by elites, the implementation of policy rests on the willingness and ability of others to do so. Such willingness and ability is an important consideration in the case of ethnic conflict.

Elites and Ethnic Conflict

The overarching question in cases of ethnic conflict is how the elites—individuals—get the masses to follow to the extent that they can organize collectively and even go to war. Are the followers being duped by the elites into embracing "false beliefs" and engaging in "actions that the followers would not want to take if they understood what the leaders were up to"?[20] Or, as instrumentalist approaches to ethnic conflict would argue, are elites using "institutional rules and norms," including constitutional rules, to attain power in the face of perceived security threats to the ethnic group?[21] Are elites able to take advantage of the everyday social interactions that produce and reproduce social identities—the social construction of identity?[22]

Scholars, such as Stuart Kaufman, have examined the role that belligerent elites play in encouraging and fostering mass hostility, and forming perceptions about others as the enemy. Leaders can stoke the hostility of the masses and rouse the security dilemma by virtue of the fact that leaders have access to government power and the media. In this way, leaders' behavior can lead to war.[23] When elites can mobilize groups by responding to their demands and grievances, such mobilization can lead to collective action, including engaging in conflict.[24] Marc Howard Ross maintains that groups and leaders utilize cultural metaphors for organization and mobilization.[25] This is so because culture provides the link between individuals and collective identity, and when such identity is perceived to be threatened, leaders can mobilize groups into action, even violent action.[26] He further notes, "Powerful metaphors [linked to how the enemy engages in a particular behavior, for example] help groups define the threats they face."[27] Relatedly, myths about one's own ethnic group and other ethnic groups provide elites with a mechanism to enhance their own power and can lead to conflict. Stephen Van Evera examines three types of chauvinist mythmaking: self-glorifying myths, self-whitewashing myths, and other-maligning myths. Self-glorifying myths are those that focus on a nation's "special virtue and competence, and false claims of past beneficence toward others." Self-whitewashing myths "incorporate false denial of past wrong-doing against others." Other-maligning myths "can incorporate claims of others' cultural inferiority, false blame of others for past crimes and tragedies, and false claims that others now harbor malign intentions against the nation." All three types mostly come from political elites, as a means to enhance their own power as well as the power of the group or nation, provide legitimacy for the elites and the regime, enable leaders "to motivate sacrifice by their citizens and to justify cruelties against others," and divert blame for domestic economic crisis to enemies.[28] A society with a weak or nonexistent free press or lack of tradition of free speech, as well as lack of free universities that can challenge the nationalist mythmakers, is a society in danger of chauvinist and misleading mythmaking.[29]

James Fearon and David Laitin find in their cases of ethnic violence that political competition between the ethnic moderates and extremists within the ethnic group motivates leaders "to 'play the ethnic card.'" Playing the ethnic card can occur in two ways. Extremist leaders or groups engage in violence as a way to compel moderate leaders and groups to strengthen their backing for more extreme (and violent) positions. Alternatively, a moderate leader, fearing a threat to his or her power base, utilizes violence as a means of securing support from the extremists or the masses at large.[30] In this way, they argue, leaders are able to construct group identities as more hostile and thus trigger "a spiral of vengeance."[31] As David Lake and Donald Rothchild claim, political entrepreneurs, motivated by power and political office rather than supporting the extremists' views, "may reflect the polarization of societies and, through their actions, propel this process further."[32] Moderates find themselves in a vulnerable position, where they must maintain or obtain power at the expense of extremists. These political entrepreneurs assert that conflict with other ethnic groups is possible. In doing so, they focus on the enemy images of other ethnic groups, undermine healthy public debate, and persuade members of their own ethnic group to support them. The quintessential example is Slobodan Milosevic in Yugoslavia.[33]

Ethnic outbidding occurs when elites, vying for power with other elites within their ethnic group, appeal to ethnic identity as the most salient identity issue for the masses. Daniel Byman distinguishes between two types of elites, political and cultural. Political elites are those leaders who are most concerned with access to power and decision making, and "may or may not care about ethnic issues." Cultural elites are concerned with ethnic issues. Byman further notes that while there are differences between the two types of elites, both seek to "enhance their position against ethnic rivals" and thus are concerned with advancing the group's status. Further, ethnic elites may be induced to encourage conflict, either because they seek power over their rivals or they believe that their cause is just and right. Defending and enhancing the group's identity provides legitimacy to the ethnic elites.[34] As noted in chapter 1, social constructivists argue that identities are malleable. Given that, elites attempt to make certain identities more salient than others, focusing on the identities that will invariably strengthen the political position of the leaders.[35] Stuart Kaufman further contributes to the discussion of ethnic outbidding by noting that "[f]or outbidding to be possible, elites require political space—i.e., the freedom to engage in outbidding." In order for outbidding to be successful, the preconditions for mass hostility or the actual existence of mass hostility are needed for the masses to respond to calls from extremists.[36] Kaufman cautions that belligerent elites and ethnic outbidding are necessary but not sufficient conditions for mobilization of the masses and thus for ethnic conflict to emerge: mass hostility and the security dilemma must also be present.[37] Such belligerent elites can come from the dominant group or from the subordinate group. When the belligerent elites come from the dominant group, they have the resources of the government at their disposal, creating "ethnic hostility and a security dilemma." When the belligerent elites come from the subordinate group, they "create rival governments aimed at seceding from or taking over the state," thereby also provoking ethnic hostility and the security dilemma. An example of this would be the Serb leaders in Croatia demanding to secede from Croatia in the early 1990s.[38]

In the diversionary theory, or hypothesis, elites use domestic problems to their advantage—namely by engaging in aggressive behavior against other states. By diverting attention from troubles at home and toward an external actor, elites can garner support. In their analyses of irredentist ethnic conflict, David Carment and Patrick James found that elites may seek to divert such domestic discord toward another state, thereby leading to conflict if the elites make claims on territory where the elites' "in-group is perceived to be oppressed."[39] As they further contend, "nationalist identities, political symbols, and ideologies" become crucial tools for elites to influence mass feeling as they seek to achieve particular foreign policy goals.[40] Lake and Rothchild remark that mobilization frequently includes an irredentist element, with ethnic elites calling for "the reunification of an often mythical but nonetheless politically salient ethnic homeland."[41]

Carment and James find that significant competition between elites within the dominant ethnic group can lead elites to put forward new issues as a means to undermine their rivals and maintain power. As noted earlier, elites also attempt to influence mass sentiment. Mass sentiment can act as a constraint on elites in their efforts to seek policies that are cooperative.[42] As a result of the emergence of new political parties pushing for a foreign policy that is more antagonistic (including irredentist claims on other states), ethnic elites engage in ethnic outbidding, opting for aggressive policies as a means of distinguishing themselves from other moderate elites.[43]

As this section demonstrates, whether through manipulating democratic freedoms,[44] endorsing and promoting mythmaking, or engaging in ethnic out-bidding, elites can and do initiate and support ethnic conflict. At the same time, elites can also foster cooperation and peace, and the resolution of ethnic conflict, which we examine in the next section.

Elites and Resolving Ethnic Conflict

Elites can play a role in managing and settling ethnic conflict. In the case of power-sharing political institutions (that is, consociationalism, federalism), elites must cooperate with elites from other groups. In order to be successful at managing ethnic tensions and conflict (rather than manipulating democratic freedoms), such elites, according to Ulrich Schneckener, must be able to induce their followers to support peaceful solutions, contain spoilers and extremists (including paramilitaries), and put together "formal and informal coalitions with moderate forces of the other side." In addition, elites must abide by the terms of the status quo agreement, as well as guarantee that all the relevant groups are able to participate in the negotiations. Managing ethnic tensions so as to lead to an agreement can also benefit everyone if elites can also look to "positive traditions of mutual understanding from the past."[45] Schneckener provides several examples of successful elite cooperation that reduced ethnic conflict, including Northern Ireland following the 1998 Good Friday Agreement (in comparison to the failed attempts at ending the conflict during the 1970s).[46] He also adds the importance of elites on both sides of a conflict being able "to present themselves vis-à-vis their followers as 'winners.' . . . [T]he terms of the agreement must help to turn a zero-sum game, typical for ethnic conflicts, into a positive-sum game (*win-win situation*)."[47]

One strategy involving the role of elites in managing and resolving conflict is the co-optation of elites by the state. If the leaders of disgruntled ethnic groups can be transformed into supporters of the status quo and peace, rather than a threat to the peace, ethnic conflict can be managed. Through inducements (bribes, jobs, status, power), governments can satisfy ethnic elites and buy them off in order to obtain their support. As Byman observes, "When co-optation is successful, grievances such as security, status, or hegemonic concerns may be widespread, but the group cannot mobilize effectively because its leaders are co-opted."[48] In terms of concerns about inter-elite competition within ethnic groups, co-optation serves to enhance the standing and power of the moderates at the expense of the extremists. Moderates are able to gain the support of their community, while extremists become marginalized.[49] There is a limit to co-optation as a strategy: if the grievances of the ethnic community are significant enough or the co-opted elites lose their status, co-optation will not succeed in ending the violence.[50]

In attempting to end ethnic conflict, however, there are always individuals who may not be satisfied with a peaceful resolution of the conflict. Stephen John Stedman examines the role of "spoilers" in peace negotiations. Spoilers fear that any peace "threatens their power, worldview, and interests" and therefore promote the continued use of violence in order to undercut the peace negotiations and possibility for an end to the conflict.[51] Stedman's work reveals the importance of recognizing the role that spoilers can play in preventing peace from being achieved. He provides a typology of spoilers that includes the position of the spoiler (a spoiler "inside" signs agreement but does not comply with the major terms of the agreement; an "outside" spoiler is not involved in the peace negotiations and employs violence in order to damage the peace process) as well as the number of spoilers (the greater the number the more difficulty in achieving the peace process).[52] Consequently, managing the spoilers, particularly by international actors, is needed in order to oversee the implementation of peace agreements. Positive inducements (such as providing the means to deal with the grievances claimed by the spoilers), socialization about the acceptable norms of behavior for those parties committed to peace and the peace process, and coercion (threat or use of punishment to deter spoilers, such as withdrawal of international involvement in the negotiations) are means to manage spoilers and promote the peace.[53]

Thus for peace negotiations to go forward, both elites and masses (followers) must buy into the agreement. As Frederic Pearson notes, "it would appear that a good balance of elite and communal involvement is likely to be necessary for peace formulae to evolve into conflict resolution."[54]

DOMESTIC LEVEL

The field of comparative politics (as well as many international relations scholars) examines the factors within states that can tell us much about particular state policies, both internal and external. There are formal institutions within a state, but also other domestic factors such as political parties, interest groups, economic sectors and factors, social movements, political culture, and other competing forces within a state that are useful to explain state behavior in general, but also ethnic conflict within and between states.

Thus, an exploration of the domestic level of analysis provides a useful tool for understanding ethnic conflict. There are many domestic sources of ethnic conflict. Consequently, there are many domestic actors and institutions that can ameliorate or exacerbate ethnic conflict. In this section of the chapter we address domestic level theories to understand the interests, powers, and organization of domestic actors through a discussion of rational interest/actor, institutionalist, and organizational theories. We explore the complexity of the state and the many political actors within it. We then turn to an examination of the underlying factors that can lead to ethnic conflict (that can also diffuse or escalate it). Finally, we consider two types of states (hegemonic and neutral) and the domestic level responses to ethnic conflict—the options available to the state to resolve or at least minimize ethnic conflict in the state, including coercive mechanisms and national institutional responses, such as federalism and consociationalism.

Domestic Level Theories: Interests, Powers, and Organization

At the domestic level, the range of possible actors from powerful individuals to mass popular participation is quite staggering. For example, the term *domestic actors* can include politicians (elites at the individual level of analysis, discussed above), political parties, interest groups, or mass social movements. Theories about these actors take into account their diversity in size and impact. Before taking a look at some very specific factors considered to be causes of ethnic conflict, we present the general theories developed by scholars about political actors in general.

It is essential to note that theories of domestic actors tend to highlight three very important aspects: their interests, their powers, and their organization. Each actor has a set of interests, commonly referred to as his or her distribution of preferences among alternatives. In other words, when presented with a choice between two or more separate alternatives (be they policies, candidates, actions, or whatever) actors have one that they prefer more than the others, one that they like the least. All other possible alternatives are ranked somewhere between the most preferred and the least preferred.[55] Different actors may have very different interests. As an example, the Protestant community in Northern Ireland generally believes that rule by the British is preferable to rule by the Republic of Ireland. The interests of the Catholic community have typically been opposite that of the Protestant community, preferring to unite with the Republic of Ireland.

Sometimes actors have similar or common interests, as when two or more groups see benefits in a single policy or action. This may occur when numerous minority groups all seek the same change in how a government operates. A good example would be a number of minority groups pressing for an expansion of civil liberties to protect each of them from the dominant group.[56]

Each actor also has a set of powers, or in other words, a distribution of resources that he or she can use to achieve his or her goals. Groups vary greatly in their ownership of powers. The distribution of powers is usually the product of broad social processes. These processes may be long-term societal changes (for example, modernization or industrialization of the economy) or short-term upheavals (for example, a political revolution). Powers are often not equally distributed among the actors, or even among the different aspects of the society, with some actors having significant economic power but little military/violent power, political power, or almost any possible combination.[57] An example would be the Chinese in Malaysia who possess a great deal of the economic wealth of the country, while the Malays maintain most of the political control and occupy the political offices.

The third factor is organization. Groups organize in a way that best suits their interests and powers. The common organizational expression of the ethnic group is the political party. Political parties exist mainly to contest elections. They do so by organizing the opinions, values, ideologies, and policy desires of the citizens into a coherent political organization.[58] Political parties are organizations that provide candidates to serve in government. In the case of democracies, political parties present the electorate with a list of candidates with party platforms. Political parties also allow for political power to alternate as leaders from different political parties run for, and win, election. This means that political parties are crucial for democracies to work. While political parties play a particularly important role in democracies, political parties are also found in nondemocracies as well.[59]

Importantly, parties that represent ethnic communities translate ethnic demands into the electoral arena. Elections are a defining moment in all societies: in a developed society they signal the continuation of authority or its transfer from one group to another; in a developing society they can signal progress toward greater democracy or a step backwards.[60] Thus, the role of ethnic political parties is the key to understanding the way ethnic conflict is managed in a society. Timothy Sisk states that when electoral institutions promote centrist, cooperative politics among competing ethnic groups, the political parties will work to reduce conflict. He labels this "centripetalism" because the idea is to get parties to find a common center. Therefore, an interaction exists between political parties, their actions, and electoral institutions.[61] Such interactions and complex relationships are examined at the domestic level of analysis. We address the role of institutions in shaping the actions of domestic actors in more detail later in the chapter.

In essence, the organization of a political party seeks to win elections and control government. However, political parties are not the only organizational expression for ethnic groups. Paramilitary organizations (or guerilla armies) also exist. These groups operate outside the acceptable democratic or constitutional framework. Paramilitaries pursue an armed resistance against the dominant ethnic group and/or the state. They use violent means (for example, assassination, terrorism, bombings) to achieve their political goals. Examples of paramilitary groups include the Irish Republican Army (IRA) in Northern Ireland and the Tamil Tigers in Sri Lanka.

Interest groups, "social or political groups that represent the interests of their constituents," can take part in the political process and thereby influence the political and economic arenas within a state.[62] Social movements are formed when people do not believe that the state or other domestic actors (namely interest groups or political parties) have attended to their interests satisfactorily and undertake collective action.[63] Examples of social movements include labor movements, peace movements, women's movements, and, of course, ethnic groups mobilized to promote their interests.

Interests, powers, and organization of any domestic actor are constrained by the "rules of the game" in the relevant polity. These rules are set by the constitution, laws, contracts, treaties, and/or the courts. The rules limit the range of possible actions and proscribe the punishment for refusing to comply. For example, the constitution of Germany forbids anyone from organizing a political party with a fascist or communist ideology. Thus, even if a domestic actor had an interest in starting such a political party, they could only do so by breaking the rules, and then would be subject to punishment (which in this instance is incarceration).

What theories can account for how the interests, powers, and organization of domestic actors behave? This section examines three theories (rational interest/actor, institutional, and organization theories) of the behavior and actions of political actors in general.

Rational Choice/Interest Theories. Rational choice theories of political participation are based on an economic model. Kenneth Arrow began the rational choice school of political thought with his seminal work examining decision making and the rules used to arrive at a collective decision. His economic model emphasizes the ability of individual decision-makers to weigh the alternatives and select the option having maximum utility.[64] Anthony Downs goes one step further and develops an economic model to explain a citizen's rationale for casting a vote in an election. In short, a citizen would become a voter if the value of casting a vote exceeded the costs involved. The value was the difference between the favored candidate and other candidates multiplied by the likelihood of that vote making a difference as to who wins.[65] Both of these founding works of the rational choice school have a model of a person as a rational, self-interested calculator. In other words, humans pursue their best interests: they take actions that maximize gains and minimize losses.

Mancur Olson builds on rational choice theory to examine an empirical paradox: collective action. Collective action is action by a group of many, which often does not occur even though a clear rational interest exists for such action. Typically this paradox occurs because the cost of the action is borne by each individual but the benefit of the action is shared collectively. For example, supporters of democracy in an authoritarian state may want to change the system. But to do so they would have to march, rally, and protest while being observed and possibly retaliated against by the oppressive state regime. Democracy is a collective good that they would all share if it came to exist, but none would receive an individual, tangible benefit. However, on the part of those protesters who are jailed, beaten, or killed, a very individual cost is paid. In other words, "[t]hough all of the members of the group . . . have a common interest in obtaining this collective benefit, they have no common interest in paying the cost of providing that collective good."[66]

Collective action lies at the heart of ethnic conflict. Ethnicities typically organize into groups of various sizes and functions in which a common identity links to common interests. We also know from history that ethnic groups do indeed press their demands and take collective action. Olson challenges the rational interest theories to explain how this collective action would occur. He argues that small groups can approximate the rational actor model because a small portion of the group can collect enough benefits to provide the common benefit for the whole group. A typical example might be a small ethnic political party that campaigns for the larger political interests. The leaders of the party would obtain benefits from holding office, such as building careers (as would be seen at the individual level of analysis). But Olson argues that large groups are less likely than small groups to act coherently in pursuing their interests.[67]

Thus, explaining mass ethnic group mobilization and action appears not to be possible with just rational interest theories. "Selective incentives" can "coerce" individuals into working for the interests of the group. In particular, Olson highlights the role of social sanctions and social rewards. Within ethnic groups, social status and social acceptance are important qualities. He states that "[i]t is in the nature of social incentives that they can distinguish among individuals: the recalcitrant individual can be ostracized," and those who cooperate can be rewarded.[68] This occurs in many instances of ethnic group action, and it is very typical of mass mobilization. For example, the ethnic mobilization in Rwanda and

"classified as political, economic, and cultural," that account for ethnic conflict.[79] Weak political institutions,[80] political and economic stratification leading to serious divisions within a society, deteriorating economic conditions,[81] as well as frustration from unmet expectations[82] can lead ethnic groups and states to engage in aggressive behavior both internally and externally as a means to improve economic and political circumstances.[83]

In an assessment of the literature on internal conflict, Michael E. Brown sets out four key categories of factors that indicate the predisposition for violence: structural factors; political factors; economic/social factors; and cultural/perceptual factors."[84] There are three structural factors that he notes scholars have addressed: "weak states; intra-state security concerns [ethnic security dilemmas]; and ethnic geography."[85]

Weak state structures often result from government corruption and ineptitude. Weakened state structures make for a more permissive atmosphere for conflict to emerge between groups. Leaders may be engaged in power struggles, extensive human rights abuses occur, there is less ability to control borders, and ethnic groups begin to push for their demands and compete with each other for resources. Consequently, a weak state is unable to respond effectively to their demands, with conflict the likely result. One can see this in the years following the Soviet withdrawal from Afghanistan in 1985 and the emergence of internal conflict between competing groups. The weak central government could not effectively respond and end the fighting.[86]

In terms of intrastate security concerns, as long as the in-group views the outgroup in negative terms (enemy image) and perceives a threat to its own identity, there will be a lack of trust between the groups. Mistrust reinforces the negative perceptions each group has of the other, especially the perception of hostile intentions, and thus each group may be inclined to threaten the other, leading to counterthreats and a spiral of escalation of the conflict. This cycle of mistrust and perception of hostile intentions results in the security dilemma, a concept found in the international relations literature within political science. In essence, when states take action to increase their own security, other states feel less secure and then take actions to increase their security in turn. In the end, all are less secure.[87] The security dilemma can also apply to ethnic and nationalist groups, as noted in chapter 1. When one group threatens another, the competition fuels the mutual mistrust that further aggravates the already tense relationship (this becomes even more of an issue when the state is weak and unable to mediate between ethnic groups). Rather than backing down in the face of threats, the other group may react with counterthreats, thereby producing a spiral of conflict. For example, in the few short years leading to the breakup of Yugoslavia, actions by both Serbs and Croats reinforced the mistrust both sides had of the other and threats to each other's identity. As noted by Barry Posen, policies undertaken by the Croatian government fueled the threats perceived by the Serbs living in the republic. For example, the Croatian government asked Serbs to take an oath of loyalty, and replaced Serbian police with Croats. The Serb minority's perception of the likelihood of further threats in the future led them to consider offensive actions against Croats.[88]

Moreover, the security dilemma and concomitant mistrust can lead to group conflict if one group is dominant over another, as is the case in Northern Ireland, where the Protestants are the majority and dominate in the areas of the police forces, professional services, government services, nonmanual labor, and overall employment. The disproportional dominance of Protestants in these various areas has led to long-term inequality and tensions with Catholics. The out-group, or minority (in this case, Irish Catholics), may perceive itself as having no recourse to address its complaints, furthering the conflict between the groups.[89]

Trying to overcome the security dilemma is crucial to resolving conflicts, including nationalist and ethnic ones. Reducing the security dilemma involves establishing trust, credible commitments, and a changed image of the enemy. If groups maintain mistrust resulting from the security dilemma, they are unlikely to be able to reach agreement in order to resolve their differences. Conversely, mutual trust makes it possible for groups and states to negotiate agreements and increase cooperation. Only over time can a group establish a reputation for being trustworthy, particularly by fulfilling its obligations.[90]

The last structural factor noted by Brown is ethnic geography. He asserts that "states with ethnic minorities are more prone to conflict than others, and certain kinds of ethnic demographics are more problematic than others."[91] Ethnic minority groups are either intermingled with each other or live in their own regions within a state. In both cases, conflict can erupt (secessionist demands for those living in their own regions, for example). Scholars repeatedly note the ethnic conflicts that emerged in the aftermath of the colonial period in Africa. When the arbitrary borders of the colonial entities were established, the newly independent states had to contend with the various ethnic divisions within their territorial boundaries. Significant numbers of ethnic groups live in the majority of African states. The problem is that many of these groups are long-time enemies, fueling the possibility of conflict.[92]

The political factors that Brown deals with include "discriminatory political institutions; exclusionary national ideologies; inter-group politics; and elite politics."[93] At the end of the day, political issues are about the control and status of territory—and which ethnic group has control of the state institutions.[94] When the political institutions of a state favor one group over another (through restrictions on the ability to vote in elections or run for public office),[95] in other words a hegemonic state,[96] the out-group is likely to feel resentment and seek to change the discriminatory institutions. The legitimacy of a state's institutions is important for reducing the chances of ethnic conflict erupting. Second, in addition to the effects of discriminatory political institutions, when a state is defined by ethnic nationalism, rather than civic nationalism, ethnic conflict is more likely to occur.[97] With ethnic nationalism, certain ethnic groups are included, and others are excluded. In civic nationalism, all people are given the same rights regardless of ethnic identity. One finds most democracies promoting civic nationalism and thus lessening the potential for conflict between groups.[98]

The third political factor Brown addresses is intergroup politics: "Conflict is especially likely if objectives are incompatible, groups are strong and determined, action is feasible, success is possible, and if inter-group comparisons lead to competition, anxiety, and fears of being dominated." Changes in the balance of power between ethnic groups can lead to instability, and increase the possibility of conflict.[99] The emergence of war in Yugoslavia resulted in many ways from fears of the shift in power from Yugoslavia's federal government, which was dominated by Serbs, to the various republics, such as Slovenia and Croatia. The shift in power meant a change in the ethnic balance of power in the state as a whole and eventually led to war when Slovenia and Croatia sought to secede in order to ensure their security and protect themselves from Serb domination.[100]

The fourth political factor Brown discusses is elite politics—the importance of politicians who take advantage of the instability in a society by exploiting ethnic sentiments.[101] We addressed elite politics, namely the elites themselves, in the individual level of analysis section, which stresses the instrumentalist explanation for ethnic conflict: elites use ethnicity as a means to maintain or gain power.

Economic and social factors encompass "economic problems" (such as the transition to a market economy that many of the states of the former Soviet bloc have experienced), "discriminatory economic systems," which can lead to resentment if one ethnic group is favored over another, and finally, "economic development and modernization" (as discussed in chapter 1 on modernization theories) in which economic and political expectations increase, which the state is often not able to meet.[102] Disputes between ethnic groups revolve around access to jobs in the government. Disputes may also result from rights related to employment in the private sector, rights "that may be regulated by rules imposed by the state."[103] These economic and social factors, in which inequities between ethnic groups are prevalent, can lead to conflict. The inequality in access to economic resources is one of the causes of the conflict in Northern Ireland between Protestants and Catholics. Protestants remain dominant in higher paying jobs, employment in the police forces, and so forth, relative to Catholics.

Finally, cultural discrimination against minority ethnic groups can serve as a trigger for conflict. For example, certain ethnic groups may be given preference for educational opportunities over another group.[104] Ethnic conflicts are often the result of conflict over language and religion—which language, which religion is the dominant one in a society.[105] In essence, such conflicts arise due to the "struggle over relative status and position in society."[106] For example, in Canada there have been periodic calls for Quebec to secede. In large part these tensions are rooted in the division between English-speakers and French-speakers. In 1969 these tensions led the federal government to recognize both as the official languages of the country. Importantly, each province is also able to endorse language policies with regard to issues that fall under the authority of the provincial governments. As a result, French is the official language of Quebec, while English is the official language in most of the other provinces.[107]

In addition to cultural factors, Brown also notes the importance of perceptual factors. By this he means the "group histories and group perceptions of themselves and others."[108] While there is definitely historical evidence of certain groups having legitimate grievances about past treatment (related to the "ancient hatreds" argument), groups also "whitewash and glorify their own histories, and they often demonize their neighbors, rivals, and adversaries."[109] As noted by Van Evera, in the case of the former Yugoslavia, Croatian politicians whitewashed the actions of the Croatian Ustashe, who had murdered significant numbers of Serbs during World War II. These actions only reinforced Serbs' perception of insecurity vis-à-vis the Croats, contributing to Serb hostility that played a significant role in the outbreak of the war between Serbia and Croatia in 1991–1992.[110] The perceptions groups have of themselves (usually favorable) and of others (enemy images) can be self-fulfilling prophecies and lead to conflict.

These cultural and perceptual factors are, in essence, about identity. While resource issues are sources of conflict, scholars increasingly note the importance of intangible factors, such as identity, as sources of conflict. This does not mean that resource issues and identity issues are mutually exclusive as causes of conflict—rather, "bargaining over those [resource] issues without prior and adequate attention first to identity issues has the effect of further polarizing the parties" to conflict.[111]

As noted in chapter 1, social identity theory provides the link between primordial sentiments and the social construction of identity. Originated by Henri Tajfel, social identity theory asserts that "humans define themselves, as well as others, largely in terms of the social groups to which they belong." In identifying with a group, individuals also distinguish themselves from those in other groups. Weldon notes that the social groups to which individuals belong endure because such groups "are also the primary vehicles for childhood and cultural socialization," molding people's views of the world.[112] Social identity theory links to an individual's psychological need to belong to a group. Moreover, belonging to a group (group identity) enhances an individual's self-esteem, especially if people believe not only that their group is different but that those differences indicate that their group is better than the other groups.[113] The collective self-esteem that comes from positive feelings about one's own group necessitates the (negative) comparison to an out-group.[114]

Importantly, in-group identity and social categorization can lead to discrimination against other groups. The lack of tolerance for minority groups (and discrimination against them) results, as recent research shows, from "strong ingroup identities, low self-esteem, and perceptions of threat."[115] Negative perceptions of the enemy (out-group) and mutual distrust fuel the perception of threat and can lead to conflict between groups. Jeff Spinner-Halev and Elizabeth Theiss-Morse observe that if an in-group believes that the natural hostility of the out-group is causing the conflict, the in-group may step up its aggressive actions preemptively as a means to gain perceived control of the situation at hand.[116]

Esman addresses psychological (perceptual) factors that contribute to ethnic conflict. However, he argues that the underlying causes of conflict are "disputes over real issues such as relative power (politics), material resources (economics), or respect (culture)."[117] What one often observes in cases of ethnic conflict is that when the conflict is underway, concerns about security and status become connected. Security fears that come from real violence tend to bolster the fear of cultural extinction of the group.[118] Lake and Rothchild declare that the most common cause of ethnic conflict is "collective fears of the future." There are two types of fears of the future. One involves the fear of "assimilation into a dominant culture and hegemonic state." The other involves the "fear for their physical safety and survival."[119] Groups experience physical insecurity, which is compounded by information failures (information about other groups' intentions and capabilities), problems of credible commitment by the government to protect the groups, and the security dilemma (inducing one group to preemptively use force against the threatening group). The information failures, security dilemma, and problems of credible commitments by the government weaken the state, and the state is no longer able to mediate between groups. A weakened state is even less able to "provide credible guarantees of protection for groups." The fear groups perceive (either real or imagined) is exacerbated. In the end, Lake and Rothchild conclude, these three strategic dilemmas lead to conflict.[120]

In support of the argument that tangible issues are sources of conflict, a recent study by Clayton Peoples found that the relationship between political discrimination against minorities and the likelihood of interethnic violence was quite strong. While the relationship between economic and cultural discrimination and interethnic violence was not statistically significant, he argues that these other types of discrimination nonetheless may have an effect on interethnic violence because of existing political discrimination. Groups facing political discrimination are unlikely to be able to overcome other types of discrimination.[121]

The above discussion of the domestic level indicates that the factors that account for the emergence of ethnic conflict are varied. What matters is determining which factors are relevant for a particular ethnic conflict. From there, one can determine which responses to ethnic conflict may be more successful, and which are likely to fail. We explore the domestic level responses to ethnic violence in the next section.

Domestic Level Responses to Violence: The State and Institutions

Inherent in this discussion of domestic level theories and factors that can lead to ethnic conflict is how the sociopolitical context creates interests, power, and organization of ethnic actors. The different theories and factors point to different reasons for ethnic conflict, but all identify ethnic actors as agents of the conflict. A number of the above theories establish that once political actors are mobilized, new interests are created and new demands occur that may alter the underlying distribution of resources. Therefore, once ethnic conflict is initiated the actors may create the conditions necessary to perpetuate the conflict, whether purposefully or unintentionally, regardless of the original cause. This claim of agency, moreover, is an important one in the eventual resolution of ethnic conflict, for addressing the problem means not only assessing the root cause but also modifying the actions of the actors. Resolving internal conflict is difficult. The political and economic systems are weak or nonexistent. Civil society needs to be rebuilt. Warring parties find it difficult to give up their weapons. Trust must be established, which is difficult when people have witnessed horrific acts of bloodshed and may want revenge instead.[122]

Governments may respond to domestic ethnic tensions and conflicts by granting minority rights, territorial autonomy, and federalism as well as by setting up consociational structures in which ethnic groups are given representation in the policy-making arena. Governments may also respond by engaging in coercion and repression against ethnic groups.[123] The governmental response to violence is predicated on whether the goal of the government is conflict management or conflict settlement. According to Adam Przeworski, conflict management is processing and reducing the severity of ethnic conflict. This is usually a short-term approach to allow for a change in conditions that may make a lasting peace more possible. As such, the conflict management approach recognizes that ethnic conflict is inherent in multicultural societies and that it may not be possible to eliminate it. When ethnic conflict occurs it is mediated and a solution to the current problem is formulated and implemented.[124]

Barbara Harff and Ted Gurr proffer three domestic level principles to manage ethnic conflict. First, the rights of minorities should be recognized and promoted by both the state and civil society. The recognition and promotion of the rights of minorities means that "groups should be free from discrimination based on race, national origin, language, or religion." Moreover, minority groups should also have the right "to organize and act politically." The ability to organize and act in the political sphere means that groups can ensure their group interests.[125] Second, to protect minority rights, institutions should both be democratic and involve power sharing. Democratic political systems enable organized minorities to use the party system as well as interest groups in order to influence the policy decisions that matter to the group. In addition, in democratic systems the peaceful resolution of conflicts is accepted and expected. Leaders of minority groups are expected to espouse moderate, rather than extreme, political goals, and to use nonviolence in achieving them.[126] Third, when conflicts involve issues of self-determination, "negotiations for autonomy within existing states," rather than secession and independence, provide the best solution. Regional autonomy, or federalism, provides for protection of group rights and increased access to decision making at the local and regional level, and even at the central government level.[127] We examine these different responses in more detail later in this section.

Conflict settlement goes further than conflict management. Stefan Wolff defines conflict settlement as aiming at establishing an institutional structure that provides a venue for ethnic groups to have their grievances heard and addressed such that groups will find it in their interest to pursue compromise rather than violence as a means to achieve their goals.[128] In the end, however, as Esman cautions, ethnic-based differences are very rarely "settled or resolved" when groups remain "under the same political roof." Without separation, the likelihood of new grievances emerging is high. As a result, at best the hope is that the management and regulation of future grievances is possible and acceptable to the various groups involved. In this way, the maintenance of peace is ensured, and ethnic differences can be minimized.[129]

State Responses to Ethnic Conflict. A state's response to ethnic conflict depends on whether the state hopes to manage the situation to the degree that outright violence and conflict is unlikely—or to achieve a stable and long-lasting settlement of the ethnic conflict. The difficulty in regard to ethnic conflict is that governmental actors and their actions vary greatly. Ilan Peleg provides a useful distinction between the neutral state that seeks to regulate conflict within its sovereignty and the hegemonic state that promotes the interests of the dominant ethnic group. The role of governmental actors is very different in these two types of states, although the actors are not.[130] Moreover, the responses to ethnic conflict by these two types of states differ.

In a hegemonic state, governmental actors are not neutral; instead, they favor and promote the rights of one ethnic group over the others. For example, during Apartheid in South Africa, the courts enforced a number of laws that were intended to strip rights away from Black South Africans. One of these laws, the Native Acts of 1956, removed the right of appeal from Blacks who were forced from their lands.[131]

Of course, when the hegemonic state is nondemocratic, the role of governmental actors in ethnic conflict is greatly increased. Without a legitimate check on their use of force (since authoritarian leaders are not accountable to the electorate and cannot be voted out of office for unpopular policies), governmental actors can effectively create and/or exacerbate ethnic conflict. "Death Squads" are a particularly horrendous example. Typically comprised of a small group of soldiers and/or police, death squads commit killings, coercion, torture, and extortion against the enemies of the state. The government denies the existence of the death squads while tacitly condoning or, at the very least, complicitly turning a blind eye to their behavior. Death squads in Central America operated in the 1980s and 1990s to terrorize indigenous populations as well as the political opposition.[132]

Thus, a hegemonic state manages conflict by transforming the state for use by the dominant ethnic group, and is thus exclusivist in nature. As Peleg points out, "having been internalized, hegemonic ethnicity is perceived as 'natural,' making the use and abuse of state power for exclusive ethnic goals normal and non-controversial."[133] The state, in essence, engages in a form of coercion, in which the dominant group pursues policies that ensure its control over other groups.[134] Likewise, the state institutions will be transformed to enshrine the hegemonic rule. Thus, the severity and duration of ethnic conflict is reduced and managed by the promotion of the dominant group's rights and the disregard for other groups' rights. It is clear that such a state is not democratic.[135]

If the state is nominally or previously democratic, it is likely to become illiberal. Peleg identifies two major variants of illiberal democracies and their approach to the management of ethnic conflict: separationist and assimilationist. In the separationist variant the dominant group "desires to keep itself separate and superior vis-à-vis the dominated group." Sri Lanka and Israel provide good examples of this type of hegemonic state (detailed in chapters 6 and 7). In both cases, the state (and its institutions) is identified exclusively with a particular dominant group (Sri Lankans and Jews, respectively).[136]

In the assimilationist variant, the dominant group tries to convert the minorities into the dominant culture. Turkey's attempt to transform the Kurdish minority is one such example.[137] Assimilationist attempts by hegemonic states can be a cause of conflict when the subordinate group does not accept assimilation, perhaps rebelling against the dominant ethnic group.[138] When the French in Algeria (a French colony from the mid-nineteenth century until independence in 1962) invoked their *mission civilisatrice* (civilizing mission), they were attempting to assimilate Algerians, to make them into Frenchmen/-women. The French believed that they had a right to rule over the Algerians, and, more important, that Algerians must become French through the dominance of the French language, laws, and so forth, at the expense of the indigenous population's culture.[139] Such a policy eventually failed, and ethnic conflict was the result, as Algerians rebelled against French colonial rule, eventually leading to Algeria's independence.

Typically, the dominant group in hegemonic states seeks to settle the conflict through the expulsion or elimination of the minority group(s). The hegemonic group tries to create a purely ethnic state. This process may entail mass expulsions and genocide.[140] In the breakup of Yugoslavia, the Serbian reliance on "ethnic cleansing" of the Croat and Muslim minorities is an example of a hegemonic state's "solution" to ethnic conflict. The mass genocidal behavior of the citizens of Rwanda and Burundi also fit into this category, as does the treatment of the African minority in Sudan by the Islamic government that rules the country.

In the end, in order "to keep the peace" once a conflict has taken place, hegemonic states engage in control policies. In doing so, Byman argues, hegemonic states attempt to lessen the security dilemma while also keeping in check the subordinate ethnic groups, but at the same time assuring the dominant groups that their dominance is guaranteed. Control policies include the use of brute force ("use of force against ethnic group members regardless of ethnic political activity," just because they are members of a group) and selective control (use of force against those who might undertake "ethnic political activity," in order to prevent them from doing so).[141] While such policies might lessen the security dilemma, these policies are inherently unstable because over time subordinate groups are likely to challenge the dominant group for access to the state institutions and an end to discriminatory policies. As subordinate groups mobilize, both politically and socially, they challenge the dominant group's hegemonic position, leading to future conflict.[142]

In a neutral state, the governmental actors do not favor one ethnicity over another; instead, they seek to regulate conflict between the groups. For example, in most Western societies with institutionalized democracy and social rights, the courts do not limit the rights of individuals on the basis of ethnicity. The role of the courts is to be "color-blind" and enforce the laws without any diminution of a person's status due to his or her ethnic background.[143] Thus, a neutral state typically follows either conflict management or settlement in a similar way: by implementing a policy or set of policies that recognize, promote, and protect minority rights. These policies may range from antidiscrimination laws, constitutional protections, and rights of political association and organization to programs to compensate for and/or reverse patterns of historical prejudice and discrimination.[144] Such states, often called accommodationist states, promote the inclusive political participation of all members of society.[145] Democratic institutions and legitimate representative bodies typically help protect minority rights. William Riker persuasively argues that only through the competition of interests in a liberal, plural, and democratic framework are the rights of all, the majority and the minorities, protected.[146] Importantly, according to Peleg, the liberal state takes a neutral position with regard to ethnicity. Ethnicity is neither promoted nor opposed. Moreover, preferential treatment of one ethnicity rather than another is not extended by the government.[147]

When confronted with violent ethnic conflict, the neutral state uses governmental resources such as the military or police to cordon off violence and protect noncombatants. Once the level of violence has decreased, the government turns its attention toward conflict settlement, usually through institutional reform.[148] A good example of this process is the resumption of democracy in Spain following the death of the dictator Francisco Franco in 1975. Confronted with nationalist calls for autonomy and the threat of violence from armed paramilitary groups, the government established a new quasi-federal distribution of authority. A number of Autonomous Communities were established to promote the rights of minorities and give them some regional authority. When paramilitary groups such as the Basque separatists ETA (Euskadi Ta Askatasuna) resume their violent campaign against the Spanish state, the government uses the legal system to prosecute the combatants. Importantly, the Spanish state remains neutral as the courts treat the separatists as ordinary criminals and not as members of an underprivileged ethnic minority.[149]

Democracy, Domestic Power-Sharing Institutions, and Conflict Management: Liberalism, Consociationalism, and Federalism. The institutional approach emphasizes the role of rules and governing bodies in modifying the behavior of individuals, elites, and groups. The study of "constitutional engineering" suggests that institutions can play a pivotal role in pushing a society toward a more stable, and, hopefully, a more democratic, structure.

As previously mentioned, a major difficulty in deeply divided societies is that relationships between groups, especially between the more dominant ethnic group and the minority groups, are often quite problematic. The domination of the state and/or government by one ethnic group complicates the working of democracy. Defining democracy is difficult, and there are many definitions offered by prominent scholars. Larry Diamond, Juan Linz, and Seymour Lipset study the working of democracy in divided societies, and thus their definition is helpful in understanding how democracy performs in divided societies.[150]

Diamond, Linz, and Lipset see democracy as a system in which three conditions are constant. First, competition between individuals and groups must be meaningful. In other words, elections and all activities surrounding them must be fair and open and produce legitimate results. Second, participation should be inclusive. Individuals and groups of all types should be able to contribute to elections, politics, and policies. Third, there need to be freedoms and liberties to ensure that participation, expression, and other rights are exercised by all individuals.[151]

Of course, producing such a democratic model requires the establishment of governmental institutions. Exclusivist models are designed to promote and enshrine the interests of only the dominant group (for example, as Apartheid did in South Africa), while accommodationist models are inclusive. The set of institutions promoted and created to establish a working democracy following the model of Diamond, Linz, and Lipset is considered an "accommodationist" model.[152]

There are two competing accommodationist democratic models: liberal and consociational. The liberal model, often referred to as the Anglo-American model, creates institutions that remain neutral in regard to ethnicity. Based on the writings of John Locke, John Stuart Mill, and others, the liberal model emphasizes individual liberties and freedoms. Citizens are equal under the law, enjoy a set of protected rights, and live under a limited government. Donald Horowitz cites a theoretical basis for electoral engineering aimed at accommodation in deeply divided societies. He argues that election rules that do not simply replicate existing ethnic groups, but rather encourage cross-group cooperation, can break down the salience of ethnic identities.[153] Sisk classifies such an approach as "centripetal."[154] The engineered institutions attempt to pull the ethnic groups and political parties toward a common center. Benjamin Reilly produces evidence that such centripetal institutions can produce promising results.[155]

Thus, the liberal institutions do not recognize any particular ethnicity as preferential, as the institutions generally do not recognize ethnicity at all! Electoral engineering favors the role of individual voters, individual candidates, and negotiation by non-ethnic groups in the legislature. This model also relies heavily on the power of constitutions and courts to regulate conflict within the system and deliver fair judgments. Further, in a liberal democracy, the state is focused on assimilation and integration of the different ethnic groups.[156]

One of the benefits of the liberal model is that it de-emphasizes ethnicity as a salient trait for political action. In order to do so, there is usually a need to supersede current ethnic identities with a common, overlapping (superordinate) identity. Supporters of the liberal model point to the United States (among other countries) as a successful application of the liberal model.[157] An "American" identity is developed and becomes more salient and dominant than the many different, and fractured, ethnic identities. In essence, the liberal model attempts to move a divided society away from division and toward consensus in a demobilization of ethnic appeals and ethnic conflict, and the emergence of a civic nationalism. Of course, critics argue that the civic-ethnic nationalism divide "is more a myth than a reality." As Spinner-Halev and Theiss-Morse note, in addressing the critics of the civic-ethnic nationalism division, "States are not merely containers of political practices; there is no such thing as a culturally neutral state. Almost all states teach a certain kind of history to their citizens; celebrate certain holidays, many with cultural and religious meanings; and use one or perhaps two languages. All of these are culturally-laden practices."[158] Furthermore, as Esman observes, complete integration takes a long time and also risks the loss of cultural diversity if people integrate fully.[159]

The consociational model differs sharply from the liberal model. Far from ignoring ethnic differences and in direct opposition to the liberal model, the consociational model recognizes the existence of distinct ethnicities (although the state itself is neutral, with no one ethnic group dominant as in the hegemonic state). Furthermore, supporters of the consociational model contend that the establishment of a stable and just society must be based on the explicit participation of the ethnic groups. Institutions should be created that allow ethnic groups to enter into agreement and accommodation. Such an agreement protects groups' rights and interests.[160] Arend Lijphart built his consociational model from his study of small, continental European nations (that is, Belgium, the Netherlands, and Switzerland). He claims that consociational institutions produced elite accommodation and the development of stable, productive societies while still preserving ethnic and group identities.[161]

Lijphart argues that in order to build a consociational model, the state must actively seek reconciliation between hostile ethnic constituencies. Also, the final agreement must be the product of negotiation between power-sharing elites, and not the product of any internal or external coercion. Elite cooperation would then ameliorate the community conflict. To arrive at this elite-driven compromise, four institutions are necessary: proportional representation, federalism, grand coalition, and mutual veto. Proportional representation for elections ensures that ethnic differences, and their representation by political parties, are replicated in the legislature. This form of election guarantees that ethnic groups have a legitimate forum to voice their concerns and interests. Federalism creates regional autonomy for ethnic groups. Mechanisms to create a "grand coalition" government promote a shared executive. The mutual veto gives each significant ethnic group the ability to halt legislation and/or executive decisions.[162]

When ethnic groups are intermingled, consociational institutions offer a solution because minority groups are represented in the central government and thus have an opportunity to engage in the act of governing.[163] I. William Zartman argues that consociational institutions can create new and overlapping identities, such as multiethnic or trans-ethnic coalitions that move beyond singularly ethnic parties and ethnic majorities.[164] Indeed, Lijphart argues that consociational institutions are responsible for the ethnic cooperation that has brought peace and harmony to divided Belgium.[165]

Federalism offers a solution to ethnic conflict when ethnic groups are territorially (regionally) concentrated because the local political institutions and competition become the focal point for the tension and hostility that would otherwise be directed at the central government.[166] Federalism can be successful if it raises the costs of secession. For example, in certain towns in Kenya, such as Nairobi and Mombasa, the Luo occupy important positions "outside their regions." Therefore, for the Luo, secession is costly because of the loss of significant opportunities in other regions in Kenya were they to secede.[167]

Some scholars argue that federalism is not necessary for power sharing and vice versa. A state could give a region territorial autonomy but not shared power at the central government level.[168] Consequently, many scholars make persuasive arguments that federalism provides the best possible government for a nation of considerable ethnic and regional disparity. Especially in territorial federations, federalism is an institutional arrangement that provides ethnic and/or regional communities with due territorial recognition.[169] Federalism may also aid in the management of conflict by providing many political centers, each of which may be the locus of resolving disputes.[170] Federalism may constrain central power, thus allowing for more regional autonomy.[171] Alexander Murphy posits that federal systems provide incentives for groups to create separate policy within their territorial unit. While such policy variance may be difficult for the state as a whole, it may eliminate, or at least ameliorate, conflict between regional units.[172] More generally, Sharda Rath goes so far as to say that federalism promotes peace, security, strength, democracy, liberty, and identity.[173]

Federalism is not without its critics. K. C. Wheare agrees that federalism is one method by which to solve ethnic conflict. However, Wheare argues that federalism may produce a constitutional crisis in some instances. Such a crisis can occur because of the built-in disequilibrium in federalism: the struggle between the imposition of common values by the central government and the jealous protection of local powers by regional units.[174] Jonathan Lemco elucidates a dozen prerequisites for federalism to be an effective method of stemming of state dissolution in multiethnic states.[175]

Federalism also suffers from the problem that minority groups within the state remain a minority in positions at the federal level.[176] For example, in the former Yugoslavia, each federal republic became ethnically based.[177] The minority groups within Serbian territory felt threatened by the increasingly ethnically focused actions of the Serbian government, and President Slobodan Milosevic in particular. Each group sought to further its interests, thereby contributing to the ethnic security dilemma within each republic. Moreover, the fear always exists that regional leaders will seek further autonomy and separation from the central government, leading to demands for independence.[178]

Thus, not everyone agrees that consociational and federal institutions are necessarily benevolent or successful. Critics make several arguments. First, one line of thought suggests that the direction of causation points the wrong way. Institutional change does not lead to social change. Rather, the moderation of cleavages (social change) allows the successful implementation of democratic institutions.[179] Conflict reduction requires mechanisms to disperse the loci of power, emphasize intra-ethnic divisions, and provide incentives for elite cooperation. Second, elite accommodation may lead to political compromise, but it does not lead to a long-term solution to the divided society, which is often the source of the conflict. For example, Cameron Ross argues that federalism allows authoritarianism to flourish in many of Russia's eighty-nine regions and republics.[180] Relatedly, Barbara Walter argues that while elites might buy into the consociational structure, the masses may not, and thus the consociational agreement is undemocratic.[181] Third, ethnic groups often do not want to cooperate with each other, but cooperation is necessary for effective government under a proportional representation system as found in consociational structures. Fourth and finally, a consociational structure can solidify (and perhaps exacerbate) ethnic divisions by making ethnicity more salient. Institutions that separate groups into hierarchical/geographic political units (for example, federalism) sharpen social divisions.[182] Political parties tend to reflect this salience by promoting themselves as ethnically based.[183] For example, as Yugoslavia's breakup occurred, political parties defined themselves in ethnic terms, and voting in elections held in 1990 reflected the nationalist/ethnic divisions within the republics. The use of the Alternative Vote in Bosnia-Herzegovina led to elections that were effectively an "ethnic census."[184] One of Lijphart's consociationalist model successes, Belgium, has faced challenges from the two dominant ethnic groups, Flemish and Walloons, in recent years. The wealthier Flemish region has demanded greater autonomy, which is resisted by the francophones living in Wallonia, the poorer region. The francophones in Wallonia worry that any reforms will lead to reductions in funding. Such a reduction in funding to the region would impact the region's economy, already declining relative to that of the Flemish region. The Flemish parties seek to split the bilingual electoral constituency, Brussels-Halle-Vilvoorde (BHV). In doing so, Halle and Vilvoorde, the Dutch-speaking components, would "become part of neighboring Flemish voting districts to the north." Constitutionally bilingual Brussels would become a discrete district.[185]

Kanchan Chandra has also noted that when "linking the politicization of ethnic divisions with the destabilization of democracy" what often happens is the "out-bidding effect." Ethnic outbidding occurs when ethnic divisions have become politicized to the extent that political parties are defined ethnically. As Chandra explains with regard to theories of ethnic outbidding, "the emergence of even a single ethnic party 'infects' the rest of the party system, leading to a spiral of extreme ethnic bids that destroy competitive politics altogether." The result can destabilize democratic states.[186] Chandra argues, however, that ethnic parties can have a positive effect on democracy, but this depends on whether the institutions are able to encourage the overlapping elements of ethnic identity (for example, different ethnic groups that share the same religion).[187] The moderation of ethnic outbidding can occur through the institutionalization of cross-cutting cleavages. Chandra provides the example of India (where there are cross-cutting cleavages in terms of religion and language that have been institutionalized in the constitution as well as in policy areas such as employment and education), in which marginal parties have engaged in ethnic outbidding, with centrist political behavior occurring afterwards.[188] An example of language laws as indicators of institutionalized cross-cutting cleavages is presented by Finland. According to Spinner-Havel and Theiss-Morse, "In Finland members of a linguistic minority (Finnish or Swedish) that constitutes at least 8 percent of a municipality have the right to speak with government officials in their native tongue; once the 8 percent threshold is met, this linguistic right can only be revoked if the minority speakers fall to 6 percent." In this way, they argue, linguistic rights are given to groups, but the set-up also provides for the change in group identities and the emergence of cross-ethnic alliances.[189]

Additionally, if the proportionality of the allocation is considered unalterable, problems may arise when the actual proportional distribution of groups changes.[190] For example, Lebanon's government was structured as a consociational democracy from the time of independence in 1943 until 1975, when civil war erupted. The relative importance of the top government positions reflected the proportion of the population of each sect: a Maronite Christian president, a Sunni Muslim prime minister, a Shiite Muslim chair of the legislature, and a Greek Orthodox deputy chair and deputy prime minister. While this arrangement worked for three decades, it faced the challenge of the changing proportionality of the population. The Christian sects had been a majority in the earlier census and thus were allocated the position of president. Over time, however, the proportion of the Muslim population overtook the Christian population, thereby leading to demands by the Muslim sects that the composition of the government reflect the changed status. Soon, periodic clashes between groups erupted into full-scale civil war.[191]

There is yet another difficulty with the consociational model: it neglects the international dimension of ethnic conflict. Consociational agreements focus exclusively on domestic institutions. Ethnic conflict often has an international component, and institutional design has to take this into account. International institutions (as noted in the section on the international level of analysis), particularly cross-border legislative or parliamentary institutions, can promote overlapping (superordinate) identities, such as people having both a European identity and national identity. Cross-cutting cleavages could encourage more moderate behavior and nonviolent conflict. Consequently, a mechanism—namely institutions—that can promote overlapping identities may afford the means to resolve, or at least reduce, conflict between opposing groups that results from inequality. In a similar fashion to the logic of the social constructivist approach, these overlapping identities may ameliorate conflict by creating forums for expression, opportunities for cooperation, and development of mutual interests.[192] The problem is that while identities are not fixed (in contradiction of the primordialist approach to ethnic identity), they are hard to change. As Byman maintains, if a person is a member of a group that has experienced violence directed at it by virtue of group identity, "that identity becomes powerful and far more salient than competing ones."[193]

These critiques of consociationalism and federalism demonstrate the limits and rarity of democratic participatory systems in ethnically divided states. In the end, attempting to transition to democracy is difficult when groups harbor significant distrust and fears of insecurity, political institutions are weak, there are fears that elections will lead to undemocratic outcomes (tyranny of the majority), and ethnic elites use their democratic freedoms (freedom of the press, etc.) to disseminate aggressive ideas and policies.[194] Although democracy may be difficult to attain, that does not mean that states should not attempt to establish democratic institutions. As Byman observes, given that democracy has a proven track record in keeping the peace within societies, democracy as a solution must be front and center in addressing ethnic conflict.[195]

In fact, in an analysis of cases of success and failure in terms of power sharing in ethnically diverse states, Schneckener proffers six structure-oriented and five actor-oriented factors that account for success. The six structure-oriented factors are (1) relative equilibrium of the various ethnic groups so that no one group is a clear majority in the state or region; (2) no considerable socioeconomic differences between the groups such that one group is at a significant disadvantage relative to the other group; (3) territorial segmentation (federalism, or even segregation of cities within a region); (4) overarching, shared identity to the region or state; (5) cross-cutting cleavages leading to overlapping identities and memberships; and (6) moderate pluralism such that ethnic groups are represented by more than one political party, thereby leading to a moderate multiparty political system.[196] The actor-oriented factors are (1) dominant elites (discussed in the individual level section); (2) respect for the existing status quo; (3) mutual understanding and traditions of compromise by the elites; (4) participation by all groups, such that they are represented at any negotiations as well as in the actual power-sharing system (this includes incorporation of paramilitary and extremist groups); and (5) a compromise solution that is arrived at internally rather than imposed from the outside.[197] Schneckener finds that the actor-oriented factors are more important than the structure-oriented ones in terms of successful management of ethnic conflict.[198] He shows that cabinet governments (rather than presidential systems), flexible proportional rules, conditional veto rights, an institutional link between the self-governing bodies and the central power-sharing body (thereby limiting segmental autonomy to certain issues), and political and judicial mechanisms should be utilized for mediating and settling conflicts.[199]

Yet, Jonathan Hearn cautions that while scholars analyze "general categories of ethnic conflict and political instability," examining particular cases may lead to the recognition of specific solutions that might not be recommended by "a single set of general prescriptions."[200] As Eiki Berg and Guy Ben-Porat argue, tackling the underlying cultural and structural causes of conflict and altering the relations between conflicting groups are the means to settle protracted conflicts.[201] In many cases, these underlying roots of conflict are found at the domestic level of analysis, and thus their solutions may be found there as well.

INTERNATIONAL LEVEL

Kenneth N. Waltz's influential book *Man, the State, and War* used the levels of analysis to understand the outbreak of international war. He argued that the international, or third, image, best captures why wars occur. The anarchic international system, in which no central authority (such as a world government) exists over states, means that states have to engage in self-help to ensure their security and survival. He asserts that "there is a constant possibility of war in a world in which there are two or more states each seeking to promote a set of interests and having no agency above them upon which they can rely for protection."[202] The other two levels (domestic and individual) can explain the immediate causes of war in the sense that a state's decision to go to war depends on several factors, such as power, interest, regime type, history, size, and location. As he contends, "States are motivated to attack each other and to defend themselves by the reason and/or passion of the comparatively few who make policies for states and of the many more who influence the few."[203]

He claims that the international system explains the outbreak of war between states. His is a realist explanation, in fact, a neorealist or structural realist explanation, because he focuses on the structure of the international system. Specifically, the structural elements of the balance of power and the anarchic environment enable war to occur: "wars occur because there is nothing to prevent them."[204] In this way, the international, or systemic, level is "the most comprehensive" level because it covers "the totality of interactions which take place within the system and its environment."[205]

As this section will demonstrate, analysis at the international level can be useful to explain ethnic conflict, both within and between states. In essence, "international conditions can provide favorable or unfavorable opportunities for access to resources, legitimacy and coalition partners."[206] For example, changes in the balance of power in the international system, such as the end of the Cold War, may lead to opportunities for ethnic groups to seek power. The case of the former Yugoslavia illustrates this well. While it was a communist country, its leader, Josip Broz Tito, broke away from the Soviet Union in the late 1940s. Thus, during the Cold War, Yugoslavia played an important strategic role for the United States as a buffer against the USSR. When the Soviet Union collapsed, ending the Cold War, the United States no longer had a need for Yugoslavia to serve as a buffer. This lack of interest by the world's only remaining superpower, as well as the deteriorating economic conditions within Yugoslavia, led to a struggle for power between the three main ethnic groups (Serbs, Croats, and Muslims in Bosnia), each seeking to gain territory and power at the expense of the others, leading to a conflict lasting more than three years.[207]

Additionally, because there is no world government in the international system, internal ethnic conflicts can become international conflicts if they spread to other countries across international borders. Moreover, when outside actors provide support to actors involved in the conflict, whether in the form of economic, diplomatic, or military support, an internal conflict becomes internationalized. Consequently, external involvement in internal ethnic conflicts from diasporas, as well as outside states intervening for strategic reasons, can contribute to the continuation of ethnic conflict.[208] At the same time, recognizing the international dynamic of ethnic conflicts (for example, significant number of refugees both within and across borders; meddling of outside powers in internal conflicts, etc.), international actors (individual states, international institutions, and nongovernmental organizations) can act to prevent, manage, or resolve such conflicts.[209] This section discusses the role that international actors can play in promoting, as well as managing, ethnic conflict.

International Level Actors in Ethnic Conflict

As noted above, international level factors can contribute to the emergence and continuation of ethnic conflict. Relevant actors include diasporas (and thus states with ethnic ties to groups within other states experiencing ethnic conflict) and states intervening for their own self-interests (as realist theory would explain).

Diasporas and Ethnic Ties across State Borders. One can view ethnic kin that live in a different state, or states, as potential international factors in ethnic conflict. These related yet foreign groups can provide material and emotional support for ethnic groups. The diaspora is thus an international actor, or external party, that can fuel ethnic conflict. Alternatively, by withholding support, the diaspora community makes it more difficult for ethnic conflict to erupt and continue.[210] In addition, kin state (home country) relations with the diaspora can affect relations with the host country in which the diaspora resides. Consequently, as noted by Yossi Shain and Aharon Barth, "Diasporas are among the most prominent actors that link international and domestic spheres of politics."[211]

Diaspora is defined as people who have migrated from one country to another. These foreign migrants, according to Esman, establish their own communities that provide a sense of connectedness in an unfamiliar and perhaps "less than friendly environment."[212] Though diaspora groups are able to acculturate into the host country, they maintain their distinctiveness. Importantly, ethnic diasporas may act as a domestic interest group within their host country to influence policies toward their home country. Actors in the home country (the government or other political actors) may urge the ethnic diaspora to provide support (economic, diplomatic, and military).[213]

States may give support to their ethnic kin residing in other states. These ethnic ties can serve as a means for intervention in the affairs of a country experiencing ethnic conflict between the ethnic kin and other ethnic groups within a state. Serbia's intervention to support Serbs living in the Krajina region of Croatia during the Balkan wars in the early 1990s is one such example. States may even go so far as to claim territory in which their ethnic kin reside (irredentism).

For example, Somalia claimed territory in Ethiopia as its own, given that Somalis resided in Ethiopia.[214]

By supporting one side in a conflict, external states "can trigger the security dilemma by threatening groups' future security," especially if the external state has a historic tie to a specific group. In one example, Iraq's Sunni Arab leadership perceived a threat from Iran's Shi'a Muslim radicalism and the 1979 Iranian revolution. The Iraqi leadership feared that the Shi'a in Iraq might foment revolution with support from Iran's Shi'a. In response, the Iraqi leadership "cracked down hard on Iraqi Shi'a," especially people with connections to Iran.[215]

Of course, there is no guarantee that having ethnic ties to groups in another state will lead to foreign policies in support of the ethnic kin. In an analysis of transstate ethnicity in the new countries established after the collapse of the Soviet Union, Charles King and Neil Melvin found that it is often difficult to mobilize around diaspora issues, as a result of several factors, including the domestic politics within the kin state.[216] If there are ethnic minorities in the kin state that are powerful enough, they can act as a "constraint on the ability of political elites to use diaspora issues as a major domestic political resource." For example, Ukraine's multiethnic composition makes it difficult for domestic actors to appeal to diaspora issues regarding Ukrainians living in other countries.[217] Also affecting diaspora–kin state relations are "the institutional strength and resources within diaspora communities themselves." How well a diaspora community is organized politically, as well as whether it has significant economic resources and whether there is a cohesive community, affects diaspora politics. King and Melvin show that the Russian, Ukrainian, and Kazakh diasporas residing in the former Soviet republics have quite weak ethnic identity and communal solidarity. As a result, the kin state has not been able to develop extensive relations with their co-ethnics.[218] Additionally, whether the kin state will engage with the diaspora depends in large part on the diaspora relations with ethnic communities within the host state. Such relations affect whether the diaspora is open to actions by the kin state.[219]

Further constraints arise from the fact that the kin state has many, and competing, foreign policy goals, only one of which may involve relations with its ethnic diaspora. In other words, the international system acts as a constraint on foreign policy behavior of the kin state.[220] Finally, King and Melvin note that kin state–diaspora relations are also affected by the economic resources of the kin state. A kin state with limited economic resources will find it more difficult to connect with its diaspora.[221]

In the end, it must be recognized that kin state–diaspora relations do matter in understanding ethnic conflict. The construction of ethnic identity reinforces the idea of a connection between kin states and the diaspora, and provides an explanation for identity-based motivations for intrastate and interstate behavior.[222]

Non-ethnic Ties and External Intervention as a Contributing Factor of Ethnic Conflict. As a result of national self-interest, external states may take actions that support one ethnic group over another in an internal ethnic conflict, as realism would argue regarding state behavior. For example, in the 1970s India's support for Bengalis in East Pakistan contributed to the breakup of Pakistan, and the creation of the new state of Bangladesh. In supporting the Bengali Muslims, India was able to weaken Pakistan, its regional rival.[223] States may see other states beset with internal conflicts as "easy targets," and thus see the opportunity "for an easy, cheap victory" by engaging in belligerent behavior against the other state, thereby escalating an internal conflict into an interstate conflict.[224] An example would be the Russian military intervention in Georgia in 1992 in support of the secessionist movement in South Ossetia (which wanted to join with North Ossetia, one of the republics in the Russian Federation). Russia's goal was twofold: to persuade Georgia to join the Commonwealth of Independent States and to gain Georgia's consent to having Russian military forces based in Georgia.[225]

External powers play a role in the emergence of ethnic conflict by virtue of the resources they can provide to extremists. Such resources can enable them to overthrow the government, engage in war, or establish an opposition government.[226] Russian support for Russian-speaking secessionists in the Dniestr region of Moldova served its strategic interests. In fact, according to Stuart Kaufman, Russia helped the Dniestrians start—and win—the war with the Moldovan government.[227]

However, as with kin state behavior noted previously, external states intervening to support an ethnic group have many foreign policy objectives, only one of which may be to support an ethnic group in conflict. The state may decide that other foreign policy goals are more important or pressing. In addition, domestic politics influence an external state's decision whether to intervene and support one side of a conflict or another.[228]

International Level Factors as a Means to Manage and Settle Ethnic Conflicts

In terms of international actors that can attempt to manage and settle ethnic conflicts, one can look at individual states, international governmental organizations, and nongovernmental organizations. Harff and Gurr argue that international actors can play a significant role in the protection of minority rights and the settlement of ethnic conflicts. In addition, international actors may need to use coercive measures, such as military intervention, in order to end ethnic conflicts, especially when such conflicts involve the mass killing of civilians.[229] As Byman observes, however, military intervention to end "the fighting and preserve peace for a short period of time while diplomats forge a political settlement and non-governmental organizations carry out humanitarian work" is problematic. Anger and hostility remain even after a civil war ends. Such anger and hostility are obstacles to production of a long-lasting political settlement as well as to success in humanitarian operations. As a result, he argues that the states in the international community need to reconsider how to intervene in civil wars.[230] Posen argues that in reconsidering approaches to intervention that will decrease the chances of conflict, external actors "must assess the local groups' strategic view of their situation." In making such an assessment, external actors should ask: "Which groups fear for their physical security and why? What military options are available to them?" Posen notes that lessening the threat perceptions of groups as well as decreasing their windows of opportunity to act aggressively may decrease the likelihood of conflict erupting.[231]

International cooperation, through international institutions, as liberalism would argue, is possible. However, as is evident in this chapter and the individual case chapters, the willingness of international institutions, such as the United Nations or European Union, to intervene depends in large part on the self-interests of the member states.[232] As Posen asserts, regional conflicts do not threaten the security or material interests of most external actors. As a result, international institutions face a credibility problem when they threaten to intervene for humanitarian reasons to safeguard groups that worry about their future.[233] Thus, while the international community can play a role in addressing ethnic conflicts, there are limits to what the international community can, and is willing to, do. In this section we examine the responses international actors can utilize in order to prevent, manage, or resolve ethnic conflict: mediation, coercive intervention and noncoercive intervention.[234]

Third-Party Mediation. Third-party mediators are external actors who attempt to resolve ethnic conflicts through negotiation and diplomacy.[235] Third-party negotiations and diplomacy can promote confidence-building measures (such as elections, autonomy, power sharing, and demonstrations of respect) for the warring parties.[236] Third parties can also persuade warring parties to accept mediation if the third party can act as the guarantor of an agreement.[237] It is important to recognize, however, that there are costs to the mediators if mediation is unsuccessful, including costs to their reputations. They may also experience economic costs if the parties to the conflict are trading partners.[238] While there are costs to the mediator, there are also costs to the warring parties. Acceptance of mediation, as

J. Michael Grieg and Patrick Regan assert, "can imply weakness, betray a lack of resolve, or convey legitimacy on a heretofore unrecognized adversary."[239]

In many ways, it is easier for individual states to mediate ethnic conflicts than for international organizations to do so. International organizations (both regional and global) must consider the positions of member states before acting. Individual states can utilize "secret 'back channel' diplomacy." Such back channel diplomacy provides the foundation for formal negotiations to take place. In order to ensure that an agreement by moderates can be enforced, individual states are also more easily able to deploy military forces against extremists who may be bent on thwarting the agreement.[240] For example, in 1995, concerned about the possibility of instability in the Balkans, the United States deployed forces to Macedonia (a state that was once a republic in the former Yugoslavia) in an attempt to prevent an outbreak of violence between the Albanian minority and the Slavic government.[241]

In considering the impact of mediation by intergovernmental organizations (IGOs), such as the European Union or the United Nations, it is important to recognize that the legitimacy of an international mediator is "one of the most effective resources" needed to get the warring parties to agree to negotiate. The "status and respect" of heads of state and other high-level officials (foreign ministers) confer legitimacy to the mediators, and may lead the warring parties to moderate their positions and make concessions.[242] Moreover, as discussed in chapter 1, international institutions can reduce the uncertainty that prevails in conflicts between parties worried about their future security. International institutions can provide "objective information about each side's capabilities, resolve, and interests."[243]

Jacob Bercovitch and Allison Houston argue that regional organizations (such as the African Union, Organization of African States) "offer the best chances of successful outcomes in international mediation," whereas more global international organizations (such as the UN) "have a very poor record in the area of mediation." The difference in outcomes may result from the fact that the members of regional organizations have "common ideals, perspectives, and interests" that may be found wanting in larger international organizations.[244]

While it may be the case that regional organizations have a better chance of a successful outcome, this does not mean that international organizations do not matter in dealing with conflict. Schrodt and Gerner's analysis of third-party mediation found that, in general, mediation "does lower the level of conflict between the antagonists."[245]

Moreover, international organizations can promote norms of acceptable behavior and condemn unacceptable behavior in addressing peace and security. UN Security Council Resolution 1325 is one such example. In October 2000, for the first time, the Security Council passed a resolution recognizing the effect of war (both intrastate and interstate) on women, particularly "as refugees and internally displaced persons, [who] increasingly are targeted by combatants and armed elements, and *recognizing* the consequent impact this has on durable peace and reconciliation." Further, the resolution *"[u]rges* Member States to ensure increased representation of women at all decision-making levels in national, regional and international institutions and mechanisms for the prevention, management, and resolution of conflict" as well as encourages the support of "local women's peace initiatives and indigenous processes for conflict resolution, and [those] that involve women in all of the implementation mechanisms of the peace agreements" (emphasis in original).[246] The resolution's call for the participation of women at the negotiating table matters for successful and inclusive mediation efforts.

In June 2008 the UN Security Council went further in its efforts to highlight the impact of war on women, particularly in the area of gender-based violence. Resolution 1820 called for the "immediate and complete halt to acts of sexual violence." The resolution further declared that "civilians account for the vast majority of those adversely affected by armed conflict; that women and girls are particularly targeted by the use of sexual violence, including as a tactic of war to humiliate, dominate, instill fear in, disperse and/or forcibly relocate civilian members of a community or *ethnic group;* and that sexual violence perpetrated in this manner may in some instances persist after the cessation of hostilities" (emphasis added). Speaking for the United States (which held the Security Council presidency that month), Secretary of State Condoleezza Rice stated that "we affirm that sexual violence profoundly affects not only the health and safety of women, but the economic and social stability of their nations." As with Resolution 1325, Resolution 1820 calls on the relevant UN agencies to consult with women and women's organizations, and include women in decision-making processes to deal with peace and the post-conflict restructuring of a country's social, economic, and political institutions and systems.[247] These two Security Council resolutions are examples of the evolution and application of an international norm of acceptable behavior (and condemnation of unacceptable behavior) promoted by an international organization in seeking to mediate conflicts, by taking into account the impact of conflicts on women and the need to include women at the peace negotiations and post-conflict social, economic, and political institutions.

Nongovernmental organizations (NGOs) are usually involved with distributing humanitarian supplies to civilian victims of ethnic conflicts. But in addition to this, in their efforts to resolve conflicts, NGOs, through the provision of "good offices," can promote dialogue between the warring parties.[248] However,

NGOs are limited in their effect because extremists often attempt to undermine agreements concluded by moderates. In that case, coercive measures may be needed, and NGOs do not have these coercive resources at their disposal.[249]

In assessing the success of mediation in internal conflicts, scholars have found that the record is mixed. Michael Brown and Chantal de Jonge Oudraat note several factors necessary for successful mediation, including "a clear strategy" of the mediators (clear political objectives, ideas of how best to achieve those objectives, including how to form an international consensus), preference of at least one side to the conflict for "talking to fighting," and mediators that have leverage over the warring parties (both inducements and punishments).[250] Even when agreement is reached, there is always the problem of implementation and enforcement of the agreement. Sometimes warring parties are not really interested in a settlement, preferring to use the negotiation process as a means to buy time for improving their military situation. Due to the significant distrust that permeates the relationship between the disputants, there is also the possibility that one or more parties to the agreement will cheat (for example, groups will withhold weapons in case they need them if fighting resumes). Additionally, leaders may not be able to control the actions of their more extremist followers, who may prefer to fight than to seek peace.[251] Finally, mediation is often unsuccessful because the international community is unwilling "to provide mediators with the economic, logistical, police, and military support needed to oversee the process of disarmament, integration of the armed forces, repatriation of refugees, and holding of general elections."[252]

Noncoercive Intervention. Noncoercive intervention involves actions by international actors that include positive and negative inducements to get the parties in conflict to end their fighting. Emphasizing international norms of acceptable behavior is needed. International actors can ostracize states and actors that do not follow these international norms.[253] Specifically, the international community can provide intelligence information to parties to the conflict they support, as well as decline to provide diplomatic support. International actors can also decide not to give economic assistance. The "denial or threatened denial of recognition" of the parties to conflict is another type of noncoercive intervention.[254]

International actors can provide inducements to groups in conflict in order to change their behavior to one of cooperation and peace. For example, following the collapse of the Soviet Union the newly independent states of Estonia and Latvia both passed citizenship laws making it hard for Russians living in those countries to become citizens. But when both Estonia and Latvia wanted to join the European Union, they reversed their restrictive citizenship laws so as not to discriminate against the ethnic Russians in their countries.[255]

International actors can offer foreign aid as a means to prevent and manage ethnic conflict. Aid can assist in development projects, such as an irrigation system as in the case of Sri Lanka, which had been enmeshed in ethnic conflict between the Sinhalese and Tamils. The Sinhalese and Tamil farmers needed to cooperate to fix the irrigation system. The farmers perceived that in cooperating to repair the system, both sides would benefit equally. As Esman notes, ethnic conflict may be prevented in cases where projects are considered to be mutually beneficial and lead to interdependence among ethnic groups.[256]

Foreign aid's influence in preventing conflict, however, is limited as donors worry that providing such aid may draw them into the politics of the country in conflict. Moreover, foreign aid often benefits one group over another, so rather than reducing conflict, foreign aid may actually increase conflict as groups perceive that they are not benefiting at the same level as another and respond with increased violence. For example, the Sri Lankan government was able to obtain foreign aid for their Mahaweli irrigation project, located in territory dominated by the Tamils. Instead of letting the project benefit the Tamils, the government relocated Sri Lankan settlers to the territory. The Tamils perceived a threat from the actions of the government, and rebelled.[257]

In general, noncoercive intervention is limited in its effects on the warring parties. On the positive side, such interventions, according to Rothchild and Lake, increase the costs to ethnic leaders in playing on ethnic sentiments as well as present the ethnic leaders with reason for accepting international norms so that they can gain "recognition, acceptance, and inclusion in the international community." But when conflicts are particularly severe, noncoercive intervention is unlikely to be successful. "The most that noncoercive intervention can do in such situations is to create a climate in which ethnic appeals and violence are perceived by all as illegitimate and, therefore, marginally less likely to be used."[258]

Coercive Intervention. Coercive intervention to end ethnic conflict includes peacekeeping operations, military assistance, arms embargoes, economic sanctions, tribunals, and military force.[259] As Byman notes, international actors "can fulfill three roles: they can protect and succor the victims of the oppressive government; they can help alter the balance of power on the ground, enabling a group to defend itself (often as a prelude to or part of a partition plan); or they can help change the government, putting in power a new regime that will be more willing and able to create peace among hostile communal groups."[260] International governmental organizations (IGOs), both regional (that is, the European Union, African Union) and global (that is, the United Nations), can be perceived as more politically legitimate, as well as better able to deal with the problems arising from burden sharing, in comparison to individual states. Concerns over the ability to build coalitions of states willing to act, over the need to obtain financing for peacekeeping operations, and over negative domestic public opinion are ever present. Yet, as Rothchild and Lake acknowledge, because intervention by definition is a shared effort, resistance both at home and abroad may be dampened.[261]

In attempting to be peacemakers, outside powers often run into difficulties in the long term. A large number of forces are needed to prevent the resumption of violence, and there are "burdensome rules of engagement." In addition, there is no clear time commitment as to how long the international forces will be deployed. Interventions focused on peacemaking do "little to foster a political settlement or nation-building."[262] Moreover, such interventions do little to end the violence, as warring parties can hide their weapons. Disarming groups does not usually increase their security, but in fact can reduce their security if they fear the future. When groups are disarmed, the balance of power can shift dramatically if even a small number of weapons are smuggled in by one group to the detriment of another.[263] Resettling people who were displaced during the conflict, another goal of intervention, is challenging. Having experienced hostile intentions of other ethnic groups, how can returnees feel safe and secure when they go home? Returnees may face violence upon their return, as was the case of those Rwandans who had fled to Zaire during the genocide. When they returned, many were killed.[264]

As noted above, coercive intervention includes actual and threatened use of military force to stop the fighting. Grieg and Regan found that warring parties were highly likely to accept offers of mediation when third parties threatened military intervention.[265] External actors can provide military support to one side for security and protection against another ethnic group, thereby shifting the balance of power between the warring parties. Military support that shifts the balance of power (usually toward the weaker side) can lead both sides to the conflict to moderate their positions.[266] When NATO intervened on behalf of the Bosnian Muslims and Croats in 1995, Bosnian Serbs moderated their demands (though the Croats, now emboldened by NATO's support, increased their demands).[267] Enforcement of an agreement can also come about from coercive intervention, as such intervention provides sorely needed credibility.[268]

Whether using coercive or noncoercive means, international actors intervene with the hopes of affecting the outcome of an internal conflict. Outcomes of a conflict include the regime type, the economic system, as well as the autonomy or independence of an ethnic group.[269] International actors need to consider intervention so as to lessen the effects of such conflicts on neighboring states. Economic instability and refugees may induce neighboring states to take advantage of the conflict and take aggressive actions for their own interests (for example, providing assistance to rebels, invading the country). Intervention by international actors can dissuade such behavior by neighboring states.[270] Importantly, as Brown and de Jonge Oudraat argue, international intervention should focus on cooperative (noncoercive) means first, given that coercive intervention "is more expensive and riskier." They contend that when the conflict has led to crimes against humanity (for example, genocide or targeting of civilians) or vital interests are at stake, then coercive means should be used.[271]

Given that internal conflicts result from insecurities of the minority, or subordinate, groups as a result of the government's policies, Kaufman argues that external actors can encourage governments to institute policies that reassure the subordinate groups that they need not fear their extinction. Policies of reassurance include economic aid to the group "conditioned on peaceful management of the ethnic dispute."[272] In cases in which one ethnic group wants dominance over the other groups, external actors can engage in deterrence, namely threatening to provide support for the subordinate groups. In doing so, they can induce both groups to moderate their demands, and thus reduce the mutual perception of threat.[273] When dealing with belligerent elites, external actors can use both inducements and punishments as means to change elite behavior, especially if such elites have engaged in ethnic outbidding. Inducements enable elites to remain in power (as instrumentalist approaches to ethnic conflict make clear, elites often use ethnicity and nationalism as means to obtain and remain in power). The problem remains, however, if the belligerent elite, having stoked mass resentment and anger, is unable to back down. Moreover, external actors may be disinclined to provide inducements to ethnic extremists out of concern for rewarding aggressive behavior.[274]

Partition as an International Response to Demands for Self-determination. The domestic level section earlier in this chapter addressed domestic institutional arrangements that may be instituted in an effort to manage and settle ethnic conflicts. In many ways, these arrangements are a function of the international community's bias in favor of maintaining territorial boundaries of states.[275] Yet, partition, in which the state's territorial boundaries are redrawn, is an option available to deal with ethnic conflict when groups seek to secede or make irredentist claims on territory in which their ethnic kin reside. Examples include the partition of Palestine that created Israel in 1948 and the establishment of a Kurdish safe haven in northern Iraq in the 1990s. Byman argues that partition may be better at reducing, if not preventing, bloodshed. As many scholars note, the historical record on the success of partition in ending violence is mixed.[276] At the same time, studies on partition find that states resulting from successful partition are more likely to move toward democracy.[277]

There are several arguments opposing partition. Partition could lead to an escalation of the conflict, particularly if civil institutions are weak and ethnic minorities are disenfranchised. Partition could lead to additional self-determination and independence movements as groups now in the new state seek to form their own state. Partition weakens the possibility of democracy as the new ethnic majorities discriminate against the minorities now residing in the new state. Population transfers needed to separate the groups are likely to be traumatic. There is the question of whether the new state will be politically and economically viable. Finally, an internal war now becomes an international war between new countries as a result of partition.[278]

The arguments in favor of partition include ending the issues that contributed to conflict between groups, as the groups are now separated. Occasionally, other options may not be possible, especially if the central government is severely weakened and unstable, and thus unable to maintain order. While domestic institutions such as federalism and consociationalism are possible (as discussed in the domestic level section), their actual implementation is often quite problematic.[279] When the identities of the population are incompatible, conflict is likely to re-escalate and democratization difficult to emerge.[280] In an analysis comparing partition, autonomy, and de facto separation of populations in conflicts from 1900 to 2002, Thomas Chapman and Philip Roeder found that the reduction of the incompatibility of national identities was more likely to happen with partition as opposed to autonomy or de facto separation. This is so because both autonomy and de facto separation embolden "ethnopoliticians as national leaders within an autonomous homeland or a de facto entity on one side of the ceasefire line" and allow for the maintenance of separate (and hardened) identities.[281] Unlike solutions that maintain existing territorial borders in which conflicting groups must make decisions together on resources, political representation, positions in the executive, etc., partition does not entail the need for joint decision making between the parties now that they no longer reside in the same territory.[282] Furthermore, partition that separates the warring parties, according to Chaim Kaufmann, decreases the motivations as well as the prospects for continued conflict. Moreover, separating the warring parties reduces the potential for ethnic cleansing.[283] As Byman contends, "Intervention to bolster such failed states is as immoral as it is hopeless. Helping deconstruct these states, on the other hand, may be the most practical and humane solution to recurring civil wars."[284]

The international community can thus play a favorable role in promoting partition as an option when all other options are not possible in order to end the fighting. Then, in addition to recognizing the new state, the international community can assist in "population transfers, provide for border security, and press for guarantees of minority rights" (as there are likely to be ethnic minorities in the newly partitioned states).[285] As Chapman and Roeder found in their study, the level of democracy was much higher for parties to partition, and democracy measures were higher in the post-conflict stage relative to the pre-conflict stage. They observed that the new states established as a result of partition "were more likely than other new states to be born democratic and to enjoy more years of postindependence democracy."[286] In the end, of course, resolving the significant ethnic tensions may not be possible; as Carter Johnson astutely remarks, "it is not clear whether this is in anyone's power." Separating the warring parties does reduce the security threat, and with the security threat reduced, moderate politicians may then have an opportunity to act.[287] Importantly, as Johnson found in his study of partitions following ethnic civil wars (1945–2004), only complete partitions, in which the warring parties are separated, are likely to lead to peace.[288]

Limitations of International Responses to End Internal Ethnic Conflict

In attempting to deal with ethnic disputes, conflicting groups often have fears for their future security, as they cannot be completely sure that the other party or parties to the conflict will not renege on the agreement and resume fighting. Ethnic conflicts become quite costly because, according to James Fearon, the majority ethnic group is unable "to make a credible commitment to the minority" ethnic group. For example, during the disintegration of Yugoslavia, Croatia's government engaged in behavior that undermined the Serb minority's security (including the use of the fascist Ustashe symbols by the new Croatian government and constitutional reforms that favored the Croatian majority). While the Croatian president, Franjo Tudjman, made verbal assurances to the Serb minority, the actual behavior of the government threatened the Serbs' security.[289] In such a case, groups will need a third party to provide a credible commitment to any agreement reached.[290] As Rothchild and Lake observe, only when the groups in conflict are convinced that the external actors are committed and willing to enforce the ethnic contract that ensures fairness for all ethnic groups "into the indefinite future" will an external guarantee succeed. The fear of the future looms large—if groups in conflict fear that the ethnic contract that protects them will not continue in the future, such groups will have little incentive to lay down their arms, and the conflict will continue.[291]

The problem, as Fearon sees it, is that "international organizations will rarely be able to make such commitments credible."[292] Countries with strong and weak interests in addressing the conflict face challenges in providing those guarantees. Strong countries intervening may be perceived as taking sides (as was the case with U.S. support for the Bosnian Muslims in opposition to the Bosnian Serbs); weak countries are likely to lack the "political stamina to enforce a new ethnic contract in the future" (for example, the African Union's efforts to mediate with regard to the conflict in Sudan in which the AU does not have the economic or military capabilities to do so).[293] However, Fearon does note that if the minority group has ethnic kin in a neighboring state that is powerful enough (for example, the Russian minority in Estonia can look to Russians in Russia, with its powerful ethnic kin), the majority ethnic group may be induced to make a credible commitment to an agreement.[294]

For peace to endure, the international community must be willing to commit for the long haul.[295] The difficulty arises, as Brown and de Jonge Oudraat contend, because international actors are not motivated to act "in the early stages of internal conflicts, when levels of violence are low and windows of opportunity are open." International actors consider taking action when the violence escalates, but at this stage, conflict management becomes more elusive.[296]

The role that external actors play in conflict prevention (focus on underlying problems that are the root of conflict and promote long-term solutions), conflict management (prevent conflicts from escalating),[297] and promotion of peace is important. While involvement by the international community is welcome, conflict management and resolution will need to be accomplished by local parties to the conflict, as they are the ones who will, in most cases, remain within existing territorial borders when the fighting ends, to solve the root causes of the conflict.[298] External intervention (mediation, noncoercive and coercive), according to Rothchild and Lake, cannot overcome the strategic dilemmas that lead to fear and violence among ethnic groups. While international actors can "facilitate communication," information failures are still possible. And security dilemmas are hard to minimize by external actors when one side to the internal conflict is faced with the incentive to engage in the preemptive use of force against another ethnic group.[299] As Kaufman astutely observes, "Third parties cannot change ethnically defined grievances, negative stereotypes, symbolic disputes, threatening demographic trends, or histories of ethnic domination in foreign countries, and they cannot eliminate the fears of extinction which may result."[300]

In the end, durable peace rests on domestic institutions established after the fighting ends. In an analysis of 111 civil wars (1944–1999), Bumba Mukherjee found that while third-party enforcement matters for encouraging "the *likelihood* of peace in the short run," it is domestic institutions such as democracy and proportional representation that play the more crucial role "for *sustaining* peace in the long run" (emphasis in original).[301]

CONCLUSION

This chapter has examined the literature at the intersection of comparative politics and international relations in an attempt to understand the causes of and solutions to ethnic conflict. Looking at individual, domestic, and international level factors demonstrates the complexity of ethnic conflicts (in fact, all conflicts). The levels of analysis framework is the foundation of the remaining chapters of the book as we explore five cases of ethnic conflict. However, one caveat the reader should keep in mind is that sometimes the distinctions between one analytical level and another may not neatly match the factors in an ethnic conflict. The division between these three levels helps us understand a conflict, but not everything will fit nicely into this categorization. In fact, it is the interaction of these levels that makes understanding ethnic conflict so difficult.

For example, Kaufman's work demonstrates that factors at different levels are necessary for ethnic conflict to emerge: mass hostility (domestic), belligerent elites (individual), and a security dilemma (domestic); he also recognizes the role played by foreign patrons—an international level factor.[302] As Harff and Gurr note, "Ethnic conflict is not solely or even mainly a consequence of domestic politics. The potential for ethnic conflict, the issues at stake, and even the lines of cleavage between contending groups have been shaped and reshaped by international actors."[303] Daniel Druckman astutely claims that group loyalty and collective action "[cross] the boundaries between levels of analysis, from individuals and small interacting groups to collectivities and nations."[304] Elites play a role in mobilizing the masses to engage in conflict (for example, through the use of domestic level factors such as ethnic political parties, socioeconomic conditions, appeals to social identity of the group), and members of the international community (individual states or international organizations) sometimes act to prevent ethnic conflict but at other times support ethnic groups in their war aims. Thus, what we propose is a multilevel analysis of ethnic conflict.[305] As will be demonstrated in the case study chapters that follow, all three levels are necessary to examine in order to understand ethnic conflict.

NOTES

1. J. David Singer, "International Conflict: Three Levels of Analysis," *World Politics* 12, no. 3 (April 1960): 453–461; J. David Singer, "The Level-of-Analysis Problem in International Relations," *World Politics* 14, no. 1 (October 1961): 77–92; Kenneth Waltz, *Man, the State, and War: A Theoretical Analysis* (New York: Columbia University Press, 1959).

2. Ole R. Holsti, "The Political Psychology of International Politics: More than a Luxury," *Political Psychology* 10, no. 3 (1989): 495–500. See also Singer, "The Level-of-Analysis Problem in International Relations," 88–89.

3. Jerel A. Rosati, "The Power of Human Cognition in the Study of World Politics," *International Studies Review* 2, no. 3 (Autumn 2000): 47.

4. Michael E. Brown, "The Causes of Internal Conflict: An Overview," in *Nationalism and Ethnic Conflict*, ed. Michael E. Brown, Owen R. Cote Jr., Sean M. Lynn-Jones, and Steven E. Miller, rev. ed. (Cambridge, Mass.: MIT Press, 2001), 17.

5. Jean Blondel, *Political Leadership: Towards a General Analysis* (London: Sage, 1987).

6. Cathy Gormley-Heenan, *Political Leadership and the Northern Ireland Peace Process: Role, Capacity, and Effect* (New York: Palgrave, 2007).

7. Lewis J. Edinger, "Approaches to the Comparative Analysis of Political Leadership," *Review of Politics* 52, no. 4 (Autumn 1990): 512–513.

8. Edinger, "Approaches to the Comparative Analysis of Political Leadership," 513–514.

9. Rosati, "The Power of Human Cognition in the Study of World Politics," 48–50. See also Edinger, "Approaches to the Comparative Analysis of Political Leadership," 509–523; Mark Shafer, "Images and Policy Preferences," *Political Psychology* 18, no. 4 (1997): 813–829.

10. Many scholars have studied leaders' impact on foreign policy decision making, recognizing the importance of the individual level of analysis. Though by no means an exhaustive list, evidence of this body of work can be found in a special issue of *International Studies Review*, which published six articles on leaders and foreign policymaking. "Leaders, Groups, and Coalitions: Understanding the People and Processes in Foreign Policymaking," *International Studies Review* 3, no. 2 (Summer 2001): 5–250.

11. Rosati, "The Power of Human Cognition in the Study of World Politics," 56–57.

12. George W. Bush, "President Delivers State of the Union Address" (January 29, 2002), http://georgewbush-whitehouse.archives.gov/news/releases/2002/01/20020129-11.html.

13. Rosati, "The Power of Human Cognition in the Study of World Politics," 66.

14. Rosati, "The Power of Human Cognition in the Study of World Politics," 67.

15. Rosati, "The Power of Human Cognition in the Study of World Politics," 59.

16. Rosati, "The Power of Human Cognition in the Study of World Politics," 60. See also Richard K. Herrmann and Michael P. Fischerkeller, "Beyond the Enemy Image and Spiral Model: Cognitive-Strategic Research after the Cold War," *International Organization* 49, no. 3 (Summer 1995): 415–450; Daniel Druckman, "Nationalism, Patriotism, and Group Loyalty: A Social Psychological Perspective," *Mershon International Studies Review* 38 (1994): 43–68.

17. Noel Kaplowitz, "Psychopolitical Dimensions of International Relations: The Reciprocal Effects of Conflict Strategies," *International Studies Quarterly* 28, no. 4 (December 1984): 376–377.

18. Druckman, "Nationalism, Patriotism, and Group Loyalty," 55.

19. Shannon Lindsey Blanton, "Images in Conflict: The Case of Ronald Reagan and El Salvador," *International Studies Quarterly* 40 (1996): 41.

20. James D. Fearon and David D. Laitin, "Violence and the Social Construction of Ethnic Identity," *International Organization* 54, no. 4 (Autumn 2000): 853–854. See also Milton J. Esman, *An Introduction to Ethnic Conflict* (Malden, Mass.: Polity Press, 2004), 33–34.

21. Fearon and Laitin, "Violence and the Social Construction of Ethnic Identity," 855. See also Ashutosh Varshney, "Nationalism, Ethnic Conflict, and Rationality," *Perspectives on Politics* 1, no. 1 (March 2003): 87–88.

22. Fearon and Laitin, "Violence and the Social Construction of Ethnic Identity," 855–856.

23. Stuart J. Kaufman, "Spiraling to Ethnic War: Elites, Masses, and Moscow in Moldova's Civil War," *International Security* 21, no. 2 (Fall 1996): 109.

24. Ted Robert Gurr, "Why Minorities Rebel: A Global Analysis of Communal Mobilization and Conflict since 1945," *International Political Science Review* 14, no. 2 (April 1993): 167.

25. Marc Howard Ross, "The Relevance of Culture for the Study of Political Psychology and Ethnic Conflict," *Political Psychology* 18, no. 2 (1997): 309.

26. Ross, "The Relevance of Culture for the Study of Political Psychology and Ethnic Conflict," 304–305. See also Gavan Duffy and Nicole Lindstrom, "Conflicting Identities: Solidary Incentives in the Serbo-Croatian War," *Journal of Peace Research* 39, no. 1 (2002): 70.

27. Ross, "The Relevance of Culture for the Study of Political Psychology and Ethnic Conflict," 319.

28. Stephen Van Evera, "Hypotheses on Nationalism and War," in *Nationalism and Ethnic Conflict*, ed. Michael E. Brown, Owen R. Cote Jr., Sean M. Lynn-Jones, and Steven E. Miller, rev. ed. (Cambridge, Mass.: MIT Press, 2001), 48–53.

29. Van Evera, "Hypotheses on Nationalism and War," 53.

30. Fearon and Laitin, "Violence and the Social Construction of Ethnic Identity," 864–865.

31. Fearon and Laitin, "Violence and the Social Construction of Ethnic Identity," 865.

32. David A. Lake and Donald Rothchild, "Spreading Fear: The Genesis of Transnational Ethnic Conflict," in *The International Spread of Ethnic Conflict: Fear, Diffusion, and Escalation*, ed. David A. Lake and Donald Rothchild (Princeton: Princeton University Press, 1998), 19.

33. Lake and Rothchild, "Spreading Fear," 20.
34. Daniel L. Byman, *Keeping the Peace: Lasting Solutions to Ethnic Conflicts* (Baltimore: Johns Hopkins University Press, 2002), 35.
35. Byman, *Keeping the Peace,* 38. See also Stephen M. Saideman, "Explaining the International Relations of Secessionist Conflicts: Vulnerability versus Ethnic Ties," *International Organization* 51, no. 4 (Autumn 1997): 721–753.
36. Kaufman, "Spiraling to Ethnic War," 109.
37. Kaufman, "Spiraling to Ethnic War," 114.
38. Kaufman, "Spiraling to Ethnic War," 117–118.
39. David Carment and Patrick James, "Internal Constraints and Interstate Ethnic Conflict," *Journal of Conflict Resolution* 39, no. 1 (March 1995): 87. See also Lake and Rothchild for a discussion of elites' use of diversionary wars, "Spreading Fear," 31.
40. Carment and James, "Internal Constraints and Interstate Ethnic Conflict," 90.
41. Lake and Rothchild, "Spreading Fear," 31.
42. Carment and James, "Internal Constraints and Interstate Ethnic Conflict," 91.
43. Carment and James, "Internal Constraints and Interstate Ethnic Conflict," 93.
44. Byman, *Keeping the Peace,* 129.
45. Ulrich Schneckener, "Making Power-Sharing Work: Lessons from Successes and Failures in Ethnic Conflict Regulation," *Journal of Peace Research* 39, no. 2 (March 2002): 224.
46. Schneckener, "Making Power-Sharing Work," 224.
47. Schneckener, "Making Power-Sharing Work," 225.
48. Byman, *Keeping the Peace,* 81.
49. Byman, *Keeping the Peace,* 82.
50. Byman, *Keeping the Peace,* 96–97.
51. Stephen John Stedman, "Spoiler Problems in Peace Processes," in *Nationalism and Ethnic Conflict,* ed. Michael E. Brown, Owen R. Cote Jr., Sean M. Lynn-Jones, and Steven E. Miller, rev. ed. (Cambridge, Mass.: MIT Press, 2001), 366.
52. Stedman also mentions the type of spoilers (limited, greedy, total) and "locus of the spoiler problem" (spoiler as leader or follower). Stedman, "Spoiler Problems in Peace Processes," 369–372.
53. Stedman, "Spoiler Problems in Peace Processes," 374–375.
54. Frederic S. Pearson, "Dimensions of Conflict Resolution in Ethnopolitical Disputes," *Journal of Peace Research* 38, no. 3 (2001): 280.
55. Kenneth Arrow, *Social Choice and Individual Values* (New York: Wiley and Sons, 1951).

56. Donald L. Horowitz, *Ethnic Groups in Conflict* (Berkeley: University of California Press, 1985), 653, 657.

57. Horowitz, *Ethnic Groups in Conflict*, 186-194.

58. Andrew Reynolds and Timothy D. Sisk, "Elections and Electoral Systems: Implications for Conflict Management," in *Elections and Conflict Management in Africa*, ed. Timothy D. Sisk and Andrew Reynolds (Washington D.C.: United States Institute of Peace, 1998), 11–36.

59. Michael J. Sodarno, *Comparative Politics: A Global Introduction* (Boston: McGraw-Hill, 2008), 274.

60. Reynolds and Sisk, "Elections and Electoral Systems: Implications for Conflict Management."

61. Timothy Sisk, *Democratization in South Africa: The Elusive Social Contract* (Princeton: Princeton University Press, 1995).

62. Gabriel A. Almond, Russell J. Dalton, G. Bingham Powell Jr., and Kaare Strom, "Interest Articulation," in *Comparative Politics Today: A World View*, ed. Gabriel A. Almond, Russell J. Dalton, G. Bingham Powell Jr., and Kaare Strom, 8th ed. (New York: Pearson Longman, 2006), 65.

63. Sodarno, *Comparative Politics*, 283.

64. Arrow, *Social Choice and Individual Values*.

65. Anthony Downs, *An Economic Theory of Democracy* (New York: Harper and Row, 1957).

66. Mancur Olson, *The Logic of Collective Action: Public Goods and the Theory of Groups* (Cambridge, Mass.: Harvard University Press, 1971), 21.

67. Olson, *The Logic of Collective Action*.

68. Olson, *The Logic of Collective Action*, 61.

69. James G. March and Johan P. Olsen, "The New Institutionalism: Organizational Factors in Political Life," *American Political Science Review* 78 (1984): 738.

70. March and Olsen, "The New Institutionalism," 742.

71. March and Olsen, "The New Institutionalism," 747.

72. George Tsebelis, *Veto Players: How Political Institutions Work* (Princeton: Princeton University Press, 2002), 2.

73. Mark Kesselman, Joel Krieger, and William A. Joseph, "Introducing Comparative Politics," in *Introduction to Comparative Politics*, ed. Mark Kesselman, Joel Krieger, and William A. Joseph, 3rd ed. (Boston: Houghton Mifflin, 2004), 8.

74. James March and Herbert Simon, *Organizations* (New York: Wiley and Sons, 1958).

75. March and Simon, *Organizations*.

76. Steven E. Lobell and Philip Mauceri, "Diffusion and Escalation of Ethnic Conflict," in *Ethnic Conflict and International Politics: Explaining Diffusion and*

Escalation, ed. Steven E. Lobell and Philip Mauceri (New York: Palgrave, 2004), 1.

77. Esman, *An Introduction to Ethnic Conflict,* 3.

78. Esman, *An Introduction to Ethnic Conflict,* 3.

79. Esman, *An Introduction to Ethnic Conflict,* 75. Stuart Kaufman argues that there are several necessary, but not sufficient, preconditions for ethnic conflict: "ethnically defined stereotypes, negative stereotypes, demographic threats, histories of ethnic domination, emotion-laden ethnic symbols, reciprocal fears of group extinction, *de facto* political anarchy, and political space and military means to act." The three proximate causes of ethnic war are mass hostility, belligerent elites, and security dilemmas. Kaufman, "Spiraling to Ethnic War," 114.

80. Jack Snyder, "Averting Anarchy in the New Europe," in *The Cold War and After,* ed. Sean M. Lynn-Jones (Cambridge, Mass.: MIT Press, 1991), 124.

81. Stephen Van Evera, "Primed for Peace: Europe after the Cold War," in *The Cold War and After,* ed. Sean M. Lynn-Jones (Cambridge, Mass.: MIT Press, 1991), 214–215.

82. Ted Robert Gurr, "The Revolution-Social-Change Nexus: Some Old Theories and New Hypotheses," *Comparative Politics* 5, no. 3 (April 1973): 359–392; Ted Robert Gurr, "Why Minorities Rebel: A Global Analysis of Communal Mobilization and Conflict Since 1945," *International Political Science Review* 14, no. 2 (April 1993): 161–201.

83. See also John Hutchinson and Anthony D. Smith, "Introduction," in *Ethnicity,* ed. John Hutchinson and Anthony D. Smith (Oxford: Oxford University Press, 1996), 3–14.

84. Brown, "The Causes of Internal Conflict," 5.

85. Brown, "The Causes of Internal Conflict," 5.

86. Brown, "The Causes of Internal Conflict," 5–6.

87. Barry R. Posen, "The Security Dilemma and Ethnic Conflict," *Survival* 35, no. 1 (Spring 1993): 28.

88. Posen, "The Security Dilemma and Ethnic Conflict," 38. See also Byman, *Keeping the Peace,* 17–22; Kaufman, "Spiraling to Ethnic War," 108–138.

89. Myron Rothbart, "Intergroup Perception and Social Conflict," in *Conflict between People and Groups: Causes, Processes, and Resolutions,* ed. Stephen Worchel and Jeffrey A. Simpson (Chicago: Nelson-Hall, 1993), 93–109.

90. Dean G. Pruitt, "Definition of the Situation as a Determinant of International Action," in *International Behavior: A Social-Psychological Analysis,* ed. Herbert C. Kelman (New York: Holt, Rinehart and Winston, 1965), 393–432; Deborah W. Larsen, "Trust and Missed Opportunities in International Relations," *Political Psychology* 18 (1997): 721. Byman argues that

the security dilemma is better understood "as an explanation for the continuation of conflict or for escalation of existing tension to violence rather than as one for why peaceful societies suddenly become violent" (*Keeping the Peace,* 19).

91. Brown, "The Causes of Internal Conflict," 6–7.
92. Brown, "The Causes of Internal Conflict," 7.
93. Brown, "The Causes of Internal Conflict," 8.
94. Esman, *An Introduction to Ethnic Conflict.* Clayton Peoples examines data for more than two hundred groups and one hundred countries, focusing on minority groups and types of discrimination and their relationship to interethnic violence. See Clayton D. Peoples, "How Discriminatory Policies Impact Interethnic Violence: A Cross-National, Group-Level Analysis," *International Journal of Sociology* 34, no. 1 (Spring 2004): 71–96.
95. Peoples, "How Discriminatory Policies Impact Interethnic Violence," 73.
96. Byman, *Keeping the Peace,* 31–32; Ilan Peleg, *Democratizing the Hegemonic State: Political Transformation in the Age of Identity* (Cambridge: Cambridge University Press, 2007).
97. Brown, "The Causes of Internal Conflict," 8.
98. Brown, "The Causes of Internal Conflict," 8–9.
99. Brown, "The Causes of Internal Conflict," 9.
100. Kristen P. Williams, "Internationalization of Ethnic Conflict in the Balkans: The Breakup of Yugoslavia," in *Ethnic Conflict and International Politics: Explaining Diffusion and Escalation,* ed. Steven E. Lobell and Philip Mauceri (New York: Palgrave, 2004), 76; Lenard J. Cohen, *Broken Bonds: The Disintegration of Yugoslavia* (Boulder: Westview Press, 1993), 266.
101. Brown, "The Causes of Internal Conflict."
102. Brown, "The Causes of Internal Conflict," 10–12. See also Peoples, "How Discriminatory Policies Impact Interethnic Violence," 73.
103. Esman, *An Introduction to Ethnic Conflict,* 79.
104. Brown, "The Causes of Internal Conflict," 12. See also Peoples, "How Discriminatory Policies Impact Interethnic Violence," 73.
105. Esman, *An Introduction to Ethnic Conflict,* 82.
106. Byman, *Keeping the Peace,* 22.
107. Esman, *An Introduction to Ethnic Conflict,* 83, 139.
108. Brown, "The Causes of Internal Conflict," 12.
109. Brown, "The Causes of Internal Conflict," 12.
110. Van Evera, "Hypotheses on Nationalism and War," 50–51.
111. Jay Rothman and Marie L. Olson, "From Interests to Identities: Towards a New Emphasis in Interactive Conflict Resolution," *Journal of Peace Research* 38, no. 3 (2001): 291.

112. Steven A. Weldon, "The Institutional Context of Tolerance for Ethnic Minorities: A Comparative, Multilevel Analysis of Western Europe," *American Journal of Political Science* 50, no. 2 (April 2006): 332.

113. Jeff Spinner-Halev and Elizabeth Theiss-Morse, "National Identity and Self-Esteem," *Perspectives on Politics* 1, no. 3 (September 2003): 519.

114. Spinner-Halev and Theiss-Morse, "National Identity and Self-Esteem," 521. See also Jeffrey R. Seul, "'Ours Is the Way of God': Religion, Identity, and Intergroup Conflict," *Journal of Peace Research* 36, no. 5 (1999): 553–569.

115. Weldon, "The Institutional Context of Tolerance for Ethnic Minorities," 333.

116. Spinner-Halev and Theiss-Morse, "National Identity and Self-Esteem," 522.

117. Esman, *An Introduction to Ethnic Conflict*, 89.

118. Byman, *Keeping the Peace*, 23.

119. Lake and Rothchild, "Spreading Fear," 7–8. See also Byman on hegemonic ambitions as a cause of ethnic conflict. He argues that hegemonic conflict is "the most difficult type of conflict to solve." This is so because the subordinate groups are expected to remain subordinate to the hegemonic ethnic group (both in terms of status and security). Byman, *Keeping the Peace*, 29–34.

120. Lake and Rothchild, "Spreading Fear," 4, 8–10. Stuart Kaufman argues that an ethnic security dilemma goes beyond the neorealist notion of a security dilemma—rather than anarchy and possible security threats leading to the dilemma, "an ethnic security dilemma [also] requires reciprocal fears of group extinction." See Kaufman, "Spiraling to Ethnic War," 112.

121. Peoples, "How Discriminatory Policies Impact Interethnic Violence," 89, 92–93.

122. Michael E. Brown and Chantal de Jonge Oudraat, "Internal Conflict and International Action: An Overview," in *Nationalism and Ethnic Conflict*, ed. Michael E. Brown, Owen R. Cote Jr., Sean M. Lynn Jones, and Steven E. Miller (Cambridge, Mass.: MIT Press, 2001), 188.

123. Byman, *Keeping the Peace*; Esman, *An Introduction to Ethnic Conflict*.

124. Adam Przeworski, *Democracy and the Market: Political and Economic Reforms in Eastern Europe and Latin America* (Cambridge: Cambridge University Press, 1991).

125. Barbara Harff and Ted Robert Gurr, *Ethnic Conflict in World Politics*, 2nd ed. (Boulder: Westview Press, 2004), 182.

126. Harff and Gurr, *Ethnic Conflict in World Politics*, 184.

127. Harff and Gurr, *Ethnic Conflict in World Politics*, 186.

128. Stefan Wolff, *Ethnic Conflict: A Global Perspective* (Oxford: Oxford University Press, 2006), 134–135.

129. Esman, *An Introduction to Ethnic Conflict*, 172.

130. Ilan Peleg, "Transforming Ethnic Orders to Pluralist Regimes: Theoretical, Comparative, and Historical Analysis," in *Democracy and Ethnic Conflict: Advancing Peace in Deeply Divided Societies,* ed. Adrian Guelke (New York: Palgrave, 2004), 7–25.

131. Peleg, "Transforming Ethnic Orders to Pluralist Regimes." On exclusionary domination, see also Esman, *An Introduction to Ethnic Conflict.*

132. Peleg, "Transforming Ethnic Orders to Pluralist Regimes."

133. Peleg, "Transforming Ethnic Orders to Pluralist Regimes," 12–13; Ilan Peleg, "Jewish-Palestinian Relations in Israel: From Hegemony to Equality?" *International Journal of Politics, Culture and Society* 17, no. 3 (Spring 2004): 426–427.

134. Elizabeth Crighton and Martha Abele Mac Iver, "The Evolution of Protracted Ethnic Conflict: Group Dominance and Political Underdevelopment in Northern Ireland and Lebanon," *Comparative Politics* 23, no. 2 (January 1991): 128.

135. Peleg, "Transforming Ethnic Orders to Pluralist Regimes," 14. Peleg distinguishes between two types of hegemonic regimes: majority and minority. A majority hegemonic regime is defined as a state in which one ethnic group is the "core nation." This "core nation" is able to use the state to maintain hegemonic rule and exclude all other groups. In the case of minority hegemonic regimes, the minority ethnic group is dominant, "negating the most basic rights of the majority, including the right of participating" in politics. In both cases, the state is exclusivist—one ethnic group (whether majority or minority) dominates the state and political institutions at the expense of other ethnic groups. Such states are undemocratic. See Peleg, "Jewish-Palestinian Relations in Israel," 429.

136. Peleg, "Transforming Ethnic Orders to Pluralist Regimes," 14; Peleg, "Jewish-Palestinian Relations in Israel," 430. Sammy Smooha and Theodor Hanf define an ethnic democracy as a state in which one ethnic group is dominant, dominance that is institutionalized. Importantly, they claim that such a democracy is different "from other types of democracy in according a structured superior status to a particular segment of the population and in regarding the non-dominant groups as having a relatively lesser claim to the state and also as being not fully loyal." They continue, "Its most outstanding manifestations are restrictions on certain individual and collective rights and on the full expression of the national identity of the non-dominant groups." The state is not neutral. Sammy Smooha and Theodor Hanf, "The Diverse Modes of Conflict-Regulation in Deeply Divided Societies," *International Journal of Comparative Sociology* 33, nos. 1–2 (1992): 32.

137. Peleg, "Transforming Ethnic Orders to Pluralist Regimes," 14; Peleg, "Jewish-Palestinian Relations in Israel," 430; Esman, *An Introduction to Ethnic Conflict,* 125–127.

138. Byman, *Keeping the Peace,* 30–31.
139. Byman, *Keeping the Peace,* 33.
140. Peleg, "Jewish-Palestinian Relations in Israel," 430.
141. Byman, *Keeping the Peace,* 44–49.
142. Byman, *Keeping the Peace,* 45–46; Crighton and Mac Iver, "The Evolution of Protracted Ethnic Conflict," 128.
143. Peleg, "Transforming Ethnic Orders to Pluralist Regimes."
144. William H. Riker, *Liberalism against Populism* (Prospect Heights, Ill.: Waveland Press, 1982).
145. Peleg, "Jewish-Palestinian Relations in Israel," 426–427.
146. Riker, *Liberalism against Populism.* See also Peleg, "Jewish-Palestinian Relations in Israel," 427.
147. Peleg, "Jewish-Palestinian Relations in Israel," 427.
148. Riker, *Liberalism against Populism.*
149. John Gibbons, *Spanish Politics Today* (Manchester: Manchester University Press, 1999).
150. Larry Diamond, Juan Linz, and Seymour Lipset, "Introduction: What Makes for Democracy?" in *Politics in Developing Countries: Comparing Experiences with Democracy,* ed. Larry Diamond, Juan Linz, and Seymour Lipset, 2nd ed. (Boulder: Lynne Rienner, 1995).
151. Diamond, Linz, and Lipset, "Introduction: What Makes for Democracy?"
152. Diamond, Linz, and Lipset, "Introduction: What Makes for Democracy?"
153. Horowitz, *Ethnic Groups in Conflict.*
154. Sisk, *Democratization in South Africa.*
155. Benjamin Reilly, *Democracy in Divided Societies: Electoral Engineering for Conflict Management* (Cambridge: Cambridge University Press, 2001).
156. Peleg, "Transforming Ethnic Orders to Pluralist Regimes"; Smooha and Hanf, "The Diverse Modes of Conflict-Regulation in Deeply Divided Societies," 33; Esman, *An Introduction to Ethnic Conflict,* 155–156.
157. Peleg, "Transforming Ethnic Orders to Pluralist Regimes."
158. Spinner-Halev and Theiss-Morse, "National Identity and Self-Esteem," 524. On this point see also Jonathan Hearn, *Rethinking Nationalism: A Critical Introduction* (New York: Palgrave Macmillan, 2006). He states that "more civic or liberal forms of nationalism are hardly a-cultural but, in fact, have evolved out of a particular culture-history and generally promote that culture" (p. 90).
159. Esman, *An Introduction to Ethnic Conflict,* 169–170.
160. Arend Lijphart, *Democracy in Plural Societies* (New Haven: Yale University Press, 1977); Smooha and Hanf, "The Diverse Modes of Conflict-Regulation in Deeply Divided Societies," 32–33.
161. Lijphart, *Democracy in Plural Societies.*

162. Lijphart, *Democracy in Plural Societies*.

163. Alicia Levine, "Political Accommodation and the Prevention of Secessionist Violence," in *The International Dimensions of Internal Conflict*, ed. Michael E. Brown (Cambridge, Mass.: MIT Press, 1996), 311-340; Esman, *An Introduction to Ethnic Conflict*, 141–142.

164. I. William Zartman, "Putting Humpty-Dumpty Together Again," in *The International Spread of Ethnic Conflict: Fear, Diffusion, and Escalation*, ed. David A. Lake and Donald Rothchild (Princeton: Princeton University Press, 1998), 317–336.

165. Arend Lijphart, *Conflict and Coexistence in Belgium: The Dynamics of a Culturally Divided Society* (Berkeley: University of California Press, 1981).

166. Levine, "Political Accommodation and the Prevention of Secessionist Violence," 331.

167. Horowitz, *Ethnic Groups in Conflict*, 626.

168. Schneckener, "Making Power-Sharing Work," 204.

169. Graham Smith, "Mapping the Federal Condition: Ideology, Political Practice and Social Justice," in *Federalism: The Multiethnic Challenge*, ed. Graham Smith (London: Longman, 1995); Horowitz, *Ethnic Groups in Conflict*.

170. David C. Nice, *Federalism: the Politics of Intergovernmental Relations* (New York: St. Martin's Press, 1987).

171. Smith, "Mapping the Federal Condition."

172. Alexander B. Murphy, "Belgium's Regional Divergence: Along the Road to Federation," in *Federalism: The Multiethnic Challenge*, ed. Graham Smith (London: Longman, 1995).

173. Sharda Rath, *Federalism Today: Approaches, Issues and Trends* (New Dehli: Sterling Publishers Private, 1984).

174. K. C. Wheare, *Federal Government*, 4th ed. (London: Oxford University Press, 1963). See also Esman, *An Introduction to Ethnic Conflict*, 141.

175. Jonathan Lemco, *Political Stability in Federal Governments* (New York: Praeger, 1991).

176. Brendan O'Leary and John McGarry, "Regulating Nations and Ethnic Communities," in *Nationalism and Rationality*, ed. Albert Breton, Gianluigi Galeotti, Pierre Salmon, and Ronald Wintrobe (Cambridge: Cambridge University Press, 1995), 245–289.

177. George Schopflin, "The Rise and Fall of Yugoslavia," in *The Politics of Ethnic Conflict Regulation*, ed. John McGarry and Brendan O'Leary (London: Routledge, 1993), 172–203.

178. Levine, "Political Accommodation and the Prevention of Secessionist Violence," 330, 332.

179. Horowitz, *Ethnic Groups in Conflict*.

180. Cameron Ross, "Federalism and Democratization in Russia," *Communist and Post-Communist Studies* 33 (2000): 403–420.

181. Barbara F. Walter, "Designing Transitions from Civil War: Demobilization, Democratization, and Commitments to Peace," in *Nationalism and Ethnic Conflict,* ed. Michael E. Brown, Owen R. Cote Jr., Sean M. Lynn-Jones, and Steven E. Miller, rev. ed. (Cambridge, Mass.: MIT Press, 2001), 430.

182. Eric A. Nordlinger, *Conflict Regulation in Divided Societies* (Cambridge, Mass.: Center for International Affairs, Harvard University, 1972); Levine, "Political Accommodation and the Prevention of Secessionist Violence," 335.

183. Levine, "Political Accommodation and the Prevention of Secessionist Violence."

184. Reilly, *Democracy in Divided Societies,* 143–144.

185. "Belgium's Pitiful Policies," *The Economist,* July 16, 2008, www.economist .com/displayStory.cfm?story_id=11739594.

186. Kanchan Chandra, "Ethnic Parties and Democratic Stability," *Perspectives on Politics* 3, no. 2 (June 2005): 235. On ethnic outbidding see James D. Fearon and David D. Laitin, "Violence and the Social Construction of Ethnic Identity," *International Organization* 54, no. 4 (Autumn 2000): 864–865.

187. Chandra, "Ethnic Parties and Democratic Stability," 236.

188. Chandra, "Ethnic Parties and Democratic Stability," 239.

189. Spinner-Halev and Theiss-Morse, "National Identity and Self-Esteem," 525.

190. Levine, "Political Accommodation and the Prevention of Secessionist Violence," 335.

191. Lijphart, *Democracy in Plural Societies,* 147–157.

192. Neal G. Jesse and Kristen P. Williams, *Identity and Institutions: Conflict Reduction in Divided Societies* (Albany: SUNY Press, 2005). See also Nina Casperson, "Good Fences Make Good Neighbours? A Comparison of Conflict-Regulation Strategies in Postwar Bosnia," *Journal of Peace Research* 41, no. 5 (2004): 569–588.

193. Byman, *Keeping the Peace,* 102.

194. Byman, *Keeping the Peace,* 126–129.

195. Byman, *Keeping the Peace,* 152.

196. Schneckener, "Making Power-Sharing Work," 211–214.

197. Schneckener, "Making Power-Sharing Work," 214–217.

198. Schneckener, "Making Power-Sharing Work," 218.

199. Schneckener, "Making Power-Sharing Work," 224.

200. Hearn, *Rethinking Nationalism,* 237.

201. Eiki Berg and Guy Ben-Porat, "Introduction: Partition vs. Power-Sharing?" *Nations and Nationalism* 14, no. 1 (2008): 31.

202. Waltz, *Man, the State, and War,* 227.

203. Waltz, *Man, the State, and War,* 232.

204. Waltz, *Man, the State, and War,* 232.
205. Singer, "The Level-of-Analysis Problem in International Relations," 80.
206. Lobell and Mauceri, "Diffusion and Escalation of Ethnic Conflict," 2.
207. Williams, "Internationalization of Ethnic Conflict in the Balkans," 75–94.
208. Esman, *An Introduction to Ethnic Conflict,* 102–103.
209. Esman, *An Introduction to Ethnic Conflict,* 119.
210. Yossi Shain and Aharon Barth, "Diasporas and International Relations Theory," *International Organization* 57, no. 3 (Summer 2003): 449–479.
211. Shain and Barth, "Diasporas and International Relations Theory," 451.
212. Esman, *An Introduction to Ethnic Conflict,* 104.
213. Esman, *An Introduction to Ethnic Conflict,* 105–106.
214. David Carment and Patrick James, "Explaining Third-party Intervention in Ethnic Conflict: Theory and Evidence," *Nations and Nationalism* 6, no. 2 (2000): 194.
215. Byman, *Keeping the Peace,* 40.
216. Charles King and Neil J. Melvin, "Diaspora Politics: Ethnic Linkages, Foreign Policy, and Security in Eurasia," *International Security* 24, no. 3 (Winter 1999/2000): 110.
217. King and Melvin, "Diaspora Politics," 131.
218. King and Melvin, "Diaspora Politics," 132.
219. King and Melvin, "Diaspora Politics," 132.
220. King and Melvin, "Diaspora Politics," 133–134.
221. King and Melvin, "Diaspora Politics," 134.
222. Shain and Barth, "Diasporas and International Relations Theory," 451, 458. See also Stephen M. Saideman, "Discrimination in International Relations: Analyzing External Support for Ethnic Groups," *Journal of Peace Research* 39, no. 1 (2002): 27–50.
223. Esman, *An Introduction to Ethnic Conflict,* 107.
224. Lake and Rothchild, "Spreading Fear," 31.
225. Matthew Evangelista, "Historical Legacies and the Politics of Intervention in the Former Soviet Union," in *The International Dimensions of Internal Conflict,* ed. Michael E. Brown (Cambridge, Mass.: MIT Press, 1996), 121–122.
226. Kaufman, "Spiraling to Ethnic War," 110, 118.
227. Kaufman, "Spiraling to Ethnic War," 110.
228. Horowitz, *Ethnic Groups in Conflict,* 273.
229. Harff and Gurr, *Ethnic Conflict in World Politics,* 188–190.
230. Byman, *Keeping the Peace,* 179.
231. Posen, "The Security Dilemma and Ethnic Conflict," 43.
232. Donald Rothchild and David A. Lake, "Containing Fear: The Management of Transnational Ethnic Conflict," in *The International Spread of Ethnic*

Conflict: Fear, Diffusion, and Escalation, ed. David A. Lake and Donald Rothchild (Princeton: Princeton University Press, 1998), 221.

233. Posen, "The Security Dilemma and Ethnic Conflict," 43–44.

234. Rothchild and Lake, "Containing Fear," 203–226.

235. Kaufman, "Spiraling to Ethnic War," 133.

236. Esman, *An Introduction to Ethnic Conflict,* 109; Rothchild and Lake, "Containing Fear," 205–211.

237. J. Michael Grieg and Patrick M. Regan, "When Do They Say Yes? An Analysis of the Willingness to Offer and Accept Mediation," *International Studies Quarterly* 52 (2008): 769.

238. Grieg and Regan, "When Do They Say Yes?" 762–763.

239. Grieg and Regan, "When Do They Say Yes?" 762.

240. Esman, *An Introduction to Ethnic Conflict,* 109–110.

241. Esman, *An Introduction to Ethnic Conflict,* 110.

242. Jacob Bercovitch and Allison Houston, "The Study of International Mediation: Theoretical Issues and Empirical Evidence," in *Resolving International Conflicts: The Theory and Practice of Mediation,* ed. Jacob Bercovitch (Boulder: Lynne Rienner, 1996), 26.

243. Sara McLaughlin Mitchell and Paul R. Hensel, "International Institutions and Compliance with Agreements," *American Journal of Political Science* 51, no. 4 (October 2007): 724.

244. Bercovitch and Houston, "The Study of International Mediation," 27.

245. Philip A. Schrodt and Deborah J. Gerner, "An Event Data Analysis of Third-Party Mediation in the Middle East and Balkans," *Journal of Conflict Resolution* 48, no. 3 (June 2004): 322.

246. United Nations Security Council Resolution 1325 (October 31, 2000).

247. United Nations, "Security Council Demands Immediate and Complete Halt to Acts of Sexual Violence against Civilians in Conflict Zones, Unanimously Adopting Resolution 1820 (2008)," Security Council SC/9364, Department of Public Information (June 19, 2008), www.un.org/News/Press/docs/2008/sc9364.doc.htm.

248. Esman, *An Introduction to Ethnic Conflict,* 114.

249. Esman, *An Introduction to Ethnic Conflict,* 115.

250. Brown and de Jonge Oudraat, "Internal Conflict and International Action," 168.

251. Brown and de Jonge Oudraat, "Internal Conflict and International Action," 168. See also Rothchild and Lake, "Containing Fear," 223–224.

252. Rothchild and Lake, "Containing Fear," 224.

253. Rothchild and Lake, "Containing Fear," 215.

254. Rothchild and Lake, "Containing Fear," 216.

255. Spinner-Halev and Theiss-Morse, "National Identity and Self-Esteem," 524.

256. Esman, *An Introduction to Ethnic Conflict,* 118.

257. Esman, *An Introduction to Ethnic Conflict,* 116–117.

258. Rothchild and Lake, "Containing Fear," 216–217.

259. Brown and de Jonge Oudraat, "Internal Conflict and International Action," 163–192.

260. Byman, *Keeping the Peace,* 178.

261. Rothchild and Lake, "Containing Fear," 221.

262. Byman, *Keeping the Peace,* 183.

263. Byman, *Keeping the Peace,* 184–185.

264. Byman, *Keeping the Peace,* 185–186.

265. Grieg and Regan, "When Do They Say Yes?" 777.

266. Posen, "The Security Dilemma and Ethnic Conflict," 44; Stephen E. Gent, "Going in When It Counts: Military Intervention and the Outcome of Civil Conflicts," *International Studies Quarterly* 52 (2008): 713–714; Rothchild and Lake, "Containing Fear," 217.

267. Rothchild and Lake, "Containing Fear," 217–18.

268. Rothchild and Lake, "Containing Fear," 218.

269. Gent, "Going in When it Counts," 715.

270. Brown and de Jonge Oudraat, "Internal Conflict and International Action," 185.

271. Brown and de Jonge Oudraat, "Internal Conflict and International Action," 188.

272. Kaufman, "Spiraling to Ethnic War," 134.

273. Kaufman, "Spiraling to Ethnic War," 135.

274. Kaufman, "Spiraling to Ethnic War," 136–137.

275. Byman, *Keeping the Peace,* 174.

276. Byman, *Keeping the Peace,* 155–169.

277. Byman, *Keeping the Peace,* 171.

278. Thomas Chapman and Philip G. Roeder, "Partition as a Solution to Wars of Nationalism: The Importance of Institutions," *American Political Science Review* 101, no. 4 (November 2007): 677; Carter Johnson, "Partitioning to Peace: Sovereignty, Demography, and Ethnic Civil Wars," *International Security* 32, no. 4 (Spring 2008): 151; Chaim Kaufmann, "Possible and Impossible Solutions to Ethnic Civil Wars," in *Nationalism and Ethnic Conflict,* ed. Michael E. Brown, Owen R. Cote Jr., Sean M. Lynn-Jones, and Steven E. Miller, rev. ed. (Cambridge, Mass.: MIT Press 2001), 478–482.

279. Byman, *Keeping the Peace,* 172–173; Johnson, "Partitioning to Peace," 151.

280. Chapman and Roeder, "Partition as a Solution to Wars of Nationalism," 679.

281. Chapman and Roeder, "Partition as a Solution to Wars of Nationalism," 679–680.
282. Chapman and Roeder, "Partition as a Solution to Wars of Nationalism," 681.
283. Kaufmann, "Possible and Impossible Solutions to Ethnic Civil Wars," 445.
284. Byman, *Keeping the Peace,* 176.
285. Byman, *Keeping the Peace,* 175; Johnson, "Partitioning to Peace," 151.
286. Chapman and Roeder, "Partition as a Solution to Wars of Nationalism," 689.
287. Johnson, "Partitioning to Peace," 151.
288. Johnson, "Partitioning to Peace," 161.
289. James D. Fearon, "Commitment Problems and the Spread of Ethnic Conflict," in *The International Spread of Ethnic Conflict: Fear, Diffusion, and Escalation,* ed. David A. Lake and Donald Rothchild (Princeton: Princeton University Press, 1998), 118–120. On the need to design credible guarantees see also Barbara Walter, "Designing Transitions from Civil War: Demobilization, Democratization, and Commitments to Peace," in *Nationalism and Ethnic Conflict,* ed. Michael E. Brown, Owen R. Cote Jr., Sean M. Lynn-Jones, and Steven E. Miller, rev. ed. (Cambridge, Mass.: MIT Press, 2001), 415–443.
290. Fearon, "Commitment Problems and the Spread of Ethnic Conflict," 107–126.
291. Rothchild and Lake, "Containing Fear," 219.
292. Fearon, "Commitment Problems and the Spread of Ethnic Conflict," 123.
293. Rothchild and Lake, "Containing Fear," 219.
294. Fearon, "Commitment Problems and the Spread of Ethnic Conflict," 123.
295. Brown and de Jonge Oudraat, "Internal Conflict and International Action," 191.
296. Brown and de Jonge Oudraat, "Internal Conflict and International Action," 184.
297. Brown and de Jonge Oudraat, "Internal Conflict and International Action," 180–181, 184.
298. Rothchild and Lake, "Containing Fear," 221–222.
299. Rothchild and Lake, "Containing Fear," 225.
300. Kaufman, "Spiraling to Ethnic War," 133.
301. Bumba Mukherjee, "Does Third-Party Enforcement or Domestic Institutions Promote Enduring Peace after Civil Wars? Policy Lessons from an Empirical Test," *Foreign Policy Analysis* 2 (2006): 428.
302. Kaufman, "Spiraling to Ethnic War," 109.
303. Harff and Gurr, *Ethnic Conflict in World Politics,* 5.

304. Druckman, "Nationalism, Patriotism, and Group Loyalty," 54. See also Pearson, "Dimensions of Conflict Resolution in Ethnopolitical Disputes," 275–287.

305. Though focusing in large part on the individual level of analysis (providing a critique of the systemic level), Deborah Welch Larson uses a multilevel approach to explain U.S. policy in the Cold War. Deborah Welch Larson, *The Origins of Containment: A Psychological Explanation* (Princeton: Princeton University Press, 1985).

CHAPTER 3

Northern Ireland: Protestants, Catholics, and "The Troubles"

On March 16, 2006, a joint hearing of two United States congressional subcommittees observed a moment of silence and prayer before the meeting began. The joint hearing was entitled "The Northern Ireland Peace Process: Policing Advances and Remaining Challenges." It was comprised of the Subcommittee on Africa, Global Human Rights, and International Operations and the Subcommittee on Europe and Emerging Threats, both of which were part of the Committee on International Relations in the United States House of Representatives. At 2:58 P.M. in room 2172, Rayburn House Office Building, the Honorable Christopher H. Smith of New Jersey presided over the moment of silence for a brave defense attorney from Northern Ireland.[1]

Rosemary Nelson was killed almost six and a half years earlier by a car bomb as she drove mere blocks away from her home. Exactly seven years before to the day of the 2006 hearing, this brave attorney from Northern Ireland gave testimony to a similar congressional committee. She described how her job representing Catholic defendants, some of whom were accused of terrorist crimes, had led to her life being threatened by the Royal Ulster Constabulatory (RUC), which was the police force of Northern Ireland at the time. She said that they had threatened her many times, both directly and through her clients. Within moments of her death, allegations of collusion by public servants circulated, pointing at the RUC, the Northern Ireland Office of the British government, the British Army, and other British state agencies. These allegations continue to this day.[2]

On November 16, 2004, the British secretary of state for Northern Ireland, the Rt. Honorable Paul Murphy, MP, announced a public inquiry into the death of Rosemary Nelson. The inquiry (known as the Rosemary Nelson Inquiry) was established under section 44 of the Police (Northern Ireland) Act of 1998. This act to reform policing in Northern Ireland was passed by the British House of Commons after the conclusion of the 1998 Good Friday Agreement in Belfast, which was agreed to by most major parties in Northern Ireland, representing the majority of both Catholic and Protestant citizens. The public inquiry was called after a retired Canadian Supreme Court judge, Peter Cory, investigated the allegations of collusion and recommended that a public inquiry would be necessary to determine the facts.[3]

The terms of reference for the inquiry are "To inquire into the death of Rosemary Nelson with a view to determining whether any wrongful act or omission by or within the Royal Ulster Constabulary, Northern Ireland Office, Army, or other state agency facilitated her death or obstructed the investigation of it, or whether attempts were made to do so; whether any such act or omission was intentional or negligent; whether the investigation of her death was carried out with due diligence; and to make recommendations."[4] In preparation for live testimonies, the inquiry gathered tens of thousands of documents. The three-member panel asked a team of former police officers to hand over all documents related to the original murder investigation, and also to prepare a report concerning the police handling of the case. Full hearings in the Rosemary Nelson Inquiry began on April 15, 2008, and are planned to continue through 2009. The inquiry had by early 2009 heard over one hundred days of testimony.[5] The end of this inquiry is still a great deal of time away and the result is uncertain.

The case of the murder of Rosemary Nelson highlights the intertwining of all levels of analysis in understanding ethnic conflict in Northern Ireland. The role of foreign governments and their governmental bodies, the actions of domestic state actors, as well as the actions and motivations of individuals, all are involved in the mysteries surrounding her death. Further, the inherent tension between the two communities in Northern Ireland is the backdrop for all of the past and current events involved in the timeline of Rosemary's murder.

NORTHERN IRELAND IN HISTORICAL CONTEXT

The Creation of Northern Ireland

To help explain the existing conflict, we provide a brief summary of the creation of Northern Ireland.[6] After French consolidation of their control on the European continent in 1540, English expansion turned from Europe toward Wales, Scotland, and Ireland. Settlement of Ireland by English and Scottish settlers was rapid. "By 1641 Protestant settlers owned 41 percent of the land in Ireland and held a majority of seats in both houses of the Irish parliament."[7] The victory of Cromwell over the Irish in 1640 led to the confiscation of Irish-owned land. This pattern repeated itself in 1690 with the defeat of the Catholic supporters of James II. The Catholic population receded into the status of a peripheral nationality on its own island.[8]

A Catholic revival in the nineteenth century led to calls for Irish independence. Prior to World War I, Irish republican political struggles created what the English parliamentarians called the "Ulster crisis." In short, the question of whether Ireland should have Home Rule was debated on both sides of the Irish

Sea. A small group of republicans felt that the outbreak of the First World War offered an opportunity to strike at British rule while the British were occupied on the European continent. The 1916 Easter Rebellion ended in defeat for the rebels, the British execution of fifteen of the republican leaders, and the subsequent turn toward terrorism by the new Irish Republican Army (IRA). The British authorities imposed martial law, which only further inflamed the republican resistance. The Anglo-Irish War lasted from 1919 to July 1921, with much violence perpetrated by both sides.[9]

Britain eventually went to the negotiating table with the idea of partition as a solution to the violence. The plan was for the nine northeastern counties in the historic area of Ulster to remain a part of Britain while the remaining counties, all predominantly Catholic, would be given Home Rule under British dominion. Eventually only six counties in Ulster would be considered for partition, and of those six, Catholics were the majority in two, Fermanagh and Tyrone, and in the city of Derry (in County Derry/Londonderry). The British Parliament passed the Government of Ireland Act in 1920, effectively dividing the north from the south. Negotiations in the remaining twenty-six counties in the South as to their status subsequently led to Home Rule and the Irish Free State, a civil war, and eventual development of a new constitution and republic in 1937.[10] For the remainder of its history to today, Northern Ireland would remain a part of the United Kingdom (Great Britain and Northern Ireland) while the Republic of Ireland (often shortened to "Republic" or sometimes "Ireland") would be an independent state. Thus, the island of Ireland is currently divided between Northern Ireland and the Republic.

From the Creation of Northern Ireland to the Present

The social and economic conditions within Northern Ireland from the 1920s to the 1960s were determined by its relationship with the rest of the United Kingdom. In essence, the British government tried to maintain parity between Northern Ireland and the other British nations. Westminster did not treat Northern Ireland as any place special or different. Despite this policy of parity, inhabitants of Northern Ireland were generally poorer than other British citizens.[11]

Sectarian relations during this time were not particularly troublesome. That does not mean, however, that there were no problems. Communal rioting in Belfast in 1935 would be a harbinger of future events. Three weeks of rioting left a dozen people dead and forced hundreds of Catholic families out of their homes. While many in the Catholic community stressed their loyalty to Britain, a smaller number agitated for exclusion. The campaign for an autonomous Republic of Ireland to the south of Northern Ireland had the mirror effect of driving northern Protestants to emphasize their "Britishness."[12]

During the Second World War (1939–1945), nationalists in the north saw an opportunity, with the British preoccupied with Germany, for ending the partition of Ireland. The Nationalist support for the Republic's foreign policy of neutrality incensed the Protestant Unionists. Efforts by the IRA to build links with Nazi Germany only made matters worse. At the same time, over 38,000 citizens of Northern Ireland enlisted in the British military and saw combat in all theaters, with over 4,700 never returning.[13]

After the war, the move to the welfare state led by British prime minister Clement Atlee extended British authority to Northern Ireland. The 1949 Ireland Act confirmed that Northern Ireland was a part of the United Kingdom and that the Republic of Ireland was not. Moreover, the Ireland Act also established that Northern Ireland could not be removed from the United Kingdom without the consent of the Northern Ireland parliament.[14]

The 1950s saw Sinn Fein (political arm of the IRA) and the IRA renew efforts to end partition through two strategies. First, Sinn Fein began to run for seats in the British House of Commons. In 1955 they named twelve candidates, half of whom were in prison, for election to Westminster. Any members elected would follow a policy of absenteeism, by which they would not swear an oath to the crown nor would they attend parliamentary sessions. The second strategy was a cross-border campaign of violence. Launching raids from strongholds in the Republic of Ireland, the IRA targeted mainly military and police barracks and personnel. This would be the start of almost six years of such raids.[15]

Civil strife began in the 1960s. The decline of staple Northern Ireland industries such as textiles, ship building, and agriculture led to economic stagnation. Income, job security, and the ability of average citizens to afford education for their children all became a concern. The Catholic community had a growing recognition of the effect of long-term discrimination in housing, education, jobs, and advancement. The result was the beginning of a civil rights movement that would argue for equality between the two communities.[16]

The Chief Constable's Office in Northern Ireland reports that from the years 1969 to 1996 there were 3,212 fatal casualties from sectarian violence in Northern Ireland.[17] Roughly two-thirds of these fatalities were civilians. The greater part of the violence occurred from 1972 through 1976. An average of over 200 civilians and more than 60 security officers (both military and police) lost their lives each year during this time. Brendan O'Leary and John McGarry figure that the responsibility for deaths from 1969 to 1989 can be distributed in the following manner: republican paramilitaries, 57.7 percent; loyalist paramilitaries, 25.3 percent; and security forces, 11.8 percent.[18] Malcolm Sutton lists every fatality from the violence, including those killed in Britain, Ireland, and elsewhere in Europe, and arrives at a fairly similar distribution of responsibility.[19]

The considerable violence in Northern Ireland led eventually to the negotiating table. In October 1973, as a response to the sectarian violence, representatives of the Catholic and Protestant parties met and agreed upon a power-sharing executive. This was followed by the Sunningdale Agreement of December 6–9, 1973, which paved the way for a Council of Ireland. The Council would allow members of the Irish (that is, the Republic's) government to meet with representatives from Northern Ireland. As a concession to the Protestant community, the Agreement also solidified that no constitutional changes in the status of Northern Ireland could occur without majority consent, in other words, the acceptance of the Protestants. Unionists disagreed with these terms, claiming that too much authority had been delegated to the Republic in the affairs of Northern Ireland. A strike by Protestant unions eventually derailed both the power-sharing executive and the Sunningdale Agreement.[20]

On November 15, 1985, the British government successfully negotiated the Anglo-Irish Agreement (AIA) between the British and Irish governments. Much like the Sunningdale Agreement, the AIA established a forum for greater participation from the Republic over affairs in Northern Ireland, while also reaffirming the role of majority consent in the north. The IRA opposed the AIA on the grounds that it solidified the view that Northern Ireland was not part of the Republic. Protestant unionists criticized the AIA as wrongly giving too much authority to the southern government. During the rest of the 1980s, violence between Protestants and Catholics continued while implementation of the AIA was hindered by both communities.[21]

The Irish Republican Army and loyalist paramilitaries declared a joint cease-fire in 1994 that led to the British government initiating inclusive, all-party talks about the future of Northern Ireland. Despite a resumption of IRA bombing in 1996, and the removal of Sinn Fein from the negotiating table, the talks moved forward with the participation of the British government, Irish government, and former U.S. senator George Mitchell as mediator. The talks also survived the IRA's new cease-fire in 1997, the re-inclusion of Sinn Fein, and the withdrawal of the Democratic Unionist Party. Eventually on April 10, 1998, the British-Irish Peace Agreement (or Good Friday Agreement as it is more commonly known) was signed by all parties. On May 22 of the same year, referenda on the Agreement passed with 71 percent in favor in Northern Ireland and 94 percent in favor in the Republic of Ireland (which had to agree to changes to its constitution to accommodate provisions of the Agreement).[22]

The Good Friday Agreement in Northern Ireland signaled a new approach to solving the intractable conflict. However, the implementation and institutionalization of the Good Friday Agreement has been problematic. Stabilizing the fundamental components of the Agreement has occurred in two stages: initial efforts at implementation (1998–2003) and meeting challenges from the results (2003–).[23]

A timetable for implementation was attached to the Agreement. However, the key components of decommissioning and disarmament did not have a specified starting date. Moreover, the completion of both would not occur until all other signatories to the Agreement fulfilled their obligations as well. It was the responsibility of the British and Irish governments to create new cross-border institutions (for example, the British-Irish Council, the North-South Ministerial Council, and the British-Irish Intergovernmental Conference). It was also primarily the obligation of the British government to see that all reforms were initiated (for example, policing and justice). It was also understood in the Good Friday Agreement negotiations that all parties to the Agreement would work toward completion of the goals of the Agreement, especially in the newly created Northern Ireland Assembly.[24]

Elections to the fledgling Assembly were held on June 25, 1998, and on July 1 it met for the first time. Progress continued to be made toward implementing the Agreement despite the massive IRA car bomb in Omagh that killed twenty-nine people and injured over three hundred more. Various paramilitary groups announced cease-fires while early in 1999 the British and Irish governments signed agreements providing the legal framework for the North-South implementation bodies.[25]

However, by April 1999 the main political parties began to miss deadlines agreed upon for devolution, or the movement of political authority from the British Parliament in London to the newly created Assembly in Northern Ireland. The sticking point was decommissioning of weapons. The IRA pointed out that loyalist groups were not disarming and that the IRA would stop doing so without assurances that all paramilitaries, not just the republican ones, were giving up their arms. The British government and loyalist organizations noted that the IRA had not unambiguously declared its war to be over and renounced violent action. On December 1, 1999, a power-sharing executive was put into place and the Assembly opened despite the continued wrangling of the political parties. In January 2000 the International Independent Commission on Decommissioning (IICD), led by the Canadian general John De Chastelain, delivered its report on the likelihood of arms decommissioning. The Protestant leader David Trimble threatened to walk out of the government, and on February 11 the secretary of state for Northern Ireland, Peter Mendelson, suspended operation of the Assembly.[26]

Thus began a pattern in which during the next three years the Assembly would be suspended over and over again. The ineffectiveness of the two moderate parties, the Social Democratic and Labour Party (SDLP) and the Ulster Unionist Party (UUP), led to growing dissatisfaction with these parties among the Catholic and

MAP 3.1
Distribution of Catholics and Protestants in Northern Ireland

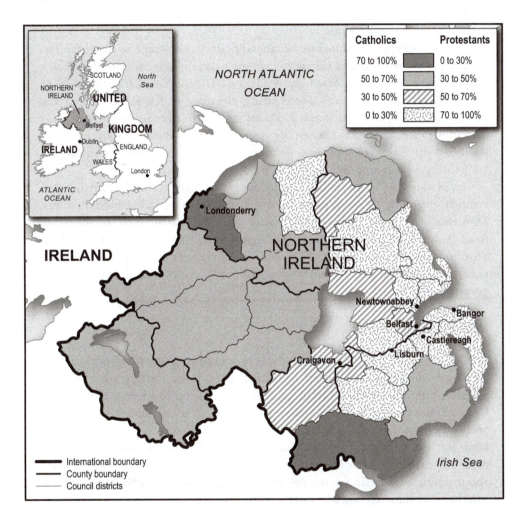

Source: Data from Paul Dixon, *Northern Ireland: The Politics of War and Peace,* (New York: Palgrave, 2001), 20, and Martin Melaugh, *Catholics and Protestants as a Percentage of the Population, District Council Areas, 1991,* CAIN, the University of Ulster, http://cain.ulst.ac.uk/images/maps/map10.htm.

Protestant communities, respectively. By the elections of November 26, 2003, the more extreme parties, Sinn Fein (SF) and the Democratic Unionist Party (DUP), became the largest parties to represent, respectively, the Irish nationalism and continued union with Britain.[27]

The 2003 elections resulted in a changed political landscape in Northern Ireland. The empowerment of the more extreme party in each community led to a lack of cooperation in the Assembly. While the DUP and Sinn Fein came close to a bargain in 2004 over the power-sharing executive, it fell through, and the Assembly was suspended through 2006. An attempt to elect an executive on May 22, 2006, failed, leaving the Assembly suspended. The March 7, 2007, elections solidified the dominance of Sinn Fein and the DUP, with the more moderate UUP losing a great amount of ground.[28]

Yet, in May 2007 both leading parties agreed to share power. The British government promptly devolved power to the Assembly. In typical fashion, however, Sinn Fein argued that policing and justice should be devolved to the Assembly from Westminster and a new deadlock began in the Northern Irish Assembly in Stormont. In the summer of 2008, Sinn Fein threatened to walk out of the executive if these two competencies were not devolved immediately by the British government.[29]

INDIVIDUAL LEVEL

The long conflict in Northern Ireland has produced its share of political leaders, be they leaders of the sectarian political parties, hunger strikers in a British prison, prime ministers of Britain and Ireland, or even former senators of the United States Congress. In this section we do not seek to examine the role of each and every important political leader involved with the conflict in Northern Ireland. Rather, we examine the role of political leadership in Northern Ireland, mainly by selecting a few illustrative examples. Moreover, we place the theories about political leadership developed in chapter 2 under the microscope and ask whether they have relevance to Northern Ireland.

Northern Ireland and Leadership Theories

There is a potential sticking point in examining the role of political leadership in Northern Ireland: that the situation has evolved from a conflict to a peace process while most of the key players have remained the same. Gerry Adams and the Reverend Ian Paisley both played a large role in the conflict stage from the late 1960s to the mid-1990s, but both have also contributed significantly to the peace process from that point forward. This presents us with a bit of a dilemma in applying leadership theories to the Northern Ireland conflict. The classic political science texts on leadership often deal with leaders faced with ongoing conflict; the peace and conflict studies literature deals more with leaders faced with conflict resolution or peace negotiations.[30]

Classic theories of leadership posit the key role played by top-level leaders who are visible, are in positions to control resources, can take positions for a group, and have great influence over their followers. John Paul Lederach has emphasized that during a peace process these leaders are less able to effect change, and especially they are less able to get their supporters to follow agreements negotiated and agreed with other top-level leaders.[31] A perfect example would be the struggles that Ulster Unionist Party leader David Trimble had following the Good Friday Agreement, which arguably was negotiated by top-level leaders. Trimble slowly and surely lost the support of his party and grassroots unionists who did not accept the Agreement and blamed him for sponsoring it. Consociational theories suffer similarly from this overemphasis on top-level political leaders and their abilities.

There is also the question of motive. Many argue that political leaders will not pursue conflict management unless it is in their individual self-interest to do so. It may be hard to find a sufficient self-interest in conflict resolution when the leader had previously been involved with years, if not decades, of self-interest in conflict. Hugh Miall, Oliver Ramsbotham, and Tom Woodhouse emphasize that one way around this dilemma is to have a change of political leadership.[32] Such is the problem in Northern Ireland: the leaders of the large sectarian communities have not changed much. Of interest also will be the "spoiler" hypothesis of leadership put forth by Stephen Stedman.[33] We will see that leaders in Northern Ireland behave very much like the "greedy spoiler" that we outlined in chapter 2.

We examine the role of long-term leaders like Gerry Adams and the Reverend Ian Paisley. We also briefly look at those with a much shorter tenure as leaders, such as John Hume and David Trimble. Lastly, we look at leaders whose involvement was bounded by external factors, such as their own tenure as prime minister or as an appointment of a foreign government. A representative of this group is former U.S. senator George Mitchell. The multilevel approach of this text allows us to tease out the effect of leadership change in the external arena. This external change will often transform the internal conflict and force the non-changing leaders in that environment to respond.

Gerry Adams and the Reverend Ian Paisley

Gerry Adams and Ian Paisley represent two extremes in Northern Ireland. Gerry Adams is president of Sinn Fein and has spent most of his adult life working toward republican goals. Ian Paisley cofounded and led the Democratic Unionist Party until 2008. He has dominated Unionist politics and was a constant and passionate defender of the continued union of Northern Ireland with Great Britain. Both men led political parties and political movements, and represented the extreme views of their respective communities. Each man has been alleged either to be a member of a paramilitary group or, at the least, to have incited groups and communities to commit violence. In a way, these two different men have followed very similar paths.

Gerry Adams was born on October 6, 1948, in West Belfast. His father had been a member of the Irish Republican Brotherhood during the Irish War of Independence. Two of his uncles were interned for suspected participation in the IRA. One author goes so far as to say that one of them was a senior leader of the IRA in the 1940s.[34] Adams's father was imprisoned from 1942 to 1950 for participating in an IRA ambush of a police patrol. Adams joined Sinn Fein in 1964. He also participated in the civil rights movement of the late 1960s through his involvement with the Northern Ireland Civil Rights Association.[35]

The transitional period for Adams from a bit-role player to a political leader occurred in the 1970s. During that decade he was interned a number of times for his involvement with Sinn Fein and also his alleged planning of the 1972 bombings in Belfast known as Bloody Friday. In his imprisonment he gained a reputation as a skilled negotiator and policymaker for Sinn Fein. He also penned a number of articles for the *Republican News* in which he urged greater political activity, especially at the local level, among republicans. He argued that political activity was a complement to the armed struggle of the IRA. In 1978 he became joint vice president of Sinn Fein. From this position, he challenged the leadership, which he saw as based in the South and dominated by southerners. During the 1981 hunger strikes he thrust Sinn Fein into the political leadership of the republican movement.[36]

In 1983 he was elected president of Sinn Fein. He subsequently won a seat in the British House of Commons, but like all representatives of his party, he followed a policy of absenteeism and refused to take his seat in the chamber. This policy coincided with the Sinn Fein belief that the only legitimate government of Northern Ireland was the IRA Army Council, as it was the successor of the last anti-Treaty parliament of the Republic in 1938. From his position as president, Adams began to move Sinn Fein away from being just a political voice of the IRA and more toward a professional political party with its own agenda.[37]

In 1998 Adams began secret talks with John Hume of the rival, Catholic community–based, Social Democratic and Labour Party. The two arrived at a negotiated settlement between the competing aims of the two parties. This settlement led to secret talks with representatives of both the British and Irish governments. Neither Westminster nor Dublin would publicly announce that they were engaged in such talks, as both had an official policy of not negotiating with terrorists.

Adams's links to the IRA had led to his being labeled a terrorist and to various restrictions on him, including limiting his freedom to travel and the sometimes humorous "voice ban" by the British government, which prevented any media broadcasting of his voice.[38]

Adams was also instrumental in supporting the 1993 Downing Street Declaration (DSD). The DSD agreement between the prime ministers of Britain and Ireland confirmed that it was for the people of Ireland alone, both North and South, to exercise their right to sovereignty and authority.[39] Adams's support of the DSD angered some republicans who claimed that it legitimized continued partition. Adams argued that it was a step forward in that it advanced movement toward a constitutional solution in Northern Ireland and that it also added the participation of the Republic of Ireland to any future agreement. The IRA cease-fire of 1994 thrust Adams back into the spotlight as he campaigned for a renewed peace process. His participation in the All-Party Talks and support for the Good Friday Agreement helped its eventual ratification.[40]

Since 1998 Adams has continued to lead Sinn Fein. He has maintained that Republican participation in the institutions of the Agreement is a transitional phase along the path to the goal of a united Ireland. Elections since 2005 have eroded the power of the SDLP and moved Sinn Fein into the position as the dominant representative of the Catholic community. In 2007 Adams met face-to-face with Ian Paisley for the first time ever. The two agreed to a power-sharing executive in which Paisley would be first minister and Martin McGuinness from Sinn Fein would be deputy first minister.[41]

Ian Paisley was born on April 6, 1926, in Armagh. His father was an Independent Baptist minister and had served in the Ulster Volunteers earlier in his life. Paisley undertook theological training at the Barry School of Evangelism (later the South Wales Bible College) and was ordained in 1946. In the 1950s Paisley established the Free Presbyterian Church of Ulster in Crossgar, County Down. Paisley preached fundamentalist Protestant views and argued against any growing links between the Catholic and Protestant churches.[42]

Paisley entered into politics through his criticism of Terrence O'Neill, the prime minister of Northern Ireland from 1963 to 1969, and O'Neill's efforts to help the Catholic community gain civil rights. His opposition to O'Neill led to the formation of the Ulster Constitution Defense Committee and the Ulster Protestant Volunteers, both of which participated in counter-demonstrations against the Catholic organization, the Northern Ireland Civil Rights Association (NICRA). In 1969 he was arrested and jailed for an illegal protest against the NICRA.[43]

In 1970 Paisley was elected to sit in the British House of Commons. In 1971 he and Desmond Boal, who had broken from the Ulster Unionist Party, formed the

Democratic Unionist Party (DUP). The DUP and Paisley immediately began what would be a long-term strategy of opposition to initiatives for change in Northern Ireland. He opposed the 1972 suspension of the Stormont parliament and he opposed the 1973 Sunningdale Agreement and the power-sharing executive. He participated in the Ulster Workers' Council Strike of 1973 and demonstrations that destabilized and eventually toppled the power-sharing government.[44]

Paisley was a leading Protestant figure in the opposition to the 1985 Anglo-Irish Agreement. He objected to the notion that a foreign government, and by this he meant the Republic of Ireland, could now interfere in the affairs of Northern Ireland. He also rejected the idea that any agreement could be enforced without a ratifying referendum of the people of Northern Ireland. He spoke to a rally of 200,000 people in front of Belfast City Hall, with the slogan of the meeting being "Ulster says No!"[45]

Paisley was also critical of the 1993 Downing Street Declaration and the 1994 IRA cease-fire, claiming that both were part of a wider scheme to destabilize Ulster. He and the DUP were initially part of the All-Party Talks in 1996. However, when the British government allowed Sinn Fein into the talks in 1997, the DUP withdrew. Subsequently, Paisley and the DUP campaigned against the Agreement's referendum ratification.[46] However, with its passage, Paisley campaigned for a seat in the new Northern Ireland Assembly. By 2000 he simultaneously held seats in three different parliaments: the British House of Commons, the Northern Ireland Assembly, and the European Parliament.

Paisley's opposition to the Good Friday Agreement reaped rewards in the 2000s. The suspension of the Assembly undermined the position of David Trimble and his Ulster Unionist Party that had supported the Agreement. Moreover, Unionist discontent over the pace of IRA decommissioning drove Protestant voters to the DUP. In the 2003 elections, the DUP campaigned on the need to renegotiate the treaty and won more seats than the UUP. Paisley immediately refused to form any power-sharing government with Sinn Fein, claiming that he would not sit down with terrorists. The British government had no option but to maintain the suspension of the Assembly.[47]

Following IRA disarmament in 2005, the British government set deadlines for the DUP and Sinn Fein to form a new executive or face direct rule from Westminster. Both parties agreed in 2006 to hold new elections. They also agreed that the two could form a new government dependent on Sinn Fein's accepting the legitimacy of the new Police Service of Northern Ireland (PSNI). The 2006 elections saw the DUP and Sinn Fein continue their leadership of their respective communities. As noted previously, in 2007 Paisley and Gerry Adams came to terms on forming a power-sharing executive with Paisley as first minister and Sinn Fein member Martin McGuinness as deputy first minister. In April 2007

Paisley traveled to Dublin and publicly shook the hand of Bertie Ahern, taoiseach (prime minister) of the Republic, something that Paisley had said that he would not do until there was peace in Northern Ireland. In March 2008 Paisley stepped down as DUP leader and first minister of the Northern Ireland Assembly.[48]

As we mentioned at the start of this section, what makes the stories of Gerry Adams and Ian Paisley difficult for most theories of political leadership to deal with is the span of time that both men have held leadership positions and the changing nature of the conflict during that span. Both went from figures who essentially led extreme movements/political parties who actively sought to inflame the conflict to leaders of parties agreeing to sit with each other in government and seek an end to the conflict. It can be argued that each pursued his own personal interest, that in fact each was a leader in order to further his own power and career, changing his policies as necessary (instrumentalist). However, by 2007 Paisley was quite old and at the end of his political career. He had very little self-interest in being an accommodationist to Sinn Fein after decades of opposing them.[49]

Cathy Gormley-Heenan emphasizes that the political leaders in Northern Ireland played many roles, primarily the interpersonal, informational, and decision-making roles.[50] She writes that when asked, most political leaders involved in the peace process could not explain their leadership. Paradoxically, she explains that academics and commentators have ascribed many attributes and are aware of the styles possessed by these leaders. But she argues that often the outside observers, and the theories that they develop, focus on only one aspect of leadership. Gormley-Heenan defines leadership in Northern Ireland as "chameleonic leadership."[51] The leadership style and role of each individual leader changed with the changing structure of the conflict. Each became the type of leader needed for the new times, and each survived.

Stedman would argue that both Adams and Paisley played the role of the "greedy spoiler." Each held "goals that expand or contract based on calculations of cost and risk."[52] When confronted with low costs and high gains, each obstructed the peace process. When presented with the reverse, each made only limited demands and helped move the peace process forward. As both were "inside spoilers," inducement and socialization were appropriate strategies employed by other actors to try and gain compliance from each man. As an example, the British inclusion of Sinn Fein in talks was an inducement to Gerry Adams, offering him a stronger personal position in the dynamics of the ethnic conflict.

John Hume and David Trimble

The story of John Hume and David Trimble is the story of how not changing can lead to an end of political leadership. Both men were very influential in the success of the negotiations leading up to the Good Friday Agreement. Hume, the leader of the SDLP, and Trimble, the leader of the UUP, were the moderate voices stuck between the extremes of Sinn Fein and the DUP.

Both men rose to a position of leadership in 1996 from more humble beginnings. Hume was a teacher who became involved in the civil rights movement of the late 1960s, becoming vice chairman of the Derry Citizens' Action Committee in 1968. He won a seat to the Stormont parliament as a member of the Nationalist Party and in 1970 helped found the SDLP. He became deputy leader and was involved in most major events of the 1970s. In 1979 he succeeded Gerry Fitt as party leader. His main change in policy during the early 1980s was to refuse to negotiate unless the Irish dimension was included in the discussions.[53]

Trimble trained as a lawyer and was a lecturer in the Faculty of Law at Queen's University Belfast. In the early 1970s he was a member of the Vanguard Unionist Progressive Party (VUPP) that campaigned for an independent Northern Ireland. When the VUPP split in the late 1970s over whether to form a coalition with the SDLP, he supported those in favor of the coalition and became deputy leader of a now smaller party. The VUPP ceased to exist in 1978, and Trimble joined the UUP. His career was relatively quiet in the 1980s but picked up steam again in the early 1990s. He was part of a UUP team that participated in the Brooke-Mayhew talks. These talks established the "three strands" approach to negotiations. The strands focused on devolved government, North-South relations, and Irish-British relations. In 1995 Trimble supported Orange Order marchers, which raised his standing among Unionists. This may have helped lead to his unexpected election as UUP party leader that same year.[54]

Hume and Trimble effectively negotiated the compromises that led to the Good Friday Agreement. In particular, Trimble allowed the Agreement to move forward despite his concern that decommissioning and disarmament of the IRA should precede any agreement. Hume moved the negotiations along despite nationalist pressure for greater autonomy for Northern Ireland and a larger role for the Republic. Each campaigned for a yes vote in the referendum, and both strongly defended the Agreement. For their efforts, both men received the Nobel Peace Prize in 1998.[55]

Unfortunately for both men, the dissatisfaction with the Agreement from both communities gained in strength as Northern Ireland moved further and further away from 1998. The Protestant community was unhappy with the slow pace of decommissioning and began to display greater electoral support for the DUP. Trimble came under pressure from within his own party to move the UUP further away from the principles of the Agreement and more toward familiar unionist positions of majority rule and reducing the role of the Irish Republic. Hume found his own party weakening by 2000 as Sinn Fein's popularity among the Catholic community continued to rise. Hume stepped down as leader in 2001, and Trimble resigned in 2005 after many years of battling with his party.[56]

As a story of political leadership, the rise and fall of John Hume and David Trimble is instructive of the difficulties of political leadership in the peace process. Both men worked for the good of Northern Ireland in the All-Party Talks and both were instrumental, and some would say necessary, in getting the Good Friday Agreement accepted. While winning international acclaim for their hard work, the political career and position of both suffered within their own communities in Northern Ireland. Quickly after 1998, both communities began to emphasize the failures of the Agreement and hold the architects accountable. As the extreme parties, in other words Sinn Fein and the DUP, sniped at the other side and espoused traditional republican and unionist positions, respectively, the center (moderate) parties felt pressure to remove their accommodationist leaders. In terms of chameleonic leadership, it was hard for Hume and Trimble to "change their colors" when their names were so associated with the Agreement.[57] It was hard at this point for Hume and Trimble to alienate the extremists, who were playing the role of spoiler. Stedman points out that "by implementing an agreement, peacemakers are vulnerable to attack from those who oppose their efforts."[58]

George Mitchell

George Mitchell wrote that the three years that he spent working toward peace in Northern Ireland was "far more demanding than the six years [he] served as majority leader of the United States Senate." He continued, "But it was well worth the effort; the outcome was the most gratifying event of my public life."[59] Mitchell's commitment to the peace process and the eventual Good Friday Agreement earned him the Liberty Medal from the National Constitution Center in Philadelphia, Pennsylvania, in 1998.[60]

It was not inevitable that George Mitchell would play such a key role in the politics of Northern Ireland. He was born on August 20, 1933, in Waterville, Maine. His father was of Irish descent, and this would help endear him to the politicians with whom he would work in Northern Ireland. He started his career as a lawyer before migrating to politics. In 1974 he ran for the governorship of Maine and lost. President Jimmy Carter appointed him the United States attorney for Maine. He held that post until being appointed to the United States District Court for the District of Maine.[61]

When Edmund Muskie resigned, Mitchell was appointed to replace him in the United States Senate. He quickly moved up the ranks in the Democratic Party, becoming the Senate majority leader in 1989. Despite his success, Mitchell did not want to make a lifetime career out of service in the Senate. He announced in

1994 that he would retire from the Senate and his position as majority leader in 1995. He wanted to return to private life and a private career. [62]

However, in November of 1994, President Bill Clinton asked if Mitchell would be interested in getting involved with Northern Ireland. Mitchell was reluctant, but after more urging from the president he agreed to accept the title of "Special Advisor to the President and the Secretary of State on Economic Initiatives in Ireland." He was to organize a trade conference, nothing more. Mitchell thought that it would only occupy a few months of his time, and Clinton said that it would only take about six months, and then he would be back in private life. In February of 1995, Mitchell took his first trip to Northern Ireland. He was impressed with the people, their energy, and their intelligence but saw the deep hatred and fear that decades of conflict had instilled in them. He also noticed the level of media attention that he received everywhere he traveled. He gained a sense of the importance of American involvement, but also the sense of fatality that Northern Ireland had grown to accept. Mitchell summed it up by saying that while people he met always offered him encouragement and thanks for being there, they also would express the fear, "You're wasting your time. We've been killing each other for centuries and we're doomed to go on killing each other forever."[63] When President Clinton asked George Mitchell to stay on longer in his position and to help the people of Northern Ireland, Mitchell said that he would.

George Mitchell spent three and one-half years working toward a peace agreement in Northern Ireland. His contributions to the eventual Good Friday Agreement are innumerable. One however stands out: the Mitchell Principles. Mitchell made it clear that in order for any party to gain admission to the all-party talks, which began in 1996, it would have to follow a doctrine of nonviolence. Through these principles he established both a means by which Sinn Fein could participate in the talks and also the prerequisite of decommissioning and disarmament for any way forward. The Mitchell Principles were the bedrock on which the Good Friday Agreement would be built.[64]

But why did George Mitchell participate at all? Mitchell himself summed it up in his writing about David Trimble. He explained that every political leader is a mix of the ideal of "wanting to do good" and of his or her own ambition, the drive "to be recognized." Mitchell said that Trimble eventually did the right thing by accepting the Agreement, even if it made his ability to hold his party together, and thus his own leadership position, more difficult. Why did George Mitchell help the people of Northern Ireland? Certainly he had very little to gain for himself, as he already had intended to give up public service to the United States. In the end, it was because he wanted to contribute to peace and an end to the violence. Mitchell expressed it himself:

The people of Ireland are sick of war. They are sick of sectarian killings and random bombings. They are sick of the sad elegance of funerals, especially those involving the small white coffins of children, prematurely laid into the rolling green fields of the Irish countryside. They want peace. . . . I have a new dream . . . to return to Northern Ireland in a few years. . . . There will be no talk of war, for the war will have long been over. There will be no talk of peace, for peace will then be taken for granted. On that day . . . I will be fulfilled.[65]

George Mitchell's steady, persistent, and patient leadership of the peace talks brought Northern Ireland one step closer to realizing that dream.

In conclusion, this section has depicted the role that individual leadership, and the leaders' motivations, attitudes, and beliefs, played in the events in Northern Ireland. It has emphasized the chameleonic nature of leadership during this phase and the difficulties in pinning certain leadership styles of motivations on individuals. As the structure and context of the political landscape changed from one of conflict to one of negotiations and then to peace settlement and beyond, the leadership style and aims of the leaders changed as well. We have also highlighted the multilevel nature of analysis by examining the role of George Mitchell in the peace process.

DOMESTIC LEVEL

The domestic level of analysis contains many actors and forces that shape the ethnic conflict in Northern Ireland. In this analysis we highlight a few of the more important ones. First, we discuss the historical construction of the two sectarian communities and their separate identities. Second, we examine the consociational nature of the executive/legislative institutions and their contribution to conflict management. Third, we address the gendered nationalism of the conflict. Fourth and finally, we look at the changing role of the British government and its position in regard to Northern Ireland.

Communities and Identities

The Protestant and Catholic communities in Northern Ireland are an example of "Communal Contenders" as defined by Barbara Harff and Ted Gurr (see chapter 1).[66] The aims of each are not necessarily "to gain autonomy or to break through discriminatory barriers but, rather, to share power."[67] The two groups are in conflict mainly because of their competing visions of how power should be shared. When an agreement is reached, it is unstable typically due to one or another leader trying to maximize his gains from the agreement at another's expense. Conflict will escalate if a stable agreement is not reached and then implemented.

Joseph Ruane and Jennifer Todd argue that understanding the objective differences between the Catholic and Protestant communities is essential to viewing the source of ethnic conflict. They emphasize that five such differences between the two communities exist: religion, ethnicity, settler-native status, concepts of progress and backwardness, and national identity and allegiance.[68]

Religious differences revolve around differences in doctrine and religious organization. Ruane and Todd note that a difference in class overlaps this religious difference. Catholics are predominantly from the lower class while Protestants range from the lowest social classes to the upper-most social classes.[69]

The ethnic differences are the direct result of colonization. British settlement brought the Scots and English to Ireland. Before British settlement the dominant ethnic people were those of Irish-Gaelic stock. As Ruane and Todd acknowledge, the close relationship between ethnicity and religion makes it difficult to specify the exact importance of ethnicity. Also related to the above two factors is that of settler-native status. The former group would eventually occupy most of Northern Ireland but does not identify with the customs, history, or culture of Ireland. The latter group feels disenfranchised from its customs, history, and culture.[70]

The concepts of progress and backwardness are important in creating the strong in-group versus out-group images. The Protestant settlers saw themselves as a modernizing force in Irish society. They came from a nation that was industrializing and had a liberal, modern, and progressive governmental structure. They viewed the Irish natives as barbaric, icon-worshipping, and backward. The Irish, on the other hand, viewed the invaders as just that, invaders, not as a modernizing and civilizing force.[71]

The last objective difference, national identity and allegiance, is based on nineteenth- and twentieth-century ideologies and concepts of the nation and state. Irish nationalism emerged in the nineteenth century alongside similar nationalist movements throughout most of Western Europe. Imported from the French Revolution, nationalism inspired ethnic groups to seek self-determination. The end desire of nationalism is the creation of a nation-state. This Irish political ambition for statehood ran counter to the desire of Protestant settlers to remain in union with Britain. Thus, the dueling ideologies of nationalism and unionism appeared.[72]

The perceived and actual differences between the two ideologies crystallized into an almost monolithic difference of "community." An observer must understand the sense of community that is so salient to an inhabitant of Northern Ireland in order to view the conflict in the correct context. Without immersion into the nature of community, it is hard for an outside observer to perceive the reasons and motivations behind the actions of many participants in the conflict.[73]

Communities are "emergent entities, products of structurally conditioned social practices which, however, possess some general properties including a level of self-consciousness, integrating organizational networks and a capacity for boundary maintenance."[74] With this definition, one can identify the main political actors at the domestic level in Northern Ireland as the dual communities of Protestants and Catholics. However, this is not to say that overlapping and multiple identities do not or cannot exist. Recent survey research demonstrates that a considerable number of both Protestants and Catholics in Northern Ireland claim a Northern Irish identity, 27 percent and 23 percent, respectively.[75] There is a class component to this identity marker, as it is the young, well-educated, and middle-class Protestants and Catholics who perceive themselves as having a Northern Irish identity. Claiming a Northern Irish identity, however, does not negate other identities: Protestants self-identifying "as Northern Irish do not differ from other Protestants in their support for the union with Great Britain, while Catholics who define themselves as Northern Irish still aspire to a United Ireland."[76]

In fact, given the existence of such overlapping and multiple identities, the development of distinct communities was a slow process, and not all communities are bounded perfectly, thereby demonstrating the social construction of identity. For example, "[p]rior to partition, Unionists classified themselves as 'Irish'—they were, after all, 'Irish' within the political context of the United Kingdom of Great Britain and Ireland."[77] Likewise, the two communities both have internal subdivisions. Protestants differ in their constitutional desire for the future of Northern Ireland. Unionists desire to remain a part of the United Kingdom while loyalists would be happy with an autonomous or independent Ulster. Likewise, the Catholic community divides among republicans, who seek a united Ireland, and nationalists, who envision an independent Northern Ireland.[78]

As an intersection between the individual level and domestic levels of analysis, the political parties in Northern Ireland represent both the community division and the intra-community segmentation. The two main Catholic parties, the Social Democratic and Labour Party (SDLP) and Sinn Fein, draw greater support from the nationalist and republican segments of the Catholic community, respectively. Moreover, the two parties' leaders (John Hume of the SDLP, Gerry Adams of Sinn Fein) have defined Irish identity differently. In an analysis of speeches by Hume and Adams in a two-year period (1984–1986), Grove and Carter found that although both leaders use the terms "Catholics," "nationalists," "Irish," and "this community," their meanings of these terms differ tremendously.[79] Prior to and following the negotiation of the 1985 Anglo-Irish Agreement (AIA), Hume stressed that the "primary political group is the community of Northern Ireland, including Protestants." When Adams refers to "this community," which is infrequently, he does not include Protestants/unionists. Thus, Hume's understanding of identity remains inclusive, while Adams's understanding is exclusive. Unlike Adams's, Hume's inclusiveness overlaps: when referring to the in-group he variously focuses on the people of Northern Ireland, people on the entire island of Ireland, people in Britain and Ireland, and people in Europe and in the world.[80]

The literature on Northern Ireland stresses many dimensions of identity difference between the two communities. Most accounts center on differences that result from four different historical processes: ethnic origin, religious indoctrination, colonialism, and ideology. Polar opposition is the usual expression of these differences: Gaelic-Irish versus English/Scottish, Catholic versus Protestant, native versus settler, or nationalism versus unionism. An example of this polarization is how each community defines its national identity. In a poll conducted in 1989, Catholics identified themselves as Irish (60 percent), Northern Irish (25 percent), British (8 percent), and Ulster (2 percent); Protestants identified themselves as British (68 percent), Northern Irish (16 percent), Ulster (10 percent), and Irish (3 percent).[81] A 2007 survey found similar results. Catholics identified themselves as Irish (62 percent), Northern Irish (23 percent), British (9 percent), and Ulster (1 percent). Protestants identified themselves as British (61 percent), Northern Irish (27 percent), Ulster (5 percent), and Irish (2 percent).[82]

The two communities have an almost exact opposite ordering of identity. As many authors point out, the tendency toward communal division emerged because of the overlap of these dimensions of differences. For example, English settlers were often supporters of Protestantism and fiercely loyal to Britain and a British identity. Native Irish were predominantly Catholic and harbored sentiments against Britain. The lack of shared identities polarized the two communities. This relationship stresses the external nature of the genesis of the sharp divisions.[83]

To Ruane and Todd the structure of dominance, dependence, and inequality in Northern Ireland highlights both the internal and external nature of the conflict. The integration of Ireland into the British state from the sixteenth to the twentieth century secured an alliance between the Protestant settlers and Britain. Both needed each other: the British crown needed the settlers to control Ireland, while the settlers needed the power of Britain to maintain their hegemony on the island. Partition in 1920 did not change this relationship much. The Protestant majority in Northern Ireland enjoys access to resources and power (economic and political) denied to the Catholic minority. The structure of Protestant dominance relies on both their numerical superiority and also the support (tacit or otherwise) of the British government. Protestant dominance has resulted in long-term inequality between the communities. The gradual ascension of the Catholic community, both numerically and substantively, slowly undermines the Protestant position of dominance by reversing the inequality. The erosion of the Protestant position forces the Protestant community to lean heavily on its dependence on British support.[84]

Consociational Institutions and Ethno-Nationalist Conflict

McGarry and O'Leary stress that the root of the conflict lies in its ethno-national nature. As such, they posit that the ascriptive group identities, such as membership in an ethnic group or nation, play more of a factor in an individual's behavior than his or her own, singular interests. In direct opposition to the individual level of analysis, McGarry and O'Leary argue that it is a fallacy to believe that the conflict is rooted in the actions and schemes of political or religious elites.[85] They assert that while "elites play an important role in mobilizing nationalist movements . . . these movements usually have some preexisting collective bases."[86]

Likewise, they reject the primordialist argument that the conflict stems from an archaic, or at least premodern, political culture. They challenge the idea that the conflict is essentially based on religious differences, an incessant obsession with the past, or even an inability of the contemporary political leaders to act in a modern, sophisticated manner. McGarry and O'Leary also refute the idea that individual discrimination or societal segregation is at the heart of the conflict. They point out that in the absence of an ethno-national conflict, the former produces petty crime and violence, while the latter produces isolation. Neither of these two is markedly observed in Northern Ireland where petty crime is not abundant and the two communities come into contact with each other constantly.[87]

In line with the consociational literature outlined in chapter 2, McGarry and O'Leary advocate consociational agreements as a way to address the fundamental ethno-national nature of the conflict. They agree that the four basic organizational principles of consociationalism do indeed address ethno-nationalist conflicts: executive power-sharing, autonomy, proportionality, and veto rights.[88] Yet, McGarry and O'Leary are also "revisionist consociationalists" in that they recognize that the basic consociational theory as developed primarily by Lijphart (see chapter 2) is not complete. In particular it suffers from an overreliance on endogenous explanations of ethno-nationalist conflict. As we have pointed out in a previous book, the ethnic conflict in Northern Ireland has an international component. The Irish identity and the conception of a united Ireland that is held by republican members of the Catholic community in Northern Ireland are derived from a history and a state that lies outside of the sovereignty of the United Kingdom.[89] McGarry and O'Leary point out that consociationalist agreements often downplay the role of external factors, neglect the input of external political actors on the implementation and operation of agreements, and rarely recognize that self-determination disputes can affect more than one state.[90] Likewise, Jesse and Williams highlight the necessity for transformative agreements to promote cross-border institutions, enlist international actors, and pool sovereignty for effective decision making.[91]

It is clear that in Northern Ireland external factors and actors played and continue to play a big part in the conflict and solving the conflict (see next section). While this is the case, the primary ethno-nationalist conflict exists in Northern Ireland. A domestic solution must be at the heart of any resolution of the conflict. The 1998 Good Friday Agreement is inherently a consociational agreement. The Assembly contains much of the same consociational devices as the earlier 1973 power-sharing Assembly, plus the new mechanism of "parallel consent." The new 108-member Assembly uses the Single Transferable Vote (STV) to elect its members. To do so, it combines existing districts used for elections to the House of Commons into larger, multimember districts. This proportional system allows for equal representation of the Northern Ireland communities. Ministers are also appointed in a proportional manner. Legislation requires a simple majority, except in decisions where a cross-community basis is required. In these instances "parallel consent" is necessary. In other words, a majority of support from representatives of both communities or a weighted majority (60 percent) of members present and voting, including at least 40 percent of each of the nationalist and unionist designations present and voting. This supermajority requirement results in de facto veto rights for each nationalist community. A power-sharing executive exists, as the posts of first minister and deputy first minister must also be decided upon by cross-community consent.[92]

McGarry and O'Leary endorse these consociational elements of the Agreement as recognizing the intrinsic ethno-nationalist nature of the conflict, but also allowing for representation through political parties to have a forum to operationalize the Agreement.[93] Unfortunately, the history of the Assembly is not a good one. As mentioned in the history section at the start of this chapter, the Assembly has been suspended for most of its existence. The sectarian political parties have not been able to reach any long-term agreement on power sharing and governing Northern Ireland.

This points to the one criticism that should be leveled at any consociationalist agreement: while it is reachable, its effective functioning is another matter altogether. McGarry and O'Leary agree that consociational agreements often consider merely political institutions, especially the executive and legislative institutions. They point out that many issues in the conflict are not about political institutions and cannot be solved by a mere changing of the legislature or executive. Such issues are important in the Northern Ireland conflict: police reform, education, demilitarization, decommissioning, and so forth.[94]

Another argument is that the conflict is essentially one of fundamental and economic deprivation. After all, indicators point out that, historically, the economic conditions in Northern Ireland are clearly more dire than in the rest of the United Kingdom.[95] In 2002–2003 unemployment in Northern Ireland was 7.3 percent, higher than any other region of the United Kingdom.[96] Recently, however, while the unemployment rate for Northern Ireland was lower than the UK average (4.3 percent for Northern Ireland; 5.7 percent UK average), in September 2008 Northern Ireland experienced an increase in joblessness that was the "biggest monthly increase in 22 years."[97] Another similar argument is that economic disparity between the two communities, typically arising from Protestant discrimination of Catholic job applications, fuels the conflict.

However, McGarry and O'Leary disagree.[98] They cite a study that shows that without ethno-nationalist identity and nationalist conflict, economic deprivation is often associated with criminal activity and not organized political violence.[99] They also point out that the upturn in violence in the late 1960s was associated with rising economic conditions and not declining ones.[100] As Jay Rothman and Marie Olson argue, "It is clear that conflicts involving identity do, in fact, contain issues of resources [such as economic resources] or other tangible interests; however . . . bargaining over those issues without prior and adequate attention first to identity issues has the effect of further polarizing the parties."[101] Therefore, while economic conditions may contribute to an overall dissatisfaction, its expression as ethnic conflict only occurs when ethno-national (identity) disputes coincide with economic deprivation.

Gendered Nationalism and Northern Ireland

As discussed in chapter 1, nationalism is gendered, and this is the case in Northern Ireland as well as elsewhere. As Fidelma Ashe observes, "The constitution of the Irish nation and its people is saturated with conservative gender narratives and familial metaphors."[102] Irish nationalism and national liberation are a function of the colonial experience in which "[t]he task of national liberation became associated with Irish men. Masculine courage, strength and sacrifice became glorified and exalted within Irish nationalist discourse. . . . Irish nationalism interlinks masculinity and the liberation of the nation. . . . Acquiescing to the colonial power was constituted as signifying the feminization of Irish men."[103] Today, the control and policing by nationalist paramilitary organizations in working-class sections of Northern Ireland are linked to nationalist masculinity. These organizations are male-dominated (women are also members but "are often viewed with suspicion and perceived as unwomanly"), and the ethnonationalist conflict itself has enabled men to remain in the public sphere, while women are relegated to the private sphere (home).[104] In Ireland, women are still expected to fulfill their duties to the nation ("Mother Ireland") that include bearing children and inculcating in them the values of their community.[105]

More recently, some of the political parties in Northern Ireland have responded to calls for more equal rights for women. Sinn Fein, for example, recognizing women's contributions to the organization (as combatants) and focusing on domestic violence, took an active policy position incorporating feminism in its ideology. The organization also made a significant commitment to gender equality.[106] However, it is still the case that "traditional discourses about gender . . . continue to influence perceptions and interpretations of women's subjectivities and roles within nationalist cultures."[107] Ashe examined the gender dynamics of the case of the sisters and partner who responded to the murder of their brother and partner, Robert McCartney, by seeking "to bring those responsible to justice."[108] McCartney was murdered in Belfast on January 30, 2005, allegedly by the Provisional Irish Republican Army (PIRA). McCartney's family claimed that the PIRA "cleaned away" forensic evidence, and that the witnesses to the murder had been intimidated by the PIRA. In response, the PIRA "'offer[ed]' to shoot any member of the organization that had been involved in the murder." The family refused the offer. Instead, they tried to pressure the PIRA and Sinn Fein to persuade "witnesses to come forward and to expose the identity of McCartney's killers."[109] The McCartney sisters and his partner then went public (even making a visit to the United States) with their claims and demands that those guilty of the murder be found and brought to justice. Going public meant crossing from the private sphere into the public sphere—the arena for men. Interestingly, though, it was "gendered and familial identities" that formed the basis of their protest—as "guardians of the family."[110] As Ashe asserts, "In contrast to their deep politicization within an Irish nationalist culture and the violent associations of the Irish Republican movement the women's gender identity allowed them to present themselves in an unthreatening and familiar way as sisters and as women concerned with the rights of family members. The campaign operated at the personal level, around the women's grief but of course that personal grief was a consequence of political factors, particularly the activities of PIRA and Sinn Fein members."[111]

What is interesting about this example is how gendered nationalism manifested itself in the nationalist/republican response to the protests by McCartney's sisters and partner. The members of the republican community became more critical of the women in response to their criticisms of the republican hierarchy. At first, Sinn Fein supported the women, but over time, concerns arose that those who opposed the republican movement had "highjacked" the McCartney campaign as a means of undermining the movement. Additionally, important leaders of Sinn Fein insinuated that "enemies outside of the nationalist community" were manipulating the women. Martin McGuinness viewed the campaign, not as a political issue, but rather a personal issue (relegated to the private sphere and thus traditionally a feminine issue), and he "urged the women to stay out of 'politics.'"[112]

Gendered nationalism manifests itself in the Protestant community, as well. As Linda Racioppi and Katherine O'Sullivan See note, "In Northern Ireland, the informal sector, where women have been much more active, has also played a role in shaping national identities, in mobilizing unionists and in influencing state policies."[113] During the peace process of the 1990s, leading to the 1998 Agreement, "the linkages between ethnic politics and gender politics became sharply delineated." Racioppi and O'Sullivan See quote David Ervine, a leader of the Progressive Unionist Party (and a former paramilitary prisoner) during a debate: "This Agreement is going down because of the macho men on both sides." They assert that "control of the state was at the heart of the negotiations over the Agreement, and 'macho men' were at the forefront of those negotiations."[114]

Moreover, during the peace negotiations, "women's issues remained marginal to [Ulster Unionist Party] politics or policies." In response, according to Racioppi and O'Sullivan See, the Ulster Women's Unionist Council (the official women's section of the Ulster Unionist Party [UUP]) created a statement on women's issues that supported equal opportunities for men and women, but also clearly underscored the importance to society of the "family unit" and of women's role as mothers.[115]

While women on both sides of the conflict have supported their communities, women have also engaged in cross-community activism, finding common ground on issues of importance to them such as domestic violence and health and child care. The Women's Information Group (WIG), founded in 1980, concentrated, not on politics or religion, but "shared issues" of health, increased rent, and juvenile criminal behavior.[116]

In addition to informal (grassroots) political activism, women in Northern Ireland have also engaged in formal politics directly related to the conflict. In 1996 women formed the Northern Ireland Women's Coalition (NIWC), a political party not tied to either ethnic community. This does not mean that the women agreed on all issues, rather that the members recognized their differences. These differences did not mean they could not work together—rather, "the NIWC worked to be as inclusive and transparent as possible, as opposed to the mainstream, male-dominated political parties."[117] The NIWC participated in the peace talks that led to the 1998 Agreement and gained seats in the new Assembly. However, after losing seats in 2003, and then failing to win any local council seats in the 2005 election, the NIWC disbanded. Importantly, the NIWC played a significant role in bringing a women's agenda into the political sphere.[118]

Consequently, while women have made some progress in the formal political sphere, they have been more successful in informal grassroots activism, reaching across the community divides. When women engage in political activism, either formally or informally, their activism is still rooted in gendered terms, in their roles as mothers and wives, further underlining the continued gendered nationalism in Northern Ireland.

The Participation of the British Government

Since Northern Ireland remains a part of the United Kingdom, it is a sovereign territory of the British Parliament. Under such a setup, acts and actions of the House of Commons are a domestic source in the ethnic conflict of Northern Ireland. Proposals from the British government to end the conflict reflect the changing British conceptions of the root of the conflict. Early proposals viewed the conflict as merely an internal one, and thus the British attempt to establish an internal solution (for example, the Stormont Parliament of 1973). When the British government changed its perception of the conflict and saw it as having not only an internal component but also an external one, the structures that it proposed became less majoritarian and more incorporative of overlapping identities.

That the actions of the British government contributed to conflict in Northern Ireland cannot be debated. Exactly how they contributed can be. Britain had conflicting goals in regard to Northern Ireland. On the one hand, Britain maintained a relationship with Northern Ireland that can be termed "postcolonial." Northern Ireland had never been fully integrated into Britain. While the Protestant majority has felt a "British" identity, the British on the mainland still refer to the Protestants as "Irish." In the perceptions of the British political elite, Northern Ireland has been seen more as an integral part of the island of Ireland than as a part of Great Britain.[119] Moreover, this view was certainly held by the British populace. Opinion polls since the 1970s have shown that a majority of the British population supports withdrawal from Northern Ireland.[120]

Further, British support of the principle of majority rule (as opposed to proportional representation) exacerbated the conflict in Northern Ireland by reinforcing the in-group (that is, Protestant) versus out-group (that is, Catholic) distinction. A hallmark of British territorial management was the belief in the right of the majority to rule. This belief was the cornerstone on which the Protestant community demanded continued British support. The majoritarian principle gave reason for the Protestants to maintain communal solidarity in the face of a growing Catholic minority. The sociodemographic dominance of the majority Protestant community has created the "dominance and dependence" relationship between it and the British government.[121]

On the other hand, Britain had certainly shown a sincere desire to reach a settlement in Northern Ireland. In the time since partition, the British government had made numerous proposals and initiatives toward ending the conflict. The changing conceptions of identity have paralleled many of the proposals. Chief among these was the short-lived consociational power-sharing Assembly of 1973 and the Sunningdale Agreement. This agreement contained all of the provisions spelled out by consociational theorists: a power-sharing executive, minority veto, legislative coalitions, and proportional representation of minority groups. In addition, it called for the creation of an all-Ireland institution, the Council of Ireland. However, the Sunningdale Agreement faced strong opposition from the Protestants. Five months after the conclusion of the agreement, the Ulster Workers Council incited strikes that led to the fall of the Assembly and the establishment of direct British rule of Northern Ireland.[122]

Perhaps due to the ease with which the two communities could criticize the agreement and take their case to the British mainland in the way of voice or violence, neither was required to accept the British-led political arrangement. Moreover, the agreement failed to induce a change in the self-image of the Unionists vis-à-vis their relationship with the nationalists. One lesson from the Sunningdale Agreement was that the external nature of the struggle in Northern Ireland prohibits any solution that relies solely on regional institutions (that is, consociational) and, in particular, does not include the Republic of Ireland.[123]

The 1985 Anglo-Irish Agreement was based on the policy that only parties acting in a constitutional manner should be privy to peace talks. The notable inclusion of the Republic of Ireland in a consultative role and the willingness of the Irish government to accept that constitutional change in Northern Ireland would require majority consent (that is, any change would need Protestant as well as Catholic approval) marked a significant turning point in the process of resolving the conflict. Thus the British-led AIA stressed the Irish external dimension, rather than an internal Northern Ireland settlement.[124]

The British government's enticement to the unionists for acceptance of the AIA rested on the diminished role in the North for the Irish government—if the unionists agreed to an internal solution with the nationalists. Yet, the 1985 agreement failed because the Unionist parties refused to participate in the negotiations. Unionists refused to accept an internal consociational agreement when the republicans would not accept the long-term constitutional stability of Northern Ireland.[125] The failure of the 1985 agreement emphasized that the republican wing of the Catholic community could not be excluded from a viable political solution. Without republican consent, the communal violence, and indeed interstate terrorism, continued.[126]

Another change in the British position regarding Northern Ireland occurred in 1993 when Britain began to acknowledge specifically the link between the internal and external causes for the conflict. The British government of Conservative prime minister John Major realized the island-wide nature of the conflict and made overtures to the Irish government in Dublin and to Sinn Fein. The goal of both governments became the inclusion of all communities (British and Irish, Catholic and Protestant) with a stake in the conflict, which marked a significant change from previous British attempts at resolution.[127]

The Downing Street Declaration of 1993 was the result of this new interstate approach. Britain declared that "it is for the people of the island of Ireland alone, by agreement between the two parts respectively, to exercise their right of self-determination on the basis of consent." The Irish government accepted that "the democratic right of self-determination by the people of Ireland as a whole must be exercised with, and subject to the agreement and consent of a majority of the people of Northern Ireland."[128] In other words, Britain protected the Protestant majority by including the majority principle.

Yet, Britain also accepted the new inclusion of both the Irish government and the Irish community, and particularly Sinn Fein. Eight months prior to the Declaration, Sinn Fein and the Social Democratic and Labour Party met in secret talks. These talks paved the way for the IRA's willingness to compromise on its demand for unification in return for the British government's offer to allow Sinn Fein a seat at the negotiating table. In response, the Republic of Ireland began to move toward a softening of the overt threat contained in articles 2 and 3 of its own constitution, the articles calling for the eventual unification of the island of Ireland. The Irish government also issued a statement commending the commitment of the IRA to accept the democratic process for constitutional change.[129]

Two years later, in February 1995, the British and Irish governments published a document titled "Frameworks for the Future." The Frameworks document contained two new proposals: devolution of British authority to a government in Northern Ireland and a new framework for agreement detailing the exact relations between Northern Ireland, the Republic of Ireland, and Great Britain. The framework specified "the creation of new cross-border institutions and the guarantee of a referendum" for any future constitutional change for the North.[130] Importantly, the Frameworks document attempted to construct a new identity for the North. The document concentrated on revising the interests and identity of the unionists away from an in-group/out-group division of Protestants versus Catholics toward an identity and interest that complemented and overlapped with those of the Irish Catholics and the Republic of Ireland.[131]

It did this in two ways. First, by proposing "devolved institutions with legislative and executive responsibilities over a wide range of areas, including security—and an elaborate system of checks and balances to protect minority interests."[132] Second, it elaborated both North-South intergovernmental bodies as well as an East-West intergovernmental conference supported by a permanent staff from both the British and Irish governments. While these cross-border institutions did not become a reality immediately, the focus on the necessity for such institutions is illustrative of the new focus on seeing the common identities. Correspondingly, the Frameworks document had broad support of most Unionist parties (with the exception of the Democratic Unionist Party) and the Catholic Social Democratic and Labour Party, and the ambiguous support of Sinn Fein.[133]

The peace talks initially failed to achieve much. Distrust of the new Irish influence led unionists to use their position in the House of Commons to push for concessions (for example, exclusion of Sinn Fein from the talks) from Major's government. Major's slim parliamentary majority left him dependent on Unionist votes. Thus, the peace talks appeared on the brink of collapse more because of the party composition in the British House of Commons than because of anything happening in Northern Ireland. Tony Blair and Labour's landslide victory in 1997 left the new prime minister with a large majority, one large enough to discount any Unionist blackmail. A change in Westminster would now open the way for a renewed effort by the British government to solve the conflict in Northern Ireland. The Good Friday Agreement of April 1998 signaled the new direction taken by Blair's Labour government.[134]

The Blair government moved quickly to a settlement of the problem in a manner consistent with its handling of other regional disputes on the British periphery, including the devolution of power to Scotland and Wales. The goal was to allow the people of Northern Ireland to run their own government and to determine the eventual fate of the six Northern counties. However, Britain would maintain an important role in the final agreement through participation in all the newly created institutions.[135]

Since 1998 many things have changed in Northern Ireland, but British involvement has remained. For example, the Assets Recovery Agency set up by the British government attempts to recover money laundered through IRA activities. The continued British suspension of the Northern Ireland Assembly highlights the fact that real change can take a long time to implement. As one example, the International Independent Commission on Decommissioning (IICD) announced in September of 2005 that the IRA had destroyed its arsenal of weapons. The IRA followed with a declaration that it was ending its armed campaign. This move led to Sinn Fein taking its position on the Policing Board, something that the DUP had blocked while the IRA's violent campaign continued.[136]

As things improve in Northern Ireland, the British government takes on more of a "normal" role. In other words, it implements policies in Northern Ireland in a manner not unlike how it implements them in the rest of the United Kingdom. For example, the reduction of violence in Northern Ireland has allowed the economy to regain its footing. A comparison of regional household income data from 2006 shows that Northern Ireland is no longer at the bottom of the United Kingdom. Households in Northern Ireland now on average earn more per year than those in the West Midlands, Tees Valley, Northumberland, and West Wales.[137]

INTERNATIONAL LEVEL

Harff and Gurr suggest that an ethnic conflict involving communal contenders is likely to induce international involvement. The conflict in Northern Ireland is no exception, as a number of external actors have become involved. Among the wide range of external actors, the greatest international involvement in the affairs of Northern Ireland has come from two sources: the Republic of Ireland and the United States. The former has been involved from the very beginning, as Northern Ireland split from Ireland. It is this split that has energized the pro-Irish feelings in the North and led to a desire for a united Ireland by communities in both the North and South of Ireland. The involvement of the South previous to the split laid the foundation for its current involvement. The role of the United States is much more recent, dating mainly from the 1960s. However, its involvement is also the product of a more distant historical event: the large-scale immigration of Irish to the United States, particularly in the 1840s. We also note the role of the European Union in encouraging reconciliation and an end to the violence.

Ireland (and the Republic of Ireland)

The history of Northern Ireland before 1920 is really the history of Ireland. The two nations are intertwined to a great degree. British conquest of Ireland was effectively completed under the military dictatorship of Oliver Cromwell in the 1600s. The deep roots of the contemporary conflict lie in the British settlement of Northern Ireland, and in particular the migration in the seventeenth century of settlers to the northeast region of Ireland known as Ulster. In 1801 Ireland was absorbed into the United Kingdom of Great Britain and Ireland, ending all sense of Irish independence from British rule. Near the start of the twentieth century, there were roughly one million Protestants in Northern Ireland compared to 2.5 million Catholics. However, over 80 percent of the Protestant population lived in Ulster while over 90 percent of the Catholic population lived elsewhere.[138]

Irish agitation for Home Rule and a devolved Irish parliament increased throughout the end of the nineteenth century. Similar to the landmark election of 1997 in which a change of party led to a change of the British position regarding

Northern Ireland, the election of 1910 put a Liberal government in power that needed the Irish Party to secure its ruling majority. The Irish Party began to push for Home Rule. Yet, it was becoming clearer that there really were two "Irish questions": what was nationalist Ireland's relationship with the United Kingdom, and what was Protestant Ireland's relationship with the Catholic Ireland? The 1914 Home Rule Act that created a devolved Irish parliament was stillborn, as it was suspended because of the outbreak of hostilities in Europe.[139]

While Britain was distracted by the First World War (1914–1918), a group of Irish nationalists tried to seize power in Dublin and establish the first Irish Republic. The Easter Rebellion of 1916 failed, with almost all of its leaders executed by the British military. One of the effects of the Easter Rebellion was the hardening of the positions of the Irish nationalists and the Protestant unionists, the former for independence from British rule and the latter for nothing less than continued union with the United Kingdom.[140]

As mentioned previously in this chapter, the 1920 Government of Ireland Act created two new jurisdictions: a six-county Northern Ireland that would remain a devolved nation with its own parliament, and a southern Ireland that would have Home Rule through its own parliament. It is at this point that the histories of Ireland and Northern Ireland diverge.

Ireland became preoccupied with its own affairs at this time. Agitation by Sinn Fein against the 1920 act led to violence and British reprisals. The 1921 Anglo-Irish Treaty effectively ended direct British involvement in Ireland. However, the 1920 act had created a division between Irish nationalists who did not want to accept the partition and those who thought that it was the best deal that could be wrested from the British. The subsequent Irish Civil War of 1921–1922 led to a split in Sinn Fein into the two political factions, and finally political parties, that are still dominant in the Republic of Ireland today: Fianna Fail and Fine Gael.[141] The former would be led by the American-born revolutionary Eamon de Valera and opposed the treaty, while the latter supported the treaty.

The Irish Free State was formed in 1922 and acted as if it was independent of the United Kingdom. In 1937 a new constitution created the Republic of Ireland. Importantly, the 1937 constitution effectively removed the provision of the British 1920 Government of Ireland Act that allowed Britain to nominally rule Ireland. Also, articles 2 and 3 of the 1937 constitution specifically defined the Irish national territory as the whole island and also made it clear that its laws would impact Northern Ireland pending its re-integration.[142] The leadership of Eamon de Valera (prime minister, 1932–1948; 1951–1954; 1957–1959; president 1959–1973) led to confrontation with Britain on numerous issues, including a trade war between the two, Irish neutrality during World War II, and Irish non-recognition of Northern Ireland's separateness.[143]

Sympathy for an end to partition continued to exist in the Republic of Ireland in the post–World War II period. It manifested itself in sporadic anti-partition movements, but these did not achieve much. The trade war had weakened economic ties between the North and South. Moreover, the struggling economies of both led each to focus on its own domestic affairs. The IRA's on-again, off-again border campaigns launched against Northern Ireland from outposts in the Republic did little to endear northern unionists to de Valera's government.[144]

A shift in the Irish government's position occurred with the ascendancy of Sean Lemass to the position of prime minister in 1959. He advocated for closer ties with Northern Ireland, and the building of common North-South interests, as a way toward an end to partition. Politicians from most southern parties embraced the emerging economic and political cooperation in Europe as a vehicle by which they could extend cooperation to North-South relations. Intrinsic to this new approach was a change in the Irish position from a belief that Britain was the primary hindrance to partition to a belief that it was Unionist opposition with which they would have to come to terms.[145]

The 1973 Sunningdale Agreement appeared to recognize the Irish dimension to the conflict in Northern Ireland and the need for more participation on the part of the Republic in any long-term solution. For politicians in the South it seemed that finally the British government recognized the need for cooperation between the two. However, the 1973 agreement did not resonate with either republicans or unionists in Northern Ireland, and thus it was a false dawn. This did not deter subsequent Irish governments from continuing to push the point home to the British that the Republic's involvement was a necessary condition for any working agreement.[146]

Taoiseach Garret Fitzgerald negotiated with British prime minster Margaret Thatcher for months in early 1985. Fitzgerald's goal was to establish a more permanent link between the Irish and British governments and to increase their understanding and cooperation regarding Northern Ireland. The 1985 Anglo-Irish Agreement did just that. It established an Intergovernmental Conference which would meet regularly to discuss legal, security, and political matters in Northern Ireland. It also allowed for the Irish government to propose legislation that would be in the interests of the Catholic community in Northern Ireland.[147]

While the Irish government hailed the agreement as a step forward, it was criticized by both sides in Northern Ireland. Republicans argued that it solidified partition and undermined their demands for the unity of the whole island. Unionists blasted the agreement and Thatcher for selling out Northern Ireland and leaving it effectively controlled by the Republic. Of course, both claims were exaggerated, as the Anglo-Irish Agreement neither endorsed the current partition nor left Northern Ireland in the hands of the Dublin government.[148]

In the early 1990s the short-lived leadership of Albert Reynolds would be consequential to future Irish involvement. As a leader of Fianna Fail, Reynolds struck up a good relationship with the new Conservative prime minister of Britain, John Major. Reynolds and Major agreed that the Republic should play a greater role in the ongoing talks and contacts occurring in Northern Ireland between John Hume of the SDLP and Gerry Adams of Sinn Fein. Reynolds became involved with these leaders and also led the Irish government into secret negotiations with paramilitaries from both sides of the conflict, republican and loyalist.[149] The contribution of Reynolds to the Irish government's participation in Northern Ireland is another example of the need for a multilevel understanding of the process. His efforts clearly stem from his own personal desire (that is, individual level), but they are channeled through the Irish government (that is, domestic level), and the policy implications are felt in Northern Ireland (that is, international level).

Reynolds and Major eventually agreed on the Downing Street Declaration of 1993. This declaration committed both governments to working toward a comprehensive framework that involved the whole of the island of Ireland and Great Britain in finding a workable solution for Northern Ireland. It also established that the will of the majority in Northern Ireland would always determine whether they remained a part of the United Kingdom or would be reunited with the Republic of Ireland. Reynolds also got included in the Declaration the provision that the citizens of the Republic also had a right to give their consent on any possible integration of the North and South.[150]

Under the leadership of Taoiseach John Bruton of Fine Gael, very little progress was made by the Irish government in negotiations in Northern Ireland.[151] However, the Bertie Ahern government in 1997 was able to press for inclusion in Northern Irish talks. Ahern got the ear of the new British prime minister, Tony Blair, and became party to the Good Friday Agreement in 1998. As mentioned previously, the Agreement required the Republic of Ireland to amend its constitution by removing its claim to Northern Ireland. Ahern led the pro-treaty campaign and helped the amendment referendum to victory.[152]

Irish involvement in the institutions established by the Good Friday Agreement are many. The North-South Ministerial Council deals with the "totality of relationships" between the governments of Northern Ireland and the Republic of Ireland. The purpose of the North-South Council is to develop consultation, cooperation, and action within the island of Ireland on an all-island and cross-border basis. This new council has the ability to make decisions on matters of implementation for common policy in the two political regions, as well as separate implementation in each jurisdiction. The British-Irish Council (BIC) comprises membership from all national and devolved assemblies on the

British Isles. Representatives of the British and Irish national governments are joined by representatives from the assemblies of Northern Ireland, Scotland, and Wales (with a provision for representatives from the Isle of Man and Channel Islands). The BIC will allow these assemblies to exchange information, discuss, and consult on cooperation on matters of mutual interest. Lastly, the British-Irish Intergovernmental Conference, comprised of the British prime minister and Irish taoiseach, meets at a summit to cooperate at all levels between the two governments regarding policies affecting Northern Ireland. Such meetings typically address security matters, rights, justice, prisons, and policing. The Intergovernmental Conference is also charged with the duty of reviewing the workings of the institutions created by the Good Friday Agreement.[153]

Clearly, the Irish government maintains an active and engaged role in the affairs of Northern Ireland. Its contemporary involvement highlights the role of international actors in the ethnic conflict, the international causes of the conflict in the first place, and the need for consociational agreements to recognize this international role.

The Involvement of the United States

The United States has been heavily involved in the conflict in Northern Ireland. Its involvement has come mainly from three separate sources: the Irish-American community, congressional action, and presidential direct involvement. Each of these has impacted the ethnic conflict in Northern Ireland in a very different way.

The United States has maintained a consul in Belfast since May 20, 1796, when Secretary of State Timothy Pickering appointed James Holmes to that position. The United States also maintained a consular appointment in Londonderry from 1830 to 1920, as well as appointments in other cities in the nineteenth century. Therefore, the State Department has been able to generate reports about the affairs of Northern Ireland almost from the inception of the United States.[154]

The primary impetus for greater U.S. involvement is of course the immigration of millions of Irish to the United States, especially during the Potato Famine of the 1840s in Ireland. Little known to most Americans is the simple fact that today for every one Irish citizen, there are ten Irish-Americans. Irish immigration was so pronounced that in the 1850 census, of a U.S. population of 24 million, 4 million openly claimed Irish ancestry.[155]

Despite this large Irish population, the United States was not paying much attention to Ireland at the start of the twentieth century. One exception was the American pleas for the British military to spare the lives of the leaders of the 1916 Irish Easter Rebellion, especially that of Eamon de Valera (who would later become prime minister and president of the Republic of Ireland). With the partition of Ireland in 1920, the U.S. government settled into a pattern of pro-British foreign policy. As such, the United States did not interfere in the British administration of Northern Ireland, nor did it question the partition as an appropriate settlement of the Irish problem. This continued through the Second World War and into the beginning of the Cold War. Irish-Americans during this time seemed indifferent to the plight of the Irish in Northern Ireland.[156]

Of course, the United States had deeper international concerns at this time. The emerging Cold War with the Soviet Union divided the international system into two camps (that is, a bipolar arrangement). The focus of foreign policy became first central Europe, and then Asia and elsewhere, as the competition between the two superpowers dictated their primary foreign policy concerns. The "special relationship" between the United States and Great Britain, as embodied in many formal treaties and organizations such as the North Atlantic Treaty Organization (NATO), aligned U.S. foreign policy with British foreign policy, particularly support of free trade, the Western defense alliances, and anticommunism.[157] In such a situation, the United States was not willing to push Britain on what was clearly its own domestic problem in Northern Ireland.

Yet, at the local level, grassroots organizing in the United States around the interests of the Catholic community mirrored the events in Northern Ireland. The Catholic community in Northern Ireland had been holding peaceful marches aimed at ending discrimination and gaining basic social rights. At the same time, the IRA was forming around a policy of confrontation with the British in order to secure a united Ireland. In June 1970 the Irish Northern Aid Committee (Noraid) was created in New York City. Its purpose was to campaign for a united Ireland. It quickly established regional organizations in most large American cities with substantial Irish-American populations (for example, Boston, Chicago). Noraid engaged in substantial fundraising in order both to lobby Congress for pro-Irish policies and to aid directly the Catholic struggle in Northern Ireland.[158]

The administration of President Richard Nixon (1969–1974) was not interested in Irish affairs. His foreign policy agenda was decidedly pro-British. His goals were to strengthen NATO and contain communism. Congress, on the other hand, was moving quicker. From 1969 to 1972 several members of Congress with pro-Irish leanings had entered comments critical of the British presence in Northern Ireland into the Congressional Record. The 1972 killings of innocent civilians in Londonderry (or Derry as the Catholic community calls it) by British troops, known as "Bloody Sunday," changed the depth of interest in Northern Ireland among Irish-Americans. House Speaker Carl Albert allowed hearings to proceed about Northern Ireland and Bloody Sunday. Further, hearings dealt with joint bills submitted to the House and Senate by pro-Irish members of Congress calling for an "immediate withdrawal of all British troops in Northern Ireland," among other things. Nothing much came of the hearings, and Nixon's policy did not change. What was clear, however, was that the pro-Irish community in the United States was lining up with pro-Irish members of Congress behind some U.S. involvement in the affairs in Northern Ireland. [159]

In 1974 the first actual Irish-American lobby was created, the Irish National Caucus (INC). Its founder, the former Irish republican priest Father Sean McManus firmly believed in the goal of a united Ireland. The strength of the INC lobby forced members of Congress to take sides on the issue. Moreover, the INC began a policy of recruiting Irish nationalists and republicans to visit America. The State Department did not support this activity. Moreover, the State Department was alarmed by the information that weapons stolen from Camp Lejeune in North Carolina had made their way to the IRA in Northern Ireland. Apparently, gunrunning from the United States to paramilitaries in Northern Ireland had picked up substantially in the few years prior. The U.S. government began surveillance of the INC, particularly given its links to Noraid and the IRA. In Congress, Sen. Ted Kennedy and Rep. Tip O'Neill had direct contact with Catholic leaders in Northern Ireland, especially those in the SDLP and particularly John Hume. Still, during this time the presidential administration of Gerald Ford (1974–1976) took no substantive action in regard to Northern Ireland.[160]

The Carter administration (1977–1980) brought new presidential action into the affairs of Northern Ireland. Jimmy Carter met with representatives of the INC before the 1976 election. In office, Carter's emphasis on humanitarianism and a reemergence of American values in foreign policy was congruent with the aims of the Irish-American lobby. In the spring of 1977, Carter sent a draft letter to the British and Irish governments saying that the sum of $100 million in U.S. aid was available to Northern Ireland if passed by Congress. The British initially resisted any outside interference in Northern Ireland as a violation of the sovereignty of the United Kingdom.[161]

Nonetheless, Carter moved forward. On August 30, 1977, his government announced that Northern Ireland "was a legitimate issue of American foreign policy." It stated that the United States would remain impartial, but that aid was available to create jobs and to benefit the people of Northern Ireland. He stated that U.S. ties to Ireland were natural given the heritage of Irish-Americans and also that U.S. businesses had already been investing directly in the region.[162]

During this time the rift widened between the State Department's pro-British stance and the increasing agitation of the pro-Irish lobby and pro-Irish members of Congress. While the State Department refused to be critical of the British military presence in Northern Ireland or its possible violations of human rights, the new Ad Hoc Congressional Committee for Irish Affairs and House Speaker O'Neill were pushing for greater American involvement.[163]

Real policy change came about during the first Reagan administration (1981–1984). This occurred not because Reagan was pro-Irish, because his administration was indeed pro-British, calling Prime Minister Margaret Thatcher's support against the communist Soviet Union essential. Rather, a series of British blunders dealing with Northern Ireland energized a pro-Irish American public to demand action. The British insensitivity to the plight of the hunger strikers in 1981, the "shoot-to-kill" policy of the British Army, and the British complacency in light of the Reverend Ian Paisley's desire to raise a loyalist paramilitary organization all incensed the pro-Irish groups in the United States.[164]

In 1981 seventy members of Congress formed the Friends of Ireland to lobby Congress and the president. The Friends pushed for a direct legislative connection between the United States and affairs in Northern Ireland. At the same time, Reagan was exploring his Irish roots with a trip to Ireland, where he met with different groups involved in the Northern Ireland conflict. In 1984 Speaker O'Neill and the president's adviser William Clark were able to get Northern Ireland on the agenda for Reagan's Camp David meeting with Margaret Thatcher. By the end of Reagan's first term, the United States was clearly engaged in trying to provide a forum in which the various actors in Northern Ireland could seek a common resolution.[165]

In Reagan's second administration (1985–1988), he listened to the urging of his staff to confront Thatcher on the issue of Northern Ireland. In particular, he encouraged the British prime minister to involve the Republic of Ireland more directly in the negotiations. How much this change in the American position contributed to the Anglo-Irish Agreement of 1985 is unclear; however, it certainly had a positive impact. But this success at the presidential level was somewhat offset by changes at the congressional level. By the end of Reagan's second administration, most of the leadership of the Friends and the Ad Hoc Congressional Committee had retired.[166]

The first Bush administration (1989–1992) committed itself to silent diplomacy with Britain. However, the academic community, as well as the larger Irish-American community, felt that U.S. concern for Northern Ireland was waning under Bush's administration, compared to Reagan's. This assessment is probably truthful. President Bush was concerned with other areas of the globe, especially given the fall of communism in Eastern Europe and the Soviet Union, and foreign policy problems in the Middle East.[167] The balance of power in the international system had changed and left the United States as the sole superpower. Without a direct competitor, the United States found itself with a new flexibility to foreign policy. Yet, the president of the United States did not yet have the time to orchestrate a new foreign policy as the 1992 presidential election ushered him out of office.

The presidency of Bill Clinton (1993–2000) brought in a sea-change in U.S. policy toward Northern Ireland. He was in a position to capitalize on the changes in the international system that left the United States with the freedom to chart a new foreign policy unhindered by Cold War zero-sum analysis. Clinton's appointment of Warren Christopher as secretary of state ushered in an emphasis on promoting democracy as a way to stabilize world regions. Establishing a democratic peace in Northern Ireland was one way to stabilize U.S.-British relations and reduce tension in Europe. A domestic impulse toward this policy was Clinton's belief that the Irish-American community voted as a single bloc in American elections.[168] Various pro-Irish interest groups quickly made contacts with the president and encouraged him to further their goals in Northern Ireland.[169]

Clinton also was a firm believer in visiting countries that were important to U.S. foreign policy, or at least having the actors involved in those countries come to the United States. As such, in spring 1992 Clinton met with the Irish taoiseach Albert Reynolds. Clinton made it clear that he would be willing to send a peace envoy to Northern Ireland to help negotiations move further along. Visits to the United States by Reynolds and the new Irish president Mary Robinson furthered Clinton's confidence that the United States could play a more active role. Moreover, the Downing Street Declaration in December 1993 reaffirmed the new neutral position of Britain toward the conflict. This left a void in which the United States could enter. In December of 1994, Clinton appointed the retiring senator George Mitchell as a special adviser to the president on Northern Ireland. The decision by Clinton in 1995 to extend a visa to Gerry Adams was controversial in the United Kingdom, but was just another signal of the president's commitment to get involved in Northern Ireland.[170]

George Mitchell's presence in the all-party talks that led to the 1998 Good Friday Agreement was key to its completion.[171] At the same time, the United States was furthering economic ties with Northern Ireland and encouraging U.S. investment in the region. After the Agreement, the Clinton administration continued to play a role, mainly by providing forums for the main players to gather and discuss issues such as decommissioning and policing reform. However, after the frustration of 1999 when progress on these issues was not being made, and with the continuing domestic problems hounding his presidency, Clinton paid less and less attention to Northern Ireland.[172]

The administration of George W. Bush (2001–2008) was characterized by much less attention to Northern Ireland. The events on September 11, 2001, focused the United States on the new threat from international terrorism. President Bush's foreign policy concentrated on the twin invasions of Afghanistan and Iraq, and the continued U.S. attempt to limit the impact of state-sponsored terrorism (for example, Afghanistan, Iraq, Iran, North Korea). The building of multinational coalitions to address the problem of global terrorism occupied much of the Bush presidency.

Furthermore, the Bush administration came to see the problems in the Northern Ireland Assembly as intractable and outside the purview of the United States' influence. While U.S. investment in the Republic of Ireland continued at a steady pace, investment in Northern Ireland was not as vibrant. Bush met with Tony Blair in 2003 to encourage devolution in Northern Ireland, but as the meeting was held immediately after the American-led invasion of Iraq, it is not clear how important Northern Ireland was in the discussions. During his farewell tour in June 2008, Bush visited Northern Ireland. Most impressions of the visit suggest that it was mainly symbolic and displayed U.S. encouragement for a solution to the crisis at Stormont.[173]

In general, U.S. participation in the ethnic conflict in Northern Ireland has waxed and waned based on three factors: the personal involvement of the American president (individual level), pressure for action from Irish-American interest groups and/or pro-Irish members of Congress (domestic level), and the changing nature of the balance of power from that of superpower competition to that of the United States as the sole world hegemon (international level). Thus, the impetus for U.S. intervention comes from many sources, some of which conflict. It is also interesting that it was the British acceptance of its own reduced position of influence to bring about positive change in Northern Ireland (as enshrined in the Downing Street Declaration) that paved the way for the direct involvement of Senator Mitchell. This is a clear example of the interconnectedness between international factors and domestic factors in promoting a solution to an ethnic conflict.

European Union

The European Union (EU) has been influential in encouraging cooperation between the British and Irish governments within the EU, and this in turn has provided the basis for cooperation at the international institutional level on the Northern Ireland conflict. The EU affords an opportunity for the representation and expression of overlapping identities as a supranational institution. Northern Ireland is a single constituency in the EU with three members in the European Parliament, which is the legislative body of the EU. Interestingly, the three members of the European Parliament (MEPs) from Northern Ireland often "speak with one voice" in the various committees on which they serve.[174] Cathal McCall argues that the EU may serve "as a potential catalyst that will effect change in communal identities in Northern Ireland."[175]

As for cross-border institutions, the EU recognizes the link between the Republic of Ireland and Northern Ireland provided by the border regions. Etian Tannam notes that groups in these regions may perceive common regional interests and identity as opposed to the interests and identities of those in the capitals of Northern Ireland, Ireland, and Great Britain. For the EU, achieving such "a Europe of the Regions" would reinforce those regional interests and identities.[176]

As liberal institutionalist theory would claim, institutions provide the mechanisms for cooperation between states, which can be extended to groups within states as well. Thus, at the EU level, two countries cooperate—the Republic of Ireland and the United Kingdom. Additionally, the two communities within Northern Ireland are a target of efforts by the EU for reconciliation through economic development, as shown by the levels of funding given to Northern Ireland from the European Union. The European Parliament affords representation for Northern Ireland through the members of the European Parliament, further enabling cooperation and supporting methods to overcome conflict.

CONCLUSION

This chapter has provided an examination of Northern Ireland as a case of ethnic conflict utilizing the levels of analysis. Individuals mattered as evidenced by the role of elites such as Gerry Adams and Ian Paisley, as well as George Mitchell. Their motivations and beliefs about the future of Northern Ireland, whether it should remain a part of the United Kingdom or unify with the Republic of Ireland, shaped their views and conduct of the conflict situation. Domestic factors mattered as well, namely political parties (SDLP, Sinn Fein, UUP, DUP), political institutions, and economic conditions, as well as the politics of identity. Finally, international actors (Republic of Ireland, the United States) played an active role in resolving the conflict (and the European Union encourages further cooperation and reconciliation). Thus, factors at all three levels of analysis are relevant for this conflict.

In terms of identity and the link to ethno-nationalist conflict, we acknowledge that primordial sentiments matter in understanding the identity of the various people in Northern Ireland. However, we also show that the people of Northern Ireland have several identities including Irish, Northern Irish, British, Protestant, and Catholic, as well as unionist, loyalist, nationalist, and republican. That people can have multiple identities, some of which are more salient than others, demonstrates that identities are fluid, and thus are constructed. The social construction of identities, rather than fixed identities, provides an opportunity for resolving the conflict.

NOTES

1. The Northern Ireland Peace Process: Policing Advances and Remaining Challenges. Joint Hearing before the Subcommittee on Africa, Global Human Rights, and International Operations and the Subcommittee on Europe and Emerging Threats of the Committee on International Relations, House of Representatives, 109th Cong., 2nd sess. March 15, 2006. Serial No. 1509-152. U.S. Government Printing Office, Washington, D.C., 2006.

2. The Northern Ireland Peace Process: Policing Advances and Remaining Challenges. Joint Hearing before the Subcommittee on Africa, Global Human Rights, and International Operations and the Subcommittee on Europe and Emerging Threats of the Committee on International Relations, House of Representatives, 109th Cong., 2nd sess. March 15, 2006. Serial No. 1509-152. U.S. Government Printing Office, Washington, D.C., 2006.

3. The Northern Ireland Peace Process: Policing Advances and Remaining Challenges. Joint Hearing before the Subcommittee on Africa, Global Human Rights, and International Operations and the Subcommittee on Europe and Emerging Threats of the Committee on International Relations, House of Representatives, 109th Cong., 2nd sess. March 15, 2006. Serial No. 1509-152. U.S. Government Printing Office, Washington, D.C., 2006.

4. The Rosemary Nelson Inquiry, www.rosemarynelsoninquiry.org.

5. The Rosemary Nelson Inquiry, www.rosemarynelsoninquiry.org.

6. There are many good sources on the history of Northern Ireland. This chapter relies primarily on Thomas Hennessey, *A History of Northern Ireland* (New York: St. Martin's Press, 1997).

7. Joseph Ruane and Jennifer Todd, *The Dynamics of Conflict in Northern Ireland: Power, Conflict, and Emancipation* (Cambridge: Cambridge University Press, 1996), 20.

8. J. G. Simms, "The Restoration and the Jacobite War (1660-1691)," in *The Course of Irish History*, ed. T. W. Moody and F. X. Martin (Cork: Mercier Press, 1967), 204-216.

9. Donal McCartney, "From Parnell to Pearse (1891-1921)," in *The Course of Irish History*, ed. T. W. Moody and F. X. Martin (Cork: Mercier Press, 1967), 294-312.

10. Patrick Lynch, "Ireland since the Treaty (1921-1966)," in *The Course of Irish History*, ed. T. W. Moody and F. X. Martin (Cork: Mercier Press, 1967), 324-342.

11. Hennessey, *A History of Northern Ireland*, 56-70.

12. Hennessey, *A History of Northern Ireland,* 70–82.

13. Hennessey, *A History of Northern Ireland,* 90.

14. Hennessey, *A History of Northern Ireland,* 97–99.

15. Hennessey, *A History of Northern Ireland,* 104–107.

16. Hennessey, *A History of Northern Ireland,* 107–110.

17. Adrian Guelke, "Political Violence and the Paramilitaries," in *Politics in Northern Ireland,* eds. Paul Mitchell and Rick Wolford (Boulder: Westview, 1999), 220–241.

18. Brendan O'Leary and John McGarry, *The Politics of Antagonism: Understanding Northern Ireland* (London: Athlone, 1993), 36.

19. Malcolm Sutton, *Bear in Mind These Dead . . . : An Index of Deaths from the Conflict in Ireland, 1969–1993* (Belfast: Beyond the Pale Publications, 1994).

20. Paul Dixon, *Northern Ireland: The Politics of War and Peace* (New York: Palgrave, 2001), 135-152.

21. Dixon, *Northern Ireland,* 190-213.

22. Dixon, *Northern Ireland,* 272–274.

23. John McGarry and Brendan O'Leary, "Stabilising the Northern Ireland Agreement," in *Devolution and Constitutional Change in Northern Ireland,* ed. Paul Carmichael, Colin Knox, and Robert Osborne (New York: Manchester University Press, 2007), 62–82.

24. McGarry and O'Leary, "Stabilising the Northern Ireland Agreement," 62–82.

25. Dixon, *Northern Ireland,* 274–277.

26. Gordon Gillespie, *Historical Dictionary of the Northern Ireland Conflict* (Lanham, Md.: Scarecrow Press, 2008), xl (Chronology).

27. Gillespie, *Historical Dictionary of the Northern Ireland Conflict,* xlii (Chronology).

28. Gillespie, *Historical Dictionary of the Northern Ireland Conflict,* xliv (Chronology).

29. "SF (Sinn Fein) Threatens to Collapse Assembly," *BBC News,* August 24, 2008, http://news.bbc.co.uk/2/hi/uk_news/northern_ireland/7580108 .stm.

30. Cathy Gormley-Heenan, *Political Leadership and the Northern Ireland Peace Process: Role, Capacity, and Effect* (New York: Palgrave, 2007).

31. John Paul Lederach, *Building Peace: Sustainable Reconciliation in Divided Societies* (Washington D.C.: United States Institute of Peace Press, 1997).

32. Hugh Miall, Oliver Ramsbotham, and Tom Woodhouse, *Contemporary Conflict Resolution: The Prevention, Management, and Transformation of Deadly Conflicts* (Oxford: Polity, 1999).

33. Stephen John Stedman, "Spoiler Problems in Peace Processes," in *Nationalism and Ethnic Conflict,* ed. Michael E. Brown, Owen R. Cote Jr., Sean M. Lynn-Jones, and Steven E. Miller, rev. ed. (Cambridge, Mass.: MIT Press, 2001), 366–414.

34. Bowyer Bell, *The Secret Army: The IRA,* 3rd ed. (New Brunswick, N.J.: Transaction, 1997).

35. Colm Keena, *A Biography of Gerry Adams* (Cork: Mercier Press, 1990).

36. Jonathan Tonge, *Northern Ireland* (Malden, Mass.: Polity Press, 2006), 107–108.

37. Tonge, *Northern Ireland,* 113–116.

38. "The 'Broadcast Ban' on Sinn Fein," *BBC News,* April 5, 2005.

39. Gillespie, *Historical Dictionary of the Northern Ireland Conflict,* 89–90.

40. Gormley-Heenan, *Political Leadership and the Northern Ireland Peace Process,* 38–39.

41. "Timeline: Northern Ireland's Road to Peace," *BBC News,* January 27, 2006, available at http://news.bbc.co.uk/2/hi/uk_news/northern_ireland/4072261.stm.

42. Gillespie, *Historical Dictionary of the Northern Ireland Conflict,* 111–112.

43. Tonge, *Northern Ireland,* 170–171.

44. Gillespie, *Historical Dictionary of the Northern Ireland Conflict,* 197.

45. Dixon, *Northern Ireland,* 195–210.

46. Dixon, *Northern Ireland,* 275-277.

47. McGarry and O'Leary, "Stabilising the Northern Ireland Agreement," 62–82.

48. "Paisley to Quit as First Minister," *BBC News,* March 4, 2008.

49. "Ian Paisley's Speech in Full," *BBC News,* May 8, 2007.

50. Gormley-Heenan, *Political Leadership and the Northern Ireland Peace Process.*

51. Gormley-Heenan, *Political Leadership and the Northern Ireland Peace Process,* 144–146.

52. Stedman, "Spoiler Problems in Peace Processes," 372.

53. Gillespie, *Historical Dictionary of the Northern Ireland Conflict,* 122–123.

54. Tonge, *Northern Ireland,* 178–204.

55. Dixon, *Northern Ireland,* 244–280.

56. Gillespie, *Historical Dictionary of the Northern Ireland Conflict,* 123, 249.

57. Gormley-Heenan, *Political Leadership and the Northern Ireland Peace Process,* 152–153.

58. Stedman, "Spoiler Problems in Peace Processes," 366.

59. George J. Mitchell, *Making Peace* (New York: Alfred A. Knopf, 1999), preface.

60. 1998 Recipient George Mitchell, Liberty Medal, National Constitution Center, www.constitutioncenter.org/libertymedal/recipient_1998.html.

61. Alberta Gould, *George Mitchell: In Search of Peace* (Farmington, Maine: Heritage, 1996).

62. Mitchell, *Making Peace,* 8.

63. Mitchell, *Making Peace,* 20.

64. Gormley-Heenan, *Political Leadership and the Northern Ireland Peace Process,* 43.

65. Mitchell, *Making Peace,* 188.

66. Barbara Harff and Ted Robert Gurr, *Ethnic Conflict in World Politics,* 2nd ed. (Boulder: Westview Press, 2004).

67. Harff and Gurr, *Ethnic Conflict in World Politics,* 28.

68. Joseph Ruane and Jennifer Todd, *The Dynamics of Conflict in Northern Ireland: Power, Conflict, and Emancipation* (Cambridge: Cambridge University Press, 1996), 22.

69. Ruane and Todd, *The Dynamics of Conflict in Northern Ireland,* 23.

70. Ruane and Todd, *The Dynamics of Conflict in Northern Ireland,* 23.

71. Ruane and Todd, *The Dynamics of Conflict in Northern Ireland,* 26–28.

72. Ruane and Todd, *The Dynamics of Conflict in Northern Ireland,* 28–29.

73. Ruane and Todd, *The Dynamics of Conflict in Northern Ireland,* 43–46.

74. Ruane and Todd, *The Dynamics of Conflict in Northern Ireland,* 9.

75. Economic and Social Research Council, "Northern Ireland Life and Times" survey 2007, www.ark.ac.uk/nilt/2007/Community_Relations/NINATID. html; Karen Trew, "The Northern Irish Identity," in *A Question of Identity,* ed. Anne J. Kershen (Aldershot: Ashgate, 1998), 60–76; Karen Trew and Denny E. Benson, "Dimensions of Social Identity in Northern Ireland," in *Changing European Identities: Social Psychological Analyses of Social Changes,* ed. Glynis M. Breakwell and Evanthia Lyons Speri (Oxford: Butterworth-Heinemann, 1996), 123–143.

76. Peter Bull, "Shifting Patterns of Social Identity in Northern Ireland," *Psychologist* 19, no. 1 (January 2006): 41.

77. Cathal McCall, *Identity in Northern Ireland* (New York: St. Martin's Press, 1999), 147.

78. Dixon, *Northern Ireland,* 7–11.

79. Andrea K. Grove and Neal A. Carter, "Not All Blarney Is Cast in Stone: International Cultural Conflict in Northern Ireland," *Political Psychology* 20 (1999): 725–765.

80. Grove and Carter, "Not All Blarney Is Cast in Stone," 733, 737.

81. Ruane and Todd, *The Dynamics of Conflict in Northern Ireland;* Edward Moxon-Browne, "National Identity in Northern Ireland," in *Social Attitudes in Northern Ireland,* ed. Peter Stringer and Jillian Robinson (Belfast: Blackstaff, 1991), 25.

82. Economic and Social Research Council, "Northern Ireland Life and Times" survey 2007, www.ark.ac.uk/nilt/2007/Community_Relations/NINATID. html.

83. Ruane and Todd, *The Dynamics of Conflict in Northern Ireland,* 49–83.

84. Dixon, *Northern Ireland,* 281–288.

85. John McGarry and Brendan O'Leary, "Five Fallacies: Northern Ireland and the Liabilities of Liberalism," in *The Northern Ireland Conflict: Consociational*

Engagements, ed. John McGarry and Brendan O'Leary (New York: Oxford University Press, 2004), 167–193.

86. McGarry and O'Leary, "Five Fallacies," 179.
87. McGarry and O'Leary, "Five Fallacies," 175–178.
88. John McGarry and Brendan O'Leary, "Introduction: Consociational Theory and Northern Ireland," in *The Northern Ireland Conflict: Consociational Engagements,* ed. John McGarry and Brendan O'Leary (New York: Oxford University Press, 2004), 1–2.
89. Neal G. Jesse and Kristen P. Williams, *Identity and Institutions: Conflict Reduction in Divided Societies* (Albany: SUNY Press, 2005).
90. McGarry and O'Leary, "Introduction," 5.
91. Jesse and Williams, *Identity and Institutions.*
92. Thomas Hennessey, *The Northern Ireland Peace Process: Ending the Troubles?* (New York: Palgrave, 2001), 175–177.
93. McGarry and O'Leary, "Introduction."
94. Hennessey, *The Northern Ireland Peace Process.*
95. David Smith and Gerald Chambers, *Inequality in Northern Ireland* (Oxford: Oxford University Press, 2001).
96. Office for National Statistics (2004), Regional Trends, London, 2004.
97. "Rise in the Number of Unemployed," *BBC News,* October 15, 2008, http://news.bbc.co.uk/go/pr/fr/-/2/hi/uk_news/northern_ireland/7671210.stm.
98. McGarry and O'Leary, "Five Fallacies," 167–193.
99. Brendan O'Duffy, "Violence in Northern Ireland, 1964–94: Sectarian or Ethnonational?" *Ethnic and Racial Studies* 18 (1995): 740–772.
100. McGarry and O'Leary, "Five Fallacies," 167–193.
101. Jay Rothman and Marie L. Olson, "From Interests to Identities: Toward a New Emphasis in Interactive Conflict Resolution," *Journal of Peace Research* 38, no. 3 (2001): 291.
102. Fidelma Ashe, "Gendering Ethno-nationalist Conflict in Northern Ireland: A Comparative Analysis of Nationalist Women's Political Protests," *Ethnic and Racial Studies* 30, no. 5 (September 2007): 768.
103. Ashe, "Gendering Ethno-nationalist Conflict in Northern Ireland," 769.
104. Ashe, "Gendering Ethno-nationalist Conflict in Northern Ireland," 769.
105. Ashe, "Gendering Ethno-nationalist Conflict in Northern Ireland," 770.
106. Ashe, "Gendering Ethno-nationalist Conflict in Northern Ireland," 770.
107. Ashe, "Gendering Ethno-nationalist Conflict in Northern Ireland," 771.
108. Ashe, "Gendering Ethno-nationalist Conflict in Northern Ireland," 767.
109. Ashe, "Gendering Ethno-nationalist Conflict in Northern Ireland," 779.
110. Ashe, "Gendering Ethno-nationalist Conflict in Northern Ireland," 779.
111. Ashe, "Gendering Ethno-nationalist Conflict in Northern Ireland," 781.
112. Ashe, "Gendering Ethno-nationalist Conflict in Northern Ireland," 783.

113. Linda Racioppi and Katherine O'Sullivan See, "'This We Will Maintain': Gender, Ethno-nationalism and the Politics of Unionism in Northern Ireland," *Nations and Nationalism* 7, no. 1 (2001): 95.
114. Racioppi and O'Sullivan See, "'This We Will Maintain,'" 101.
115. Racioppi and O'Sullivan See, "'This We Will Maintain,'" 103.
116. Joyce P. Kaufman and Kristen P. Williams, *Women, the State, and War: A Comparative Perspective on Citizenship and Nationalism* (Lanham, Md.: Lexington, 2007), 177.
117. Kaufman and Williams, *Women, the State, and War,* 183.
118. Kaufman and Williams, *Women, the State, and War,* 184
119. Brendan O'Leary, "Public Opinion and Northern Irish Futures," *Political Quarterly* 63 (1992): 143–170.
120. Dixon, *Northern Ireland,* 301.
121. Ruane and Todd, *The Dynamics of Conflict in Northern Ireland.*
122. Arend Lijphart, *Democracy in Plural Societies* (New Haven: Yale University Press, 1997).
123. Dixon, *Northern Ireland,* 142–157.
124. Dixon, *Northern Ireland,* 190–214.
125. Hennessey, *The Northern Ireland Peace Process,* 18.
126. Dixon, *Northern Ireland,* 190–214.
127. Dixon, *Northern Ireland,* 235–240.
128. Arthur Aughey, "Northern Ireland," in *Developments in British Politics,* ed. P. Dunleavy, A. Gamble, I. Holliday, and G. Peele, 5th ed. (New York: St. Martin's Press, 1997), 241–252.
129. Dixon, *Northern Ireland,* 228.
130. Bill McSweeney, "Security, Identity, and the Peace Process in Northern Ireland," *Security Dialogue,* 27 (1996): 167–178.
131. McSweeney, "Security, Identity, and the Peace Process in Northern Ireland," 167–178.
132. Ruane and Todd, *The Dynamics of Conflict in Northern Ireland,* 50.
133. Ruane and Todd, *The Dynamics of Conflict in Northern Ireland,* 297–300.
134. Colin McKeogh, "Northern Ireland: The Good Friday Solution," *New Zealand International Review* 23 (1998), 2–6.
135. Polls in both 1996 and 1997 showed that the proposed solution (a local Northern Irish parliament with power-sharing and cross-border institutions shared with the Republic of Ireland) was more highly favored by Catholics than Protestants. In 1997 the poll asked respondents if any of the proposed solutions were "unacceptable." Only 2.7 percent of Catholics responded yes, while 15.5 percent of Protestants agreed. The source for the 1996 poll is Market Research Bureau of Ireland (MRBI) on behalf of the

Sunday Times, September 1996. The source for the 1997 poll is Coopers and Lybrand for BBC, September 1997.

136. McGarry and O'Leary, "Stabilising the Northern Ireland Agreement," 80.
137. Office for National Statistics (online), www.statistics.gov.uk.
138. T. W. Moody and F. X. Martin, eds., *The Course of Irish History* (Cork: Mercier Press, 1967).
139. Hennessey, *A History of Northern Ireland,* 1–2.
140. McCartney, "From Parnell to Pearse (1891–1921)," 294–312.
141. Peter Mair, *The Changing Irish Party System* (London: Pinter, 1987), 13.
142. Michael Gallagher, "The Changing Constitution," in *Politics in the Republic of Ireland,* ed. John Coakley and Michael Gallagher, 3rd ed. (New York: Routledge, 1999), 71–98.
143. Dixon, *Northern Ireland,* 51–53.
144. Hennessey, *The Northern Ireland Peace Process,* 104–107.
145. Dixon, *Northern Ireland,* 60–64.
146. Brian Girvin, "Northern Ireland and the Republic," in *Politics in Northern Ireland,* ed. Paul Mitchell and Rick Wilford (Boulder: Westview, 1999): 220–241.
147. Hennessey, *The Northern Ireland Peace Process,* 270–273.
148. Hennessey, *The Northern Ireland Peace Process,* 273–276.
149. Gillespie, *Historical Dictionary of the Northern Ireland Conflict,* 220–221.
150. Aughey, "Northern Ireland," 241–252.
151. Gillespie, *Historical Dictionary of the Northern Ireland Conflict,* 48–49.
152. Gormley-Heenan, *Political Leadership and the Northern Ireland Peace Process,* 37.
153. McGarry and O'Leary, "Introduction," 10–13.
154. Francis M. Carroll, *The American Presence in Ulster: A Diplomatic History, 1796–1996* (Washington, D.C.: Catholic University of America Press, 2005).
155. Joseph E. Thompson, *American Policy and Northern Ireland: A Saga of Peacebuilding* (Westport, Conn.: Praeger, 2001), 8.
156. Thompson, *American Policy and Northern Ireland,* 14–15.
157. Walter LaFeber, *America, Russia, and the Cold War: 1945–1990,* 6th ed. (New York: McGraw-Hill, 1991).
158. Thompson, *American Policy and Northern Ireland,* 30–31.
159. Thompson, *American Policy and Northern Ireland,* 38.
160. Thompson, *American Policy and Northern Ireland,* 48–69.
161. Thompson, *American Policy and Northern Ireland,* 71–74.
162. Thompson, *American Policy and Northern Ireland,* 77.
163. Thompson, *American Policy and Northern Ireland,* 75–93.
164. Thompson, *American Policy and Northern Ireland,* 109–110.
165. Thompson, *American Policy and Northern Ireland,* 117–120.

166. Thompson, *American Policy and Northern Ireland,* 123–141.
167. Thompson, *American Policy and Northern Ireland,* 143–161.
168. Thompson, *American Policy and Northern Ireland,* 166.
169. Thompson, *American Policy and Northern Ireland,* 163–166.
170. Thompson, *American Policy and Northern Ireland,* 179.
171. For a firsthand account, see Mitchell, *Making Peace.*
172. Thompson, *American Policy and Northern Ireland,* 192–215.
173. "President Leaves NI (Northern Ireland) after Visit," *BBC News,* June 16, 2008, http://news.bbc.co.uk/2/hi/uk_news/northern_ireland/7455806.stm.
174. Paul Bew and Elizabeth Meehan, "Regions and Borders: Controversies in Northern Ireland about the European Union," *Journal of European Public Policy* 1 (1994): 104.
175. McCall, *Identity in Northern Ireland,* 86.
176. Etian Tannam, *Cross-Border Cooperation in the Republic of Ireland and Northern Ireland* (New York: St. Martin's Press, 1999), 109.

CHAPTER 4

Bosnia: War in the Balkans

The dissolution of Yugoslavia, culminating in the 1992–1995 Bosnian war, offers an illustrative case of ethnic conflict in the immediate post–Cold War period. The Bosnian war's end led to the creation of five new states (Bosnia, Croatia, Macedonia, Serbia, and Slovenia).[1] Following the secession of Slovenia and Croatia from Yugoslavia in 1991 and a short war in Slovenia, the emergence of war in Croatia, and the 1992 referendum in Bosnia that called for an independent Bosnia, war broke out between Bosnian Serbs, Bosnian Croats, and Muslims (Bosniaks) in Bosnia proper.[2] Bosnian Croats garnered support from the newly independent state of Croatia, while Bosnian Serbs were aided by Serbia (the dominant republic in what was left of Yugoslavia, which now consisted of Serbia and the republics of Macedonia and Montenegro). Fighting was intense, as witnessed by significant refugee flows and ethnic cleansing. The spread of the conflict (from Slovenia, to Croatia, and then to Bosnia) demonstrates the diffusion of the conflict, while escalation occurred as other states (such as Serbia and the new neighboring state of Croatia) and non-state actors intervened as Yugoslavia fell apart.[3] The war ended in 1995 with the signing of the Dayton Accords (so called because the agreement was signed in Dayton, Ohio) by the representatives of the republics of Bosnia, Croatia, and Serbia, representing the three main ethnic groups. Bosnia became a confederation of two entities: Bosnian Serb Republic (Republika Srpska, 49 percent of the territory), with a predominantly Bosnian Serb population; and a Muslim-Croat Federation (51 percent of the territory).[4]

International intervention came in the form of an international Implementation Force (IFOR) sent to Bosnia, and a UN-established "transitional administration" in Croatia. The Dayton Accords led to an end to violent conflict in the region, but tensions between the three main ethnic groups still remain.[5] Roberto Belloni argues that the Bosnian Serbs and the Bosnian Croats persist in their efforts to increase the autonomy of their respective entities rather than support the joint political institutions. In contrast, the goal of the Bosnian Muslims is to bolster the Bosnian state. In doing so, they face accusations that they are attempting to gain control and power through the state-level joint institutions.

MAP 4.1
Ethnic Distribution in Bosnia and Herzegovina

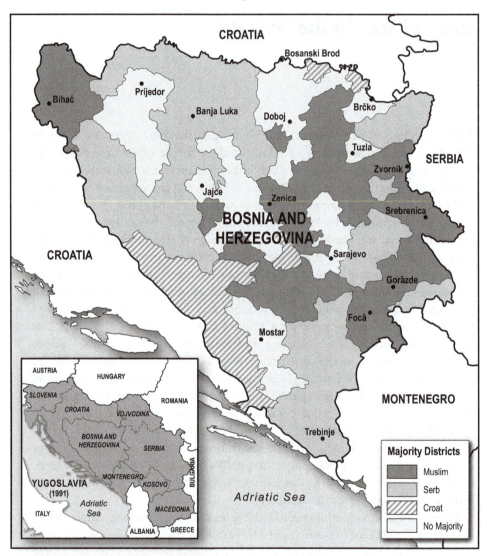

CROATIA

Bosanski Brod

Bihać

Prijedor

Banja Luka

Doboj

Brčko

Tuzla

SERBIA

Zvornik

Jajce

Zenica

Srebrenica

BOSNIA AND HERZEGOVINA

CROATIA

Sarajevo

Gorázde

Foča

Mostar

MONTENEGRO

Trebinje

AUSTRIA

HUNGARY

SLOVENIA

ROMANIA

CROATIA

VOJVODINA

BOSNIA AND HERZEGOVINA

SERBIA

MONTENEGRO

KOSOVO

YUGOSLAVIA
(1991)

Adriatic Sea

BULGARIA

ITALY

MACEDONIA

ALBANIA

GREECE

Adriatic Sea

Majority Districts

- Muslim
- Serb
- Croat
- No Majority

Source: Data from Susan L. Woodward, *Balkan Tragedy: Chaos and Dissolution after the Cold War* (Washington, DC: Brookings Institution, 1995), 28.

The international community intervenes at the local level of politics that then plays a role in "the 'political irresponsibility' of local leaders."[6]

This chapter begins with an overview of the historical background of the creation of Yugoslavia and origins of the Bosnian war that began in 1992. The chapter then moves to a discussion of the individual level factors that mattered for an understanding of the war's origins. We look at the role and motivations of Serbian leader Slobodan Milosevic, Croatian leader Franjo Tudjman, and Bosnian Muslim leader Alija Izetbegovic. Each of these elites sought to solidify his power, engaging in ethnic outbidding through his appeals to his respective ethnic group (Serbs, Croats, and Muslims). The next section of the chapter focuses on the domestic level factors, including public opinion, parties and elections, criminals, media, gendered nationalism, economic and political conditions as related to the ethnic balance of power, and religion. International level factors are then examined—namely the role of the international community in responding to the breakup of Yugoslavia and attempting to resolve the crisis and prevent the subsequent war. The next section covers the post-Dayton peace in Bosnia, which continues to face challenges from ethnic nationalism and the possibility of resumption of ethnic conflict. The concluding section reiterates the interplay between the three levels as explanations for the origins of and solutions to the conflict.

BOSNIA IN HISTORICAL CONTEXT

Yugoslavia ("south Slavs") as an independent country did not exist prior to 1919. Before its creation, parts of the territory were ruled by either the Ottoman Empire or the Austro-Hungarian Empire. Only in the case of Serbia did independence come before the beginning of the twentieth century. In the nineteenth century, Croatia was part of the Austro-Hungarian Empire, while Bosnia proper had been a protectorate of the Ottoman Empire since the fifteenth century. Importantly, during the nineteenth century, Croatian and Serbian nationalism increased. It was during the period of Bosnia's annexation by the Austro-Hungarian Empire beginning in 1908 that one finds the emergence of Croatian and Serbian nationalist movements. These nationalist movements within Bosnia sought to incorporate Bosnian territory "into a Greater Croatia and a Greater Serbia, respectively."[7]

At the conclusion of World War I, and the defeat of both the Ottoman and Austro-Hungarian Empires, a new state was created that included Croatia, Serbia, and Bosnia. This new state, Yugoslavia, came into being in 1919 and was known as the "Kingdom of Croats, Serbs and Slovenes." The Slavic background of the various peoples made it possible to unify the territory into an independent state. The reality of unification, however, proved more difficult, given the different historical experiences as well as different religious identities of those living in the country. The dominance of Serbs in positions of authority (king, army, police, and political institutions) led to resentment by the other ethnic groups in the state. This resentment would become pronounced in the next world war.[8]

During World War II, Yugoslavia's geographic location in the center of Europe meant that it was to be a battleground of war. In a Yugoslavia occupied by Germany and Italy, civil war erupted between Serbs, Croats, and Muslims, with Bosnia "the theatre of conflict." The civil war was marked by significant atrocities carried out by Serbian Chechnik and Croatian Ustashe fascist forces—memories of which would not be forgotten in the 1980s and 1990s.[9] With the war's end, a new government came to power—the Yugoslav Communist Party—led by Josip Broz Tito, a partisan who fought in World War II.

Tito attempted to address the tensions between the various ethnic groups and republics within Yugoslavia by devising a federal structure.[10] However, his policy, according to Gavan Duffy and Nicole Lindstrom, "was always unstable, as he constructed it over tenuous faultlines."[11] Tensions between the major ethnic groups, namely Serbs and Croats, concerned both political and economic power. The Serbs sought to redistribute wealth from Croatia and Slovenia, the two wealthiest republics, to the less developed republics in the country. Moreover, Serbs also wanted to reassert their hegemony and centralize the political system in their favor. Croats, of course, had opposing claims, primarily curbing assistance to projects deemed unprofitable in Serbia and other republics in the south of the country. Additionally, Croats sought to dismantle central planning and decentralize decision making on economic issues.[12] These opposing demands led to tensions that were not addressed to the satisfaction of either ethnic group. Duffy and Lindstrom focus on two periods to demonstrate the instability of Tito's policy: the Reform Struggle of 1962–1965 and the "Croatian Crisis" of 1970–1971. The Reform Struggle crisis resulted from the federal government's actions in Split, the tourist town on the Croatian coast, and concerned two economic issues: the Yugoslav central bank's decision to take the hard-currency profits generated from Split's tourism, and the building of tourist hotels in the region by Serb construction firms.[13] These issues led to calls by Croatia and Slovenia for economic reform (Macedonia joined Croatia and Slovenia in these calls). In response, in 1965 Tito's government instituted a series of economic reforms including the "abolition of the federally controlled General Investment Fund and devolution of some power from the federal government to individual republics and their banks."[14]

In the case of the Croatian Crisis of 1970–1971, Croatian cultural demands were transformed into calls for political and economic reform—to such an extent that calls for secession became "mainstream sentiment in Croatia." Croats complained that Serbs retained more political power than Croats, in terms of a predominance of ethnic Serbs in the Croatian Communist Party as well as in the Croatian police force and army officer corps. In addition, Croatian leaders were distressed by the fact that hard-currency profits earned in Croatia were being used to improve Serbia's economy. Tito's government viewed Croatia's secession demands as a direct challenge to the legitimacy of Yugoslavia's political institutions. Students engaged in strikes in Croatia in November 1971; in response, the federal government threatened to send Yugoslav army troops to end the strikes as well as to stop Croatia from seceding. The government was able to get the Croatian Communist Party leadership to resign the next month, thereby ending the crisis.[15]

After the crisis ended, the government recognized that tensions between the republics remained and sought to deal with Croatian demands for more economic and political autonomy. The government did so through the 1974 Yugoslav constitution, in which power within the Yugoslav federation devolved to the six constituent republics, so that the federal government had authority in areas of foreign policy and defense, while the republics were allowed to have their own judicial entities, central bank, schools, and police. Serbia's authority over Vojvodina and Kosovo, two provinces within the Serb republic, was removed. The two provinces were then each given "power to nominate officials to federal bodies and votes in the Yugoslav Presidency."[16] A further important consequence of the new constitution was the elevated status of Bosnian Muslims in the Bosnian republic, people who were now "considered a distinct community" or "nation." Bosnian Muslims now found themselves "as the dominant group when competing with Bosnian Croats and Serbs for administrative and legislative positions."[17]

Tensions lessened, but only because of Tito's leadership and exclusive control. With his death in 1980 those tensions came to the forefront. Serbs' resentment about their diminished power, given the 1974 constitution, continued to the extent that in the perception of many Serbs the new constitution was intended to undermine their power. Elites, such as Slobodan Milosevic, who came to power in 1989, appealed to popular sentiment by focusing on national identity and fears of the continued erosion of Serb power.[18] At the same time, Croatian lack of trust of, and resentment toward, the Yugoslav federal government had not dissipated with the end of the Croatian Crisis in 1971. Rather, Croatian leaders, such as Franjo Tudjman, saw an opportunity to push for further demands.[19]

By the late 1980s the various republics focused on gaining and maintaining political and economic power. Serbia was able to regain control over the two provinces, Vojvodina and Kosovo. With the control of the two provinces' votes as well as Montenegro's vote, Serbia had half of the votes (four out of eight) necessary for the presidency. Importantly, having obtained these four votes shifted the balance of power in Serbia's favor to the extent that it could block any demands Croatia or Slovenia made for further devolution of power. For example, at the Fourteenth Communist Party Congress, held in January 1990, Serbia was able to defeat all the amendments to the Communist Party rules put forward by Croatia or Slovenia. As a result, Slovenia's delegation left the congress entirely. The Slovenian action led to the downfall of the Yugoslav Communist Party. By the next summer, referenda on secession were held in Croatia and Slovenia. These referenda were passed overwhelmingly by their respective populations, prompting both republics to declare independence on June 25, 1991. These declarations of independence, in turn, were met with resistance by the federal army, whose troops were sent to Slovenia to maintain Yugoslavia's territorial borders. The conflict lasted ten days, at which time the federal troops were withdrawn, in large part as a result of threats of political and economic sanctions by the European Community.[20]

The end of conflict between the federal army and the wayward republics did not last long. While Slovenia was able to secede and become a new state, such a fate would not come easily for Croatia. Given the sizeable minority of ethnic Serbs living within the Croatian republic, Milosevic would not permit Croatian secession, as this would thwart his goal of a Greater Serbia that united all Serbs in one territorial entity. Conflict erupted between Croatians and the Yugoslav national army, dominated by Serbs, in September 1991. An external actor, the United Nations, intervened and negotiated a cease-fire in December of that same year. Croatia's independence was recognized by the international community. Yet, by January the federal army controlled almost a third of Croatian territory.[21]

Following the independence declarations of Croatia and Slovenia, Bosnia held a referendum on secession in 1992. Bosnian Serbs boycotted the referendum, which passed when Bosnian Croats and Muslims voted in favor of independence. Bosnia's independence had ramifications for the balance of power between the ethnic groups. Both the Bosnian Serbs and Croats were now ethnic minorities rather than "members of the dominant Croat and Serb nations within Yugoslavia."[22] Ethnic nationalism became even more pronounced, at the expense of democratic institutions, to the extent that overt war broke out, a war that would last for three years. Interestingly, as J. Andrew Slack and Roy R. Doyon observe, the Yugoslav constitution allowed for each republic to have a referendum for self-determination, but that process actually led to the demise of the country.[23]

How can the origins of ethnic conflict in Bosnia be explained by the theories discussed in chapter 1? Frank P. Harvey argues that primordialism does not provide a satisfactory explanation for the conflict. He argues that "it is almost impossible for people in the region to trace the ethnic line of most inhabitants." Given the widespread intermarriage in the region, one cannot detect any "physical differences among people of different ethnic origins."[24] He notes that ethnic differences existed both in times of war and peace, and thus those differences cannot be sources of conflict. Instead, other factors must be at work.[25] Additionally, he argues that there is nothing "unique" about the ethnic divisions within Yugoslavia that necessarily led to conflict. In many parts of the world there are comparable "levels of ethnic and religious division," but the outcomes have not been ethnic cleansing or civil war.[26] Harvey also notes that while the conventional wisdom places the blame for the breakup of the country on the linguistic and religious divisions already there, he argues that the breakup actually led to and intensified the discord and violence between the groups.[27]

While primordialist sentiments were present, a social constructivist explanation is more accurate. Tito's attempt at constructing a Yugoslav identity that would unify the various groups became problematic.[28] The Croatian crises of the 1960s and 1970s and the burgeoning fears of the future for the minority groups within the particular republics in the late 1980s and early 1990s led to ethnic security dilemmas and contributed to constructions of identity that reinforced the divisions and differences among the various ethnic groups. As Joyce Kaufman and Kristen Williams note, "As Yugoslavia disintegrated in the early 1990s, nationalist leaders focused on constructing ethnically 'pure' states, thereby determining who could be a citizen, i.e., who belonged. The drive for ethnically based states challenged the very essence of Yugoslavia as a multiethnic country."[29]

Rather than a primordial explanation for the outbreak of war in the region, Harvey asserts that the causes of the conflict "can also be viewed in terms of a combination of necessary and sufficient conditions: (1) economic, political and military threats to the identity and/or existence of the ethnic group (primordial attachments), (2) elites with the political skills and resources to play on those fears (instrumentalist forces) and (3) third-party military, political or economic support for at least one side in the dispute."[30] Harvey's three necessary and sufficient conditions are, in essence, factors found at the three levels of analysis. Importantly, factors at all three levels of analysis interacted in such a way as to contribute to the outbreak of war. The next section examines individual level factors to understand the Bosnian conflict.

INDIVIDUAL LEVEL

As chapter 2 discusses, individuals make decisions about policies and behavior—such as whether to go to war or not. Tito's death in 1980 changed the political landscape of Yugoslavia. In the power vacuum that ensued, political entrepreneurs were able to mobilize support by appealing to nationalist sentiments and tensions. By capitalizing on these nationalist tensions, elites were able to trigger "new rounds of intergroup conflict."[31] The ethnic and nationalist tensions that played a direct role in the dissolution of Yugoslavia and the outbreak of war in the Bosnian republic can be explained by the actions of many individuals, but the three that are most representative are Slobodan Milosevic, Franjo Tudjman, and Alija Izetbegovic, and it is they who are the focus of this section of the chapter.[32]

Slobodan Milosevic

Slobodan Milosevic is probably the name most synonymous with the war in the Balkans and the disintegration of Yugoslavia. Milosevic rose to power in 1989 when he ousted the Serbian president, Ivan Stambolic, and became the president of the republic. Though a banker by training (he had moved up the ladder of the economic bureaucracy in Yugoslavia beginning in the late 1960s), he was also active in party politics as early as during his college years. His political activism continued, and he joined the League of Communists of Yugoslavia (LCY) in 1969.[33] By the mid-1980s he entered politics full time when he became the leader of the Belgrade (capital of Serbia) city committee, and in 1986, when his mentor (and later, rival) Stambolic left his position as the head of the Central Committee of the League of Communists of Serbia (LCS), Milosevic took over as chairman.[34] While Stambolic served as Milosevic's mentor, there were also differences in their views on Serbian nationalism. In response to Albanian riots in Kosovo and the subsequent fleeing of Montenegrins and Serbs from Kosovo, Stambolic indicated his support for the Serbian nationalist position that the 1974 Yugoslav constitution (which removed Serbian authority over Kosovo and diluted Yugoslavia's federal structure, of which Serbia had been dominant) was unfair to Serbs. However, as Sabrina Ramet notes, "he also warned that 'certain individuals' were 'coqueting' with Serbian nationalism."[35] Milosevic, on the other hand, placed his support squarely with the Serbs living in Kosovo.[36] Conservatives, headed by Milosevic, were able to use the cause of Kosovo's Serbs to undermine reformists within Serbia specifically and Yugoslavia in general.[37]

A meeting of three hundred LCY party delegates (mostly ethnic Albanians) in Kosovo Polje (a suburb of Pristina, Kosovo's capital) in April 1987 became the lightning rod for Serbian discontent. Although the meeting was closed to the public (only the party delegates were to attend), approximately 15,000 Serbs and Montenegrins attempted to enter the building. The police responded by "beating them back with clubs." As a member of the LCY, Milosevic was attending the meeting, and "raised his hands, signaling the police to let the Serbs through." He then said to the crowd, "Nobody, either now or in the future, has the right to beat you."[38] As Ramet asserts, "These words assured Milosevic a place in Serbian mythology."[39] Moreover, he did not leave the building until the next morning as he listened to the complaints of Serbs about their plight. The Serbs made it clear that they held the Albanian leaders responsible for the declining conditions in Kosovo. Ramet quotes a Serbian journalist who had known Milosevic for quite some time: "After that night, suddenly there was a psychological change in him. All at once, he discovered he had this power over people."[40]

His appeal to the ethnic identity of Serbs as a means to secure his leadership position fits very well with an instrumentalist approach to understanding ethnicity and nationalism.[41] As Dusko Sekulic and his coauthors argue, the political elites were able to tap into nationalist ideology and historical memories, as well as the "political resentment and dissatisfaction of Serbian elites," in order to mobilize support of the masses.[42] Thus, such an appeal to Serbian nationalism enabled Milosevic to further his power and oust Stambolic so that by the middle of December 1988 Stambolic was ousted as the Serbian president. On May 8, 1989, Milosevic secured his position of power when he became the new Serbian president.[43]

Milosevic's "political program" was focused not on reform but fostering conflict, especially given that it was framed in terms of nationalism. According to Ramet, he had four goals: he aimed to establish complete control in Serbia, to reestablish Serbian control over Kosovo and Vojvodina, to overturn the 1974 constitution, and to create a Serbian-dominated country "that would have a semi-free market and a semidemocratic communist party."[44]

In terms of his first goal, Milosevic appealed to Serb nationalism in order to gain control of Serbia. Ramet notes, "His rule has been one continuous celebration of Serbia—he talks of Serbia's place in the world, of its struggles, of its enemies, of its needs." Importantly, he was able to encourage Serb nationalism through the creation of a "cult of personality," control of the media, and the support of the Serbian Orthodox church.[45] His "cult of personality" was cultivated with his populist style, which was such that many Serbs put their trust in him. In doing so, the political institutions were undermined. Some Serbs expressed criticism of Tito for having reduced Serbia's power in the country, telling "foreigners that they had never been free under Tito, but were with 'Slobo' at their head 'completely free as never before.'"[46] With this cult of personality, Milosevic was able to use the Serbian party apparatus for his own power. He would circumvent the party structure if it hindered his instrumentalist goals of consolidating and maintaining his rule. He did not permit any public criticism of his rule; those who did criticize him faced the possibility of losing their jobs.[47]

Milosevic used both the media and the Serbian Orthodox church to his advantage. He willingly fired editors and journalists who did not support his policies or his rule. As a result, major daily newspapers and weekly publications "became mere mouthpieces for Milosevic's policies."[48] With regard to the

Serbian Orthodox church, for example, in June 1989, Milosevic and several church leaders held a joint commemoration of the 600th anniversary of the Battle of Kosovo (where the Serbs were defeated by the Ottomans in 1389). The Battle of Kosovo figures prominently in Serbian mythology as it "symbolically captures the essence of the tragedy of Serbia's conquest and occupation by Turkey."[49] (The media and religion are discussed in more detail in the domestic level section.)

Milosevic's second goal, reasserting Serbian control over the two autonomous provinces, Kosovo and Vojvodina, was obtained by mobilizing Serbs and Montenegrins living in the provinces, according to Ramet. In 1988 he had established the Committee for the Protection of Kosovo Serbs and Montenegrins, which organized several rallies in both provinces with tens of thousands of people.[50] He was also able to mobilize people in Novi Sad (Vojvodina's capital), which led to the resignation of the Vojvodina leadership. Milosevic used this opportunity to put his own supporters in these leadership positions, including the positions of Vojvodina party chief and president.[51]

A similar turn of events occurred in Kosovo itself. Given Kosovo's particularly important role in Serbian nationalism, Milosevic sought to reestablish Serbian control over the province. He was able to do so by obtaining the resignations of the Kosovar leadership—all of whom were ethnic Albanians—and putting his own supporters in their place. He orchestrated the adoption of Serbo-Croatian as the only official language in Kosovo, so that Albanian could no longer be used for official matters. He also set forth a series of constitutional amendments that would end Kosovo's autonomy. Milosevic encountered some opposition, but in the end he prevailed.[52] The Serbian parliament suspended Kosovo's Provincial Assembly as well as the Provincial Executive Council. The Serbian parliament now gained "full and direct control of the province."[53] Although members of the Kosovar Assembly, many of whom were ethnic Albanians, met in secret and drafted a new constitution that stated Kosovo's rights as a republic and declared Albanian as the official language of Kosovo, in the end Milosevic succeeded in gaining Serbian control of the territory.[54]

Overturning the 1974 Yugoslav constitution was Milosevic's third goal. His claims that the constitution effectively reduced Serbia's power within the federation became a rallying cry for Serbs. He thus sought to reassert Serbia's dominance in the federation and revise the constitution to reflect that goal. He did so by orchestrating protests in Montenegro in mid-late 1988 and early 1989 that led to unrest in that republic and the resignation of the Montenegrin collective presidency. As was his modus operandi, Milosevic replaced these people with his own supporters.[55] Milosevic's attempts to change the 1974 constitution and rouse Serbian nationalism led to "anti-Serbian solidarity between Bosnian Croats and Bosnian Muslims." With the Serbian media focused "on 'the alleged imperilment of Serbs in Bosnia-Herzegovina,'" the Bosnian leadership responded by seeking support from Croatia and Slovenia as a means to oppose Milosevic's policies that threatened the country.[56]

Milosevic's fourth, and final, goal was to centralize Yugoslavia under Serb domination. With Slovenia and Croatia both declaring sovereignty (but not independence) in July 1988, followed by Bosnia's declaration in August, the prospect of these republics withdrawing from the federation loomed large. Bosnia, Macedonia, and Montenegro planned to hold multiparty elections.[57] In response, Milosevic and other Serb leaders agreed to multiple parties in Serbia. Interestingly, two parties, "expressly nationalist in character," were established in January 1990. The platform of the Party of Serbian National Renewal (SNR), a monarchist party, sought the return of the Serbian monarchy (Karadjordjevic dynasty) to lead Greater Serbia. Territory of Serbia, Kosovo, Macedonia, Montenegro, and Vojvodina was to be part of Greater Serbia, along with parts of Bosnia and Croatia whose populations were dominated by Serbs.[58] The SNR opposed Milosevic and called for his resignation, arguing that "instead of being the president of all Serbs, (Milosevic) has become a factor of division of the Serbian people."[59] The second party was the Democratic Freedom Party (DS); this party (though claiming to support Yugoslavia's inclusion in the European Community and promoting democracy) sought to eliminate Kosovo and Vojvodina as territorial entities. The party also sought to force ethnic Albanians to leave Yugoslavia. Serb property that Serbs lost when they were driven from Kosovo during World War II was to be returned. The party called for the "maximum extension of Serbia's borders" if Yugoslavia did break apart. All of these policies demonstrated the party's nationalist character.[60]

When multiparty elections were held in December 1990, Milosevic won the majority of votes and thus was named president of Serbia. His Socialist Party of Serbia (SPS, created in June 1990 when the League of Communists of Serbia and the Socialist Alliance of Working People of Serbia united) succeeded in winning a significant number of seats in the Serbian Parliament.[61] Milosevic's control of the media meant that opposition parties were given very little access to television, and this helped the SPS win.[62] Ramet quotes the December 11 issue of the *New York Times,* which reported that his "victory 'sent a defiant signal to Yugoslavia's other five republics, particularly Slovenia.'"[63]

In March 1991 Milosevic met with Croatian president Franjo Tudjman to discuss dividing Bosnia between Serbia and Croatia. In June, Milosevic put pressure on Serbs living in Croatia to negotiate with the Croatian regime. The Croatian Serbs "refused to reach an agreement."[64] As V. P. Gagnon notes, however, Milosevic's strategy also continued to focus on inciting ethnic tensions.[65] He quotes Milosevic as calling protestors the "enemies of Serbia," and emphasized "great foreign pressures and threats" against Serbia.[66]

Milosevic expanded his strategy from appealing to Serbian nationalism in regard to Kosovo to appealing to Serbian nationalism in the country at large, including Serbs in Croatia and Bosnia.[67] The Bosnian Serbs had already been witness to the "recent upsurge of Croatian and Moslem nationalism," which only reinforced their perception of threat. For the Bosnian Serbs, the need to make direct connections with Serbia proper became more apparent.[68] Because the Bosnian Serbs were concentrated in particular areas of the republic, Bosnian Serb leaders were more easily able to mobilize the population. In fact, by mid-1990 the Croatian-based Serbian Democratic Party (SDS) had established a branch in Bosnia-Herzegovina.[69] By the fall of 1990 the Serbian Democratic Party in Croatia and Bosnia, supported by many Serbs, worried about Serbs in these two republics being separated from the Serbian republic if reforms succeeded in structuring the country in a confederation.[70]

With tensions continuing regarding the future of Yugoslavia, on March 16, 1991, Milosevic went on television to state that "the failure of the presidency to take action against Slovenia and Croatia illustrated that 'the plan for the destruction of Yugoslavia had entered its final agonizing stage.'" He argued that threats to Serbia's vital interests led him to mobilize Serbia's police reserve units. He also appealed to the various political parties to unify and "to ignore their 'mutual disputes and differences in the interests of Serbia.'"[71]

On March 25, 1991, Tudjman and Milosevic met in Karadjordjevo (on the Serb-Croat border) to discuss Yugoslavia's future.[72] During this meeting (and others in April 1991), the two leaders attempted to figure out a way to divide Bosnia between Serbia and Croatia.[73] The meeting did not lead to any compromise between the two nationalist leaders. Relations between Croatia and Serbia continued to deteriorate.[74] Rabia Ali and Lawrence Lifschultz note that the "common goal" between Tudjman and Milosevic happened "a full year before Bosnia-Hercegovina declared its independence." They write, "As far as Milosevic and Tudjman were concerned, Bosnia's fate was settled regardless of whether or not it declared its independence from Yugoslavia."[75]

Milosevic continued to focus on the preservation of Yugoslavia as a federal state and promoted Serbian dominance. He remained committed to protecting and supporting Serb communities in the other republics, particularly in Croatia and Bosnia. For him, these "were crucial bargaining chips in discussions about Yugoslavia's future."[76] Moreover, his position was that republics could secede, but then Serbs living within those republics could secede as well. By spring 1991 he indicated that he would not challenge Slovenia's secession from the country, especially given that there were not significant numbers of Serbs residing in the republic.[77]

By July 1991 Serbian arms were reaching Serb militias in Bosnia. Milosevic met with Radovan Karadzic, the Bosnian Serb leader, in August. At their meeting, they talked about their Bosnian strategy—the use of force in order to seize Bosnian territory. Non-Serbs living in those areas would either be expelled or killed. In September 1991 the Serbian Autonomous Region of Herzegovina was established by the Yugoslav federal army.[78] Fighting between Serbs and non-Serbs started in August 1991, with the Serb attack on Bosnia starting "in earnest" in April 1992.[79] Milosevic's strategy to reassert Serbian control over Yugoslavia contributed to the outbreak of war and the collapse of the country.

Franjo Tudjman

A historian on the faculty of a university in Zagreb, Croatia, as well as a communist official, Franjo Tudjman was expelled from the League of Communists of Yugoslavia due to his activism in nationalist politics in the late 1960s. During the 1970s and 1980s he was sent to prison for his nationalist stance.[80] By the late 1980s, Tudjman was the leader of the Croatian Democratic Alliance (HDZ), having broken from the Communist Party because of his nationalist views. This was by far "the largest and best financed alternative political party" (particularly from the Croatian diaspora). The HDZ soon had branches in communities in Bosnia-Herzegovina and Vojvodina dominated by Croatians.[81]

Tudjman's primary focus was on "Croatian identity and sovereignty." In order to pursue that goal, he sought to reform Yugoslavia from a federal structure to a confederation that would be, in essence, an "alliance of states." In this confederation, any central authority would have very little power. His conception of a confederation implied (as he did not openly call for secession) that he envisioned Croatia as an independent entity within a newly structured Yugoslavia.[82] In mobilizing the Croatian population to support his platform, Tudjman promoted the idea of Croatian self-determination and national pride, as well as the end to discrimination against Croats (given the overrepresentation of Serbs in the republic's administrative positions). To do so, he sought to revitalize Croatian cultural symbols and make Croatian the official language of the republic.[83]

This platform became problematic for other ethnic groups residing in Bosnia (he considered Muslims as Islamicized Croats) and Croatia (especially the Serbian minority). Tudjman claimed that Croatians and Muslims in Bosnia should be incorporated into the Croatian sovereign entity, which entailed possible territorial border revisions to reflect that position. His sentiments were in keeping with those of much of the Croatian population living in Croatia. Soon after the election in 1990, Tudjman stated that "Croatia and Bosnia constitute a geographical and political unity, and have always formed a joint state in history."[84]

Tudjman did attempt to reassure the Serbs in Croatia. Lenard Cohen notes that Tudjman made it clear that Serbs "would be granted democratic rights should his party attain power, and that any changes to Bosnia-Hercegovina's status could only follow a democratic referendum in that republic." But while Tudjman tried to reassure the Serbs in Bosnia and Croatia, the fact is that pressure from the more extremist elements in the HDZ party led to government policies that proved otherwise.[85] His government's actions included resurrecting the wartime Ustashe fascist regime symbols and instituting constitutional reforms that were detrimental to Serbs in Croatia, which further illustrated the lack of a credible commitment to protect the Croatian Serbs.[86] As Barry Posen points out, in the spring of 1990, Serbs living in Croatia were now considered a minority (no longer "a constituent nation") and the Serb minority was not offered cultural autonomy. They were also asked to take an oath of loyalty. Croats replaced Serbian police and local officials. The Croatian government did not offer cultural autonomy to the Serb minority. In total, the government policies only served to increase the fears of the future for the Serbs.[87] Yugoslav critics of Tudjman's appeals to Croatian nationalism and means to garner support from Croats "referred to Tudjman as the 'Croatian Milosevic' whose 'Croatianism' would be a 'bomb planted under the republic.'"[88]

When the election was held in 1990, Tudjman's HDZ party won overwhelmingly. However, most Croatian Serbs voted against the party. Instead, they voted for the Serbian Democratic Party (SDS) or the communist party.[89] In the end, Tudjman became the republic's president.[90] Tudjman's nationalist policies pleased Croats, but threatened Serbs in Croatia, who worried that Tudjman's policies (whether the confederation or Croatian secession from Yugoslavia) would further put the Serb minority in a precarious position.[91]

Consequently, in July 1990 the Serbian Democratic Party in Croatia, led by Jovan Raskovic, "rejected the draft amendments to the Croatian constitution, characterizing them as an attack on the Serbian people."[92] The Croatian Serbs adopted the "Declaration on the Sovereignty and Autonomy of the Serbian People" the next month. The Serbian leadership declared that if Croatia remained part of Yugoslavia, Croatian Serbs should have cultural autonomy. If Croatia seceded from the country, Croatian Serbs should have political autonomy.[93] The Croatian leadership perceived Serbian positions as a threat to Croatia and was convinced of the role of Serbia proper in fomenting discord in the Croatian republic.[94] Tudjman made it clear when he stated that "[t]erritorial autonomy for the Serbs is out of the question . . . we will not allow it."[95]

As James Fearon notes, polarization of the ethnic groups, and thus conflict in Croatia, resulted from the commitment problem between the Croat majority and Serb minority. He writes that following Croatia's declaration of independence in

1991, "Serbs in Croatia, whether extremist or utterly indifferent to such things, faced the prospect of entering the new state of Croatia with no credible guarantees on their political status, or economic and even physical security."[96] Moreover, Croatian Serb leaders faced pressure from Serbian authorities not to participate in the new Croatian government. For example, "Raskovic turned down an invitation to join the new Croatian government as a deputy prime minister."[97] Tensions simmered down after the July-August 1990 crisis in Croatia but, as Cohen notes, a stalemate emerged between the Croatian government and the Serb minority. Serbian leaders, both in Croatia and Serbia proper, looked to Bosnia, with its significant Serb diaspora.[98]

In terms of Croatia's relationship with Bosnia, by the latter part of 1991, as Susan Woodward notes, western Herzegovina "was well integrated into the Croatian state." Bosnian Croats had already been given many of the benefits of ties to Croatia in 1990, including dual citizenship in Croatia and the right to vote in Croatian elections. The Bosnian Croats "used Croatian educational curricula, currency, state symbols (such as the flag and crest), police uniforms, and car registration plates."[99] Further reinforcing the ties with the Bosnian Croats, "Tudjman staged a coup in the leadership of the Bosnian Croats (a wing of Tudjman's HDZ)" in order to replace Stjepan Kljuic, the party's elected leader. Kljuic's position in support of Bosnia's territorial integrity was at odds with Tudjman's project to incorporate parts of Bosnia-Herzegovina into Croatia proper. Tudjman replaced Kljuic with Mate Boban, who then declared "a separate Croat state in western Herzegovina, Herzeg-Bosnia."[100] Importantly, Tudjman's actions occurred one week after Croatia's declaration of independence went into effect in mid-January 1992.[101] Thus, in July 1992, with the support of Tudjman's government, the Republic of Herceg-Bosnia was established by the Croats of the HDZ (the area was majority Croat), only a few months after the Bosnian Serbs had declared the Serbian Republic.[102]

Alija Izetbegovic

Alija Izetbegovic, a lawyer before becoming the leader of the Bosnian republic, was a religious person who identified himself as a Muslim, an identity he carried through his youth into his adult years. He believed in the idea of a Muslim nation in Bosnia that coincided with a territorial entity. During World War II he belonged to the Young Muslims organization, which had connections with the Ustashe (fascist) youth movement. As a strong anticommunist, his political activities were considered threatening to the ruling communist party in Yugoslavia. As a result, in 1946 he was arrested for his membership in the Young Muslims and spent three years in jail. In 1983 he was arrested for his distribution of the manifesto *Islamic Declaration* in 1970. He again was sentenced to jail, serving two years of a fourteen-year sentence. The *Islamic Declaration* was perceived as a threat to Serbs in that they read the document as an indication of Izetbegovic's desires to make Bosnia an Islamic state.[103] The perceived threat of the Serbs resonated when the country began to fall apart later in the decade.

With Yugoslavia in turmoil in the late 1980s, Izetbegovic established the Muslim-dominated Party of Democratic Action (SDA) in March 1990. There were divisions within the party between those conservatives who were inclined to support a partitioned Bosnia (which would entail a Muslim Bosnia) and the liberal secularists who supported a unified, multiethnic, and democratic Bosnia.[104] The Muslim nationalist extremists within the SDA, led by Izetbegovic, challenged their secular members, eventually leading the moderates to split from the party and form their own party, the Muslim Bosniak Organization (MBO).[105] The strong nationalist element within the SDA sought to ensure the Bosnian Muslims' "relative majority status" in the republic and to promote Muslim "religious values." When tensions mounted as the country began to disintegrate and Bosnia moved toward independence, Izetbegovic and the SDA looked to predominantly Muslim areas of Bosnia for territorial claims, particularly the area of Sandjak. This area had been divided in 1945 between Montenegro and Serbia, but Izetbegovic and the SDA (which had set up a branch in June 1990 in Sandjak) asserted that the Sandjak Muslims would insist on cultural and political autonomy if Montenegro and Serbia unified in a confederation or a new Yugoslav federation.[106] At the same time, Izetbegovic recognized that a coalition government would be needed, given Bosnia's multiethnic composition and the likelihood "that no single party was likely to obtain a majority in the upcoming election." As a result, Izetbegovic stressed the complex ethnic composition of the Bosnian republic. He also recognized the necessity of maintaining the republic's current territorial borders.[107] As president of Bosnia as well as the leader of the SDA, he attempted to keep Bosnia as a multiethnic entity as the ethnic tensions mounted. Yet, he faced challenges emanating from the Bosnian Serbs and Bosnian Croats, who sought to unite with Serbia and Croatia, respectively. He thought he could maintain Bosnia's independence, as illustrated by the fact that, as Ramet observes, "on the very eve of Serbia's attack on Bosnia, Bosnian President Izetbegovic told the Zagreb weekly *Danas* that he was convinced that Bosnia would neither be attacked nor slide into war."[108] Cohen quotes Izetbegovic: "Bosnia has lasted 1,000 years. I do not see any reason to break it up now. Bosnia is impossible to divide, because it is such a mixture of nationalities, just like the apartment bloc where I live."[109]

Thus, in many ways, Izetbegovic saw his role as a balance between Serbs and Croats in Yugoslavia at large and Bosnia in particular. He stated: "The Croats and the Serbs determined the character of Yugoslavia, and will to a large extent determine it in the future. We must adopt a balancing posture in that situation, and thereby maintain our national interests. . . . Intelligent and conscious people in Bosnia desire to maintain their independent position toward both Croatia and Serbia. Moslem national consciousness is the only answer to the great-state pretensions from both sides. We are neither Serbs nor Croats, and that must be clear."[110] Over time, however, Izetbegovic was unable to maintain this balance, as challenges to Bosnian Muslim nationalism from Serbian nationalists continued.[111] Further, the war in Croatia beginning in 1991 meant that the eruption of war in Bosnia was only a matter of time. In the end, the militias and the governments in Croatia and Serbia were able to provide resources to their respective ethnic kin in Bosnia. Woodward comments on the "reciprocal networks" that the various political parties had, in regard to militaries that were ethnically based, as well as the Croat and Serb refugees who crossed over into Croatia and Serbia, respectively. These "reciprocal networks" of political parties, ethnically based armies, and refugees, she notes, "kindled tensions along partisan, ethnic, and military lines."[112] The Bosnian Muslims did not have such a network, and thus formed a National Defense Council in June 1991. Izetbegovic formed this council "as an arm of his party, and was illegally purchasing weapons from Slovenia during the fall."[113] Given this situation, Izetbegovic and the SDA looked to the outside world for support in maintaining Bosnia as a multiethnic territorial entity, even as the country was falling apart (international intervention is discussed in more detail in the international level section of the chapter). As the historical background section made clear, Izetbegovic's goal was very difficult to maintain in light of the Serbian and Croatian demands for Greater Serbia and Greater Croatia, respectively, which meant these two republics sought to incorporate Bosnian territory into their own.

Ethnic Outbidding

As discussed in chapter 2, moderates are often drowned out by the extremists using the strategy of ethnic outbidding. Stephen Saideman asserts that outbidding on ethnic issues was a successful strategy of politicians in large part "because changing political institutions and the perils of economic reform caused most ethnic groups to perceive threats to their economic, political, and physical well-being." Groups engaged in efforts to ensure their own security, which only increased the insecurity of the other ethnic groups, resulting in an ethnic security dilemma.[114] Nationalist ideology often takes on a life of its own. This is true in the case of Bosnia. As Woodward observes, "Even when nationalist leaders did not stir up nationalist fervor, they were not easily able to escape the role they had created. Establishing their credentials as national protectors, nationalist politicians had to respond in kind when challenged by more extreme nationalists in order to keep their constituency." Opposition nationalists were able to present challenges to Milosevic's leadership, questioning whether he was a nationalist and repre-sented the Serb nation. As a result of ethnic outbidding, Serbs living in other republics became "pawns in this competition, in which any commitment to republican borders and guaranteed minority rights for Serbs in other states—the terms necessary to end the war in Croatia and in Bosnia-Herzegovina according to the approach adopted by the international community—was declared a betrayal of the Serb nation."[115]

Extreme Croatian nationalists from the HDZ party in Bosnia challenged the less nationalist politicians, with some arguing that Croatia should annex the Bosnian territory dominated by Croats located in western Herzegovina. If annex-ation was not possible, these extremists argued, Bosnian Croats should obtain significant political autonomy.[116]

In the end, both Milosevic and Tudjman ran into difficulties when they actively promoted right-wing radicals (in their respective political parties and those individuals more to the right on the political spectrum) in order to dem-onstrate their own moderate positions relative to the extremists. Their actions were also meant to show moderate positions to the international community (see the international level factors section for the detailed discussion of the international community's role). Such a moderate stance would serve to weaken opposition nationalist parties.[117] The difficulties arose when the more radical groups engaged in "terrorist, semilegal, and criminal activities in Croatia and in Bosnia-Herzegovina, including campaigns of 'ethnic cleansing' that continued into 1994."[118]

Izetbegovic's government also encouraged these radical elements within Bos-nia at the expense of the government's ability to control, to some extent, the course of events in the conflict. For example, during 1992 the government invited foreign *mujahedin* (Muslim militants) to come to Bosnia. Yet, these muja-hedin engaged in "terrorist, illegal, and shock-troop activities" that in the end became difficult for the government to control, such that "[b]y 1994 this was becoming a matter of serious concern." The mujahedin's actions undermined the various negotiated cease-fires. Their teaching of Islamic fundamentalism undermined the prospects for peace. In the end, the local populations continued to live in fear.[119]

In sum, what transpired over the course of a few years is that the tensions between the ethnic groups in Bosnia increased with ethnic outbidding by extrem-ists in all three ethnic groups. With Yugoslavia's future uncertain, extremists were able to capitalize on that uncertainty by intimating "the specter of immi-nent civil war among the country's different ethnic groups and regions." Serb nationalists worried about an Islamic-Catholic conspiracy emanating from Cro-ats and Muslims in Bosnia. Militant Croats perceived a threat from Bosnian

Serbs who sought sovereignty, with the support of the Serbian government and Serbian Orthodox church.[120] In the end, the ethnic outbidding led to the movement of the political center toward the right. Opposition parties that were overtly antinationalist faced difficulties in trying to gain support from their respective populations, further challenged by the lack of access to the media dominated and controlled by the nationalist parties. As the war in Croatia and Bosnia continued, leaders found it difficult to negotiate for peace, as the governments became "more radical than leaders." As Woodward states, "Governmental policy appeared to remain intransigent, or to move further away, from the policies necessary to bring an end to the conflict."[121]

DOMESTIC LEVEL

Domestic level factors that account for the breakup of Yugoslavia and the origins of the Bosnian war include public opinion, politics, criminal elements, media, gendered nationalism, economics, and religion. The results of the 1990 multiparty elections in the country reflected, as Woodward claims, "the process of disintegration over a decade of economic crisis and constitutional conflict."[122] As Cohen remarks, "it was a classic case of Croatian and Serbian nationalism feeding upon one another, a pattern that had tragically emerged several times before in Balkan and Yugoslav history."[123] In essence, domestic level factors interacted with the decisions and policies of political elites who appealed to nationalism.[124]

Public Opinion, Parties, and Elections

Analyses of the elections held in the republics in 1990 reveal that the nationalist parties won, not because they were more popular but "from their ability to manipulate the system and from the disarray of their opposition." For example, Tudjman's nationalist party (the HDZ) in Croatia was able to win the election because of its ability to spend much more than the opposition. Much of its funds came from the Croatian diaspora, primarily living in North America, who were militant in their views. Moreover, the electoral system's structure favored Tudjman's nationalist party—it won only 42 percent of the vote, but garnered 69 percent of the seats. Interestingly, the Serb minority in Croatia did not vote overwhelmingly in favor of the Serb nationalists—in fact, the Croatian Serb nationalist party received less than a fourth of the Serbian vote.[125]

Milosevic's party, the SPS (Socialist Party of Serbia), also did well in the elections of the early 1990s, in large part because of his control of the media and ability to use public funds illegally to buy votes. John Mueller notes that his use of the media and public funds demonstrates that the Serb nationalist party itself did not have widespread appeal.[126] As with Tudjman's nationalist party's success in gaining a higher percentage of seats than of the popular vote, Milosevic's party obtained 78 percent of the seats, and yet received less than 50 percent of the vote.[127]

What this evidence indicates is that at the outset of the 1990s, the nationalist parties did not enjoy significant popular support. Mueller cites a poll conducted in the summer and autumn of 1990 in Yugoslavia that tells us much about people's views about maintaining Yugoslavia as a country. The question asked: "Do you agree that every (Yugoslav) nation should have a national state of its own?" While 23 percent either agreed completely (16 percent) or to some extent (7 percent), with 10 percent undecided, 67 percent answered that they did not agree "in part" (6 percent) or "at all" (61 percent).[128]

In the case of Bosnia, nationalist parties representing the three ethnic groups eclipsed the communists and reformists. The three ethnically based parties, the Serbian Democratic Party (SDS), the Croatian Democratic Alliance (Tudjman's HDZ, based in Zagreb, Croatia), and the Bosnian Muslims' Party of Democratic Action (SDA) "expressed general support for the continuation of Bosnia-Hercegovina's unique multiethnic and multiconfessional makeup as well as a commitment to the termination of communist rule."[129] At the same time, the three parties differed in their concerns about what Yugoslavia might look like in the future, and Bosnia's position in that future entity. As Cohen observes, "For the Serbs in the SDS, Bosnia-Hercegovina's separation from the Yugoslav federal system was a threatening prospect, whereas most nationalist Moslems in the SDA and Croats in the HDZ found the idea of a confederation, with or without Serbia, as an option worthy of consideration." The Bosnian Croats were most supportive of a confederation, as they were the smallest of the three ethnic groups in Bosnia and thus "viewed their group's expanded participation with Croatia and Slovenia as a means to offset their minority situation."[130]

The elections of November and December 1990 in Bosnia resulted in significant wins for the nationalist parties to such an extent that 202 of 240 seats (84 percent) were awarded to the three principal ethnic parties (Muslim Party of Democratic Action, SDA; Serbian Democratic Party, SDS; and the Croatian Democratic Alliance, HDZ). The communists and reformers fared poorly.[131] The elections reinforced the fact that Bosnia's electorate was now polarized along ethnic lines. This polarization threatened the unity of Yugoslavia as a whole.[132] The leaders of the ethnic parties did try to maintain the unity of Bosnia by forming a coalition government that distributed ministerial and administrative positions on an ethnic basis. Alija Izetbegovic was elected president, an HDZ Croat became prime minister, and an SDS Serb became president of Bosnia's legislature. The coalition government, however, had an extremely difficult time trying to govern the republic.[133]

Criminals and Militias

In 1990, when Yugoslavia faced severe challenges economically and politically, public opinion overwhelmingly favored maintaining unity. How can we reconcile the fact that the public supported a unified country and yet the course of events led to the spiral to war in Bosnia and the breakup of Yugoslavia so soon after?

Mueller argues that rather than "a frenzy of nationalism" that led to war, it was the "actions of recently empowered and unpoliced thugs." The political elites played a role in actually initiating the wars and stoked the feelings of hatred. But the political elites looked to "thugs and hooligans" for committing the violence.[134] When the conflicts in Croatia and Bosnia erupted, the Yugoslav army (dominated by Serbs) fell apart. Serb members of the army "often mutinied or deserted en masse." Moreover, rather than face conscription, many young Serb males left the country "or went underground." As Mueller observes, "only 50 percent of Serbian reservists and only 15 percent in Belgrade obeyed orders to report for duty."[135] Without large numbers of Serbian men willing to fight Croatia and Bosnia, the Serbian military armed Serbs living in Croatia and Bosnia.[136] Yet, the Serbian military leaders expressed concern about the effect on "military morale," because those engaged in the violence were "notably composed not of committed nationalists or ideologues, nor of locals out to get their neighbors, nor of ordinary people whipped into a frenzy by demagogues and the media, but rather of common criminals recruited for the task."[137] It was the politicians, the political entrepreneurs, who looked to these criminals and hooligans to do the dirty work of war. Many of these criminals did join the Serb army, while others joined paramilitary groups (Arkan's Tigers is one of the most notorious) or became warlords in particular areas.[138] And the Serbs were not the only ones to utilize these criminal elements to do the fighting, as Bosnian and Croatian forces were also comprised "of small bands of criminals and violent opportunists recruited or self-recruited from street gangs and organized mobs."[139]

Mueller concludes that the Bosnia war (and the war in Croatia) was not actually an ethnic war, but rather "something far more banal: the creation of communities of criminal violence and pillage."[140] Those engaging in the fighting were able to silence their co-ethnics, whether through forcing them to flee or, in some cases, killing them. Mueller cites a UN report that clearly noted the threat to the local Serbs when the paramilitary groups came to an area. Local residents were threatened by these paramilitary groups to the point that they shunned their Muslim neighbors or sometimes even engaged in aggressive behavior toward them.[141] In one example, in Srebrenica (a Muslim enclave in Bosnia), the Muslim warlord Orib and his supporters "controlled the few jobs in town, lived in the larger homes, and had more food than others."[142] By inflating the actual size of the population, Orib's men were able to obtain more humanitarian aid,

which they then hoarded, leading to an increase in prices. The goods were eventually sold on the black market at inflated prices. If any Muslims dared challenge
Orib and his followers about the situation, they faced retribution, including
death.[143] Orib's men also prevented Muslims from leaving Srebrenica as they
were "used as human shields to protect" Orib's and his men's income and property. Orib and his followers did not take steps to better the lives of those living in
the city "unless it brought personal profit to the ruling gang."[144]

To support further his argument about the "banality of ethnic war," Mueller
notes that the various thugs and criminals engaging in the violence used ethnicity when it served their purposes, but that such criminals were also willing to
jeopardize the lives of their co-ethnics if doing so enriched them. For example,
because the Serbs in Bosnia were able to obtain weapons from Serbia proper, they
were quite well armed. When the war in Bosnia became less intense, many Bosnian Serb leaders sought to make a profit by selling excess weapons—and they
were willing to sell them to the Croats and Muslims in Bosnia. These weapons
were then used against Serbs in Bosnia and Croatia. The Croats also looked to
profit from the war. Croatia sold fuel to Bosnian Serbs, which aided their war
with the Bosnian Croats.[145]

According to Mueller, rather than being "a crucial motivating force," ethnicity
became the vehicle for mobilizing support for the elites and thugs as they orchestrated and conducted the war.[146] One cannot discount the interactive role
between the nationalist elites and the criminals in their use of ethnicity and
nationalist ideology to mobilize the masses.

Media, Intellectuals, and the Democratization Process

The news media played an important role in stoking the nationalist sentiments of
the masses. Given that the republic governments of Serbia and Croatia had almost
a complete monopoly of the news media, they had an outlet for their nationalist
ideological message. Their access to the media enabled them to silence the views
of the liberal opposition within each republic. As Jack Snyder and Karen Ballentine assert, the Serbian elite feared the democratization process occurring in
Yugoslavia at the time. With a weakened central government, the possibility arose
for a multiparty system that challenged the dominance of the League of Communists of Yugoslavia (LCY), dominated by Serbs. For those elites (intellectuals,
journalists, and politicians), the democratization process threatened their power
base, and thus they used the media to appeal to Serbian nationalist myths.[147]

Accordingly, journalists and intellectuals mattered quite a bit in stoking the
ethnic flames. Some were doing so before Milosevic "played the ethnic card," with
a particular focus on the Albanian threat to Serbs in Kosovo. Members of the
Serbian Academy of Sciences published a memorandum in 1986 in which they
discussed the "genocide" of Serbs in Kosovo. The Serbian Central Committee, as

well as the mainstream press in Belgrade, condemned the memorandum in large part out of concern for the content of the memorandum. Snyder and Ballentine note that such a response may also have resulted from the need of the "elites to reposition themselves on a new foundation of ideological legitimacy in the context of the waning of centralized communist authority." What this case reveals is the division between nationalist journalists and those committed to a continued liberalization and a free press. The nationalist journalists won out.[148]

Serbian television coverage described Serbs as the victims and showed images of dead Serbs to reinforce the point of victimization of the Serb population. For the elites, as Snyder and Ballentine observe, the depiction of Serbs as the victims and defenseless people "was thought to strike the right chord in a people who glorify a defeat at the hands of the Turks half a millennium ago in the battle of Kosovo." Croatian television took a completely opposite approach in its depiction of Croatia. Rather than showing defeats (such as towns in Croatia destroyed by enemy forces), the government instructed Croatian media in their coverage of the battles, including defeats, to end their reporting with positive and upbeat pronouncements. Given that Croatia, unlike Serbia, did not have "a firm tradition of statehood," the Croatian government worried that media coverage of defeats might lead the Croatian masses to "give up hope if they knew the odds they faced."[149]

In the case of Bosnia proper, for a period of six months, the Serbs had a monopoly over television coverage in the northern part of the republic. The Serbian elites were able to use this monopoly of the media in order to prepare the Serbian masses for the "ethnic cleansing" policy of 1992. The media were able to claim that Bosnian Muslims sought to transform Bosnia into an Islamic fundamentalist country.[150]

The Bosnian government used the Western media in order to highlight the precarious situation faced by Bosnian Muslims—as victims of Serbian aggression. The Western media outlets, for the most part, genuinely felt for the difficulties Muslims confronted, all the while not recognizing that the Bosnian government sought to influence the media coverage of the war.[151] In fact, for the Bosnian Muslims, Izetbegovic's SDA embarked on a domestic and international "propaganda campaign" to convey Bosnia as an independent historical entity through "the creation of new state symbols." In doing so, the Bosnian government sought to separate itself from Croatia and Serbia and justify its demands for independence.[152]

Interestingly, all three nationalist parties who shared power after the November 1990 elections in Bosnia cooperated to set about pushing for legislation that would enable them to establish state control of the media. This control would come in the form of each party appointing "one-third of the governing boards and editors in TV and newspapers." This legislation was deemed unconstitutional by the courts. Why this is important to consider, though, is that the legislation was a means for the three parties to keep their intra-ethnic rivals at bay.[153]

Gendered Nationalism

With the economic and political situation in Yugoslavia worsening in the 1980s, women's position in the society also deteriorated. Women found it difficult to remain employed and to hold political positions.[154] In the elections held in 1990, when the nationalist parties came to power in all the republics, women fared poorly in terms of their election to the parliaments in Serbia and Croatia.[155]

Consequently, as Yugoslavia began to disintegrate, women's traditional gender roles were reinforced by the nationalist discourse emerging at the time. As Miranda Alison notes in the case of Serbia, "Nationalist ideals linking Serbian masculinity with militarism were constructed alongside the 'woman-as-mother' image, illustrating the significance of women as biological and social reproducers."[156] With ethnic differences between groups increasingly reinforced in the public discourse, gender roles became increasingly solidified. As reproducers of the ethnic group and as "heroic mothers," women were "to accept the maternal role as the 'natural' outcome of their gender and ethnic-national destiny." The expectation for men, on the other hand, was "to engage in socially sanctioned violence for the 'good of the nation' and their manhood."[157]

Nationalist leaders sought to have legislation passed that underlined the role that women played as biological and social reproducers of the particular ethnic group, whether through laws on citizenship, religious edicts, or laws on reproduction (abortion for those of the "Other" ethnic groups, but laws and norms encouraging women of the in-group to have more children).[158]

Such a process invariably led to systematic and mass rape of women, as well as forced impregnation and pregnancy, by all the ethnic groups.[159] What is particularly striking is the role that mass rapes and impregnation played in the furthering of nationalist goals. The goal of rape was twofold: to send a signal to the woman's ethnic group as well as "to affect the individual woman herself."[160] Forced impregnation became a mechanism for the ethnic groups to ensure the reproduction of their particular group, because the child's ethnicity was perceived to come from the father, not the mother.[161] The problem for all the ethnic groups involved was that the mother's ethnic identity needed to be denied. Having children of mixed ethnic identity became problematic in a conflict in which "ethnic identity became the point of reference for all social and political interaction."[162] In fact, women in ethnically mixed marriages were in an exceptionally difficult position given the focus on ethnicity and the creation of ethnically pure states. These women faced violence from their own husbands. They also were targeted by their co-ethnics.[163]

What this shows is that women did not make the decision to go to war, but were very much affected by it. Their ethnic identity or that of their husbands made them targets for violence. In such a patriarchal society, men's military and political goals—namely the creation of ethnic states through the use of force—meant that women became the recipients of sexual and physical violence by the other ethnic groups. They could not rely on their husbands and fathers to protect them from this violence—protection that defines in many ways a traditional and patriarchal society.[164]

Many women opposed the nationalist leaders' call for war and rejected nationalism. Before the war, many pushed for women's equal rights in the political and economic spheres. As nationalist fervor increased, women peace activists, such as the members of the Yugoslav Women's Party (ZEST), protested against the militarization of Yugoslavia. Antiwar protests by women's groups were held throughout Yugoslavia in 1991. Women peace activists crossed ethnic lines to form networks of people opposed to the nationalist wars looming in the country. For example, the Women in Black Against War, formed by feminists in Serbia, held vigils in Serbia. Women in Black took the lead in condemning rapes against women, which were being reported in the media.[165] The feminist peace activists faced challenges in maintaining their cross-ethnic work and unity as the wars progressed. In the end, the women's groups were unable to continue their cooperation, as their gender identity became "subsumed under their ethnic identity."[166]

Women also responded to the war by supporting the nationalist leaders through the formation of all-women militia units in Serbia, Croatia, and the Muslim-dominated army in Bosnia, as well as nationalist women's groups that emphasized women's traditional roles as mothers and wives in support of their ethnic group.[167] Women in combat roles in the Bosnian government army, such as the Seventeenth Brigade, were often considered to be very effective.[168]

Interestingly, when the war in Bosnia ended with the Dayton Accords, it is striking how gender still mattered. No Bosnian women were present at the negotiations, and the Accords did not cover issues dealing with women or gender. With the war's end, women remained in positions of inferiority to men, economically and politically. Women still have higher rates of unemployment and lower political representation in the formal political arena.[169]

Economic and Political Conditions and the Ethnic Balance of Power

The 1980s was a "pivotal period" for Yugoslavia's future that enabled politicians to use ethnicity to appeal to constituents. According to Saideman, two economic conditions were particularly important: the significant deterioration of the country's economy as well as uneven development across the country, in which some republics were more economically developed than others. Jobs, technology, wealth, and projected economic growth were all uneven. Croatia, Slovenia, and Vojvodina were the wealthiest of the republics, and they resented their subsidization of the poorer republics.[170]

At the same time, the economic conditions and the shifting ethnic balance of power in Yugoslavia in general led to demands from different republics for changes in the country. Conservatives in Serbia, in order to maintain their dominance at the federal level, sought to create a larger Serbia. A larger territorial entity with a significant number of Serbs relative to other ethnic groups would provide the mechanism for appealing to Serb nationalism and thus political interests that would serve the Serbs.[171]

As Fearon observes, "In the case of Yugoslavia, Tito's construction had solved the nested commitment problems by relying implicitly on a balance of power—Slovenia and Croatia balanced Serbia." This balance of power was undermined once Slovenia declared its independence from Yugoslavia, and Croatia would be a minority relative to Serb dominance in the country if it remained a federation. For Croatia, such a situation was untenable and thus propelled the Croats to declare independence in turn. With the Croatian declaration of independence, the security of the Croatian Serbs was threatened, and thus a commitment problem arose for them.[172]

The Serbs in Croatia were not the only ones to be alarmed by the changing ethnic demographics. Within Bosnia, the two decades from 1971 to 1991 saw a shift in the demographic balance of power between Serbs and Muslims. The Bosnian Muslim population increased, while the Bosnian Serb population decreased. The demographic change had detrimental effects for the Serbs, given the Yugoslav "ethnic key" policy. According to Slack and Doyon, "This policy allocated political power and jobs based on the percentage of each ethnic group as counted by the census . . . at all levels of government, but most importantly at the municipal level. . . . As the numbers of Muslims in the population increased while the Serbs declined, there would have been a transfer of jobs from Serbs to Muslims."[173] Concerns arose for Bosnian Serbs, as they perceived a threat to their economic and political security resulting from these demographic changes. In fact, the ethnic competition between Bosnian Serbs and Muslims was the result. This ethnic competition became a vehicle for mobilization of the respective populations along ethnic lines.[174]

Religion and Nationalism

One of the most interesting aspects of the conflict that erupted in Bosnia is the role that religion played. As Michael Sells observes, religion mattered in two ways. In the first place, people were targeted largely by virtue of their religious affiliation (Croatian Catholics, Muslims, and Serb Orthodox) because for the most part differences based on "appearance, language, or clothing" were not readily apparent.[175] Religion mattered in a second way in that the justification for the violence and destruction was linked explicitly to religious institutions and symbols. Sells asserts that the Serb (Orthodox) nationalists and Croat (Catholic) nationalists engaged in violence, including ethnic cleansing, "based upon religiously informed ideologies and constructions of difference."[176]

The connection between the nationalist parties and their respective religious communities was strong. As Mitja Velikonja argues, "national, political, and, ultimately, military mobilization could not be achieved without religious legitimation." And the religious communities needed the nationalist parties in order to accomplish their goals.[177]

All three sides in the Bosnian conflict demonized their opponents, using religious terms, so that, for instance, Izetbegovic was labeled the "world's foremost soldier of the jihad." Croatian religious nationalists perceived a threat from Muslims in Bosnia, arguing that they sought to establish an Islamic state. Bosnian Muslims perceived a threat from the Croats and Serbs, fearful of "Crusades" by the two other groups or "a Christian Europe." Serbs considered Bosnian Muslims *"jihad fighters"* who sought to make Bosnia "an *Islamic fundamentalist state*" (emphasis in original).[178]

As evidence of the connection between religion and nationalism, one need only look to the words of Izetbegovic, a little more than a year before the outbreak of war, when he remarked that the Muslims/Bosnians were a "religious nation."[179] The "Muslim" nation was created by the Yugoslav government in the 1980s as a way to give Slavic Muslims (including Bosniaks, those Muslims living in Bosnia) equal footing as a nation with Bosnian Croats and Serbs. The contradiction, as Sells points out, is that the factors that define nationality and ethnicity did not differ for Croats, Muslims (Bosniaks), and Serbs. He notes that "they spoke the same language (that is, they understood each other when speaking, though for historical and political reasons they called the language by different names), shared a great many cultural features, and traced their descent to the same medieval South Slavic tribes."[180]

Given that the Yugoslav federal government promoted the idea of a "Muslim" nation, Bosnia's Muslims began to assert their ethnic and political identity. Bosnian Muslims benefited from the legal rulings that supported proportional representation based on ethnic composition within the republic and federal levels. The proportional representation on this ethnic basis threatened the Serbs, in Bosnia specifically and at the federal level in general.[181] The perceived threat to the Serbs then became couched in religious nationalist terms, particularly as related to Kosovo. Serb Orthodox bishops as well as intellectuals and church-affiliated journals claimed that Kosovar Albanians were engaging in "mass rape, annihilation of Serb shrines, and genocide."[182]

The use of religious ideology combined with nationalism fueled the tensions emanating throughout Yugoslavia in such a way that when conflict erupted in Bosnia, religious identity became the target of Serb violence. For example, mosques were deliberately targeted.[183]

Religion was utilized by Croatian nationalists, as well, in justifying the nationalist ideology and support for a Croatian state and Bosnian Croats. In Bosnia in 1992, Croatian nationalists attacked Bosnian Muslims and Serbs in Croat-dominated areas of Herzegovina and Western Bosnia (Mostar). These areas were to be included in Greater Croatia, a Catholic Greater Croatia.[184] Croatian forces attacked Muslim religious buildings, such as mosques, as well as Orthodox churches throughout Bosnia. Sells notes that the targets were chosen as a result of the "participation of an educated elite as advisors, including, according to reports, local Catholic art historians and professors."[185]

During the wars in Croatia and Bosnia, religious structures were targeted by all three sides' forces. Velikonja cites estimates of the destruction of 340 Orthodox churches, 450 Roman Catholic churches and monasteries, and from 1,000 to 1,100 mosques when the wars finally ended.[186] Velikonja also observes that the linkage of religious symbols and structures with nationalism and ethnicity is evident from the post-conflict period when "sacral buildings (churches, mosques, etc.) were among the first objects to be restored and rebuilt."[187]

The tight connection between religion and nationalism manifested itself also in the militaries of the various warring groups. Velikonja notes that Christian and Muslim chaplains existed in most military units. Moreover, "religious practices, customs, and symbols were introduced to military life, barracks, and units." Local religious leaders conducted religious rituals and services (and included "the blessing of units and weapons"). Clergy "visited their troops in the 'liberated territories,'" at which time "the images of (erstwhile) political leaders and military commanders were displayed alongside icons, symbols, and images of important religious personalities."[188]

INTERNATIONAL LEVEL

Responding to the Outbreak of War

At the international level, various states (particularly the major European states, such as Britain, France, Germany, and Russia, as well as the United States) and international organizations (the United Nations, the European Community—which became the European Union in 1993) were concerned about the rising tensions in Yugoslavia during the late 1980s and early 1990s. At the outbreak of conflict in Croatia in 1991 and then the intensification of nationalist hostilities, the international community responded primarily with diplomatic efforts. Later, as the conflict in Bosnia continued unabated, the international community, through the United Nations and NATO, intervened militarily to provide for humanitarian assistance and the introduction of peacekeeping forces. What is particularly striking about the international involvement in the breakup of Yugoslavia is that the international community faced a challenge: on the one hand there was the tendency to blame Serbia for the outbreak of war and the collapse of the country (and thus pursue strategies and policies to coerce the Serbs to end their use of force), but on the other hand, the international community was willing to support the violation of the norm of territorial sovereignty by recognizing the independence (secession) of Slovenia, Croatia, and Bosnia.[189] The UN's ever-increasing role in Bosnia, from humanitarian assistance to establishing and guaranteeing safe havens, enabled the Bosnian government to secede from Yugoslavia, again challenging the very norm of territorial integrity fundamental to international relations.[190]

Accordingly, the international community, namely the European Community/ Union and United Nations, failed to end the conflict in Bosnia and prevent the breakup of Yugoslavia.[191] In fact, the unwillingness to commit troops for a military intervention led to further bloodshed. When the European Community members were unsuccessful in preventing the breakup of the country, the United Nations was the next responder. Britain and France, as permanent members of the UN Security Council, took the lead. Britain and France both worried about an escalation of the fighting, given that both had troops on the ground as part of the various UN peacekeeping forces. The British and French view (which represented much of the stance of other European states) was at odds with the Bush administration in the United States. Focused on the larger balance of power, namely U.S.-Soviet relations and the collapse of communism in the USSR, the U.S. government's position supported the territorial integrity of Yugoslavia.[192] Bill Clinton, as presidential candidate, campaigned that the U.S. should take a stronger role, but did not support the introduction of U.S. ground troops. The new Clinton administration did try to end the international arms embargo on Bosnia, as a means to help the Bosnian Muslims, in 1993. The Europeans rejected the U.S. proposal. In response, the United States supported France's proposal to establish safe havens in Bosnia.[193] Given Russia's support for its Slavic kin, the Bosnian Serbs, Russia opposed UN intervention beyond humanitarian assistance. The decision to use significant force (as the United States and its allies increasingly came to recognize was needed as a means to end the conflict) came about only when the decision making on the crisis shifted from the UN to NATO in mid-1995. In this way, Russia was no longer an obstacle, given that it was not a member of NATO.[194] In assessing the international response to the crisis, as Saideman remarks, "[n]o international organization could develop a consistent policy during the crisis due in part to the complexity of the conflict (groups seeking to secede from seceding republics), but also because bargaining among member nations generated the policies of international organizations."[195]

Peace Plans

The international community made several attempts at resolving the Bosnian conflict that had diffused from Croatia, in a series of peace plans from early 1992 through 1995. The peace plans attempted to prevent Bosnia's breakup into separate states, reach an accommodation with the three main ethnic groups, and maintain Bosnia as a multiethnic and unified state. While the peace plans sought to end the conflict, they actually contributed to the escalation, as more external actors became involved.[196] Moreover, through these various attempts at diplomacy and negotiations to achieve a peaceful resolution to the conflict, the international community continued to negotiate with the various nationalist leaders (Milosevic, Tudjman, and Izetbegovic, among others), who were able to maintain their power and overcome any challenges from more moderate elites within their respective ethnic communities.[197] Thus, domestic level factors interacted with international level ones.

The first peace plan was reached in March 1992, which occurred prior to Bosnia's recognition as an independent state by the international community. The plan set out to create a federal structure of three national territorial units, thereby reassuring the ethnic minorities living in the Muslim-dominated republic.[198] Bosnian Serb leader Radovan Karadzic supported the plan, but Izetbegovic did not.[199] As a result of this failed peace plan, the European Community sought to initiate another peace conference. The leaders of the new Republic of Yugoslavia (Serbia and Montenegro) would not attend. Izetbegovic refused to meet with the Bosnian Croat and Bosnian Serb leaders. The Conference on Security and Cooperation in Europe (CSCE) placed the blame for the war squarely on Serbia and expressed this sentiment to Yugoslavia. More harsh actions (sanctions) were threatened by the CSCE if Yugoslavia did not cease its campaign of ethnic cleansing of Croats and Muslims.[200] At the International Conference on the Former Yugoslavia (ICFY), hosted by the European Community and UN in August 1992 in London, support for territorial integrity and sovereignty was promoted. The conference also called for a cease-fire. The Serbs made concessions, including agreeing to CSCE monitors in Kosovo. Yet, they also violated the commitments they had agreed to. In response, the United Nations expelled the new Yugoslavia from the body and approved the deployment of more troops to Bosnia. In order to address the atrocities being committed in the course of the war, the UN established a War Crimes Commission.[201] At the same time, the major states (including the United States) did not want to increase their military commitment—the use of force—to the conflict as a means to deter the Serbs.[202]

The second peace plan, the 1993 Vance-Owen plan, created a unitary federal Bosnia. The state would be comprised of ten semiautonomous regions based on ethnic composition. There would be a weak central government with regional representatives based in the capital. The plan was rejected by the Bosnian Serbs, given that they sought independence; they did not want to remain part of Bosnia. The Bosnian Croats liked the plan because they would gain additional territory since Western Herzegovina was now firmly in their control. The Muslims would gain some territory. After several months of negotiations, the Bosnian Croats and Muslims agreed to the plan. The impact of international sanctions on the new Yugoslavia, as well as challenges to his domestic support, compelled Milosevic to pressure Karadzic to accept the plan. The Bosnian Serbs finally agreed to do so, but at that time Tudjman's Croatian forces were fighting against Bosnian Muslim forces, as well as against Serb forces in Croatia.[203] The plan failed.

The UN continued its involvement in the conflict with the passage of various resolutions for its UNPROFOR operation to provide humanitarian assistance. "No-fly" zones over Bosnia (with NATO's enforcement) and safe havens were established. NATO's role in the peacekeeping operation increased, although the amount of force authorized by the UN Security Council was still quite limited. The conflict actually escalated when Bosnian Serbs took UN peacekeepers as hostages in response to NATO air strikes.[204]

By the middle of 1993, the international community recognized the facts on the ground in Bosnia—that the partition of Bosnia into three republics would be the most viable solution to end the conflict. By this time, Bosnia was already partitioned along ethnic lines—each ethnic group had its own administrative structure and military forces. The third plan, the Owen-Stoltenberg Plan, reflected that reality (it also looked a lot like the March 1992 plan). Both the Bosnian Croats and Serbs accepted the plan, but the Bosnian government rejected it. Negotiations were at a standstill. For the Bosnian Muslims, the creation of a Muslim state, rather than a multiethnic one, was the goal.[205]

Differing policy responses by the major powers, such as the United States (who did not want to put troops on the ground but did support sanctions against Yugoslavia), France and Britain (both of whom threatened to withdraw their troops), and international organizations such as the UN and EU, led to unsuccessful mediation efforts, and the fighting continued.[206] Only with the February 1994 shelling of a market in Sarajevo did the West take a stronger position. President Clinton and NATO gave an ultimatum to the Bosnian Serbs. They demanded that all the Bosnian Serb heavy artillery that surrounded the Bosnian capital be removed or put under UN control. If the Serbs refused, NATO would launch air attacks. The Muslim forces were also expected to put their artillery under UN control (which they did). Russian pressure on the Bosnian Serbs secured their agreement with the NATO/Clinton ultimatum. A cease-fire for Sarajevo was reached, indicating a successful UN/NATO strategy. Yet, the Bosnian Muslims then increased their demand for more territory. The Bosnian Serbs responded— they secured their territorial borders in Bosnia. These actions pitted the external actors against each other, given that the United States supported the Bosnian Muslim claims and would not pressure the Bosnian government to agree to the partition of Bosnia.[207]

The actions of the Contact Group (comprised of Britain, France, Germany, Russia, and the United States, the Contact Group was created in 1994) led to the fourth and final peace plan. The Washington Framework Agreement, concluded on March 1, 1994, created a Bosnian federation. The agreement maintained Bosnia as a unified state (which the Bosnian government supported), being a confederation of a Bosnian-Muslim and Croat federation and a Bosnian Serb republic. Instead of peace resulting from the agreement, the Bosnian Muslim forces went on the offensive in spring 1994.[208] NATO threatened the use of force against the Serbs to end the war, but when NATO did in fact use air strikes, Bosnian Serb forces took more UN peacekeepers as hostages. In the end, the Bosnian Serb strategy did not succeed, as the UN force increased its combat capability, thereby improving its position in Bosnia. A Croatian offensive succeeded in ending Serb control of territory in Croatia proper (Croatia then "cleansed" the territory of Serbs). With the joining of Croatian forces with Bosnian forces in Bosnia, the Serbs began to lose territory in Bosnia. The Bosnian Serbs were also faced with lack of support from Serbia. The Bosnian Serb leaders looked to Milosevic to help them negotiate an end to the conflict. With that, the Dayton Accords were signed in November 1995, which ended the war after three years.[209] Interestingly, the Accords were not accepted by the Bosnian Serbs or the Croats. The people of Bosnia did not get to vote on the agreement because it was not subject to the ratification process.[210]

When the war ended, Izetbegovic remained in power as the Muslim member of the multiethnic presidency in Bosnia (he had been the head of the country's collective presidency since 1990). While he did sign the Dayton Accords (along with Tudjman and Milosevic), he also stated, "To my people I say—this may not be a just peace, but it is more just than a continuation of the war."[211] (He eventually stepped down as president in 2000 due to ill health, but remained as leader of the Party of Democratic Action [SDA] for another year, before continuing as the honorary chairman of the party until his death in 2003.)[212]

POSTWAR BOSNIA

International Actors and Agreements

With the war's conclusion, the international community remained committed to promoting Bosnia's peace and stability. NATO implemented the military terms of the Dayton Accords with the Implementation Force (IFOR) which lasted until 1996. IFOR was replaced with the Stabilization Force (SFOR) in December 1996. SFOR's mandate ended in 2004, replaced by the 2,500-strong European Union force, Operation Althea. NATO still maintains a presence in Sarajevo engaged in counterterrorism operations and detaining people indicted for war crimes; Bosnia became a member of NATO's Partnership for Peace in December 2006.[213] The goal of the EU with regard to Bosnia is to move the country "beyond peace implementation towards European integration." The EU Special Representative (EUSR) is considered "the lynchpin" for the EU's involvement in Bosnia.[214] The EU and Bosnia signed the Stabilization and Association Agreement (SAA) on June 16, 2008. The SAA will enter into force once the ratification process has concluded. On the same day, an Interim Agreement on Trade and Trade-Related Issues was signed (it entered into force on July 1, 2008).[215] The SAA has several objectives, including "supporting efforts to strengthen the rule of law in Bosnia and Herzegovina," "contributing to political, economic and institutional stability in BiH [Bosnia-Herzegovina] and in the wider region," and "supporting efforts to complete the transition to a market economy."[216]

Recognizing the significant atrocities committed in Bosnia and Croatia during the course of the wars, the UN Security Council passed Resolution 827, which established the International Criminal Tribunal for the former Yugoslavia (ICTY) in May 1993 (the tribunal was the first of its kind since the war crimes tribunals in Nuremburg, Germany, and Tokyo, Japan, that were established at the end of World War II). Individuals, not states, can be arrested and tried for crimes against humanity and genocide at the ICTY. While the majority of those that have been arrested and tried are Serbs or Bosnian Serbs, the ICTY has also tried Croats and Muslims for war crimes (including rape and torture).[217]

Given Bosnia's interest in having closer ties with the EU and NATO (eventually leading to membership), the Bosnian Federation has supported the ICTY. However, the Bosnian Serb Republic has been less inclined to do so. It was not until January 2005 that it finally arrested an indicted war crimes suspect.[218] Extremist nationalist Serb elites in both the Bosnian Serb Republic and those in positions in Serbia's political institutions (such as the military) played a major part in Milosevic's reluctance to capture and deliver to the Tribunal the Bosnian Serb leaders Ratko Mladic and Radovan Karadzic when the war ended. Lack of enthusiasm to support the Tribunal's work carried over after Milosevic was ousted from power in 2000. Vojislav Kostunica, who succeeded him, was also not inclined to provide assistance to the Tribunal. In fact, Kostunica refused to hand over Milosevic, who had been indicted by the Tribunal in 1999. In doing so, he made clear his opposition to the ICTY's authority. (Milosevic was finally arrested in 2001 and died in 2006 while standing trial for war crimes and genocide.)[219] Karadzic was finally caught in July 2008. The government turned him over in large part because of the desire for increased cooperation and assistance from the European Union. Pro-European parties won in the general election held in May 2008. The president, Boris Tadic, leader of the Democratic Party, was able to establish a pro-European coalition government. In doing so, he was able to force out Prime Minister Kostunica. Two weeks later, Serbian security forces captured Karadzic.[220]

Even with such a significant international involvement and presence, which continues today, most scholars argue that the Dayton Accords did not actually resolve the ethnic conflict, as the domestic political structures and institutions remain ethnically based. Moreover, as long as the international community continues its presence in Bosnia (particularly its troop presence), the stability of the country may be undermined. According to Duffy and Lindstrom, "The conflict only deepened longstanding ethnic animosities in the region."[221] Belloni observes that the positions and demands of the three ethnic groups have not changed. The Serbian and Croatian governments seek to bolster the autonomy of the Bosnian Serb Republic and the Croatian parts of Bosnia, respectively, rather than strengthening the joint political institutions. At the same time, the Bosnian Muslims continue in their attempts to bolster the Bosnian state. They face accusations of attempting to dominate the state through the political institutions. Given that the international community's presence in the country is so pervasive (its micromanagement), Belloni notes that "ethnic leaders can effectively take advantage of this situation." The leaders are not forced to be responsible political actors, improving the country's economic and political situation.[222] For example, the international community remained critical of Izetbegovic's inability or unwillingness to deal with corrupt SDA officials. Such officials had been accused of profiting from international reconstruction aid. Moreover, the international community expressed concerns that Izetbegovic was supporting the Bosnian Muslims, which only fostered ethnic and national discord rather than promoting the reintegration of Bosnian society after the war.[223]

What many scholars argue, therefore, is the need for political leadership in Bosnia that reaches across ethnic boundaries.[224] One can argue that without the parties on the ground as significant players in the postwar reconstruction of society, the possibility of conflict erupting (or demands for secession by the Bosnian Croats and Serbs) remains. This means that the role of elites matters for the stability of the state because they must convince their followers to support the new, postwar structure. As Schneckener observes, for conflict regulation and peace to prevail, there must be "a strong commitment to cooperation and the principles of shared rule by elites."[225] The problem, however, is that there is a widespread norm of authoritarianism, according to Zupanov and his coauthors, which makes it difficult for democracy and non-ethnically based parties and institutions to take root.[226]

Political Institutions

Political institutions in Bosnia have been designed to prevent the recurrence of conflict. And yet, the ethnic focus of postwar Bosnia continues through the power-sharing political institutions, ethnically defined political parties, and the elites who lead those parties. Each of the two entities, the Bosnian Serb Republic and the Bosnian Federation, has its own president, as well as government and parliament. The state, the Republic of Bosnia and Herzegovina, is a decentralized one. The government has few powers, basically foreign policy, defense policy, and trade.[227] The Bosnian presidency is a three-person presidency, and each member comes from one of the three main ethnic groups. As the structure of the Bosnian presidency demonstrates, ethnicity is the defining factor for political identity and representation in the political institutions.[228] As a result, Bosnia's political structure is one in which the nationalist parties continue to dominate. The Bosniak SDA, the Croatian HDZ, and the Serbian SDS remain dominant although public attitudes have moderated. The Social Democratic Party (SDP), formerly the Communist Party, is the only major party that can appeal to all the ethnic groups. Yet, it tends to gain votes only from Bosniaks, and not the Croats or Serbs.[229] Following the 2000 election, there were attempts to encourage interethnic alliances, as for instance through the appointed mayors. The major ethnic parties also "offered coalition agreements to parties from other ethnic groups." But the major parties did not establish any cross-ethnic partnerships prior to the elections. The SDP was the lone major party that deliberately attempted to attract voters from the different ethnic groups.[230] Thus, there are few, if any, incentives for politicians to cross ethnic lines and appeal to voters from the other ethnic groups. Instead, as Belloni asserts, the nature of the consociational democracy in Bosnia means that the three ethnic groups are assured representation at all levels. Each group is quite autonomous. Moreover, each ethnic group can employ a minority veto that enables the "vital interests" of its group to be defended. The problem, as many scholars observe, is that the framework established by the constitution played an important role in ending the conflict as well as enabled the peaceful transition to democracy, but it also supported and maintained "the existing ethnic order." Further, there is a lack of transparency and accountability on the part of politicians, leading to persistent party patronage.[231]

Having two entities that comprise the state, that are in essence separate, means a de facto partition.[232] Importantly, the Dayton Accords permitted each entity (Croat and Serb) to establish its own citizenship. Each entity was also allowed "to maintain 'special parallel relationships' with neighboring states (i.e., Croatia and Serbia)."[233] As a result, as Duffy and Lindstrom observe, Croat and Serb nationalists within Bosnia continue to seek to unify with Croatia and Serbia, proper, respectively. Rather than bringing about a political structure that encourages stability and peace, the focus on "group rights and ethnic representation" leads to a situation in which "the Dayton constitution itself obstructs peace." There is the concern that the Bosnian Croat and Serb nationalists will push for secession in the future.[234]

CONCLUSION

This chapter demonstrates that the levels of analysis provide a useful framework for understanding the origins of the collapse of Yugoslavia and the Bosnian war. Elites, such as Milosevic, Tudjman, and Izetbegovic, mattered in utilizing nationalist ideology to gain support from the masses. Elites need to motivate people to follow them in order to maintain their power and control. Nationalism provided the mechanism for those elites to do so, as an instrumentalist approach would explain. At the same time, leaders mattered in ending the conflict and constructing the postwar settlement. All three leaders remained in power when the war ended in 1995, but also faced challenges in the subsequent years. For example, Tudjman faced two competing demands. The international community opposed the annexation of Bosnian territory and the Herzegovian Croats wanted to secede and join Croatia. Tudjman was unable to take a strong position on one side or the other. As Duffy and Lindstrom remark, "this pleased no one."[235]

Whether due to death or loss of an election, these leaders have all been replaced in their respective countries (Serbia, Croatia, and Bosnia). In Serbia and Croatia today, focus on their own countries' economic and political development remains paramount, rather than seeking to unite with their Bosnian Serb and Croatian kin, respectively. As for Bosnia itself, *The Economist* sums up the situation: "Bosnia ticks over on a day-to-day basis, but seems paralysed when it comes to bigger issues over its future. The EU has been demanding reforms to make it more coherent and efficient, but they have mostly been blocked by Milorad Dodik, leader of Republika Srpska, the Bosnian Serb entity, who is reluctant to cede any more power to the central state in Sarajevo. Nor is he the only leader whom Mr. Lajcak [the international high representative in Bosnia, who resigned in February 2009] deems obstructive. He [Lajcak] has often said that its *politicians* are Bosnia's biggest problem" (emphasis added).[236]

In addition to the role of elites, domestic level factors mattered, whether the emergence of nationalist political parties, economic and political conditions, changes in the ethnic balance of power, gendered nationalism, or religion. The case demonstrates that when economic conditions are poor and political structures and institutions are weak, nationalism becomes a forceful tool for mobilizing the public. Religion and nationalism were a potent mix in Bosnia, as the group identity of each ethnic group was tied to its religious affiliation. As the war progressed, religious institutions and structures were deliberately targeted by the militaries of all three sides. Gender roles became increasingly polarized, with women expected to play their roles as nurturers, reproducers of the ethnic group identity, and so forth. The intentional targeting of women from the other ethnic groups, whether in the form of rape or other violence, became a signal to the enemy that they could not protect their women.

In terms of international factors, the international community failed to prevent the outbreak of war. When it did engage in diplomacy through the various peace plans proposed, or through military intervention, the international community was tasked with reconciling the goal of maintaining the norm of territorial integrity of Yugoslavia as a country with the demands for independence of the various republics. The differences in policy positions of the major external actors, such as the European countries and the United States, were reflected in the lack of consensus on how to respond to the crisis and, in many ways, prolonged the fighting. Since the conflict ended, the international community remains very much a part of the fabric of Bosnia's domestic politics, given the European Union's troop presence as well as the focus on economic development. The International Criminal Tribunal for the former Yugoslavia continues to indict and try individuals for war crimes and genocide in order to bring to justice those who carried out atrocities.

In the end, all three levels of analysis are important to examine to understand both the origins of the Bosnian war as well as the postwar period.

NOTES

1. With the war's end in 1995, Montenegro, one of the six Yugoslav republics, remained united with Serbia, only becoming independent, and thus a member of the United Nations, in June 2006. Its official title is The Former Yugoslav Republic of Montenegro. United Nations, *United Nations Member States*, www.un.org/en/members/index.shtml.
2. The republic is called Bosnia-Herzegovina, but for ease of use, we refer to it as Bosnia.
3. Kristen P. Williams, "Internationalization of Ethnic Conflict in the Balkans: The Breakup of Yugoslavia," in *Ethnic Conflict and International Politics: Explaining Diffusion and Escalation*, ed. Steven E. Lobell and Philip Mauceri (New York: Palgrave, 2004), 75, 81.
4. Kristen P. Williams, *Despite Nationalist Conflicts: Theory and Practice of Maintaining World Peace* (Westport, Conn.: Praeger, 2001), 106–107; Williams, "Internationalization of Ethnic Conflict in the Balkans," 75; Roberto Belloni, "Civil Society and Peacebuilding in Bosnia and Herzegovina," *Journal of Peace Research* 38, no. 2 (2001): 164.

5. Gavan Duffy and Nicole Lindstrom, "Conflicting Identities: Solidary Incentives in the Serbo-Croatian War," *Journal of Peace Research* 39, no. 1 (2002): 80–81.
6. Roberto Belloni, "Civil Society and Peacebuilding in Bosnia and Herzegovina," *Journal of Peace Research* 38, no. 2 (2001): 166.
7. J. Andrew Slack and Roy R. Doyon, "Population Dynamics and Susceptibility for Ethnic Conflict: The Case of Bosnia and Herzegovina," *Journal of Peace Research* 38, no. 2 (2001): 141.
8. Joyce P. Kaufman and Kristen P. Williams, *Women, the State, and War: A Comparative Perspective on Citizenship and Nationalism* (Lanham, Md.: Lexington, 2007), 80; Williams, *Despite Nationalist Conflicts,* 89.
9. Slack and Doyon, "Population Dynamics," 141.
10. Slack and Doyon, "Population Dynamics," 142.
11. Duffy and Lindstrom, "Conflicting Identities," 73.
12. Duffy and Lindstrom, "Conflicting Identities," 73.
13. Duffy and Lindstrom, "Conflicting Identities," 73.
14. Duffy and Lindstrom, "Conflicting Identities," 73.
15. Duffy and Lindstrom, "Conflicting Identities," 74.
16. Duffy and Lindstrom, "Conflicting Identities," 74. See also Kaufman and Williams, *Women, the State, and War,* 81.
17. Slack and Doyon, "Population Dynamics," 142.
18. Duffy and Lindstrom, "Conflicting Identities," 74-75.
19. Duffy and Lindstrom, "Conflicting Identities," 74.
20. Duffy and Lindstrom, "Conflicting Identities," 75. See also Kaufman and Williams, *Women, the State, and War,* 82.
21. Duffy and Lindstrom, "Conflicting Identities," 75.
22. Slack and Doyon, "Population Dynamics," 142–143.
23. Slack and Doyon, "Population Dynamics," 143.
24. Frank P. Harvey, "Primordialism, Evolutionary Theory and Ethnic Violence in the Balkans: Opportunities and Constraints for Theory and Policy," *Canadian Journal of Political Science* 33, no. 1 (March 2000): 42–43. For another critique of the primordialist approach as an explanation of the conflict in Yugoslavia, see Dusko Sekulic, Garth Massey, and Randy Hodson, "Ethnic Intolerance and Ethnic Conflict in the Dissolution of Yugoslavia," *Ethnic and Racial Studies* 29, no. 5 (September 2006): 800–801.
25. Harvey, "Primordialism," 43.
26. Harvey, "Primordialism," 44.

27. Harvey, "Primordialism," 44.
28. James D. Fearon and David D. Laitin, "Violence and the Social Construction of Ethnic Identity," *International Organization* 54, no. 4 (Autumn 2000): 850.
29. Kaufman and Williams, *Women, the State, and War,* 80.
30. Harvey, "Primordialism," 56.
31. Duffy and Lindstrom, "Conflicting Identities," 74.
32. For an excellent review of memoirs published by various principals involved in the dissolution of Yugoslavia, see Sabrina P. Ramet, "Views from Inside: Memoirs concerning the Yugoslav Breakup and War," *Slavic Review* 61, no. 3 (Fall 2002): 558–580.
33. Sabrina P. Ramet, "Serbia's Slobodan Milosevic: A Profile," *Orbis* 35, no. 1 (Winter 1991): 93. See also Sabrina Petra Ramet, "War in the Balkans," *Foreign Affairs* 71, no. 4 (Fall 1992): 79–98; Lenard J. Cohen, *Broken Bonds: The Disintegration of Yugoslavia* (Boulder: Westview Press, 1993), 51.
34. Ramet, "Serbia's Slobodan Milosevic," 94.
35. Ramet, "Serbia's Slobodan Milosevic," 94.
36. Ramet, "Serbia's Slobodan Milosevic," 94.
37. V. P. Gagnon, "Ethnic Nationalism and International Conflict: The Case of Serbia," *International Security* 19, no. 3 (Winter 1994–1995): 148.
38. Ramet, "Serbia's Slobodan Milosevic," 94–95. See also Cohen, *Broken Bonds,* 52.
39. Ramet, "Serbia's Slobodan Milosevic," 95.
40. Ramet, "Serbia's Slobodan Milosevic," 95.
41. Stephen M. Saideman, "Explaining the International Relations of Secessionist Conflicts: Vulnerability versus Ethnic Ties," *International Organization* 51, no. 4 (Autumn 1997): 741.
42. Sekulic et al., "Ethnic Intolerance and Ethnic Conflict in the Dissolution of Yugoslavia," 801.
43. Ramet, "Serbia's Slobodan Milosevic," 95.
44. Ramet, "Serbia's Slobodan Milosevic," 95.
45. Ramet, "Serbia's Slobodan Milosevic," 96.
46. Ramet, "Serbia's Slobodan Milosevic," 96.
47. Ramet, "Serbia's Slobodan Milosevic," 97.
48. Ramet, "Serbia's Slobodan Milosevic," 97.
49. Ramet, "Serbia's Slobodan Milosevic," 97.
50. Ramet, "Serbia's Slobodan Milosevic," 98. See also Duffy and Lindstrom, "Conflicting Identities," 75.

51. Ramet, "Serbia's Slobodan Milosevic," 98. See also Gagnon, "Ethnic Nationalism and International Conflict," 150.
52. Ramet, "Serbia's Slobodan Milosevic," 99.
53. Ramet, "Serbia's Slobodan Milosevic," 99.
54. Ramet, "Serbia's Slobodan Milosevic," 99–100.
55. Ramet, "Serbia's Slobodan Milosevic," 100. See also Gagnon, "Ethnic Nationalism and International Conflict," 150; Barry R. Posen, "The Security Dilemma and Ethnic Conflict," *Survival* 35, no. 1 (Spring 1993): 37.
56. Ramet, "Serbia's Slobodan Milosevic," 102.
57. Ramet, "Serbia's Slobodan Milosevic," 103.
58. Ramet, "Serbia's Slobodan Milosevic," 103.
59. As quoted in Ramet, "Serbia's Slobodan Milosevic," 103.
60. Ramet, "Serbia's Slobodan Milosevic," 104.
61. Ramet, "Serbia's Slobodan Milosevic," 104–105.
62. Gagnon, "Ethnic Nationalism and International Conflict," 154.
63. Ramet, "Serbia's Slobodan Milosevic," 105.
64. Gagnon, "Ethnic Nationalism and International Conflict," 158.
65. Gagnon, "Ethnic Nationalism and International Conflict," 158.
66. Gagnon, "Ethnic Nationalism and International Conflict," 158.
67. Cohen, *Broken Bonds,* 140.
68. Cohen, *Broken Bonds,* 140–141.
69. Cohen, *Broken Bonds,* 141.
70. Cohen, *Broken Bonds,* 143.
71. As quoted in Cohen, *Broken Bonds,* 202.
72. Cohen, *Broken Bonds,* 205.
73. Susan L. Woodward, *Balkan Tragedy: Chaos and Dissolution after the Cold War* (Washington, D.C.: Brookings Institution, 1995), 172.
74. Cohen, *Broken Bonds,* 206.
75. Rabia Ali and Lawrence Lifschultz, "Why Bosnia?" *Third World Quarterly* 15, no. 3 (1994): 377–378. Interestingly, the leaders of the Bosnian Croats (Mate Boban of the Croatian Democratic Alliance ([HDZ]) and Bosnian Serbs (Radovan Karadzic of the Serbian Democratic Party [SDS]) met in early May 1991 to discuss the territorial division of Bosnia-Herzegovina. Ali and Lifschultz, "Why Bosnia?" 378.
76. Cohen, *Broken Bonds,* 207.
77. Cohen, *Broken Bonds,* 207.
78. Ramet, "Views from Inside," 573.
79. Ramet, "Views from Inside," 573–574.
80. Cohen, *Broken Bonds,* 110, fn. 45.

81. Cohen, *Broken Bonds,* 95.
82. Cohen, *Broken Bonds,* 96.
83. Duffy and Lindstrom, "Conflicting Identities," 79.
84. As quoted in Cohen, *Broken Bonds,* 97.
85. Cohen, *Broken Bonds,* 97–98.
86. James D. Fearon, "Commitment Problems and the Spread of Ethnic Conflict," in *The International Spread of Ethnic Conflict: Fear, Diffusion, and Escalation,* ed. David A. Lake and Donald Rothchild (Princeton: Princeton University Press, 1998), 119.
87. Posen, "The Security Dilemma," 37–38.
88. Cohen, *Broken Bonds,* 98.
89. Cohen, *Broken Bonds,* 98–99.
90. Cohen, *Broken Bonds,* 101.
91. Cohen, *Broken Bonds,* 130–131.
92. Cohen, *Broken Bonds,* 131.
93. Cohen, *Broken Bonds,* 132.
94. Cohen, *Broken Bonds,* 132-133.
95. As quoted in Cohen, *Broken Bonds,* 133.
96. Fearon, "Commitment Problems and the Spread of Ethnic Conflict," 116.
97. Cohen, *Broken Bonds,* 131.
98. Cohen, *Broken Bonds,* 135.
99. Woodward, *Balkan Tragedy,* 230–231.
100. Woodward, *Balkan Tragedy,* 194.
101. Woodward, *Balkan Tragedy,* 279.
102. Ali and Lifschultz, "Why Bosnia?" 378.
103. The *Islamic Declaration,* according to Steven L. Burg and Paul S. Shoup, was an appeal for the "regeneration of the Muslim world." Steven L. Burg and Paul S. Shoup, *The War in Bosnia-Herzegovina: Ethnic Conflict and International Intervention* (Armonk, N.Y.: M.E. Sharpe, 2000), 67. See also Cohen, *Broken Bonds,* 144.
104. Burg and Shoup, *The War in Bosnia-Herzegovina,* 66–68.
105. Cohen, *Broken Bonds,* 144.
106. Cohen, *Broken Bonds,* 144–145.
107. Cohen, *Broken Bonds,* 144–145.
108. Ramet, "War in the Balkans," 87.
109. As quoted in Cohen, *Broken Bonds,* 145.
110. As quoted in Cohen, *Broken Bonds,* 145.
111. Cohen, *Broken Bonds,* 145.
112. Woodward, *Balkan Tragedy,* 253.
113. Woodward, *Balkan Tragedy,* 253.

114. Stephen M. Saideman, "Is Pandora's Box Half Empty or Half Full? The Limited Virulence of Secessionism and the Domestic Sources of Disintegration," in *The International Spread of Ethnic Conflict: Fear, Diffusion, and Escalation*, ed. David A. Lake and Donald Rothchild (Princeton: Princeton University Press, 1998), 147.

115. Woodward, *Balkan Tragedy*, 355.

116. Cohen, *Broken Bonds*, 144.

117. Woodward, *Balkan Tragedy*, 355. See also Fearon and Laitin, "Violence and the Social Construction of Ethnic Identity," 845–877.

118. Woodward, *Balkan Tragedy*, 356.

119. Woodward, *Balkan Tragedy*, 356–357.

120. Cohen, *Broken Bonds*, 144.

121. Woodward, *Balkan Tragedy*, 357.

122. Woodward, *Balkan Tragedy*, 118.

123. Cohen, *Broken Bonds*, 101.

124. Woodward, *Balkan Tragedy*, 118.

125. John Mueller, "The Banality of 'Ethnic War,'" in *Nationalism and Ethnic Conflict*, ed. Michael E. Brown, Owen R. Cote Jr., Sean M. Lynn-Jones, and Steven E. Miller, rev. ed. (Cambridge, Mass.: MIT Press, 2001), 100.

126. Mueller, "The Banality of 'Ethnic War,'" 100.

127. Mueller, "The Banality of 'Ethnic War,'" 100–101.

128. Mueller, "The Banality of 'Ethnic War,'" 101.

129. Cohen, *Broken Bonds*, 143.

130. Cohen, *Broken Bonds*, 143.

131. Cohen, *Broken Bonds*, 146.

132. Cohen, *Broken Bonds*, 147.

133. Cohen, *Broken Bonds*, 147.

134. Mueller, "The Banality of 'Ethnic War,'" 102.

135. Mueller, "The Banality of 'Ethnic War,'" 102–103.

136. Mueller, "The Banality of 'Ethnic War,'" 103.

137. Mueller, "The Banality of 'Ethnic War,'" 104.

138. Mueller, "The Banality of 'Ethnic War,'" 104–105.

139. Mueller, "The Banality of 'Ethnic War,'" 105.

140. Mueller, "The Banality of 'Ethnic War,'" 108.

141. Mueller, "The Banality of 'Ethnic War,'" 108–109.

142. Mueller, "The Banality of 'Ethnic War,'" 111.

143. Mueller, "The Banality of 'Ethnic War,'" 111–112.

144. Mueller, "The Banality of 'Ethnic War,'" 112.

145. Mueller, "The Banality of 'Ethnic War,'" 113.

146. Mueller, "The Banality of 'Ethnic War,'" 117.

147. Jack Snyder and Karen Ballentine, "Nationalism and the Marketplace of Ideas," in *Nationalism and Ethnic Conflict,* ed. Michael E. Brown, Owen R. Cote Jr., Sean M. Lynn-Jones, and Steven E. Miller, rev. ed. (Cambridge, Mass.: MIT Press, 2001), 81–82.

148. Snyder and Ballentine, "Nationalism and the Marketplace of Ideas," 83–84.

149. Snyder and Ballentine, "Nationalism and the Marketplace of Ideas," 85–86.

150. Snyder and Ballentine, "Nationalism and the Marketplace of Ideas," 84.

151. Burg and Shoup, *The War in Bosnia-Herzegovina,* 162–163.

152. Woodward, *Balkan Tragedy,* 234.

153. Woodward, *Balkan Tragedy,* 230.

154. Branka Andjelkovic, "Reflections on Nationalism and Its Impact on Women in Serbia," in *Women in the Politics of Postcommunist Europe,* ed. Marilyn Rueschemeyer (Armonk, N.Y.: M. E. Sharpe, 1998), 236–237; Kaufman and Williams, *Women, the State, and War,* 83.

155. Wendy Bracewell, "Women, Motherhood, and Contemporary Serbian Nationalism," *Women's Studies International Forum* 19, nos. 1–2 (1996): 26; Carol S. Lilly and Jill A. Irvine, "Negotiating Interests: Women and Nationalism in Serbia and Croatia, 1990–1997," *East European Politics and Societies* 16, no. 1 (2002): 137; Kaufman and Williams, *Women, the State, and War,* 84.

156. Miranda Alison, "Wartime Sexual Violence: Women's Human Rights and Questions of Masculinity," *Review of International Studies* 33 (2007): 85.

157. Alison, "Wartime Sexual Violence," 85.

158. V. Spike Peterson, "Gendered Nationalism: Reproducing 'Us' versus 'Them,'" in *The Women and War Reader,* ed. Lois Ann Lorentzen and Jennifer Turpin (New York: New York University Press, 1998), 43; Kaufman and Williams, *Women, the State, and War,* 87. See also Cynthia Enloe, "All the Men Are in the Militias, All the Women Are Victims: The Politics of Masculinity and Femininity in Nationalist Wars," in *The Women and War Reader,* ed. Lois Ann Lorentzen and Jennifer Turpin (New York: New York University Press, 1998), 50-62.

159. Alison, "Wartime Sexual Violence," 85.

160. Inger Skjelsbaek, "Is Feminism Inherently Peaceful? The Construction of Femininity in War," in *Gender, Peace and Conflict,* ed. Inger Skjelsbaek and Dan Smith (London: Sage Publications, 2001), 55.

161. Alison, "Wartime Sexual Violence," 86.

162. Skjelsbaek, "Is Feminism Inherently Peaceful?" 55.

163. Vesna Nikolic-Ristanovic, "Physical Abuse and Homicide," in *Women, Violence and War: Wartime Victimization of Refugees in the Balkans,* ed. Vesna

Nikolic-Ristanovic (Budapest, Hungary: Central European University Press, 2000), 91.

164. Vesna Nikolic-Ristanovic, "Conclusion," in *Women, Violence and War: Wartime Victimization of Refugees in the Balkans,* ed. Vesna Nikolic-Ristanovic (Budapest, Hungary: Central European University Press, 2000), 195.

165. Lepa Mladjenovic and Vera Litricin, transcribed by Tanya Renne, "Belgrade Feminists 1992: Separation, Guilt and Identity Crisis," *Feminist Review* 45 (1993): 115; Laura Pitter and Alexandra Stiglmayer, "Will the World Remember? Can the Women Forget?" *Ms.*, March/April 1993, 21; Cynthia Cockburn, *The Space between Us: Negotiating Gender and National Identities in Conflict* (London: Zed Books, 1998), 168–169, 171; Kaufman and Williams, *Women, the State, and War*, 92-93.

166. Kaufman and Williams, *Women, the State, and War,* 95.

167. Bracewell, "Women, Motherhood, and Contemporary Serbian Nationalism," 45; Lilly and Irvine, "Negotiating Interests," 139, 141; Obrad Kesic, "Women and Gender Imagery in Bosnia: Amazons, Sluts, Victims, Witches, and Wombs," in *Gender Politics in the Western Balkans: Women and Society in Yugoslavia and the Yugoslav Successor States,* ed. Sabrina P. Ramet (University Park: Pennsylvania State University Press, 1999), 189.

168. Inger Skjelsbaek and Dan Smith, "Introduction," in *Gender, Peace and Conflict,* ed. Inger Skjelsbaek and Dan Smith (London: Sage Publications, 2001), 7.

169. Maja Korac, "Gender, Conflict and Peace-Building: Lessons from the Conflict in the Former Yugoslavia," *Women's Studies International Forum* 29 (2006): 511–512; Sophie Wittenberg, "Security Council Resolution 1325 and CEDAW: Combating Gender-Based Discrimination and Violence in Bosnia and Herzegovina," *A PeaceWomen Project Analysis,* June 2006, 2, www.peacewomen.org/un/ecosoc/CEDAW/35th_Sesssion/SCR1325_CEDAW.html; Martha Walsh, "Profile: Bosnia and Herzegovina," in *Women and Civil War: Impact, Organizations, and Action,* ed. Krishna Kumar (Boulder: Lynne Rienner, 2001), 61, 63–65; Kaufman and Williams, *Women, the State, and War*, 103.

170. Saideman, "Is Pandora's Box Half Empty or Half Full?" 140.

171. Gagnon, "Ethnic Nationalism and International Conflict," 164.

172. Fearon, "Commitment Problems," 125–126.

173. Slack and Doyon, "Population Dynamics and Susceptibility for Ethnic Conflict," 148–150.

174. Slack and Doyon, "Population Dynamics and Susceptibility for Ethnic Conflict," 150–153.

175. Michael Sells, "Crosses of Blood: Sacred Space, Religion, and Violence in Bosnia-Hercegovina," *Sociology of Religion* 64, no. 3 (2003): 309.

176. Sells, "Crosses of Blood," 310. See also Mitja Velikonja, *"In Hoc Signo Vinces: Religious Symbolism in the Balkan Wars 1991–1995," International Journal of Politics, Culture and Society* 17, no. 1 (Fall 2003): 25–39.

177. Velikonja, *"In Hoc Signo Vinces,"* 27–28.

178. Velikonja, *"In Hoc Signo Vinces,"* 32–33.

179. Velikonja, *"In Hoc Signo Vinces,"* 28.

180. Sells, "Crosses of Blood," 310–311.

181. Cohen, *Broken Bonds,* 140.

182. Sells, "Crosses of Blood," 311.

183. Sells, "Crosses of Blood," 314.

184. Sells, "Crosses of Blood," 316–317.

185. Sells, "Crosses of Blood," 318.

186. Velikonja, *"In Hoc Signo Vinces,"* 33–34.

187. Velikonja, *"In Hoc Signo Vinces,"* 34.

188. Velikonja, *"In Hoc Signo Vinces,"* 30.

189. Michael Moodie, "The Balkan Tragedy," *Annals of the American Academy of Political Sciences* 542 (September 1995): 105-115.

190. Saideman, "Explaining the International Relations of Secessionist Conflicts," 742.

191. Duffy and Lindstrom, "Conflicting Identities," 75; Moodie, "The Balkan Tragedy," 110.

192. Moodie, "The Balkan Tragedy," 111.

193. Moodie, "The Balkan Tragedy," 111-112.

194. Saideman, "Explaining the International Relations of Secessionist Conflicts," 743.

195. Saideman, "Explaining the International Relations of Secessionist Conflicts," 743.

196. Williams, "Internationalization of Ethnic Conflict," 87; Williams, *Despite Nationalist Conflicts,* 102–107.

197. Woodward, *Balkan Tragedy,* 360.

198. Aleksa Djilas, "Fear Thy Neighbor: The Breakup of Yugoslavia," in *Nationalism and Nationalities in the New Europe,* ed. Charles A. Kupchan (Ithaca: Cornell University Press, 1995), 99.

199. John Mearsheimer and Stephen Van Evera, "When Peace Means War: The Partition That Dare not Speak Its Name," *New Republic,* December 18, 1995, 16.

200. Keith Webb with Vassiliki Koutrakou and Mike Waters, "The Yugoslav Conflict, European Mediation, and the Contingency Model: A Critical Perspective," in *Resolving International Conflict: The Theory and Practice of Mediation,* ed. Jacob Bercovitch (Boulder: Lynne Rienner, 1996), 179; Williams, *Despite Nationalist Conflicts,* 102.

201. Cohen, *Broken Bonds,* 243; James Gow, "Coercive Cadences: The Yugoslav War of Dissolution," in *Strategic Coercion: Concepts and Cases,* ed. Lawrence Freedman (Oxford: Oxford University Press, 1998), 284; Robert L. Hutchings, *American Diplomacy and the End of the Cold War: An Insider's Account of U.S. Policy in Europe, 1982–1992* (Washington, D.C.: Woodrow Wilson Center Press, 1997), 316–317; Williams, *Despite Nationalist Conflicts,* 102–103.

202. Cohen, *Broken Bonds,* 243; Ivo Daalder, "Fear and Loathing in the Former Yugoslavia," in *The International Dimensions of Internal Conflict,* ed. Michael E. Brown (Cambridge, Mass.: MIT Press, 1996), 65–66; Woodward, *Balkan Tragedy,* 307–308; Williams, *Despite Nationalist Conflicts,* 103.

203. Cohen, *Broken Bonds,* 243–244, 248–253; Dusko Doder, "Yugoslavia: New War, Old Hatreds," *Foreign Policy* 91 (1993), 20–21; Mearsheimer and Van Evera, "When Peace Means War," 16; Webb et al., "The Yugoslav Conflict," 181; Woodward, *Balkan Tragedy,* 307–308. See also Williams, *Despite Nationalist Conflicts,* 103.

204. Age Eknes, "The United Nations' Predicament in the Former Yugoslavia," in *The United Nations and Civil War,* ed. Thomas G. Weiss (Boulder: Lynne Rienner, 1995), 117–118; Frank Harvey, "Deterrence and Compellence in *Protracted Crisis:* Methodology and Preliminary Findings," *International Studies Notes* 22 (1997): 12; Frank Harvey, "Deterrence and Ethnic Conflict: The Case of Bosnia-Herzegovina, 1993-94," *Security Studies* 6 (1997): 194; Williams, *Despite Nationalist Conflicts,* 104.

205. Djilas, "Fear Thy Neighbor," 103–104; Harvey, "Deterrence and Ethnic Conflict," 198; Mearsheimer and Van Evera, "When Peace Means War," 16; Woodward, *Balkan Tragedy,* 310–312; Williams, *Despite Nationalist Conflicts,* 104.

206. Woodward, *Balkan Tragedy,* 312–313.

207. Djilas, "Fear Thy Neighbor," 104–105; Gow, "Coercive Cadences," 288–290; Susan L. Woodward, "Redrawing Borders in a Period of Systemic Transition," in *International Organizations and Ethnic Conflict,* ed. Milton J. Esman and Shibley Telhami (Ithaca: Cornell University Press, 1995), 216–217; Williams, *Despite Nationalist Conflicts,* 105.

208. Spyros Economides and Paul Taylor, "Former Yugoslavia," in *The New Interventionism 1991–1994: United Nations Experience in Cambodia, Former Yugoslavia, and Somalia,* ed. James Mayall (Cambridge: Cambridge University Press, 1996), 86–87; Gow, "Coercive Cadences," 292; Woodward, *Balkan Tragedy* 314–315, 320–321; Williams, *Despite Nationalist Conflicts,* 105.

209. Gow, "Coercive Cadences," 292–295.

210. Robert M. Hayden, "Bosnia's Internal War and the International Criminal Tribunal," *Fletcher Forum of World Affairs* 22, no. 1 (1998): 47, 49.

211. Gabriel Partos, "Bosnia War: Main Players," *BBC News,* October 14, 2000, http://news.bbc.co.uk/2/hi/europe/969131.stm; "On This Day—1995: Balkan Leaders Agree to Peace," *BBC News,* November 21, 1995, http://news .bbc.co.uk/onthisday/hi/dates/stories/november/21/newsid_2549000/ 2549809.stm.

212. "Former Bosnian President Dies," *BBC News,* October 19, 2003, http:// news.bbc.co.uk/go/pr/fr/-/2/hi/europe/3205392.stm.

213. "Peace Support Operations in Bosnia and Herzegovina," NATO, www.nato .int/cps/en/natolive/topics_52122.htm.

214. European Union Special Representative in Bosnia and Herzegovina, "EUSR Introduction" (May 17, 2007), www.eusrbih.eu/gen-info/?cid=1012,1,1, and "EUSR Mandate" (October 8, 2007), www.eusrbih.eu/gen-info/?cid=2000,1,1; European Union, "Bosnia and Herzegovina—Relations with the EU," http://ec.europa.eu/enlargement/potential-candidate-countries/bosnia_ and_herzegovina/eu_bosnia_and_herzegovina_relations_en.htm.

215. European Union, "Bosnia and Herzegovina—Relations with the EU."

216. Council of the European Union, "EU Signs Stabilization and Association Agreement with Bosnia and Herzegovina" (June 16, 2008), www.consilium .europa.eu/uedocs/cms_data/docs/pressdata/en/er/101233.pdf.

217. International Criminal Tribunal for the Former Yugoslavia, "About the ICTY," www.icty.org/sections/AbouttheICTY.

218. Julie Kim, "Bosnia: Overview of Issues Ten Years after Dayton," *Report for Congress,* November 14, 2005, 4, Congressional Research Service document (RS22324).

219. Duffy and Lindstrom, "Conflicting Identities," 84; "Obituary: Slobodan Milosevic," *BBC News,* March 11, 2006, http://news.bbc.co.uk/2/hi/europe/ 655616.stm.

220. "Karadzic Caught," *The Economist,* July 24, 2008.

221. Duffy and Lindstrom, "Conflicting Identities," 81.

222. Belloni, "Civil Society and Peacebuilding in Bosnia," 166.

223. "Former Bosnian President Dies," *BBC News,* October 19, 2003, http://news. bbc.co.uk/go/pr/fr/-/2/hi/europe/3205392.stm.

224. Duffy and Lindstrom, "Conflicting Identities," 88.

225. Ulrich Schneckener, "Making Power-Sharing Work: Lessons from Successes and Failures in Ethnic Conflict Regulation," *Journal of Peace Research* 39, no. 2 (March 2002): 224.

226. Josip Zupanov, Dusko Sekulic, and Zeljka Sporer, "A Breakdown of the Civil Order: The Balkan Bloodbath," *International Journal of Politics, Culture and Society* 9, no. 3 (Spring 1996): 416, 419.

227. Schneckener, "Making Power-Sharing Work," 209; Burg and Shoup, *The War in Bosnia-Herzegovina,* 367.

228. Burg and Shoup, *The War in Bosnia-Herzegovina,* 370.

229. Nina Caspersen, "Good Fences Make Good Neighbours? A Comparison of Conflict-Regulation Strategies in Postwar Bosnia," *Journal of Peace Research* 41, no. 5 (September 2004): 575.

230. Caspersen, "Good Fences Make Good Neighbours?" 579.

231. Belloni, "Civil Society and Peacebuilding in Bosnia," 172.

232. Burg and Shoup, *The War in Bosnia-Herzegovina,* 368.

233. Schneckener, "Making Power-Sharing Work," 209.

234. Duffy and Lindstrom, "Conflicting Identities," 87–88.

235. Duffy and Lindstrom, "Conflicting Identities," 85.

236. "The Western Balkans: A Stuck Region," *The Economist,* February 12, 2009.

CHAPTER 5

Sudan: Arabs versus Africans and Darfur in Crisis

In February 2003 rebels attacked the government garrison town of Golu, Sudan, and killed two hundred soldiers.[1] In April rebels from Darfur attacked numerous police stations and the airport in El Fasher, the capital of North Darfur, as well as the town of Nyala.[2] Most of the attacks were carried out by two rebel groups, the Justice and Equality Movement (JEM) and the Sudan Liberation Army (SLA).[3] Rebel attacks continued in the next few months of 2003, with rebels killing hundreds of government soldiers, capturing hundreds of prisoners, and destroying aircraft and government installations.[4] The rebels explained their action as a response to decades of economic and political marginalization and deprivation. In particular, they launched their attacks against the ruling National Islamic Front (NIF). The rebels claimed that the government had systematically targeted African Muslim ethnic groups in Darfur since the 1990s.[5] The NIF dismissed the rebels' claims and labeled them terrorists.

The response from the government was severe. The Sudanese government armed local Arab tribes and militias (known as the "Janjaweed" or "men on horseback") and set them against the population of Darfur. The government also deployed the Popular Defense Force (PDF) to hunt down the rebel groups.[6] The two worked in conjunction: the Janjaweed would make surprise attacks, destroying villages and forcing the population to flee, while the military would provide air support and transportation.[7] In these attacks, the Janjaweed engaged in a campaign of terror against civilians that included the systematic destruction of homes and property, mutilations, torture, executions, rape, and forced relocation.[8]

There is no clear consensus about the extent of the atrocities in Darfur, but that they have occurred is not in doubt. International agencies have condemned the violence, but they disagree on how to categorize the atrocities. The United Nations lists the events as "crimes against humanity."[9] Human Rights Watch went further, labeling the atrocities as "ethnic cleansing."[10] The United States State Department estimated that by August 2004 over 400 villages were destroyed, 200,000 refugees had crossed into neighboring Chad, and perhaps

1.2 million refugees were displaced within Western Sudan.[11] The Sudanese government denied the reports of atrocities. They claimed that Western media bias against Arabs was the source of the reporting.[12]

By February 2004 the government announced victory in a military campaign against the JEM and SLA.[13] However, the Janjaweed attacks against civilians continued for months, forcing thousands into neighboring Chad. Peace negotiations between the Sudanese government, the JEM, and the SLA began in April 2004. Two problems plagued these agreements: the increasingly divided leadership of the rebels and the continued Janjaweed activity.[14] Throughout 2004 and 2005 these efforts toward peace were undermined by a continuation of violence, albeit at low levels, in Darfur. During this same time, the United States began to react to the crisis. It began to provide humanitarian assistance and a small amount of funding to assist an African peacekeeping operation.[15] The United States also established a Disaster Assistance Response Team (DART) specifically for Darfur. In June 2004, the United States secretary of state Colin Powell met with Sudan's president Omar Hassan al-Bashir and emphasized the need to dismantle the Janjaweed.[16] In testimony before a Senate committee in September 2004, Secretary Powell said that the atrocities were genocide.[17]

Other international actors also responded to the crisis, although quite slowly. The African Union sent an observer mission in May 2004 to the region and also began to help with cease-fire negotiations.[18] In October 2004 the African Union sent 3,320 personnel (with up to 2,300 being military personnel) into Darfur to monitor compliance with a previously signed cease-fire agreement and to help protect humanitarian aid workers who were being victimized by both sides in the conflict.[19] Attacks on the African Union mission in 2005 caused a number of deaths, and dozens of personnel were abducted. Importantly, the Sudanese government would not allow the expansion of the mission to include the protection of civilians. This restriction made the vulnerable citizens in Western Sudan doubt the credibility of the African Union mission.[20]

The United Nations Security Council passed a resolution in July 2004 demanding that the government of Sudan disarm and disband the Janjaweed.[21] In July 2005 a UN delegation determined that the government had not pursued a policy of genocide, although it did report that the government and the Janjaweed had committed crimes against humanity. In March 2005 the UN Security Council established a UN mission in Sudan (UNMIS). However, the Sudanese government opposed any UN role, and for the time being the African Union force was the only one in Western Sudan.[22] In January 2006 the African Union called on the UN to replace them, which was refused by the Sudanese government.

At the same time, in 2006, the government was negotiating with one of the more powerful factions within the SLA. On May 5, 2006, the Darfur Peace

Agreement (DPA) was signed between the government and the SLA in Abuja.[23] In August 2006 the UN Security Council passed Resolution 1706 that expanded the UNMIS mandate to deploy peacekeepers to Darfur in order to assist in the implementation of the Darfur Peace Agreement.[24] Recognizing that a greater international presence was necessary to address the crisis in Darfur, the UN Security Council passed another resolution, Resolution 1769, in July 2007, establishing the UN African Union/United Nations Hybrid operation in Darfur (UNAMID). The mandate of this joint African Union/United Nations peacekeeping operation is manifold and includes the "restoration of necessary security conditions for the safe provision of humanitarian assistance and to facilitate full humanitarian access throughout Darfur" and "monitor, observe compliance with and verify the implementation of various ceasefire agreements signed since 2004, as well as assist with the implementation of the Darfur Peace Agreement and any subsequent agreements."[25]

Despite the rather lengthy peace agreement, the humanitarian crisis in Darfur has not abated, and the clashes between rebel forces and the government continue. In addition, the conflict has spread to neighboring Chad, a case of diffusion. With support and armaments from the Sudanese government, Chadian rebels from West Darfur have attempted to overthrow the Chadian government. The Darfur JEM has supported the Chadian president in his fight with the Chadian rebels.[26] Also, government attacks in West Darfur in February 2008 and North Darfur in late 2008 signaled that President al-Bashir was willing to continue the fighting despite international condemnation.[27] According to the United Nations, in October 2008 more than 2 million people were in need of humanitarian assistance. This number does not include the nearly 2.7 million internally displaced people (IDPs) also in need of assistance.[28]

THE DARFUR CRISIS IN HISTORICAL CONTEXT

While the current humanitarian crisis in Western Sudan has attracted a great deal of media and celebrity attention, the roots of the crisis stretch into the North-South wars in Sudan since 1983, and back even further to the wars immediately after independence in 1956. Like many other African nations, current race and ethnic relations are partially a result of colonial state formation.[29] Measured in geographical size, Sudan is the largest country in Africa. It is also ethnically diverse with over twenty-eight million people speaking more than four hundred languages.[30] Most of Sudan is underdeveloped, and grievances started immediately after independence. The first in a long line of civil wars began in 1955 with the mutiny of soldiers in Southern Sudan. Demands by the southern populations for federalism and devolved authority clashed with the

Muslim administration of the northern areas.[31] On November 17, 1958, the fledgling Sudanese government collapsed under the strife of civil war in the South. General Ibrahim Abboud declared emergency rule, and the Supreme Council of the Armed Forces took control.[32]

The civil war lasted until 1972, with most of the South divided along ethnic lines into numerous guerilla armies.[33] The Addis Ababa Agreement of that year gave the South institutional autonomy through a regional assembly and a high executive council.[34] During the 1970s the Northern leaders were criticized by Arab groups for conceding too much authority to the South, while the Southern leaders were criticized by their Southern political opponents for taking subordinate positions to the Northern leaders.

The increasing shift toward Islamic government in the early 1980s coincided with new demands from the South regarding oil resources, borders, and regional development.[35] Drought in the west (mainly in Darfur) drove refugees into the South, leading to ethnic conflict and displacement.[36] The civil war in Chad impacted the situation in Sudan. The Pan-Arabism ideology generated by the Arab minority in Chad spread into Sudan, as did weapons from the Chadian conflict (leading to an escalation of the conflict in Sudan).[37] The declaration of *sharia* law in Khartoum also focused much of the Southern resistance against the threat of an Islamic government.[38] The civil war in the South of Sudan eventually spread into the North, with tribes using the influx of weapons to arm militias. The development of militias targeting civilian populations, primarily to steal livestock and people, while burning settlements and crops, plagued the pastoral population of much of the country. Complicating the civil war was the introduction of mutinous army units, based in Ethiopia, who formed together as the Sudan People's Liberation Army (SPLA) as a military wing of the Sudan People's Liberation Movement (SPLM). The SPLA quickly became one of the main challengers for power in Sudan.[39]

The Koka Dam Agreement in 1986 sought to end the various conflicts in the country, but was rejected by the NIF.[40] The government abandoned the agreement in 1987, and a state of emergency was declared. The various conflicts continued until 1989, when Lt. Gen. Omar Hassan al-Bashir led a military coup and assumed power. The military government banned all political parties, but in truth it was backed by the NIF.[41] Later that year, al-Bashir's government passed the Popular Defense Act establishing the Popular Defense Force (PDF), a paramilitary organization. On December 31, 1990, al-Bashir announced sharia law in Northern Sudan. In an effort to destroy the various enemy combatants in the nation, the state directed violence against the population of the country, primarily in the South.[42] The state thus began a pattern of providing material benefits, primarily land, loot, and military support, to those who would engage in state-directed violence. This pattern laid the groundwork for the atrocities in Darfur after the turn of the twenty-first century.[43]

The various civil wars continued into the 1990s. Numerous peace attempts aimed at stopping the decades-long North-South conflicts ended in failure during that decade. A locus of contention was the increasing desire of the South to gain complete independence from the Northern government.[44] The Nairobi Declaration of 2004 between the government and the SPLM established partial autonomy in the South and power sharing in the Sudanese government. Implementation of the Nairobi Declaration was sidetracked by the new crisis in Darfur.[45] Finally, in 2005, Sudan's twenty-one-year-long civil war between the North and South ended after successful negotiations led to the Comprehensive Peace Agreement (CPA). The National Congress Party (with its origins in the NIF) and the Sudanese People's Liberation Movement party formed the Government of National Unity, with elections set for 2009, and a referendum on autonomy for the South to be held by 2011.[46] While the parties to the conflict were able to sign an agreement to end the civil war, the conflict in Darfur continued.

The crisis in Darfur is tied to the decades of conflicts in Sudan, primarily between the Arab North and African South. Thus, the "war in Darfur is the most recent manifestation of a pattern of extreme political violence."[47] The setting for the conflict in Darfur is more complicated than it may at first appear. Darfur, literally "homeland of the Fur people," is the furthest west republic of the Sudan. Darfur had a pre-conflict population of about six million out of the estimated forty million in the whole of Sudan.[48] It is mainly hot desert in the north, a dry savannah in the center, and a wetter, woodland savannah in the south. There are about eighty ethnic groups in Darfur, of which the Fur is the largest African tribe, with roughly one million people.[49]

The government's explanation for the conflict is that competition for scarce resources led the people of Darfur to resort to violence. This explanation points to the activities of the rebel JEM and SLA.[50] The conflict has also been defined as between the Muslim and non-Muslim population of Darfur. It may be more accurate to point to the more salient difference between Arab and African, as many African tribes are indeed Muslim.[51] And yet the Arab and African identities are very much socially constructed, as is the case of the identities of people in the North-South conflict. The people in the north "are really Africans who assimilated into Arab culture. Their constructed identity serves to block a north-south national integration in Sudan that could resolve the bloody conflict."[52] Thus, the identity of each side in the conflict is more complicated than what is typically reported in the Western media.[53] Further, the recent cycle of violence has disrupted a stable system of land tenure, mainly established by the Fur prior to British intervention in 1916.[54] Arab groups, supported by the violence of the

Janjaweed, covet the northern migratory routes and also a portion of the well-watered southern lands. The forced dislocation of African groups from these areas has upset the nomadic and pastoral traditions in the area. Lastly, the lack of a strong state government in Khartoum, and its marginalization and underdevelopment of Darfur, works both to fuel the rebels' campaign against the government and also to give ambitious Arab groups the freedom to seize land.[55]

Today, the civil war between the North and the South can be said to be dormant, especially in light of the signing of the Comprehensive Peace Agreement, though its implementation has not proceeded in a timely manner. In Darfur, perhaps because of international condemnation, the overt displacement of tribes by the government-supported Janjaweed has slowed. The NIF-led government has promised to disarm the Janjaweed, but has not done so yet.[56]

In July 2008, likely reacting to the threat of an arrest warrant by the International Criminal Court (ICC) for crimes against humanity and genocide, President al-Bashir announced the "People of Sudan Initiative" as a means to resolve the Darfur conflict, focusing on several factors of the conflict, including development, reconciliation, refugees, and security, as well as the international aspect of the crisis. The ruling party in the southern region of the country, the Sudan People's Liberation Movement, supports the initiative, but the leaders of the Darfur rebel groups refuse to attend the talks.[57]

Clashes between the government forces and rebels continue in the region, leading to further displacement of the population.[58] The extent of the humanitarian crisis for the population in Darfur cannot be minimized. Though the number of dead and displaced from the conflict in Darfur is still disputed,[59] reports on estimated deaths from academics, government organizations (such as the United States Department of State), and nongovernmental organizations (such as the World Health Organization) place the number of deaths in Darfur from 35,000 to close to 400,000.[60] Estimates on the number of displaced are around 1.85 million people. The total number of affected residents is near 4 million (including the displaced), or roughly two out of every three pre-conflict residents of Darfur.[61]

Humanitarian aid to Darfur has come from a number of state and non-state actors. The United States has provided over $1 billion in aid. Most of this has been food delivered through the United Nations World Food Programme and the International Committee of the Red Cross.[62] The rest of the world has provided roughly a similar amount. The ability of nongovernmental organizations (NGOs) and various United Nations agencies to get aid to the displaced has been hampered by the continued violence in the region. The hindrance of humanitarian aid has been primarily due to interference from the Sudanese government, although the rebel groups have also created a hindrance.[63] The ability of the UNAMID operation to provide substantial assistance has also been affected by

MAP 5.1
Ethnic Distribution in Sudan

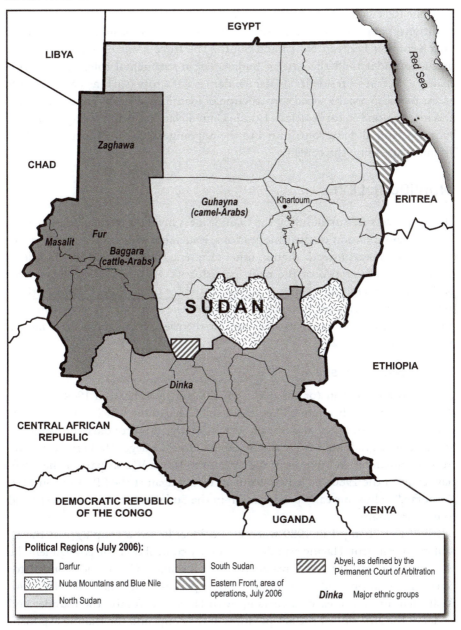

Political Regions (July 2006):

Darfur

Nuba Mountains and Blue Nile

North Sudan

South Sudan

Eastern Front, area of operations, July 2006

Abyei, as defined by the Permanent Court of Arbitration

Dinka   Major ethnic groups

Source: Data from *Regions of Sudan,* United Nations Office for the Coordination of Humanitarian Affairs, http://www.reliefweb.int/rw/fullMaps_Af.nsf/luFullMap/8AC5353DE81D0EEB852576880058BDB2/$Fil e/map.pdf?OpenElement; *Reference Map of Sudan,* United Nations Cartographic Section, http://www .un.org/Depts/Cartographic/map/profile/sudan.pdf; and the Library of Congress Country Studies Series, http://lcweb2.loc.gov/frd/cs/sudan/sd02_03a.pdf.

limited capabilities, including shortfalls in numbers of troops as well as in transportation equipment such as helicopters.[64]

While the civil war that lasted decades has been halted, the destruction of the traditional people of Darfur appears to have been accomplished as a side effect of the conflict between North and South. The three levels of analysis are also useful to understand the case of Sudan. The instrumental roles of elites (for example, Sudan's president, al-Bashir), domestic factors (such as conflicts over access to resources; the social construction of identities as Arabs versus Africans), and international actors (African Union; United Nations; neighboring countries, such as Chad) all have contributed to the ongoing conflict in Darfur as well as attempts at ending the conflict.

INDIVIDUAL LEVEL

Due to the secrecy surrounding the main leaders involved in the Sudanese conflicts, an examination of their motivations, leadership styles, and behaviors will necessarily be less in-depth than in other chapters. However, this does not deter us from looking at two of the main participants, President Omar Hassan al-Bashir and General John Garang de Mabior, leader of the SPLA. Each of these men offers an interesting portrait of the role of the individual in the turmoil in Sudan, and each allows us to examine our theories of individual level factors generated in chapter 2.

Omar Hassan al-Bashir

Omar Hassan al-Bashir (or Umar Hassan al'Bashir) was born in 1944 in Hoshe Bannaga near Shendi, about 150 miles north of Khartoum, which at the time was in the Kingdom of Egypt and Sudan. After primary and secondary education, he attended and graduated from the Sudan Military College. He became a paratroop commander and fought in the 1973 Arab-Israeli War as part of the Egyptian army. In the 1980s he led government troops against the SPLA in southern Kordofan.[65] Thus, his early participation in the Sudanese conflict was restricted to military affairs.

All of this changed in 1989 when as a colonel he led a coup against the al-Mahdi government. Having established military control over the government, he abolished the constitution, created the Revolutionary Command Council for National Salvation, and banned all political parties other than the NIF.[66] Al-Bashir fell into an uneasy partnership with Hassan al-Turabi, the founder and leader of the NIF, one of the key planners of the coup, and the leading exponent of Islamic law. Turabi eventually gained the position of Speaker of the Council and used it as a platform to subtly alter the government's policy.[67]

Al-Bashir's leadership fits the mold of the typical military dictator. He did not abide dissent, closing down opposition newspapers and trade unions. A failed military coup attempt in April 1990 met with over two dozen executions. He also continued the civil war against the South, despite his assertions when he led his coup that he would seek peace negotiations to end the war. He sought aid from Iran, Iraq, and China, which placed his foreign policy in contrast to that of the United States and its Western allies. More controversially, al-Bashir supported Islamic terrorist groups, allowing them to conduct some of their operations out of Sudan.[68]

To quell his domestic dissenters, al-Bashir allowed for a new, more representative and democratic constitution. The new governmental structure would have a directly elected president, a directly elected National Assembly, and a Speaker to lead the government. The 1996 elections, which most international observers agree were neither free nor fair, led to al-Bashir winning the presidency and al-Turabi winning the position of Speaker.[69] Despite this return to the status quo, al-Bashir allowed for greater freedom of the press and the return of a number of former political parties to the assembly.

The tension between al-Turabi and al-Bashir erupted into open conflict in December 1999. Al-Turabi introduced into the National Assembly a series of constitutional changes that would effectively shift a great degree of executive power from the president to the Speaker. Al-Bashir predictably moved swiftly to end this threat. He dissolved the Assembly, removed a number of local governors, and arrested al-Turabi as an enemy of the state (al-Turabi had signed a memorandum of agreement with the SPLM).[70] In the subsequent presidential election of 2000 amid an opposition boycott, al-Bashir won 86.5 percent of the vote.[71]

Former U.S. ambassador Donald Petterson describes al-Bashir as "a typical Sudanese, in that he is open, friendly, and good humored."[72] He is of "medium height and medium coloring and . . . look[s] fit," usually dressed in either an olive-green military uniform or the traditional white jellabiya (gown) worn by Sudanese men.[73] Petterson also says that while al-Bashir was "pleasant and attentive" in conversation, he was also "inflexible when he expressed his disagreements with U.S. foreign policies."[74]

One particular trait that most observers have noted about al-Bashir is his determination to defend the Sudanese government against charges of abuse. When pressed, he denies any wrongdoing. In 1992 when asked by Ambassador Petterson about the climate of fear his security police were creating in the capital, al-Bashir replied, "None of this is true, the opposition . . . [is] spreading false rumors. . . . We respect human rights in Sudan . . . perhaps our understanding of human rights differs from your government's."[75] In a 1994 exchange with U.S. secretary of state Madeleine Albright, Bashir again denied "that his government was guilty of any wrongdoing" and accused the United States of being hostile to him because of his support of Islam.[76]

Al-Bashir dealt harshly with the uprising in Darfur in 2003. His immediate response to the JEM and SLA attacks was to say that the "army would now be 'unleashed'" against them.[77] Al-Bashir, and the Sudanese government, then denied that any atrocities had taken place or were taking place in Darfur. In a sly twist of words when criticized that the government was supporting and linked to the Janjaweed, Bashir said that in order to "rein in" the Janjaweed they had "been incorporated in[to] . . . the armed forces and the police."[78] That al-Bashir knew of the atrocities is not debatable. In December 2003 during a rally of the Popular Defense Force, he asked them to "shed the blood of political opponents" and to defeat the "renegades, traitors, and highwaymen of Darfur."[79] Al-Bashir continues to deny access to the region to external relief groups and decries the genocide label as a Western fiction. Following the death of John Garang in 2005, al-Bashir and the Sudanese government are trying to eliminate all their opposition in Darfur.[80]

In July of 2008 the chief prosecutor of the International Criminal Court (ICC) asked the judges to issue an arrest warrant against al-Bashir for crimes against humanity. Opposition to the issuing of this warrant came mainly from China, the Arab League, and the African Union, while most of the West supported it.[81] On March 4, 2009, the ICC did indeed issue an arrest warrant for al-Bashir on five counts of crimes against humanity and two counts of war crimes.

In summary, we can say that al-Bashir's role in encouraging and fostering mass hostility fits with the model of Kaufman and others outlined in chapter 2. By playing on cultural stereotypes, myths, and metaphors, al-Bashir helped mobilize collective action to enhance his own political position and power. That al-Bashir has little reason to end the conflict can be understood through the lens of domestic politics. Without any significant internal opposition (since 2000 when al-Turabi was silenced), al-Bashir does not have any strong "outbidder" who can challenge his role as the leader of the ethnic group (in this case the Arab Sudanese). Al-Bashir is optimistic that he and his National Congress Party (NCP) will win the elections called for by the Comprehensive Peace Agreement, including winning the majority of the votes of Darfurians. As El Tahir Adam El Faki (Speaker of the Legislative Council of JEM) observes, "Al-Bashir is very keen for the elections and seeks re-election for both legitimacy as well as a weapon against the ICC and the Prosecutor Moreno-Ocampo, to demonstrate that he has the support of all Sudanese, Darfurians included. These reasons alone entail the NCP to mobilise all the power and machineries of the state at its disposal to secure winning the elections [in 2010] at all costs."[82] Free from internal dissension, he does not have to compromise with any internal political institutions and thus can remain defiant of external actors and play a spoiler role in the peace process.

John Garang de Mabior (SPLA)

John Garang was born in Wagkulei, a small village in southern Sudan in the Bor district populated by the largest ethnic group in Sudan, the Dinkas. He grew up relatively poor, and both his parents died in his early childhood.[83] He went to high school in Tanzania. He traveled to the United States and attended Grinnell College, earning his B.A. in 1971. Returning to Sudan, he joined the Anya-Nya, a military organization in Southern Sudan separate from the Sudanese military and seeking the secession of the South. After the 1972 Addis Ababa Agreement, the Anya-Nya was integrated into the national armed forces, and so was Garang, who took the rank of captain. General Joseph Lagu, previously the commander of Anya-Nya, assumed the position of the military leader of the South, and he named Garang his chief aide.[84]

Former U.S. ambassador to Sudan Donald Petterson describes John Garang as follows: "Like most Dinka he is tall, well over six feet, but unlike most Dinka, he is not thin."[85] Petterson also says that Garang is "a well-spoken man, [and] is a master at avoiding answering difficult questions."[86] Francis Deng describes Garang as inflexible, driven by principle, and callous.[87] Thus, Garang is a typical example of a strongman who rises to power in a weak state. He is physically impressive, well-educated, well-spoken, but also brutal and ambitious.

In 1974 Garang returned to the United States to complete military training at Fort Benning, Georgia (the United States routinely trains military officers of foreign countries). He followed this by earning a Ph.D. in agricultural economics from Iowa State University.[88] He returned to Sudan and taught simultaneously at the University of Khartoum and the Khartoum Military School. He maintained his position in the military and rose to the rank of colonel before the uprisings of 1983 broke out. President Nimeiri ordered Garang to lead troops in the South. Specifically, he was to travel to Bor and end a mutiny of Southern troops that were being reassigned to the North. Instead of putting down the rebellion, he mutinied and joined the rebels.[89]

With Garang as leader, on March 3, 1984, the SPLA was founded. Garang made it clear that the SPLA was not just a secessionist movement, but one that wanted to liberate all Sudanese people from the dictatorship in Khartoum, promote economic development of the poorer regions of Sudan, and revoke the application of Islamic law.[90] Garang became both the military commander of the SPLA and part of the governing board (along with civilian politicians) of the SPLM. In 1984 and 1985 the SPLA achieved a number of military successes in the South, especially in the Upper Nile area. After the 1985 coup that brought down the Nimeiri government, Garang refused to meet for peace talks, claiming that while Sadiq al-Mahdi was an elected prime minister, the real power behind the government was still the military and General Suwar al-Dahab. Garang also rejected the al-Mahdi state as Islamic and refused to negotiate until Islamic law was lifted.[91]

Garang's leadership of the SPLA was not without controversy. Other figures in the SPLA leadership, particularly those of the second largest ethnic group, the Neur, felt marginalized and resented Garang's dictatorial leadership style.[92] The period of Southern unity lasted only during the late 1980s. Challenges to his leadership hit a peak in 1996 when a number of Neur leaders sought to undermine his authority and many of them were killed. Other SPLA leaders shifted their allegiance to the government, including Riek Machar. By 1998 Garang was effectively the only major leader of the SPLA.[93]

Garang continued his war against the Khartoum government, but by the early 2000s he also sought a means to resolve the endless fighting while holding true to the principle of a self-governed South and eventual self-determination. On September 25, 2003, the SPLA signed the framework agreement that assured the South of exactly these things. In 2004 the government and Garang negotiated a cease-fire, which was quickly followed by a power-sharing agreement. General Garang certainly did well in the agreement, as he would be appointed the First Vice President of Sudan (there would be two vice presidents) and president of the Southern government, while retaining his position as commander of the SPLA.[94]

As noted previously, the Sudanese government and the SPLM signed the Comprehensive Peace Agreement (CPA) in spring of 2005. Sensitive to the opportunity for his critics to claim that he abandoned the objectives for which the South had been fighting for decades, Garang announced that the CPA was a step forward for all Sudanese and 2005 would be a year of peace.[95] This would not come to pass. On July 30, 2005, General Garang was killed in a helicopter crash. Southerners in the capital of Khartoum rioted, suspicious that the crash was no accident.[96] Commentators lamented the possibility that Garang's death would stall the movement toward peace, but others suggested that without his repressive leadership style and forceful personality, more moderate and diplomatic SPLM leaders could build a consensus among the tribes in the South.[97]

Interestingly, Garang is an example of a leader who clearly sought his own personal aggrandizement but also served larger principles (for example, self-determination for the South). In congruence with the idea of the "greedy spoiler" from chapter 2, he acted very selfishly by seeking to expand violence if it meant a greater role for him in the SPLA. His ruthless expulsion or killing of competing leaders and brutality against all who stood in his way defined his leadership. He sanctioned SPLA attacks on UN compounds and routinely stole food and supplies from the starving so that he could feed his soldiers and officials.[98] His eventual acceptance of a high position in the Sudanese government mirrored his earlier movement into the national military in 1972. When the gains of participating in the government were higher than the risks of rebellion, he joined; when it was the reverse, he was in rebellion. Therefore, we can conclude that his adherence to self-determination for the South was instrumental; in other words, as long as advancing that cause advanced his position of power, he would champion it.

DOMESTIC LEVEL

Communities and Identities

Identity in Darfur is complicated by two general factors: there are many different ethnic groups living in the region, and the continuous history of state formation over the centuries has led to overlapping processes of identity formation. These two factors are, of course, tied together. The development of the many different identities today is connected intimately to the historical development of the Sudanese state.

Alex de Waal traces the development of four different processes of identity formation in Darfur, each associated with a different era of history. First are the Sudanic identities, which developed previous to the twentieth century and are associated with the development of the Darfur Sultanate. The second is the Islamic identity, which is a product of the development of Islam over a number of recent centuries. The third is the administrative tribalism created by British rule at the start of the twentieth century. The last is the recent polarization of the communities into Arab versus African identities.[99]

The area of the Darfur Sultanate is home to many different ethnicities. De Waal identifies two dozen major non-Arab groups, almost a similar number of Arab groups, and a dozen or so separate ethnic groups in the region of South Darfur.[100] Within this ethnic diversity, prior to the recent century, the dominant groups were mainly the Fur and the Keira.[101] The construction of a Sudanic identity by these groups was a means to provide legitimacy for their rule.[102] These central and dominant groups subjugated nomadic groups to the north and assimilated many of them into a Fur identity. To the south, the Fur often dispatched soldiers to plunder and obtain slaves for the Egyptian slave markets. Thus, a constant state of war in the area both mingled the ethnic groups, and also created a dominant Fur identity versus the subject identities.[103]

Of particular significance is the distinction that arose during the Turco-Egyptian state of 1821–1884. For the rest of Sudan, the difference between an Arab North and an African South would become important. For Darfur, however, this distinction meant nothing. Darfurians comprised many identities, including African, nomadic, and cultural Arabs.[104] Thus, a Darfurian identity separate from the emerging Sudanese state existed in Darfur.

The formation of an Islamic identity overlaps with the latter period of the development of the Darfurian identity. From the fourteenth to the eighteenth century, Islam migrated with groups entering Darfur from the west.[105] As a result, most of the Arab groups in Darfur have weak historic claims to territory. The nineteenth century can be divided between Turkish rule (1821–1881) and the Mahdiyya state (1881–1898).[106] The first emerged due to the Egyptian conquest of what is now Northern Sudan in 1821 and the eventual conquest of the Southern Sudan in the 1860s. Under Turco-Egyptian rule, the first central state administration occurred, with a semblance of centralized taxation. Further, Islamic orthodoxy replaced the multiple Islamic practices in the region, and Quranic schools were established.[107] The Mahdist state emerged from the jihad of Muhammad Ahmad ibn Abdallah al-Mahdi against corrupt Muslims and all nonbelievers. In 1881 al-Mahdi and his band of supporters escaped the Nile Valley and migrated to Western Sudan. From there, they conquered Khartoum and ended the Turco-Egyptian rule.[108] This change in rule led to disputes between the Shayqiyya who participated in the Turkish rule and the Baqqara who claimed power during the Mahdiyya. The southern, non-Muslim tribes continued to suffer under the new rule as they had under the Turkish rule.[109]

Therefore, the Islamization of Sudan was a very long process and not a coherent one. Many different Arab groups embrace different forms of Islam. Further, the relationship of a group to dominance of the state or subjugation by the state also factors into hostility or accommodation between different Islamic groups.[110] These differences will gain renewed importance in the twenty-first century under the rule of the National Islamic Front/National Congress Party.

The third process of identity formation happened during the British domination of Sudan in 1899 and continued until independence in 1956. The 1899 Anglo-Egyptian Condominium declared that Britain would build a new form of government for Sudan. This new administration would "be based on low taxation, the toleration of domestic slavery, and the encouragement of Orthodox Islam . . . [and] encourage tribal leadership."[111] De Waal calls this the period of "Administrative tribalism" and "Native Administration."[112] The British used this arrangement to tidy up the confusion of multiethnic allegiances and tribal confrontations. Included in this "tidying up" was relocation of some tribes in order to form a single tribe and the creation of artificial boundaries, exemplified by the division of the Darfur Sultanate into four provinces.[113] Jay O'Brien argues that the British simplification of the identities of the people over which they ruled was Darwinian, emphasizing the differences between hunters, pastoralists, and cultivators, and their relative position on a social evolutionary scale.[114] R. S. O'Fahey goes so far as to say that "a consciously institutionalized Islamic policy in the Sudan is a British invention," laying the seeds of the future polarization of Arab versus African identity at the feet of the British.[115]

The fourth process of identity formation is very recent. The incorporation of the rich and diverse Darfur region into mainstream Sudanese politics and the Sudanese state (as well as the larger Middle Eastern political development, globalization and its spread into Africa, and the emerging tension between the Arab and Western worlds) has led to an oversimplification of the diversity in Darfur. The creation of a polarized Arab versus African distinction does not do justice to the complexity in Darfur, but it does fit nicely into contemporary understandings of ethnic relations.[116] As mentioned at the start of this chapter, the Pan-Arabism of the 1970s and 1980s led to a sense of Islamic superiority vis-à-vis other identities. The spread of Islam from Khartoum to Darfur carried with it this new politicized Arab identity. It also carried with it a militant strand, consistent with the Mahdi past but also with the new Pan-Arabism, especially that espoused by Muammar Gaddafi, leader of Libya.[117]

The development of an Arab/Islamic identity by the ruling NIF is also quite calculated. This new identity is an instrument to legitimize the existence of an Islamic state.[118] The NIF has "correlated the division between the north and south with the distinction between Arab and African, while also associating Islam with Arabism."[119] The corresponding creation of the African identity is closely tied to the resistance groups, and especially John Garang and the SPLA.[120] In contradiction to the NIF claims of Sudan as an Islamic nation, Garang emphasized that an African majority exists in Sudan. Thus, the construction of an African identity coincided with the instrumental need for a political alliance of many tribes against the Islamic government in the capital. Much as the new "Arab" identity is a recruiting tool for the NIF both domestically and internationally, the new "African" identity has a ring both internally and externally. Witness to its power is the use of the term "genocide" by the United States State Department and the simplification by many NGOs that the Arab Sudanese are slaughtering the African Sudanese.

In general, the ethnic divisions within Sudan are many. Elfatih A. A/Salam summarizes the division by categorizing the four different types of division: social pluralism (that is, division into 500+ ethnic groups), linguistic pluralism (that is, the 113+ different languages), religious pluralism (mainly Muslim, Christian, and Pagan), and administrative pluralism (as a reference point for identification).[121] This multitude of identities has served as a means to obtain material privilege, as a source of honor, dignity, self-esteem, and lastly, as a way to further political goals. The increasing politicization is tied to the accelerated process of nation-building over the last few decades.

Gendered Nationalism

With the overthrow of Sadiq al-Mahdi in 1989, the National Islamic Front (NIF) party seized power (the NIF is the forerunner to the National Congress Party, currently in power along with the SPLM, as part of the ruling Government of National Unity). The NIF's version of Islamic fundamentalism "subordinates and discriminates against women." Women are expected to remain in "the margins of public life" and thus are limited in their access to economic, political, and social resources.[122] For example, in September 2000 Mazjoub al-Khalifa, the governor of the state of Khartoum (he was the former minister of social planning), imposed a ban preventing "women from working in public places where they come into direct contact with men."[123] Women, therefore, are not allowed to work in places such as gas stations, hotels, and restaurants. Human Rights Watch quoted the governor, in his justification for the ban, as saying that the ban is "'intended to honor women,' to uphold their status in line with Islamic law, and to respect the values and the traditions of the nation."[124] Both Muslim and non-Muslim women living in the North "are regulated and restricted by Shari'a law."[125] As Sondra Hale writes, "In the name of the ideal woman, as morally central to the ideal family, women's behaviour is thus ideologically manipulated by male-controlled religio-political institutions."[126]

This evidence of gendered nationalism is all the more troubling in light of the impact the many years of civil war in Sudan have had on women. Given that the conflict has meant that the men are off fighting, women are left to provide for their families. If women do not have access to jobs, they cannot earn money needed to live.[127] Thus, the North-South conflict has affected women and men differently. Audrey Macklin notes that for women and their children the conflict meant that they were forcibly removed and displaced. For men it meant that they left their homes to fight, to find jobs, or to avoid the violence.[128]

Besides suffering constraints on their ability to work, women also find it difficult to participate in the political and military spheres. Women were not present at the peace negotiations in mid-2000 held by the Inter-Governmental Authority on Development (IGAD), an intergovernmental organization (IGO) comprised of East African countries, in which the different parties to the North-South conflict worked to achieve a settlement to end the civil war.[129] Women's groups, such as the Sudanese Women's Peace Initiative, lobbied IGAD for access to the peace negotiations as representatives. The women's lobbying efforts sought to draw attention to the plight of women as they are affected by the conflict. The women also stressed the need to have women in political leadership positions and "the integration of women's perspectives in governance." The need for health and education policies was also forefront in their requests.[130] The impact of the war in the South on women demonstrates the critical need for a peace settlement that provides for adequate health care. While women, men, and children "suffer the same health risks," women's "socialized role as mothers often relegates their needs to the lowest priority."[131]

As noted throughout this chapter, rape and sexual violence were, and are, prevalent in the North-South civil war as well as the conflict in Darfur. Gender-based violence is further evidence of gendered nationalism. The parties to the conflict engage in sexual violence, targeting the women and girls of the enemy group. As Macklin observes, "The ubiquitous threat of violence—attack, abduction, rape, looting, and death—hangs in the air in Southern Sudan."[132] Further, as Macklin astutely contends, "sexual violence—whether perpetrated by attacking militia, by male authorities in IDP [internally displaced peoples] camps who extort sex in exchange for food, or by soldier-husbands demanding sexual services in the name of 'reproducing the nation'—inflicts special damage on women's physical and mental health."[133] It is important to recognize that sexual violence demonstrates the government's inability to provide security for women.[134]

The Comprehensive Peace Agreement (CPA) of January 2005 that ended the twenty-one-year civil war between the North and South sought to bring peace to Africa's longest civil war. While there were some women present in the peace negotiations that led to the CPA, their impact was not significant in terms of promoting women's participation or recognizing the need for a women's peace agenda. As Anne Itto, one of the Sudan People's Liberation Movement/Army (SPLM/A) female negotiators, observes, the leadership of the SPLM/A "nominated a handful of women leaders as members of the delegation," but "this did not necessarily enable their strong participation." She continues, "the women were often co-opted to these delegations at short notice with very little opportunity to consult with each other and develop a women's peace agenda; they were expected to contribute to the overall party position which was gender-blind to begin with; and they were always a minority, ill-prepared for debates with seasoned politicians who ridiculed or intimidated anyone who dared to spend much time on gender issues." During the negotiations "when women were consulted about gender issues or directly included in the peace negotiations, it was only a gesture to showcase democracy and inclusiveness: their perspectives and their experiences in peacebuilding and negotiation were not recognized or fully utilized."[135]

In the case of Darfur, women's groups were involved in the final peace negotiations that led to the Darfur Peace Agreement (DPA) in 2006, signed by one of the rebel groups (there are three) and the Sudanese government. Yet, women "are vastly under-represented on key committees and decision-making bodies, and their interests often are overlooked in policy-making." In the negotiations on the DPA, women's involvement was found mainly as "consulting experts" and as a "very small minority of members of formal negotiating delegations."[136] However, unlike the CPA, the DPA does include more than seventy sections that explicitly refer to women (such as "recognition of gender-based violence and the recommendation that women be involved in drafting legislation"). Tellingly, men are responsible for the implementation of both the CPA and DPA.[137]

Recognizing that women's voices still need to be heard for any lasting peace in Sudan, women's groups continue to lobby for gender-based policies and inclusion in political decision making. For example, in January 2008 the first-ever African Women's Consultation on Darfur forum was held in Addis Ababa, Ethiopia. The nearly one hundred women in attendance (from Darfur and other parts of Sudan, and other African countries) met to draft a Darfuri Women Plan of Action for Peace. In this way, the Consultation's participants hoped to highlight the need for women's participation in the peace process and post-conflict society. After the meeting ended, the Plan of Action for Peace was presented to the African Union Heads of State and Government's Ordinary Session with the hope that the members of the organization would consider the Plan as negotiations on the Darfur crisis continued.[138]

However, it is not surprising that the terms of both the CPA and DPA have not been fully implemented, and conflict, particularly in Darfur, continues. Crucial deadlines of the CPA have been missed; a UN-led peace process initiated in late 2007 "fell apart almost immediately."[139] Women continue to suffer gender-based sexual violence and struggle to protect their families in the face of continued fighting. Itto's personal observations reiterate the point that by not including women at the negotiation table or by including and yet marginalizing them, not establishing significant gender-based policies for a post-conflict reconstruction of society, and not including significant numbers of women in positions in political institutions, the country is unlikely to achieve a lasting and effective peace.

Ethno-Nationalist Conflict and Domestic Political Institutions

Sudan is a good example of Peleg's definition of a hegemonic state. The government, run by the National Islamic Front, actively pushes its position in the conflict, supporting and arming one side. Its long-term facilitation of the Janjaweed has intensified the devastation in Darfur and created an asymmetrical distribution of the means of violence. Understanding the motivations and behavior of the National Islamic Front can help uncover the source of the continuing humanitarian crisis in Darfur.

Roger Winter describes the ruling National Congress Party in Sudan as "controlled by an intellectually capable, radically committed, conspiratorial, and compassionless nucleus of individuals, long referred to as the National Islamic Front."[140] The military coup in 1989 that brought al-Bashir to power led to a government that was both Islamic and Arab-centrist. The new government injected an ideological and racist dimension into the various conflicts in Sudan.[141] Responsibility for the crisis falls on the National Congress and its ruling party, the National Islamic Front. In particular, Hassan al-Turabi, the former Speaker of the State Parliament and secretary-general of the NIF, issued a decree stating that the NIF "aims to support the Arab tribes by . . . displacement of the Fur . . . complete disarming of the Fur people," replacing them with Arab tribes and the arming and financing of the Arab tribes.[142]

After the 1989 military coup, the new government moved to empower the NIF as the sole ruling party. It suspended the state constitution, dissolved parliament, and banned all other political parties. The NIF thus established an authoritarian government that could effectively purge the army, police, civil service, and other government agencies of all opponents.[143] The Revolutionary Command Council then moved to silence the media, outlaw labor unions, and withdraw from any commitment to the previous peace agreements. General Omar Hassan al-Bashir became prime minister while Hassan al-Turabi led the NIF and chaired the Committee of Forty, which set official government policy. The two leaders struggled with each other and their individual ambitions, with al-Turabi initially gaining ascendency. He was successful in creating the Popular Defense Force (PDF) as a rival to the newly purged National Army.[144]

Al-Turabi realized the need to find a vehicle to control the will of the people and bend their support to the new regime. The NIF held local meetings and elections from 1992 to 1995 in which it slowly set up a series of puppet organizations and institutions. Eventually, al-Bashir was elected president and became the nominal head of the government. Power was effectively centralized into Khartoum while the NIF's vision of Islam was exported to all corners of the state. In economics, the NIF pushed privatization of public property. These measures allowed NIF officials and supporters to gain ownership of a great deal of enterprises and land.[145]

In 1999 the split between al-Bashir and al-Turabi intensified and boiled over. In December al-Bashir declared a state of emergency and moved against al-Turabi and the NIF. Al-Turabi formed a new political party based on regional leaders of the NIF and entered into opposition to al-Bashir and the NIF that remained loyal to him. He did this primarily by establishing an allegiance between his supporters and the SPLA in the South, but he also rallied anti-Bashir Arabs in Darfur.[146] Al-Turabi led a coup attempt against the government in 2004 but was unsuccessful.[147]

One scholar argues that the dismissal of al-Turabi "demarcates the first decade of the Islamists' project" in which they "tried their very best to keep the totalitarian regime intact."[148] Importantly, the fall of al-Turabi exposes the authoritarian underpinnings of the al-Bashir regime and the desire of the state-directed regime to "demolish . . . other autonomous institutions that normally act independently within the sphere of the civil, religious and political societies."[149] The role of the Islamist state is to "develop a uniform bureaucracy that can help control and monopolize the political, religious, economic and social markets," and to "serve the ideological and political program of the Islamists."[150] Religion gained an authoritarian or totalitarian disposition to enforce the political ideology of the new regime. In this light, systematic terror against resistant Sudanese populations is part of the regime's "project" to control all aspects of the society in the name of order and governance. The NIF and the government of Sudan are said to be directly responsible for "gross human rights violations, such as genocide and extrajudicial killing, tortures, acts of slavery and ethnic cleansing, confiscation of private property [and] arbitrary arrest."[151]

The role of Islam in the current civil war and as an underpinning for the current regime is thus not entirely clear. Islam has been disproportionally a part of civil wars in Africa and also the post–World War II world.[152] Monica Toft identifies three factors that explain the congruence between Islam and civil war, of which two are important for our understanding of its role in Sudan: the co-location of Islamic holy sites to petroleum reserves and the role of jihad in Islam. She argues that the West's dependence on petroleum and its hegemony over the Middle East and North Africa, combined with the growing antipathy of the Arab populations toward the West and its policies in the region, make the geographical occurrence of civil war correlate with the presence of Islam. Second, the role of jihad as a defense of a community against external nonbelievers fuels and legitimizes civil struggles.[153]

Toft further argues that religion moved from being a peripheral to a central element in the Sudanese civil wars when elites attempted to outbid each other to "increase their religious legitimacy with an internal and, in many but not all cases, external audience."[154] In short, Northern leaders, threatened by military successes of the SPLA/SPLM in the South, sought religion as a means to prop up and legitimize their continued hegemonic rule from the North. Al-Turabi and his role as leader of the NIF exemplify this process of outbidding. Religious authority is both a goal of ambitious elites and also a tool that they use to mobilize support and legitimize their rule. In this context, Islam is only as central as needed by the leaders or the state to maintain their hegemony.

In summary, President al-Bashir and the NIF organized the post-1989 Sudanese government into an authoritarian, one-party regime. This centralization of power and authority into the capital of Khartoum allowed them to propel both their war against rebels in the South and also their "Islamification" of the entirety of Sudan. This pro-Arab and pro-Islamic ideology allies the resources of the state with the political will of the rulers, and allows them to brand their opponents as opponents of the state and Islam. This hegemonic position creates few opportunities for domestic opponents other than outright rebellion against the center. Of course, any rebel attacks provoke the Khartoum government to respond with state-sponsored violence and repression, all in the name of preserving order. While the NIF–National Congress Party (NCP) formed the Government of Unity with the SPLM following the signing of the Comprehensive Peace Agreement, the NIF/NCP expects to remain in power and maintain control of the country.

The explosion of violence in Darfur in 2003 follows this pattern exactly. Darfur was a longtime supporter of the previous ruling Umma Party, and thus was not a friend of the ruling NIF elites. The slow displacement and disenfranchisement of the Darfurians in the 1990s fueled the JEM and SLA uprising. These attacks provided an excuse for the NIF to respond with military aggression against the rebels. But the financing of any government response is costly, and cost has hampered the ability of the Sudanese government to end insurrections against it for decades. This has limited the direct role of the National Army/Popular Defense Force. Moreover, the army has so far proven ineffective in ending the violence in the South, so its ability to project a sustained amount of force into Darfur is questionable.[155]

Therefore, one of the ways that the NIF has fought its war against the people of Darfur is through direct and indirect arming and supporting of the Janjaweed operations. The previous Sudanese government had armed Arab tribes to fight against the rebels in the South, but there was very little actual control of these groups. In 1989 the NIF incorporated the Arab tribes into government militias, thus organizing them into a more coherent force and also allowing greater supply from the government. In 2003 it was suggested that the Sudanese Army organized a number of the Janjaweed militias into actual military brigades.[156]

Direct involvement is most evident through the use of government aircraft to support the violence in Darfur. Aerial bombing of villages in Darfur, primarily in Northern Darfur, by Antonov military transport aircraft, helicopters, and MiG fighter jets occurred for many years starting in roughly 2003 or 2004.[157] The bombings were used not only to terrorize the civilian population to discourage their assistance to the rebel groups, but also to displace them and destroy crops, both of which would also undermine the rebels.[158]

Indirect assistance includes the use of governmental aircraft in aerial reconnaissance. These flights occurred both before and after Janjaweed attacks. Apparently, these flights were used to confirm the presence of targets and also to confirm the success of the attacks. Another use of governmental aircraft is that of supplying the Janjaweed. Various deliveries of arms and supplies to

Janjaweed camps outside of villages have been reported.[159] It has also been reported that government ground vehicles have been involved in Janjaweed raids and attacks.[160]

Only after 2003 has the Sudanese government been able to support the Janjaweed, due to the increasing expenditure on the military. By 2004 Sudan was spending the seventh-largest amount in Africa on its military.[161] Despite an incremental increase in oil output in the first decade of the twenty-first century, since 2002 the Sudanese government has taken in almost $700 million a year, mainly due to the run-up in the global price of oil.[162] Correspondingly, it is estimated that in 2003 the Sudanese government allocated $700 million of the state budget to the military.[163]

Nongovernmental Domestic Actors

The number of nongovernmental domestic actors in Sudan could fill volumes. We have chosen to highlight three that demonstrate key aspects of the conflict. First, the Janjaweed are a civil militia that operates mainly in Western Sudan and Darfur. As such, its activities have been central to the atrocities committed in that region. Second, the SPLA/SPLM are the main rebel military opposition to the government and have been a strong factor in the continued civil wars between the North and the South. Third, the SLA is one of the main rebel groups in Darfur.

Janjaweed. Any examination of the conflict in Sudan must seek an understanding of the role of the Janjaweed. This collection of semi-organized horsemen represents a clear example of a "civil militia" and the role that such militias play not only in Sudanese politics, but also in the rest of Africa. Civil militias typically "comprise citizens, including young people and unemployed youths, marginalized and dissatisfied with the . . . state . . . mostly with no constitutional provision or legislation legalizing their existence."[164] Such militias serve a particular interest of a mobilizing leader or subgroup and thus are susceptible to political manipulation and subversion. In a weak or failed state that cannot maintain a monopoly of force or violence, the proliferation of civil militias may occur. Direction or guidance of civil militias can be a tool for a weak state that cannot or does not wish to project its power directly.

The Janjaweed in Sudan fit this definition. The Janjaweed did not spontaneously generate due to the 2003 rebellion in Darfur. Rather, they are the product of the long-term instability and civil war in Sudan. Reports by Amnesty International from the 1980s identified civil militias as partly responsible for human rights violations and killings.[165] In fact, the Janjaweed are just one of three important groups of militias that operate in Sudan. The other two groups are urban militias under the direction of a particular political party or individual, and rebel groups in the South that rival the SPLA. The nomadic Arabs in Western Sudan were initially organized into Murahaleen militias in the 1980s by the Sadiq al-Mahdi government.[166] This formation underscores the use of civil militias to further a political goal, in this instance, the desire of the al-Mahdi government to have a counter force against SPLA/SPLM incursions into Western Sudan.

The NIF incorporated the Murahaleen into the new PDF. It encouraged the expansion and arming of the various nomadic militias into the larger force known as the Janjaweed. That Darfur became the new theater of conflict in the long-running Sudanese civil wars fueled the government's interest in maintaining a dominant role in the region. However, it should be emphasized that the ethnic divisions between the mostly Arab militias and the mostly African tribes in Darfur play a role in the willingness of the Janjaweed to act. They are not merely being "duped" by the NIF into committing the atrocities; they are a willing participant. Also, the economic deprivation of Western Sudan gives a criminal incentive to the militias to steal land and resources from their weaker neighboring tribes.[167]

The composition, organization, and structure of the Janjaweed are not completely known, but key characteristics are generally agreed upon. They number at least 20,000, are one hundred percent Arab, and are drawn from both Chadian and Sudanese Arab tribes. Most of the leadership is drawn from the Arab tribal leadership, with most identified leaders holding positions appointed by the government in the regional and ethnic reorganization of the 1990s.[168] While the Janjaweed are not stationed in the same barracks as the state military, they receive a wage from the state, wear uniforms and insignia similar to the state military, and often mobilize in abandoned or decommissioned state military facilities.[169]

Attacks and counter-insurgent operations by the Janjaweed are ethnically motivated and typically aimed at cleansing a village or area of a targeted non-Arab group, such as the Fur or Masalit.[170] The level of violence and atrocity has drawn international condemnation and includes "indiscriminate attacks against civilians; rape and other forms of sexual violence; destruction of property and pillage; forced displacement; disappearances; and persecution and discrimination."[171]

SPLA/SPLM. The Sudan People's Liberation Army (SPLA) and its political wing, the Sudan People's Liberation Movement (SPLM), has sought to expel the Northern rule from the South since the early 1980s. In doing so, it became the main political and military opposition to the Khartoum regime. Originally led by General John Garang, the SPLA/SPLM seeks not only to seize government resources by force, but also to "employ political resources and violence to sustain, reformulate, or destroy the foundation of legitimacy" of the Northern regime.[172]

SPLA/SPLM opposition to the government began in 1983 with the Northern subdivision of the South into three regions, and the subsequent Islamification project initiated in the South. Initially, most recruits to the new movement sought retribution against local Muslims and in return for raids by Arabs from the North.[173] Also of consequence was the Ethiopian support for SPLM during its genesis. This would allow the Northern government to brand the SPLM as a foreign group and seek to expel its armed troops from Sudan. Under the guidance of the politically astute Garang, the SPLA became a single vehicle for many divergent Southern tribes and interests. Therefore, one of the initial and long-lasting goals of the SPLA has been the creation of a "New Sudan." This vision of a New Sudan has typically meant either an independent South or the dominance of the entire Sudanese state by Southern elite.[174]

The ambiguous and sometimes contradictory aims of the SPLA/SPLM during the 1980s led to divisions within the movement by the 1990s. The strength of the SPLM changed dramatically in 1991 with the fall of the Mengistu government in Ethiopia. SPLM troops that had camped in Ethiopia were forced to move into Equitoria Sudan and northern Uganda. Mengistu had been a major patron of Garang, and now his position was weakened vis-à-vis his adversaries internal to the SPLA.[175] In particular, Commander Riek Machar challenged the dictatorial leadership of Garang, before eventually leaving the movement altogether, joining with the NIF-led government, and becoming an appointed governor in South Sudan.[176]

In 1994 the SPLA held a national convention and tried to endorse liberal methods of governance and calls for self-determination for the South. The convention created a separation of the political and military wings of the movement, allowing the former to dissociate itself clearly from any violent actions of the latter. In essence, the convention confirmed the SPLA as not just a liberation movement, but also as a pro-democracy movement. Given the shift in the international environment in the early 1990s toward democratic norms, one could reasonably question the sincerity of the pro-democratic shift of the SPLA.[177]

By the late 1990s the SPLA had captured a number of towns and maintained a position of strength in the South. In 2000 the SPLA had effectively blockaded the Nile River, stopping barge traffic between the North and the South. This increased the ability of the SPLA to threaten and harass oil production.[178] In 2004, after years of intense and increased fighting, the government and the SPLM signed three protocols on power sharing, the Nuba Mountains, and

Southern Blue Nile.[179] These interim protocols recognized the eventual need for self-determination in the South, but until then, a quasi-federal system would grant some degree of regional autonomy under the Khartoum government. This system was based on "the right of the South to control and govern affairs in their region; full and equal participation in the National Government; a shared common heritage . . . ; the sharing of wealth . . . ; [and] the freedom of belief and absence of distinction based on religion."[180] The constitutional power sharing contained in the protocols is a prime example of a consociational arrangement (as defined in chapter 2).

The three protocols were quickly followed by the Nairobi Declaration on June 5, 2004, which declared that the parties agreed to a long list of negotiations from the previous three years. In January 2005 the NIF and SPLM signed the Comprehensive Peace Agreement (CPA), effectively ending the North-South civil war.[181] The CPA contained self-determination for the South, stating that in 2011 the region could hold a referendum on its future. The CPA contains 1,100 specific tasks, and while that is too large a number to address in this limited format, some of the most important provisions are the following: a North-South unity government, a new Government of South Sudan, joint integrated military units, division of oil revenues, and an independent judiciary.[182] The CPA creates a new unity government, much in accordance with consociational principles of power sharing between rival groups. Of course, while the civil war in the South was abating, the war in the West intensified. Currently, the SPLA/SPLM contributes to the government, as per the CPA. The president of Southern Sudan and the vice president of the Sudanese Government is Salva Kiir Mayardi, the leader of the SPLA.[183]

SLA. The Sudan Liberation Army (SLA) is one of the two main rebel groups in Darfur. The origins of the SLA lie in a group of educated Darfurians who sought to organize villages into self-defense communities against the allies of the NIF. These defense communities were set up in the 1990s among Fur, Zaghawa, and Masalit villages. They were poorly equipped and coordinated, often refusing to help defend each other when attacked by Arab militias.[184] Disagreements between Zaghawa and Masalit leaders led to a lack of any coherent organization. This would change after 2001 when back-and-forth raids between the Arab Awlad Zeid tribe and the Zaghawa led to a spiral of armed escalation of conflict.[185]

Julie Flint and Alex de Waal place the genesis of the SLA at July 21, 2001. On that date Fur and Zaghawa delegations met at Abu Gamra and "swore a solemn oath on the Qur'an to work together to foil Arab supremacist policies in Darfur."[186] A later meeting with a Masalit group led to the formation of the Darfur Liberation Front (DLF), which was a defense pact between the three communities. The DLF sought assistance from Chad and the SPLA/SPLM. The former became an important source of weapons and vehicles, while the latter contributed weapons and training, and added a sense of developing a nationwide agenda and nationwide coordination of resistance to the Khartoum government.[187]

With the idea of a nationwide agenda in mind, the DLF changed its name to the Sudan Liberation Army (SLA) in February 2003. It was in that year that the SLA (at the same time as the JEM) managed a number of stunning military victories over the military and police. The tactics of the SLA rely on "small, loosely organized but highly mobile units of 4x4 pick-ups armed with heavy machine guns."[188] The NIF-led government took this threat seriously, retaliating with attacks, coordinated with the Janjaweed, against Darfurian villages. The resulting combat saw the dispersal of the SLA. It reconstituted into a force of roughly 10,000 strong by 2005. Presently, it remains divided along ethnic lines, primarily between the Zaghawa and Fur, as well as divided over a proper strategy to challenge the government.[189]

One of the Zaghawa leaders, Minni Minawari, was a signatory of the May 5, 2006, Darfur Peace Agreement (DPA). Since that time, Minni's position within the SLA has diminished while he officially is the fourth highest ranking official in the Sudanese government.[190] One of the reasons is that the Fur and Masalit tribes disagreed with the strategy of compromise embedded in the DPA and did not want any part of participating in an Arab-directed government. The second reason is that the level of violence and displacement in Darfur has continued to increase.[191] Since 2006 the SLA has splintered into a number of rival groups, with a general level of distrust between them that prevents effective coordination.

INTERNATIONAL LEVEL

The scope and number of international actors involved in the decades-long conflicts in Sudan are too great for an examination of all of them in any level of detail. This section selects a number of the more important international factors affecting primarily the Second Civil War (1983–2005) between the North and South, and also the current conflict and humanitarian crisis in Darfur and the Western Sudan (2003–). It highlights the international arming of the Sudanese government and rebels, the role of the United States both during and after the Cold War, the international condemnation of the Sudanese government's actions in Darfur, the participation of the African Union in peacekeeping missions, and examples of some more minor actors.

Military Supply of the Sudanese Government

The supply of military and dual-use aircraft to the Sudanese government has come from many sources. Amnesty International reports that Belarus supplied a half-dozen attack helicopters to Sudan in 1996, the People's Republic of China sold Sudan dozens of fighter aircraft and military helicopters, Iran helped finance the Sudanese purchase of military and transport aircraft, a company in Lithuania was involved with the repair of a number of Sudanese aircraft, Russia sold a dozen MiG-29 fighter aircraft, and a British company and a Ukrainian company entered into a contract to deliver cargo planes to Sudan.[192]

The supply of military ground vehicles and artillery by foreign countries is also prevalent. Belarus supplied the Sudanese government with close to four dozen military vehicles and over thirty artillery pieces, most of which were of Russian origin.[193] Most of these shipments occurred from 2001 to 2003. Bulgaria also delivered eighteen self-propelled howitzers, along with components of these and similar weapons, to the Sudanese government in 2001. In 1998 the sale of fifty T-55 tanks by Poland to Sudan was halted by pressure from the United States. However, in 1999 twenty T-55 tanks were transferred from Poland to Yemen and later illegally re-exported to Sudan. The Polish government, again under pressure from the United States, reported that while its delivery of a remaining thirty tanks was "to Yemen," it would cancel the delivery.[194] Finally, in 2004, a number of arms dealers in the Republic of Ireland and the United Kingdom were involved in the sale of rocket launchers, T-72 main battle tanks, armored personnel carriers, armored fighting vehicles, 130mm field guns, aircraft, and small arms to Sudan.[195] As mentioned in the previous section on domestic sources, the Sudanese government has paid for these weapons with its oil wealth.

Small arms, light weapons, and ammunition have been supplied by numerous countries. Included in the list of major contributors are the People's Republic of China, France, Iran, Saudi Arabia, Switzerland, Ukraine, the United Kingdom, and Brazil. Minor exporters of weapons to Sudan also include Cyprus, Greece, Germany, Austria, United Arab Emirates, Egypt, Yemen, Kuwait, and Qatar, perhaps underscoring the pervasive nature of the global arms trade.[196]

Arming of the opposition groups has been more sparse, mainly because of their inability to pay. Rebel groups have typically obtained arms by taking them from the Janjaweed, government forces, and police stations.[197] Arms from Chad and Libya have certainly been smuggled to the rebel groups. The NIF accuses Eritrea and Israel of shipping arms to the rebels, but these allegations have not been substantiated.[198]

European Union Arms Embargo

The European Union (EU) was quick to react to the outbreak of violence during the Second Civil War. The EU "Common Position 94/165/CFSP, adopted on 16 March 1994," slapped an arms embargo on Sudan. The embargo covered all weapons, ammunition, ancillary equipment, parts, repair, maintenance, and transfer of military material. Thus, the sale and/or transfer of material from an EU member-state to Sudan was prohibited.[199]

United States

While the September 9, 2004, testimony by U.S. secretary of state Colin Powell before the Senate Foreign Relations Committee declaring that the atrocities in Darfur were indeed genocide stands out as a moment in which U.S action played a role in the conflict, the truth is that the United States has been involved in Sudan for a very long time.[200] During the Nimeiri regime, and as part of the Cold War and the larger U.S. foreign policy stance toward the Horn of Africa, the United States (along with Egypt) provided military support to Sudan. This was done as a check against both Libya and Ethiopia.[201] Also, the United States Agency for International Development (USAID) maintained an office in Khartoum, even into the 1990s when there was no other direct U.S. representation in Sudan.[202]

The period from 1989 to 1995 was characterized by the United States responding to the pro-Islamic foreign policy of the NIF.[203] Initially the United States was neutral on the new al-Bashir–led government, but the Sudanese alignment with Iran in 1990 led to the United States declaring Sudan a supporter of terrorism.[204] The 1995 assassination attempt against the Egyptian president Mubarak led to the United States seeking sanctions against Sudan. While the United Nations took up the suggestion of sanctions, the resolutions that the UN finally passed were not severe and not as strong as desired by the United States. The difficulty for the United States was what to do next: support efforts to bring the Islamic regime to the negotiating table or to encourage and/or support the growing military confrontation with the South?[205]

In 1996 the United States "announced $20 million worth of military aid . . . to Eritrea, Ethiopia, and Uganda."[206] It appeared that this aid was to meet the perceived threat of Sudan. That some of the weapons might end up with the SPLA, especially given the group's connection to both Uganda and Ethiopia, was a certainty. The new, harder line of the United States was crystal clear when U.S. secretary of state Madeleine Albright met with SPLA leader General John Garang in Uganda in 1997.[207]

Attacks on U.S. embassies in Kenya and Tanzania in 1998 led to a U.S. response against Sudan. Suspecting Sudanese support for the terrorist acts, the United States launched Tomahawk cruise missiles at a pharmaceutical plant in

Khartoum, destroying it.[208] The United States had been aware of the Sudanese support of Islamic terrorist networks, including the al-Qaeda network of Osama bin Laden, who had been in Sudan until 1996, when he fled to Afghanistan fearing that the Sudanese government might turn him over to the United States.

The United States also stepped up its humanitarian assistance to Sudan following 1998. In 2000 it gave over $93 million in aid, and that number rose to more than $600 million by 2005, with $380 million in the Southern Sudan and at least $200 for Darfur.[209] The Bush administration in 2002 added the Southern Sudan Agricultural Revitalization Project and the Sudan Basic Education Program to its assistance programs. At the same time, the United States supported the talks sponsored by the Intergovernmental Authority on Development (IGAD) and the Comprehensive Peace Agreement between the Sudanese government and the Southern rebels. Thus, the United States pursued a dual-tactic approach to Sudan: humanitarian aid and support for peace initiatives while also taking a hard line toward the government's support of terrorism and providing tacit aid for the government's opponents. The conversion of the al-Bashir government to cooperation with the United States against terrorism in 2002 probably has little to do with any change in the Sudanese government's thinking about global Islamic movements and more to do with political survival vis-à-vis pressure from the United States.[210] In 2004 the State Department removed Sudan from the "non-cooperative" list in the war against terrorism, but President Bush maintained economic sanctions, mainly because of the continuing deterioration of conditions in Darfur.[211] The administration of President Barack Obama maintains the policy of seeking an end to the humanitarian crisis in Darfur. It endorses the implementation of a comprehensive peace agreement to ensure the long-term stability of Sudan.[212]

International Condemnation

The United Nations acted in 2004 through UN Security Council Resolution 1556 calling for an arms embargo against the Janjaweed.[213] This embargo was not very effective since it only prohibited direct sales to the Janjaweed. As long as the Sudanese government was the main supplier of the Janjaweed, weapons would still get to them. UN Security Council Resolution 1564 in September of 2004 called for the Sudanese government to protect civilians and to bring all Janjaweed to justice. The resolution even threatened UN sanctions against Sudan's petroleum industry if it did not comply.[214]

As noted earlier in the chapter, the UN Security Council did act more forcefully in August 2006 when it passed Resolution 1706. Resolution 1706 expanded the UNMIS mandate to deploy peacekeepers to Darfur in order to assist in the implementation of the Darfur Peace Agreement.[215] The UN Security Council responded further when it passed another resolution (1769) in July 2007 that created the UN African Union/United Nations Hybrid operation in Darfur (UNAMID). The mandate of this peacekeeping operation includes restoring security conditions such that humanitarian assistance can be provided throughout Darfur. In addition, the operation will ensure compliance with the various cease-fire agreements and help implement the terms of the Darfur Peace Agreement as well as any other future agreements.[216]

It should be noted that many members of the UN, especially Pakistan and China, were not convinced initially that the humanitarian crisis was sufficient to warrant a violation of Sudanese sovereignty. Russia argued that there was not enough reason to challenge the Sudanese government's position that it was safeguarding its citizens.[217] China and Russia maintained that only genocide would trump sovereignty, and international reluctance to use that word delayed UN action. When U.S. secretary of state Colin Powell announced that genocide was occurring in Darfur, it mobilized the international community.[218]

African Union

The African Union (AU) responded to the growing crisis in Darfur in 2003. It became involved first with the cease-fire negotiations and then in 2004 sent a delegation to Chad to participate more directly.[219] In April 2004 an agreement between the Sudanese Government, SLA, and JEM tasked the AU to establish a commission to oversee the cease-fire. In August 2004 the African Union deployed the African Mission in the Sudan (AMIS), which comprised 305 troops, to Darfur in order to monitor the cease-fire.[220]

As hostilities resumed shortly thereafter in 2004, the AU condemned the violation of the cease-fire, but its small force was incapable of effectively maintaining the cease-fire, let along monitor it. The AU agreed in late 2004 to extend the size of the AMIS by up to 3,500 troops. However, by January 2005 the AU was calling on the United Nations and other international parties "to exert constant pressure on all the parties [that is, the Sudanese government and the rebel groups] so that they abide by their commitments and extend full cooperation to AU efforts."[221] Despite squabbling among the members of the AU, and severe financial constraints, the AU had over 450 monitors and over 1,600 troops in Darfur by the end of 2005.[222]

The reaction to AU involvement has been mixed. It has been praised "for its leadership role and engagement in one of Africa's complex and dangerous conflicts . . . and for taking bold steps to stop fighting and stem the humanitarian crisis in Darfur."[223] One report cites the AMIS use of preventive deployments to villages to prevent future attacks, its use of accompaniment to protect women and children, its role in mediation, assistance to human rights officers, positive influence on local police, and advocacy against the use of child soldiers, as well as other positive contributions.[224] However, its weaknesses and failures include the inability to get AU members to contribute enough personnel and finances, its poor command and control, lack of rules of engagement, absence of standard operating procedures, poor coordination with other international groups, and insufficient impact of its monitoring functions, among other things.[225]

Other International Involvement: Some Minor Actors

Lord's Resistance Army. A number of other groups play a small part in the troubles in Sudan. One example is the Lord's Resistance Army (LRA). This rebel group has operated in resistance to the government of Uganda since 1987. Led by Joseph Kony, a self-described messenger of God, this armed group of roughly three thousand has terrorized both Northern Uganda and Southern Sudan. In the 1990s the Khartoum government tolerated the presence of the LRA "to undermine the SPLM, and to retaliate against the government of Uganda for its support of the SPLM/A."[226] The International Criminal Court (ICC) has issued arrest warrants for Kony and most of the LRA leaders. In 2005–2006 the government of Southern Sudan tried to mediate between the LRA and Uganda. In 2007 President al-Bashir "demanded the group's departure from the country."[227]

The LRA is a good example of how porous borders and movements can be in Africa. Because most states are weak and cannot effectively control their borders, rebel or governmental paramilitaries from one country can easily cross over into another without repercussion. Moreover, the existence of ethnic relations between groups living on either side of the border can lend support to these migrating militias. Thus, armed opposition to a government can often be seen as the creation of, or at least related to, the weakness of a neighboring state.[228] Such is the case with the LRA and, correspondingly, the SPLM. The Ugandan government accuses Sudan of supporting the LRA, while the Sudanese government accuses Uganda of allowing the SPLM to base in Uganda at best, and actually using Ugandan armed forces personnel in the SPLM at worst.[229]

People's Republic of China. China's interest in Africa expanded greatly with the end of the Cold War. Specifically, China launched a "corporate engagement" strategy toward Africa that picked up steam after 2000. Through this strategy, China combines "economic assistance, debt relief, and expanding market access for African states" to get more engagement with African states.[230] By 2007 China had at least 7,000 enterprises operating in 160 countries, including ten centers for the promotion of trade in Sub-Saharan Africa. Specific to Sudan, "13 of the 15 largest foreign companies operating are Chinese, primarily in the oil industry."[231]

This connection between China and Sudan created international pressure on China to help deal with the conflict in Darfur. Officially, China supports the African Union and the AMIS. However, it still uses its position on the United Nations Security Council to prevent any actions by the United States or United Kingdom calling for greater sanctions against the Sudanese government.[232]

NGOs. A number of international nongovernmental organizations (NGOs) operated within Sudan prior to the recent conflict in Darfur. For example, Operation Lifeline Sudan (which was established by the UN in 1989) and Norwegian People's Aid were in Southern Sudan during the Second Civil War.[233] NGOs have typically provided humanitarian relief, but they have a complex relationship in the Sudanese conflicts. Both the government forces and the rebels have diverted aid to their supporters and armies. Moreover, both view relief agencies as a political presence "as if competing with a rival power or even [a] hostile enemy."[234]

Action since 2004 has taken many different forms. Efforts to either provide relief in Darfur or to move governments to take more direct action have been put forth by the NAACP, Save Darfur Coalition, Amnesty International, International Medical Corps, American Red Cross, International Rescue Community, UNICEF, Medecins sans Frontieres, and dozens of others.

Other African Nations. It should be clear from the discussion above that Ethiopia, Chad, and Uganda have certainly been involved in funding and/or supporting various rebel movements in Sudan. In particular, the Ethiopian support of the SPLA was clear, with Ethiopian forces being implicated in the bombing of a town in the South to help rebel forces.[235] The overthrow of Mengistu in Ethiopia in 1991 led to the eviction of SPLA forces from Ethiopian land and a rapprochement between Sudan and Ethiopia. The assassination attempt against Mubarak in 1995 led to distancing between the two governments and renewed Ethiopian assistance to the SPLA. In 1997 Sudanese president al-Bashir accused Ethiopia of sending hundreds of troops across the border into Sudan to assist the SPLA, a charge that Ethiopia denied.[236] The deterioration of Ethiopia into the status of a failed state in the 2000s has led to a decline in the Ethiopian concern with events in Sudan.

CONCLUSION

This chapter has provided an examination of the many conflicts in Sudan with an eye toward the use of the levels of analysis as an organizing guide. While the crisis in the Darfur region gets international attention, the complexity of the decades-long North vs. South civil wars and the Arab vs. African, tribe vs. tribe, and Muslim vs. the rest dimensions of this conflict should now be a bit better understood. The context of the humanitarian crisis in Darfur is structured by these long-term antagonisms, and a solution to the ethnic conflict and cycles of violence can only succeed if it addresses the many factors that drive the societies in Sudan toward war.

In particular, we examined the leadership styles of two of the major figures (President al-Bashir and General Garang) in the context of the leadership theories in chapter 2. We identified the spoiler role that each plays and how that has prolonged the conflict. Much as in Northern Ireland, the Comprehensive Peace Agreement (and the Protocols that preceded it) contains consociational elements. The new power-sharing government and the semi-autonomous nature of the new government of South Sudan are clearly intended to promote cooperation among elites while maintaining a degree of cultural/ethnic/regional distinction. In chapter 2 we highlighted the critics who refute the usefulness of consociational agreements, especially Horowitz and his argument that ethnofederalism only promotes the breakup of the state. In this light, it remains to be seen whether the new CPA can bring harmony to the North-South division in Sudan.

At the international level, intervention by the African Union as a third-party mediator did not resolve the crisis in Darfur. International organizations often find it much more difficult to successfully mediate conflicts than an individual state actor. The failure of the United Nations and the African Union to commit sufficient resources and peacekeepers to Darfur and to end the violence is a good example of this limit. Moreover, the pattern of coercive intervention by international actors, such as the European Union's arms embargo and the United Nations' sanctions, has had little impact on the NIF-led government's policy toward Darfur.

NOTES

1. M. W. Daly, *Darfur's Sorrow: A History of Destruction and Genocide* (Cambridge: Cambridge University Press, 2007), 281.
2. William R. Jeffries, "Timeline of Darfur Events," in *The Darfur Crisis,* ed. William R. Jeffries (New York: Nova Science Publishers, 2008), Appendix 2.
3. Molly J. Miller, "The Crisis in Darfur," in *Mediterranean Quarterly* 18, no. 4 (2007): 112–130.
4. Daly, *Darfur's Sorrow,* 281–282.

5. Ted Dagne and Bathsheaba Everett, "Sudan: The Darfur Crisis and the Status of the North-South Negotiations," in *The Darfur Crisis,* ed. William R. Jeffries (New York: Nova Science Publishers, 2008), 1–2.

6. Dagne and Everett, "Sudan: The Darfur Crisis and the Status of the North-South Negotiations," 3.

7. Daly, *Darfur's Sorrow,* 283.

8. Daly, *Darfur's Sorrow,* 283–284.

9. United Nations, International Commission of Inquiry on Darfur, *Report to the Secretary-General,* Geneva, January 25, 2005.

10. Human Rights Watch, "Darfur Destroyed: Ethnic Cleansing by Government and Militia Forces in Western Sudan," *Human Rights Watch* 16, no. 6A (May 2004).

11. Daly, *Darfur's Sorrow,* 284.

12. Daly, *Darfur's Sorrow,* 285.

13. Dagne and Everett, "Sudan: The Darfur Crisis and the Status of the North-South Negotiations," 4.

14. Miller, "The Crisis in Darfur," 112–130.

15. Dagne and Everett, "Sudan: The Darfur Crisis and the Status of the North-South Negotiations," 6.

16. Dagne and Everett, "Sudan: The Darfur Crisis and the Status of the North-South Negotiations," 10.

17. Dagne and Everett, "Sudan: The Darfur Crisis and the Status of the North-South Negotiations," 14.

18. Dagne and Everett, "Sudan: The Darfur Crisis and the Status of the North-South Negotiations," 7.

19. Jeffries, "Timeline of Darfur Events," Appendix 2.

20. Dagne and Everett, "Sudan: The Darfur Crisis and the Status of the North-South Negotiations," 8.

21. Dagne and Everett, "Sudan: The Darfur Crisis and the Status of the North-South Negotiations," 12.

22. Daly, *Darfur's Sorrow,* 300–301.

23. Daly, *Darfur's Sorrow,* 302.

24. United Nations Mission in the Sudan, "Sudan—UNMIS—Background" (United Nations, 2008), 9–10, www.un.org/depts./dpko/missions/unmis/background.html.

25. UNAMID: African Union/United Nations Hybrid Operation in Darfur, "Darfur—UNAMID—Mandate" (United Nations, 2008), 1, www.un.org/depts/dpko/missions/unamid/mandate.html.

26. "Peacekeepers into the Fray," *The Economist*, March 13, 2008, www .economist.com/world/middleeast-africa/displaystory.cfm?story_id= E1_TDRVPJRS.

27. Human Rights Watch, "They Shot at Us as We Fled: Government Attacks on Civilians in West Darfur in February 2008" (New York: Human Rights Watch, May 2008), www.hrw.org/en/reports/2008/05/18/they-shot-us-we-fled; Office of UN Deputy Special Representative of the UN Secretary-General for Sudan, UN Resident and Humanitarian Co-ordinator, *Darfur Humanitarian Profile No. 33* (United Nations, October 1, 2008), www.un sudanig.org/docs/DHP33_narrative_1%20October%202008.pdf, 3.

28. Office of UN Deputy Special Representative of the UN Secretary-General for Sudan, UN Resident and Humanitarian Co-ordinator, *Darfur Humanitarian Profile No. 32* (United Nations, July 1, 2008), 3; and *Darfur Humanitarian Profile No. 33* (United Nations, October 1, 2008), 3.

29. Francis M. Deng, *War of Visions: Conflicts of Identities in the Sudan* (Washington, D.C.: Brookings Institution, 1995).

30. Peter Verney, *Sudan: Conflict and Minorities* (London: Minority Rights Group, 1995), 5.

31. Verney, *Sudan,* 12.

32. Daly, *Darfur's Sorrow,* 183.

33. Verney, *Sudan,* 12.

34. Verney, *Sudan,* 12.

35. Verney, *Sudan,* 13.

36. Douglas H. Johnson, "Darfur: Peace, Genocide, and Crimes against Humanity in Sudan," in *Violence, Political Culture and Development in Africa,* ed. Preben Kaarsholm (Athens: Ohio University Press, 2006), 94.

37. Johnson, "Darfur," 94.

38. Verney, *Sudan,* 14.

39. Verney, *Sudan,* 14–16.

40. Verney, *Sudan,* 15.

41. Verney, *Sudan,* 16–17.

42. Johnson, "Darfur," 99–101.

43. Johnson, "Darfur," 10.

44. Johnson, "Darfur," 97–98.

45. Dagne and Everett, "Sudan: The Darfur Crisis and the Status of the North-South Negotiations," 16.

46. Hunt Alternatives Fund, "Sudan," www.huntalternatives.org/pages/7656_sudan.cfm.

47. Alex de Waal, "Sudan: The Turbulent State," in *War in Darfur and the Search for Peace*, ed. Alex de Waal (Cambridge, Mass.: Harvard University, Global Equity Initiative, 2007), 1.

48. United States Government Accountability Office (GAO), "Darfur Crisis: Death Estimates Demonstrate Severity of Crisis, but Their Accuracy and Credibility Could Be Enhanced" (Washington, D.C.: GAO, November 2006), 5.

49. Fouad Ibrahim, "Introduction to the Conflict in Darfur/West Sudan," in *Explaining Darfur: Four Lectures on the Ongoing Genocide*, ed. Agnes van Ardenne–van der Hoeven et al. (Amsterdam: Vossiuspers UvA, 2006), 12.

50. Ibrahim, "Introduction to the Conflict in Darfur/West Sudan," 13.

51. Jerome Tubiana, "Darfur: A Conflict for Land?" in *War in Darfur and the Search for Peace*, ed. Alex de Waal (Cambridge, Mass.: Harvard University, Global Equity Initiative, 2007), 70.

52. James D. Fearon and David D. Laitin, "Violence and the Social Construction of Ethnic Identity," *International Organization* 54, no. 4 (Autumn 2000): 858.

53. Deborah Murphy, "Narrating Darfur: Darfur in the U.S. Press, March–September 2004," in *War in Darfur and the Search for Peace*, ed. Alex de Waal (Cambridge, Mass.: Harvard University, Global Equity Initiative, 2007), 314–336.

54. Tubiana, "Darfur: A Conflict for Land?" 73.

55. Tubiana, "Darfur: A Conflict for Land?" 90–91.

56. Chandra Lekha Sriram, *Peace as Governance: Power-Sharing, Armed Groups, and Contemporary Peace Negotiations* (New York: Palgrave, 2008), 126.

57. "An End to the War?" *The Economist*, October 22, 2008, www.economist .com/agenda/PrinterFriendly.cfm?story_id=12454123. In 2005 the UN Security Council requested that the ICC investigate al-Bashir's actions in Darfur to determine whether he was responsible for crimes against humanity, genocide, and war crimes. In July 2008 the ICC prosecutor presented evidence that al-Bashir was indeed criminally responsible for these actions and requested an arrest warrant. International Criminal Court, "ICC Prosecutor Presents Cases against Sudanese President, Hassan Ahmad AL BASHIR, for Genocide, Crimes against Humanity and War Crimes in Darfur" (July 14, 2008), www.icc-cpi.int/menus/icc/situations%20and%20 cases/situations/situation%20icc%200205/press%20releases/a.

58. Office of UN Deputy Special Representative of the UN Secretary-General for Sudan, UN Resident and Humanitarian Co-ordinator, *Darfur Humanitarian Profile No. 32*, 4.

59. United States Government Accountability Office (GAO), "Darfur Crisis," 1–2, 20.

60. United States Government Accountability Office (GAO), "Darfur Crisis," 1–2.

61. United States Government Accountability Office (GAO), "Darfur Crisis," 1.

62. United States Government Accountability Office (GAO), "Darfur Crisis," 10–11.

63. United States Government Accountability Office (GAO), "Darfur Crisis," 65–66.

64. UNAMID, "Darfur—UNAMID—Background" (United Nations, 2008), www.un.org/depts/dpko/missions/unamid/background.html.

65. Richard A. Lobban Jr., Robert S. Kramer, and Carolyn Fluehr-Lobban, *Historical Dictionary of the Sudan*, 3rd ed. (Lanham, Md.: Scarecrow Press, 2002), 449.

66. Lobban et al., *Historical Dictionary of the Sudan*, 49.

67. Deng, *War of Visions*, 169–179.

68. Lobban et al., *Historical Dictionary of the Sudan*, 50.

69. Lobban et al., *Historical Dictionary of the Sudan*, 50.

70. Lobban et al., *Historical Dictionary of the Sudan*, 298.

71. Lobban et al., *Historical Dictionary of the Sudan*, 51.

72. Donald Petterson, *Inside Sudan: Political Islam, Conflict, and Catastrophe* (Boulder: Westview Press, 1999), 15.

73. Petterson, *Inside Sudan*, 15.

74. Petterson, *Inside Sudan*, 15.

75. Petterson, *Inside Sudan*, 39.

76. Petterson, *Inside Sudan*, 105.

77. Daly, *Darfur's Sorrow*, 281.

78. Nsongurua J. Udombana, "When Neutrality Is a Sin: The Darfur Crisis and the Crisis of Humanitarian Intervention in Sudan," *Human Rights Quarterly* 27 (2005): 1156.

79. Mahgoub El-Tigani Mahmoud, "Inside Darfur: Ethnic Genocide by a Governance Crisis," *Comparative Studies of South Asia, Africa, and the Middle East* 24, no. 2 (2004): 7.

80. Roger P. Winter, "Sudan and the National Congress Party," *Mediterranean Quarterly* 18, no. 2 (2007): 64.

81. "Warrant Issued for Sudan's Leader," *BBC*, March 4, 2009, http://news.bbc.co.uk/2/hi/7923102.stm.

82. El Tahir Adam El Faki, "Why Is the National Congress Party So Keen for Elections?" SSRC Blogs, Making Sense of Darfur (November 7, 2008), www.ssrc.org/blogs/darfur/2008/11/07/why-is-the-national-congress-party-so-keen-for-elections/.

83. Lobban et al., *Historical Dictionary of the Sudan*, 106–107.

84. Lobban et al., *Historical Dictionary of the Sudan*, 106–107.

85. Petterson, *Inside Sudan,* 59.
86. Petterson, *Inside Sudan,* 59.
87. Deng, *War of Visions,* 172–173.
88. Lobban et al., *Historical Dictionary of the Sudan,* 107.
89. Deng, *War of Visions,* 173
90. Lobban et al., *Historical Dictionary of the Sudan,* 279.
91. Verney, *Sudan,* 14.
92. Lobban et al., *Historical Dictionary of the Sudan,* 280.
93. Lobban et al., *Historical Dictionary of the Sudan,* 281.
94. Sriram, *Peace as Governance,* 119.
95. Sriram, *Peace as Governance,* 120.
96. Sriram, *Peace as Governance,* 122.
97. Sriram, *Peace as Governance,* 122.
98. Petterson, *Inside Sudan,* 53–59.
99. Alex De Waal, "Who Are the Darfurians? Arab and African Identities, Violence and External Engagement," *African Affairs* 104 (2005): 181–205.
100. De Waal, "Who Are the Darfurians?" 186–187.
101. De Waal, "Who Are the Darfurians?" 185.
102. Amir H. Idris, *Conflict and Politics of the Identity in Sudan* (New York: Palgrave, 2005), 15.
103. De Waal, "Who Are the Darfurians?" 183–86.
104. De Waal, "Who Are the Darfurians?" 186–87.
105. De Waal, "Who Are the Darfurians?" 188.
106. Gabriel Warburg, "Religious and Ethnic Conflict in Sudan: Can National Unity Survive?" in *Ethnic Conflict and International Politics in the Middle East,* ed. Leonard Binder (Gainesville: University Press of Florida, 1999), 110–128.
107. Warburg, "Religious and Ethnic Conflict in Sudan," 110–111.
108. Warburg, "Religious and Ethnic Conflict in Sudan," 111.
109. Warburg, "Religious and Ethnic Conflict in Sudan," 110–111.
110. Heather J. Sharkey, "Arab Identity and Ideology in Sudan: The Politics of Language, Ethnicity, and Race," *African Affairs* 107, no. 426 (2008): 21–43.
111. Warburg, "Religious and Ethnic Conflict in Sudan," 110–115.
112. De Waal, "Who Are the Darfurians?" 192.
113. De Waal, "Who Are the Darfurians?" 193.
114. Jay O'Brien, "Power and the Discourse of Ethnicity in Sudan," in *Ethnicity and the State in Eastern Africa,* ed. M. A. Mohamed Salih and John Markakis (Uppsala, Sweden: Nordiska Afrikainstitutet, 1998), 62–71.
115. R. S. O'Fahey, "Islam and Ethnicity in the Sudan," *Journal of Religion in Africa* 26, no. 3 (1996): 260.
116. De Waal, "Who Are the Darfurians?" 197.

117. De Waal, "Who Are the Darfurians?" 198.
118. Warburg, "Religious and Ethnic Conflict in Sudan," 119–123.
119. M. A. Mohamed Salih, "Political Narratives and Identity Formation in Post-1989 Sudan," in *Ethnicity and the State in Eastern Africa,* ed. M. A. Mohamed Salih and John Markakis (Uppsala: Nordiska Afrikainstitutet, 1998), 74.
120. De Waal, "Who Are the Darfurians?" 194.
121. Elfatih A. A/Salam, "The Politicization of Ethnic Sentiments in the Sudan: Implications for Nation-Building," *Journal of Third World Studies* 25, no. 1 (2008): 118.
122. Audrey Macklin, "Like Oil and Water, with a Match: Militarized Commerce, Armed Conflict, and Human Security in Sudan," in *Sites of Violence: Gender and Conflict Zones,* ed. Wenona Giles and Jennifer Hyndman (Berkeley: University of California Press, 2004), 83. It was in 1983 that the leader, Nimeiri, passed the "September Laws." These laws declared the country an Islamic republic and inaugurated enforcement of sharia law. With Nimeiri's overthrow in 1985, the Islamic "project" was left unfinished. The NIF's rule attempted to complete the Islamicization of the country. Sondra Hale, "The Rise of Islam and Women of the National Islamic Front in Sudan," *Review of African Political Economy* 54 (July 1992): 30, 32.
123. Macklin, "Like Oil and Water, with a Match," 83; Human Rights Watch, "Sudan Blasted on Women's Ban" (September 8, 2000), www.hrw.org/en/news/2000/09/08/sudan-blasted-womens-ban.
124. Human Rights Watch, "Sudan Blasted on Women's Ban."
125. Macklin, "Like Oil and Water, with a Match," 83.
126. Hale, "The Rise of Islam and Women of the National Islamic Front in Sudan," 28.
127. Human Rights Watch, "Sudan Blasted on Women's Ban."
128. Macklin, "Like Oil and Water, with a Match," 91.
129. Macklin, "Like Oil and Water, with a Match," 83.
130. Macklin, "Like Oil and Water, with a Match," 84.
131. Macklin, "Like Oil and Water, with a Match," 94.
132. Macklin, "Like Oil and Water, with a Match," 87.
133. Macklin, "Like Oil and Water, with a Match," 94.
134. Sam Dealey, "Who Speaks for Her?" *Time*, August 28, 2005, www.time.com/time/magazine/article/0,9171,1098951,00.html.
135. Anne Itto, "Guests at the Table? The Role of Women in Peace Processes," *Conciliation Resources* (2006), www.c-r.org/our-work/accord/sudan/women.php.
136. Hunt Alternatives Fund, "Sudan," www.huntalternatives.org/pages/7656_sudan.cfm. For an overview of the DPA, and the challenges still present for

its implementation, see International Crisis Group, "Darfur: Revitalizing the Peace Process" (April 30, 2007), www.crisisgroup.org/home/index .cfm?id=4769.

137. Itto, "Guests at the Table?"

138. Femmes Africa Solidarite, "FAS Brings Sudan Women to the African Union, Advocates for Gender-Sensitive Peace Process" (January 2008), 1, 4, www.fasngo.org/assets/files/publicatons/FAS%20News%20January%20 2008.pdf.

139. Shashank Bengali, "For Africa, 2008 a Year to Forget," *Christian Science Monitor*, January 2, 2009, www.csmonitor.com/2009/0102/p25s07-woaf .html.

140. Roger P. Winter, "Sudan and the National Congress Party," *Mediterranean Quarterly* 18, no. 2 (2007): 61.

141. El-Tigani Mahmoud, "Inside Darfur," 3–17.

142. El-Tigani Mahmoud, "Inside Darfur," 6.

143. Daly, *Darfur's Sorrow*, 248–249.

144. Daly, *Darfur's Sorrow*, 248–249.

145. Daly, *Darfur's Sorrow*, 261.

146. Gerard Prunier, *Darfur: The Ambiguous Genocide* (Ithaca: Cornell University Press, 2007), 81–91.

147. Daly, *Darfur's Sorrow*, 290.

148. Abdullahi A. Gallab, "The Insecure Rendezvous between Islam and Totalitarianism: The Failure of the Islamist State in the Sudan," *Arab Studies Quarterly* 23, no. 2 (Spring 2001): 87.

149. Gallab, "The Insecure Rendezvous between Islam and Totalitarianism," 87.

150. Gallab, "The Insecure Rendezvous between Islam and Totalitarianism," 98.

151. Maghoub El-Tigani Mahmoud, "Solving the Crisis of Sudan: The Right of Self-Determination versus State Torture," *Arab Studies Quarterly* 23, no. 2 (Spring 2001): 41.

152. Monica Duffy Toft, "Getting Religion? The Puzzling Case of Islam and Civil War," *International Security* 31, no. 4 (2007): 97–131.

153. Toft, "Getting Religion?" 97–131.

154. Toft, "Getting Religion?" 124.

155. El-Tigani Mahmoud, "Inside Darfur," 7.

156. Human Rights Watch, "Darfur Destroyed," 44–45.

157. Amnesty International, *Sudan: Arming the Perpetrators of Grave Abuses in Darfur* (London: Amnesty International, November 2004), 10–11.

158. Amnesty International, *Sudan: Arming the Perpetrators of Grave Abuses in Darfur*, 11–13.

159. Amnesty International, *Sudan: Arming the Perpetrators of Grave Abuses in Darfur,* 15.

160. Amnesty International, *Sudan: Arming the Perpetrators of Grave Abuses in Darfur,* 20-21.

161. Amnesty International, *Sudan: Arming the Perpetrators of Grave Abuses in Darfur,* 41.

162. Amnesty International, *Sudan: Arming the Perpetrators of Grave Abuses in Darfur,* 41.

163. Amnesty International, *Sudan: Arming the Perpetrators of Grave Abuses in Darfur,* 41.

164. David J. Francis, "Introduction," in *Civil Militia: Africa's Intractable Security Menace?* ed. David J. Francis (Aldershot: Ashgate, 2005), 2.

165. Usman Tar, "Counter-Insurgents or Ethnic Vanguards? Civil Militia and State Violence in Darfur Region, Western Sudan," in *Civil Militia: Africa's Intractable Security Menace?* ed. David J. Francis (Aldershot: Ashgate, 2005), 135.

166. Tar, "Counter-Insurgents or Ethnic Vanguards?" 135-136.

167. Tar, "Counter-Insurgents or Ethnic Vanguards?" 138-140.

168. Tar, "Counter-Insurgents or Ethnic Vanguards?" 147.

169. Tar, "Counter-Insurgents or Ethnic Vanguards?" 148.

170. Tar, "Counter-Insurgents or Ethnic Vanguards?" 149.

171. Tar, "Counter-Insurgents or Ethnic Vanguards?" 149.

172. Claire Metelits, "Reformed Rebels? Democratization, Global Norms, and the Sudan People's Liberation Army," *Africa Today* 11, no. 1 (Fall 2004): 66.

173. Metelits, "Reformed Rebels?" 70.

174. Ruth Iyob and Gilbert M. Khadiagala, *Sudan: The Elusive Quest for Peace* (Boulder: Lynne Rienner, 2006), 167-177.

175. Verney, *Sudan,* 16.

176. Metelits, "Reformed Rebels?" 71.

177. Metelits, "Reformed Rebels?" 78.

178. International Crisis Group (ICG), "Sudan: Organising for Peace as the War Escalates," Africa Report 48 (Nairobi/Brussels: ICG, June 27, 2002).

179. Dagne and Everett, "Sudan: The Darfur Crisis and the Status of the North-South Negotiations," 15.

180. Marc Weller, "Self-Governance in Interim Settlements: The Case of Sudan," in *Autonomy, Self-Governance, and Conflict Resolution: Innovative Approaches to Institutional Design in Divided Societies,* ed. Marc Weller and Stefan Wolff (New York: Routledge, 2005), 166.

181. Daly, *Darfur's Sorrow,* 273.

182. Timothy Carney, *Some Assembly Required: Sudan's Comprehensive Peace Agreement,* Special Report 194 (Washington D.C.: United States Institute of Peace, November 2007), 7–8

183. CIA World Factbook Online, https://www.cia.gov/library/publications/the-world-factbook/geos/su.html

184. Victor Tanner and Jerome Tubiana, *Divided They Fall: The Fragmentation of Darfur's Rebel Groups* (Geneva: Small Arms Survey, 2007), 17.

185. Tanner and Tubiana, *Divided They Fall,* 18–19.

186. Julie Flint and Alex de Waal, *Darfur: A Short History of a Long War* (London: Zed Books, 2005), 76.

187. Tanner and Tubiana, *Divided They Fall,* 21–22.

188. Tanner and Tubiana, *Divided They Fall,* 37.

189. Tanner and Tubiana, *Divided They Fall,* 25–29.

190. Tanner and Tubiana, *Divided They Fall,* 40.

191. Tanner and Tubiana, *Divided They Fall,* 42–43.

192. Amnesty International, *Sudan: Arming the Perpetrators of Grave Abuses in Darfur,* 16–20.

193. Amnesty International, *Sudan: Arming the Perpetrators of Grave Abuses in Darfur,* 21–22.

194. Amnesty International, *Sudan: Arming the Perpetrators of Grave Abuses in Darfur,* 23–24.

195. Amnesty International, *Sudan: Arming the Perpetrators of Grave Abuses in Darfur,* 24–25.

196. Amnesty International, *Sudan: Arming the Perpetrators of Grave Abuses in Darfur,* 30–33.

197. Amnesty International, *Sudan: Arming the Perpetrators of Grave Abuses in Darfur,* 36–37.

198. Amnesty International, *Sudan: Arming the Perpetrators of Grave Abuses in Darfur,* 36–37.

199. Amnesty International, *Sudan: Arming the Perpetrators of Grave Abuses in Darfur,* 8.

200. Dagne and Everett, "Sudan: The Darfur Crisis and the Status of the North-South Negotiations," 14.

201. Verney, *Sudan,* 14.

202. Peter Woodward, *US Foreign Policy and the Horn of Africa* (Aldershot: Ashgate, 2006), 5.

203. Woodward, *US Foreign Policy and the Horn of Africa,* 93.

204. Verney, *Sudan,* 19.

205. Woodward, *US Foreign Policy and the Horn of Africa,* 97.

206. Woodward, *US Foreign Policy and the Horn of Africa*, 97.

207. Woodward, *US Foreign Policy and the Horn of Africa*, 98–99.

208. Woodward, *US Foreign Policy and the Horn of Africa*, 104.

209. Ted Dagne and Bathsheaba Everett, "Sudan: Humanitarian Crisis, Peace Talks, Terrorism, and U.S. Policy," in *The Darfur Crisis*, ed. William R. Jeffries (New York: Nova Science Publishers, 2008), 31–32.

210. Greg Collins, "Incorporating Africa's Conflicts into the War on Terror," *Peace Review: A Journal of Social Justice* 19 (2007): 399.

211. Dagne and Everett, "Sudan: Humanitarian Crisis, Peace Talks, Terrorism, and U.S. Policy," 39.

212. "Foreign Policy," Office of the President, United States Government, www.whitehouse.gov/issues/foreign-policy.

213. Amnesty International, *Sudan: Arming the Perpetrators of Grave Abuses in Darfur*, 8.

214. Amnesty International, *Sudan: Arming the Perpetrators of Grave Abuses in Darfur*, 9.

215. United Nations Mission in the Sudan, "Sudan—UNMIS—Background," 9–10.

216. UNAMID, "Darfur—UNAMID—Mandate," 1.

217. Alex J. Bellamy and Paul D. Williams, "The UN Security Council and the Question of Humanitarian Intervention in Darfur," *Journal of Military Ethics* 5, no. 2 (2006): 150.

218. Hugo Slim, "Dithering over Darfur? A Preliminary Review of the International Response," *International Affairs* 80, no. 5 (2004): 811–828.

219. Dagne and Everett, "Sudan: The Darfur Crisis and the Status of the North-South Negotiations," 7.

220. Dagne and Everett, "Sudan: The Darfur Crisis and the Status of the North-South Negotiations," 1.

221. African Union, "Communique of the Twenty-Third Meeting of the Peace and Security Council, 10 January 2005," *The African Union and the Conflict in the Darfur Region of the Sudan* (Addis Ababa: African Union), 61.

222. African Union, "Appendix A," *The African Union and the Conflict in the Darfur Region of the Sudan* (Addis Ababa: African Union), 91.

223. Peter Kagwanja and Patrick Mutahi, "Protection of Civilians in African Peace Missions: The Case of the African Union Mission in Sudan, Darfur," ISS Paper 139 (Pretoria: Institute for Security Studies, May 2007), 14.

224. William G. O'Neill and Violette Cassis, "Protecting Two Million Internally Displaced: The Successes and Shortcomings of the African Union in Darfur," occasional paper (University of Bern, November 2005), 22–34.

225. O'Neill and Cassis, "Protecting Two Million Internally Displaced," 34–42.

226. Sriram, *Peace as Governance*, 133.

227. Sriram, *Peace as Governance*, 134.

228. Samson S. Wasara, "Conflict and State Security in the Horn of Africa: Militarization of Civilian Groups," *African Journal of Political Science* 7, no. 2 (2002): 39–59.

229. Wasara, "Conflict and State Security in the Horn of Africa," 48–49.

230. Bates Gill and James Reilly, "The Tenuous Hold of China Inc. in Africa," *Washington Quarterly* 30, no. 3 (2007): 38.

231. Gill and Reilly, "The Tenuous Hold of China Inc. in Africa," 40.

232. Collins, "Incorporating Africa's Conflicts into the War on Terror," 401.

233. Volker Riehl, *Who Is Ruling in South Sudan? The Role of NGOs in Rebuilding Socio-Political Order* (Uppsala, Sweden: Nordiska Afrikainstitutet, 2001), 6.

234. Riehl, *Who Is Ruling in South Sudan?* 7.

235. Yhudit Ronen, "Ethiopia's Involvement in the Sudanese Civil War: Was It as Significant as Khartoum Claimed?" *Northeast African Studies* 9, no. 1 (2002): 111.

236. Ronen, "Ethiopia's Involvement in the Sudanese Civil War," 118.

CHAPTER 6

Sri Lanka: Protracted Rebellion

In the Pakistani city of Lahore on March 3, 2009, a group of gunmen fired upon a tour bus carrying the Sri Lankan national cricket team to the Gaddafi Stadium, which was just a short distance away from where the attack occurred at the Liberty Square circle. The result of the attack was six dead Pakistani policemen and bus driver while eight members of the Sri Lankan cricket team were injured. In the aftermath of the attacks, the Pakistani president, Asif Ali Zardari, vowed to punish those who participated in the attacks. He also said that while the attack was a serious setback, it would not harm relations between Pakistan and Sri Lanka.[1]

Just about a month earlier and a short distance away on the island of Sri Lanka, the Sri Lankan Army captured the city of Mullaitivu, the last of the strongholds held by the Tamil in the northeast of the country.[2] The city was the center of the Tamil's military power, estimated to be roughly a few thousand soldiers or, as they are colloquially known, the "Tigers."[3] The fall of Mullaitivu came a few weeks after the Sri Lankan Army's conquest in early January of Kilinochchi, the de facto capital of the Liberation Tigers of Tamil Eelam (LTTE).[4] In both instances, the rebel Tigers had melted away into the jungle along with the civilian population of the area, leaving the towns deserted. The Sri Lankan military offensive in early 2009 effectively pushed the rebels into a small piece of territory. The rebels, who at one time controlled 15,000 square kilometers of territory, held only 300 square meters (or 3,230 square feet) by mid-May 2009.[5] On May 17, 2009, Selvarasa Pathmanathan, the LTTE's head of International Diplomatic Relations, announced on the pro-Tamil website, TamilNet.com, "Despite our plea to the world to save the thousands of people in Vanni from the clutches of death, the silence of the international community has only encouraged the Sri Lankan military to execute the war to its bitter end. . . . To save the lives of our people is the need of the hour. Mindful of this, we have already announced to the world our position to silence our guns to save our people."[6] The following day, Monday, May 18, 2009, the Sri Lankan government declared that the leader of the LTTE, Velupillai Prabhakaran, was killed by military forces (as well as other leaders of the organization).[7] With this declaration, the government proclaimed the end of the twenty-six-year civil war.

The Norwegian-brokered cease-fire of 2002 was ended by the government in 2008, which foreshadowed the early 2009 military offensive. The cease-fire led to on-again, off-again talks between the Sri Lankan government and the representatives of the rebel Tamil minority. In a breakthrough, the LTTE abandoned its demand for a separate Tamil state.[8] The Tigers had pulled out of the talks twice, and both sides accused the other of acts that breached the cease-fire on numerous occasions.

The start of the recent round of violence most likely linked back to the November 2005 election and Sri Lankan president Mahinda Rajapaksa's declaration ruling out any Tamil autonomy in the north and east of the island. The military offensives of 2007 and 2008 made progress, eliminating some Tamil control of both the north and east. The offensive of 2009 generated more success than the previous governmental campaigns—the Tamils announced the end of military rebellion against the government. The reasons for this appeared to be increased government spending on the military, international help in cutting off funding for the Tamil rebels, and greater joint Sri Lanka–India naval patrols to stop gun-running to the island.[9]

Of course, there is a dramatic civilian toll of this latest round of violence. The United Nations estimates that between 70,000 and 200,000 civilians are caught in the current war zones. The international organization also estimates that thousands of civilians have been killed.[10] India announced that it would send a medical team to the region to aid displaced populations. This would be the first official Indian presence since the end of its failed peacekeeping mission in 1987–1990.[11]

Then there is the matter of what is next for the rebels. The LTTE was born as a guerilla movement in the 1970s seeking independence for the Tamil minority, and it very well could return to guerilla warfare against the government assuming new leaders come to the fore. There is also the matter of a political settlement of the disputes between the Tamil minority and the Sinhalese majority. Without some sort of agreement between the former separatists and the government, any government military victory may be short-lived. There is also the issue of internal repression, with human rights groups deploring the government's ransacking of media offices and the shooting death of an outspoken editor critical of the government.[12] Thus, questions arise as to the future of Sri Lanka now that the fighting is over: Will the underlying causes of the conflict be addressed? Or will conflict resume at some future time?

THE SRI LANKAN CRISIS IN HISTORICAL CONTEXT

The current ethnic conflict between the Indian Tamil minority and the Sinhalese majority has been raging since the 1980s. However, the historical roots of the conflict go much further back. Sri Lanka is an island slightly larger than the

MAP 6.1
Ethnic Distribution in Sri Lanka

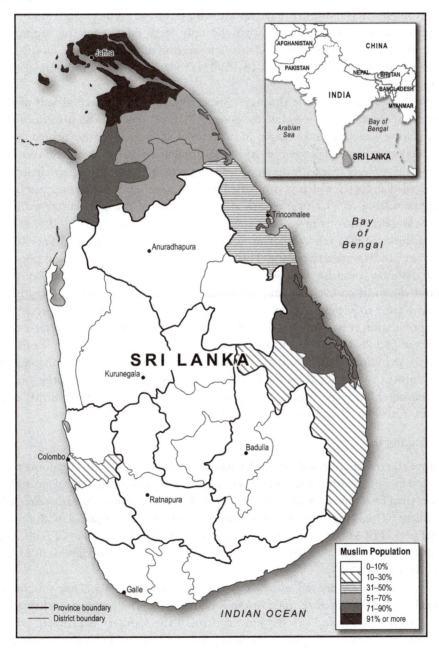

Muslim Population
- 0–10%
- 10–30%
- 31–50%
- 51–70%
- 71–90%
- 91% or more

— Province boundary
— District boundary

Source: Data from *Ethnic communities and religions*, http://www.lib.utexas.edu/maps/islands_oceans_poles/sri_lanka_charts_76.jpg; *Sri Lanka*, U.S. Central Intelligence Agency, http://www.lib.utexas.edu/maps/middle_east_and_asia/sri_lanka_pol01.jpg; and *Province, District and DS boundaries of Sri Lanka: 2001*, Sri Lanka Department of Census and Statistics, http://www.statistics.gov.lk/misc/slmap.pdf.

U.S state of West Virginia, and it sits off the southeastern coast of India. It contains both rolling plains and a mountainous, jungle interior.[13] The nation has a very long history and until 1972 was known as Ceylon.[14] The population of the country is around 21 million, with the only large city being the capital of Colombo, with over 650,000 residents (and around 400,000 more in suburbs).[15] These numbers are estimates, as the civil war made taking an accurate census impossible.[16]

Sri Lanka has also gone through a modernization in the second half of the twentieth century. At the end of the Second World War, nearly 85 percent of the population was rural and engaged in subsistence agriculture or indentured work. By 2000 more than 20 percent of the population lived in urban areas, and even the rural villages were markedly developed. The agricultural workforce participates in export-led industry which is diversified and modernized.[17] Education has been made available to all citizens, with the percentage of the population without schooling dropping from 41.8 percent in 1953 to 8.6 percent in 1996–1997.[18]

Anthropologists report that around the fifth century B.C., migrants from northern India settled the island. This group would become the Sinhalese population that now comprises three-quarters of the population of Sri Lanka.[19] Roughly about the third century B.C., migration from the Tamil population of southern India started to populate the northern region of Sri Lanka. Just over 7 percent of the population is Muslim, a legacy of the Arab seafaring merchants of later centuries, especially the tenth century onward.[20] Both Sinhala and Tamil are official languages in Sri Lanka, although linguistic division is the reality. The language of government is Sinhala, the elite typically can also speak English, and the Tamils in the north and east speak Tamil almost exclusively.[21] A religious divide also exists, as the Tamils are mostly Hindus and the Sinhala are Buddhists.

Colonialism

Before the colonial period Sri Lanka had a number of different kingdoms that existed in close proximity to each other. A Tamil kingdom existed in the north for more than four centuries, until the arrival of the Portuguese in the early sixteenth century.[22] This Tamil nation centered in the northern city of Jaffna, with only a brief period of Muslim rule in the fourteenth century.[23] A number of Sinhalese principalities dominated the south during the period from the thirteenth to fifteenth century.[24]

The Portuguese arrived on the coast of Sri Lanka in 1505. They sought to establish and monopolize trade in the Indian Ocean. The Portuguese displaced the Muslim traders and slowly gained control of the southern Sri Lankan ports. The net effect was to displace Sinhalese principalities and push them inland.[25] Disputes between the Portuguese and the different Sri Lankan kingdoms led to a slow domination of all Sri Lankan authorities except the Kingdom of Kandy in the interior highlands.[26]

European intervention in Sri Lankan affairs took a decidedly different turn in the mid-seventeenth century, when the Kandy leader negotiated with the Dutch East India Company (VOC) for protection against the Portuguese. In return for driving out the Portuguese from the island, the VOC was handed a monopoly on the lucrative spice trade.[27] The Dutch used the pretense of having to pay for the war with the Portuguese as grounds to invade the Jaffna Kingdom and to gain control over the cinnamon trade. The Kandyan Kingdom was reduced in size and could not effectively repel the Dutch gains made at its expense.[28]

By the late eighteenth century, the steadily declining Kandyan Kingdom again turned toward external aid to help in its plight against a European power. As the British power in the Indian Ocean increased, the Kandyan leaders enticed the English East India Company (EIC) to expel the Dutch. However, the English were not interested. The Dutch reacted with great anger to this overture and invaded the Kandyan Kingdom, forcing the latter into a treaty that landlocked the Sri Lankan kingdom and effectively reduced it into servitude.[29]

Events in Europe would create a change in the colonial administration of Sri Lanka. Napoleon's conquest of the Netherlands in 1796 alarmed the British, who now feared that the French fleets would attempt to gobble up all the Dutch possessions. A British naval expedition to Sri Lanka quickly dispatched the Dutch defenders. In 1798 the British Parliament declared Sri Lanka (with the exception of the Kandyan Kingdom) to be a crown colony of the British Empire.[30] In 1815 the British annexed the declining Kandyan Kingdom, thus gaining control of the entire island, but allowed Kandyan administrative institutions to remain.[31] A Kandyan rebellion in 1818 was brutally repressed by the British, who now extended administrative control over the entire colony and abolished all Sri Lankan administrations.[32]

The British occupation laid the roots for the ethnic conflict that now exists. British ideas of racial superiority and nationalism combined with the ethnic differences that already existed on the island.[33] The Colebrooke-Cameron Reforms of the Sri Lankan administration initially created a legislative council that contained one Sinhala, one Tamil, and one European (referred to as Burghers).[34] The development of an education system that promoted English gave preference to those elites who were willing to learn and speak the colonizer's language.[35] The Dutch Burghers initially held advantages in this respect, but eventually they were outnumbered by the Sinhala and Tamil. As Colombo and other southern ports became the center of British trade and administration, the power of the Sinhala grew in proportion.[36]

The revival of Sinhalese Buddhism in the late nineteenth century led to challenges to British rule. The first Buddhist riot occurred in 1883 and was aimed at Catholics, who had slowly converted during the years of Portuguese rule.[37] Buddhist riots against Catholics also happened in 1890, 1891, 1897, 1899, 1902, and 1903, displaying the level of animosity between the two religions and their believers.[38] The Buddhists also turned their attention to the Muslim traders who held key positions in retail trade in the coastal ports.[39] A number of anti-Muslim riots in 1915 spread from the Kandyan interior to the coastal cities, leading to destruction of thousands of shops, burning of mosques, looting of Christian churches, and the deaths of dozens of Muslims.[40] The British governor, Robert Chalmers, declared martial law, with the resulting arrests of thousands and shooting deaths of hundreds of protestors.[41] As a result of this crackdown, the Sinhala began to question the necessity of British rule, while the Muslim population started to side with the British administration.

Thus, while the British remained neutral to local populations, their encouragement of the separation of different communities was having the unintended effect of instilling nationalism and nationalist pride.[42] Interesting to note is that in the first two censuses held under British rule (1814 and 1824) the only distinguishing categories were caste and religion.[43] Only in the censuses of 1871 and 1881 did the term race appear, as did national categories.[44] In fact, prior to the twentieth century, it appeared that a single Sri Lanka nationalism might appear, rather than what eventually became a divided number of separate nationalisms.

During the 1920s Sri Lanka experienced a bit of an economic boom as a steady rise in exports led to growth, especially in agriculture as irrigation schemes began to transform the "dry zone" into farmable land. However, the Great Depression dropped the price of export crops.[45] The plantation system of farming had exported too much labor during the expansion, and now these laborers found themselves unemployed. Moreover, a great deal of the immigrant labor had come from Tamil regions in India. In the southern ports and cities, Sinhalese railway and shipyard workers also were being released from employment.[46] Race relations took a nasty turn as Sinhalese politicians enacted legislation to entitle only Sinhala to "land ownership, rice cultivation, retail trade, and gem mining."[47]

A very fateful constitutional reform may indeed have exacerbated the growing tensions between the nationalities. The British advanced the Donoughmore Constitution in 1931.[48] This new constitution established a fifty-member State Council to administer the colonial government. Unfortunately, the division into numerous electoral districts encouraged politicians to campaign as individuals and to appeal to local constituents. The resulting dominance of the State Council by Sinhalese elite set the stage for the development of two nationalisms: Sinhala and Tamil.[49] The lesson that the Sinhala took from this experience was that consociational agreements with the Tamils were not necessary; the Sinhala could rule as a majority without Tamil input.

After the elections of 1936, Sinhalese politicians dominated the legislative committees and appointed only Sinhala to the Board of Ministers, a body that negotiated with the British government. By the late 1930s the tide of anti-Indian legislation reached a crescendo. A State Council resolution led to the compulsory retirement of thousands of workers of Indian origin, whether a temporary resident or not. Reform of the voting rolls tossed thousands of those of Indian origin (some Tamil, others recent immigrants) from the list of registered voters. Non-Sinhalese businesses were subsequently required by law to hire Sinhalese workers and had to pay double taxation under the Income Tax Ordinance of 1942.[50] The state of India fought back against this clearly discriminatory legislation, banning emigration of unskilled Indians to Sri Lanka.[51]

Sri Lankan independence from British rule on February 4, 1948, led to the creation of political parties to contest elections and control of the government.[52] However peaceful and uneventful the transfer of power was, it did not resolve the underlying problem of lack of minority representation.[53] The United National Party (UNP) under the leadership of the Sinhala Don Stephen Senanayake won the elections of 1947. The UNP formed a government with the help of independents, the main opposition being a collection of leftist and Marxist parties. Interesting to note is that while at this time all of the main parties included politicians from all the main ethnic groups, all of the leaders were Sinhala and English-educated. Of political importance was the overrepresentation of Kandyan Sinhala who comprised a landowning class that was both anti-urban and anti-laborer. Legislative acts of the late 1940s continued the trend of the State Council period by reducing the rights of Indian-origin laborers and even disenfranchising them from land that their families had held for generations.[54]

The 1956 election revolved around two key issues. First, a great debate arose about what to make the official language(s) of the state. The UNP adopted a Sinhala-only stance, while Muslim and Tamil groups advocated Sinhala as the official language of government business as long as English and Tamil were recognized as languages.[55] The second issue was the role of Buddhism. Buddhist leaders accused the UNP of neglecting the religion. Activist Buddhist leaders began to work with villages to encourage them to focus on virtue (which meant temperance), education, and crime reduction. Other activists tried to influence the political process, mainly by arguing that the current political regime had led to the decline of Buddhist life.[56]

The 1956 election ushered in a left-led government and saw the UNP decline into second party status. The ruling Mahajana Eksath Peramuna (MEP) "promised to restore Buddhism, Sinhalese culture, and Sinhala to a predominant position in the nation."[57] Moreover, over 80 percent of the seats in the parliament were in Sinhalese hands, emphasizing that to rule the government a party needed only to campaign to the Sinhalese voters. And for the first time since independence, the government contained "Muslims, Burghers, and Christians . . . but no Tamils."[58]

The new government solved the language question by passing a "Sinhala only" bill, which made Sinhala the language of government business immediately. While Tamils led demonstrations and protests, Sinhalese mobs violently murdered hundreds of Tamils across Sri Lanka.[59] In 1958 a wave of anti-Tamil riots led to the deaths of hundreds more Tamils. The nation's economy sank as wave after wave of protest came from Buddhists, Tamils, disgruntled politicians on the left as well as the right, and even Sinhalese nationalists.[60] In 1959 a Buddhist monk assassinated the prime minister, plunging the country into chaos. By the middle of 1960 it appeared that parliamentary democracy would crumble, with most anticipating a coup removing the government.[61]

The widow of the slain prime minister regrouped the government and on the last day of 1960 passed a bill making Sinhala the only official language throughout all of Sri Lanka. This set off a wave of mass protests by the Tamil minority.[62] Further inflaming the issue was the nationalization of schools, particularly in the north. State schools could now only teach Sinhala, even in Jaffna where Tamils made up the overwhelming population in the schools. The Official Language Act provoked a series of grievances from the Tamil population against government organizations that now seemed to discriminate on the basis of language, with the resulting lack of resource allocation to the Tamil population.[63]

Politics in Sri Lanka would now "see-saw" back and forth between a leftist government and its nationalization program (1960–1965; 1970–1971) and the UNP, which sought to reverse nationalization (1965–1969). By the 1970 election this back and forth had damaged the economy severely. Poverty was growing and unemployment was rampant, even in the countryside. Further, despite the attempts at making Sinhala the official language, most of the elite were still comprised of an Anglicized class who spoke English. Many Sri Lanka youth became radicalized during this period. Especially troubling was the attraction of the Marxist parties and movements, such as the Janatha Vimukthi Peramuna (JVP, People's Liberation Front), to young Sinhala. In 1971 a JVP uprising led mainly by students and activists attempted to overthrow the government by seizing police stations. The prime minister declared a state of emergency and mobilized the police and army to resist. After days of fighting, the uprising was ended with the jailing of tens of thousands and the deaths of anywhere from 1,000 to 10,000.[64]

The lasting consequence of the Marxist uprising was the permanent state of emergency, which continued until 1977. The government increased spending and the size of the armed forces. The new 1972 constitution that changed the name of the island from Ceylon to Sri Lanka also lessened constitutional restraints on the government, introduced socialist principles, and gave both Sinhala and Buddhism a dominant position.[65] Committed to socialist, Sinhalese, and Buddhist ideals, the leftist government promptly standardized both secondary and higher education. The net effect was to make it harder for Tamils to gain employment, as they did not score as well on standardized tests.[66] In effect, Tamils were being denied admission to university-level education, which then exacerbated discrimination in employment.[67] By the 1970s the Tamil population's perception of their opportunities, compared to those of the Sinhalese majority, brought them into conflict in five areas: "language, education, employment, distribution of land and land settlement, and devolution of power."[68]

What now occurred was a change from Tamil politicians and activists seeking a federal relationship with the south to demands for separatism based on nationalist appeals.[69] The main Tamil political party, Illankai Tamil Arasu Kadchi (ITAK), no longer participated in government and thus lost its voice. As such, a host of smaller Tamil parties combined with ITAK to form the new Tamil United Front (TUF) to contest elections (the TUF changed its name in 1976 to the Tamil United Liberation Front [TULF]).[70] Moreover, the TULF moved its position away from a moderate line and more toward a separatist sentiment.[71] This shift toward self-determination for the Tamil people signaled the "abandoning of the concept of a singular state" in which Tamils and Sinhala could live together.[72]

Events after 1972 spiraled out of control of the major actors. Bombings in 1972, the 1973 assassination of a former Jaffna mayor, more assassinations in 1975, and brutal police activity toward the Tamils pushed the region toward desperation. The TUF (now the TULF) national convention in 1976 called for the "sovereign socialist state of Tamil Eelam" (Eelam is the Tamil name for their proposed state).[73] What was ethnic conflict was soon to become ethnic and civil war. On May 5, 1976, a small activist group changed its name to the Liberation Tigers of Tamil Eelam (LTTE) and became the first paramilitary expression of the new Tamil nationalism.[74] The disaffected and radicalized youth were now turning toward militancy as an answer.

The 1977 election confirmed the new divide between Tamils and Sinhala as the TULF won every single seat in Tamil areas and the UNP decisively defeated a fragmented left.[75] Riots and running battles in Jaffna between police and civilians followed the election. In the south, Sinhala burned and looted Tamil properties. The UNP government instituted a new constitution in 1978 that created a directly elected president and proportional representation for the (now) unicameral legislature. In an attempt at some reconciliation with minority groups, the 1978 constitution contained language that allowed for greater linguistic and religious liberty.[76]

Against a backdrop of communal violence from 1979 to 1982, President Jayewardene used a technicality to hold an early election for president in October 1982. After winning this election, he held a public referendum that allowed him to extend the term of the parliament to 1989, which was five years later than when its current term would have run out.[77] The net effect was to keep the left from power by maintaining the UNP's grip on both the presidency and parliament.

Civil War

Without any political solution to Tamil nationalism, and with a government more concerned with maintaining control over the state, the ethnic conflict eventually boiled over into civil war. The night after an LTTE ambush of a military patrol, mob violence against Tamils started. A week-long orgy of violence ensued, in which Tamils and their property were targeted. While the official number of deaths was only 367, the actual number may be ten times as high.[78] Moreover, since the violence took place mainly in Colombo and other cities, the Tamils who suffered at the hands of their neighbors had typically been the more moderate ones who supported working with and through the government for reform. Tamil and Indian businesses were burned, even those that employed thousands of workers and provided an economic engine for Sri Lanka.[79] President Jayewardene immediately passed a bill through parliament making the advocacy of a separatist state illegal, forcing TULF out of parliament. The ouster of the moderate Tamil politicians and the violence directed at the Tamils by the Sinhalese mobs provided moral argument for the Tamil militants to gain control of the nationalist movement. The LTTE would now intensify the fight against the government.[80]

Under the leadership of Velupillai Prabhakaran, the LTTE first crushed all opposition to its dominance of the militant, nationalist cause. In 1983 and 1984 it increased its strength to over two thousand militants, obtained weapons and external funding, and systematically used brutal tactics to kill other militant Tamil leaders and destroy their nascent organizations.[81] The LTTE established an international network based in cities with large communities of Tamil expatriates, such as London and Madras. The LTTE also stepped up attacks against the government, using bombings, assassinations, ambushes, kidnappings, and other methods to kill members of the government security forces. Government reprisals against Tamil targets inflamed the passions of the militants, pushing them onward.[82]

In 1984 both sides turned toward harsher methods of conducting the war. The LTTE terrorist bombings and killings now included unarmed civilian targets. The government forces began rounding up political opponents who were not heard from again, creating a wave of "disappearances."[83] Peace attempts in 1985 between the LTTE and the government were inconclusive and the fighting continued. In 1986 President Jayewardene tried to defuse the conflict by presenting a new set of proposals to the parliament. These proposals called for the creation of provincial councils that would provide some measure of autonomy for the north and east provinces. While government forces were steadily pushing the LTTE back toward Jaffna, parliament was approving the new proposals. With the country still under martial law, elections to the new provincial councils were held in 1988. The TULF did not contest the elections, stating that they could not legitimately claim to be a nonviolent party.[84] The Eelam People's Revolutionary Liberation Front (EPRLF) won all the seats in the Northern Province and half of the seats in the Eastern Province.[85]

Fighting between the government forces and the LTTE intensified in the east during this time. Actions by both sides were increasing the suffering of the civilian population. Aerial bombings by government forces and the LTTE use of civilian hostages were particularly nasty developments. India was not oblivious to the plight of the Tamils, and after the Sri Lankan government refused to provide humanitarian aid to the north, the Indian government air-dropped food and medicine to the Tamil population.[86] A peace accord between India and Sri Lanka was signed on July 29, 1987.[87] An Indian Peacekeeping Force (IPKF) was now inserted into the Jaffna Peninsula to disarm the LTTE. The latter did not agree to such an arrangement, and battles between the Indian peacekeepers and the LTTE ensued. The Indian troops were under orders to refrain from killing civilians and to limit the overall number of casualties; the LTTE had no such orders. The Indian government eventually committed over 72,000 troops and spent upwards of $1.25 billion trying unsuccessfully to disarm the LTTE.[88] By March 1990 all the Indian troops had left Sri Lanka, their mission unaccomplished. Almost immediately, the LTTE regained control of the north and began to forcibly expel Muslims, a process that has been described as ethnic cleansing.[89]

During this time the government lifted a ban on the Janatha Vimukthi Peramuna (JVP), a Sinhalese extremist party. The JVP turned immediately toward militancy, using sabotage and assassination to prevent elections in 1988.[90] Colombo was particularly hard hit by the violence, with hundreds of people being killed in 1988 alone.[91] President Premadasa (who followed Jayewardene) organized his security forces and allowed them to ruthlessly seek out and destroy the JVP and its supporters. Estimates range from 12,000 to 60,000 victims of government death squads.[92]

In 1991 the civil war picked up again once the Indian peacekeepers left. Fierce fighting between the LTTE and government forces in 1991–1992 left the population in the Tamil areas at the mercy of the brutal pattern of retaliations. The typical pattern was for the numerically superior government forces to capture towns while the Tigers fled into the jungles and highlands, only to return when the government troops left. The end result was that the civilian population suffered as the villages and towns shifted control from one group to the other. The resumption of the civil war also apparently had consequences in India, as the LTTE was implicated in the assassination of the Indian prime minister, Rajiv Gandhi. Assassinations picked up in Sri Lanka as well. President Premadasa was implicated in eliminations of rival politicians, but he himself fell to a suicide bicycle bombing at the hands of a Tamil in 1993.[93]

In 1994 the new president, Chandrika Bandaranaike Kumaratunga, promised to find a way to end the war that had claimed over 60,000 lives. She represented the People's Alliance (PA) and its peace platform. The parliament was in the hands of a regrouped left that sought a negotiated settlement with the LTTE and campaigned against the corruption and violence of the UNP regime.[94] In October 1994 the government entered into a round of talks with the LTTE during a cease-fire agreement. The LTTE used the time to rearm and build up its strength to over 14,000 fighters.[95] The LTTE unilaterally withdrew from the negotiations and resumed the civil war, which had now entered its third phase of prolonged conflict.

A government offensive captured Jaffna in 1995, but this did not end the LTTE rebellion. The Tigers launched numerous attacks on government offices, military bases, and other related sites. While many of these were unsuccessful, the LTTE did bomb the Central Bank in Colombo and overran the government military base at Mullaitivu in 1996. In 1997 the LTTE also successfully set off a bomb in the Colombo Fort, which symbolized the ability of the Tigers to hit the military even in its most secure areas. The LTTE continued its terrorist acts, bombing temples, assassinating political figures, and, in perhaps its most sensational act, launching a suicide attack at the Sri Lanka International Airport that destroyed both military and commercial aircraft and terrorized the masses who used such transportation.[96]

President Kumaratunga tried to settle the dispute through a call for devolution of powers to the Tamil areas. However, such calls were met with great resistance from the Sinhalese and Buddhist nationalists, who were opposed to any movement away from the unitary state. The UNP opposed the proposal, even though it was substantively similar to one that they had proposed while they were in power.[97] Clearly, the opposition preferred to prevent any negotiated settlement that the president could use to bolster her position among the Sinhalese voters.

Battle fatigue led to a cease-fire in 2002 and a fragile truce. In a move that had great implications for the unity of the Tamil resistance, the LTTE in 2003 abandoned its call for a separatist Tamil state, announcing its willingness to accept a form of devolution and regional autonomy.[98] Peace talks brokered by Norway and held in Japan began in 2003. The decision by the LTTE to negotiate with the government led to a split in the Tamil resistance and the resumption of violence by Tiger splinter groups.[99]

In December 2004 a massive tsunami struck Sri Lanka, killing more than 30,000 as a gigantic wave devastated coastal villages and communities. Despite the possibility of collaboration in the wake of a humanitarian crisis, the government and the LTTE administered recovery in their areas as if each lived in a separate nation-state.[100] This clearly showed the lack of trust between the two and the distance that still had to be spanned in order to reach an agreement. In 2005 the foreign minister was assassinated, and a Tamil was implicated. The LTTE and the government reaffirmed the cease-fire, but this did not stop the violence from mounting. In 2006 a number of Tiger attacks on government bases and the navy resumed the direct confrontation between the government forces and the Tamils.[101]

The violence quickly escalated with a government offensive in late 2006 against the LTTE in the east province. Through 2006 and 2007 the government made headway while the Tigers resorted to terrorist attacks against southern ports, visiting diplomats, and civilian targets. In 2007 the government forces removed the Tigers from the east and started moving toward the Jaffna Peninsula. The Tigers launched a series of air raids against government targets that same year, a first for the Tamil resistance, forcing two international airlines to suspend flights to Sri Lanka.[102]

In 2008 the Tigers launched a number of attacks that killed a government minister, killed civilians in Colombo, and terrorized many throughout the island.[103] The government responded by allowing the cease-fire to expire and intensifying attacks in the north. An international panel invited by the government to monitor human rights abuses left the country, citing government interference as preventing them from completing their work. In 2009 the government offensive successfully captured more Tiger villages, effectively driving them into the jungles and highlands.[104]

INDIVIDUAL LEVEL

Examining the role of individual leaders in the Sri Lankan conflict is not an easy task. The numerous political leaders of the Sri Lankan government offer a veritable cornucopia from which to choose. The selection of any one can only tell part of the story. Finding a representative leader of the Tamils is much harder, not because one cannot be identified, but because of the secrecy surrounding the

Tigers. Given these constraints we focus on two individuals: Chandrika Bandaranaike Kumaratunga, prime minister of Sri Lanka from August to November 1994 and then president of Sri Lanka from November 1994 to 2005, and Velupillai Prabhakaran, the leader of the LTTE. At the end of this section, we briefly outline how ethnic outbidding also contributes to the continuing conflict in Sri Lanka.

Common to the literature on the Sri Lankan conflict is the idea of the failure of political leadership.[105] In particular, leaders have more often sought support within their ethnic group, which has led to the leaders taking extreme positions vis-à-vis the opposing ethnic group (ethnic outbidding), than support in a multiethnic framework.[106] Extending this argument is the idea that leaders operate more on greed than grievance, seeking to enhance their power and riches than actually seeking a remediation of their grievances.[107] As such, we use these themes as a framework for our examination of two important leaders in the Sri Lankan conflict.

Chandrika Bandaranaike Kumaratunga

Chandrika Bandaranaike Kumaratunga is the former prime minister (August 19, 1994, to November 14, 1994) and two-term president (November 12, 1994, to November 19, 2005) of Sri Lanka. She was the first woman to hold the position of president and the second woman to be prime minister. Bandaranaike Kumaratunga is the daughter of Sirimavo Bandaranaike, the first woman to be prime minister (July 1960–March 1965; May 1970–July 1977), and Soloman West Ridgeway Dias Bandaranaike (often abbreviated S.W.R.D. Bandaranaike), who himself was prime minister until assassinated (April 1956–September 1959). Her husband, Vijaya Kumaratunga, was a movie actor who founded in 1984 the Sri Lanka Mahajana Pakshaya (SLMP), a leftist political party. He was assassinated in 1988, and Bandaranaike Kumaratunga has not remarried.[108]

Bandaranaike Kumaratunga is an educated woman who earned a degree in political science at the University of Paris.[109] She was pursuing her doctorate when she returned to Sri Lanka to enter politics in the early 1970s. Initially a member of the Sri Lanka Freedom Party (SLFP), she eventually switched to supporting her husband's party, the SLMP. During this time, the SLMP merged with other leftist parties to become the United Left Front (ULF).[110] After the assassination of her husband, Bandaranaike Kumaratunga left for the United Kingdom and did not return until 1993. Upon her return, she defeated her brother to become the leader of the SFLP. In the 1993 elections, the People's Alliance, an alliance of leftist parties including the SFLP, won provincial council elections in the west and south. After the assassination of Premadasa in 1993 and the dissolution of parliament in 1994, Bandaranaike Kumaratunga and the PA narrowly won parliamentary elections.[111]

Bandaranaike Kumaratunga became prime minister and used this office as a launching pad in the presidential election of 1994. She subsequently won over 62 percent of the vote, the most ever accumulated by a single candidate.[112] Her campaign emphasized a need for peace and reaching out to the Tamils. She also campaigned against the corruption and violence so endemic to Premadasa's government. She also promised to abolish the executive presidency, the position that she now held, and to limit the number of cabinet positions in order to reduce government expenditures on these expensive appointments.[113]

Once in power, Bandaranaike Kumaratunga reversed course on all of these promises, except for trying to negotiate with the Tamils. She not only did not abolish the presidency, she used its prerogative powers to call for early presidential elections in 1999. She expanded the cabinet greatly, nearly doubling the number of members. Also, she appointed her aging mother as prime minister, and Sirimavo Bandaranaike served in that position until 2000. The defeat of the PA government to the UNP in 2000 led to a period of "cohabitation" with a UNP prime minister who opposed Bandaranaike Kumaratunga until 2004.[114]

In regard to the Tamil problem, Bandaranaike Kumaratunga did indeed initially reach out to the LTTE. However, she was distracted in the early 1990s by the faltering Sri Lankan economy and a surge in inflation. Her initial calls in 2000 for devolution in the north and east met legislative gridlock. The eventual decline of her parliamentary majority forced the governing coalition to add the JVP in 2001. The JVP was unwavering in its opposition to any cooperation with the Tamils and used its power to check any overtures from the president.[115] In the run-up to the 2000 election, the opposition UNP now took the position of negotiating with the LTTE while the president, now forced to act tough due to reliance on the JVP, took a more hard-line stance. The UNP-led governments after 2000 secretly negotiated with the LTTE and even arranged a cease-fire against the wishes of Bandaranaike Kumaratunga in 2002.[116]

When Bandaranaike Kumaratunga stepped down in 2005, her goals of 1994 remained unmet. While domestic politics played a key part in this (and we explore this in the section on domestic factors later in this chapter), one factor is that Bandaranaike Kumaratunga was an opportunistic leader who often used her position to retain power rather than seek an end to political conflict.[117] Her suspension of elections, use of emergency powers, failure to rein in extremist parties (instead actually including them in her governing coalitions), and her battles with the opposition prime ministers highlight her preoccupation with the politics of the government and not the politics of the state. There are also accusations about the government's bullying of the press, media, and investigators, as well as continued corruption and abuse of power. However, given all of this, she did return Sri Lanka to a more democratic process than her predecessor.[118]

Velupillai Prabhakaran

Velupillai Prabhakaran was the leader of the Liberation Tigers of Tamil Eelam (LTTE) until his death by government forces in May 2009. He was born in 1954, two years after the Official Language Act that made Sinhala the only official language. He grew up in a time when Tamils were repressed and marginalized by the Sri Lankan central government. He dropped out of school at sixteen and began to organize with other militant youth, quickly rising to informal positions of leadership. His first recognized act of violence was quite shocking: the assassination of the mayor of Jaffna in July 1975. The next year he renamed his fledgling militant group the Liberation Tigers of Tamil Eelam, more popularly known as the Tamil Tigers.[119]

Prabhakaran's leadership of the LTTE turned it into "arguably the most disciplined, dedicated, and ruthless guerrilla organization in the world."[120] Prabhakaran led the group as the sole decision-maker. He has been described both as "a murderous megalomaniac and as a brilliant strategist."[121] He had the "unswerving loyalty from his men and from his large following of young Tamil men and women."[122] In his pursuit of a Tamil homeland, he authorized the LTTE to use whatever means necessary to achieve its goal. Under him, the Tigers systematically eliminated all competing Tamil militant groups and used murder, assassination, suicide bombings, torture, and other techniques of terrorism. The early elimination of other Tamil militant organizations allowed Prabhakaran to establish the LTTE as the de facto "state" in Tamil areas.[123] Thus, atrocities carried out by the LTTE can almost certainly be attributed to orders from Prabhakaran. The International Criminal Police Organization (INTERPOL) in 2001 named him as one of their most wanted criminals, accusing him of offenses of "crimes against life and health, organized crime/transnational crime, terrorism, and terrorism conspiracy."[124]

What is known about this elusive leader is sparse, mainly because of his rare public appearances. In 1990, only a week after the Indian Peacekeeping Force (IPKF) had withdrawn from Sri Lanka, Prabhakaran spoke to a number of journalists in Jaffna. His next press conference was in 2002 at a remote location near the city of Kilinochchi.[125] At the time he denied that the LTTE were terrorists, a comment in direct response to the inclusion of the organization on the lists of terrorist groups by the United States and other nations. Instead, he called his Tigers "Freedom Fighters" and insisted that the LTTE was committed to peace.[126] The conference exposed very little about this mysterious leader of the LTTE who is said to personally select the members of the Black Tigers, the elite cadre of suicide bombers.[127]

While Prabhakaran talked peace during interviews and in negotiations with the government, he always resorted to violence to pursue his and the LTTE's goals. Criticism of his leadership centered on two aspects: his autocratic mode of decision making and his quick resort to violence, even against Tamils, in order to ensure the ascendency of the LTTE. In this way, he appears to fit the model of a leader who is more interested in monopolizing power than in obtaining the nationalist goals, as an instrumentalist approach would argue.[128]

Ethnic Outbidding

Another individual level aspect of the conflict that keeps the two sides from reconciliation is ethnic outbidding, that is, the process by which "politicians strive to outdo one another by playing on their . . . community's fears and ambitions."[129] The majoritarian system left behind by the British encouraged the dominance of government by the majority group, in this instance the Sinhala. The ability to rule without significant contribution from minority groups creates an environment for politicians within the "in-group" to outbid each other for the loyalty of that group's community. A good example would be the switch of both the UNP and SLFP from the early 1950s to the late 1950s on the issue of the inclusion of the Tamil language. Both parties supported a role for the Tamil language, but after fierce parliamentary competition between the two Sinhalese parties, each took an exclusionary stance before the 1956 election.[130] Ethnic outbidding also seems to have been a force in the radicalization of Buddhist youths and the rise of the JVP on at least two separate occasions.

Likewise, outbidding can occur among the minority group as well. Because of the lack of access to government, those politicians and activists who were more moderate eventually were "outbid" for the loyalty of Tamil youth. The LTTE, the most ruthless of the resistance groups, gained in recruitment the more hard-line its position became toward the nonnegotiability of a Tamil homeland (that is, Eelam). When in the mid-2000s the LTTE weakened its demand to regional autonomy, it began to be outbid by splinter Tiger groups.[131]

Generally, four conditions facilitate ethnic outbidding: a conducive political structure, poor leadership, social/ethnic/economic grievances, and territoriality.[132] All of these conditions are present in Sri Lanka. The majority-dominated political system represents mainly Sinhalese interests and creates an "us versus them" attitude toward minority groups. The leadership in Sri Lanka has been particularly prone to messianic appeals to extremist groups. The list of grievances is quite lengthy, and the territorial concentration of the Tamils in the north and east makes the group more easily targeted. The confluence of many factors facilitating ethnic outbidding has embedded the practice into Sri Lankan politics.[133] This pattern makes any peaceful solution in Sri Lanka less likely.

DOMESTIC LEVEL

A multiplicity of domestic level factors contributes to the ethnic conflict in Sri Lanka. In this section we attempt to sort out some of the more important factors, pointing out their relationship to the continued ethnic violence. The lack of significant international intervention (which we will explore in the section on international factors) allows the domestic factors and actors to have a greater impact on the course of the Sri Lankan conflict than perhaps they do in the other conflicts covered in this book.

Communities and Identities

Over 90 percent of the population of Sri Lanka belongs to one of two ethnic communities: Sinhalese Buddhists or Tamil Hindus. Another 7 to 9 percent are Muslims, who are also referred to as Ceylon Moors. As mentioned in the historical introduction to this chapter, there are also a number of citizens of European descent, known as Burghers, who make up a very small fraction of the population and are primarily centered in Colombo. Thus, Sri Lanka is a polyethnic and multireligious state.[134]

The Sinhalese majority "developed a distinct consciousness of themselves as a people by at least the tenth century . . . rooted in Buddhist religion."[135] This historical development of an independent ethnic identity fits the primordialist approach to ethnic conflict described in chapter 1. Despite this long-standing identity, it was only with the beginning of European occupation of Sri Lanka that "Sinhalese consciousness underwent a radical transformation."[136] In successive waves, the Portuguese, Dutch, and British marginalized the Buddhist religion and its practitioners.[137] By the late nineteenth century, Buddhist monks began to mobilize the Sinhalese population to resist the Christian missionary efforts of the British. Key to the resistance was the idea that Buddhism and the Sinhalese identity were superior to the religions and identities of the British, and also by proxy of the Tamils and Hindu.[138] Despite the emergence of a single "Sinhalese" identity, there is actually no single origin of the present-day Sinhalese population. Many diverse groups and migrants to Sri Lanka, including Dravidians, Chetties, Tamils, and others, have assimilated over time into the Sinhalese population.[139]

In the 1980s "Buddhist discourses began to authorize a particular Buddhist image of the 'fearless' young monk who would march to the 'battlefront' and lay down his life to rescue and lead the Buddhist nation facing the threat of 'terrorism.'"[140] Thus, Sinhalese and Buddhist identity in the 1980s and 1990s saw no incompatibility between religious belief and the use of violence. In fact, the Buddhist temple had long been a source of political resistance in Sri Lanka, and even the wider area of South Asia.[141] Capturing this idea of social and political resistance, the Buddhist monks were instrumental in focusing the Sinhalese identity in opposition to the Tamils, and in particular in calling for an escalation of the ethnic conflict in order to assert this identity.[142] In some sense, the creation of a new Sinhalese identity in the 1980s indicates that constructivist theories of identity formation (outlined in chapter 1) can help explain the resumption of ethnic conflict in the 1980s.

The Sinhala-only movement and similar pro-Sinhala initiatives strengthened the Sinhalese identity as superior and distinct from any other Sri Lankan identity. Thus, the development of an exclusive, as opposed to inclusive, identity for the majority began early in Sri Lankan history and gained steam during the colonial period and extended its momentum in the twentieth century. This singular identity has gradually replaced the historical distinction between Low Country Sinhala and Kandyan Sinhala.[143]

In opposition to the dominant Sinhalese identity is the minority Tamil nation. During three centuries of colonial rule, the Tamil identity remained. This is despite not having any constitutional representation during this period, whereas the tendency in the modern age has been for non-state identities to wither.[144] In spite of the strength of this single identity, the Tamil population is really two separate nations. The Sri Lanka Tamils (or Ceylon Tamils) are a Hindu nation that has been on the island for as long as the Sinhalese population. The Sri Lanka Tamils number roughly 1.8 million. The Indian Tamils (also referred to as "up-country" Tamils) immigrated in the nineteenth and twentieth centuries to work on the Sri Lankan plantations, are also Hindu, and number roughly 1.1 million. Together, these two Tamil nations constitute close to one-fifth of the Sri Lankan population.[145]

The two Tamil nations differ substantially from each other.[146] The Sri Lanka Tamils live mainly in the north and east, but have a significant presence in Colombo and other southern cities. The Sri Lanka Tamils are also economically prosperous and educated. The Indian Tamils mainly populate the tea growing highlands in the center of the island. While a good portion of them are field workers who typically lack substantial education and are much poorer than their Ceylon kin, a generation of youths is now overeducated and underemployed.[147] Also of note is that the Indian Tamils have largely not been involved in the LTTE or overall Tamil militancy. The many reasons for this include the lack of a nationalist ideology among the Indian Tamils, their general support of the government, a lack of external support, and the complicity of their elite with the political and economic systems in a pattern of co-optation.[148]

The Sri Lanka Tamils began to develop a distinct identity primarily in opposition to the Sinhalese identity and its push for a single, official Sri Lankan language. The exclusionary policies of the majority created a shift in Tamil nationalism toward separatism and the development of its own history and identity.[149] Especially in the north and east among the Sri Lankan Tamils, the creation of an identity separate from the Sinhalese majority gained significant ground. Because they lived in or near majority Sinhalese communities, the Indian

Tamils were not developing a separate identity. Yet, and somewhat paradoxically, the proximity of the Indian Tamils to the Sinhalese population centers "contributed to and reconfirmed Sinhalese perceptions" of the Tamils as an alien population and essentially as foreigners in Sri Lanka.[150] Indeed, it is this proximity to Sinhalese communities that led the Indian Tamils to be victims of ethnic riots in 1977, 1981, and 1983.

The fact that by the 1980s Sinhalese and Tamil identities both grew into distinct and exclusionary identities divided the nation of Sri Lanka into irreconcilable camps. In particular, the political construction of identity, which divides Sri Lanka into two separate nationalist movements, creates polarized "identity politics."[151] The "us versus them" mentality that naturally grows out of this separateness contributes to brutal retaliation and revenge and an unending cycle of violence.[152] The partition of Sri Lanka into two states (that is, a government-controlled Sri Lanka and the LTTE-controlled areas of Sri Lanka) reinforced the distinct identities and promulgated the conflict. Secessionist demands by the Tamil leadership lent a political realism to the separate identities.

Of note is also the slow development of the Muslim (or Sri Lanka Moor) identity separate from the other two. The nascent political distinction of Muslims in the state government coincided with the development of a separate national identity. As an example, prior to 1889 the Muslim population was represented in the Legislative Council by a "government-appointed Tamil."[153] The British preoccupation with "race" as a distinguishing factor led to the promotion of the Moor community as separate from the Tamils, despite the shared use of the Tamil language. During the twentieth century the Muslim identity existed in a tenuous middle ground between some assimilation into the dominant Sinhalese majority (especially in the west) and the re-emergence of a distinct Muslim identity, especially in the east, where violence directed at the Muslim community from both the Sri Lankan Army and the LTTE brutalized the Muslim population.[154]

Competing Ideas of State Formation

Jayadeva Uyangoda argues that the on-again, off-again civil war between the government and the Tigers resulted from competing ideas of state formation.[155] He asserts that the ethnic war in Sri Lanka represents two different and irreconcilable definitions of the Sri Lankan state. The Tigers pursue space for a separate Tamil nation, while the government seeks to enforce its view of a single, unitary Sri Lankan state built around Buddhism and Sinhala. Therefore, the LTTE's pursuit of a Tamil "homeland" is a far cry from the possible role of addressing issues of poverty, discrimination, inequality, and so forth.[156] In other words, the LTTE and the government used the war as the means by which they hoped to achieve their differing views of the state.

Ethnic nationalism in this regard spurred the nationalism of the competing groups. The more that the Sinhalese population created a unitary state during the postcolonial period, the more it stoked the desire of the Tamil population to resist such a state.[157] The more that the Tamil (and even the Muslim) population pushed for reform, the more it was refused by the Sinhalese majority, who subsequently imposed state reform of their own design. Each is locked into an ethnic security dilemma, much as is discussed in chapter 2. The pursuit of security by each group leads to insecurity in the other, and the result is a backlash by each against any compromise. That the LTTE views the conflict in Sri Lanka as a civil war between two competing states is easy to ascertain by the terminology that they use to describe the conflict. The Tamil history divides the battle with the Sri Lankan government into "three phases: Eelam War I (1983–1987), Eelam War II (1990–1994) and Eelam War III (1995–2002)."[158] Thus, to the LTTE, the struggle has been about the existence of a separate, Tamil state.

In a controversial interpretation of the conflict, Uyangoda states that "it may not be an exaggeration to describe peace negotiations in Sri Lanka as continuation of the war for state formation by other means."[159] Only with the negotiations beginning in 2002 was the formation of the state included in any possible settlement. The Oslo Formula and the discussions of a federal state that occurred that year, before LTTE withdrawal from the peace process, were the first steps toward addressing the competing views of the state.[160] However, even moderate Tamil proposals would probably have been met with resistance, as "a credible offer would far exceed what the Sinhalese political class could constructively consider, precisely because it would envisage a radical reconstitution of the existing state."[161] Thus, any proposal that envisions state reform is unacceptable to the Sinhalese majority and any proposal without state reform is unacceptable to the Tamil population.

Consociationalism versus the Hegemonic State in Sri Lanka

The Lijphart model of consociationalism is an institutional theory. As outlined in chapter 2, the consociational model comprises a set of institutions that when in place can help reduce conflict in divided societies and bring stability to government. However, Lijphart emphasizes that political elites must cooperate in these institutions and not compete. The history of Sri Lanka demonstrates how elites can undermine a consociational arrangement.[162]

As noted in the first section of this chapter, Sri Lanka used the British model of plurality elections from 1948 to 1977, comprising eight elections.[163] The results of these elections followed typical patterns seen across the world. First, there was an alternation of power between a party on the right (UNP) and a party-led coalition on the left (SLFP). Second, the system manufactured a majority for the ruling party.[164] Third, rural areas gained a sense of power over the government, typically because of overrepresentation of their interests.[165] Fourth, the results of the elections led to the gradual exclusion and marginalization of ethnic minorities.[166]

The constitution of August 16, 1978, changed the electoral system to proportional representation. The total number of parliamentarians was increased to 196. Of the 196 seats, 160 are apportioned based on population while the remaining 36 are distributed 4 apiece to each of nine districts. A 5 percent threshold prevents extremely small parties from obtaining any seats. Predictably, the large parties no longer can count on a manufactured majority. Coalition government is the norm, with the resulting tendency of small parties to hold immense bargaining power during government formation negotiations.[167]

While it would appear that the 1978 constitution and its consociational elements would lead to greater ethnic participation in governance, this did not happen in Sri Lanka. It is true that the party representing the Muslim minority (the Sri Lanka Muslim Congress) did join a governing coalition in 2000, but in general the marginalization of the ethnic parties continued.[168] In particular, the Tamil leadership had been so discredited by its inability to defend Tamil interests that the constitutional change came too late. Turnout in the Tamil areas declined steadily from the middle 1970s, and so did the number of seats held by the TULF and its allied parties.[169] Thus, the consociational elements of proportional representation elections and coalition governments did not actually create a multiethnic government nor improve interethnic relations. Proposals for reform in the 1990s and again after 2002 contained the consociational element of federalism, or at least more regional autonomy, especially for the Tamil minority. Unfortunately, these proposals have never been implemented.

Chapter 2 discussed the hegemonic state theory of Ilan Peleg.[170] To reiterate, the hegemonic state is not neutral in the ethnic conflict. Rather, it acts usually in a nondemocratic fashion to favor and promote the rights and interests of one ethnic group, usually the majority group. Ian Lustick distinguishes the hegemonic state by labeling it a "control model" versus the consociational model.[171] The 1978 constitution strengthened the power of the president. In fact, the incumbent, President Jayewardene, who was the chief architect of the constitution, expressly wanted a strong presidency in order to counter the power of the parliament.[172] The movement of power into the presidency went a great distance in negating any consociational elements by institutionalizing Sinhala-Buddhist nationalism in the role of the president.[173] The movement of even more authority into the presidency after 1983 centralized control even more.[174] The end result is that while the government functions well and appears democratic, it acts like an authoritarian state and maintains little actual territorial control.[175] The typical pattern is that "emergency regulations promulgated for 'national security' reasons have increasingly eclipsed due process and the rule of law."[176]

The hegemonic state has also led to a change in civil-military relations in Sri Lanka. The political economy of continued conflict has created a new role for the military. The military now "has increased its sphere of control over traditionally civilian posts and administrative duties in the war zones."[177] While command and control of the military, and especially the Sri Lankan Navy, remains in the hands of the democratically elected president, the continuous conflict has given rise to a hidden economy comprised of arms deals, bribes, fees, trafficking, and other related economic activity.[178]

Negotiating from Power Balance or Power Asymmetry

A number of studies of negotiation underscore that power asymmetry between the main competitors is a hindrance to a successful agreement. The logic is that the strong party(-ies) to the negotiations will not feel a strong compulsion to negotiate, while the weak party(-ies) will be fearful of the results of any negotiations.[179] A study of major agreements in Sri Lanka from the 1950s to the 1980s suggests that power asymmetry played a role in the lack of implementation of those agreements.[180] Importantly, the main flaw in these agreements was that Tamil input was not sought by the strong power(s). An example would be the Nehru-Kotelawala Pact in 1954 between India and Sri Lanka. India agreed to stop immigration to Sri Lanka, and the Sri Lankan government would register all adults who remained on the island. Neither of these strong powers consulted with the Tamil population (that is, the weak negotiator) during the negotiations. The Sri Lankan government unilaterally stopped registering Tamils as residents, as it felt no need to actually carry out its half of the Pact.[181]

Moreover, the two main combatants in Sri Lanka hold antagonistic views of what constitutes a good strategic position from which to bargain. The rebels preferred to negotiate from a state of power symmetry.[182] The LTTE preferred to bargain with the government only after it had proven its capability to gain and maintain control of a significant portion of the north and east of the island. In essence, the LTTE negotiated when it looked the most like a "state." The government rather preferred to negotiate from a position of power asymmetry.[183] It sought to undermine militarily the LTTE's argument about its ability to represent a Tamil homeland and then force upon the rebels the *fait accompli* of a unitary state. Consecutive military offensives to take Jaffna and other key cities away from the Tigers remained part of a government strategy to force the LTTE to the bargaining table with a weak hand.[184]

Economic Roots of the Conflict

While ethnicity certainly plays a central part in the conflict in Sri Lanka, some observers point to economics as a contributing factor.[185] In particular, they address the change in Sri Lanka from having a promising and developing economy at the end of the Second World War to one by the 1970s that was underdeveloped and declining. Strikingly, while the 1960s and early 1970s saw Sri Lanka's economic expansion lead to improvements in income distribution and overall wealth, the liberal trade policy that was friendly to Western businesses also created unintended displacements of workers and a dependence on international markets and export prices.[186] The leftist turn in the late 1970s exacerbated the economic difficulties by focusing on further economic redistribution and stifling economic growth. By 1977 "some 20% of the labor force was unemployed."[187]

Sirimal Abeyratne points to the "twin political conflict" (that is, the ethnic conflict between the Tamil minority and Sinhalese majority, and the militant uprisings of Sinhala-Buddhist youth versus the government) and how economic difficulties have contributed to both. In particular, Abeyratne argues that "an increasingly restrictive trade regime in a welfare-oriented state" created development policy errors and social exclusion of an emerging generation of youth.[188]

Gendered Nationalism in Sri Lanka

The conflict between the Sri Lankan government and the LTTE has impacted women.[189] For example, women who were widowed because of the war have become heads of household. Yet, a society that values men as the heads of household, and women as mothers and housewives, means that widows confront the challenge, in addition to having to cope with the loss of their spouses, of struggling "for economic stability, privacy, physical safety, and most important, self-worth and social dignity."[190] Notably, the war led to important changes in the gender roles within the family unit, and yet, this does not mean that women were then able to enter the public sphere.[191] Moreover, according to Malathi de Alwis, "Sri Lankan women, be they Sinhala, Tamil, or Muslim, continue to be constructed as the reproducers, nurturers, and disseminators of 'tradition,' 'culture,' 'community,' and 'nation.'"[192] These gendered constructions of women's roles in Sri Lankan society are relevant for understanding the impact of war on women, and their responses to the war. Some women responded by forming organizations that stressed their maternal roles, others formed explicitly feminist organizations, and others responded by fighting.

In terms of organizations that explicitly focused on women's maternal roles and identity, branches of the women's organization Mothers' Front were created. The first branch was formed in 1984 as a protest against the mass arrests of Tamils by the government. Women of all classes comprised the group's membership.[193] Another branch of the Mothers' Front was established in 1990 in the south as a response to the state's oppressive actions against Sinhalese youth of the Janatha Vimukthi Peramuna (JVP) party who rebelled.[194] This branch was formed in July 1990 by middle-class Sinhalese women protesting human rights violations by the state—namely the disappearance of around 60,000 men (Sinhalese men began protesting against the government, which then responded by arresting them); and the women defined their cause in traditional terms, as mothers and wives.[195] As quoted by Malathi de Alwis, they demanded that the government provide "a climate where we can raise our sons to manhood, have our husbands with us and lead normal women's lives."[196] The opposition political party, the SLFP, mobilized and funded the group, and "these women were never pushed to break out of their gender and class stereotypes or to form links with other women's groups."[197] The Sri Lankan government responded by banning demonstrations by the group, and even organized women's rallies to counter the Mothers' Front protests.[198] Militant groups opposed the organization to the point where the Mothers' Front leader was assassinated.[199]

Women in Sri Lanka have also engaged in violent actions in the course of the ethnic conflict that marked the past two decades. Women in the LTTE have had a combat role, as members of the women's wing, Birds of Freedom, including as suicide bombers.[200] According to Miranda Alison, "The women's military wing is a well-organised and highly disciplined force. . . . [T]he LTTE's naval force, the Sea Tigers, is primary female and the suicide squad, known as the Black Tigers, has a large number of women in it."[201] In order to mobilize women to fight, the LTTE has used slogans such as "Women! Break barriers, expedite liberation," but at the same time, for the most part, very few women have significant decision-making positions in the organization.[202] What has changed is the image of a Tamil woman from, as Rita Manchanda defines, "auspicious, married, fecund." She notes that "LTTE women's freedom of movement and equality of social and political commitment have challenged the stifling rituals and practices that oppressed the Tamil woman in a social system marked by caste, dowry, seclusion of the unmarried woman and sequestration of menstruating women."[203] In fact, the Women's Front of the LTTE actively seeks to highlight "the unequal position of Tamil women in their society." In doing so the hope is to rectify that inequality. Thus, the national liberation movement is linked explicitly to women's liberation.[204]

The feminist movement in Sri Lanka also responded to the anti-Tamil riots that occurred in 1983, as well as the outbreak of civil war.[205] Feminists argued for a peaceful resolution to the conflict and drew attention to "the shared suffering of both Tamil and Sinhala women as a result of this war."[206] The media and certain parts of the Sinhalese public reacted negatively to the feminist peace activists, asserting that these feminists were "not only discrediting their own country, but their race and religion as well."[207]

The Sri Lankan feminist movement did play a role in pushing for inclusion of a gender perspective in the peace negotiations that emerged with the 2002 cease-fire. In terms of actual negotiations to end the ethnic conflict between the government and Tamil rebels, facilitated by Norway in late 2002, the Sub-Committee on Gender Issues (SGI) was created.[208] As in other cases of ethnic conflict that attempt to address women's interests and gender (and follow from the mandates of UN Security Council Resolution 1325), however, while the mandate of the subcommittee seeks to incorporate "a gender perspective and women's interests and concerns" in the peace negotiation process, the fact remains that the SGI has not had a significant impact on the peace process.[209] The problem is the lack of provision to force parties to the agreement to comply with any of the relevant recommendations set forth by the SGI.[210]

As noted at the outset of this section, women in Sri Lanka, regardless of their ethnic group identity (Sinhalese, Tamil, or Muslim), are still defined by their gendered roles as mothers and wives. Some women, such as those in the Mothers' Front, have embraced those roles in their protests against the government's actions. Women in the feminist movement have tried to challenge those roles, only to be accused of being a threat to their nation/ethnic group. Thus, gendered nationalism remains an ever-present factor in Sri Lanka.

The discussion of the various domestic level factors above tells us much about the ethnic and class tensions, which highly resemble those in Northern Ireland. Ethnic discrimination from a majority-dominated government and/or majority ethnic group leads to minority grievances. When the grievances are not satisfied, or, as is the case in Sri Lanka, not addressed, radicalization of the minority ethnic group leads to confrontation, conflict, and eventually violence.

INTERNATIONAL LEVEL

Despite the decades-long ethnic conflict in Sri Lanka, international interventions into the conflict have been minimal. The Indian peacekeeping force in the late 1980s is the only tangible, direct involvement of any foreign power. Most direct intervention was in the historical period before the outbreak of ethnic conflict. After that time, a host of NGOs have been present in Sri Lanka, and some countries have become involved with the various peace initiatives, yet the overall level of international involvement is generally less than in the other countries in this text. Given this, in this section we discuss how Sri Lanka's geo-strategic position might explain the lack of foreign intervention. We then discuss various other international level factors that play a role in the ethnic conflict.

Sri Lanka's Importance to the Cold War and Post–Cold War World

Sri Lanka occupies a strategic sea lane between the West and the South/Southeastern Asian countries. Furthermore, it exports a number of important goods such as tea and rubber. Sri Lanka's significance is obvious from the successive European nations, and later the United States, that have taken advantage of its position to further their own interests. This section concentrates on the postcolonial experience and the relationship between Sri Lanka and the United States.

Before 1948 Sri Lanka had only a marginal level of trade with the United States, most of it generated from the trade preferences of Britain. After independence, Sri Lankan trade with the United States blossomed rapidly. As part of President Truman's program to assist underdeveloped nations, the United States and Sri Lanka entered into a mutual cooperation agreement in 1950–1951.[211] This economic and development cooperation was not by chance. The bipolar nature of the brewing Cold War provided incentive for the relationship: the United States gained access to Sri Lankan ports while the latter gained access to the U.S. economy. The mutual benefit was obvious immediately as Sri Lankan harbors were available for the U.S. Navy during the Korean War and Sri Lanka quickly realized a positive trade balance with the superpower.[212]

Despite disagreements over Sri Lanka's rubber exports to the nascent People's Republic of China in the early 1950s, the Sri Lankan commitment to anticommunism placed it firmly within the U.S. sphere of influence.[213] However, this sympathy did not extend as far as Great Britain. The leftist government of the SLFP that won the 1956 elections promptly expelled the British naval bases from Sri Lanka. Prime Minister S.W.R.D. Bandaranaike also moved Sri Lanka toward nonalignment in international affairs. Despite this attitude and some disagreements over the Suez Crisis, relations between the United States and Sri Lanka remained cordial from 1956 to 1961, with trade between the two increasing.[214]

In 1961 the Sri Lankan government nationalized some refining assets belonging to Western oil companies; included among these were two U.S. and one British company.[215] After nationalizing these plants, Sri Lanka began to import oil from the Soviet Union, the United Arab Republic, and Romania. Under a new act passed by the U.S. Congress, the United States demanded that the oil companies receive due compensation, threatening to suspend all aid to Sri Lanka unless it acquiesced. Relations between the two countries deteriorated rapidly in 1963, with Sri Lanka denying the U.S. Seventh Fleet entry into its territorial waters and even protesting its presence in the Indian Ocean. Despite the frosty relationship and Sri Lanka's leftist government, the relationship improved in 1964 as both countries concentrated on the continuing trade and swept political disagreements under the rug.[216]

The return of the UNP to power in 1965 led to improved U.S.–Sri Lankan relations. Despite a number of strains between the two countries over the Vietnam War, the Arab-Israeli conflict, the Sri Lankan support of China's admission to the United Nations, and the continuing Sri Lankan foreign policy of nonalignment, the general pro-West position of the UNP fostered an atmosphere of agreement.[217] With the 1970 election victory of Senanayake and the United Front (UF), a left-leaning government fostered a dramatic change in Sri Lankan foreign policy. The government immediately recognized East Germany, North Vietnam, and North Korea, while also suspending diplomatic relations with Israel.[218] Despite these bold moves in international diplomacy, the UF government made it clear that it was not anti–United States. In fact, during the 1970–1977 period of UF leadership, a number of bilateral trade agreements between the two countries were signed.[219]

Since the outbreak of open warfare between the government and the Tamil Tigers in 1983, the United States has maintained trade relations with Sri Lanka while simultaneously pushing for a peaceful resolution. Visits of Sri Lankan leaders to the White House stopped in 1984. Moreover, as the Sri Lankan government slowly turned illiberal, the United States began to complain about deteriorating human rights and government accountability. The United States hoped that Sri Lanka would return to good government.[220] In essence, the United States treats the conflict as one that should be settled at the regional level. During the 1980s and 1990s, India took a more leading role in the Sri Lankan crisis (see the section below on India and noncoercive intervention). Therefore, the United States does not commit itself or its resources to brokering or mediating an end to the conflict.[221] In fact, some of its actions may have contributed to the conflict. In 1984 the United States arranged contact between the Sri Lankan government and Israeli security forces.[222]

In 1997 the U.S. State Department labeled the LTTE a foreign terrorist organization as part of President Clinton's antiterrorism efforts. Experts debate the effects of this move by the United States, especially whether it forced the LTTE into talks with the government or because of the limits of neutral venues it precluded effective talks.[223] The events of September 11, 2001, and President Bush's "War on Terror" continued this movement and thrust Sri Lanka back into the spotlight of American foreign policy. In 2002 the U.S. president met with the Sri Lankan prime minister in Washington, D.C., and pledged American economic and military support.[224] This set off a chain of events that led to joint military exercises, integration of intelligence communities, and increased U.S. foreign assistance (roughly $8.4 million in 2002).[225] The resumption of sustained violence in 2006 created consternation in Congress over the U.S. support of the Sri Lankan government, especially military aid and collaboration.

With the Sri Lankan military offensive in 2009, the Barak Obama administration and the U.S. Department of State called for the Sri Lankan government's offensive to stop, for the Tamil Tigers to surrender their arms to a third party, for a limited amnesty for the Tigers, and for the resumption of talks to incorporate the Tamils in the operation of the Sri Lanka government.[226] In a joint meeting on May 12, 2009, Secretary of State Hillary Clinton and the UK foreign secretary, David Miliband, "call[ed] for a political solution that reconciles all Sri Lankans, and establishes a meaningful role for Tamil and other minorities in national political life."[227] The next day, President Obama made an official statement and reiterated his concerns about the civilians caught in the conflict zone and impending humanitarian crisis, and thus the need for their safe passage. He called on the LTTE "to lay down their arms and let civilians go." He also called on the government not to use heavy weapons and to allow UN humanitarian agencies and the International Committee of the Red Cross into the territory. He stated, "The United States stands ready to work with the international community to support the people of Sri Lanka in this time of suffering. I don't believe that we can delay. Now is the time for all of us to work together to avert further humanitarian suffering. Going forward, Sri Lanka must seek a peace that is secure and lasting, and grounded in respect for all of its citizens. More civilian casualties and inadequate care for those caught in resettlement camps will only make it more difficult to achieve the peace that the people of Sri Lanka deserve."[228]

International Intervention

Despite the fact that the ethnic conflict in Sri Lanka was one of the longest-running ones in the modern world, and the tens of thousands of deaths and hundreds of thousands displaced rank it as one of the most violent, there was very little international intervention. The friendly relationship of Sri Lanka to the Western great powers (and especially the United States and Britain) placed Sri Lankan domestic politics a bit low on the agenda for international intervention. While this might seem paradoxical, the fact that both Britain and the United States have such firm and secure relations with Sri Lanka, and that the Soviet Union did not challenge these relationships during the Cold War, has given Sri Lanka some latitude to operate independently of great power politics. Under such circumstances, the most significant international actor to intervene in the Sri Lankan conflict has been India.

Diffusion (as addressed in chapter 2) of the conflict to include India depends on the extent to which India's leaders are willing to intervene in the Sri Lankan crisis (addressed in the next section). However, diffusion also occurs because of links to drug trafficking, contacts between Tamil leaders, especially those living outside of Sri Lanka, and leaders of other dissident and terrorist groups, and also ties to international gun runners.[229] Escalation of the conflict occurred in the 1980s when India decided to intervene directly by sending a peacekeeping force into the north and east of the island (detailed below).

India and Noncoercive Intervention

As should be apparent, the "geographical, political, cultural and ethnic juxta-position with India" shapes Sri Lanka's development.[230] The relative size of the Indian economy and its hegemony over the Indian Ocean plays an important role in the Indo–Sri Lankan relationship. In particular, after 1971 and the creation of Bangladesh, India inserted itself more forcefully into the politics of its neigh-bors.[231] Some believe that Indian "imperialism" in the Indian Ocean (or the Rajiv doctrine as it was called by some) led India to interfere in the domestic politics of Sri Lanka. A more sober understanding of Indian foreign policy asserts that India often reacted in an ad hoc manner to Sri Lankan events and that it did not have any designs on the island.[232]

The historical context of the relationship between India and Sri Lanka is complicated, but revolves around the status of the Indian Tamils. Issues of citizenship, migration (both emigration and immigration), and trade between the Tamil population and India have been the main focus. Regarding international issues, India and Sri Lanka "espoused a common approach," including "the issue of national liberation generally, disarmament, and resistance to military pact."[233] Both the Nehru-Kotelawala Pact of 1954 and the Sirimavo-Shastri Pact of 1964 dealt with issues of Indian citizenship and employment in Sri Lanka.[234] Economic competition between the two countries around tea exporting led to cooperation in the 1960s and 1970s to influence the global price of that commodity. The two countries have also disagreed over maritime boundaries, the protection of fishing, and the island of Kachcha Thivu.[235]

The explosion of violence after the 1983 riots led to a different Indian approach to Sri Lanka. India began to pursue a noncoercive intervention policy designed to accomplish three goals: stabilization/reduction of the internal Sri Lankan conflict, protection of the Tamils, and prevention of external, international intervention that could undermine Indian regional hegemony.[236] Relations between Sri Lanka and India would be strained by accusations that the Indian military and security forces were covertly arming and aiding the LTTE.[237] Yet, Indian foreign policy respected Sri Lankan sovereignty, and direct Indian intervention did not occur. At the same time, Sri Lanka changed its foreign policy toward India, taking a more defensive stance. Sri Lanka made overtures to the United Kingdom, United States, and others to provide military assistance to Sri Lanka in case of an Indian invasion.[238]

The 1987 Indo–Sri Lankan Peace Accord changed everything. India would now directly insert peacekeepers into the north and east of Sri Lanka. Why did the Indian government change course at this time? Two factors seem to present themselves. First, by 1987 the situation of the Tamil population was worsening. Indian air-dropping of supplies was not alleviating the deteriorating economic and humanitarian conditions in Tamil areas.[239] International humanitarian intervention by the United States, China, or any other nation was not forthcoming, mainly because of international concern with being seen as supporting the LTTE against the Sri Lankan government. India was presented with a decision of whether to abandon support for the Tamil liberation movement in order to support the Tamil civilian population. Second, the pro-Western lean of the Sri Lankan government was troublesome to the new Indian prime minister, Rajiv Gandhi, son of the slain Indira Gandhi, who wanted to maintain Indian hegemony in the region.[240]

Thus, Indian foreign policy settled on abandonment of the LTTE cause, protection of the Tamil civilians, and preemptive intervention to deter any other international intervention. The signing of the accord was met bitterly by the Sinhalese majority in Sri Lanka, who felt that their government had betrayed their interests to the Indians.[241] The LTTE complained about the treaty because it was not consulted as a third party to the negotiations. Here again the Tigers' desire to be treated as a separate state in Sri Lanka was not confirmed by the other parties. Prabhakaran begrudgingly agreed to the treaty, but also undermined elements of it.[242] The overall Tamil population was generally responsive to any events that would bring relief from the fighting.

The day after the accord was signed (July 30, 1987), "four Indian Infantry Brigades, consisting of approximately 3,000 troops, landed in Sri Lanka."[243] The Indian Peacekeeping Force (IPKF) was to replace the Sri Lankan military in Tamil areas (that is, north and east) and to disarm the LTTE within seventy-two hours. The use of the IPKF would change India's role from mediator of the ethnic warfare in Sri Lanka to guarantor of the Tamil population.[244] The Sri Lankan government was happy to release control of these areas to the IPKF, as the Sri Lankan troops were needed in the south to deal with the JVP uprising.[245] Two factors contributed to the breakdown of the IPKF mission in less than two months: open violence between the LTTE and rival Tiger resistance groups, and the inability of the IPKF to disarm by force the LTTE.[246] In what became a tangled web of relations, joint Indo–Sri Lankan military cooperation angered the LTTE, while the appearance of LTTE-Indian massacres of Sri Lankan troops inflamed the Sri Lankan government. What was clear to all was the impunity with which the LTTE was attacking all rivals for the establishment of Eelam, including the IPKF.[247]

On October 10, 1987, the IPKF launched "Operation Pawan" in an attempt to break the LTTE by capturing Jaffna. The peacekeeping force had now become a peace "enforcing" mission. After a grueling assault, the IPKF captured Jaffna at the cost of over six hundred casualties, while the LTTE faded into the countryside to harass the IPKF.[248] Operation Pawan was a victory for the Indian troops, but it accomplished nothing in the long run. The LTTE was temporarily on the defensive, but it would regroup quickly. Meanwhile, the Indian troops now found themselves in an all-out war against the LTTE, with the Tamil population caught in the middle. This was a far cry from the original intent of the IPKF to protect the Tamil civilians from LTTE versus Sri Lankan government fighting.[249]

Things would change rapidly in 1988. Ranasinghe Premadasa won the Sri Lankan presidential election of that year. Premadasa had always been against the accord and on July 31, 1989, he ordered the IPKF to leave Sri Lanka.[250] Indian prime minister Rajiv Gandhi refused to remove the IPKF, instead arguing that their presence was necessary to protect the Tamil minority.[251] However, later in 1989 Gandhi was under domestic pressure to reduce costs associated with the IPKF, and in response he began to remove some Indian troops. The election of V.P. Singh as prime minister of India on December 2, 1989, signaled the end of the Indian mission in Sri Lanka. Singh had always thought that the IPKF was a mistake. He promptly withdrew all Indian forces in 1990.[252] Within a few months, the LTTE attacked a number of government-held police stations in the east and the civil war between the Tigers and the government resumed.

Indian intervention in Sri Lanka failed because it was comprised of two separate actions that did not seek to accomplish the same goal. First, the covert sponsorship of the Tigers allowed the LTTE to continue its fight against the government and seek its goal of a Tamil state. Second, the IPKF direct intervention also sought to support the Tamils, but it hindered the goal of a Tamil state by replacing the Sri Lankan government with the Indian occupiers. In such a scenario, the actions of the Indian occupation ran counter to its covert actions. Perhaps this strange paradox exposes the lack of any consistent (over time or otherwise) and coherent Indian foreign policy toward Sri Lanka. Unfortunately, it also exposes how a misguided international intervention can cause even greater suffering in the state already suffering from ethnic warfare.

Prior to the announcement of the end of hostilities in May 2009, Indian officials met with the Sri Lankan president and requested a truce in the fighting. India agreed with the United States that the LTTE should surrender its weapons to a third party and that a United Nations humanitarian team should be allowed into Sri Lanka to care for civilians. India had no plans to directly intervene in the conflict.[253] On the day of the announcement that Prabhakaran had been killed by Sri Lankan military forces, the Indian government "asked Sri

Lanka to take political steps to ensure 'effective devolution of power' so that Tamils in the island nation could live with dignity." The Indian External Affairs Ministry issued a statement later that day (May 18, 2009) noting that "it is our view that as the conventional conflict in Sri Lanka comes to an end, this is the moment when the root cause of conflict in Sri Lanka can be addressed. This would include political steps towards the effective devolution of power within the Sri Lankan Constitution so that Sri Lankans of all communities, including the Tamils, can feel at home and lead lives of dignity of their own free will."[254]

Norway's Role in the Peace Process

The small Scandinavian state of Norway was a key facilitator and mediator of peace talks between the government and the LTTE from the year 2002 to the year 2006. This Norwegian involvement in Sri Lanka did not arise out of thin air, but emerged from three factors in Norway's history. First, the Scandinavian countries had been monitoring the conflict in Sri Lanka for quite some time and had been "promoting low-key peace-making initiatives" for years.[255] In fact, Norway had approached the LTTE in the 1990s offering its services as a mediator, but this led the government to question the Norwegian intentions. Second, Norway was "well-known for having played a leading role in the brokering of the Oslo Accords in the Israel/Palestine conflict up until 1993, and more discreetly in peace processes such as those in Guatemala (1996), Haiti, Sudan, Cyprus, Kosovo (1999), and Colombia (2000)."[256] Third, "Norway already had a strong NGO presence in Sri Lanka" and was familiar with the extent of the conflict.[257]

In 2000 President Kumaratunga formally asked Norway to act as a third party to peace negotiations, to which the Norwegians agreed in February of that year. Why Norway would want to participate says a great deal about the roles available to small states. One generally accepted theory is that Norway acts as a "norm entrepreneur," exporting its ideas and ideals of humanitarian assistance, peaceful resolution of conflict, and sustainable development. Another accepted theory is that a small state like Norway tries to carve out a niche in the international system to demonstrate its relevance, giving the small Scandinavian state a presence larger than it might have otherwise.[258]

The Norwegian delegation played the role of facilitator between the government and LTTE, helping broker the 2002 cease-fire. The impartiality of the Norwegians impressed both sides, even if it did not exactly fit their preconceived perceptions of the role the Norwegians should play (for example, the LTTE wanted the Norwegians to act as mediators who could push for Tamil causes).[259] The 2004 tsunami created a new challenge to the Norwegians' role, and perhaps the lack of coordination between the LTTE and the government following the catastrophe demonstrates the limited extent to which the Norwegian facilitation brought the two warring sides together. The resumption of conflict in 2006 and the failed peace talks in Geneva that same year ended the Norwegian efforts at facilitation. In summary, while one cannot say that the Norwegians failed, it perhaps is clear in hindsight that without a fundamental understanding of both the LTTE and government as to the division of state power, any brokered peace agreement was bound to fail.[260]

NGOs and IGOs

Nongovernmental organizations (NGOs) have been active in Sri Lanka for many decades. For example, the Sri Lanka Red Cross Society was active as early as the late 1950s in providing humanitarian and charitable relief.[261] However, the growth in foreign aid and funding to such organizations in the 1980s and 1990s saw their presence in Sri Lanka expand greatly.[262] A first generation of NGOs typically consists of voluntary welfarist associations. Most of those in Sri Lanka existed before the conflict began and have a religion-based, welfare and/or charity background.[263] A second generation of NGOs entered Sri Lanka during the 1980s and 1990s in response to the conflict. The International Committee of the Red Cross and Amnesty International began working in Sri Lanka during this period.[264] Also among this group are the usual humanitarian aid agencies, but this generation also includes groups who advocate on behalf of certain populations or for peace-building.[265] Examples of second generation NGOs include the British Oxfam and Save the Children Fund, as well as the Norwegian Forut (Campaign for Development and Solidarity) and Red Barna (Save the Children).[266]

Initial studies of the impact of NGOs illustrate the difficulty of the task that they face in war-torn Sri Lanka. Community surveys identify the NGOs' largest impact as "mitigating the effects of the conflict on the most vulnerable" (for example, women, children, displaced).[267] Those same surveys stress that "NGOs have a limited impact on the local dynamics of the conflict."[268] In particular, NGOs that play an advocacy role find it challenging to make an impact. Typically, such groups have pursued two strategies: lobbying the combatants and lobbying international actors who can pressure the combatants.[269] One of the difficulties is maintaining the reality or perception of neutrality by the NGOs. For example, the Norwegian NGOs suffered from the perception that they are connected to the foreign aid, foreign policy, and facilitator role of the Norwegian government.[270]

Another complication is the role that international financial institutions (IFIs) (which are international governmental organizations, or IGOs) play in funding NGOs. The three largest IFIs in Sri Lanka are the Asian Development Bank, the International Monetary Fund, and the World Bank.[271] The IFIs have an agenda that is usually focused on producing a "peace dividend," or in other words, some tangible economic benefit and development from the aid and a continuance of peace. The IFIs often portray this peace dividend as a reason for the combatants not to return to violence.[272] One study finds that the promotion of the peace dividend often creates confusion for aid organizations that are typically following a more basic humanitarian mission. Also, it can reduce collaboration and create competition between NGOs for the funding of the IFIs.[273]

The resumption of conflict in 2006 appears to undermine the argument of the peace dividend as a key to peace-building in Sri Lanka. A recent analysis finds that aid is "too blunt an instrument to influence the short-term dynamics and incentive systems of conflict and peace" in Sri Lanka.[274] In fact, the Sri Lankan government criticized the role of NGOs for rebuilding the capacity of LTTE areas during the gap in conflict, allowing the Tigers to recruit, regroup, and regain their footing for a continuation of the civil war. In 2009 NGOs were still operating in Sri Lanka during the government's offensive. Their mission to protect civilians and champion humanitarian causes has not changed. Human Rights Watch maintains that the government offensive of 2008–2009 put civilians at risk and created a no-fire zone that is "one of the most dangerous places in the world."[275] The International Committee of the Red Cross (by 2009 the only NGO working in the war zone, as permitted by the government) described the conflict zone in 2009 as "an unimaginable humanitarian disaster."[276] The future of NGO activity in Sri Lanka is uncertain at this time, given that the LTTE has now put down its arms.

The major IGO, the United Nations, has not taken an active role in ending the Sri Lankan conflict in terms of military intervention. One explanation for this is that the United Nations itself, particularly since the 1990s, has found it difficult to intervene in humanitarian crises.[277] The UN Security Council issued a press statement in mid-May 2009 regarding Sri Lanka, as the government forces were in the final days of defeating the LTTE. Security Council president Vitaly Churkin of the Russian Federation read the statement in which he "expressed grave concern" in regard to the deteriorating humanitarian crisis. The statement further "called for urgent action by all parties to ensure the safety of civilians." The Security Council and the secretary general of the UN, Ban Ki-moon, focused on the need for UN and other humanitarian aid workers to enter the conflict zone and help the civilians trapped in the fighting.[278] The UN Security Council did not call for UN intervention. Rather, the UN action has typically been through the Office of the United Nations High Commissioner for Refugees (UNHCR) and aimed at neutral, protective humanitarian relief programs. This pattern of participation continued in 2009 with the Central Emergency Response Fund (CERF) of the UN allocation of $10 million to feed, build shelters for, and provide medical aid to those displaced by the violence.[279] The World Food Programme (WFP), another UN agency, provides food for displaced people in government screening points on their way to temporary transit facilities in cities such as

Jaffna. In May 2009 the WFP provided food for nearly 200,000 internally displaced people in the north of the country.[280] As in the past two decades, the UN did not consider military intervention to end the fighting.

CONCLUSION

This chapter has provided an examination of the two-decades-long ethnic conflict in Sri Lanka by utilizing the levels of analysis framework. While suicide bombings and other acts of terrorism get widespread attention in the international media, the roots and complexities of this conflict that extend past these acts of violence should now be better illuminated. The contestation of the Tamil minority for control over the Sri Lankan state, or at least to carve out an independent Tamil nation, lies at the heart of the conflict.

The domestic level factors examined illustrate that competing claims over representation and authority in the central government have pushed the two sides into irreconcilable positions. Ethnic outbidding in an electoral system and governmental system that rewards a "winner take all" mentality has empowered extremists on both sides while marginalizing moderates. Outbursts of mob violence and brutality have only confirmed the worst fears of both the Sinhala and Tamil nations.

At the individual level, the weak and self-interested leadership has found it useful to continue war while talking peace. At the international level, foreign powers were reluctant to get involved and the peace mission undertaken by India in the late 1980s proved disastrous. The successful mediation of the conflict by an outside, third party (in this instance, Norway) proved much more difficult than imagined. The resulting cease-fire did not lead to long-lasting peace, but only a temporary period in which the contestants rearmed and prepared to resume conflict.

After the intensive government offensive in May 2009 that resulted in the defeat of the LTTE, with its leadership killed and significant numbers of civilians displaced, uncertainty remains as to how the tensions between the ethnic groups will be managed and whether conflict will resume in the future.

NOTES

1. "Gunmen Shoot Sri Lanka Cricketeers," *BBC World News,* March 3, 2009, http://news.bbc.co.uk/2/hi/south_asia/7920260.stm.
2. "Sri Lanka Army in Ghost Tiger Town," *BBC World News,* January 28, 2009, http://news.bbc.co.uk/2/hi/south_asia/7857247.stm.

3. "Is the End Near for Sri Lanka's Rebels?" *BBC World News,* January 9, 2009, http://news.bbc.co.uk/2/hi/south_asia/7820188.stm.

4. "Ruined Remains of Rebel 'Capital,'" *BBC World News,* January 5, 2009, http://news.bbc.co.uk/2/hi/south_asia/7811360.stm.

5. "Sri Lanka's Rebel Leader 'Killed,'" *BBC News,* May 18, 2009, http://news.bbc.co.uk/go/pr/fr/-/2/hi/south_asia/8055015.stm.

6. "Dignity and Respect for Our People Is All We Ask—Pathmanathan," *Tamil-Net* (May 17, 2009), http://tamilnet.com/art.html?catid=13&artid=29389.

7. "Sri Lanka: Tamil Leader Has Been Killed," *CNN.com,* May 18, 2009, www.cnn.com/2009/WORLD/asiapcf/05/18/sri.lanka.conflict/index.html.

8. "Q&A: Sri Lanka Conflict," *BBC News,* May 19, 2009, http://news.bbc.co.uk/2/hi/south_asia/2405347.stm.

9. "Q&A: Sri Lanka Conflict," *BBC News,* May 19, 2009.

10. "Many Dead in Sri Lanka, Says UN," *BBC World News,* March 6, 2009, http://news.bbc.co.uk/2/hi/south_asia/7927774.stm.

11. "The Last Battle?" *The Economist,* September 27, 2008, 55–58.

12. "Is the End Near for Sri Lanka's Rebels?" *BBC World News,* January 9, 2009.

13. CIA World Factbook, https://www.cia.gov/library/publications/the-world-factbook.

14. Patrick Peeples, *The History of Sri Lanka* (Westport, Conn.: Greenwood Press, 2006), 1. To avoid confusion, we use the term Sri Lanka for the entirety of the nation's history. The most correct way would be to use Ceylon during the period of colonial administration of the island (1505–1948) and to refer to different kingdoms before that.

15. Peeples, *The History of Sri Lanka,* 3.

16. Peeples, *The History of Sri Lanka,* 6.

17. Weligamage D. Lakshmanan and Clement A. Tisdell, "Sri Lanka's Development since Independence," in *Sri Lanka: Current Issue and Historical Background,* ed. Walter Nubin (New York: Nova Science Publishers, 2002), 14–15.

18. Lakshmanan and Tisdell, "Sri Lanka's Development since Independence," 17.

19. Peeples, *The History of Sri Lanka,* 6.

20. Peeples, *The History of Sri Lanka,* 7, 33.

21. Peeples, *The History of Sri Lanka,* 7.

22. V. P. Vaidik, *Ethnic Crisis in Sri Lanka: India's Options* (New Delhi: National Publishing, 1986), 8.

23. Peeples, *The History of Sri Lanka,* 31–32.

24. Peeples, *The History of Sri Lanka,* 29–31.

25. Peeples, *The History of Sri Lanka,* 34.
26. Peeples, *The History of Sri Lanka,* 35.
27. Peeples, *The History of Sri Lanka,* 37.
28. Lakshmanan and Tisdell, "Sri Lanka's Development since Independence," 57–64.
29. Lakshmanan Sabaratnam, *Ethnic Attachments in Sri Lanka: Social Change and Cultural Continuity* (New York: Palgrave, 2001), 54–66.
30. Peeples, *The History of Sri Lanka,* 47.
31. Peeples, *The History of Sri Lanka,* 48.
32. Peeples, *The History of Sri Lanka,* 50–51.
33. Nira Wickramasinghe, *Sri Lanka in the Modern Age: A History of Contested Identities* (Honolulu: University of Hawai'i Press, 2006), 44.
34. Peeples, *The History of Sri Lanka,* 51–52.
35. Peeples, *The History of Sri Lanka,* 65.
36. Wickramasinghe, *Sri Lanka in the Modern Age,* 26–28.
37. Vaidik, *Ethnic Crisis in Sri Lanka,* 1.
38. R. L. Stirrat, "The Riots and the Roman Catholic Church in Historical Perspective," in *Sri Lanka in Change and Crisis,* ed. James Manor (New York: St. Martin's Press, 1984), 196.
39. Peeples, *The History of Sri Lanka,* 74–81
40. Peeples, *The History of Sri Lanka,* 80–81.
41. Peeples, *The History of Sri Lanka,* 81.
42. A. Jeyaratnam Wilson, *Sri Lankan Tamil Nationalism: Its Origins and Development in the Nineteenth and Twentieth Centuries* (Vancouver: University of British Columbia Press, 2000), 2.
43. Wickramasinghe, *Sri Lanka in the Modern Age,* 47.
44. Wickramasinghe, *Sri Lanka in the Modern Age,* 48.
45. Peeples, *The History of Sri Lanka,* 89–90.
46. Peeples, *The History of Sri Lanka,* 90.
47. Peeples, *The History of Sri Lanka,* 90.
48. Wickramasinghe, *Sri Lanka in the Modern Age,* 162–167.
49. Peeples, *The History of Sri Lanka,* 84–94.
50. Peeples, *The History of Sri Lanka,* 92.
51. Peeples, *The History of Sri Lanka,* 92.
52. Peeples, *The History of Sri Lanka,* 93.
53. Peeples, *The History of Sri Lanka,* 99.
54. Peeples, *The History of Sri Lanka,* 100.
55. Peeples, *The History of Sri Lanka,* 104–105.
56. Peeples, *The History of Sri Lanka,* 105.
57. Peeples, *The History of Sri Lanka,* 106.

58. Peeples, *The History of Sri Lanka,* 107–108.

59. Peeples, *The History of Sri Lanka,* 110.

60. Peeples, *The History of Sri Lanka,* 111–112.

61. Wickramasinghe, *Sri Lanka in the Modern Age,* 209–215.

62. Peeples, *The History of Sri Lanka,* 112–113.

63. Neil DeVotta, *Blowback: Linguistic Nationalism, Institutional Decay, and Ethnic Conflict in Sri Lanka* (Palo Alto: Stanford University Press, 2004), 129–130.

64. Peeples, *The History of Sri Lanka,* 119–120.

65. Wickramasinghe, *Sri Lanka in the Modern Age,* 183.

66. Peeples, *The History of Sri Lanka,* 120–121.

67. Wilson, *Sri Lankan Tamil Nationalism,* 102–103.

68. Vaidik, *Ethnic Crisis in Sri Lanka,* 68.

69. Wilson, *Sri Lankan Tamil Nationalism,* 101.

70. Peeples, *The History of Sri Lanka,* 127; "Tamil United Liberation Front," U.S. Library of Congress, http://countrystudies.us/sri-lanka/69.htm.

71. Wilson, *Sri Lankan Tamil Nationalism,* 103–104.

72. Wilson, *Sri Lankan Tamil Nationalism,* 105.

73. Wilson, *Sri Lankan Tamil Nationalism,* 110.

74. Peeples, *The History of Sri Lanka,* 127.

75. Peeples, *The History of Sri Lanka,* 128–129.

76. Peeples, *The History of Sri Lanka,* 131–132.

77. Peeples, *The History of Sri Lanka,* 134–135.

78. Peeples, *The History of Sri Lanka,* 135.

79. Unknown Author (identity withheld for security reasons), "Sri Lanka's Week of Shame: An Eyewitness Account," *Race and Class: A Journal for Black and Third World Liberation,* special issue on "Sri Lanka: Racism and the Authoritarian State," 26 (1984): 40–42.

80. Wickramasinghe, *Sri Lanka in the Modern Age,* 285–288.

81. Peeples, *The History of Sri Lanka,* 152–153.

82. K. M. de Silva, *Managing Ethnic Tensions in Multi-Ethnic Societies: Sri Lanka 1880–1985* (Lanham, Md.: University Press of America, 1986), 342–347.

83. Peeples, *The History of Sri Lanka,* 153–154.

84. Peeples, *The History of Sri Lanka,* 156.

85. Peeples, *The History of Sri Lanka,* 156.

86. Peeples, *The History of Sri Lanka,* 157.

87. Wickramasinghe, *Sri Lanka in the Modern Age,* 190.

88. Peeples, *The History of Sri Lanka,* 158.

89. Peeples, *The History of Sri Lanka,* 161.

90. Wickramasinghe, *Sri Lanka in the Modern Age,* 239.

91. Peeples, *The History of Sri Lanka,* 159.

92. Peeples, *The History of Sri Lanka*, 159.

93. Peeples, *The History of Sri Lanka*, 161–163.

94. Peeples, *The History of Sri Lanka*, 163–165.

95. Peeples, *The History of Sri Lanka*, 168.

96. Peeples, *The History of Sri Lanka*, 168–170.

97. Peeples, *The History of Sri Lanka*, 171–172.

98. Peeples, *The History of Sri Lanka*, 172–173.

99. Jason Motlagh, "Tamil Tiger Trap," *New Statesman*, September 22, 2008, 20.

100. Jayadeva Uyangoda, "Ethnic Conflict, the State, and the Tsunami Disaster in Sri Lanka," *Inter-Asia Cultural Studies* 6 (2005): 341–352.

101. "Timeline: Sri Lanka," *BBC World News*, July 17, 2008.

102. "Timeline: Sri Lanka," *BBC World News*, July 17, 2008.

103. Motlagh, "Tamil Tiger Trap," 20.

104. "Many Dead in Sri Lanka, Says UN," *BBC World News*, March 6, 2009.

105. A. Jeyaratnam Wilson, "Nation-Building in a Demotic State: The Failure of Political Leadership in Sri Lanka," in *The Post-Colonial States of South Asia: Democracy, Development, and Identity*, ed. Amita Shastri and A. Jeyaratnam Wilson (New York: Palgrave, 2001), 88–113.

106. DeVotta, *Blowback*, 182.

107. Benedikt Korf, "Functions of Violence Revisited: Greed, Pride, and Grievance in Sri Lanka's Civil War," *Progress in Development Studies* 6 (2002): 109–122.

108. Peeples, *The History of Sri Lanka*, 159–160, 182–194.

109. "Profile: Chandrika Kumaratunga," *BBC News*, August 25, 2005, http://news.bbc.co.uk/2/hi/south_asia/3239821.stm.

110. Peeples, *The History of Sri Lanka*, 159–160.

111. Peeples, *The History of Sri Lanka*, 163.

112. Peeples, *The History of Sri Lanka*, 164.

113. Laksiri Jayasuriya, *The Changing Face of Electoral Politics in Sri Lanka, 1994–2004* (Singapore: Marshall Cavendish, 2005), 25–44.

114. Peeples, *The History of Sri Lanka*, 165–166.

115. Peeples, *The History of Sri Lanka*, 166.

116. Jayasuriya, *The Changing Face of Electoral Politics in Sri Lanka, 1994–2004*, 75–83.

117. DeVotta, *Blowback*, 184.

118. Peeples, *The History of Sri Lanka*, 167.

119. DeVotta, *Blowback*, 169.

120. DeVotta, *Blowback*, 170.

121. DeVotta, *Blowback*, 170.

122. Wilson, *Sri Lankan Tamil Nationalism*, 132.
123. Suthaharan Nadarajah and Dhananjayan Sriskandarajah, "Liberation Struggle or Terrorism? The Politics of Naming the LTTE," *Third World Quarterly* 26 (2005): 93.
124. "Wanted: Velupillai Prabhakaran," INTERPOL, 2001. This wanted listing was posted on INTERPOL Web site www.interpol.int.
125. "Reclusive Tamil Rebel Leader Faces Public," *BBC News*, April 10, 2002, http://news.bbc.co.uk/2/hi/south_asia/1922478.stm.
126. "Reclusive Tamil Rebel Leader Faces Public," *BBC News*, April 10, 2002.
127. DeVotta, *Blowback*, 173–176.
128. Korf, "Functions of Violence Revisited."
129. Neil DeVotta, "Illiberalism and Ethnic Conflict in Sri Lanka," *Journal of Democracy* 13 (2002): 84.
130. DeVotta, "Illiberalism and Ethnic Conflict in Sri Lanka," 86–88.
131. DeVotta, "Illiberalism and Ethnic Conflict in Sri Lanka," 88–91.
132. Neil DeVotta, "From Ethnic Outbidding to Ethnic Conflict: The Institutional Bases for Sri Lanka's Separatist War," *Nations and Nationalism* 11 (2005): 143–144.
133. DeVotta, "From Ethnic Outbidding to Ethnic Conflict," 154.
134. DeVotta, *Blowback*, 22.
135. DeVotta, *Blowback*, 27.
136. R. A. L. H. Gunawardana, "The People of the Lion: The Sinhala Identity and Ideology in History and Historiography," in *Sri Lanka: History and the Roots of the Conflict*, ed. Jonathan Spencer (London: Routledge, 1990), 70.
137. DeVotta, *Blowback*, 27–29.
138. DeVotta, *Blowback*, 31.
139. Satchi Ponnambalam, *Sri Lanka: National Conflict and the Tamil Liberation Struggle* (London: Zed Books, 1983), 20–21.
140. Ananda Abeysekara, "The Saffron Army, Violence, Terror(ism): Buddhism, Identity, and Difference in Sri Lanka," *Numen* 48 (2001): 5.
141. Rohan Bastin, "Hindu Temples in the Sri Lankan Ethnic Conflict: Capture and Excess," *Social Analysis* 49 (2005): 45–66.
142. H. L. Seneviratne, "Buddhist Monks and Ethnic Politics: A War Zone in an Island Paradise," *Anthropology Today* 17 (2001): 15–21.
143. Oddvar Hallop, "Ethnic Identity, Violence, and the Estate Tamil Minority in Sri Lanka," *Round Table* 323 (1992): 5.
144. V. Nithi Nithiyanandam, "Changing Scenarios of Tamilian Culture: Some Thoughts on the Cultural Dimensions of the Ethnic War in Sri Lanka," *Asian Ethnicity* 2 (2001): 35–54.

145. Walter Schwarz, *The Tamils of Sri Lanka* (London: Minority Rights Group, 1975), 5; Elizabeth Nissan, *Sri Lanka: A Bitter Harvest* (London: Minority Rights Group, 1996), 7–9.

146. Schwarz, *The Tamils of Sri Lanka*, 5.

147. Daniel Bass, "Paper Tigers on the Prowl: Rumors, Violence, and Agency in the Up-Country of Sri Lanka," *Anthropological Quarterly* 81 (2008): 269–295.

148. Bass, "Paper Tigers on the Prowl," 272–273. The theory of co-optation is Daniel Byman's, as discussed in chapter 2. Daniel L. Byman, *Keeping the Peace: Lasting Solutions to Ethnic Conflicts* (Baltimore: Johns Hopkins University Press, 2002).

149. Hallop, "Ethnic Identity, Violence, and the Estate Tamil Minority in Sri Lanka," 2.

150. Hallop, "Ethnic Identity, Violence, and the Estate Tamil Minority in Sri Lanka," 8.

151. Camilla Orjuela, *Civil Society in Civil War: Peace Work and Identity Politics in Sri Lanka* (Göteborg: Göteborg University, 2004), esp. 85–97.

152. Purnaka L. de Silva, "Combat Modes, Mimesis, and the Cultivation of Hatred: Revenge/Counter-Revenge Killings in Sri Lanka," in *Imagined Differences: Hatred and the Construction of Identity*, ed. Gunther Schlee (New York: Palgrave, 2002), 215–239.

153. Dennis B. McGilvray, *Crucible of Conflict: Tamil and Muslim Society on the East Coast of Sri Lanka* (Durham: Duke University Press, 2008), 314.

154. McGilvray, *Crucible of Conflict*, 317–329.

155. Jayadeva Uyangoda, *Ethnic Conflict in Sri Lanka: Changing Dynamics* (Washington D.C.: East-West Center, 2007), 10.

156. Uyangoda, *Ethnic Conflict in Sri Lanka*, 10.

157. Lakshmanan Sabaratnam, "Sri Lanka: The Lion and the Tiger in the Ethnic Archipelago," in *State Violence and Ethnicity*, ed. Pierre L. van den Berge (Boulder: University Press of Colorado, 1990), 187–220.

158. Sumantra Bose, *Contested Lands: Israel-Palestine, Kashmir, Bosnia, Cyprus, and Sri Lanka* (Cambridge, Mass.: Harvard University Press, 2007), 29.

159. Uyangoda, *Ethnic Conflict in Sri Lanka*, 11.

160. Uyangoda, *Ethnic Conflict in Sri Lanka*, 15–16.

161. Uyangoda, *Ethnic Conflict in Sri Lanka*, 18–19.

162. A. Jeyeratnam Wilson, "Sri Lanka: Ethnic Strife and the Politics of Space," in *The Territorial Management of Ethnic Conflict*, ed. John Coakley (London: Frank Cass, 2003), 173.

163. Sunil Bastian, "The Political Economy of Electoral Reform: Proportional Representation in Sri Lanka," in *Can Democracy Be Designed? The Politics of Institutional Choice in Conflict-Torn Societies*, ed. Sunil Bastian and Robin Luckham (New York: Zed Books, 2003), 201.

164. Bastian, "The Political Economy of Electoral Reform," 204.

165. Bastian, "The Political Economy of Electoral Reform," 206–207.

166. Jayasuriya, *The Changing Face of Electoral Politics in Sri Lanka, 1994–2004*, 14–16.

167. Bastian, "The Political Economy of Electoral Reform," 210.

168. Bastian, "The Political Economy of Electoral Reform," 218.

169. Jayasuriya, *The Changing Face of Electoral Politics in Sri Lanka, 1994–2004*, 30–34.

170. Ilan Peleg, "Transforming Ethnic Orders to Pluralist Regimes: Theoretical, Comparative, and Historical Analysis," in *Democracy and Ethnic Conflict: Advancing Peace in Deeply Divided Societies*, ed. Adrian Guelke (New York: Palgrave, 2004), 7–25.

171. Ian Lustick, "Stability in Deeply Divided Societies: Consociationalism versus Control," *World Politics* 31 (1979): 325–344.

172. Bastian, "The Political Economy of Electoral Reform," 206–207.

173. Maya Chadda, "Between Consociationalism and Control," in *Managing and Settling Ethnic Conflicts: Perspectives on Successes and Failures in Europe, Africa, and Asia*, ed. Ulrich Schneckener and Stefan Wolff (New York: Palgrave, 2004), 110.

174. Jonathan Spencer, "A Nationalism without Politics? The Illiberal Consequences of Liberal Institutions in Sri Lanka," *Third World Quarterly* 29 (2008): 611–629.

175. Erin K. Jenne, "Sri Lanka: A Fragmented State," in *State Failure and State Weakness in a Time of Terror*, ed. Robert I. Rotberg (Washington, D.C.: Brookings Institution Press, 2003), 219–244.

176. Darini Rajasingham-Senanyake, "Sri Lanka: Transformation of Legitimate Violence and Civil-Military Relations," in *Coercion and Governance: The Declining Political Role of the Military in Asia*, ed. Muthiah Alagappa (Palo Alto: Stanford University Press, 2001), 295.

177. Rajasingham-Senanyake, "Sri Lanka," 309.

178. Rajasingham-Senanyake, "Sri Lanka," 309.

179. Jeffrey Z. Rubin and I. William Zartman, "Asymmetric Bargaining," *Negotiation Journal* 11 (1995): 349–64.

180. Lloyd Jensen, "Negotiations and Power Asymmetries: The Cases of Bosnia, Northern Ireland, and Sri Lanka," *International Negotiation* 2 (1997): 21–41.

181. Jensen, "Negotiations and Power Asymmetries," 36–37.

182. Uyangoda, *Ethnic Conflict in Sri Lanka*, 9.

183. Uyangoda, *Ethnic Conflict in Sri Lanka*, 9–10.

184. Bruce Matthews, "Counter-Insurgency and the State in Modern Sri Lanka," in *The Counter-Insurgent State: Guerilla Warfare and State Building in the Twentieth Century*, ed. Paul B. Rich and Richard Stubbs (New York: St. Martin's Press, 1997), 88.

185. Sirimal Abeyratne, "Economic Roots of Political Conflict: The Case of Sri Lanka," *World Economy* 27 (2004): 1295–1314; Benedikt Korf and Kalinga Tudor Silva, "Poverty, Ethnicity, and Conflict in Sri Lanka" (paper presented at the conference "Staying Poor: Chronic Poverty and Development Policy," University of Manchester, April 7–9, 2003).

186. S. J. Tambiah, *Sri Lanka: Ethnic Fratricide and the Dismantling of Democracy* (Chicago: University of Chicago Press, 1986), 54–55.

187. Tambiah, *Sri Lanka*, 57.

188. Abeyratne, "Economic Roots of Political Conflict," 1296.

189. Rita Manchanda, "Ambivalent Gains in South Asian Conflicts," in *The Aftermath: Women in Post-Conflict Transformation*, ed. Sheila Meintjes, Anu Pillay, and Meredith Turshen (London: Zed Books, 2001), 112.

190. Malathi de Alwis, "The Changing Role of Women in Sri Lankan Society," *Social Research* 69, no. 3 (Fall 2002): 681.

191. Manchanda, "Ambivalent Gains in South Asian Conflicts," 113.

192. De Alwis, "The Changing Role of Women in Sri Lankan Society," 675–676.

193. De Alwis, "The Changing Role of Women in Sri Lankan Society," 683.

194. De Alwis, "The Changing Role of Women in Sri Lankan Society," 679, 684.

195. Manchanda, "Ambivalent Gains in South Asian Conflicts," 113; Malathi de Alwis, "Motherhood as a Space of Protest: Women's Political Participation in Contemporary Sri Lanka," *Nivedini—A Sri Lankan Feminist Journal* 9, no. 1 (June 2001): 3.

196. De Alwis, "The Changing Role of Women in Sri Lankan Society," 684.

197. De Alwis, "Motherhood as a Space of Protest," 17.

198. De Alwis, "Motherhood as a Space of Protest," 9.

199. Manchanda, "Ambivalent Gains in South Asian Conflicts," 113.

200. Manchanda, "Ambivalent Gains in South Asian Conflicts," 114; de Alwis, "The Changing Role of Women in Sri Lankan Society," 682; Yasmin Tambiah, "Sexuality and Women's Rights in Armed Conflict in Sri Lanka," *Reproductive Health Matters* 12, no. 23 (2004): 80. During the JVP rebellion of 1987–1989, women also participated, but very few. De Alwis, "The Changing Role of Women in Sri Lankan Society," 681.

201. Miranda Alison, "Cogs in the Wheel? Women in the Liberation Tigers of Tamil Eelam," *Civil Wars* 6, no. 4 (Winter 2003): 39.

202. Manchanda, "Ambivalent Gains in South Asian Conflicts," 114; see also Alison, "Cogs in the Wheel?" 47.

203. Manchanda, "Ambivalent Gains in South Asian Conflicts," 115. See also de Alwis on the phases of mobilization of women in the LTTE, with women being viewed as "warrior mother," and then later as the "new woman," by which women's liberation was explicitly connected with national liberation. De Alwis, "The Changing Role of Women in Sri Lankan Society," 682.

204. Alison, "Cogs in the Wheel?" 44–45.

205. De Alwis, "The Changing Role of Women in Sri Lankan Society," 686.

206. De Alwis, "The Changing Role of Women in Sri Lankan Society," 686.

207. De Alwis, "The Changing Role of Women in Sri Lankan Society," 686.

208. Simon Harris, "Gender, Participation, and Post-conflict Planning in Northern Sri Lanka," *Gender and Development* 12, no. 3 (November 2004): 62; Tambiah, "Sexuality and Women's Rights in Armed Conflict in Sri Lanka," 80.

209. Tambiah, "Sexuality and Women's Rights in Armed Conflict in Sri Lanka," 80.

210. Harris, "Gender, Participation, and Post-conflict Planning in Northern Sri Lanka," 63.

211. Ramashish Prasad Sinha, *Sri Lanka-United States Relations* (New Delhi: Commonwealth Publishers, 1992), 20.

212. Sinha, *Sri Lanka-United States Relations*, 19–21.

213. Sinha, *Sri Lanka-United States Relations*, 23–30.

214. Sinha, *Sri Lanka-United States Relations*, 40–43, 45–75.

215. Sinha, *Sri Lanka-United States Relations*, 75.

216. Sinha, *Sri Lanka-United States Relations*, 76–78, 81–82.

217. Sinha, *Sri Lanka-United States Relations*, 95–119.

218. Sinha, *Sri Lanka-United States Relations*, 131.

219. Sinha, *Sri Lanka-United States Relations*, 149.

220. Political Crisis in South Asia: Pakistan, Bangladesh, Sri Lanka, and Nepal. Hearing before the Subcommittee on the Middle East and South Asia of the Committee on Foreign Affairs. House of Representatives, 110th Cong., 1st sess. August 1, 2007. Serial No. 110-132. U.S. Government Printing Office, Washington, D.C., 2007.

221. K. Alan Kronstadt, "Sri Lanka: Background and U.S. Relations," *Report for Congress*, April 3, 2003, Congressional Research Service document (CRS-2003 RL31707).

222. Alan J. Bullion, *India, Sri Lanka, and the Tamil Crisis, 1976–1994: An International Perspective* (New York: Pinter, 1995), 84.

223. Nadarajah and Sriskandarajah, "Liberation Struggle or Terrorism?" 98.

224. Kronstadt, "Sri Lanka: Background and U.S. Relations," 9.

225. Kronstadt, "Sri Lanka: Background and U.S. Relations," 10.

226. "U.S. Wants Tamil Tigers to Surrender to Third Party and Sri Lanka to Offer Rebels Amnesty–State Department Official," *Asian Tribune*, May 7, 2009.

227. "United States and United Kingdom Joint Statement on the Humanitarian Situation in Sri Lanka," U.S. Department of State (May 12, 2009), www.state.gov/r/pa/prs/ps/2009/05/123288.htm.

228. "Statement by the President on the Situation in Sri Lanka and Detainee Photographs," Office of the Press Secretary (May 13, 2009), www.white

house.gov/the_press_office/Statement-by-the-President-on-the-Situation-in-Sri-Lanka-and-Detainee-Photographs/.

229. Robert C. Oberst, "The Impact of International Diffusion on the Escalation of the Sri Lankan Conflict," in *Ethnic Conflict and International Politics: Explaining Diffusion and Escalation*, ed. Steven E. Lobell and Philip Mauceri (New York: Palgrave, 2004), 165–179.

230. Bullion, *India, Sri Lanka, and the Tamil Crisis, 1976–1994*, 1.

231. Bullion, *India, Sri Lanka, and the Tamil Crisis, 1976–1994*, 41.

232. Bullion, *India, Sri Lanka, and the Tamil Crisis, 1976–1994*, 43.

233. Shelton U. Kodikara, *Foreign Policy of Sri Lanka: A Third World Perspective* (Delhi: Chanakya Publications, 1982), 26.

234. Bullion, *India, Sri Lanka, and the Tamil Crisis, 1976–1994*, 46–48.

235. Ravi Kant Dubey, *Indo-Sri Lankan Relations with Special Reference to the Tamil Problem* (New Delhi: Deep and Deep Publications, 1993), 80–81.

236. Bullion, *India, Sri Lanka, and the Tamil Crisis, 1976–1994*, 51.

237. Bullion, *India, Sri Lanka, and the Tamil Crisis, 1976–1994*, 55.

238. Dubey, *Indo-Sri Lankan Relations with Special Reference to the Tamil Problem*, 85.

239. Bullion, *India, Sri Lanka, and the Tamil Crisis, 1976–1994*, 107–108.

240. Bullion, *India, Sri Lanka, and the Tamil Crisis, 1976–1994*, 107–108.

241. Bullion, *India, Sri Lanka, and the Tamil Crisis, 1976–1994*, 111.

242. Bullion, *India, Sri Lanka, and the Tamil Crisis, 1976–1994*, 113.

243. Bullion, *India, Sri Lanka, and the Tamil Crisis, 1976–1994*, 122.

244. Dubey, *Indo-Sri Lankan Relations with Special Reference to the Tamil Problem*, 112.

245. Bullion, *India, Sri Lanka, and the Tamil Crisis, 1976–1994*, 123.

246. Bullion, *India, Sri Lanka, and the Tamil Crisis, 1976–1994*, 125.

247. Bullion, *India, Sri Lanka, and the Tamil Crisis, 1976–1994*, 125.

248. Bullion, *India, Sri Lanka, and the Tamil Crisis, 1976–1994*, 127–128.

249. Bullion, *India, Sri Lanka, and the Tamil Crisis, 1976–1994*, 126–28.

250. Bullion, *India, Sri Lanka, and the Tamil Crisis, 1976–1994*, 133–35.

251. Bullion, *India, Sri Lanka, and the Tamil Crisis, 1976–1994*, 135–36.

252. Bullion, *India, Sri Lanka, and the Tamil Crisis, 1976–1994*, 137–138.

253. "India Presses for Sri Lanka Truce as Casualties Rise," *Reuters*, April 24, 2009, www.reuters.com/article/asiaCrisis/idUSCOL318519.

254. As quoted in "Ensure 'Effective Devolution of Power': India to Sri Lanka," *The Hindu*, May 18, 2009, www.hindu.com/thehindu/holnus/00020090518 1985.htm.

255. John Stephen Moolakkattu, "Peace Facilitation by Small States: Norway in Sri Lanka," *Cooperation and Conflict* 40 (2005): 390.

256. Alan Bullion, "Norway and the Peace Process in Sri Lanka," *Civil Wars* 4 (2001): 76.

257. Moolakkattu, "Peace Facilitation by Small States: Norway in Sri Lanka," 391.

258. Moolakkattu, "Peace Facilitation by Small States: Norway in Sri Lanka," 386.

259. Moolakkattu, "Peace Facilitation by Small States: Norway in Sri Lanka," 392–396.

260. Uyangoda, *Ethnic Conflict in Sri Lanka*, 10-19.

261. Neelan Tiruchelvam, "Sri Lanka's Ethnic Conflict and Preventive Action: The Role of NGOs," in *Vigilance and Vengeance: NGOs Preventing Ethnic Conflict in Divided Societies*, ed. Robert I. Rotberg (Washington, D.C.: Brookings Institution Press, 1996), 154.

262. Jonathan Goodhand and Nick Lewer, "Sri Lanka: NGOs and Peace-Building in Complex Political Emergencies," *Third World Quarterly* 20 (1999): 73.

263. Goodhand and Lewer, "Sri Lanka: NGOs and Peace-Building in Complex Political Emergencies," 73-74.

264. Tiruchelvam, "Sri Lanka's Ethnic Conflict and Preventive Action," 157–159.

265. Goodhand and Lewer, "Sri Lanka: NGOs and Peace-Building in Complex Political Emergencies," 74–80.

266. Marit Haug, "Combining Service Delivery and Advocacy within Humanitarian Agencies: Experiences from the Conflict in Sri Lanka," International Working Papers #10 (London School of Economics, 2001), 1.

267. Goodhand and Lewer, "Sri Lanka: NGOs and Peace-Building in Complex Political Emergencies," 79.

268. Goodhand and Lewer, "Sri Lanka: NGOs and Peace-Building in Complex Political Emergencies," 80.

269. Haug, "Combining Service Delivery and Advocacy within Humanitarian Agencies," 12.

270. Haug, "Combining Service Delivery and Advocacy within Humanitarian Agencies," 9.

271. Vance Culbert, "Civil Society Development versus the Peace Dividend: International Aid in the Wanni," *Disasters* 29 (2005): 50.

272. Culbert, "Civil Society Development versus the Peace Dividend," 48–49.

273. Culbert, "Civil Society Development versus the Peace Dividend," 53–54.

274. Jonathan Goodhand and Bart Klem, *Aid, Conflict, and Peacebuilding in Sri Lanka, 2000–2005* (Colombo: The Asia Foundation, 2005), 93.

275. "Army to Rescue Trapped Civilians but NGO Says People Still at Risk," *Radio France Internationale*, April 10, 2009.

276. "LTTE Chief Prabhakaran Killed: Lanka Govt," *The Times of India*, May 18, 2009.

277. William Clarence, *Ethnic Warfare in Sri Lanka and the UN Crisis* (London/Ann Arbor: Pluto Press, 2007).

278. United Nations, "Sri Lanka: Thousands Caught in Conflict" (May 13, 2009), http://ochaonline.un.org/News/Features/ThousandsCaughtinSriLanka Conflict/tabid/5362/language/en-US/Default.aspx.

279. "CERF Allocates Nearly $10 Million for Emergency Humanitarian Assistance in Sri Lanka," Central Emergency Response Fund/United Nations, February 27, 2009.

280. World Food Programme, "WFP Providing Meals to Thousands of Sri Lankans Fleeing Civil Conflict" (May 15, 2009), www.wfp.org/news/news-release/wfp-providing-meal-thousands-sri-lankans-fleeing-civil-conflict.

CHAPTER 7

Israel and Palestine: Two Peoples, One Land

On December 17, 2008, Israel initiated "Operation Cast Lead," a military offensive into the Gaza Strip, a tiny sliver of land that Israel acquired after winning the Arab-Israeli war in 1967. Along with the West Bank, Gaza is defined as "occupied Palestinian territory" (while Israel unilaterally withdrew from Gaza in 2005, Gaza is still considered "occupied territory" by the United Nations, the United States and other countries, and Palestinians themselves).[1] The Israeli military offensive against Hamas, the Islamist Palestinian political party that has governed Gaza since it ousted the Palestinian Authority (PA, which is dominated by the secular political party, Fatah) in 2007, targeted government buildings, mosques, police stations, roads, and tunnels used to smuggle weapons into Gaza.[2] The Israeli military also shelled a UN school set up as a temporary refuge for the civilian population.[3] The air, sea, and ground offensive lasted for twenty-two days, ending on January 18, 2009, when Hamas and Israel each initiated a unilateral cease-fire.

The UN claims that more than 1,400 people were killed, and another 5,000 injured.[4] The Israeli military claims that 1,166 Palestinians were killed, of which 709 "were identified as Hamas terror operatives, among them several from various other terror organizations," 295 were civilians, and the remaining 162 "have not yet been attributed to any organization." Overall, the military argues that of the total number of Palestinians killed, the "vast majority" were "terror operatives."[5] In contrast to the Israeli military's numbers, the Palestinian Center for Human Rights (PCHR) maintains that 1,417 Palestinians were killed, of which 926 were civilians, 255 were "non-combatant" police officers, and 236 "took 'an active part in hostilities.'"[6] In many ways, this dispute about numbers of killed underscores the competing narratives about what is at stake in the conflict.

Since "Operation Cast Lead" ended, the plight of the 1.5 million people who live in Gaza remains dire. Given that Gaza's borders remain closed, there is no longer adequate food for children, medicine is increasingly unavailable,[7] unemployment and poverty levels remain high,[8] and access to electricity and water are limited. Approximately 90 percent of the population is affected by power cuts, and the other 10 percent has no electricity. Approximately 100,000 people "get water once in every two or three days." In addition, according to UN agencies working in Gaza, 4,100 houses were destroyed and more than 15,000 damaged, leaving thousands homeless and living in refugee camps (also damaged during the three weeks of fighting). Israel maintains sanctions placed on Gaza after Hamas came to power in the territory.[9]

Israel justified its actions by arguing that it was responding to years of rocket attacks into southern Israel from Palestinian militants in Gaza, and such a formidable response would restore Israel's deterrent power and capability.[10] Moreover, in terms of specific targets, Israel claimed that Hamas (which it considers a terrorist organization) had used civilian buildings, including the UN school and hospitals, in its attacks on Israeli forces. While regretting the loss of civilian life, Israel maintained that Hamas's actions left it no choice but to hit these targets.[11]

The international community responded to the Gaza conflict when it began, calling on both parties to halt their actions. Israel was expected to end its offensive, and Hamas was expected to end its rocket attacks on southern Israel. Both were expected to agree to a cease-fire. Moreover, in light of concerns about the Israeli military's conduct during the conflict (including the possible use of white phosphorous munitions in civilian populated areas, which is illegal under international law, and the disproportionate use of force in response to militant rocket attacks on Israeli territory) and Hamas's actions (including firing of rockets into civilian areas within Israel as well as offensives carried out within the civilian populated parts of Gaza), the United Nations launched an investigation into whether violations of international law (such as war crimes) were committed by both sides. In April 2009 the UN's Human Rights Council appointed a four-person team, led by Justice Richard Goldstone (who had previously served as chief prosecutor of the International Criminal Tribunals for the former Yugoslavia and Rwanda), to examine whether such violations of international law occurred.[12] Israel refused to cooperate with the UN Human Rights Council investigation, while Hamas informed Goldstone that it would provide "full and transparent cooperation."[13] Released on September 15, 2009, the Goldstone Report, as it is called, concluded that both Israel and Hamas committed violations of international law, including war crimes and crimes against humanity. The report urges both parties to conduct credible, impartial, and comprehensive investigations into whether such crimes were in fact committed. The report further recommends that if the two parties cannot or will not conduct such investigations and prosecutions, the UN Security Council should consider sending the matter to the International Criminal Court. Both Hamas and Israel disagreed with the report's findings that civilians were deliberately targeted. The Israeli government rejected the report's findings, while the Hamas leadership stated it would conduct investigations.[14]

The three-week-long Gaza conflict is a recent example of the ongoing conflict between Israeli Jews and Palestinians, both of whom make claims for control over the same land. The case is an example of both escalation (Arab states have provided logistical, financial, and political support for Palestinians, and are thus drawn into the conflict) and diffusion (Israel has engaged in actions against states that have provided refuge for Palestinian militants, such as Lebanon). Attempts at peace have occurred over the years, but more than six decades after Israel's independence, conflict between these two national-ethnic groups remains.

This chapter seeks to explore and examine the causes of the conflict, as well as the various peace proposals to end the conflict (and why they have failed). These two ethnic groups continue to hold enemy images of each other, with concomitant mistrust that prevents movement toward a durable peace. The conflict is complicated by the fact that some Palestinians reside in Israel proper, and are therefore Israeli citizens, while others reside in the occupied (Israel calls them "disputed") territories of the West Bank, East Jerusalem, and Gaza. Israel maintains control over all access points (air, roads, sea) to Gaza even after its unilateral withdrawal, except Gaza's border with Egypt. Those Palestinians living in the occupied territories are not Israeli citizens, as Israel has not formally annexed the territories (Palestinians living in East Jerusalem are considered residents, not citizens). At the same time, however, Israel maintains control over most of the West Bank with checkpoints and roadblocks throughout the territory and the construction of a security wall to prevent Palestinian terrorist attacks on Israel. Moreover, Israeli Jewish settlements continue to be built in the West Bank and East Jerusalem (dominated by Palestinian Arabs). Today approximately 280,000 Israelis live in settlements in the West Bank (121 settlements are officially recognized by the Israeli government; there are 102 unauthorized settlements in the West Bank not recognized by the government), and 190,000 live in settlements in East Jerusalem.[15]

While the conflict is often focused on the specifics of control of the land, as David Makovsky notes, "the conflict runs far deeper. Palestinians and Israelis have radically different historical narratives. These predate the occupation that began in 1967; they go to each side's self-conception as a historical victim, and they have engendered much mutual hatred."[16] What solution, therefore, to this ongoing ethnic conflict is possible? Following the 1967 Arab-Israeli war, the UN Security Council passed Resolution 242, which called for a two-state solution, with the formation of a viable Palestinian state in the territories Israel occupied in 1967 ("land for peace"). Forty plus years later, the two-state solution continues

MAP 7.1
Ethnic Distribution in Israel and Palestine

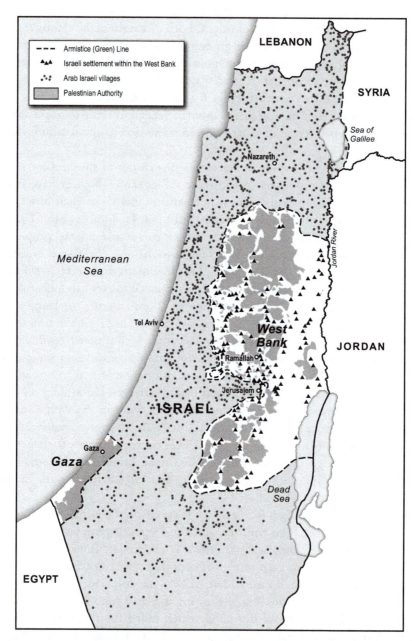

Source: Data from The Palestinian Return Center, http://www.prc.org.uk/mapmain.php, and the United Nations Office for the Coordination of Humanitarian Affairs, http://www.ochaopt.org/documents/OCHAoPt_ClsrMp_WB0106_En.pdf.

to be supported by the international community, and most Israelis and Palestinians, as the best solution to resolve the crisis, and yet its attainment has proved difficult, as this chapter will show.

Jeffrey Helsing accurately captures the essence of the Israeli-Palestinian conflict: "a unique ethnic conflict because it has always been a highly internationalized conflict born of two world wars and focused on a small area of land with much broader regional and global implications."[17] The chapter thus begins with an overview of the historical background to the conflict and the various attempts at peace by the international community. Using the levels of analysis framework,[18] the chapter then moves to a discussion of individual Palestinian and Israeli leaders who affected the course of the conflict, followed by a discussion of the domestic level factors. The next section explores the role of international level actors who have attempted to resolve the conflict. The chapter concludes with a recap of the main themes of the chapter and a discussion of the future of the conflict.

ISRAEL AND PALESTINE IN HISTORICAL CONTEXT

The Ottoman Empire ruled over the territory of what is now Israel and the occupied territories from the sixteenth century until the early twentieth century.[19] Immigration of Jews to Palestine began in earnest in the late nineteenth century, particularly followers of the Zionist movement for the creation of a Jewish homeland in "historic and biblical Jewish lands."[20] With the defeat of the Ottoman Empire's military forces in 1917, Britain gained control of the territory.[21] During World War I, Britain's policies in the region directly affected the rising tensions between Arabs and Jews in Palestine (as well as affecting the rest of the Middle East region). The British promised Arab independence and encouraged the Arabs to revolt against their Ottoman rulers. Yet, the British sought support from Jews. The 1917 Balfour Declaration, announced by the British government, "was a pledge to support a national homeland for Jews in Palestine."[22]

With the defeat of the Ottoman Empire, British control of the territory, known as the British Mandate, began in 1920 and ended in 1948 when Israel became independent. During the period of the British Mandate, "Arabs comprised 92 percent of the population and owned 98 percent of the land."[23] With Hitler in power in Germany, Jews sought to escape and looked to Palestine as their destination, given that very few countries were willing to accept Jewish immigration. With the dramatic increase in the numbers of Jews immigrating to Palestine, Arabs living in the region expressed their discontent violently and revolted.[24] Tensions between Jews and Arabs were kept in check by the British presence in Palestine. Once Britain withdrew, following the end of World War II, it was not clear who would govern the territory: Jews or Arabs? The problem was that neither group was willing to give up their hegemonic ambitions. Both groups perceived a threat from the other, leading to an ethnic security dilemma. Thus, when the British finally did withdraw, conflict was the outcome, not peace.[25]

Conflict over the Land

The international community became involved in the conflict before Israel became an independent state (but while the territory was still part of the British Mandate). In November 1947 the United Nations General Assembly passed Resolution 181, which called for the partition of the territory into two states, one Arab and one Jewish. Jerusalem would be made an internationally protected city.[26] Concerned that they would no longer control the territory and that the Zionist leadership would not comply with a future compromise, the Palestinians and the Arab countries rejected the partition plan.[27] In fact, David Ben-Gurion (who would become Israel's first prime minister) spoke at a Zionist meeting in 1938: "I favor partition of the country because when we become a strong power after the establishment of the state, we will abolish partition and spread throughout all of Palestine."[28]

Soon, war broke out between the two groups, with the involvement of armies from neighboring Arab states (Egypt, Jordan, Lebanon, and Syria) who fought on the side of the Palestinian Arabs. Approximately 10,000 Arabs and 6,000 Jews died in the 1948 war. In addition to those that died, more than a million people were displaced from their homes.[29] In the end, the Zionists prevailed, the new Israeli state was established, and an armistice signed in 1949 between the four Arab countries and Israel divided the territory of the former British Mandate (the West Bank and East Jerusalem controlled by Jordan, the Gaza Strip controlled by Egypt, and Israel). At the same time, the war led to the creation of a Palestinian diaspora seeking a return to their homeland. The plight of the Palestinians and the call for an independent Palestinian state "became a rallying cry in much of the Arab world," which would resonate for many years that followed and, indeed, continues today.[30] The *nakba* (Arabic for "catastrophe") and the desire to return would define Palestinians' identity.

Though most Palestinians fled, either by choice or force (even before the invasion of Israel by the Arab states in 1948), many did stay (it is estimated that of a population of 900,000 before the war, upwards of 750,000 Palestinians no longer resided in the territory of the new state of Israel). Importantly, anywhere from one-sixth to one-half of those Palestinians who stayed became internal refugees. These internal refugees lost their homes and their land. With the loss of such a large percentage of the prewar population, as well as the loss of land and homes, the Arabs who remained were clustered geographically into three main areas of the country, and in small numbers in predominantly Jewish cities or ethnically mixed cities. Mutual hostility and mistrust continued between the Palestinians and Jews residing in the same country, but violent clashes did not continue after the wars of 1947–1949.[31] Israeli Arabs were granted Israeli citizenship. At the same time, Israeli Jews perceived a threat to Israel's existence as a result of concerns that Israeli Arabs identified both with the larger Arab community as well as the plight of the Palestinians, and the irredentist claims emanating from the Arab countries in the region. Palestinian Arabs now lived in a state in which Jewish identity and community dominated.[32]

Faced with a weakened but hostile Arab population (now approximately 20 percent of the total Israeli population), the Israeli government engaged in coercive policies to control the Arabs living in Israel, concerned with maintaining a Jewish majority. Beginning in 1948, the government imposed military rule in Arab areas, including policies such as administrative detention and censorship, as well as restricting the free movement of the Arab population.[33] Military rule, which lasted until 1966, maintained and strengthened Jewish dominance in the state, weakened the Arabs, and prevented the outbreak of violence between Jews and Arabs. Yet, hostility between the ethnic groups did not dissipate.[34]

At the same time that the Israeli government faced a hostile Arab population within its borders, it also faced a Palestinian population desperate to return to its homeland outside its borders. Now living in refugee camps in Arab countries, such as Syria, Lebanon, and Jordan, the Palestinian diaspora, with the support of these countries, sought to regain their territory. Cross-border attacks by Palestinians occurred even after the 1948 war. The Israeli government responded with military strikes against Palestinian targets. While the Arab states lessened their support for the Palestinian cross-border attacks, Arab nationalism grew. The Palestinians sought the support of the Arab states for their liberation.[35] In 1964 the Palestine Liberation Organization (PLO) was established, headed by Yasser Arafat. He would remain the most prominent spokesperson for Palestinian independence for the next four decades until his death in 2004 (see the individual level of analysis).

The 1967 Arab-Israeli war, in which Israel launched a preemptive attack against the Arab states that it perceived as a serious and immediate threat, led to the defeat of the Arab militaries and the Israeli occupation of the West Bank and East Jerusalem (formerly under Jordan's control), Gaza (Egyptian territory), and the Golan Heights (Syrian territory). With the conclusion of the war, Palestinians engaged in cross-border strikes, originating from Jordan. In response, the Israeli government took action, striking Palestinian targets and also pressuring Jordan to control the Palestinians residing in that country. Concerns about instability within Jordan led the government to clamp down on the Palestinians in September 1970, known as "Black September." The Palestinian nationalist movement was expelled, forced to find a new home, this time in Lebanon. Cross-border strikes by Palestinians from Lebanon into Israel met with reprisals from the

Israeli government. The Israeli raids contributed to the instability of Lebanon and the eruption of civil war in that country. The Palestinian strikes did not end, as the Lebanese government could not control the militants. Israel responded in 1982 with an invasion of the country (which lasted until 2000 when Israel withdrew its forces from southern Lebanon).[36]

Palestinians living in the West Bank, East Jerusalem, and Gaza now found themselves in "occupied territory" following Israel's victory in the 1967 war. For these Palestinians, life was "severely restricted" by the Israeli military administration that ruled the territories. Palestinians were limited in their freedom of association, freedom of expression, and freedom of the press.[37]

In the years after the 1967 war, Palestinians and Israelis acknowledged the need to reach a compromise. The Palestinians called for an independent state, with territorial claims over territory occupied by Israel. The international community responded. The UN Security Council passed resolutions 242 and 338. Both resolutions called on Israel to withdraw from the occupied territories.[38] Palestinian nationalist demands for liberation and an end to Israeli discriminatory policies continued in the subsequent decades, with terrorist attacks against Israel. By the late 1980s, the situation became increasingly problematic within the occupied territories. As a result, on December 9, 1987, Palestinians rebelled— the first *intifada*. With the intifada well underway, the PLO responded, as was highlighted in Arafat's speech to the United Nations General Assembly on December 13, 1988, in which he endorsed the idea of the two-state solution. This was a marked evolution in the PLO's platform. Its platform from its creation in 1964 focused on the liberation of all Palestinian territory, and such liberation necessitated the end of Israel's existence. Yet, beginning in the 1960s, the PLO's platform began to modify. By 1988 the PLO accepted the two-state solution, and thus recognized the existence of Israel, as the solution to the conflict. The Palestinian leadership would accept an independent Palestinian state created in Gaza and the West Bank. East Jerusalem would be the capital. The PLO further agreed that such a state would be demilitarized, and endorsed the presence of an international peacekeeping force along the new Palestinian-Israeli border. Moreover, the PLO agreed to cease terrorism and other attacks on Israel, while also agreeing to "a token return" of Palestinian refugees to Israel (rather than a large-scale return that would undermine the Jewish majority in Israel).[39] The intifada finally ended in 1992, and the movement toward peace negotiations directly between Palestinians and Israelis began.

Attempts at Peace

In response to the deteriorating situation with the intifada, the 1990s witnessed a flurry of diplomatic activity between Israel and its neighbors, including, for the first time, the Palestinians. It was also in the 1990s that peace negotiations occurred directly between Israelis and Palestinians. The 1991 Madrid Conference was the first such conference, focusing on peace based on resolutions 242 and 338 (the conference was between Israel and Syria, but Palestinians were also present). In 1993 secret face-to-face negotiations were mediated by Norway between Israeli and Palestinian representatives. These secret negotiations led to the 1993 Oslo Accords/Declaration of Principles (DOP) (which called for the mutual recognition of Israel and the PLO), signed in Washington, D.C., when President Bill Clinton, Israeli prime minister Yitzhak Rabin, and PLO leader Yasser Arafat shook hands on the White House lawn—a monumental historical event. An interim agreement, the DOP established a transitional period of Palestinian self-rule in the West Bank and Gaza (with the idea that negotiations on the final status of the territories would go forward). Between May 1994 and September 1999, a series of agreements, such as the Oslo II (1995) interim agreement, led to the transfer of some (security and civilian police) powers from Israel to the Palestinian Authority (PA) (which had been created in 1994) in those areas populated by Palestinians.[40]

While the series of agreements were signed, the expectations of the Palestinians, following the signing of the Oslo Accords for an independent Palestinian state, were dashed. As Jerome Slater remarks, "The achilles heel of Oslo was that it postponed the most difficult issues—the borders of the Palestinian state, the Israeli settlements, the Jerusalem problem, the division of West Bank water, and the refugee issue—until the final settlement that was to be negotiated by May 1999."[41] In the meantime, for example, there was no halt to Israeli settlement expansion or the requirement to dismantle existing ones.[42] Prime Minister Shimon Peres increased the settlement process and opposed Palestinian independence. In response to the Israeli government's "assassination of a Palestinian activist accused of terrorism," Palestinian militants bombed urban centers in Israel, which killed many Israeli civilians. Palestinian violence as well as the failed intervention in Lebanon led to the loss of support for Peres by the Israeli public. In 1996 a new election brought an end to Peres's leadership and the rise of Benjamin Netanyahu to power. With Netanyahu, a hard-liner from the Likud Party, the Oslo peace process effectively stalled and the Israeli occupation of the West Bank and Gaza continued, settlements continued to expand, and the deadline for the completion of the final status settlement of 1999 passed.[43]

In turn, Netanyahu lost the election to Ehud Barak, who took office in 1999. At the invitation of President Clinton, in July 2000, PA leader Arafat and Israeli prime minister Barak met at Camp David, Maryland, to restart the peace negotiations. While both sides made concessions at the summit, in the end it failed when Arafat rejected the proposal. Scholars have examined the positions of the parties to the negotiations and concluded that the conventional U.S. and Israeli narrative, that the Palestinians rejected the generous Israeli offers, is flawed. Rather, the Palestinian narrative better reflects the reality of what transpired at the talks.[44] Importantly, when Israelis and Palestinians worked on the maps based on the proposals set forth, it was clear that the two occupied territories would remain divided. Within each of the territories, as Slater observes, were further divisions "into enclaves by the Israeli settlements, highways, and military positions, the links between which 'would always be at the mercies of Israel, the Israeli Defense Forces, and the settlers.'" Moreover, as the Palestinians would have "little or no control over [Palestine's] water resources" nor "independently controlled border access to neighboring countries," the economic dependence of the new Palestinian state on Israel would be significant.[45] According to Jeremy Pressman, the Israeli territorial proposal was "less forthcoming than it initially appeared." For example, the Israelis offered 91 percent of the West Bank as defined by Israel. The specific offer differed "by approximately 5 percentage points from the Palestinian definition."[46] Additionally, the territory that the Israelis were offering at the summit was not "contiguous"; instead, the West Bank would be separated "into two, if not three, separate areas."[47] Moreover, while willing to divide Jerusalem, Barak was unwilling to permit Palestinian sovereignty over Arab villages in East Jerusalem. What Palestinians would receive was "functional autonomy . . . in core Arab neighborhoods of East Jerusalem." Thus, Israel would maintain sovereignty over Arab areas of the city.[48] This would make it difficult to have a viable and independent state. Given the actual implications of the proposal facing the Palestinians, Arafat's response was one of rejection.

Following the breakdown of the negotiations, the situation on the ground for Palestinians did not improve. In fact, the situation worsened two months later when Palestinians perceived Knesset (Israeli parliament) member Ariel Sharon's September 28, 2000, visit to the Al-Aqsa mosque at the Haram al-Sharif/Temple Mount in Jerusalem with more than a thousand Israeli police as offensive. In response, unarmed Palestinians demonstrated. The demonstrators faced a large number of Israeli police who responded by firing on them. The government also instituted further closures that restricted the goods and people in the West Bank and Gaza. The confrontation triggered a series of Palestinian demonstrations and was the start of the second uprising, or intifada, in the occupied territories. The Israeli government claims that the intifada was orchestrated by the PLO/PA leadership in order to gain the upper hand in diplomatic negotiations and sympathy from the international community.[49]

The international community responded. In October 2000 U.S. president Clinton as well as representatives from Israel, Egypt, Jordan, the PA, the EU, and the UN attended the Middle East Peace Summit at Sharm el-Sheikh, Egypt. At this summit, Clinton announced the formation of a fact-finding mission to examine the causes of the second intifada and provide recommendations for resuming peace talks. On April 30, 2001, the Sharm el-Sheikh Fact-Finding Committee, headed by former senator George Mitchell (who led the peace negotiations in Northern Ireland that culminated in the 1998 Good Friday Agreement), presented its report. The Mitchell Report, as it was called, recommended three steps to address the lack of trust: end the violence, rebuild confidence (for example, Israel halt settlement activity, the PA take concrete measures to prevent terrorist operations and punish those engaging in terrorist activity), and resume negotiations. The report stated that in recognizing the increased perception "of futility and despair" and increased use of violence, "[p]olitical leaders on both sides must act and speak decisively to reverse these dangerous trends, they must rekindle the desire and the drive for peace. That will be difficult. But it can be done and it must be done, for the alternative is unacceptable and should be unthinkable."[50]

The Arab Peace Initiative, initiated by Saudi Arabia, was presented by the members of the Arab League at its summit in March 2002. The document called for an Israeli withdrawal from the territories captured in 1967 (thus implementing UN resolutions 242 and 338) and Israel's acceptance of an independent Palestinian state (with East Jerusalem as its capital). The Arab states also declared that they would "establish normal relations" with Israel in return, as the Arab states would "consider the Arab-Israeli conflict over, sign a peace agreement with Israel, and achieve peace for all states in the region."[51]

In April 2003 the "Quartet" (the EU, Russia, the United States, and the UN) created the "performance-based roadmap" (in three phases) that would lead to a settlement of the Israeli-Palestinian conflict by 2005. Importantly, the Road Map was structured such that the final settlement would be the two-state solution. The Road Map affirmed that "[t]he settlement will resolve the Israeli-Palestinian conflict, and end the occupation that began in 1967, based on the foundations of the Madrid Conference, the principle of land for peace, UNSCRs 242, 338 and 1397, agreements previously reached by the parties, and the initiative of Saudi Crown Prince Abdullah—endorsed by the Beirut Arab League Summit—calling for acceptance of Israel as a neighbor living in peace and security, in the context of a comprehensive settlement."[52] Continued violence and claims by both sides that the other side was not meeting the commitments to the Road Map phases led to the postponement of the 2005 date for an agreement on the permanent status.[53]

During this time, Arafat was under siege by the Israeli government at his compound in Ramallah in the West Bank.[54] The siege had begun in 2002; Arafat remained in power until late 2004, when he died, replaced by Mahmoud Abbas following an election in the West Bank and Gaza in January 2005. To get the peace process going again, in February 2005 the PA and Israel agreed to the Sharm el-Sheikh Commitments. Later that year, in September, Israel unilaterally withdrew its military forces and settlers from Gaza (as well as settlers and soldiers from four West Bank settlements in the north), but maintained control over all access points to Gaza.[55] Following Hamas's election victory in 2006 and its ouster of the PA from Gaza in 2007, the PA and Hamas have been unable to form a unity government, and thus Gaza and the West Bank are governed by two different Palestinian factions.[56]

Another attempt at moving the peace process forward occurred at a meeting held in Annapolis, Maryland, in November 2007. Abbas and Israeli prime minister Ehud Olmert (he had become prime minister in March 2006) agreed to restart negotiations that would lead to a final settlement of the conflict.[57] However, the main ("final status") issues of contention between Israelis and Palestinians remain: the status of Jerusalem, Jewish settlements in the West Bank and East Jerusalem, borders of the possible Palestinian state, the Israeli security wall/fence, water rights, and the right of return for more than three million Palestinian refugees.[58] Peace remains elusive and the conflict continues.

INDIVIDUAL LEVEL

This section examines key individuals on both sides who have been instrumental in the peace negotiations (both their success and failure). From the outset of Israeli independence, Israeli leaders have been motivated to ensure the Jewish state's continued existence and Israel's security in a region with neighbors seeking the country's destruction. The consistent policy of ensuring Israel's security and a Jewish majority has dominated the agenda of all Israeli prime ministers, regardless of whether they came from political parties on the left, center, or right. Israeli prime ministers have been willing to enter into negotiations with Israel's Arab neighbors. Direct negotiations between the Palestinians and Israelis, however, did not begin in earnest until the early 1990s. This section, therefore, focuses on two Israeli prime ministers (Yitzhak Rabin and Ehud Barak) who participated in these peace talks, one that led to an agreement (Oslo) and one that did not (Camp David).

Among Palestinian leaders, the section examines Yasser Arafat. As leader of the Palestine Liberation Organization from the 1960s onward, as well as the president of the governing body, the Palestinian Authority (PA), Arafat was by far the most dominant and representative figure for the Palestinians. He represented the Palestinians at the negotiations leading to both the Oslo Accords and the Camp David summit.

What will be evident in the discussion of both Palestinian and Israeli leaders is the presence of extremists and spoilers who have made the conclusion of a final peace settlement difficult. Extremists on the Israeli side demand the right to construct settlements in any land considered biblical Israel, even in areas in which Palestinians already reside. Moreover, the expectation is that the Israeli Defense Forces (IDF) will protect the settlers. Extremists on the Palestinian side demand the right of return for all those Palestinians who were expelled or who left during the 1948 war, and their descendants. The right of return is perceived as a threat to Israelis, as the return of Palestinians would change the demographic makeup of Israel, in that it would no longer be a Jewish state. Both sides engage in violent actions, as Palestinian militants carry out terrorist attacks. The Israeli response is to engage in military raids on places from which the Palestinian violence emanates. In the end, as Milton Esman points out, "the cycle of violence and reprisals continue."[59] How the leaders from both sides have been able to deal with the extremists within their own groups (and thus ethnic outbidding), as well as each other, reveals much about the role that individuals play in ethnic conflict.

Yitzhak Rabin

Born in Jerusalem in 1922, Yitzhak Rabin began his professional life in the military. He served in the Israeli military for nearly three decades, including holding the position of Chief of Staff of the IDF. He held this position during the 1967 War, and retired from the IDF in 1968. Appointed as the Israeli ambassador to the United States until 1973, he was able to strengthen the U.S.-Israeli relationship. In terms of party politics, he became involved with the Labor Party after his tenure as ambassador ended, beginning with a position as minister of labor in April 1974 in Prime Minister Golda Meir's government. Following the resignation of her government, he became prime minister on June 2, 1974. His focus was in large part domestic politics: improve the economy and address social problems. He also sought to strengthen the IDF, and he pursued an active foreign policy, concluding an interim agreement with Egypt in 1975 (the United States mediated). The signing of this agreement led to the first Memorandum of Understanding between Israel and the United States, thereby solidifying the close relationship between these two countries. His tenure as prime minister lasted until May 1977 when elections led to the defeat of the Labor Party. He continued to hold political positions; for example, he was the minister of defense in the National Unity Government (1984–1990). From 1990 until 1992 he was an opposition member of the Knesset. He was elected prime minister again with the Labor win in the 1992 elections. While focused on domestic issues, he was also focused on foreign policy, seeking peace with the Palestinians as well as Arab countries. His foreign policy led to the support for the secret Oslo negotiations that culminated in the Oslo Accords in 1993. He followed that agreement with the signing of the Gaza-Jericho agreement (which dealt with the implementation of the first stage of the DOP) and the Israel-Jordan Peace Treaty in 1994. Along with Israeli foreign minister Shimon Peres and Yasser Arafat, Rabin received the Nobel Peace Prize in 1994.[60]

While campaigning for election in 1992 he more than once asserted the possibility of a peace agreement with the Palestinians "within six to nine months."[61] At the same time, his first few months in office did not move the peace process along, as the government was preoccupied with internal politics given the nature of the coalition government (Labor had to join forces with Shas, the ultraorthodox religious party, and Meretz, a secular-dovish party, to form a governing coalition).[62] Yet, Rabin's role in the negotiation of the Oslo Accords cannot be overstated. The decision to recognize the PLO as the legitimate representative of the Palestinians was a significant development in Israeli-Palestinian relations. His willingness to agree to territorial partition represented a change in Israeli policy. The Israeli religious right's long-term goal of a Greater Israel that encompassed significant territory was dashed with Oslo.[63] He explained his reasoning for moving forward with the peace process that resulted from the negotiations: "I'm fed up. It's time to bring something new to our children. We belong to a generation that has had to fight. And though there is a deeply held feeling that this is Israel's fate, I must try to change it. We must either close the door to this feeling or close the door to the whole world, for the whole world supports the peace process."[64]

At the same time, however, Rabin refused to accept the Palestinian demand for a freeze on settlements. In fact, he supported the continued expansion of Jewish settlements.[65] Yet, he made it clear that there was a difference between settlements in pre-1967 areas and post-1967 areas. In 1995 he stated that "settlements add nothing, absolutely nothing, to Israel's security. They are a liability rather than an asset."[66] With regard to Jerusalem, on September 2, 1993, at the Knesset, Rabin remarked: "This government, like all of its predecessors, believes there is no disagreement in this House concerning Jerusalem as the eternal capital of Israel. United Jerusalem will not be open to negotiation. It has been and will forever be the capital of the Jewish people, under Israeli sovereignty, a focus of dreams and longings of every Jew."[67]

While the Oslo Accords were meant to open a new period of peace between Israelis and Palestinians, Rabin's closure policy of the occupied territories earlier in the year, in March 1993, made life more difficult for Palestinians. For example, approximately 120,000 Palestinians worked in Israel. The closure policy prevented these workers from entering Israel, thereby leading to significant unemployment.[68] The "general closure" separated Gaza from the West Bank and East Jerusalem. The Israeli government installed a fence around Gaza. The Jewish settlers living in Gaza were protected by Israeli military forces. The PA controlled the remaining territory within Gaza (approximately "1.3 million Palestinians and eight refugee camps").[69] Moreover, two years after the closure policy was first instituted, at Rabin's direction, Moshe Shahal, Israel's energy minister, began to draft plans for a "security fence" to "run more or less parallel to the West Bank Green Line" (the Green Line, or Armistice Line, is the border resulting from the 1967 war).[70]

The Oslo Accords, in essence, called for Israel's "direct cooperation with an Arab security force, specifically the Palestinian Authority police." Rabin's view was that Israel's military was sufficient to ensure Israel's self-defense. Cooperating with other actors, such as the PA, did not threaten that self-defense. During the 1992 election campaign, he made it clear that Israel's continued rule over the Palestinians was a security threat. The way to reduce that threat was through a policy of separation from the Palestinians; in other words, Israel would end its occupation of the territories. For him, according to Danny Ben-Moshe, security meant a "strong economy, foreign investment, absorption and employment, all of which peace would help facilitate."[71]

Internal divisions within the Labor Party, however, plagued the peace process when Rabin planned to bring the Interim Agreement with the Palestinians (Oslo II) to the Knesset for a vote in October. The agreement passed with the slimmest of margins, 61 in favor, but 59 opposed.[72] During the debate on the agreement in the Knesset in August 1995, Rabin stated: "this Government does not believe in Greater Israel, nor does it want to rule another people."[73]

In his speech to the Knesset on October 5, 1995, he continued to lay out his plans, noting that the Jordan River would serve as Israel's security border. According to Slater, "Israel would retain settlements and military bases in the Jordan River valley, deep inside Palestinian territory." Rabin explained that the Palestinian "entity" comprised the "home to most of the Palestinian residents living in the Gaza Strip and the West Bank. . . . We would like this to be . . . less than a state."[74] This Palestinian entity would effectively be "a series of isolated enclaves on less than 50 percent of the West Bank and Gaza, cut off from each other and surrounded by Israeli settlers and military bases." Rabin's plans went forward, including increased Jewish settlements in Jerusalem. Palestinian homes were confiscated and destroyed so that the government could construct roads for access to Jewish settlements.[75] In fact, as Slater observes further, expansion of Jewish settlements during Rabin's term "was greater than it had been under the previous hardline Likud government of Yitzhak Shamir."[76]

Rabin's vision of a settlement with the Palestinians came to a halt following his assassination on November 4, 1995, by a right-wing Israeli Jewish man, and Palestinian suicide bombings in Israel proper, which led to the election of Benjamin Netanyahu of the Likud Party in 1996. During his tenure as prime minister, the peace process lost momentum, only to be restarted with the election of Ehud Barak in 1999.[77]

Ehud Barak

Born in 1942 in British Mandate Palestine, Barak began his career in the military. He served for thirty-six years in the IDF until 1995 when he entered politics. His career in the IDF culminated in his position of Chief of the General Staff, which included the responsibility of implementing the security arrangements as well as the redeployment of Israeli forces in Gaza and Jericho following the signing of the 1994 Gaza-Jericho agreement. With his retirement from the IDF, Prime Minister Rabin asked him to serve as minister of the interior, which he readily accepted. He then became minister of foreign affairs when Peres assumed the position of prime minister following Rabin's assassination. By the late 1990s, he became head of the Labor Party; following the election in 1999 he became the prime minister.[78]

Barak's victory over Netanyahu, and the return to power of the Labor Party, resulted, in large part, from Netanyahu's policies regarding the Palestinians. He signed the 1998 Wye River Memorandum, mediated by the United States, that outlined the implementation process for the agreements that Arafat and Rabin had signed earlier, but Netanyahu actually did nothing to carry out the agreement's terms. As a result, the Israeli public who supported the continuing peace efforts was disenchanted with him, while those who opposed the peace process "felt betrayed by him" for having signed the memorandum in the first place. Domestic pressure forced Netanyahu to run for election, only to be defeated and replaced by Barak.[79]

Upon entering office, Barak was committed to resolve "the entire Arab-Israeli conflict within a year." As Makovsky notes, there were three main points to his promise: he indicated he was willing to make significant concessions to the Palestinians, sought to deal with the threat from Iraq and Iran (as rising regional powers), and would maintain the extremely positive relationship he had with Clinton.[80] At the same time, he sought to improve relations with Syria, but those talks, having failed in spring 2000, expended precious time in his first eight months in office. Those eight months made it problematic to reach a deal with the Palestinians within his one-year deadline.[81]

At the Camp David summit in June 2000 with Clinton and Arafat, he made significant concessions to the Palestinians. Yet as Slater observes, "It is true that Barak's proposal went further than any other previous Israeli offer to the Palestinians, especially in agreeing to a Palestinian state and to the sharing of at least part of Jerusalem. On the other hand, it is no less true that Barak's proposals fell far short of a genuinely fair compromise that would result in a viable Palestinian state. Within a few weeks of Camp David, a number of Israel political analysts had reached this conclusion."[82] For example, his offers were verbal, as he would not allow an officially written record. With regard to Jerusalem, he proposed that Greater Jerusalem would encompass all Jewish settlements constructed throughout East Jerusalem and its suburbs since 1967. These settlements "extend far into the West Bank." The Arab areas of East Jerusalem with no Jewish settlements would be under Palestinian sovereignty, and the Muslim Quarter in the Old City (but not the other parts of the Old City) of Jerusalem. The capital of the new state of Palestine could then be established within these areas: the Muslim Quarter of the Old City and Arab neighborhoods in East Jerusalem. As for other settlements in the West Bank and Gaza with significant numbers of Palestinians, Slater asserts that Barak did not take a position on whether they would be included in the new Palestinian state, be dismantled, or "be under nominal Palestinian sovereignty but actual Israeli military control."[83] While at Camp David, he was working on the Israeli government's 2001 budget that stipulated financial assistance to encourage Israelis to relocate to settlements in the West Bank and East Jerusalem.[84] As for Palestinian refugees, Barak made it clear he would not admit Israel's "moral or historical responsibility" for the massive refugee situation. He would not agree to any right of return for these refugees, beyond a token 10,000 who could return "as part of a family reunification program."[85]

With the failure of the summit and the outbreak of violence by Palestinians in the second intifada, Barak resigned. In the election of 2000, the Likud Party came to power and Ariel Sharon became the new prime minister in February 2001. Barak left politics shortly thereafter, having failed to secure peace with the Palestinians.[86] One of his legacies, carried out further by his successor, was the notion of "unilateral separation" as a means to resolve the conflict. In this way, a separation wall annexing territories in the West Bank that Israel wanted to retain under its control, along with a unilateral "withdrawal from those deemed expendable, especially the Gaza Strip," would determine Israel's borders.[87] A month after the outbreak of the intifada, Barak authorized the construction of the wall/barrier in the northern end of the West Bank as a way to prevent Palestinian militants from attacking Israel. Sharon's government pursued the permanent wall plan "along the length of the border," which was endorsed by the cabinet in 2001.[88] In this case, a Labor prime minister initiated serious plans to construct such a barrier, which were implemented by a Likud prime minister. Israeli policy from leaders from two different political parties demonstrates consistency in addressing the conflict with the Palestinians.

Yasser Arafat

Born in Cairo, Egypt, in 1929, Arafat was drawn to grassroots activism to liberate Palestine. He founded Fatah (Movement for the Liberation of Palestine) some time after Israel's independence. He headed the militant arm of Fatah, launching attacks against Israel from neighboring countries, such as Lebanon and Jordan. Following the 1967 war, Fatah remained as "the only credible force left fighting Israel." Two years later, he was elected chairman of the PLO's executive committee. Following a series of attacks on Israelis, the Jordanian government expelled the PLO, which then moved to Lebanon. Arafat directed PLO attacks against Israel from Lebanon, and eventually the Israeli invasion of Lebanon in 1982 led to the PLO's expulsion from that country. The leadership then moved to Tunisia.[89]

By the late 1980s and early 1990s Arafat and the PLO leadership moved from demanding all of Palestine and the destruction of Israel toward negotiations with the Israelis in a "land for peace" deal. On December 13, 1988, at the UN General Assembly, he laid out a Palestinian peace initiative in which he stated, "The PLO will seek a comprehensive settlement among the parties concerned in the Arab-Israeli conflict, including the State of Palestine, Israel, and other neighbors, within the framework of the international conference for peace in the Middle East on the basis of resolutions 242 and 338 and so as to guarantee equality and the balance of interests, especially our people's rights, in freedom, national independence, and respect the right to exist in peace and security for all."[90] Following his speech at the UN, he continued to push for the "land for peace" plan (in 1991 he had said, "We are not asking for the moon"). At the White House signing ceremony of the Oslo Accords, he stated, "Our people do not consider that exercising the right to self-determination could violate the right of their neighbours or infringe on their security. Rather, putting an end to their feelings of being wronged and of having suffered an historic injustice is the strongest guarantee to achieve coexistence and openness between our two peoples and future generations. Our two peoples are awaiting today this historic hope, and they want to give peace a real chance."[91] With this acceptance in 1993 of a two-state solution, the Palestinians "renounced all sovereign claims to 78% of their ancestral homeland, including the territory allotted to 'the Arab state' under the 1947 UN partition plan."[92]

In signing the agreement, the PLO was officially recognized by the Israeli government. Hamas and other militant groups expressed their opposition to the agreement by committing acts of terrorism such as bombing busses, killing Israeli civilians.[93]

With the establishment in 1994 of the PA, with Arafat as its leader, the move toward peace continued, but haltingly so. Makovsky argues that Arafat's leadership was lacking to such an extent that it had a negative impact on the peace process. For example, Arafat did not renounce violence as a bargaining tool in negotiations with the Israelis. He also did not "equate peace with reconciliation." Therefore, the prospect of the two sides coming together to conclude a durable peace were slim.[94] While part of the Oslo agreement included the establishment of an armed PA as a security force in the occupied territories, Arafat failed to use the security force to suppress Hamas, which continued to launch attacks against Israeli civilians.[95]

With Netanyahu's election in 1996, the peace process stalled (due to continued Palestinian extremist violence and the hard-line position of Netanyahu's Likud Party), only to resume again in 2000 with the new Israeli prime minister Barak. As noted earlier, Barak and Arafat attended the Camp David summit, where Arafat rejected Barak's proposal.[96] With the failure of the summit and the eruption of the second intifada, Arafat faced internal challenges to his leadership from Hamas and other militant groups, which led him to implement institutional and constitutional reforms. The Israelis did not, however, agree to withdraw their forces from Palestinian cities that they had reoccupied in the wake of the second intifada. As a result, Arafat's leadership was challenged yet again, and reforms were put on hold. With the 2003 Road Map, Arafat indicated his willingness to consider reforms of the PA. When Abbas became the new Palestinian prime minister, his government made sincere attempts at institutionalizing reforms. As in the past, the reform process "fell short," because Arafat undermined Abbas's government, a government supported by 61 percent of the Palestinian public.[97] Israel's refusal to withdraw from Palestinian territory as well as freezing construction of the settlements did not help to bolster Abbas's credibility and legitimacy. Added to this, Arafat, under siege by the Israeli government, was unable to move about freely. In the end, with the Palestinian public's support for Abbas dwindling in light of the continued deterioration in economic and political conditions, Abbas resigned in September 2003.[98] Arafat remained in power until his death in November 2004, and a final agreement proved elusive once again.

Extremists, Spoilers, and Ethnic Outbidding

Extremists on both sides have attempted to thwart the peace process, at times successfully so. Opposition to both Rabin and Arafat from their respective ethnic groups became problematic for the peace process in the 1990s. Jewish extremists, as asserted by Louis Kriesberg, perceive the conflict as one that revolves around religious nationalism, in that God gave the Land of Israel to the Jews. Palestinian extremists, both Islamic activists as well as Palestinian ethno-nationalist activists, view a Jewish state on perceived Palestinian territory "as an unacceptable Western intrusion."[99]

While surveys showed that the majority of the Israeli public approved of the Rabin government's decision to sign the Oslo Accords (52 percent said "yes," while 36 percent were opposed),[100] following the signing of the Accords, extremist opposition within Israel to the agreement came to the fore, to the extent that some sought to undermine the agreement. There were attacks against Palestinians by religious extremists, including the massacre by Baruch Goldstein of Muslims praying at a mosque in Hebron.[101] The ultimate expression of extremist opposition was Rabin's assassination. His successor, Peres, faced a serious challenge in the 1996 election that led to the victory of Netanyahu. The election demonstrated that the majority of the Israeli public was willing to abandon the peace process given the increased incidence of terrorist attacks by a small number of Palestinian extremists.[102]

[Those who hold extremist views about peace with Israel comprise a minority of Palestinians but they can have a significant impact when they keep the peace process from moving forward.[103] In the course of the peace process in the 1990s and early 2000s, Arafat faced challenges from these extremists as he attempted to find a middle ground with the Israelis.]He was unable to prevent terrorist attacks in the mid-1990s, but Israelis questioned whether he was unable and/or unwilling to prevent the outbreak of the second intifada. Interestingly, according to Andrew Kydd and Barbara Walter's analysis of the peace process from 1993 to 2001, his "weakness actually saved the peace process in the early 1990s by shielding him from accusations of untrustworthiness in the wake of early terrorist attacks, and his more recent perceived strength has significantly lowered Israel's trust by convincing Israel that Arafat could stop the renewal of the intifada but has chosen not to."[104] Extremist attacks against Israel were successful in disrupting the peace process, first in the period from February to April 1996, contributing to the election success of Netanyahu, and also bringing an end to significant peace negotiations with Arafat. Again, in December 2000 Hamas attacks also contributed to the decision by Labor Party prime minister Barak to withdraw from politics and the election of Likud Party member Ariel Sharon as the new prime minister. Sharon, a very hawkish prime minister, did not favor the Oslo peace accords.[105]

It is interesting to note, however, that Hamas attacks at other times (such as during the signing of the Oslo agreement and the 1998 Wye River Memorandum) did not succeed in ending the peace process.[106] Kydd and Walter note that even after Hamas militants had detonated bombs in October and November 1993, Rabin and Arafat continued with peace talks. Both the Israelis and Palestinians began to carry out the terms of the accord. Rabin's Labor Party considered peace essential to such an extent that it was willing to withstand terrorist attacks and still continue with the peace process. For Rabin and his supporters, dealing with the PLO that was moderate and secular was a much better option than trying to work with an Islamic fundamentalist organization unwilling to negotiate. Moreover, the majority of Israelis were not convinced that Arafat could contain all terrorist incidents; they felt that, in essence, he was weak. Israelis were inclined to continue to support the peace efforts, recognizing that Arafat was doing what he could to deal with Palestinian extremists, such as arresting some Hamas militants.[107] In 1998 Hamas initiated attacks on Israel, but these attacks did not prevent Netanyahu from signing the Wye accord. By this time, Israeli public opinion had moved back toward support for the peace process, given that Arafat had made significant attempts at preventing terrorist attacks on Israel (and polls showed that Israelis viewed Netanyahu as an obstacle to that peace, an opinion which may have induced him to move forward with an agreement).[108]

DOMESTIC LEVEL

Domestic level factors, such as Zionism and Palestinian nationalism, gendered nationalism, economic and political conditions in the occupied territories, public opinion, and political parties, all affect the evolution of the conflict and the failure to obtain a comprehensive and durable peace settlement. According to Oren Barak, "Both Jews and Palestinians are human groups whose needs for identity and security went unfulfilled." Zionism and Palestinian nationalism are the dominant narratives of each group and encompass their interests and identities. For Jews, Zionism meant more than a need for identity and security of Jews; Zionism became "a political interest" in the sense that a Jewish homeland needed to be established—in Palestine. Palestinian nationalism demanded the liberation of Palestine.[109] The conflict for both sides is marked by perceptions of their constructed identity where each group "sees itself as a people, and each has formulated goals based on ethno-nationalist thinking." Importantly, each group's identity is linked intimately with the same territory.[110] The identity and interests of both groups are directly tied to the domestic factors under consideration.

Nationalism and National Identity

Zionism. The Zionist movement, according to Helsing, led to "a reawakening of Jews, even a national awakening as a people, by creating in the minds of Jews everywhere, as well as in the international community, the notion of a national homeland for Jews." In order to succeed as a nationalist movement, Zionism promoted the idea of Jewish immigration "to historic and biblical Jewish lands." More than just immigration to this land, Zionism called for the development of an infrastructure (economic and political institutions) that would support and promote the Jewish homeland. The Zionist project constructed a particular Jewish identity, for example, through the restoration of Hebrew as a spoken language. Moreover, "Jewish identity would be cast as a Middle Eastern identity that was linked to the ancient lands of Israel and the city that had always symbolized Judaism, Jerusalem." Rather than perceiving themselves as a diaspora, Jews would now have a homeland of their own.[111]

One of the leaders of the Zionist movement, David Ben-Gurion (who would become Israel's first prime minister), explicitly placed "the state at the center of Zionism." As a result, the Zionist movement prior to independence was willing to give up some of the land deemed the "historic Jewish homeland," including Jerusalem, in order to establish the state of Israel.[112] Nonetheless, this willingness to compromise on Jerusalem has not diminished Jerusalem's symbolic meaning for Zionism. Mainstream Israelis have not opposed the government's policy of expanding Israel's border to include East Jerusalem, and the Knesset passed a series of decrees and laws supporting the expansion of Israeli territory into East Jerusalem.[113] Ian Lustick notes that "[o]n the symbolic level, the day of East Jerusalem's conquest [in 1967] by Israeli forces has been declared a national holiday—'Jerusalem Day.'"[114] He further points out that while both Likud and Labor politicians have supported the unity of Jerusalem under Israeli control, in fact there have been Israeli politicians who have publicly asserted the position of an Israeli withdrawal to the 1967 borders as well as the partition of Jerusalem.[115]

While both sides of the political spectrum, left and right, agree that there is a direct link between identity and the land and borders, opinions on "the role and status of those borders, and the type of Jewish-Zionist identity and State within those borders" differ, and those differences relate to the peace process.[116] These different views manifested themselves in three ways, according to Danny Ben-Moshe. First, the question of the timing of the negotiation and agreement of the Oslo Accords occurred at a period of time in which the idea of post-Zionism posed a direct challenge to the Jewish/Zionist identity. Post-Zionism is considered "a political-cultural process that seeks to de-Judaise and de-Zionise Israel."[117] The peace process at Oslo provided an opportunity for the Israeli public and elites to consider Israel's "internal character."[118] Second, Zionist ideology specifically called for the expansion of the Jewish presence, in the form of settlements, in Greater Israel. The Likud Party supported this Zionist mission. For Zionists, Rabin's willingness to negotiate and sign the Oslo agreement meant an end to the notion of Greater Israel.[119] Third, negotiation with the Palestinians, as occurred with the Oslo process, indicated a shift in the Zionist idea of self-defense of the state.[120]

As successive Israeli governments sought to promote the peace process with the Palestinians, they confronted the challenges of the religious Zionist movement in Israel. Thus, when Barak was at Camp David, the Zionists framed their demonstrations opposing negotiations with the Palestinians around security issues (instead of using the rhetoric of Jewish biblical claims). Slogans such as "This agreement will obliterate the state" and "A secure future for our children is in the entirety of the Land of Israel under Israeli sovereignty" were utilized to put pressure on Barak against making concessions.[121] With Sharon's electoral win in 2001, Likud came to power, but needed to share power with Labor in order to form a governing coalition. The National Religious Party did not join the government until April 2002, with provisions established by Sharon. Sharon's decision to establish the security fence squarely challenged the position of the religious Zionists, as the fence could, in essence, institutionalize the borders of the state, rather than permitting continued expansion into areas deemed by Zionists as part of the Land of Israel.[122]

Importantly, even with the debates within Israel regarding religious and secular Zionism, as a political ideology it remains very much part of the nationalist discourse regarding Israel as the Jewish homeland.[123]

Palestinian Nationalism. Palestinian nationalism is defined by territorial nationalism, rather than religiously inspired nationalism. Palestinian nationalism revolves around the right of return for Palestinian refugees who currently reside in the occupied territories and the diaspora (those living in refugee camps in Lebanon, Syria, and Jordan), as expressed in UN Resolution 194, passed in December 1948. For Palestinians, their claims are based on international law.[124] Today, most Palestinians support the establishment of a Palestinian state in the territories conquered by Israel in 1967. The Palestinian national movement also makes claims for the establishment of its future capital in East Jerusalem.[125] Yet, the secular Palestinian nationalism of the PLO is contested by the rise of Islamic fundamentalism, as represented by Hamas and Islamic Jihad.[126]

The Palestinian nationalist movement "was largely shattered" in the course of the 1948 war. The formation of the PLO revitalized the movement. With a number of political groups representing Palestinians, the Fatah leadership permitted these groups to become members of the PLO, thus the organization was "a forum for decision-making." As a result of this structure, other Palestinian groups, such as the Popular Front for the Liberation of Palestine (PFLP) and the Democratic Front for the Liberation of Palestine (DFLP), challenged the Fatah/PLO leadership. Given that Fatah had more resources and more members, the other groups struggled to gain power. To do so, they often chose more aggressive language and actions, including attacks on Israel, as a way to impact the politics within the Palestinian movement.[127]

The PLO's movement toward diplomacy in the 1970s, following the 1973 Arab-Israeli war in which the Arab states experienced yet another military defeat at the hands of the Israeli forces, as well as its contention that it represented all Palestinians and its attempts at undermining the influence and position of other Palestinian factions, led these other groups to engage in spoiler behavior.[128] This move toward diplomacy did not mean that the Fatah leaders would not consider the option of violence to obtain their goals, given the concern for Palestinian refugees and the desire for a Palestinian homeland. As Wendy Pearlman asserts, Fatah's leaders clearly recognized that it was in the movement's interest to pursue the peace process. Yet, the internal politics of the Palestinian movement pushing for the continuation of violent actions against Israel made this diplomatic policy position problematic.[129]

By the early 1990s the Oslo peace process was in full swing, yet the PLO and Arafat faced internal challenges to their dominance of the Palestinian national movement. The 1987 intifada demonstrated this most clearly, as an uprising from within, rather than from the PLO leadership based in Tunisia. The new generation of activists in the nationalist movement living in the occupied territories posed a direct challenge to Arafat's leadership and representation of the Palestinians as a whole. In response to this challenge, Arafat took the lead in pushing forward with peace negotiations with the Israelis.[130] Pearlman points out that for Arafat, a peace agreement would give him international recognition of the PLO, with him as leader. The negotiations leading to the conclusion of the Oslo Accords did just that—Israel and the United States acknowledged Arafat "as the only person able to act authoritatively in the name of the Palestinian struggle."[131] The Oslo Accords also allowed Fatah/PLO/Arafat to gain at the expense of the Islamic movement. In response, Hamas carried out terrorist attacks against Israel, in light of the continued occupation and discrimination against Palestinians, as a means to gain public support.[132]

In mid-2000, before the start of the second intifada, public opinion clearly favored the Islamist parties relative to the moderate nationalists.[133] As Khalil Shikaki writes, following the second intifada "a split between the old and young guard within the nationalist movement" emerged that effectively constrained the PA in its attempts at responding to the internal crisis and to negotiate with Israel. Moreover, the nationalists had been losing ground to Hamas and other Islamist Palestinian groups.[134] Many Palestinians realized the widespread corruption endemic in the Palestinian Authority.[135] Conflict between Hamas and Fatah continued through the second intifada, and the two parties have been unable to form a unity government that would govern all of the occupied territories. Both continue to compete for representation of Palestinian nationalism.

Borders, Naming, and National Identity. Borders and national identity are linked to ethnic conflicts, and this is evident in the case of the Israeli-Palestinian conflict. Artificial constructs that are not just definitions of a physical space, borders have a symbolic meaning related to a group's identity. Elites use borders as representations of group identity in order "to establish control and to generate legitimacy," as argued by Gad Barzilai and Ilan Peleg.[136] For an example of how the national identity of both ethnic groups is contested, one need only examine the process of naming of events, boundaries, and markers that reflects the differing identities. Thus, Israel views the war of 1948 as the war of independence. Palestinians call this same event the catastrophe. Each side, according to Julie Peteet, formed a narrative to explain the event. For the Israelis, the victory of a small number of Jewish forces over the coordinated military offensive by Arabs became their narrative embedded in the historical record. For the Palestinians, their loss resulted from the efforts of "a well armed, well trained and well supported military" against the "disorganized, ideologically disparate, under-armed and leaderless Palestinians and an insufficient and weak set of Arab forces with outdated weaponry."[137] Naming of events, places, and so forth is closely tied to the construction of identity, collective memories, and traditions. As Peteet further states, for there to be "a sense of a collective present and future," the creation of "narratives of a past" are needed.[138] The Israeli naming process is linked to the Zionist project of making biblical historical claims to territory for a particular people—Jews. This naming process is also a deliberate attempt at negating the presence of a historical claim for Palestinians to the same territory. The Palestinian naming process is linked to the notion of "mass displacement, dispossession and a sustained resistance movement." Thus, the naming strategy reflects an attempt at maintaining and promoting "legitimate rights to reside there."[139]

Naming of the other ethnic group also served a purpose in making claims for territory. For the Zionists to succeed in their goal of creating a Jewish state in Palestine, language mattered (hence the revival of Hebrew as a spoken language). Relatedly, the Israeli project negated the identity of Palestinians, referring to them as Arabs. Not until the 1990s did official Israeli documents use the word "Palestinian people." Former prime minister Golda Meir once stated, "There is no such thing as a Palestinian." Her words reflected the Israeli narrative that Palestinians did not exist as a separate identity, and thus could not make legitimate claims to the land.[140] The acknowledgment of the identity of Palestinians came to the fore as a result of the first intifada. Alongside speech referring to the Arab-Israeli conflict, the term "Israeli-Palestinian conflict" entered into the common discourse.[141]

The Palestinians did not refer to Israel as Israel, but "as the Zionist entity or occupied Palestine." In the late 1980s the use of "Zionist entity" or "Occupied Palestine" became less prominent as the peace process moved forward and the PLO recognized Israel.[142] Even with these changes, names still matter in the context of the conflict. The concepts of return and refugees "are hotly contested." As part of the national narrative, Israel maintains that Palestinians "abandoned" their homes and territory in 1948. Invoking the term "abandoned" implies that Palestinians gave up their rights to the land, and thus Israelis could rename these areas and make legitimate claims. Yet, Palestinians have sought to return to their homes, as a right recognized by international law. While Israeli laws specify the right of return for any Jew, this same right is not extended to Palestinians.[143]

Gendered Nationalism

Gendered nationalism is reflected in both communities, where traditional stereotypes of women's roles dominate (women need to be protected; women's central role is the family). Yet, there are women's organizations in both communities who recognize the harmful impact of conflict on women and have acted independently and jointly in pushing for a peaceful resolution to the conflict. For example, Jerusalem Link, a women's organization that links two women's centers, Jerusalem Center for Women (Palestinian) and Bat Shalom (Israeli), formed in 1994 and is an explicitly feminist organization. Jerusalem Link specifically promotes equality and peace for women and their societies, and supports ongoing dialog between the two sides.[144]

In 2005, Israeli, Palestinian, and other women came together and formed the International Women's Commission for a Just and Sustainable Peace between Israel and Palestine (IWC). In a statement issued on May 3, 2006, the IWC stated, "As women, who are deeply engaged in the politics of our respective communities, we oppose the continuation of violence, collective punishment, coercion, and continuous threats to personal rights which also threaten our own freedom. The IWC is dedicated to ending the Israeli occupation, to achieving a just peace and a two-state solution based on international law, human rights and equality." The statement, in recognizing the continued omission of women from the peace negotiations, also noted that "as women we are absent from the spaces of power where men are taking decisions that will impact Palestinians and Israelis for generations to come. Despite the fact that Israel, Palestine and members of the Quartet have all pledged to implement Security Council Resolution 1325, which calls for increased engagement of women at all levels of decision-making in conflict resolution, this intention has still to be translated into practice."[145]

The IWC and Jerusalem Link are only two examples of women's organizations dedicated to resolving the Israeli-Palestinian conflict. In fact, women's movements exist with differing positions with regard to the conflict in both communities. Some women's organizations are explicitly defined as feminist and peace activists (such as Women in Black, in Israel, and the Women's Affairs Technical Committee in the occupied territories), while others focus on women's traditional roles as they express their support for their respective governments' policies.

Israel. Zionism's goal of the establishment of a Jewish state in Palestine was very much a masculine endeavor. The security and survival of the new state, born of war and conflict, "was constructed around the myth of the masculine hero who was fighting for the 'mother country.'"[146] As Sara Helman observes, "Participation in war and military service was identified as the ultimate token of political obligation as well as the highest contribution to the enhancement of collective goals."[147] In fact, in the Zionist project Jewish women's roles were front and center as wives and mothers. The need to reproduce more citizens as the new state of Israel developed solidified women's status in terms of their mothering role. After independence was declared, women were marginalized in many ways, as evidenced by marriage laws (determined by the religious authorities, not the state) and participation in the military (while both men and women are obligated to serve in the Israeli military, men are in the higher ranking positions).[148] As Nitza Berkovitch explains, the Israeli-Palestinian conflict is in many ways linked to the demographic balance between Jews and Arabs. In order to fulfill the Zionist ideology of a Jewish majority in Israel, producing Jewish children "is celebrated as having a major national significance."[149] Women have, for the most part, been excluded from formal politics.[150]

Feminist peace activists responded to the militarization of Israeli society and the ongoing conflict with the Palestinians. For example, in January 1988, one month after the start of the first intifada, a group of women in Jerusalem protested against the Israeli government's occupation of the Palestinian territories. The group, Women in Black, continues to oppose the occupation.[151] The goal of the Coalition of Women for Peace (established in November 2000) is to end Israel's occupation, bring to an end the "excessive militarization of Israeli society," as well as promote the "equality, inclusion, and justice for Palestinian citizens of Israel."[152]

Women's organizations, such as the IWC noted earlier, have been at the forefront in pushing the government to include women in peace negotiations to end the conflict. As recently as December 2008, several "Israeli women's groups filed a complaint to the United Nations Security Council." The complaint accused the government of failure to implement Resolution 1325. In 2005 the Knesset adopted 1325, but the government had yet to appoint women in any senior decision-making positions. Interestingly, the complaint noted that "rumors of a major IDF operation in Gaza in the near future" were circulating, and thus there was all the more reason to include women in any decision to go to war.[153] During the December 2008–January 2009 Israeli offensive against Gaza, women's organizations sought to be present in the peace process.[154]

While women's organizations (both feminist and more traditional in orientation) have protested the government's policies in the occupied territories, other women have also expressed support for the state's goals in terms of expansion of Jewish settlements and refusal to withdraw to the 1967 borders. Examples of such groups are the Merry Wives of Windsor and the Women of the First Circle.

These groups have appealed to women's roles as mothers and wives, focused on norms of femininity. Moreover, these groups did not challenge the state's policies with regard to Israel's security in relation to the Palestinians.[155]

Palestine. Palestinian women have organized, since the outset of the twentieth century, in support of the Palestinian nationalist cause.[156] Following Israel's independence, women continued to organize, seeking an increase in women's political participation and the improvement of women's rights, as well as offering overall support for the liberation of Palestine. However, Palestinian nationalism is very much one defined by masculinity. Women, therefore, are assumed to need protection by men, especially as women's traditional gendered roles, as wives and mothers and the locus of the family, remained crucial for the nationalist project. Thus, while women were used as symbols for the nationalist liberation cause, they were not permitted to enter the political sphere. Adding to the situation are the differing views of women's organizations, as Maria Holt observes, some of which argue for national liberation first, and then women's rights, while others argue that national liberation and women's rights should move in tandem. Some women's organizations supported the peace process, first established by Oslo, while other women's groups did not. Some women support Hamas and the other Islamic organizations, while other women's groups worry that the Islamic movement "has had largely negative implications for women."[157]

With the eruption of the first intifada, the women's movement responded to the calls for independence by mobilizing women, with a focus on both "national and social liberation."[158] For example, the Women's Affairs Technical Committee (WATC), established in 1992, brought together various women's organizations in support of the peace process. In doing so, the WATC was able to increase the representation of women on several of the negotiating teams (including education and the environment).[159] Following the intifada and the Oslo Accords, the General Union of Palestinian Women (a body within the PLO, established in 1965, representing Palestinian women) and the primary women's organizations backed the Women's Charter (Declaration of Palestinian Women's Rights) of 1994. The Charter referred to the 1988 Palestinian Declaration of Independence's principle of "equality between the sexes," in stressing the "national, political, social and economic rights for women, thus putting forward a new gender (and social) contract for Palestinian society," as noted by Penny Johnson and Eileen Kuttab. Yet, the women's organizations were unable to mobilize the population to support these goals as the peace process moved along haltingly in the mid- to late 1990s, and eventually women's activism was significantly depoliticized, especially by the time of the second intifada.[160]

A proposal to create a Ministry of Women's Affairs was rejected by the Palestinian Authority when it was first established in 1994. In response, the WATC decided to focus on bringing other women's organizations together to form "a broad women's coalition . . . that could respond to the expectations of Palestinian women once independence is achieved."[161] The push by women's organizations for inclusion in politics eventually succeeded in the creation of the Ministry of Women's Affairs in 2003. While women's organizations persist in their goals of promoting women's rights in education, economics, and so forth, traditional stereotypes endure and continue to impede women's liberation. Men continue to dominate the political parties and in education and employment opportunities, while women experience domestic violence (considered acceptable by social norms and traditions) and unequal treatment by the legal system (that is, property rights, marriage laws, citizenship). The ongoing Israeli occupation of the West Bank and Gaza adds another layer of difficulty for women in their attempts to improve women's status and conditions within the territories, particularly as the closure policies have led to deteriorating economic and social conditions on the ground.[162]

In addition to efforts to work within the political system, some women have engaged in violence as a means to end the occupation. Following the second intifada, several women became suicide bombers starting in January 2002. Female members of the al-Aqsa Brigades (the militant arm of the Fatah movement) as well as Islamic Jihad have taken part in these bombings. While women have participated in suicide bombings, this participation has not translated into higher levels of representation in the various Palestinian organizations that endorse suicide bombings.[163]

Though Israeli and Palestinian women peace activists have pushed for an end to the conflict and have sought inclusion at the peace process negotiations, they have not had a seat at the negotiating table. During the Oslo peace process, women were excluded from the respective negotiating teams.[164] Women's organizations continue to push both the Israeli and Palestinian governments to include women in the decision-making process as well as a gender analysis in their policies.

Political Parties

Israeli Political Parties. Currently, there are more than thirty political parties in Israel, whose ideologies cover a wide range, including the right (that is, Likud, National Unity, Yisrael Beiteinu), the center (Center Party, Shinui, Kadima), religious (Shas), left (Labor, Meretz), and even Arab (Hadash, Balad).[165] But only two parties have dominated Israel's government since its founding in 1948—Likud and Labor.

The secular political parties in Israel engage in power sharing with the religious parties, given the structure of the parliamentary political system in the country, in which coalitions are formed. From the outset of Israel's independence, the Labor Party shared power with the NRP (National Religious Party, comprised of the Mizrahi and Hapoel Hamizrahi Party—the religious Zionists). This power-sharing arrangement lasted until 1967 when the NRP members pushed the government to annex territory considered to be part of historic Israel. The Labor governments were willing to permit some settlements to be built, but only in areas of Gaza, the West Bank, and Golan Heights that were considered strategic. The religious Zionists were unsatisfied, and thus abandoned their alliance with Labor and forged a relationship with Likud. In doing so, the religious Zionists were able to push for territorial expansion with the establishment of settlements in the West Bank and Gaza. Yet, even Likud was disinclined to expand too far.[166] With Rabin's Labor government back in power in 1992, a significant change occurred in relation to how strong the connection between the secular party and religious movement would continue to be. As Hillel Frisch and Shmuel Sandler note, Rabin decided not to include the NRP in a governing coalition. While this was the first time in Israeli history that the NRP was not included, Rabin took this course of action out of concern for the role that religion had increasingly played in Israeli foreign policy, a role that he believed should be minimized. What is interesting is that Rabin's Labor Party entered into a power-sharing agreement with Shas, a new ultraorthodox party. Shas's spiritual leader "ruled that territorial compromise [with Arabs] was religiously acceptable for the sake of peace and security." Shas's position enabled Rabin's Labor government to enter into negotiations with the PLO—the first time in Israeli government history—which opened the way for the Oslo Accords.[167]

It was only in the early 1990s, however, that a major Israeli political party changed its views about the PLO, as Labor did right before it won the 1992 election.[168] With regard to the occupied territories, both the Likud Party and the Labor Party supported maintaining control of Gaza and the West Bank "until real progress was made on the diplomatic front." For both parties, the territories matter for strategic and diplomatic purposes. Strategically, the territories provide a buffer for the Israeli government for self-defense against a conventional attack. Diplomatically, the territories are useful as a bargaining chip.[169] Both parties also support the concept of separation—Israel on one side and the Palestinian territories on the other. Both parties eventually supported the unilateral withdrawal from Gaza and the construction of a security fence around the West Bank.[170] The two parties formed the National Unity Government that ruled Israel from 1984 until 1990 (with one of the two parties' leaders as prime minister).

A consensus of both parties developed that supported a federal solution in dealing with the Palestinians. Neither party supported an independent Palestinian state at this time, but they did support autonomy (in May 1989 the Likud-Labor government made a proposal for free elections in the occupied territories that would produce a Palestinian group that could enter into negotiations on autonomy).[171] Today, leaders in both major secular parties have expressed support for an independent Palestinian state.

Palestinian Political Parties: The PLO and Hamas. Fatah dominated the PLO from the outset and was by far the most prominent of the various Palestinian groups at the time.[172] In 1974 the Palestinian parliament in exile, the Palestine National Council (PNC), began to consider a two-state solution as a viable option, rather than demanding the liberation of all of Palestine and the destruction of Israel. Fourteen years later, Arafat would publicly proclaim an independent Palestinian state in the occupied territories, a more limited territorial demand.[173]

Since Arafat's death, the PA, dominated by Fatah/PLO, remains in control of the West Bank. Yet, the PA is perceived by most Palestinians as corrupt. Recent survey data indicate that 68 percent of those polled said yes in response to the question: "Do you think that there is corruption in PA institutions under the control of President Abu Mazin [Abbas]?"[174]

The PA/PLO faces a continual challenge from Hamas, which came into its own during the first intifada. In December 1987 it issued its first communiqué in which it claimed "Islam as the solution and the alternative." In addition to Islam as the central identity of the organization, Hamas also invokes resistance as a means to liberate Palestine from Israel.[175] An outgrowth of the Muslim Brotherhood in Egypt, Hamas, while Islamic, is at its base a Palestinian nationalist organization that seeks to end the Israeli occupation.[176] In order to end the occupation, Hamas focuses on jihad as both a national and a religious obligation.[177] Consequently, Hamas engages in attacks against Israeli military as well as civilian targets. Unlike Fatah/PLO, Hamas refuses to recognize Israel officially. At the same time, however, Hamas indicated its "willingness to work within a 1967 framework." For example, in the fall of 1997, one of its leaders spoke of conditions for a truce that included the dismantling of Jewish settlements and a complete Israeli withdrawal from the West Bank and Gaza. By 2004 Hamas's West Bank leader also noted the possibility of a long-term truce if a Palestinian state was established on the basis of the 1967 borders.[178] As recently as mid-2009, Hamas's exiled leader, Khaled Meshaal, stated at a press conference in Egypt that Hamas "will not obstruct" any deal that establishes a Palestinian state along the 1967 borders with Israel.[179]

Yet, Hamas has also challenged the peace process, as noted in the section on extremists and spoilers, engaging in bombings following the Oslo Accords, the Camp David summit, and the second intifada. Hamas's electoral power increased when it ran for elections in 2006, and its influence in Palestinian society increased even further with its ouster of the PA from Gaza the next year. Even without legitimacy and recognition from the international community (the United States and the EU, as well as Israel, call it a terrorist organization), Hamas remains a significant player in Palestinian society. Hamas's rule in Gaza is marked by intra-Palestinian violence as well, as militants target Palestinians it claims are collaborating with Israel or are members of Fatah.[180] A recent poll (May 2009) showed that if an election were held, 33 percent of potential voters support Hamas (41 percent support Fatah). Polls also show that the continued tension between Hamas and Fatah "is causing anxiety among the majority," worried about harm to themselves or their family.[181] The question becomes what impact the Hamas-Fatah conflict may have on the Israeli-Palestinian peace process and prospects for the two-state solution.

Public Opinion

The perceived intractableness of the conflict has produced collective fears for survival and security for Israel's Jews. As Daniel Bar-Tal observes, "The conflict has been on Israel's public agenda daily, occupying a central place in news and public debates. Many threatening events have left their impact on the Israelis."[182] The "collective memory of the Jewish history," whether through the experience of the Holocaust or generations of anti-Semitism, remains front and center in the public discourse about Israel's right to exist as a homeland for Jews. Moreover, this collective memory "encouraged the maintenance of a siege mentality."[183] As a result, literature, school textbooks, and the media contributed to the emergence and continuation of the collective fear of Israeli society. Only recently have there been changes in these areas in an attempt to overcome negative stereotypes of Arabs/Palestinians. More criticisms of government policy are found in the media, but even as recently as the early 1990s the official government position was reflected in the Israeli media's reporting.[184] The importance of the continued collective fear is that it hinders the forward movement of the peace process, contributing to further mistrust between the two groups.[185]

Yet, polling data from the 1980s onward demonstrate that the Israeli Jews are increasingly less supportive of the territorial status quo that followed after the 1967 war. The Israeli Jewish public increasingly supports either federal (autonomy) interim solutions or permanent solutions. In 1990, two years before the 1992 elections, for example, Israeli Jewish public opinion expressed recognition of Palestinian political self-determination.[186] Given that Zionists on both the left and right of the political spectrum oppose a binational state (in other words, one in which Israel would not be defined as a Jewish state), the public has increasingly conveyed support for separation of Israelis and Palestinians (for many, but by no means all, this means autonomy, not independence for Palestinians).[187]

This sentiment—in favor of separation and Palestinian self-determination—is reflected in support by both communities for the two-state solution. According to recent poll data (commissioned by the nongovernmental organization One-Voice in 2009), a significant majority of Palestinians (74 percent) and Israelis (78 percent) support the idea of a two-state solution.[188] At the same time, however, majorities of both Israelis and Palestinians express pessimism that a final settlement can be achieved and a Palestinian state created in the near future (next five years). While a slim majority (52 percent of Israelis, 50 percent of Palestinians) supports the mutual (national identity) recognition of Palestine as the state of the Palestinian people and Israel as the state of the Jewish people after an independent Palestinian state has been created and all unresolved issues are dealt with, this support has declined over time. Interestingly, 50 percent of Israelis (this includes Israeli Arabs) support talks with Hamas if it will lead to a peace agreement, and 62 percent of Israelis support talks with a joint Hamas-Fatah national unity government (if one was reestablished).[189]

Israel as Hegemonic Democracy/Ethnocracy

As discussed in chapter 2, some states are defined as hegemonic democracies in which one ethnic group dominates. Ilan Peleg argues that Israel fits the exclusivist model of hegemonic democracy because the country's identity is an exclusive one—Jewish nationality and/or religion.[190] Jews are the majority and hold economic, political, and cultural power relative to the country's Israeli Arabs.[191] Oren Yiftachel defines Israel as an ethnocracy, "a specific expression of nationalism that exists in contested territories where a dominant ethnos gains political control and uses the state apparatus to ethnicize the territory and society in question."[192] He argues that Israel, as an ethnocracy, is not a democracy, given that it breaches most democratic principles.[193] He explains that while Israel does have elections, a free press, an independent judiciary, and human rights laws, when looking at "the deeper structure" one finds that an ethnocratic regime is one in which it is not democratic "because [it] promotes the seizure of territory and the public realm by one ethnos, thus undermining key democratic principles such as civil and legal equality, the protection of minorities, and the maintenance of equality and proportionality among the collectivities making up the state."[194] Yiftachel further remarks that Israel is not democratic because of the lack of separation between church and state. Approximately twenty laws have been passed that "discriminate formally between Jews and Arabs." In refusing to define its borders, as well as occupying and building Jewish settlements in Palestinian territories (in violation of international law), Israel has not "established the legal-territorial basis for democracy."[195] The implication for this in the context of the conflict is that the regime's discriminatory policies vis-à-vis Israeli Arab (Palestinian) citizens impact its treatment of Palestinians in the occupied territories (Palestinians living in Jerusalem are considered "residents" whereas Palestinians living in the occupied territories are not, nor are they Israeli citizens). Jewish settlers living in the occupied territories are citizens of Israel.[196] The perception that Israel is a Jewish state for the Jewish people explicitly implies that non-Jews are not considered part of the body politic.

While Israeli Arabs have the right to vote, to elect members of the Knesset, attend Israeli universities, obtain health care from excellent hospitals, and so forth, they still continue to experience significant discrimination. As Esman observes, "In effect, Palestinians are second-class citizens, leading separate but unequal lives."[197] There is marked discrimination in land policy (land is exclusively under Jewish control), education, and employment.[198] Consequently, Israeli Arabs would favor a power-sharing (consociational) system that reflects a binational state comprised of Palestinians and Jews with equal status.[199]

Israeli Arabs perceive themselves as Palestinians, but, according to Peleg, "a separate group of Palestinians." Israeli Arabs support the creation of an independent Palestinian state in the West Bank and Gaza, but do not necessarily see themselves immigrating to the new state. Moreover, they do not favor the annexation of their towns and villages by the new Palestinian state; rather, they prefer to stay in Israel as Israeli citizens.[200]

Israel's Arabs are in a bind. If they sympathize with their Palestinian kin in the occupied territories, they are accused of being a threat by Israel's Jewish population (as occurred when Israeli Arabs demonstrated in support of the second intifada). If they do not openly support the Palestinians in the occupied territories, they are accused of being traitors by Palestinians.[201]

Economic and Political Factors in the Occupied Territories

In the case of the occupied territories, two separate laws apply to the two separate peoples living there. Jewish settlers are bound by Israeli law, whereas Palestinians are bound by military and Jordanian laws. Israeli Jews in the occupied territories have sovereignty even though the territory is in dispute and occupation violates international law. Robert Blecher notes that more than a hundred Palestinian villages are "extra-territorialized"—going unrecognized by Israel to the extent "that they do not appear on Israeli maps."[202]

Even with the emergence of the peace process in the 1990s, conditions on the ground for Palestinians in the occupied territories remained problematic. The dependence of Palestinians on Israel was significant. Land and water resources were controlled by the government. Israeli companies supplied electricity, telephones, and water. This dependence was reinforced with the closure policy instituted by the Israeli government in 1991 during the first Gulf War, but made more widespread in 1993, at the same time the peace process was underway.[203] Because of the significant level of integration of the Palestinian economy with that of Israel, the impact of the closure was extremely harmful.[204] Economic growth in the occupied territories became difficult. With the decline in the economy, and concomitant problems of access to education, health services, and so forth, the potential for Palestinian violence increased. The result of the closure policy was to separate and isolate Palestinian communities, increase the unemployment rate (Palestinians lost their jobs in Israel because they could not cross into Israel proper), and decrease Palestinian trade (there were fewer exports relative to imports, and little access to markets beyond Israel). Both agricultural and industrial production decreased. Sara Roy remarks that poverty and child-labor rates increased "to levels not before seen during the entire period of Israeli occupation."[205] After the outbreak of the second intifada, the Israeli government continued the closure policy by establishing more than five hundred military checkpoints in both Gaza and the West Bank, leading to further economic decline in the territories.[206] By the middle of 2007 the World Bank estimated that the territory had been divided into ten isolated areas.[207]

As Sarah Leah Whitson, the Middle East director of Human Rights Watch, wrote in June 2009, "The economic and social cost of Israeli settlements to the Palestinian population, stemming in part from Israel's need to protect them, are enormous. The 634 (at last count) roadblocks, barriers and checkpoints erected to control the movement of lawful residents of the territory make travel an ordeal. Sometimes even getting to work, school or the home of a relative is impossible for Palestinians. Every day, they must wait in line for hours to show their IDs, and some days they are randomly rerouted, told to go home or, worse, detained for questioning." She states further, in regard to the security wall, "the fact that Israel is building 87% of its projected 450-mile 'security barrier' on Palestinian territory has less to do with protecting Israel from suicide bombers—which could have been accomplished by erecting a wall on the Green Line—than it does with putting 10% of West Bank territory, including most settlers, on the Israeli side."[208]

The continued decline in economic and social standards in both Gaza and the West Bank has led to a significant reliance on donors for international aid. Since 2001 development assistance from states and multilateral donors amounts to more than $1.1 billion annually (from 1995 to 2007 the amount was $14.3 billion total).[209] There is a direct relationship between the economic and political conditions, and the prospect for peace. Without a lasting political settlement and a durable peace, the Palestinian economy will continue to spiral downward, as Palestinians will experience little or no access to international markets for their exports, rising poverty levels, rising unemployment levels, and restrictions on the movement of goods, labor, and capital.[210]

INTERNATIONAL LEVEL

Given the internationalization of the Israeli-Palestinian conflict, and the continued mistrust of both sides, scholars argue that external actors are needed to get the parties to the negotiating table and a peaceful solution to the conflict. The concern, of course, is that outside involvement does not guarantee success, as demonstrated by the breakdown of the Oslo peace process with the eruption of the second intifada seven years later.[211] This has not prevented states and international organizations from promoting the peace process. While many NGOs are active in addressing the conflict, it is individual states and international institutions (IGOs) that have been the most instrumental in getting the two sides to the negotiating table. This section briefly examines several international actors: the United States, the United Nations, Norway, and the European Union.

United States

The close relationship between Israel and the United States has existed since Israel's independence, reinforced over time by successive presidential administrations, both Republican and Democratic. The American public and Congress consistently express their support for Israel, viewed as a liberal, democratic state in a region marked by authoritarian regimes bent on Israel's destruction. The Holocaust profoundly influenced American support for the new state.[212] In addition, the Middle East became an area of contestation between the United States and the Soviet Union during the Cold War, as both recognized its strategic value given its oil wealth. As Helsing notes, "Because the Arab-Israeli conflict became the critical foreign policy issue in the region, it also became the critical issue for the superpowers."[213]

After the 1967 war and then the end of the Cold War (and the change in the balance of power in the international system), some American elites and groups began to question the close relationship the United States maintained with Israel, claiming that uncritical support of its ally came at the expense of the United States' relationship with Arab states. Concerns for U.S. interests drove the change in unqualified support for Israel, as the realist approach would assert. Israel, in response, looked to other groups within the United States for support, namely evangelical Protestants. For these Protestants, support for

Israel was crucial, as Israel's existence was "the fulfillment of God's plan and a prerequisite for the end times."[214]

Congress has backed the American public's support for Israel, passing a series of resolutions expressing support for Israel when it has responded to terrorist actions, for example in 2002 at the time of the second intifada.[215] In their study of Senate support for Israel from 1993 to 2002, Beth Rosenson et al. found that conservatives and Jews were "Israel's staunchest advocates in the Senate."[216] They also found that *"elite* identification as an evangelical" was a predictor of strong support, rather than an elite's response to evangelical constituents' support for Israel.[217]

While U.S. support for Israel has been unwavering for six decades[218] (U.S. aid to Israel amounts to more than $2 billion per year, including both economic and military assistance—cumulatively it has received far more in U.S. assistance than any other country since the Second World War),[219] the United States has also acted to promote the peace process. It is seen as the only state with the resources (foreign aid) and power (only superpower remaining in the international system) to mediate between the two parties and bring them to the negotiating table. Public opinion polls consistently show Israeli approval of U.S. leadership is higher than the Palestinian approval of U.S. leadership. Yet, the Palestinians recognize that the United States is the only country that can induce a change in Israeli behavior toward resolving the conflict, given the close relationship between the two countries (although they would prefer other countries taking the lead, namely in the Arab world, which the Israelis oppose).[220]

U.S. efforts in the Middle East peace process began as early as the 1978 Camp David Accords, leading to a peace agreement between Egypt and Israel (while also acknowledging that the end to the Arab-Israeli conflict was closely connected to the Palestinian issue). After that, not much momentum for the peace process occurred until the first intifada.[221] During the late 1980s and early 1990s, the United States took a more active role. During the George H. W. Bush (Republican) and Clinton (Democratic) administrations, U.S. policy toward the peace process fluctuated, according to Makovsky, "depending on who held power in Israel." When a Likud government was in power, the United States "took an active stance." In doing so, the United States worried that a hard-line Israeli government's actions might actually lead to a regional conflict, which would be harmful to U.S. national interests. This activism is evident in the 1991 Madrid conference and 1998 Wye River Memorandum. With a Labor government in power, the U.S. role (regardless of which political party held the presidency in the United States) has been that of facilitator. In this role, Israel "set the pace" for negotiations, with the United States playing a background role. The Oslo Accords, brokered by Norway, without U.S. involvement, is a case in point.[222]

The Camp David summit was, however, an example of the United States taking a more active role with a Labor government in power in Israel. Clinton and his negotiating team "shuttled" between Barak and Arafat, neither of whom met each other alone during the entire summit, which lasted twelve days.[223]

For the George W. Bush administration, the Middle East peace process was not a priority in terms of a leading role for the United States (Bush did initiate a fact-finding mission: the "Mitchell Report"). Even in the aftermath of the September 11, 2001, terrorist attacks, the administration did not make a Middle East peace agreement the focus of its foreign policy; rather, such a peace process was considered "part of the war on terrorism."[224] Interestingly, Bush was the first U.S. president to express explicit support for an independent Palestinian state, in a June 24, 2002, speech. He noted that peace between the two groups could only be achieved when "the Israeli occupation that began in 1967 will be ended through a settlement negotiated between the parties, based on UN Resolutions 242 and 338, with Israeli withdrawal to secure and recognized borders."[225] For the Palestinians, Bush's words meant an independent Palestinian state in the occupied territories.[226] Bush then pushed for the 2003 Road Map, which became the blueprint for a resolution to the conflict that included an end to all settlement construction as well as a two-state solution by 2005. However, as that deadline came and went, the subsequent impasse in the movement toward peace brought the parties together at Annapolis in 2007, which gave rise to "a new role for the United States as 'judge' of Israel's and the Palestinians' fulfillment of their commitments" of the Road Map.[227] Importantly, U.S. policy supporting Israel, as a country with a special relationship with the United States, remained consistent with that of previous administrations.

The new administration of Barak Obama in January 2009 clearly showed that the peace process would be a top priority, as reflected in the comments by the secretary of state–designate Hillary Clinton in the week before the inauguration, in which she expressed U.S. support for a secure Israel and an independent Palestinian state (a continuation of U.S. policy). Obama's strong commitment was evident when he appointed George Mitchell as the U.S. Special Envoy to the Middle East two days after the inauguration.[228] Since his appointment, Mitchell has met with Israeli and Palestinian leaders about the need to return to peace talks, suspended during Bush's term in office and hampered further by the twenty-two-day Israeli offensive against Gaza.[229] The United States made it clear that while the country would remain Israel's staunch ally, it was also in Israel's (and the United States') interest to end settlement building (both existing and new) and resolve the outstanding issues between Israelis and Palestinians. The United States continued its support for the PA, while making it clear it would not negotiate with Hamas as long as the organization did not acknowledge Israel's right to exist (again, a consistent U.S. policy). In an interview with the *Jerusalem Post* in December 2008, Mitchell remarked, "I believe that neither [Israel nor Palestine] can attain its objective by denying to the other side its objectives. Israelis are not likely to have sustainable security if the Palestinians don't have a state, and Palestinians will never achieve a state until the people of Israel have some security."[230] In response to U.S. pressure, on June 14, 2009, Israeli prime minister Netanyahu gave a speech in which he articulated his endorsement of an independent Palestinian state, but on the condition that Palestinians would accept Israel as a Jewish state, Jerusalem would remain undivided as the capital of Israel, Palestine would be demilitarized, and Israel would have control of Palestinian airspace.[231] In late June 2009, also in response to U.S. pressure, as well as the increased security role taken by the police forces of the PA, Israel began to dismantle several dozen West Bank roadblocks in order to ease the restrictions of Palestinian movements in the occupied territory and improve economic conditions.[232] At the same time, the Netanyahu government refuses to end settlement expansion, in defiance of U.S. demands. As in previous administrations, the United States continues to promote the peace process and offers to mediate even though its efforts have not always succeeded nor has mediation led to a lasting peace settlement.

United Nations

The United Nations Security Council and General Assembly (GA) addressed the conflict even prior to Israel's independence, beginning with the first resolution in 1947 (UNGA Resolution 181) which called for the partition of Palestine. Subsequent to this resolution, the UN passed resolutions 242 (1967) and 338 (1973), which form the basis of the Palestinian claims for territory and an end to Israeli occupation of territory acquired in the 1967 war ("land for peace"). The Security Council passed resolutions since 242 and 338 that reaffirm its call for an end to Israeli occupation of the territories as well as call on Israel to follow international law with regard to protecting civilians in time of war (Resolution 1322, October 2000); it has endorsed the 2003 Road Map (Resolution 1515, November 2003) and has called for a cease-fire during the Israeli offensive in Gaza (Resolution 1860, January 2009). The UN General Assembly has also passed resolutions in regard to the conflict, including Resolution ES-10/8 (December 2001) calling on Israel and Palestine to implement the 2001 Mitchell Report recommendations, and Resolution ES-10/15 (August 2004) recognizing the International Court of Justice ruling that Israel's separation wall is illegal under international law.[233]

The UN position has been consistent, as evidenced by statements as recent as May 11, 2009. Unanimously, all fifteen members of the Security Council approved that statement. U.S. ambassador to the UN Susan Rice commented that President Obama was determined to get the peace talks back on track and a comprehensive peace settlement concluded in the near future. The Security Council statement directed its comments to both the Israelis and Palestinians, urging Israel to push forward with a two-state solution and for the Palestinian factions to end their intra-Palestinian divisions, repudiate violence, and recognize Israel. The statement further noted its support for the Road Map, as well as the Arab peace plan. The Israeli ambassador to the UN, Gabriela Shalev, however, made it clear that the Israeli government's position was that there should be bilateral talks and not the involvement of the Security Council.[234]

While the United Nations has passed resolutions encouraging peace between the parties and supports the efforts of the United States, Norway, and other states, it has been unable to take a leading role in large part due to the United States. The United States has vetoed or abstained from votes cast in the Security Council critical of Israel. As a result, the UN has primarily focused on humanitarian efforts to ease the plight of the Palestinians, as evidenced by the ongoing work of the United Nations Relief and Works Agency for Palestine Refugees in the Near East (UNRWA), established in 1949 by the UNGA (Resolution 302) following the 1948 war. UNRWA's mandate is to provide housing, clothing, education, and health care for those Palestinians made refugees after the war (those Palestinians who lost their homes and livelihood and who lived in Palestine between June 1, 1946, and May 15, 1948, and the descendants of the fathers). While originally created as a temporary agency, UNRWA continues to operate. The General Assembly renews the mandate, with its most recent extension to June 30, 2011. Today, UNRWA assists more than 4.6 million Palestinian refugees living in several countries and territories, including the West Bank and Gaza.[235] The United States is the largest bilateral donor to the agency, having provided $184.7 million in 2008.[236]

Norway

Norway played a particularly vital role in moving the negotiations forward in the early 1990s, hosting the secret negotiations in 1992 that led to the 1993 Oslo Accords. Norway, as "a trusted ally and NATO partner of the United States" that was acceptable to both sides of the conflict, was able to mediate between the two parties. As early as 1979, and again in the 1980s, Arafat sought out Norway as a mediator.[237] By 1992 Norway offered to host secret talks between the Israelis and the PLO (occurring at the same time as talks being held in Washington). The Israelis accepted, because in doing so Israel could "explore the views held by the PLO without any commitment," according to Hilde Waage. Thus, by January 1993, the "back channel" began, starting with two Israeli academics and three PLO officials. The talks were "informal and exploratory," though the Palestinian side was represented by PLO members.[238] The Norwegians viewed their role as facilitators, rather than mediators, in the process. Norway's representatives contributed to the talks by "getting the parties together, booking flights and hotels, paying the bills, arranging meetings and, not least, keeping the negotiations going and secret." Their actions in large part involved promoting trust between the two parties through the informal environment that would enable the Israelis and Palestinians to build friendships. The Norwegians hoped that their role as facilitator would alter the parties' negative stereotypes of the other (enemy images) as well as address any misunderstandings.[239] The final status issues were not addressed, which the Israelis liked, and the PLO was willing to put these issues off for a later time.[240] By May 1993 the talks moved from the informal level to formal negotiations for the first time between the two parties. The major components of the draft declaration became sources of contention in the formal talks with Israel, which was concerned that a trusteeship over Gaza would set "a precedent for future UN involvement in Israeli administration of the occupied territories," for example. Likewise, at this time, the Israeli government did not support the creation of an independent Palestinian state.[241] The Palestinians responded with their own demands, including Israeli "recognition of the national rights of the Palestinian people." The Palestinians also wanted "a self-governing structure that could lead to a future Palestinian state."[242]

The impasse between the two sides led Norway to elevate its role from facilitator to mediator. The Norwegian government appointed a new foreign minister to play an active role in the negotiations. The Israelis were particularly interested in mutual recognition from the PLO representatives: Israel would recognize the PLO as the official representative of the Palestinians, and the PLO, in turn, would recognize Israel. The Israelis also demanded that the PLO renounce violence and the use of terror.[243] Eventually both sides responded to Norway's active mediator role, as the Norwegian foreign minister's hands-on approach pushed the two sides to come to an agreement. The final agreement became the Oslo Accords, but the agreement was basically "an initial agreement on principles." The Norwegians viewed the agreement as "a starting point" for future negotiations on the final status issues. Yet, the agreement was silent about an independent Palestinian state in the future, and the national rights of the Palestinian people were not acknowledged. Though resolutions 242 and 338 were noted, the wording of the resolutions is open to different interpretations. As Waage concludes, "On their road to an agreement, the Palestinians had given up many of their initial demands. Israel, on the other hand, had withdrawn many of the concessions it had made in the first rounds. What was left was a timetable in which difficult matters were postponed to the future, and the timetable itself depended wholly on mutual faith and trust between the parties."[244] Norway's role was heavily dependent on Israel's continued participation in the talks, given the power asymmetry between the Israelis and Palestinians. The Israelis could always walk away from the talks and still have the status quo, which the Palestinians desperately wanted to change. Waage concludes, "There is no evidence to suggest Norwegian attempts to persuade the Israelis to see the Palestinian point of view or to tell the PLO negotiators where there might be some 'give' in Israeli positions or what counter proposals might prove fruitful."[245] The Israelis threatened to end their participation in the talks if Norway informed the United States that the negotiations were in progress. The Norwegians complied. Moreover, the Norwegians had a propensity to blame the PLO representatives for any delays in the talks, favoring the Israeli positions instead. In this case, Norway did not have the power to force the Israelis to negotiate from a position of equal power with the Palestinians. As a result peace was not achieved. In order to achieve peace, "strong muscles are needed. Norway had none."[246]

European Union

For most of the time, the peace process excluded the European countries. Israel traditionally opposed European and UN intervention, determined to have the United States in the leading role, given the long-standing relationship between the United States and Israel. Israel perceived the European countries and the UN as having a pro-Arab stance. Yet, Israel also sought to enhance its economic ties with the EU in the 1990s, through an improvement of the EU-Israeli trade agreement of 1975. At the 1991 Madrid Conference, Israel agreed to the European presence as "participant" in the talks ("one step up from the 'observer' status permitted the UN"). The Oslo negotiations represented a greater role for Europe, even though the Norwegians involved in the negotiations were not invited to the White House reception following the signing ceremony.[247] During the period of the signing of the agreement, the EU proposed an aid plan for the occupied territories amounting to $600 million over five years, as well as additional funding for setting up administrative offices in Gaza and Jericho.[248] The Europeans also showed their support for the process through their observer role in the 1996 Palestinian elections to ensure the elections were fair.[249] The EU did attempt to play a bigger role in the peace process when it proposed a joint EU-U.S. initiative to restart the peace process in April 1997. The United States rejected the proposal.[250]

The EU position with regard to the two parties to the conflict is twofold: economic and political support for the Palestinians, including endorsement of an independent state comprised of the territory occupied since 1967, but also an insistence on the recognition of Israel.[251] The EU has reaffirmed its commitment to a two-state solution over the years, based on the various UN Security Council resolutions. It also is a major donor to the UNRWA in order to ensure financial support for the agency's various services. The EU's Middle East policy has been put forth in a series of statements over the years: for example, the Venice Declaration (1980), which "recognized the right to security and existence for all states in the region including Israel, and the need to fulfill the legitimate rights of the Palestinian people." The Berlin Declaration (1999) made "an explicit commitment" to the establishment of a Palestinian state. The EU expressed its support for the Arab Peace Initiative and cosponsored the Road Map, reinforced by the Annapolis summit. The EU continues to support the peace process and expresses the need for both parties to address the final status issues (the EU opposes the settlements in the West Bank and East Jerusalem). The EU also has made clear its commitment to contribute to post-conflict building once a comprehensive agreement that resolves all issues has been concluded.[252]

Overall, international actors have had some success in their mediation efforts in bringing the two parties to the negotiating table. However, as the above discussion makes clear, mediation is limited, as evidenced by the lack of a comprehensive agreement to date. The two parties look to different external actors for support for their respective positions: the Israelis prefer the United States, while the Palestinians look to the UN, EU, and Arab states. What is interesting to note, however, is that the external actors discussed above all support the two-state solution. Getting the two parties to achieve that goal, however, has proved difficult.

CONCLUSION

As Makovsky observes, "Israel has no military solution to Palestinian nationalism, and the Palestinians can never eliminate Israel through force. The two sides must live together."[253] This chapter illustrates the complexity of the conflict, the competing narratives, and the challenges for achieving a durable and lasting peace. Analysis of the conflict at the individual level highlights the role that leaders on both sides have played in framing the conditions for a comprehensive settlement, as well as the role of those extremists who have attempted to thwart the peace process. At the domestic level, ethnic/national identities and interests remain salient in this conflict, as expressed through nationalism, political parties, economic and political conditions, and public opinion. Finally, the international community has responded to the conflict, in its efforts to mediate, sometimes successfully (in the case of the Oslo Accords) and sometimes not (Camp David, 2000). Even with these peace agreements negotiated and, sometimes, concluded, a comprehensive peace settlement between Israelis and Palestinians remains elusive as long as the final status issues (refugees, territorial borders, settlements, resources, and so forth) are not settled and both sides are unwilling to compromise.

NOTES

1. Josh Levs, "Is Gaza 'Occupied' Territory?" *CNN.com*, January 6, 2009, www.cnn.com/2009/WORLD/meast/01/06/israel.gaza.occupation.question/index.html.
2. "Where Will It End?" *The Economist*, January 8, 2009, www.economist.com/world/mideast-africa/displaystory.cfm?story_id=12903402.
3. "Where Will It End?"
4. "Health Conditions Worsening in Gaza as Borders Remain Closed—UN Agency," UN News Service (May 22, 2009), www.un.org/apps/news/story.asp?NewsID=30899&Cr=gaza&Cr1=.
5. As quoted in CNN, "Israel Says Gaza Death Toll Lower than Claimed," *CNN.com*, March 26, 2009, www.cnn.com/2009/WORLD/meast/03/26/israel.gaza.death.toll/index.html.
6. CNN, "Israel Says Gaza Death Toll Lower than Claimed."
7. "Health Conditions Worsening in Gaza as Borders Remain Closed—UN Agency."
8. CIA, "The World Factbook: Gaza Strip," https://www.cia.gov/library/publications/the-world-factbook/geos/gz.html.
9. "Not Nearly Back to Normal," *The Economist*, April 30, 2009, www.economist.com/world/mideast-africa/displaystory.cfm?story_id=13578934.
10. "The Outlines of a Settlement," *The Economist*, January 15, 2009, www.economist.com/world/middleeast-africa/displaystory.cfm?story_id=E1_TNJQVDTR.
11. Israel Ministry of Foreign Affairs, "Responding to Hamas Attacks from Gaza—Issues of Proportionality" (December 29, 2008), www.mfa.gov.il/MFA/Government/Law/Legal+Issues+and+Rulings/Responding+to+Hamas+attacks+from+Gaza+-+Issues+of+Proportionality+-+March+2008.htm. After the conflict ended, the United Nations sought compensation ($11 million) from Israel for the damage incurred to UN buildings by the Israeli military during the conflict. "UN Seeks $11m for Israeli Raids," *BBC News*, May 6, 2009, http://news.bbc.co.uk/go/pr/fr/-/2/hi/middle_east/8036054.stm.
12. BBC News, "UN Seeks $11m for Israeli Raids"; Human Rights Watch, "US: Ask Israel to Cooperate with Goldstone Inquiry" (May 17, 2009), www.hrw.org/en/news/2009/05/17/us-ask-israel-cooperate-goldstone-inquiry.
13. As quoted in Human Rights Watch, "US: Ask Israel to Cooperate with Goldstone Inquiry."
14. Nathan Guttman, "Israel, U.S. Working to Limit Damage of Goldstone Report," *Haaretz.com*, September 27, 2009, www.haaretz.com/hasen/

spages/1117314.html; Barbara Plett, "Legal Row over Gaza Report Intensifies," *BBC News*, November 6, 2009, http://news.bbc.co.uk/go/pr/fr/-/2/hi/middle_east/8347861.stm; Joe Stork, "Moving beyond the Goldstone Report," *Human Rights Watch* (November 9, 2009), www.hrw.org/en/news/2009/11/09/moving-beyond-goldstone-report; Stephen Zunes, "The Goldstone Report: Killing the Messenger," *Foreign Policy in Focus* (October 7, 2009), www.fpif.org/fpiftxt/6485.

15. "Israel Rejects US Call over Settlement Work," *BBC News*, May 28, 2009, http://news.bbc.co.uk/go/pr/fr/-/2/hi/middle_east/8071491.stm; Israel Ministry of Foreign Affairs, "Disputed Territories: Forgotten Facts about the West Bank and Gaza Strip" (February 1, 2003), www.mfa.gov.il/MFA/MFAArchive/2000_2009/2003/2/DISPUTED+TERRITORIES-+Forgotten+Facts+About+the+We.htm.

16. David Makovsky, "Middle East Peace through Partition," *Foreign Affairs* 80, no. 2 (March/April 2001): 30.

17. Jeffrey W. Helsing, "The Regionalization, Internationalization, and Perpetuation of Conflict in the Middle East," in *Ethnic Conflict and International Politics: Explaining Diffusion and Escalation,* ed. Steven E. Lobell and Philip Mauceri (New York: Palgrave, 2004), 134.

18. Donald Sylvan et al. specifically focus on applying the levels of analysis to the Israeli-Palestinian conflict in an article that tests international relations theories and experts on the Middle East in forecasting outcomes with regard to Israeli-Palestinian relations. See Donald A. Sylvan, Jonathan W. Keller, and Yoram Z. Haftel, "Forecasting Israeli-Palestinian Relations," *Journal of Peace Research* 41, no. 4 (2004): 445–463.

19. "Early History: Palestine History," Palestine Facts, www.palestinefacts.org/pf_early_palestine_brief_history.php; Beshara B. Doumani, "Rediscovering Ottoman Palestine: Writing Palestinians into History," *Journal of Palestine Studies* 21, no. 2 (Winter 1992): 5-28; Human Rights Watch, "A Question of Security: Violence against Palestinian Women and Girls" (New York: Human Rights Watch, November 2006), 10, www.hrw.org/en/reports/2006/11/6/question-security.

20. Helsing, "The Regionalization, Internationalization, and Perpetuation of Conflict in the Middle East," 155.

21. Human Rights Watch, "A Question of Security," 10; Helsing, "The Regionalization, Internationalization, and Perpetuation of Conflict in the Middle East," 155.

22. Helsing, "The Regionalization, Internationalization, and Perpetuation of Conflict in the Middle East," 155. Jerome Slater makes the point that the Balfour Declaration promised the Jews a national homeland in Palestine, but "did not promise Jewish sovereignty over Palestine." Jerome Slater,

"What Went Wrong? The Collapse of the Israeli-Palestinian Peace Process," *Political Science Quarterly* 116, no. 2 (2001): 173.

23. Daniel L. Byman, *Keeping the Peace: Lasting Solutions to Ethnic Conflicts* (Baltimore: Johns Hopkins University Press, 2002), 157.

24. Helsing, "The Regionalization, Internationalization, and Perpetuation of Conflict in the Middle East," 155.

25. Byman, *Keeping the Peace,* 159.

26. Global Policy Forum, "Israel, Palestine, and the Occupied Territories," www.globalpolicy.org/security-council/index-of-countries-on-the-security-council-agenda/israel-palestine-and-the-occupied-territories.html.

27. Slater, "What Went Wrong?" 173.

28. Quoted in Slater, "What Went Wrong?" 174.

29. Byman, *Keeping the Peace,* 159–160.

30. Byman, *Keeping the Peace,* 160.

31. Byman, *Keeping the Peace,* 51, 53–54; Slater, "What Went Wrong?" 174.

32. Byman, *Keeping the Peace,* 53.

33. Byman, *Keeping the Peace,* 55.

34. Byman, *Keeping the Peace,* 54, 56, 61.

35. Byman, *Keeping the Peace,* 160–162.

36. Byman, *Keeping the Peace,* 162.

37. Human Rights Watch, "A Question of Security," 10.

38. Global Policy Forum, "Israel, Palestine and the Occupied Territories."

39. Slater, "What Went Wrong?" 176.

40. CIA, "The World Factbook: Israel," https://www.cia.gov/library/publications/the-world-factbook/geos/is.html; CIA, "The World Factbook: Gaza Strip," https://www.cia.gov/library/publications/the-world-factbook/geos/gz.html. Agreements signed in this period include the May 1994 Gaza-Jericho agreement, the August 1994 Agreement on Preparatory Transfer of Powers and Responsibilities, the September 1995 Israeli-Palestinian Interim Agreement on the West Bank and the Gaza Strip (this was the first stage of the DOP), and the October 1998 Wye River Memorandum. Israel Ministry of Foreign Affairs, "Israel-Palestinian Negotiations," www.mfa.gov.il/MFA/Peace+Process/Guide+to+the+Peace+Process/Israel-Palestinian+negotiations.htm.

41. Slater, "What Went Wrong?" 177.

42. Slater, "What Went Wrong?" 177.

43. Slater, "What Went Wrong?" 178–179. Oren Barak argues that the failure of the Oslo peace process can be situated in the fact that "an intergroup conflict between Israelis and Palestinians was construed and treated as an interstate conflict" and this affected how the conflict was framed, and made the possibility of successful negotiation problematic. In essence, he

argues that there was "an interstate bias towards the conflict, which ultimately hindered its successful treatment." Oren Barak, "The Failure of the
Israeli-Palestinian Peace Process, 1993–2000," *Journal of Peace Research* 42,
no. 6 (2005): 733.

44. Slater, "What Went Wrong?" 182–188; Jeremy Pressman, "Visions in Collision: What Happened at Camp David and Taba?" *International Security* 28,
no. 2 (Fall 2003): 5–43.

45. Slater, "What Went Wrong?" 184.

46. Pressman, "Visions in Collision," 16.

47. Pressman, "Visions in Collision," 17.

48. Pressman, "Visions in Collision," 18.

49. European Union, "Sharm El-Sheikh Fact-Finding Committee Report:
'Mitchell Report'" (April 30, 2001) www.consilium.europa.eu/ueDocs/
cms_Data/docs/pressdata/EN/reports/ACF310.pdf.

50. European Union, "Sharm El-Sheikh Fact-Finding Committee Report."
Israeli and Palestinian negotiators met again in mid-January 2001 in
Taba, Egypt, to discuss Clinton's plan that emerged from the Camp David
summit (the plan called for a Palestinian state in 97 percent of the West
Bank and the whole of the Gaza Strip; Jerusalem would have Palestinian
and Israeli control over their respective religious sites; Palestinian refugees
would have the right of return to the new Palestinian state, as well as financial compensation; Israel would concede the suffering Palestinians experienced in 1948). With Barak's defeat by Ariel Sharon in the February 2001
elections, the new government decided not to continue with high-level
talks with the Palestinians. Pressman, "Visions in Collision," 8–9.

51. Global Policy Forum, "Saudi-Initiated Peace Plan Document" (March 25,
2002), www.globalpolicy.org/component/content/article/189/38003.html.

52. Global Policy Forum, "A Performance-Based Roadmap to a Permanent
Two-State Solution to the Israeli-Palestinian Conflict" (2003), www.global
policy.org/images/pdfs/roadmap122002.pdf.

53. CIA, "The World Factbook: Gaza Strip."

54. Khalil Shikaki, "The Future of Palestine," *Foreign Affairs* 83, no. 6 (Novem-
ber/December 2004): 51.

55. In November the two sides signed an agreement that authorized the
Rafah border crossing between Egypt and Gaza reopened. The Rafah border
crossing would be controlled jointly by Egypt and the PA. CIA, "The World
Factbook: Gaza Strip." Ghazi-Walid Falah argues that Prime Minister Ariel
Sharon's "disengagement plan" is a form of "enclavisation"—"a strategy of
territorial control that can be enacted here by turning an entire geographical
bloc of Palestinian settlement into a closed zone. . . . confining and drastically
weakening the population economically, politically, and socially—in effect

'neutralizing' its challenge as a potential opponent." Ghazi-Walid Falah, "The Geopolitics of 'Enclavisation' and the Demise of a Two-State Solution to the Israeli-Palestinian Conflict," *Third World Quarterly* 26, no. 8 (2005): 1344.

56. CIA, "The World Factbook: Gaza Strip."

57. CIA, "The World Factbook: Gaza Strip."

58. Falah, "The Geopolitics of 'Enclavisation,'" 1342, 1349; Makovsky, "Middle East Peace through Partition," 38; Slater, "What Went Wrong?" 187.

59. Milton J. Esman, *An Introduction to Ethnic Conflict* (Cambridge: Polity, 2004), 75.

60. Government of Israel, Prime Minister's Office, "Yitzhak Rabin—The Fifth Prime Minister," www.pmo.gov.il/PMOEng/History/FormerPrime Minister/YitzhaRabin.htm.

61. As quoted by Reuven Y. Hazan, "Intraparty Politics and Peacemaking in Democratic Societies: Israel's Labor Party and the Middle East Peace Process, 1992–96," *Journal of Peace Research* 37, no. 3 (2000): 366.

62. Hazan, "Intraparty Politics and Peacemaking in Democratic Societies," 366.

63. Makovsky, "Middle East Peace through Partition," 28-29; Hazan, "Intraparty Politics and Peacemaking in Democratic Societies," 372.

64. As quoted in Danny Ben-Moshe, "The Oslo Peace Process and Two Views on Judaism and Zionism, 1992–1996," *British Journal of Middle Eastern Studies* 32, no. 1 (May 2005): 18.

65. Makovsky, "Middle East Peace through Partition," 34.

66. As quoted in Ben-Moshe, "The Oslo Peace Process," 23.

67. As quoted in Ian S. Lustick, "Reinventing Jerusalem," *Foreign Policy* 93 (Winter 1993–1994): 50.

68. Interestingly, Rabin's military aides tried to discourage him from instituting the closure policy, but the public, concerned about continued Palestinian violence, influenced his decision. Yehudith Auerbach and Charles W. Greenbaum, "Assessing Leader Credibility during a Peace Process: Rabin's Private Polls," *Journal of Peace Research* 37, no. 1 (2000): 43.

69. Graham Usher, "Unmaking Palestine: On Israel, the Palestinians, and the Wall," *Journal of Palestine Studies* 35, no. 1 (Autumn 2005): 31.

70. Usher, "Unmaking Palestine," 32.

71. Ben-Moshe, "The Oslo Peace Process," 22–23.

72. Hazan, "Intraparty Politics and Peacemaking in Democratic Societies," 370.

73. Ben-Moshe, "The Oslo Peace Process," 19. For Rabin, his willingness to sacrifice Greater Israel for peace was a step forward, as indicated in his comments on Israel radio on Independence Day 1994. He said: "I don't propose we look at the Bible as the map of the State of Israel. In my eyes, the Bible is the religion, faith, values and heritage of the Jews. This is the way I studied the book of books." As quoted in Ben-Moshe, "The Oslo Peace Process," 20.

74. As quoted in Slater, "What Went Wrong?" 177.
75. Slater, "What Went Wrong?" 177.
76. Slater, "What Went Wrong?" 177–178.
77. Louis Kriesberg, "Mediation and the Transformation of the Israeli-Palestinian Conflict," *Journal of Peace Research* 38, no. 3 (2001): 377, 386.
78. Government of Israel, Prime Minister's Office, "Ehud Barak—The Tenth Prime Minister," www.pmo.gov.il/PMOEng/History/FormerPrimeMinister/EhudBarak.htm.
79. Kriesberg, "Mediation and the Transformation of the Israeli-Palestinian Conflict," 390.
80. Makovsky, "Middle East Peace through Partition," 37.
81. Makovsky, "Middle East Peace through Partition," 37.
82. Slater, "What Went Wrong?" 184.
83. Slater, "What Went Wrong?" 182–183.
84. Slater, "What Went Wrong?" 181.
85. Slater, "What Went Wrong?" 183.
86. Government of Israel, Prime Minister's Office, "Ehud Barak—The Tenth Prime Minister."
87. Usher, "Unmaking Palestine," 32-33.
88. Usher, "Unmaking Palestine," 33.
89. "Obituary: Yasser Arafat," *BBC News,* November 11, 2004, http://news.bbc.co.uk/go/pr/fr/-/2/hi/middle_east/890161.stm.
90. Global Policy Forum, "Yasser Arafat, Speech at UN General Assembly" (December 13, 1988), www.globalpolicy.org/images/pdfs/arafatga121988.pdf. See also Slater, "What Went Wrong?" 176.
91. As quoted in "Arafat: Words of War and Peace," *BBC News*, November 11, 2004, http://news.bbc.co.uk/2/hi/middle_east/4003823.stm.
92. Usher, "Unmaking Palestine," 26.
93. Kriesberg, "Mediation and the Transformation of the Israeli-Palestinian Conflict," 386, 389.
94. Makovsky, "Middle East Peace through Partition," 30–31.
95. Makovsky, "Middle East Peace through Partition," 31.
96. Slater, "What Went Wrong?" 178-179; Kriesberg, "Mediation and the Transformation of the Israeli-Palestinian Conflict," 377. See also Akram Hanieh's papers on the negotiations at the Camp David summit from the Palestinian perspective (Hanieh was a special adviser to Arafat and a member of the Palestinian negotiating team). Akram Hanieh, "Special Document: The Camp David Papers," *Journal of Palestine Studies* 30, no. 2 (Winter 2001): 75–97. Dennis B. Ross, lead negotiator during the Clinton administration, provides an opposing view; see Dennis B. Ross, "Yasir Arafat," *Foreign Policy* 131 (July-August 2002): 18–26.

97. Shikaki, "The Future of Palestine," 50–51.
98. Shikaki, "The Future of Palestine," 51.
99. Kriesberg, "Mediation and the Transformation of the Israeli-Palestinian Conflict," 384.
100. Auerbach and Greenbaum, "Assessing Leader Credibility during a Peace Process," 48.
101. Kriesberg, "Mediation and the Transformation of the Israeli-Palestinian Conflict," 389.
102. Andrew Kydd and Barbara F. Walter, "Sabotaging the Peace: The Politics of Extremist Violence," *International Organization* 56, no. 2 (Spring 2002): 263.
103. Kydd and Walter, "Sabotaging the Peace," 266.
104. Kydd and Walter, "Sabotaging the Peace," 276.
105. Kydd and Walter, "Sabotaging the Peace," 280.
106. Kydd and Walter, "Sabotaging the Peace," 280.
107. Kydd and Walter, "Sabotaging the Peace," 282–283.
108. Kydd and Walter, "Sabotaging the Peace," 286–287.
109. Barak, "The Failure of the Israeli-Palestinian Peace Process, 1993–2000," 727.
110. Kriesberg, "Mediation and Transformation of the Israeli-Palestinian Conflict," 384.
111. Helsing, "The Regionalization, Internationalization, and Perpetuation of Conflict in the Middle East," 155.
112. Interestingly, during the war of 1948, the Israeli leaders' war strategy did not include conquering Jerusalem; instead, the leadership determined that the Negev, a significant strategic area, was more important than the Old City, the location of the Temple Mount. As a result, the military focused its efforts there. Hillel Frisch and Shmuel Sandler, "Religion, State, and the International System in the Israeli-Palestinian Conflict," *International Political Science Review* 25, no. 1 (2004): 81–82.
113. Lustick, "Reinventing Jerusalem," 43, 45. Several laws specifically related to Jerusalem include the 1980 Basic Law on Jerusalem and the March 1990 resolution that reaffirmed "that united Jerusalem is under Israeli sovereignty and there will be no negotiations on its unity and status." Yitzhak Shamir's Likud government also created the Ministry for Jerusalem Affairs in 1990; it was disbanded with the return of the Labor Party to power. See Ian Lustick, "Reinventing Jerusalem," 53–55.
114. Lustick, "Reinventing Jerusalem," 43. He also writes, "The June 1967 demarcating Jerusalem's boundary was not only unprecedented, but also devoid of any religious, historical, or emotional justification. It was drawn as a compromise between minimalist and maximalist positions advanced by various Israeli bureaucrats, military officers, and politicians. . . . an accidental shape whose only rationale was that it maximized the acquisition of

Arab land while minimizing the number of Arabs who would become Israeli residents." Lustick, "Reinventing Jerusalem," 45–46.

115. Lustick, "Reinventing Jerusalem," 48. As early as Israel's founding in 1948, several of the Israeli "founding fathers" "opposed making any part of Jerusalem Israel's capital, not only because of fear of provoking the international community, but because of disdain for the city itself compared to the comforts and 'appropriate climate' of Tel Aviv." Lustick, "Reinventing Jerusalem," 57.

116. Ben-Moshe, "The Oslo Peace Process," 14.

117. Ben-Moshe, "The Oslo Peace Process," 14.

118. Ben-Moshe, "The Oslo Peace Process," 14–15.

119. Ben-Moshe, "The Oslo Peace Process," 14-15.

120. Ben-Moshe, "The Oslo Peace Process," 14.

121. Frisch and Sandler, "Religion, State, and the International System in the Israeli-Palestinian Conflict," 87–88.

122. Frisch and Sandler, "Religion, State, and the International System in the Israeli-Palestinian Conflict," 89.

123. Israel Ministry of Foreign Affairs, "Aliyah" (October 29, 2002), www.mfa .gov.il/MFA/MFAArchive/2000_2009/2002/10/Aliyah.htm.

124. Frisch and Sandler, "Religion, State, and the International System in the Israeli-Palestinian Conflict," 85, 89–90. Helga Baumgarten examines the three "faces/phases" of Palestinian nationalism since 1948, starting with the Movement of Arab Nationalists (MAN), then Fatah/PLO, and finally Hamas. MAN revolved around Pan-Arabism, while the latter two focus more specifically on Palestinian nationalism. Helga Baumgarten, "The Three Faces/Phases of Palestinian Nationalism, 1948–2005," *Journal of Palestine Studies* 34, no. 4 (Summer 2005): 25–48.

125. Frisch and Sandler, "Religion, State, and the International System in the Israeli-Palestinian Conflict," 90.

126. Shlomo Ben-Ami, "A War to Start All Wars: Will Israel Ever Seal the Victory of 1948?" *Foreign Affairs* 87, no. 5 (September/October 2008): 155–156.

127. Wendy Pearlman, "Spoiling Inside and Out: Internal Political Contestation and the Middle East Peace Process," *International Security* 33, no. 3 (Winter 2008/2009): 86–87.

128. Pearlman, "Spoiling Inside and Out," 87, 90.

129. Pearlman, "Spoiling Inside and Out," 94-95.

130. Pearlman, "Spoiling Inside and Out," 97; Khalil Shikaki, "Palestinians Divided," *Foreign Affairs* 81, no. 1 (January/February 2002): 93–94.

131. Pearlman, "Spoiling Inside and Out," 97.

132. Pearlman, "Spoiling Inside and Out," 98–100.

133. Shikaki, "The Future of Palestine," 46.

134. Shikaki, "Palestinians Divided," 90.

135. Shikaki, "The Future of Palestine," 47.

136. Gad Barzilai and Ilan Peleg, "Israel and Future Borders: Assessment of a Dynamic," *Journal of Peace Research* 31, no. 1 (February 1994): 59–60.

137. Julie Peteet, "Words as Interventions: Naming in the Palestine-Israel Conflict," *Third World Quarterly* 26, no. 1 (2005): 155–156.

138. Peteet, "Words as Interventions," 157.

139. Peteet, "Words as Interventions," 158. Peteet notes that in the 1930s the Zionists established the Names Committee, which was then replaced with the Israel Place-Names Committee upon Israel's independence. The committee was responsible for changing names to either national/Zionist ones or biblical ones. The Palestinians in refugee camps named their new village areas after their original villages. Peteet, "Words as Interventions," 158–159.

140. Peteet, "Words as Interventions," 161.

141. Peteet, "Words as Interventions," 162.

142. Peteet, "Words as Interventions," 163.

143. Peteet, "Words as Interventions," 165.

144. Bat Shalom, "Who We Are," www.batshalom.org/about.php.

145. International Women's Commission, "Statement Issued by the International Women's Commission for a Just and Sustainable Peace between Israel and Palestine" (May 3, 2006), www.iwc-peace.org/.

146. Joyce P. Kaufman and Kristen P. Williams, *Women, the State, and War: A Comparative Perspective on Citizenship and Nationalism* (Lanham, Md.: Lexington, 2007), 124.

147. Sara Helman, "From Soldiering and Motherhood to Citizenship: A Study of Four Israeli Peace Protest Movements," *Social Politics* 6, no. 3 (Fall 1999): 298.

148. Tamar Rapoport and Tamar El-Or, "Cultures of Womanhood in Israel: Social Agencies and Gender Production," *Women's Studies International Forum* 20, nos. 5/6 (1997): 575.

149. Nitza Berkovitch, "Motherhood as a National Mission: The Construction of Womanhood in the Legal Discourse in Israel," *Women's Studies International Forum* 20, nos. 5/6 (1997): 607, 616.

150. Kaufman and Williams, *Women, the State, and War,* 124.

151. Helman, "From Soldiering and Motherhood to Citizenship," 306.

152. Coalition of Women for Peace, "The Coalition: General Info," http://coalitionofwomen.org/home/english/about/general_info/.

153. Maayana Miskin, "Israeli Women's Groups Complain to UN—Against Israel," *IsraelNationalNews.com*, December 22, 2008, www.israelnational-news.com/news/news.aspx/128981.

154. Mary Honeyball, "Will Women Be Excluded from the Gaza Peace Process?" *New Europe*, January 12, 2009, www.neurope.eu/articles/91858.php.

155. Kaufman and Williams, *Women, the State, and War,* 130.

156. General Union of Palestinian Women, "The National Strategy for the Advancement of Palestinian Women," http://web.archive.org/web/2008020 5051246/http://www.gupw.net/publications/st1.htm.

157. Maria Holt, "Palestinian Women, Violence, and the Peace Process," *Development in Practice* 13, nos. 2–3 (May 2003): 224, 228. See also Tami Amanda Jacoby, "Feminism, Nationalism, and Difference: Reflections on the Palestinian Women's Movement," *Women's Studies International Forum* 22, no. 5 (1999): 511–523.

158. Penny Johnson and Eileen Kuttab, "Where Have All the Women (and Men) Gone? Reflections on Gender and the Second Palestinian Intifada," *Feminist Review* 69 (Winter 2001): 27.

159. Women's Affairs Technical Committee, "WATC's Beginnings," http://watcpal.org/english/display.asp?DocID=7.

160. Johnson and Kuttab, "Where Have All the Women (and Men) Gone?" 28–29.

161. "WATC's Beginnings."

162. Freedom House, "Palestine (Palestinian Authority and Israeli-Occupied Territories)," www.freedomhouse.org/template.cfm?page=180; United Nations, "Press Conference on Situation of Women in Occupied Palestinian Territory," United Nations Department of Public Information (March 4, 2009), www.un.org/News/briefings/docs/2009/090304_OPT.doc.htm; Palestinian Women's Research and Documentation Center, UNESCO, "Violence against Women in Palestine: National Campaign against Violence against Women" (November 25–December 10, 2006), www.pwrdc.ps/site_files/Violence%20against%20Women.pdf.

163. Claudia Brunner, "Female Suicide Bombers—Male Suicide Bombing? Looking for Gender in Reporting the Suicide Bombings of the Israeli-Palestinian Conflict," *Global Society* 19, no. 1 (January 2005): 29–48.

164. There is one glaring exception: Hanan Ashrawi. Ashrawi was the official spokesperson for the Palestinian delegation to the Middle East peace process initiated by President George H. W. Bush in 1991. During the Oslo Accords peace process she led the Preparatory Committee of the Palestinian Independent Commission for Citizens' Rights in Jerusalem. She was elected to the Palestinian Legislative Council in 1996 as a member of the Third Way party, a rival to Fatah and Hamas. "Hanan Ashrawi," *Encyclopedia Britannica,* www.britannica.com/EBchecked/topic/38365/Hanan-Ashrawi.

165. Israel Ministry of Foreign Affairs, "Elections in Israel—February 2009" (February 10, 2009), www.mfa.gov.il/MFA/History/Modern+History/Historic+Events/Elections_in_Israel_February_2009.htm.

166. Frisch and Sandler, "Religion, State, and the International System in the Israeli-Palestinian Conflict," 83.

167. Frisch and Sandler, "Religion, State, and the International System in the Israeli-Palestinian Conflict," 84.
168. Hazan, "Intraparty Politics and Peacemaking in Democratic Societies," 374.
169. Barry Rubin, "Israel's New Strategy," *Foreign Affairs* 85, no. 4 (July/August 2006): 113.
170. Rubin, "Israel's New Strategy," 120.
171. Gad Barzilai, Giora Goldberg, and Efraim Inbar, "Israeli Leadership and Public Attitudes toward Federal Solutions for the Arab-Israeli Conflict before and after Desert Storm," *Publius: The Journal of Federalism* 21 (Summer 1991): 194.
172. Baumgarten, "The Three Faces/Phases of Palestinian Nationalism," 29, 31.
173. Baumgarten, "The Three Faces/Phases of Palestinian Nationalism," 35–36.
174. Palestinian Center for Policy and Survey Research, "Palestinian Public Opinion Poll No. (32): While Abbas's popularity improves and while a majority of Palestinians accepts Fateh's position that a national unity government must accept agreements signed with Israel, and while a majority supports the two-state solution, pessimism prevails regarding the peace process and the chances for Fateh-Hamas reconciliation" (May 2009), www.pcpsr.org/survey/polls/2009/p32e.html.
175. Baumgarten, "The Three Faces/Phases of Palestinian Nationalism," 37.
176. Baumgarten, "The Three Faces/Phases of Palestinian Nationalism," 37–39.
177. Baumgarten, "The Three Faces/Phases of Palestinian Nationalism," 40.
178. Baumgarten, "The Three Faces/Phases of Palestinian Nationalism," 41.
179. As quoted in "Hamas 'Will Not Obstruct' 1967 Borders Deal," *BBC News*, June 10, 2009, http://news.bbc.co.uk/go/pr/fr/-/2/hi/middle_east/8091377.stm.
180. "Hamas 'Killing' Palestinian Foes," *BBC News*, April 20, 2009, http://news.bbc.co.uk/go/pr/fr/-/2/hi/middle_east/8007756.stm.
181. Palestinian Center for Policy and Survey Research, "Palestinian Public Opinion Poll No. (32)."
182. Daniel Bar-Tal, "Why Does Fear Override Hope in Societies Engulfed by Intractable Conflict, as It Does in the Israeli Society?" *Political Psychology* 22, no. 3 (September 2001): 611.
183. Bar-Tal, "Why Does Fear Override Hope," 611.
184. Bar-Tal, "Why Does Fear Override Hope," 612–617.
185. Bar-Tal, "Why Does Fear Override Hope," 619.
186. Barzilai and Peleg, "Israel and Future Borders," 65.
187. Barzilai and Peleg, "Israel and Future Borders," 66.
188. "Poll: Most Palestinians, Israelis Want Two-State Solution," *Haaretz.com*, April 22, 2009, www.haaretz.com/hasen/spages/1080267.html.

189. Palestinian Center for Policy and Survey Research, "Pessimism among Israelis and Palestinians regarding the prospects for a settlement and a Palestinian state in the next few years, but majorities on both sides support a two-state solution" (June 14, 2009), www.pcpsr.org/survey/polls/2009/p32ejoint.html.

190. Ilan Peleg, "Jewish-Palestinian Relations in Israel: From Hegemony to Equality?" *International Journal of Politics, Culture, and Society* 17, no. 3 (Spring 2004): 430.

191. Peleg, "Jewish-Palestinian Relations in Israel," 419.

192. Oren Yiftachel, "'Ethnocracy' and Its Discontents: Minorities, Protests, and the Israeli Polity," *Critical Inquiry* 26 (Summer 2000): 730. See also Oren Yiftachel, "Israeli Society and Jewish-Palestinian Reconciliation: 'Ethnocracy' and Its Territorial Contradictions," *Middle East Journal* 51, no. 4 (Autumn 1997): 505–519; "Democracy or Ethnocracy? Territory and Settler Politics in Israel/Palestine," *Middle East Report* 207 (Summer 1998): 8–13; "The Shrinking Space of Citizenship: Ethnocratic Politics in Israel," *Middle East Report* 223 (Summer 2002): 38–45.

193. Yiftachel, "'Ethnocracy' and Its Discontents," 732.

194. Yiftachel, "'Ethnocracy' and Its Discontents," 733.

195. Yiftachel, "'Ethnocracy' and Its Discontents," 737.

196. Yiftachel, "'Ethnocracy' and Its Discontents," 741.

197. Esman, *An Introduction to Ethnic Conflict,* 130.

198. Peleg, "Jewish-Palestinian Relations in Israel," 421–425.

199. Esman, *An Introduction to Ethnic Conflict,* 177. See also Byman, *Keeping the Peace,* 135; Yiftachel, "'Ethnocracy' and Its Discontents," 755.

200. Peleg, "Jewish-Palestinian Relations in Israel," 421.

201. Byman, *Keeping the Peace,* 138–139. See also Robert Blecher, "Citizens without Sovereignty: Transfer and Ethnic Cleansing in Israel," *Comparative Studies in Society and History* 47, no. 4 (October 2005): 725–754.

202. Blecher, "Citizens without Sovereignty," 754.

203. Barak, "The Failure of the Israeli-Palestinian Peace Process," 731.

204. Sara Roy, "The Palestinian-Israeli Conflict and Palestinian Socioeconomic Decline: A Place Denied," *International Journal of Politics, Culture and Society* 17, no. 3 (Spring 2004): 367.

205. Roy presents data showing that in the years 1993–1996 (the same time as the Oslo peace process was well underway), "the Israeli government imposed 342 days of total closure in the Gaza Strip and 291 days in the West Bank." She further notes, "That is, for almost one-third of each year between 1993 and 1996, Palestinians were denied the right to leave [the West Bank and Gaza] or to engage in economic activity across their

borders. And for the remaining portion of those years, Palestinians were subject to closure in a less extreme form." Roy, "The Palestinian-Israeli Conflict and Palestinian Socioeconomic Decline," 368.

206. Roy, "The Palestinian-Israeli Conflict and Palestinian Socioeconomic Decline," 369.

207. Cited in "Palestinian Growth 'Obstructed,'" *BBC News*, May 9, 2007, http://news.bbc.co.uk/go/pr/fr/-/2/hi/business/6638241.stm.

208. Sarah Leah Whitson, "Israel's Settlements Are on Shaky Ground," *Human Rights Watch* (June 28, 2009), www.hrw.org/en/news/2009/06/28/israels-settlements-are-shaky-ground.

209. The Palestinian economy is comprised, in essence, of "three distinct and isolated zones." The first zone is Ramallah, the headquarters of the PA. The second is the rest of the West Bank, which is heavily dependent on farm income and assistance from Ramallah (given all the checkpoints and roadblocks, the economy is one "of largely informal markets"). The third is Gaza, an area with few natural resources and with no access to external markets. Gaza's situation is compounded by the fact that it has one of the highest fertility levels globally. Navtej Dhillon, "Beyond Reconstruction: What Lies Ahead for Young Palestinians?" Brookings Institution (March 10, 2009), www.brookings.edu/opinions/2009/0310_west_bank_gaza_dhillon.aspx.

210. Dhillon, "Beyond Reconstruction."

211. Helsing, "The Regionalization, Internationalization, and Perpetuation of Conflict in the Middle East," 161.

212. Beth Rosenson, Elizabeth A. Oldmixon, and Kenneth D. Wald, "U.S. Senators' Support for Israel Examined through Sponsorship/Cosponsorship Decisions, 1993–2002: The Influence of Elite and Constituent Factors," *Foreign Policy Analysis* 5 (2009): 73–74.

213. Helsing, "The Regionalization, Internationalization, and Perpetuation of Conflict in the Middle East," 156.

214. Rosenson et al., "U.S. Senators' Support for Israel," 74.

215. Rosenson et al., "U.S. Senators' Support for Israel," 74–75.

216. Rosenson et al., "U.S. Senators' Support for Israel," 85.

217. Rosenson et al., "U.S. Senators' Support for Israel," 86.

218. See John J. Mearsheimer and Stephen M. Walt for a critical examination of the role of the Israeli lobby in influencing U.S. policy toward the Middle East, particularly support for Israel. Mearsheimer and Walt, *The Israel Lobby and U.S. Foreign Policy* (New York: Farrar, Straus and Giroux, 2007).

219. For nearly thirty years (1976–2004), Israel received more U.S. foreign assistance annually than any other country, surpassed by Iraq following the U.S.

invasion of that country in 2003. See the CRS Report for Congress on more details of U.S. financial support to Israel. "CRS Report for Congress: U.S. Foreign Aid to Israel," Congressional Research Service (January 2, 2008), http://fpc.state.gov/documents/organization/100102.pdf.

220. Lydia Saad, "Palestinians Have Little Faith in U.S. as Peace Broker," Gallup News Service (June 20, 2006), www.gallup.com/poll/23377/Palestinians-Little-Faith-US-Peace-Broker.aspx.

221. Helsing, "The Regionalization, Internationalization, and Perpetuation of Conflict in the Middle East," 157.

222. Makovsky, "Middle East Peace through Partition," 39.

223. Makovsky, "Middle East Peace through Partition," 39.

224. The overall lack of a strong commitment was reflected in the failure of Secretary of State Colin Powell to appoint a special Middle East envoy. Condoleezza Rice also did not appoint a special envoy during her tenure as secretary of state in Bush's second term. Rather, following the Israeli withdrawal from Gaza in 2005, she mediated an accord that reopened the Egyptian-Gaza border crossing, and in 2007 she sought the support of moderate Sunni Arab states in order to counter Iran. For the moderate Arab states, the Palestinian-Israeli issue directly impacts regional stability. Carol Migdalovitz, "Israeli-Arab Negotiations: Background, Conflicts, and U.S. Policy," Congressional Research Service (March 9, 2009), 7, http://fpc.state.gov/documents/organization/120969.pdf.

225. As quoted in David Makovsky, "Gaza: Moving Forward by Pulling Back," *Foreign Affairs* 84, no. 3 (May/June 2005): 55.

226. Makovsky, "Gaza," 55.

227. Migdalovitz, "Israeli-Arab Negotiations," 7.

228. Migdalovitz, "Israeli-Arab Negotiations," 4.

229. "US Urges Quick Return to Mid-East Talks," *BBC News*, June 9, 2009, http://news.bbc.co.uk/go/pr/fr/-/2/hi/middle_east/8090761.stm.

230. As quoted in Alex Altman, "Middle East Envoy George Mitchell," *Time*, January 22, 2009, http://www.time.com/time/world/article/0,8599,1873532,00.html.

231. "Benjamin Netanyahu: Full Speech on Palestinian State," *Telegraph.co.uk*, www.telegraph.co.uk/news/worldnews/middleeast/israel/5535664/Benjamin-Netanyahu-full-speech-on-Palestinian-state.html.

232. Amos Harel and Avi Issacharoff, "Israel Removes Dozens of West Bank Roadblocks," *Haaretz.com*, June 24, 2009, http://haaretz.com/hasen/spages/1095231.html.

233. Global Policy Forum, "UN Documents," www.globalpolicy.org/security-council/index-of-countries-on-the-security-council-agenda/israel-palestine-and-the-occupied-territories/38296.html.

234. Edith M. Lederer, "Security Council Calls for Two-State Solution," *Boston Globe*, May 12, 2009.

235. "Establishment of UNRWA," UNRWA, www.un.org/unrwa/overview/index .html; "History and Establishment of UNRWA," UNRWA, www.un.org/ unrwa/overview/qa.html.

236. "U.S. Government Contributes $55 million to UNRWA," UNRWA, www .un.org/unrwa/news/releases/pr-2009/jer_10jun09.html.

237. Hilde Henrikson Waage, "Norway's Role in the Middle East Peace Talks: Between a Strong State and a Weak Belligerent," *Journal of Palestine Studies* 34, no. 4 (Summer 2005): 7.

238. Waage, "Norway's Role in the Middle East Peace Talks," 8.

239. Waage, "Norway's Role in the Middle East Peace Talks," 8–9.

240. Waage, "Norway's Role in the Middle East Peace Talks," 9.

241. Waage, "Norway's Role in the Middle East Peace Talks," 10–11.

242. Waage, "Norway's Role in the Middle East Peace Talks," 11.

243. Waage, "Norway's Role in the Middle East Peace Talks," 11–15.

244. Waage, "Norway's Role in the Middle East Peace Talks," 17.

245. Waage, "Norway's Role in the Middle East Peace Talks," 19.

246. Waage, "Norway's Role in the Middle East Peace Talks," 20.

247. Robert K. Olson, "Partners in the Peace Process: The United States and Europe," *Journal of Palestine Studies* 26, no. 4 (Summer 1997): 79–80.

248. Olson, "Partners in the Peace Process," 80.

249. Olson, "Partners in the Peace Process," 85.

250. Olson, "Partners in the Peace Process," 86.

251. Lydia Saad and Steve Crabtree, "Israel/Palestine: Support for Potential Peace Brokers," Gallup (January 26, 2007), www.gallup.com/poll/26290/ IsraelPalestine-Support-Potential-Peace-Brokers.aspx.

252. European Union, "The EU in the Middle East Peace Process" (February 27, 2009), http://europa.eu/rapid/pressReleasesAction.do?reference=MEMO/ 09/88&format=HTML&aged=0&language=EN&guiLanguage=en; Council of the European Union, "Council Conclusions on Middle East Peace Process" (June 15, 2009), www.consilium.europa.eu/uedocs/cms_Data/docs/ pressdata/en/gena/108500.pdf.

253. Makovsky, "Middle East Peace through Partition," 30.

CHAPTER 8

Conclusion

The aim of this book was to understand and analyze the causes and continuation of ethnic conflict as well as the resolution of such conflicts. We sought to integrate literature from two major subfields in the political science discipline: comparative politics with its emphasis on internal factors, and international relations with its emphasis on systemic factors. In chapter 1 we defined ethnic conflict, and identified the major theories of ethnicity, nationalism, and international relations. Later in this chapter, we return to these theories and discuss how the case studies (chapters 3 through 7) illustrate them.

In chapter 2 we presented our framework for integrating these two subfields and the causes of ethnic conflict that each presents. Using a levels of analysis framework, we sought to categorize the various causes and factors of ethnic conflict into three separate levels: international, domestic, and individual. We expanded upon each level, presenting the numerous factors contained in each. We ended that chapter by explaining that some elements of ethnic conflict might not fit neatly into a single level of analysis, and that it is precisely the interaction between the levels that makes understanding, and thus solving, ethnic conflict so difficult.

In chapters 3 through 7 we presented five case studies of ethnic conflict. Each presented a brief history of the conflict before applying the levels of analysis framework. In each case, we outlined the presence of various factors in these conflicts. While trying to be exhaustive, we selectively emphasized factors that we felt were more relevant to each case. An examination of all five case study chapters reveals certain similarities among the cases, as well as differences.

This conclusion provides an overview of the case study chapters. By organizing the information presented earlier into comparative charts, we highlight the similarities and differences that we believe exist in our five case studies. We emphasize two approaches: applying the theories from chapter 1 to explaining the emergence of ethnic conflict and exploring the presence or absence of the factors detailed in chapter 2.

REVISITING THEORIES OF ETHNICITY AND NATIONALISM

As mentioned in chapter 1, scholars are in disagreement over which factors best explain the origins of ethnicity, nation, and nationalism. The two broad theoretical categories are primordialism and constructivism. Primordialism argues that human nature creates unchangeable (and thus fixed or given) identities. Group consciousness and socialization reinforce these identities over time, creating natural "us" versus "them" distinctions. Therefore, ethnic conflict results from "natural" disputes between ethnic groups.

Constructivism argues that identities are created and thus can change over time. Ethnicity is a social phenomenon that is generated by centers of power and human behavior. People form ethnicities as part of an "imagined community." Thus, ethnicity is not inherently conflictual. Yet, when violence is possible, the social construction of competing ethnicities can lead to conflict. Constructivist approaches can be divided into two separate subcategories: instrumental theories and modernization theories. Instrumentalism highlights agent-driven construction of identity. Political elites mold identity/ethnicity/nationalism in order to further a political goal and to gain political benefit. Identity is a means to an end. Ethnic conflict may result when political elites find that it furthers their individual ambition. Modernization theories posit that the imagined community results from the homogenizing process of modern development. As the state, economy, and society centralize and move toward uniformity, this very transformation highlights social fragmentation and competing mobilization. Fragmentation and mobilization lead to multiple demands upon the state and the rise of ethnic nationalism. Table 8.1 outlines these theories.

Feminist scholars have contributed to the literature on nationalism and ethnicity, noting that as ethnicity and nationalism/national identity are socially constructed, so too is gender a social construction. Moreover, nationalism and ethnicity are gendered. In their efforts at promoting a particular national/ethnic identity, ethnic and national leaders reinforce the symbolic role that women play as mothers and wives, as women are considered the biological reproducers of the ethnic and national group.

Finally, social identity theory offers a bridge between primordial sentiments and the social construction of ethnic and national identity. Individuals have a psychological need to belong to a group, and that belonging is often expressed in an ethnic and/or national group. The ethnic/national group identity takes

TABLE 8.1
Theories of Origin of Ethnicity, Nations, and Nationalism

	Theory		
	Primordialism	Constructivism: Instrumentalism	Constructivism: Modernization
Source of Identity	Natural differences; socialization	Selective history, images, icons	Social fragmentation (for example, class)
Agent	Group/community	Political elites	Economic transformation
Origin of Conflict	Natural	Manufactured	Part of the process of change

on characteristics that are considered fixed, even if they are actually socially constructed.

INTERNATIONAL RELATIONS THEORIES ON ETHNIC CONFLICT

In chapter 1 we outline three main theories in the field of international relations: realism, liberalism/liberal institutionalism, and constructivism. Each of these three primarily addresses how states act in the international system. Yet, scholars have extended these theories to analyze ethnic conflict.

Realists highlight the anarchical nature of the international system and the high priority on security. A security dilemma exists when one group feels that it is threatened by another group or by the system in general. The group then responds by taking actions that are considered threatening by another group, making all less secure. This can particularly occur during times of state transformation or breakdown. Liberalism/liberal institutionalism emphasizes the ability of actors (that is, states or ethnic groups) to cooperate, even in an anarchical, self-help system. These actors can create institutions to promote further cooperation through either enforceable agreements or bundles of institutions that work toward some singular end (that is, regimes). Constructivism points to the manufacturing of identity and threats by groups and/or the state. It uncovers how shared norms and culture, particularly those aligned with the state, can lead to conflict between groups.

Table 8.2 illustrates the differences between these three theories.

TABLE 8.2
International Relations Theories

	Theory		
	Realism	Liberalism	Constructivism
View of International System	Anarchical; self-help	State-driven	Social structure
Key Factor	Power	Institutions	Norms
Concern of Actors	Security	Cooperation	Identity

LEVELS OF ANALYSIS

In chapter 2 we developed our levels of analysis framework to examine the causes and factors involved in ethnic conflict. Each of the three separate levels, individual, domestic, and international, contains a characteristic set of factors. While realizing that some factors may overlap two or even all three levels, we identified in chapter 2 the most common factors that comprise each level of analysis. In this conclusion, we look for the presence or absence of those factors in the five cases.

Individual Level

The individual level of analysis emphasizes the role of decisions by elites. It focuses on human cognition, psychology, and motivation. We categorize the multitude of factors involved with this level into two broad categories. The first is political leadership, comprised of the style, beliefs, images, and attitudes that political elites bring to their decision making. An individual's cognitive abilities to recognize self-interests and to determine costs and benefits or perception and misperception, and to accurately choose appropriate strategies are important. The limits and style of cognitive processing by an elite shape their subsequent choices and behavior, rendering the individual an important element in any structural context. The second category of factors deals with elites and ethnic outbidding. It includes how elites lead and potentially manipulate ethnic groups. Elites do so in an effort to further a shared ethnic objective and/or to further their own individual desires (for example, for power, wealth). Of interest is the role of political competition between intra-ethnic elites. As each seeks power and authority, their combined efforts to represent the ethnic group lead to appeals to the more radical and extreme elements of the group. Elites thus construct groups in a more violent and antagonistic manner, not because it is the most beneficial organization, but rather to derail and defeat intra-ethnic competitors.

Throughout our cases we saw the role of political leadership and leadership styles, but it was particularly relevant to two cases. In Northern Ireland, Gerry Adams and Ian Paisley both played the role of "greedy spoiler" during many decades of the conflict, leading to a lack of compromise between the Catholic and Protestant communities. However, and as we detail in chapter 2, leaders and their leadership style can also play a key role in conflict reduction and/or conflict resolution. Both Adams and Paisley moved toward conciliatory positions in the recent decade, leading to more intersectarian compromise. While their change of behavior may be solely self-beneficial and instrumental, nonetheless it has contributed to a reduction in the ethnic conflict. Leadership style played an important role among the Tamil Tigers in Sri Lanka. Velupillai Prabhakaran's autocratic and brutal leadership of the Tigers inspired his followers and intimidated rival Tamil organizations. His unending and unyielding pursuit of a Tamil state left almost no ground for compromise with the Sri Lankan government.

Ethnic outbidding occupies a key position as a dominant factor in four out of the five cases. The ability of extremists to encourage, entice, or intimidate elites into taking more extreme positions seems to be a hallmark of ethnic conflict. In Bosnia, Milosevic purposely played to Serb nationalism and extremism in order both to rally the Serb population behind his political goals and also to limit Serb challengers to his central position of power. Leaders on both sides of the Israel-Palestine conflict find it difficult to remain moderate when extremists have the power to remove them from political office. In both Sri Lanka and Northern Ireland, extremist political parties used nationalist positions to strip moderate leaders and parties of authority and derail interethnic compromise or negotiation. The case of the Sudan is a more difficult one to classify. As mentioned in chapter 5, the extreme secrecy around the Khartoum government makes it almost impossible to get reliable information about how and why governmental decisions are made. Moreover, it obfuscates any examination of leadership styles and/or ethnic outbidding.

Rational choice theorists would model this pattern of ethnic outbidding as a Prisoner's Dilemma. Leaders realize that mutual compromise would be mutually beneficial, but extremists force the leader to "defect" from any interethnic agreements. In essence, the structure of the "game" is such that elites who compromise lose their positions as leaders due to extremist dissatisfaction (and thus remove the ability to deliver on any compromise) and elites who appease extremists cannot compromise. The social outcome is suboptimal, in other words, a continuation of the conflict to the benefit of only a small, extreme minority. It would seem that institutions to insulate leaders from their followers are needed, giving the elites the ability to compromise.

Domestic Level

The domestic level of analysis deals with perhaps the greatest number of idiosyncratic factors. The possible factors include regime type, small organizations and groups, political parties, the armed forces, and social movements. Three separate schools of thought inform any examination of domestic factors. The rational choice approach emphasizes that individual actors have defined interests and preferences. As such, they act in a logical and strategic manner upon those interests by choosing and taking action. The institutional approach highlights the autonomous nature of institutions and their ability to "act" as if they were individual actors. Last, the organizational approach focuses on the interactions within a political actor (for example, within a bureaucratic organization) and how operating procedures, rules of procedure, and norms can affect the behavior of that actor. Thus, domestic level factors must take into account not only "who" is acting and why, but also "in what way" is that actor making decisions and following through with action.

Domestic Factors Contributing to Conflict. Given the diversity of local actors and ways of acting, it is necessary to categorize and draw general insights. In chapter 2, we drew upon Michael Brown's classification of the most common factors likely to contribute to internal conflict, including ethnic/national conflict: structural, political, economic/social, and cultural/perceptual.[1] In this section we explore the incidence of these factors in our five case studies. We also note that in each case, gendered nationalism was present.

Structural factors include weak states, ethnic security dilemmas, and ethnic geography. Weak, or weakening states, often permit ethnic conflict to emerge. Weak states are less likely to provide necessary social services, are more prone to corruption, are less able to control their borders, and are less capable of meeting ethnic demands for resources, access, etc.[2] Four of our cases display this tendency. Over time, communist Yugoslavia transformed into a loose confederation, which led to a weakening of the central state. Ethnic groups in the different republics had much more room to make ethnic demands and mobilize populations for conflict. The result was the three-year-long war in Bosnia. In the Sudan, the incapacity of the government in Khartoum to deal effectively with the decades-long North-South civil war led to its weakening in general. The severe deprivation of the Darfur region encouraged ethnic demands. Moreover, the lack of sovereign control over the territory also meant that armed militias (such as the Janjaweed) could operate with impunity against the Fur population. Sri Lanka is another case of a weak centralized state. The government in Colombo could not or would not provide necessary social services to the Tamil population. This "space" allowed the Tamil Tigers to fill the void, effectively creating a quasi-state within a state and mobilizing the Tamil population for resistance. The weak state is also present in the Israel/Palestine conflict. The Palestinian territories, dominated by Hamas in Gaza and the PA in the West Bank, have no unity government, so instead each entity is a quasi-state and legitimizes itself in the process. The lack of a unified government is likely to make any future independent Palestinian state quite weak.

Security dilemmas can also lead to ethnic conflict.[3] If one group feels threatened by another, the resort to violence in the name of security can often push the other group to retaliate and/or escalate the violence. The resulting spiral of violence can be hard to check. A threat from one group, whether real or perceived, leads to new threats by the other group. In the presence of a hegemonic state (that is, the state is run by and for the interests of one ethnic group) the security dilemma for the excluded ethnic groups can be both real and severe. Northern Ireland exemplifies this problem. The Protestant majority aligns with the ruling British government. The Catholic minority felt that they were discriminated against in all aspects of social, political, and economic life and that the British parliament acted like a hegemonic state toward the Catholic community. The militant IRA turned to violence and began to target the Protestant majority and the British military. The Protestant community then felt threatened, demanding from the British government protection against the IRA and forming volunteer militias to combat the IRA. As the British intervened and their presence increased, the Catholic community felt more threatened and the violence escalated. Only after decades of cease-fires, peace initiatives, elections, international mediation, and devolution of authority to Northern Ireland did the vicious cycle of violence end. The Bosnian conflict also contained a security dilemma. The ethnic demands by Bosnian Croats, Bosnian Serbs, and Bosnian Muslims all led to the others feeling threatened. Mistrust and threat became the dominant interaction between the different ethnic groups. In the Israeli-Palestinian conflict, each side's quest for absolute security has led to a complete lack of trust between the two communities. The tit-for-tat violence between the two only exacerbates the security dilemma. Resolving the mistrust and fear to break the cycle of retaliatory violence must precede any meaningful negotiations.

Ethnic geography also plays a role in some of the cases.[4] When ethnic groups exist side-by-side or intermingled into an arbitrary arrangement, the proximity and contact may lead to violence. Our cases highlight that the "checkerboard" arrangement of ethnic groups in Northern Ireland, Bosnia, Sri Lanka, and Israel-Palestine puts volatile populations into contact with each other, leading to violence. The case of Sudan is a troubling one for the theory because while there is great ethnic diversity in the Darfur region, the ethnic groups had lived side-by-side for centuries without true ethnic conflict. Only in the past two decades have the different groups turned on each other. Also, the ethnic geography of Northern Ireland has not changed much in the past few decades, yet the two communities are now less prone to inflict violence on each other. Thus, ethnic geography might be necessary for ethnic conflict, but it certainly is not sufficient to explain it.

Political factors were present in all of our cases. In all five instances, at least one minority group is discriminated against by the state political institutions, whether it is the Catholics in Northern Ireland, Croats and Muslims in Bosnia, Fur in Sudan, Tamils in Sri Lanka, or the Palestinians in Israel and the occupied territories. National ideologies that exclude certain ethnic groups based on either ethnicity, language, culture, religion, or some other characteristic also exist in all cases to varying degrees. For example, sharp distinctions in citizenship based on ethnicity characterized the chaos in the republics of the former Yugoslavia as the state was breaking up. Israeli Arabs/Palestinians are excluded from political authority in Israel even though they are citizens. Palestinians in the occupied territories are even further excluded. Religion is connected to the ethnic/national identity in all cases, even if religion itself is not the primary arena for competition. There is a direct connection, however, between religion and nationalist ideology. In all these instances, the state acts in a hegemonic way toward the minority group, excluding them from participation in the political spheres.

Economic/social factors encompass transitions and transformations of the economic system and/or society.[5] Economic discrimination against an ethnic group is present in all cases. The end of the Communist system in Yugoslavia also saw the end of the fragile ethnic compromise that Tito had managed for decades. The end of the state-controlled economy contributed to an economic free-for-all that heightened tension between the ethnic groups, with some ethnic groups faring better economically than others. The rise of the Islamic government in the Sudan also was a radical departure from the previous governments, and there are economic disparities between the groups in conflict. While the movement to Islamic law was, and is, still incomplete, the reshaping of society based on the Islamists' ideas fundamentally altered the existing social contract between the ethnic groups. Economic discrimination plays a significant role in exacerbating conflict in Northern Ireland, Sri Lanka, and Israel-Palestine as well, with one group benefitting from economic policies relative to another (dominant) group.

Cultural/perceptual factors encompass the link between identity, social constructions, events, and perceptions.[6] Social identity theory (SIT) asserts that as individuals define themselves in a positive way, this can lead to discriminatory action against and a negative identification of other groups. Once security dilemmas, economic disparity, political demands, or any other factors lead to the beginning of distrust, the perception of others as "different" and the group's fear of the other exacerbate the violence. Group fear can be that of being assimilated by a dominant group and/or fear for physical safety and survival. Thus, cultural perceptions can build upon real, tangible factors and/or events to perpetuate conflict.

For example, the Colombo riots, the Tamil suicide bombers, and the government reprisals against demonstrators, all were events that reinforced the perception on each side of the conflict that the other side could not be trusted. The cycle of revenge killings and bombings in Northern Ireland reinforced negative perceptions of the other community for decades. The tit-for-tat violent response between Palestinian militants and the Israeli military continues to bolster the negative perceptions of each group, making a peaceful settlement increasingly elusive.

Much of the literature on nationalism and ethnic conflict omits gender as an analytical category (as demonstrated by the classification above). And yet, as each of the cases in this book illustrates, nationalism and ethnic conflict are gendered. In all five cases, women are expected to fulfill their duty to the nation/ethnic group that includes bearing children and supporting the ethnic group's goals. Leaders refer to women's roles as mothers and wives in promoting the group's nationalist cause. It is interesting to note, too, that many women in each of these societies oppose the patriarchal structure and militarized societies through the formation of organizations whose goals are to end the conflict and promote a more just and equal society that improves women's lives. In addition, the challenge for women in all these cases is getting a seat at the negotiating table in order to resolve the conflict. Women continue to be marginalized in the formal political process.

Domestic Factors in Managing and Resolving Conflict. In chapter 2, we outline three possible internal institutional approaches to ameliorating and/or solving ethnic conflict popular in the scholarly literature: liberalism, consociationalism, and federalism. To reiterate, liberalism argues for an ethnically neutral state based on the Anglo-American model; consociationalism involves a host of institutions all designed to accommodate interethnic, elite accommodation; and federalism is the geographical division of state power into subnational units. Our case studies provide some evidence as to which of these approaches works best.

Northern Ireland provides an interesting example of both the liberalism and the consociationalism approaches. The British state moved from a hegemonic position regarding Northern Ireland to a neutral position during the late 1980s. This paved the way for eventual all-party elections and all-party talks that led to the 1998 Good Friday Agreement. That agreement contains many institutions that are consociational in nature: division of the Assembly into community representation (that is, Protestants and Catholics), minority veto, and grand coalition. While the Assembly has been less than fully functional, it has nonetheless survived to this day. The Dayton Accords that ended the fighting in Bosnia produced a three-person presidency, along the lines of a consociational grand coalition. As we mention in chapter 4, while this arrangement seems to have ended the previous conflict, it maintains the existing ethnic order. Croat and Serb nationalists in Bosnia continue to agitate for inclusion into Croatia and Serbia, respectively. The seeds for future conflict remain. In Sudan a power-sharing structure was considered for the North-South conflict, but not for Darfur. Israeli politicians have considered a federal interim solution for the Palestinians, but this has not come to pass (and the Palestinians oppose such a structure as long as the state defines itself as a Jewish state). In the Sri Lanka case, no power-sharing structure is present.

The single example of a liberal approach is not sufficient for us to make any sweeping judgments. Moreover, the mixed nature of consociational approaches also continues the debate about the usefulness of that approach. Federalism has been used in only one of the cases (Bosnia with the separation into two territorial entities: the Bosnian Serb Republic [Republika Srpska] and the Croat-Muslim Federation). As of yet, federalism has not been pursued seriously in four of our five cases. This does not necessarily mean that political actors in these conflicts reject this option, but it does highlight that its acceptance among academics may be greater than among practitioners. The three cases of the Sudan, Sri Lanka, and Israel/Palestine cannot offer us much insight as to the veracity of our theories of conflict resolution.

International Level

Analysis at the international level illuminates how the international system and international actors can impact ethnic conflict within a single state. This level focuses on such factors as the nature of the international system, the structure of power within the system, international organizations, international regimes, and diffusion/escalation of conflict. Typically, the international level looks at factors that are either international in composition (for example, the United Nations) or that cross international boundaries (for example, the Kurdish ethnic group that exists in both Iraq and Turkey).

In chapter 2, we identified a number of key factors related to the international level. The first is ethnic ties across borders. This occurs in two ways: a diaspora when an ethnic group migrates (whether voluntarily or involuntarily) and historical ethnic groups divided by a recognized border. In both instances, the presence of a similar ethnic community outside of the state experiencing ethnic conflict often exacerbates that conflict. In our five cases, we have three good examples of ethnic ties across borders. In Northern Ireland, the Irish Catholic community shares its ethnicity with the Irish nation to its south. Moreover, the Irish disaspora, particularly to the United States, has created a significant Irish community living abroad. The Irish Republican Army/Sinn Fein has used these ethnic ties to maintain funding for its campaigns, to recruit volunteers, and to provide political allies against the British government. In the Bosnian conflict, the presence of a Serb community in Bosnia helped motivate Serbia to take action and was a rallying cry for Serbian nationalists. Likewise, the historical link between India and the Tamils in Sri Lanka prompted the Indian government to intervene in the Sri Lankan ethnic conflict. The Palestinians living in Arab countries, such as Lebanon, have launched terrorist attacks against Israel in their attempts to end the occupation of Palestinian territory.

A second factor is national self-interest. Other states, or other political actors within those states, may intervene in an ethnic conflict if they perceive an interest to do so. This happens especially in instances of diffusion, where ethnic conflict spills out of its borders and into neighboring countries. However, it is also possible solely through the escalation of the ethnic conflict by third-party intervention. Realist international relations theory would predict that such intervention would be relatively common. Yet, in our five cases, direct intervention is actually quite rare. In Sudan, non-state militias from both Libya and Uganda have crossed the border, but neither is a major player in the conflict. The relatively peripheral nature of both Northern Ireland and Sri Lanka has precluded escalation by other powers. The conflict in Bosnia is perhaps a counterexample. The ethnic tensions between the Bosnian inhabitants drew both Serbia and Croatia into a protracted civil war. The Israel/Palestine conflict is yet another counterexample. Arab intervention, especially in the 1967 and 1973 wars, and Arab support of the PLO, as well as continuous American military and political support of Israel, demonstrate the role international involvement can have in an ethnic conflict. Yet, even with Arab intervention, the major states in the international system have not intervened militarily in the Israel-Palestine conflict.

Third, the presence of third-party mediation (whether individual states or international institutions) should be beneficial toward an amelioration of the conflict. International mediation has been successful in two of our cases (Northern Ireland and Bosnia), limited in its success in two (Sri Lanka and Israel/Palestine), and absent in one (Sudan). In Northern Ireland, American mediation through former senator George Mitchell was instrumental in concluding the Good Friday Agreement. Likewise, the Dayton Accords and United Nations intervention contributed to the end of violent conflict in Bosnia. Norwegian efforts in Sri Lanka did not bring the warring parties together, and numerous American efforts at peace between Israel and Palestine have not had lasting impact as the two-state solution has not come to fruition. International mediation has not been possible in Sudan, mainly because the Sudanese government refuses any international intervention. While liberal institutionalism claims that international institutions can lead to cooperation and peace, in ethnic conflict this may prove not to be the case, or at the very least very difficult to bring about.

Fourth, coercive or noncoercive direct international intervention can be a factor. Typically, noncoercive intervention has a larger impact when conflict is less severe, where it can help delegitimize violence. Coercive intervention can succeed as a means to end severe conflict. The presence of international nongovernmental organizations (NGOs) in a number of our cases (for example, Sri Lanka, Sudan, Bosnia, occupied Palestinian territories) shows how noncoercive involvement is almost always present in one way or another. Typically, these efforts aim at relieving humanitarian concerns and do not directly alter the shape or outcome of the conflict. Coercive intervention is much rarer. Two of our cases have direct, coercive intervention: Bosnia and Sri Lanka. In Bosnia, the international Implementation Force (IFOR) and other United Nations actions altered the balance of power on the ground. The establishment and guarantee of safe havens, as well as the support for an independent Bosnian government, made the Serbian demand for a unified, Serb-led Bosnia impossible. Moreover, the threat of NATO airstrikes in 1994 and increased UN peacekeeper combat capability limited the ability of the Serb armed forces to succeed in the conflict. Unlike the NATO/UN intervention in Bosnia, the Indian military intervention in Sri Lanka was a complete disaster. Designed to protect the Tamils against government incursion, the Indian peacekeepers actually ended up caught between the two warring factions. In the end, it was the Tamil Tigers who forcefully expelled the Indian troops, as the Tigers had seen Indian intervention as a direct challenge to their own hegemony over the Tamil population.

CONCLUSION

The dilemma of ethnic outbidding is a good place to start when looking at how the three levels of analysis interact, and also how any process of conflict resolution needs to be structured with the levels in mind. Typical solutions to the problems of cooperation and coordination revolve around a neutral third party to help the two sides develop trust, compromise, and carry through with their commitments. International organizations, external states, a liberal (and neutral) centralized state, or even an impartial moderator can all play this role. The ability of elites to marginalize extremists and seek peace can also be transformative.

Thus, international, domestic, and individual factors can all play a role in conflict resolution. The answer in Bosnia was coercive international intervention, and eventual replacement of Milosevic and Tudjman in Serbia and Croatia, respectively. The answer in Northern Ireland was the movement of Conservative governments to a neutral, liberal position, third-party mediation, and new domestic power-sharing institutions. The conflict in Sri Lanka appears to have been resolved by a massive, governmental military campaign, although it remains to be seen whether the Tamil resistance has merely been pushed into the countryside, to appear again in years or decades. There has been no solution in Sudan and in Israel/Palestine.

The purpose of this book was to show how the levels of analysis can help us uncover the multiple factors contributing to ethnic conflict (see table 8.3).

TABLE 8.3
Applying the Levels of Analysis to the Cases

	Levels		
	Individual	Domestic	International
Northern Ireland	Gerry Adams John Hume Ian Paisley David Trimble George Mitchell Spoiler roles Leadership style (chameleonic leadership) Ethnic outbidding	Protestant and Catholic communities Polarized and sectarian political parties (DUP, UUP, Sinn Fein, SDLP) Power-sharing institutions Gendered nationalism Economic, political, and social discrimination	Republic of Ireland United States Irish diaspora European Union
Bosnia	Alija Izetbegovic Slobodan Milosevic Franjo Tudjman Ethnic outbidding Elite mobilization	Public opinion Political parties Gendered nationalism Economic disparity between republics Shifting ethnic balance of power between republics and federal institutions Religion and nationalism	International peace plans proposed by EU, UN NATO intervention Contact Group
Sudan	Omar Hassan al-Bashir John Garang de Mabior Elite mobilization Spoiler roles	Arab and non-Arab communities Gendered nationalism Hegemonic political institutions Janjaweed (civil militia) Rebel political parties (SPLM; SLA)	United States European Union African Union China Lord's Resistance Army (based in Uganda)
Sri Lanka	Chandrika Bandaranaike Kumaratunga Velupillai Prabhakaran Ethnic outbidding Leadership style (failed leadership)	Sinhalese and Tamil communities Economic conditions Gendered nationalism Hegemonic state (Sinhalese domination of political institutions)	India Norway UNHCR

(Continued)

TABLE 8.3
Applying the Levels of Analysis to the Cases (Continued)

	Levels		
	Individual	Domestic	International
Israel-Palestine	Yitzhak Rabin Ehud Barak Yasser Arafat Ethnic outbidding Spoiler roles	Nationalist ideology (Zionism; Palestinian nationalism) Gendered nationalism Polarized and sectarian political parties (Likud, Labor, Kedima, PLO, Hamas) Economic and political discrimination in occupied territories	United States United Nations Norway European Union Arab League

An exploration of how each level points to different, yet potentially linked, causes enables a greater appreciation of how difficult the resolution of ethnic conflict can be. As such, we hope that it has answered more questions than it has created. No single book on the subject can contain the definitive solution to ethnic/national conflicts. We have presented what we consider to be the most important theories and explored their relevance with a number of illustrative (but by no means exhaustive) cases. We remain optimistic that through research and knowledge, solutions to ethnic conflict can be found.

NOTES

1. Michael E. Brown, "The Causes of Internal Conflict: An Overview," in *Nationalism and Ethnic Conflict*, ed. Michael E. Brown, Owen R. Cote Jr., Sean M. Lynn-Jones, and Steven E. Miller, rev.ed. (Cambridge, Mass.: MIT Press, 2001), 3–25.
2. Brown, "The Causes of Internal Conflict," 5.
3. Brown, "The Causes of Internal Conflict," 5–6.
4. Brown, "The Causes of Internal Conflict," 6–7.
5. Brown, "The Causes of Internal Conflict," 10–12.
6. Brown, "The Causes of Internal Conflict," 12.

"Abbas to Attend Gaza Truce Talks." *BBC News*, February 2, 2009. http://news .bbc.co.uk/go/pr/fr/-/2/hi/middle_east/7864265.stm.

Abeyratne, Sirimal. "Economic Roots of Political Conflict: The Case of Sri Lanka." *World Economy* 27 (2004): 1295-1314.

Abeysekara, Ananda. "The Saffron Army, Violence, Terror(ism): Buddhism, Identity, and Difference in Sri Lanka." *Numen* 48 (2001): 1-46.

"About the ICTY." *International Criminal Tribunal for the Former Yugoslavia*. www .icty.org/sections/AbouttheICTY.

African Union. "Communique of the Twenty-Third Meeting of the Peace and Security Council, 10 January 2005." In *The African Union and the Conflict in the Darfur Region of the Sudan*. Addis Ababa: African Union, 2005.

Ali, Rabia, and Lawrence Lifschultz. "Why Bosnia?" *Third World Quarterly* 15, no. 3 (1994): 367-401.

"Alija Izetbegovic: Bosnian Muslim Leader Who Led His Country to Independence." *The Independent*, October 20, 2003.

Alison, Miranda. "Wartime Sexual Violence: Women's Human Rights and Questions of Masculinity." *Review of International Studies* 33 (2007): 75-90.

Almond, Gabriel A., Russell J. Dalton, G. Bingham Powell Jr., and Kaare Strom. "Interest Articulation." In *Comparative Politics Today: A World View*, 8th ed., edited by Gabriel A. Almond, Russell J. Dalton, G. Bingham Powell Jr., and Kaare Strom, 62-80. New York: Pearson Longman, 2006.

Altman, Alex. "Middle East Envoy George Mitchell." *Time*, January 22, 2009. www.time.com/time/printout/0,8816,1873532,00.html.

Amnesty International. *Sudan: Arming the Perpetrators of Grave Abuses in Darfur*. London: Amnesty International, November 2004.

Anderson, Benedict. *Imagined Communities: Reflections on the Origin and Spread of Nationalism*. London: Verso, 1991.

Andjelkovic, Branka. "Reflections on Nationalism and Its Impact on Women in Serbia." In *Women in the Politics of Postcommunist Europe*, edited by Marilyn Rueschemeyer, 235-248. Armonk, N.Y.: M. E. Sharpe, 1998.

Anthias, Floya, and Nira Yuval-Davis. "Introduction." In *Woman-Nation-State*, edited by Nira Yuval-Davis and Floya Anthias, 1-15. London: Palgrave Macmillan, 1989.

"Arafat: Words of War and Peace." *BBC News*, November 11, 2004. http://news .bbc.co.uk/2/hi/middle_east/4003823.stm.

Arrow, Kenneth J. *Social Choice and Individual Values*. New York: Wiley and Sons, 1951.

A/Salam, Elfatih A. "The Politicization of Ethnic Sentiments in the Sudan: Implications for Nation-Building." *Journal of Third World Studies* 25, no. 1 (2008): 111–135.

Ashe, Fidelma. "Gendering Ethno-Nationalist Conflict in Northern Ireland: A Comparative Analysis of Nationalist Women's Political Protests." *Ethnic and Racial Studies* 30, no. 5 (September 2007): 766–786.

Auerbach, Yehudith, and Charles W. Greenbaum. "Assessing Leader Credibility during a Peace Process: Rabin's Private Polls." *Journal of Peace Research* 37, no. 1 (2000): 31–50.

Aughey, Arthur. "Northern Ireland." In *Developments in British Politics*, 5th ed., edited by P. Dunleavy, A. Gamble, I. Holliday, and G. Peele, 241–252. New York: St. Martin's Press, 1997.

Axtmann, Roland. "The State of the State: The Model of the Modern State and Its Contemporary Transformation." *International Political Science Review* 25, no. 3 (2004): 259–279.

Barak, Oren. "The Failure of the Israeli-Palestinian Peace Process, 1993–2000." *Journal of Peace Research* 42, no. 6 (2005): 719–736.

Barrington, Lowell W. "'Nation' and 'Nationalism': The Misuse of Key Concepts in Political Science." *PS: Political Science and Politics* 30, no. 4 (December 1997): 712–716.

Bar-Tal, Daniel. "Why Does Fear Override Hope in Societies Engulfed by Intractable Conflict, as It Does in the Israeli Society?" *Political Psychology* 22, no. 3 (September 2001): 601–627.

Barzilai, Gad, and Ilan Peleg. "Israel and Future Borders: Assessment of a Dynamic Process." *Journal of Peace Research* 31, no. 1 (1994): 59–73.

Barzilai, Gad, Giora Goldberg, and Efraim Inbar. "Israeli Leadership and Public Attitudes toward Federal Solutions for the Arab-Israeli Conflict before and after Desert Storm." *Publius: The Journal of Federalism* 21 (Summer 1991): 191–209.

Bass, Daniel. "Paper Tigers on the Prowl: Rumors, Violence, and Agency in the Up-Country of Sri Lanka." *Anthropological Quarterly* 81 (2008): 269–295.

Bastian, Sunil. "The Political Economy of Electoral Reform: Proportional Representation in Sri Lanka." In *Can Democracy Be Designed? The Politics of Institutional Choice in Conflict-Torn Societies*, edited by Sunil Bastian and Robin Luckham, 196–219. New York: Zed Books, 2003.

Bastin, Rohan. "Hindu Temples in the Sri Lankan Ethnic Conflict: Capture and Excess." *Social Analysis* 49 (2005): 45–66.

Bat Shalom. "Who We Are." www.batshalom.org/about.php.

Baumgarten, Helga. "The Three Faces/Phases of Palestinian Nationalism, 1948–2005." *Journal of Palestine Studies* 34, no. 4 (Summer 2005): 25–48.

"Belgium's Pitiful Policies." *The Economist*, July 16, 2008. www.economist.com/displayStory.cfm?story_id=11739594.

Bell, Bowyer. *The Secret Army: The IRA*. 3rd ed. New Brunswick, N.J.: Transaction, 1997.

Bellamy, Alex J., and Paul D. Williams. "The UN Security Council and the Question of Humanitarian Intervention in Darfur." *Journal of Military Ethics* 5, no. 2 (2006): 144–160.

Belloni, Roberto. "Civil Society and Peacebuilding in Bosnia and Herzegovina." *Journal of Peace Research* 38, no. 2 (2001): 163–180.

Ben-Ami, Shlomo. "A War to Start All Wars: Will Israel Ever Seal the Victory of 1948?" *Foreign Affairs* 87, no. 5 (September/October 2008): 148–156.

Ben-Moshe, Danny. "The Oslo Peace Process and Two Views on Judaism and Zionism, 1992–1996." *British Journal of Middle Eastern Studies* 32, no. 1 (May 2005): 13–27.

Bengali, Shashank. "For Africa, 2008 a Year to Forget." *Christian Science Monitor*, January 2, 2009. www.csmonitor.com/2009/0102/p25s07-woaf.html.

"Benjamin Netanyahu: Full Speech on Palestinian State." Telegraph.co.uk. www.telegraph.co.uk/news/worldnews/middleeast/israel/5535664/Benjamin-Netanyahu-full-speech-on-Palestinian-state.html.

Berg, Eiki, and Guy Ben-Porat. "Introduction: Partition vs. Power-sharing?" *Nations and Nationalism* 14, no. 1 (2008): 29–37.

Berkovitch, Nitza. "Motherhood as a National Mission: The Construction of Womanhood in the Legal Discourse in Israel." *Women's Studies International Forum* 20, no. 5/6 (1997): 605–619.

Bew, Paul, and Elizabeth Meehan. "Regions and Borders: Controversies in Northern Ireland about the European Union." *Journal of European Public Policy* 1 (1994): 95–113.

Blanton, Shannon Lindsey. "Images in Conflict: The Case of Ronald Reagan and El Salvador." *International Studies Quarterly* 40, no. 1 (March 1996): 23–44.

Blecher, Robert. "Citizens without Sovereignty: Transfer and Ethnic Cleansing in Israel." *Comparative Studies in Society and History* 47, no. 4 (October 2005): 725–754.

Blondel, Jean. *Political Leadership: Towards a General Analysis*. London: Sage, 1987.

Bose, Sumantra. *Contested Lands: Israel-Palestine, Kashmir, Bosnia, Cyprus, and Sri Lanka*. Cambridge, Mass.: Harvard University Press, 2007.

Bracewell, Wendy. "Women, Motherhood, and Contemporary Serbian Nationalism." *Women's Studies International Forum* 19, no. 1–2 (1996): 25–33.

Brewer, Marilynn. "Ingroup Identification and Intergroup Conflict: When Does Ingroup Love Become Outgroup Hate?" In *Social Identity, Intergroup Conflict, and Conflict Reduction*, edited by Richard D. Ashmore, Lee Jussim, and David Wilder, 429–444. Oxford: Oxford University Press, 2001.

_____. "The Social Psychology of Intergroup Relations: Can Research Inform Practice?" *Journal of Social Issues* 53 (1997): 197–211.

Brewer, Marilynn B., and Wendi Gardner. "Who Is This 'We'? Levels of Collective Identity and Self-Representations." *Journal of Personality and Social Psychology* 71 (1996): 83–93.

Brown, Michael E. "The Causes of Internal Conflict: An Overview." In *Nationalism and Ethnic Conflict*, rev. ed., edited by Michael E. Brown, Owen R. Cote Jr., Sean M. Lynn-Jones, and Steven E. Miller, 3–25. Cambridge, Mass.: MIT Press, 2001.

Brown, Michael E., and Chantal de Jonge Oudraat. "Internal Conflict and International Action: An Overview." In *Nationalism and Ethnic Conflict*, rev. ed., edited by Michael E. Brown, Owen R. Cote Jr., Sean M. Lynn-Jones, and Steven E. Miller, 163–192. Cambridge, Mass.: MIT Press, 2001.

Brubaker, Rogers, and David D. Laitin. "Ethnic and Nationalist Violence." *Annual Review of Sociology* 24 (1998): 423–452.

Brunner, Claudia. "Female Suicide Bombers—Male Suicide Bombing? Looking for Gender in Reporting the Suicide Bombings of the Israeli-Palestinian Conflict." *Global Society* 19, no. 1 (January 2005): 29–48.

Bull, Peter. "Shifting Patterns of Social Identity in Northern Ireland." *The Psychologist* 19, no. 1 (January 2006): 40–43.

Bullion, Alan J. *India, Sri Lanka, and the Tamil Crisis, 1976–1994: An International Perspective*. New York: Pinter, 1995.

_____. "Norway and the Peace Process in Sri Lanka." *Civil Wars* 4 (2001): 70–92.

Burg, Steven L., and Paul S. Shoup. *The War in Bosnia-Herzegovina: Ethnic Conflict and International Intervention*. Armonk, N.Y.: M. E. Sharpe, 2000.

Bush, George W. "President Delivers State of the Union Address." January 2, 2002. http://georgewbush-whitehouse.archives.gov/news/releases/2002/01/20020129-11.html.

Byman, Daniel L. *Keeping the Peace: Lasting Solutions to Ethnic Conflict*. Baltimore: Johns Hopkins University Press, 2002.

Carment, David, and Patrick James. "Explaining Third-Party Intervention in Ethnic Conflict: Theory and Evidence." *Nations and Nationalism* 6, no. 2 (2000): 173–202.

_____. "Internal Constraints and Interstate Ethnic Conflict." *Journal of Conflict Resolution* 39, no. 1 (March 1995): 82–109.

Carney, Timothy. *Some Assembly Required: Sudan's Comprehensive Peace Agreement.* Special Report 194. Washington, D.C.: United States Institute of Peace, November 2007.

Carroll, Francis M. *The American Presence in Ulster: A Diplomatic History, 1796–1996.* Washington, D.C.: Catholic University of America Press, 2005.

Casperson, Nina. "Good Fences Make Good Neighbours? A Comparison of Conflict-Regulation Strategies in Postwar Bosnia." *Journal of Peace Research* 41, no. 5 (2004): 569–588.

Cerulo, Karen A. "Identity Construction: New Issues, New Directions." *Annual Review of Sociology* 23 (1997): 385–409.

Chadda, Maya. "Between Consociationalism and Control." In *Managing and Settling Ethnic Conflicts: Perspectives on Successes and Failures in Europe, Africa, and Asia,* edited by Ulrich Schneckener and Stefan Wolff, 94–114. New York: Palgrave, 2004.

Chandra, Kanchan. "Cumulative Findings in the Study of Ethnic Politics." *APSA-CP Newsletter* 12, no. 1 (Winter 2001): 7–25.

———. "Ethnic Parties and Democratic Stability." *Perspectives on Politics* 3, no. 2 (June 2005): 235–252.

Chapman, Thomas, and Philip G. Roeder. "Partition as a Solution to Wars of Nationalism: The Importance of Institutions." *American Political Science Review* 101, no. 4 (November 2007): 677–691.

CIA. "The World Factbook: Gaza Strip." https://www.cia.gov/library/publica tions/the-world-factbook/geos/gz.html.

———. "The World Factbook: Israel." https://www.cia.gov/library/publications/the-world-factbook/geos/is.html.

———. "The World Factbook: Sudan." https://www.cia.gov/library/publications/the-world-factbook/geos/su.html.

Coalition of Women for Peace. "The Coalition: General Info." http://coalitionof women.org/home/english/about/general_info/.

Cohen, Lenard J. *Broken Bonds: The Disintegration of Yugoslavia.* Boulder: Westview Press, 1993.

Collins, Greg. "Incorporating Africa's Conflicts into the War on Terror." *Peace Review: A Journal of Social Justice* 19 (2007): 397–406.

Comaroff, John L., and Paul C. Stern. "New Perspectives on Nationalism and War." *Theory and Society* 23 (1994): 35–45.

Congressional Research Service. "CRS Report for Congress: U.S. Foreign Aid to Israel." January 2, 2008. http://fpc.state.gov/documents/organization/100102 .pdf.

Connor, Walker. *Ethno-Nationalism: The Quest for Understanding.* Princeton: Princeton University Press, 1994.

Conversi, Daniele. "Reassessing Current Theories of Nationalism: Nationalism as Boundary Maintenance and Creation." *Nationalism and Ethnic Politics* 1, no. 1 (Spring 1995): 73–85.

Council of the European Union. "Council Conclusions on Middle East Peace Process." June 15, 2009. www.consilium.europa.eu/uedocs/cms_Data/docs/pressdata/en/gena/108500.pdf.

_____. "EU Signs Stabilization and Association Agreement with Bosnia and Herzegovina." June 16, 2008. www.consilium.europa.eu/uedocs/cms_data/docs/pressdata/en/er/101233.pdf.

Crighton, Elizabeth, and Martha Abele Mac Iver. "The Evolution of Protracted Ethnic Conflict: Group Dominance and Political Underdevelopment in Northern Ireland and Lebanon." *Comparative Politics* 23, no. 2 (January 1991): 127–142.

Culbert, Vance. "Civil Society Development versus the Peace Dividend: International Aid in the Wanni." *Disasters* 29 (2005): 38–57.

Daalder, Ivo. "Fear and Loathing in the Former Yugoslavia." In *The International Dimensions of Internal Conflict*, edited by Michael E. Brown, 35–67. Cambridge, Mass.: MIT Press, 1996.

Dagne, Ted, and Bathsheaba Everett. *Sudan: The Darfur Crisis and the Status of the North-South Negotiations*. Washington D.C.: Congressional Research Service, 2008.

Dagne, Ted, and Bathsheaba Everett. "Sudan: The Darfur Crisis and the Status of the North-South Negotiations." In *The Darfur Crisis,* edited by William R. Jeffries, 1–24. New York: Nova Science Publishers, 2008.

Dagne, Ted, and Bathsheaba Everett. "Sudan: Humanitarian Crisis, Peace Talks, Terrorism, and U.S. Policy." In *The Darfur Crisis,* edited by Williams R. Jeffries, 25–41. New York: Nova Science Publishers, 2008.

Daly, M. W. *Darfur's Sorrow: A History of Destruction and Genocide*. Cambridge: Cambridge University Press, 2007.

Dawisha, Adeed. "Nation and Nationalism: Historical Antecedents to Contemporary Debates." *International Studies Review* 4, no. 1 (Spring 2002): 3–22.

Deng, Francis M. *War of Visions: Conflicts of Identities in the Sudan*. Washington, D.C.: Brookings Institution, 1995.

de Silva, Purnaka L. "Combat Modes, Mimesis, and the Cultivation of Hatred: Revenge/Counter-Revenge Killings in Sri Lanka." In *Imagined Differences: Hatred and the Construction of Identity*, edited by Gunther Schlee, 215–239. New York: Palgrave, 2002.

Deutsch, Karl W. *Nationalism and Social Communication: An Inquiry into the Foundations of Nationality*. Cambridge, Mass.: MIT Press, 1953.

DeVotta, Neil. *Blowback: Linguistic Nationalism, Institutional Decay, and Ethnic Conflict in Sri Lanka*. Palo Alto: Stanford University Press, 2004.

_____. "From Ethnic Outbidding to Ethnic Conflict: The Institutional Bases for Sri Lanka's Separatist War." *Nations and Nationalism* 11 (2005): 141–159.

_____. "Illiberalism and Ethnic Conflict in Sri Lanka." *Journal of Democracy* 13 (2002): 84–98.

de Waal, Alex. "Sudan: The Turbulent State." In *War in Darfur and the Search for Peace*, edited by Alex de Waal, 1–38. Cambridge, Mass.: Harvard University, 2007.

_____. "Who Are the Darfurians? Arab and African Identities, Violence and External Engagement." *African Affairs* 104 (2005): 181–205.

Dhillon, Navtej. "Beyond Reconstruction: What Lies Ahead for Young Palestinians?" Brookings Institution (March 10, 2009), www.brookings.edu/opinions/2009/0310_west_bank_gaza_dhillon.aspx.

Diamond, Larry, Juan Linz, and Seymour Martin Lipset, eds. *Politics in Developing Countries*. 2nd ed. Boulder: Lynne Rienner, 1995.

Dixon, Paul. *Northern Ireland: The Politics of War and Peace*. New York: Palgrave, 2001.

Djilas, Aleksa. "Fear Thy Neighbor: The Breakup of Yugoslavia." In *Nationalism and Nationalities in the New Europe*, edited by Charles A. Kupchan, 85–106. Ithaca: Cornell University Press, 1995.

Doder, Dusko. "Yugoslavia: New War, Old Hatreds." *Foreign Policy* 91 (1993): 3–23.

Doumani, Beshara B. "Rediscovering Ottoman Palestine: Writing Palestinians into History." *Journal of Palestine Studies* 21, no. 2 (Winter 1992): 5-28.

Downs, Anthony. *An Economic Theory of Democracy*. New York: Harper, 1957.

Druckman, Daniel. "Nationalism, Patriotism, and Group Loyalty: A Social Psychological Perspective." *Mershon International Studies Review* 38 (1994): 43–68.

Dubey, Ravi Kant. *Indo-Sri Lankan Relations with Special Reference to the Tamil Problem*. New Delhi: Deep and Deep Publications, 1993.

Duffy, Gavan, and Nicole Lindstrom. "Conflicting Identities: Solidarity Incentives in the Serbo-Croatian War." *Journal of Peace Research* 39, no. 1 (2002): 69–90.

Economides, Spyros, and Paul Taylor. "Former Yugoslavia." In *The New Interventionism 1991–1994: United Nations Experience in Cambodia, Former Yugoslavia, and Somalia*, edited by James Mayall, 59–93. Cambridge: Cambridge University Press, 1996.

Edinger, Lewis J. "Approaches to the Comparative Analysis of Political Leadership." *Review of Politics* 52, no. 4 (Autumn 1990): 509–523.

Eknes, Age. "The United Nations' Predicament in the Former Yugoslavia." In *The United Nations and Civil War*, edited by Thomas G. Weiss, 109–126. Boulder: Lynne Rienner, 1995.

"An End to the War?" *The Economist*, October 22, 2008. www.economist.com/agenda/displaystory.cfm?story_id=12454123.

Esman, Milton J. *An Introduction to Ethnic Conflict.* Cambridge: Polity, 2004.

European Union. "Bosnia and Herzegovina—Relations with the EU." http://ec .europa.eu/enlargement/potential-candidate-countries/bosnia_and_herze govina/eu_bosnia_and_herzegovina_relations_en.htm.

_____. "The EU in the Middle East Peace Process." February 27, 2009. http://europa .eu/rapid/pressReleasesAction.do?reference=MEMO/09/88&format= HTML&aged=0&language=EN&guiLangagues=en.

_____. "Sharm El-Sheikh Fact-Finding Committee Report: 'Mitchell Report.'" April 30, 2001. http://ec.europa.eu/external_relations/mepp/docs/mitchell_ report_2001_en.pdf.

European Union Special Representative in Bosnia and Herzegovina. "EUSR Introduction." May 17, 2007. www.eusrbih.org.

_____. "EUSR Mandate." October 8, 2007. www.eusrbih.org.

Evangelista, Matthew. "Historical Legacies and the Politics of Intervention in the Former Soviet Union." In *The International Dimensions of Internal Conflict,* edited by Michael E. Brown, 108–140. Cambridge, Mass.: MIT Press, 1996.

Falah, Ghazi-Walid. "The Geopolitics of 'Enclavisation' and the Demise of a Two-State Solution to the Israeli-Palestinian Conflict." *Third World Quarterly* 26, no. 8 (2005): 1341–1372.

Farrell, Theo. "Constructivist Security Studies: Portrait of a Research Program." *International Studies Review* 4, no. 1 (Spring 2002): 49–72.

Fearon, James D. "Commitment Problems and the Spread of Ethnic Conflict." In *The International Spread of Ethnic Conflict: Fear, Diffusion, and Escalation,* edited by David A. Lake and Donald Rothchild, 107–126. Princeton: Princeton University Press, 1998.

Fearon, James D., and David D. Laitin. "Violence and the Social Construction of Ethnic Identity." *International Organization* 54, no. 4 (Autumn 2000): 845–877.

Flint, Julie, and Alex de Waal. *Darfur: A Short History of a Long War.* London: Zed Books, 2005.

"Former Bosnian President Dies." *BBC News,* October 19, 2003. http://news.bbc .co.uk/go/pr/fr/-/2/hi/europe/3205392.stm.

Francis, David J. "Introduction." In *Civil Militia: Africa's Intractable Security Menace?* edited by David J. Francis, 1–30. Aldershot: Ashgate, 2005.

Freedom House. "Palestine (Palestinian Authority and Israeli-Occupied Territories)." www.freedomhouse.org/template.cfm?page=180.

Frisch, Hillel, and Shmuel Sandler. "Religion, State, and the International System in the Israeli-Palestinian Conflict." *International Political Science Review* 25, no. 1 (2004): 77–96.

Gagnon, V. P. "Ethnic Nationalism and International Conflict: The Case of Serbia." *International Security* 19, no. 3 (Winter 1994–1995): 130–166.

Gallab, Abdullahi A. "The Insecure Rendezvous between Islam and Totalitarianism: The Failure of the Islamist State in the Sudan." *Arab Studies Quarterly* 23, no. 2 (Spring 2001): 87–108.

Gallagher, Michael. "The Changing Constitution." In *Politics in the Republic of Ireland*, 3rd ed., edited by John Coakley and Michael Gallagher, 71–98. New York: Routledge, 1999.

"Gaza Conflict Enters Third Week." *BBC News*, January 10, 2009. http://news .bbc.co.uk/go/pr/fr/-/2/hi/middle_east/7821646.stm.

Gellner, Ernest. *Nations and Nationalism*. Ithaca: Cornell University Press, 1983.

General Union of Palestinian Women. "Mission Statement." http://web.archive .org/web/20080126070631/http://www.gupw.net/about/about.htm.

——. "The National Strategy for the Advancement of Palestinian Women." http://web.archive.org/web/20080205051246/http://www.gupw.net/ publications/st1.htm.

Gent, Stephen E. "Going in When It Counts: Military Intervention and the Outcome of Civil Conflicts." *International Studies Quarterly* 52 (2008): 713–735.

Gibbons, John. *Spanish Politics Today*. Manchester: Manchester University Press, 1999.

Gill, Bates, and James Reilly. "The Tenuous Hold of China Inc. in Africa." *The Washington Quarterly* 30, no. 3 (2007): 37–52.

Gillespie, Gordon. *Historical Dictionary of the Northern Ireland Conflict*. Lanham, Md.: Scarecrow Press, 2008.

Gilley, Bruce. "Against the Concept of Ethnic Conflict." *Third World Quarterly* 25, no. 6 (2004): 1155–1166.

Girvin, Brian. "Northern Ireland and the Republic." In *Politics in Northern Ireland*, edited by Paul Mitchell and Rick Wilford, 220–241. Boulder: Westview Press, 1999.

Global Policy Forum. "Israel, Palestine, and the Occupied Territories." www .globalpolicy.org/security-council/index-of-countries-on-the-security- council-agenda/israel-palestine-and-the-occupied-territories.html.

——. "A Performance-Based Roadmap to a Permanent Two-State Solution to the Israeli-Palestinian Conflict." 2003. www.globalpolicy.org/images/pdfs/ roadmap122002.pdf.

——. "Saudi-Initiated Peace Plan Document." March 25, 2002. www.global policy.org/component/content/article/189/38003.html.

——. "UN Documents." www.globalpolicy.org/security-council/index-of- countries-on-the-security-council-agenda/israel-palestine-and-the-occupied- territories/38296.html.

——. "Yasser Arafat, Speech at UN General Assembly." December 13, 1998. www .globalpolicy.org/images/pdfs/arafatga121988.pdf.

Goodhand, Jonathan, and Bart Klem. *Aid, Conflict, and Peacebuilding in Sri Lanka, 2000–2005*. Colombo: Asia Foundation, 2005.

Goodhand, Jonathan, and Nick Lewer. "Sri Lanka: NGOs and Peace-Building in Complex Political Emergencies." *Third World Quarterly* 20 (1999): 69–87.

Gormley-Heenan, Cathy. *Political Leadership and the Northern Ireland Peace Process: Role, Capacity, and Effect.* New York: Palgrave, 2007.

Gould, Alberta. *George Mitchell: In Search of Peace.* Farmington, Maine: Heritage, 1996.

Government of Israel, Prime Minister's Office. "Ehud Barak—The Tenth Prime Minister." www.pmo.gov.il/PMOEng/History/FormerPrimeMinister/Ehud Barak.htm.

———. "Yitzhak Rabin—The Fifth Prime Minister." www.pmo.gov.il/PMOEng/History/FormerPrimeMinister/YitzhaRabin.htm.

Gow, James. "Coercive Cadences: The Yugoslav War of Dissolution." In *Strategic Coercion: Concepts and Cases*, edited by Lawrence Freedman, 276–296. Oxford: Oxford University Press, 1998.

Grieg, J. Michael, and Patrick M. Regan. "When Do They Say Yes? An Analysis of the Willingness to Offer and Accept Mediation." *International Studies Quarterly* 52 (2008): 759–781.

Grove, Andrea K. and Neal A. Carter. "Not All Blarney Is Cast in Stone: International Cultural Conflict in Northern Ireland." *Political Psychology* 20 (1999): 725–765.

Guelke, Adrian. "Political Violence and the Paramilitaries." In *Politics in Northern Ireland*, edited by Paul Mitchell and Rick Wolford, 220–241. Boulder: Westview Press, 1999.

Gunawardana, R. A. L. H. "The People of the Lion: The Sinhala Identity and Ideology in History and Historiography." In *Sri Lanka: History and the Roots of the Conflict*, edited by Jonathan Spencer, 45–86. London: Routledge, 1990.

"Gunmen Shoot Sri Lanka Cricketeers." *BBC World News.* http://news.bbc.co.uk/2/hi/south_asia/7920260.stm.

Gurr, Ted Robert. "The Revolution-Social-Change Nexus: Some Old Theories and New Hypotheses." *Comparative Politics* 5, no. 3 (April 1973): 359–392.

———. "Why Minorities Rebel: A Global Analysis of Communal Mobilization and Conflict Since 1945." *International Political Science Review* 14, no. 2 (April 1993): 161–201.

Guttman, Nathan. "Israel, U.S. Working to Limit Damage of Goldstone Report." *Haaretz.com,* September 27, 2009. www.haaretz.com/hasen/spages/1117314 .html.

Hallop, Oddvar. "Ethnic Identity, Violence, and the Estate Tamil Minority in Sri Lanka." *Round Table* 323 (1992): 315–338.

"Hamas 'Will Not Obstruct' 1967 Borders Deal." *BBC News*, June 10, 2009. http://news.bbc.co.uk/go/pr/fr/-/2/hi/middle_east/8091377.stm.

"Hamas 'Killing' Palestinian Foes." *BBC News*, April 20, 2009. http://news.bbc.co.uk/go/pr/fr/-/2/hi/middle_east/8007756.stm.

"Hanan Ashrawi." *Encyclopedia Britannica*. www.britannica.com/EBchecked/topic/38365/Hanan-Ashrawi.

Hanieh, Akram. "Special Document: The Camp David Papers." *Journal of Palestine Studies* 30, no. 2 (Winter 2001): 75–97.

Harel, Amos, and Avi Issacharoff. "Israel removes dozens of West Bank roadblocks." *Haaretz.com*, June 24, 2009. http://haaretz.com/hasen/spages/1095231.html.

Harff, Barbara, and Ted Robert Gurr. *Ethnic Conflict in World Politics*. 2nd ed. Boulder: Westview Press, 2004.

Harvey, Frank P. "Deterrence and Compellence in *Protracted Crises*: Methodology and Preliminary Findings." *International Studies Notes* 22 (1997): 269–294.

———. "Deterrence and Ethnic Conflict: The Case of Bosnia-Herzegovina, 1993–94." *Security Studies* 6 (1997): 180–210.

———. "Primordialism, Evolutionary Theory and Ethnic Violence in the Balkans: Opportunities and Constraints for Theory and Policy." *Canadian Journal of Political Science* 33, no. 1 (March 2000): 37–65.

Haug, Marit. "Combining Service Delivery and Advocacy within Humanitarian Agencies: Experiences from the Conflict in Sir Lanka." International Working Papers 10. London School of Economics, 2001.

Hayden, Robert M. "Bosnia's Internal War and the International Criminal Tribunal." *The Fletcher Forum of World Affairs* 22, no. 1 (1998): 45–64.

Hazan, Reuven Y. "Intraparty Politics and Peacemaking in Democratic Societies: Israel's Labor Party and the Middle East Peace Process, 1992–96." *Journal of Peace Research* 37, no. 3 (2000): 363–378.

"Health Conditions Worsening in Gaza as Borders Remain Closed—UN Agency." UN News Service, May 22, 2009. www.un.org/apps/news/story.asp?NewsID=30899&Cr=gaza&Cr1=.

Hearn, Jonathan. *Rethinking Nationalism: A Critical Introduction*. New York: Palgrave Macmillan, 2006.

Heavens, Andrew. "China Urges Deferral of Bashir War Crimes Case." *Reuters*, January 7, 2009.

Helman, Sara. "From Soldiering and Motherhood to Citizenship: A Study of Four Israeli Peace Protest Movements." *Social Politics* 6, no. 3 (Fall 1999): 292–313.

Helsing, Jeffrey W. "The Regionalization, Internationalization, and Perpetuation of Conflict in the Middle East." In *Ethnic Conflict and International Politics:*

Explaining Diffusion and Escalation, edited by Steven E. Lobell and Philip Mauceri, 133–163. New York: Palgrave, 2004.

Hennessey, Thomas. *A History of Northern Ireland*. New York: St. Martin's Press, 1997.

———. *The Northern Ireland Peace Process: Ending the Troubles?* New York: Palgrave, 2001.

Hermann, Margaret G., ed. *Leaders, Groups, and Coalitions: Understanding the People and Processes in Foreign Policymaking*. Special issue, *International Studies Review* 3, no. 2 (Summer 2001).

Herrmann, Richard K., and Michael P. Fischerkeller. "Beyond the Enemy Image and Spiral Model: Cognitive-Strategic Research after the Cold War." *International Organization* 49, no. 3 (Summer 1995): 415–450.

Hobsbawm, Eric J. *Nations and Nationalism since 1780: Programme, Myth, Reality*. Cambridge: Cambridge University Press, 1990.

Hogg, Michael A., Deborah J. Terry, and Katherine M. White. "A Tale of Two Theories: A Critical Comparison of Identity Theory with Social Identity Theory." *Social Psychology Quarterly* 58 (1995): 255–269.

Holsti, Ole R. "The Political Psychology of International Politics: More than a Luxury." *Political Psychology* 10, no. 3 (1989): 495–500.

Holt, Maria. "Palestinian Women, Violence, and the Peace Process." *Development in Practice* 13, nos. 2–3 (May 2003): 223–238.

Honeyball, Mary. "Will Women Be Excluded from the Gaza Peace Process?" January 12, 2009. www.neurope.eu/articles/91858.php.

Hopf, Ted. "The Promise of Constructivism in International Relations Theory." *International Security* 23, no. 1 (Summer 1998): 171–200.

Horowitz, Donald. *Ethnic Groups in Conflict*. Berkeley: University of California Press, 1985.

Horowitz, Shale. "Identities Unbound: Escalating Ethnic Conflict in Post-Soviet Azerbaijan, Georgia, Moldova, and Tajikistan." In *Ethnic Conflict and International Politics: Explaining Diffusion and Escalation*, edited by Steven E. Lobell and Philip Mauceri, 51–74. New York: Palgrave, 2004.

Human Rights Watch. "Darfur Destroyed: Ethnic Cleansing by Government and Militia Forces in Western Sudan." *Human Rights Watch* 16, no. 6A (May 2004).

———. "EU: Press Croatia to Continue Cooperation with Yugoslav Tribunal." February 20, 2009. www.hrw.org/en/news/2009/02/19/eu-press-croatia-continue-cooperation-yugoslav-tribunal.

———. "A Question of Security: Violence against Palestinian Women and Girls." *Human Rights Watch* 18, no. 7 (November 2006).

_____. "They Shot at Us as We Fled: Government Attacks on Civilians in West Darfur in February 2008." May 18, 2008. www.hrw.org/en/reports/2008/05/18/they-shot-us-we-fled.

_____. "US: Ask Israel to Cooperate with Goldstone Inquiry." May 17, 2009. www.hrw.org/en/news/2009/05/17/us-ask-israel-cooperate-goldstone-inquiry.

Huntington, Samuel P. *Political Order in Changing Societies*. New Haven: Yale University Press, 1968.

Hutchings, Robert L. *American Diplomacy and the End of the Cold War: An Insider's Account of U.S. Policy in Europe, 1982–1992*. Washington, D.C.: Woodrow Wilson Center Press, 1997.

Hutchinson, John, and Anthony D. Smith. "Introduction." In *Ethnicity*, edited by John Hutchinson and Anthony D. Smith, 3–14. Oxford: Oxford University Press, 1996.

"Ian Paisley's Speech in Full." *BBC News*, May 8, 2007. http://news.bbc.co.uk/2/hi/uk_news/northern_ireland/6636139.stm.

Ibrahim, Fouad. "Introduction to the Conflict in Darfur/West Sudan." In *Explaining Darfur: Four Lectures on the Ongoing Genocide*, edited by Agnes van Ardenne-van der Hoeven, Mohamed Abdel Rahim Mohamed Salih, Nick Grono, and Juan E. Méndez, 9–18. Amsterdam: Vossiuspers UvA, 2006.

Idris, Amir H. *Conflict and Politics of the Identity in Sudan*. New York: Palgrave, 2005.

International Criminal Court, "ICC Prosecutor Presents Cases against Sudanese President, Hassan Ahmad Al Bashir, for Genocide, Crimes against Humanity and War Crimes in Darfur." www.icc-cpi.int/menus/icc/situations%20and%20cases/situations/situation%20icc%200205/press%20releases/a.

International Crisis Group. *Sudan: Organising for Peace as the War Escalates*. Africa Report 48. Nairobi/Brussels: ICG, June 2002.

International Women's Commission. "Statement Issued by the International Women's Commission for a Just and Sustainable Peace between Israel and Palestine," May 3, 2006. www.iwc-peace.org/.

Israel Ministry of Foreign Affairs. "Aliyah." October 29, 2002. www.mfa.gov.il/MFA/MFAArchive/2000_2009/2002/10/Aliyah.htm.

_____. "Disputed Territories: Forgotten Facts about the West Bank and Gaza Strip." February 1, 2003. www.mfa.gov.il/MFA/MFAArchive/2000_2009/2003/2/DISPUTED+TERRITORIES-+Forgotten+Facts+About_the+We.htm.

_____. "Elections in Israel—February 2009." February 10, 2009. www.mfa.gov.il/MFA/History/Modern+History/Historic+Events/Elections_in_Israel_February_2009.htm.

_____. "Israel-Palestinian Negotiations." www.mfa.gov.il/MFA/Peace+Process/Guide+to+the+Peace+Process/Israel-Palestinian+negotiations.htm.

_____. "Responding to Hamas Attacks from Gaza—Issues of Proportionality." December 29, 2008. www.mfa.gov.il/MFA/GOvernment/Law/Legal+Issues+ and+Rulings/Responding+to+Hamas+attacks+from+Gaza+-+Issues+of+ Proportionality+-+March+2008.htm.

"Israel Rejects US Call over Settlement Work." _BBC News_, May 28, 2009. http:// news.bbc.co.uk/go/pr/fr/-/2/hi/middle_east/8071491.stm.

"Israel Says Gaza Death Toll Lower than Claimed." _CNN.com_, March 26, 2009. www.cnn.com/2009/WORLD/meast/03/26/israel.gaza.death.toll/index .html.

"Is the End Near for Sri Lanka's Rebels?" _BBC News_, January 9, 2009. http://news .bbc.co.uk/2/hi/south_asia/7820188.stm.

Iyob, Ruth, and Gilbert M. Khadiagala. _Sudan: The Elusive Quest for Peace_. Boulder.: Lynne Rienner, 2006.

Jacoby, Tami Amanda. "Feminism, Nationalism, and Difference: Reflections on the Palestinian Women's Movement." _Women's Studies International Forum_ 22, no. 5 (1999): 511–523.

Jaeger, David A., and M. Daniele Paserman. "Israel, the Palestinian Factions, and the Cycle of Violence." _American Economic Review_ 96, no. 2 (May 2006): 45–49.

Jayasuriya, Laksiri. _The Changing Face of Electoral Politics in Sri Lanka, 1994–2004_. Singapore: Marshall Cavendish, 2005.

Jeffries, William R. "Timeline of Darfur Events." In _The Darfur Crisis_, edited by William R. Jeffries, Appendix 2. New York: Nova Science Publishers, 2008.

Jenne, Erin K. "Sri Lanka: A Fragmented State." In _State Failure and State Weakness in a Time of Terror_, edited by Robert I. Rotberg, 219–244. Washington, D.C.: Brookings Institution Press, 2003.

Jensen, Lloyd. "Negotiations and Power Asymmetries: The Cases of Bosnia, Northern Ireland, and Sri Lanka." _International Negotiation_ 2 (1997): 21–41.

Jervis, Robert. _Perception and Misperception in International Relations_. Princeton: Princeton University Press, 1976.

Jesse, Neal G., and Kristen P. Williams. _Identity and Institutions: Conflict Reduction in Divided Societies_. Albany: SUNY Press, 2005.

Jeyaratnam, Wilson A. "Nation-Building in a Demotic State: The Failure of Political Leadership in Sri Lanka." In _The Post-Colonial States of South Asia: Democracy, Development, and Identity_, edited by Amita Shastri and A. Jeyaratnam Wilson, 88–113. New York: Palgrave, 2001.

_____. "Sri Lanka: Ethnic Strife and the Politics of Space." In _The Territorial Management of Ethnic Conflict_, edited by John Coakley, 173–198. London: Frank Cass, 2003.

_____. *Sri Lankan Tamil Nationalism: Its Origins and Development in the Nineteenth and Twentieth Centuries.* Vancouver: University of British Columbia Press, 2000.

Johnson, Carter. "Partitioning to Peace: Sovereignty, Demography, and Ethnic Civil Wars." *International Security* 32, no. 4 (Spring 2008): 140–170.

Johnson, Douglas H. "Darfur: Peace, Genocide, and Crimes against Humanity in Sudan." In *Violence, Political Culture and Development in Africa*, edited by Preben Kaarsholm, 92–104. Athens: Ohio University Press, 2006.

Johnson, Penny, and Eileen Kuttab. "Where Have All the Women (and Men) Gone?" *Feminist Review* 69 (2001): 21–43.

Kagwanja, Peter, and Patrick Mutahi. "Protection of Civilians in African Peace Missions: The Case of the African Union Mission in Sudan, Darfur." Paper 139. Pretoria: Institute for Security Studies, May 2007.

Kandiyoti, Deniz. "Women, Ethnicity and Nationalism." In *Ethnicity*, edited by John Hutchinson and Anthony D. Smith, 311–316. Oxford: Oxford University Press, 1996.

Kaplowitz, Noel. "Psychopolitical Dimensions of International Relations: The Reciprocal Effects of Conflict Strategies." *International Studies Quarterly* 28, no. 4 (December 1984): 373–406.

"Karadzic Caught." *The Economist*, July 24, 2008.

Katz, D. "Nationalism and Strategies of International Conflict Resolution." In *International Behavior: A Social-Psychological Analysis*, edited by Herbert C. Kelman, 356–390. New York: Holt, 1964.

Katzenstein, Peter J., Robert O. Keohane, and Stephen D. Krasner. "*International Organization* and the Study of World Politics." *International Organization* 52, no. 4 (Autumn 1998): 645–685.

Kaufman, Joyce P., and Kristen P. Williams. *Women, the State, and War: A Comparative Perspective on Citizenship and Nationalism.* Lanham, Md.: Lexington, 2007.

Kaufman, Stuart J. "Spiraling to Ethnic War: Elites, Masses, and Moscow in Moldova's Civil War." *International Security* 21, no. 2 (Fall 1996): 108–138.

Kaufmann, Chaim. "Possible and Impossible Solutions to Ethnic Civil Wars." In *Nationalism and Ethnic Conflict*, rev. ed., edited by Michael E. Brown, Owen R. Cote Jr., Sean M. Lynn-Jones, and Steven E. Miller, 444–483. Cambridge, Mass.: MIT Press 2001.

Keena, Colma. *A Biography of Gerry Adams.* Cork: Mercier Press, 1990.

Keohane, Robert O., and Lisa L. Martin. "The Promise of Institutionalist Theory." *International Security* 20 (1995): 39–51.

Kesic, Obrad. "Women and Gender Imagery in Bosnia: Amazons, Sluts, Victims, Witches, and Wombs." In *Gender Politics in the Western Balkans: Women and Society in Yugoslavia and the Yugoslav Successor States*, edited by Sabrina P. Ramet, 187–202. University Park: Pennsylvania State University Press, 1999.

Kesselman, Mark, Joel Krieger, and William A. Joseph. "Introducing Comparative Politics." In *Introduction to Comparative Politics*, 3rd ed., edited by Mark Kesselman, Joel Krieger, and William A. Joseph, 3–23. Boston: Houghton Mifflin, 2004.

Kim, Julie. "Bosnia: Overview of Issues Ten Years after Dayton." *Report for Congress*, November 14, 2005, Congressional Research Service document (RS22324).

King, Charles, and Neil J. Melvin. "Diaspora Politics: Ethnic Linkages, Foreign Policy, and Security in Eurasia." *International Security* 24, no. 3 (Winter 1999/2000): 108–138.

Kodikara, Shelton U. *Foreign Policy of Sri Lanka: A Third World Perspective.* Delhi: Chanakya Publications, 1982.

Korac, Maja. "Gender, Conflict and Peace-Building: Lessons from the Conflict in the Former Yugoslavia." *Women's Studies International Forum* 29 (2006): 510–520.

Korf, Benedikt. "Functions of Violence Revisited: Greed, Pride, and Grievance in Sri Lanka's Civil War." *Progress in Development Studies* 6 (2002): 109–122.

Korf, Benedikt, and Kalinga Tudor Silva. "Poverty, Ethnicity, and Conflict in Sri Lanka." Paper presented at the conference, "Staying Poor: Chronic Poverty and Development Policy," University of Manchester, April 7–9, 2003.

Krause, Keith, and Michael C. Williams. "Broadening the Agenda of Security Studies: Politics and Methods." *Mershon International Studies Review* 40, no. 2 (October 1996): 229–254.

Kriesberg, Louis. "Mediation and the Transformation of the Israeli-Palestinian Conflict." *Journal of Peace Research* 38, no. 3 (2001): 373–392.

Kronstadt, K. Alan. "Sri Lanka: Background and U.S. Relations." *Report for Congress*, April 3, 2003, Congressional Research Service document (CRS-2003 RL31707).

Kydd, Andrew, and Barbara F. Walter. "Sabotaging the Peace: The Politics of Extremist Violence." *International Organization* 56, no. 2 (Spring 2002): 263–296.

"Labour Market Statistics: Regional (Statistical Bulletin)." Office for National Statistics. www.statistics.gov.uk/statbase/Product.asp?vlnk=5838.

LaFeber, Walter. *America, Russia, and the Cold War: 1945–1990.* 6th ed. New York: McGraw-Hill, 1991.

Lake, David A., and Donald Rothchild, eds. *The International Spread of Ethnic Conflict: Fear, Diffusion and Escalation.* Princeton: Princeton University Press, 1998.

———. "Spreading Fear: The Genesis of Transnational Ethnic Conflict." In *The International Spread of Ethnic Conflict: Fear, Diffusion, and Escalation*, edited by

David A. Lake and Donald Rothchild, 3–32. Princeton: Princeton University Press, 1998.

Lakshman, Weligamage D., and Clement A. Tisdell. "Sri Lanka's Development since Independence." In *Sri Lanka: Current Issues and Historical Background*, edited by Walter Nubin, 13–28. New York: Nova Science Publishers, 2002.

Larson, Deborah Welch. *The Origins of Containment: A Psychological Explanation*. Princeton: Princeton University Press, 1985.

Larson, Deborah W. "Trust and Missed Opportunities in International Relations." *Political Psychology* 18 (1997): 701–734.

Lederach, John Paul. *Building Peace: Sustainable Reconciliation in Divided Societies*. Washington D.C.: United States Institute of Peace Press, 1997.

Lederer, Edith M. "Security Council Calls for Two-State Solution." *The Boston Globe*, May 12, 2009.

Lemco, Jonathan. *Political Stability in Federal Governments*. New York: Praeger, 1991.

Levine, Alicia. "Political Accommodation and the Prevention of Secessionist Violence." In *The International Dimensions of Internal Conflict*, edited by Michael E. Brown, 311–40. Cambridge, Mass.: MIT Press, 1996.

Levs, Josh. "Is Gaza 'Occupied' Territory?" *CNN.com*, January 6, 2009. www.cnn.com/2009WORLD/meast/01/06/israel.gaza.occupation.question/index.html.

Lijphart, Arend. *Conflict and Coexistence in Belgium: The Dynamics of a Culturally Divided Society*. Berkeley: University of California Press, 1981.

_____. *Democracy in Plural Societies: A Comparative Exploration*. New Haven, Conn.: Yale University Press, 1977.

Lilly, Carol S., and Jill A. Irvine. "Negotiating Interests: Women and Nationalism in Serbia and Croatia, 1990–1997." *East European Politics and Societies* 16, no. 1 (2002): 109–144.

Lobban Jr., Richard A., Robert S. Kramer, and Carolyn Fluehr-Lobban. *Historical Dictionary of the Sudan*. 3rd ed. Lanham, Md.: Scarecrow Press, 2002.

Lobell, Steven E., and Philip Mauceri. "Diffusion and Escalation of Ethnic Conflict." In *Ethnic Conflict and International Politics: Explaining Diffusion and Escalation*, edited by Steven E. Lobell and Philip Mauceri, 1–10. New York: Palgrave, 2004.

Lustick, Ian. "Reinventing Jerusalem." *Foreign Policy* 93 (Winter 1993/1994): 41–59.

_____. "Stability in Deeply Divided Societies: Consociationalism versus Control." *World Politics* 31 (1979): 325–344.

Lynch, Patrick. "Ireland since the Treaty (1921–1966)." In *The Course of Irish History*, edited by T. W. Moody and F. X. Martin, 324–342. Cork: Mercier Press, 1967.

Mahmoud, Mahgoub El-Tigani. "Inside Darfur: Ethnic Genocide by a Governance Crisis." *Comparative Studies of South Asia, Africa, and the Middle East* 24, no. 2 (2004): 3–17.

_____. "Solving the Crisis of Sudan: The Right of Self-Determination versus State Torture." *Arab Studies Quarterly* 23, no. 2 (Spring 2001): 41–59.

Mair, Peter. *The Changing Irish Party System*. London: Pinter, 1987.

Makovsky, David. "Gaza: Moving Forward by Pulling Back." *Foreign Affairs* 84, no. 3 (May/June 2005): 52–62.

_____. "Middle East Peace through Partition." *Foreign Affairs* 80, no. 2 (March/April 2001): 28–45.

"Many Dead in Sri Lanka, Says UN." *BBC News,* March 6, 2009. http://news.bbc.co.uk/2/hi/south_asia/7927774.stm.

March, James, and Herbert Simon. *Organizations*. New York: Wiley and Sons, 1958.

March, James G., and Johan P. Olsen. "The New Institutionalism: Organizational Factors in Political Life." *American Political Science Review* 78, no. 3 (1984): 734–749.

Marshall, Monty G. "Major Episodes of Political Violence 1946–2009." Center for Systemic Peace. www.systemicpeace.org/warlist.htm.

Marshall, Monty G., and Benjamin R. Cole. "Global Report on Conflict, Governance and State Fragility 2008." *Foreign Policy Bulletin* (Winter 2008): 3–21.

Marx, Anthony D. "The Nation-State and Its Exclusion." *Political Science Quarterly* 117, no. 1 (Spring 2002): 103–126.

Matthews, Bruce. "Counter-Insurgency and the State in Modern Sri Lanka." In *The Counter-Insurgent State: Guerilla Warfare and State Building in the Twentieth Century*, edited by Paul B. Rich and Richard Stubbs, 72–96. New York: St. Martin's Press, 1997.

McCall, Cathal. *Identity in Northern Ireland*. New York: St. Martin's Press, 1999.

McCartney, Donal. "From Parnell to Pearse (1891–1921)." In *The Course of Irish History*, edited by T. W. Moody and F. X. Martin, 294–312. Cork: Mercier Press, 1967.

McDowell, David. *A Modern History of the Kurds*. Rev. 3rd ed. London/New York: I.B. Tauris, 2004.

McGarry, John, and Brendan O'Leary. "Five Fallacies: Northern Ireland and the Liabilities of Liberalism." In *The Northern Ireland Conflict: Consociational Engagements*, edited by John McGarry and Brendan O'Leary, 167–193. New York: Oxford University Press, 2004.

_____. "Introduction: Consociational Theory and Northern Ireland." In *The Northern Ireland Conflict: Consociational Engagements*, edited by John McGarry and Brendan O'Leary, 1–61. New York: Oxford University Press, 2004.

_____. "Stabilising the Northern Ireland Agreement." In *Devolution and Constitutional Change in Northern Ireland*, edited by Paul Carmichael, Colin Knox, and Robert Osborne, 62–82. New York: Manchester University Press, 2007.

McGilvray, Dennis B. *Crucible of Conflict: Tamil and Muslim Society on the East Coast of Sri Lanka*. Durham: Duke University Press, 2008.

McKeogh, Colin. "Northern Ireland: The Good Friday Solution." *New Zealand International Review* 23 (1998): 2–6.

McSweeney, Bill. "Security, Identity, and the Peace Process in Northern Ireland." *Security Dialogue* 27 (1996): 167–178.

Mearsheimer, John J. "Back to the Future." In *The Cold War and After: Prospects for Peace*, edited by Sean M. Lynn-Jones, 141–192. Cambridge, Mass.: MIT Press, 1991.

_____. "The False Promise of International Institutions." *International Security* 19, no. 3 (Winter 1994/1995): 5–49.

Mearsheimer, John J., and Stephen M. Walt. *The Israel Lobby and U.S. Foreign Policy*. New York: Farrar, Straus and Giroux, 2007.

Mearsheimer, John J., and Stephen Van Evera. "When Peace Means War: The Partition That Dare Not Speak Its Name." *The New Republic*, December 18, 1995, pp. 16–21.

Metelits, Claire. "Reformed Rebels? Democratization, Global Norms, and the Sudan People's Liberation Army." *Africa Today* 11, no. 1 (Fall 2004): 65–82.

Miall, Hugh, Oliver Ramsbotham, and Tom Woodhouse. *Contemporary Conflict Resolution: The Prevention, Management, and Transformation of Deadly Conflicts*. Oxford: Polity, 1999.

Migdalovitz, Carol. "Israeli-Arab Negotiations: Background, Conflicts, and U.S. Policy." Congressional Research Service, March 9, 2009. http://fpc.state.gov/documents/organization/120969.pdf.

Miller, Molly J. "The Crisis in Darfur." *Mediterranean Quarterly* 18, no. 4 (2007): 112–130.

Milton-Edwards, Beverley, and Alistair Crooke. "Elusive Ingredient: Hamas and the Peace Process." *Journal of Palestine Studies* 33, no. 4 (Summer 2004): 39–52.

Miskin, Maayana. "Israeli Women's Groups Complain to UN—Against Israel." *IsraelNationalNews.com*, December 22, 2008. www.israelnationalnews.com/news/news.aspx/128981.

Mitchell, George J. *Making Peace*. New York: Alfred A. Knopf, 1999.

Moodie, Michael. "The Balkan Tragedy." *Annals of the American Academy of Political Sciences* 542 (1995): 101–115.

Moolakkattu, John Stephen. "Peace Facilitation by Small States: Norway in Sri Lanka." *Cooperation and Conflict* 40 (2005): 385–402.

Mostov, Julie. "Sexing the Nation/Desexing the Body: Politics of National Identity in the Former Yugoslavia." In *Gender Ironies of Nationalism: Sexing the Nation*, edited by Tamar Mayer, 98–102. London: Routledge, 2000.

Moxon-Browne, Edward. "National Identity in Northern Ireland." In *Social Attitudes in Northern Ireland*, edited by Peter Stringer and Jillian Robinson, 23–30. Belfast: Blackstaff, 1991.

Mueller, John. "The Banality of 'Ethnic War.'" In *Nationalism and Ethnic Conflict*, rev. ed., edited by Michael E. Brown, Owen R. Cote Jr., Sean M. Lynn-Jones, and Steven E. Miller, 97–125. Cambridge, Mass.: MIT Press, 2001.

Mukherjee, Bumba. "Does Third-Party Enforcement of Domestic Institutions Promote Enduring Peace after Civil Wars? Policy Lessons from an Empirical Test." *Foreign Policy Analysis* 2 (2006): 405–430.

Murphy, Alexander B. "Belgium's Regional Divergence: Along the Road to Federation." In *Federalism: the Multiethnic Challenge*, edited by Graham Smith, 73–100. London: Longman, 1995.

Murphy, Deborah. "Narrating Darfur: Darfur in the U.S. Press, March-September 2004." In *War in Darfur and the Search for Peace*, edited by Alex de Waal, 314–336. Cambridge: Harvard University, 2007.

Nadarajah, Suthaharan, and Dhananjayan Sriskandarajah. "Liberation Struggle or Terrorism? The Politics of Naming the LTTE." *Third World Quarterly* 26 (2005): 87–100.

Nagel, Joane. "Ethnicity and Sexuality." *Annual Review of Sociology* 26 (2000): 107–133.

"Netanyahu Speech—Key Excerpts." *BBC News*, June 14, 2009. http://news.bbc .co.uk/go/pr/fr/-/2/hi/middle_east/8099749.stm.

Nice, David C. *Federalism: The Politics of Intergovernmental Relations*. New York: St. Martin's Press, 1987.

Nikolic-Ristanovic, Vesna, ed. *Women, Violence and War: Wartime Victimization of Refugees in the Balkans*. Budapest, Hungary: Central European University Press, 2000.

"1998 Recipient George Mitchell, Liberty Medal." National Constitution Center. www.constitutioncenter.org.

Nissan, Elizabeth. *Sri Lanka: A Bitter Harvest*. London: Minority Rights Group, 1996.

Nithiyanandam, V. Nithi. "Changing Scenarios of Tamilian Culture: Some Thoughts on the Cultural Dimensions of the Ethnic War in Sri Lanka." *Asian Ethnicity* 2 (2001): 35–54.

Nordlinger, Eric A. *Conflict Regulation in Divided Societies*. Cambridge, Mass.: Center for International Affairs, Harvard University, 1972.

"Northern Ireland Life and Times Survey 2007." Economic Social and Research Council. www.ark.ac.uk/nilt/2007/Community_Relations/NINATID.html.

"Not Nearly Back to Normal." *The Economist*, April 30, 2009. www.economist.com/world/mideast-africa/displaystory.cfm?story_id=13578934.

"Obituary: Slobodan Milosevic." *BBC News*, March 11, 2006. http://news.bbc.co.uk/go/pr/fr/-/2/hi/europe/655616.stm.

"Obituary: Yasser Arafat." *BBC News*, November 11, 2004. http://news.bbc.co.uk/go/pr/fr/-/2/hi/middle_east/890161.stm.

O'Brien, Jay. "Power and the Discourse of Ethnicity in Sudan." In *Ethnicity and the State in Eastern Africa*, edited by M. A. Mohamed Salih and John Markakis, 62–71. Uppsala: Nordiska Afrikainstitutet, 1998.

O'Duffy, Brendan. "Violence in Northern Ireland, 1964–94: Sectarian or Ethnonational?" *Ethnic and Racial Studies* 18 (1995): 740–772.

O'Fahey, R. S. "Islam and Ethnicity in the Sudan." *Journal of Religion in Africa* 26, no. 3 (1996): 258–267.

O'Leary, Brendan. "Public Opinion and Northern Irish Futures." *The Political Quarterly* 63 (1992): 143–70.

O'Leary, Brendan, and John McGarry. *The Politics of Antagonism: Understanding Northern Ireland*. London: Athlone, 1993.

_____. "Regulating Nations and Ethnic Communities." In *Nationalism and Rationality*, edited by Albert Breton, Gianluigi Galeotti, Pierre Salmon, and Ronald Wintrobe, 245–289. Cambridge: Cambridge University Press, 1995.

Olson, Mancur. *The Logic of Collective Action: Public Goods and the Theory of Groups*. Cambridge, Mass.: Harvard University Press, 1971.

Olson, Robert K. "Partners in the Peace Process: The United States and Europe." *Journal of Palestine Studies* 26, no. 4 (Summer 1997): 78–89.

O'Neill, William G., and Violette Cassis. "Protecting Two Million Internally Displaced: The Successes and Shortcomings of the African Union in Darfur." Occasional Paper. Washington, D.C.: Brookings Institution/University of Bern, November 2005.

Orjuela, Camilla. *Civil Society in Civil War: Peace Work and Identity Politics in Sri Lanka*. Göteborg: Göteborg University, 2004.

"The Outlines of a Settlement." *The Economist*, January 15, 2009. www.economist.com/world/middleeast-africa/displaystory.cfm?story_id=E1_TNJQVDTR.

"Paisley to Quit as First Minister." *BBC News*, March 4, 2008. http://news.bbc.co.uk/2/hi/uk_news/northern_ireland/7277886.stm.

Palestinian Center for Policy and Survey Research. "Joint Israeli-Palestinian Poll: Pessimism among Israelis and Palestinians regarding the prospects for a settlement and a Palestinian state in the next few years, but majorities on both sides support a two-state solution." June 14, 2009. www.pcpsr.org/survey/polls/2009/p32ejoint.html.

_____. "Palestinian Public Opinion Poll No. (32): While Abbas's popularity improves and while a majority of Palestinians accepts Fateh's position that a national unity government must accept agreements signed with Israel, and while a majority supports the two-state solution, pessimism prevails regarding the peace process and the chances for Fateh-Hamas reconciliation." May 2009. www.pcpsr.org/survey/polls/2009/p32e.html.

"Palestinian Growth 'Obstructed.'" *BBC News*, May 9, 2007. http://news.bbc.co.uk/go/pr/fr/-/2/hi/business/6638241.stm.

Palestinian Women's Research and Documentation Center, UNESCO. "Violence against Women in Palestine: National Campaign against Violence against Women." November 25–December 10, 2006. www.pwrdc.ps/site_files/Violence%20against%20Women.pdf.

"PEACE III: EU Programme for Peace and Reconciliation 2007–2013 Northern Ireland and the Border Region of Ireland: Operational Program." Special EU Programmes Body. www.seupb.eu/programmes2007-2013/peaceiii programme/overview.aspx.

"Peacekeepers into the Fray." *The Economist*, March 13, 2008. www.economist.com/world/middleeast-africa/displaystory.cfm?story_id=E1_TDRVPJRS.

"Peace Support Operations in Bosnia and Herzegovina." NATO. www.nato.int/cps/en/natolive/topics_52122.htm.

Pearlman, Wendy. "Spoiling Inside and Out: Internal Political Contestation and the Middle East Peace Process." *International Security* 33, no. 3 (Winter 2008/2009): 79–109.

Pearson, Frederic S. "Dimensions of Conflict Resolution in Ethnopolitical Disputes." *Journal of Peace Research* 38, no. 3 (2001): 275–287.

Peeples, Patrick. *The History of Sri Lanka*. Westport, Conn.: Greenwood Press, 2006.

Peleg, Ilan. *Democratizing the Hegemonic State: Political Transformation in the Age of Identity*. Cambridge: Cambridge University Press, 2007.

_____. "Jewish-Palestinian Relations in Israel: From Hegemony to Equality?" *International Journal of Politics, Culture and Society* 17, no. 3 (Spring 2004): 415–437.

_____. "Transforming Ethnic Orders to Pluralist Regimes: Theoretical, Comparative, and Historical Analysis." In *Democracy and Ethnic Conflict: Advancing Peace in Deeply Divided Societies*, edited by Adrian Guelke, 7–25. New York: Palgrave, 2004.

Peoples, Clayton D. "How Discriminatory Policies Impact Interethnic Violence." *International Journal of Sociology* 34, no. 1 (Spring 2004): 71–96.

Peretz, Don, and Gideon Doron. "Israel's 1996 Elections: A Second Political Earthquake?" *Middle East Journal* 50, no. 4 (Autumn 1996): 529–546.

Peretz, Don, Rebecca Kook, and Gideon Doron. "Knesset Election 2003: Why Likud Regained Its Political Domination and Labor Continued to Fade Out." *Middle East Journal* 57, no. 4 (Autumn 2003): 259–273.

Peteet, Julie. "Words as Interventions: Naming in the Palestine-Israel Conflict." *Third World Quarterly* 26, no. 1 (2005): 153–172.

Peterson, V. Spike. "Gendered Nationalism: Reproducing 'Us' versus 'Them.'" In *The Women and War Reader*, edited by Lois Ann Lorentzen and Jennifer Turpin, 41–49. New York: New York University Press, 1998.

_____. "Sexing Political Identities/Nationalism as Heterosexism." *International Feminist Journal of Politics* 1, no. 1 (June 1999): 34–65.

Peterson, V. Spike, and Anne Sisson Runyan. *Global Gender Issues*. 2nd ed. Boulder: Westview Press, 1999.

Petterson, Donald. *Inside Sudan: Political Islam, Conflict, and Catastrophe*. Boulder: Westview Press, 1999.

Plett, Barbara. "Legal Row over Gaza Report Intensifies." *BBC News*, November 6, 2009. http://news.bbc.co.uk/go/pr/fr/-/2/hi/middle_east/8347861.stm.

Ponnambalam, Satchi. *Sri Lanka: National Conflict and the Tamil Liberation Struggle*. London: Zed Books, 1983.

Posen, Barry R. "The Security Dilemma and Ethnic Conflict." *Survival* 35, no. 1 (Spring 1993): 27–47.

"President Leaves NI (Northern Ireland) after Visit." *BBC News*, June 16, 2008. http://news.bbc.co.uk/2/hi/uk_news/northern_ireland/7455806.stm.

Pressman, Jeremy. "Historical Schools and Political Science: An Arab-Israeli History of the Arab-Israeli Conflict." *Perspectives on Politics* 3, no. 3 (September 2005): 577–582.

_____. "Visions in Collision: What Happened at Camp David and Taba?" *International Security* 28, no. 2 (Fall 2003): 5–43.

"Profile: Chandrika Kumaratunga." *BBC News*, August 25, 2005. http://news.bbc.co.uk/2/hi/south_asia/3239821.stm.

"Profile: Mahmoud Abbas." *BBC News*, January 10, 2005. http://news.bbc.co.uk/go/pr/fr/-/2/hi/middle_east/1933453.stm.

Pruitt, Dean G. "Definition of the Situation as a Determinant of International Action." In *International Behavior: A Social-Psychological Analysis*, edited by Herbert C. Kelman, 393–432. New York: Holt, Rinehart and Winston, 1965.

Prunier, Gerard. *Darfur: The Ambiguous Genocide*. Ithaca: Cornell University Press, 2007.

Przeworski, Adam. *Democracy and the Market: Political and Economic Reforms in Eastern Europe and Latin America*. Cambridge: Cambridge University Press, 1991.

"Q&A: Sri Lanka Conflict." *BBC News,* May 19, 2009. http://news.bbc.co.uk/2/hi/south_asia/2405347.stm.

Quinn, John James. "Diffusion and Escalation in the Great Lakes Region: The Rwandan Genocide, the Rebellion in Zaire, and Mobutu's Overthrow." In *Ethnic Conflict and International Politics: Explaining Diffusion and Escalation,* edited by Steven E. Lobell and Philip Mauceri, 111–131. New York: Palgrave, 2004.

Racioppi, Linda, and Katherine O'Sullivan See. "'This We Will Maintain': Gender, Ethno-nationalism and the Politics of Unionism in Northern Ireland." *Nations and Nationalism* 7, no. 1 (2001): 93–112.

Rajasingham-Senanyake, Darini. "Sri Lanka: Transformation of Legitimate Violence and Civil-Military Relations." In *Coercion and Governance: The Declining Political Role of the Military in Asia,* edited by Muthiah Alagappa, 294–316. Palo Alto: Stanford University Press, 2001.

Ramet, Sabrina P. "Serbia's Slobodan Milosevic: A Profile." *Orbis* 35, no. 1 (1991): 93–105.

_____. "Views from Inside: Memoirs concerning the Yugoslav Breakup and War." *Slavic Review* 61, no. 3 (2002): 558–880.

_____. "War in the Balkans." *Foreign Affairs* 71, no. 4 (1992): 79–98.

Rapoport, Tamar, and Tamar El-Or. "Cultures of Womanhood in Israel: Social Agencies and Gender Production." *Women's Studies International Forum* 20, nos. 5/6 (1997): 573–580.

Rath, Sharda. *Federalism Today: Approaches, Issues and Trends.* New Delhi: Sterling Publishers Private, 1984.

"Reclusive Tamil Rebel Leader Faces Public." *BBC News,* April 10, 2002. http://news.bbc.co.uk/2/hi/south_asia/1922478.stm.

Reilly, Ben. *Democracy in Divided Societies: Electoral Engineering for Conflict Management.* New York: Cambridge University Press, 2001.

Reynolds, Andrew, and Timothy D. Sisk. "Elections and Electoral Systems: Implications for Conflict Management." In *Elections and Conflict Management in Africa,* edited by Timothy D. Sisk and Andrew Reynolds, 11–36. Washington D.C.: United States Institute of Peace, 1998.

Riehl, Volker. *Who Is Ruling in South Sudan? The Role of NGOs in Rebuilding Socio-Political Order.* Uppsala, Sweden: Nordiska Afrikainstitutet, 2001.

Riker, William H. *Liberalism against Populism.* San Francisco: W.H. Freeman, 1982.

"Rise in the Number of Unemployed." *BBC News,* October 15, 2008. http://news.bbc.co.uk/go/pr/fr/-/2/hi/uk_news/northern_ireland/7671210.stm.

Ronen, Yhudit. "Ethiopia's Involvement in the Sudanese Civil War: Was It as Significant as Khartoum Claimed?" *Northeast African Studies* 9, no. 1 (2002): 103–126.

Rosati, Jerel A. "The Power of Human Cognition in the Study of World Politics." *International Studies Review* 2, no. 3 (Autumn 2000): 45-75.

The Rosemary Nelson Inquiry. www.rosemarynelsoninquiry.org.

Rosenson, Beth, Elizabeth A. Oldmixon, and Kenneth D. Wald. "U.S. Senators' Support for Israel Examined through Sponsorship/Cosponsorship Decisions, 1993-2002: The Influence of Elite and Constituent Factors." *Foreign Policy Analysis* 5 (2009): 73-91.

Ross, Cameron. "Federalism and Democratization in Russia." *Communist and Post-Communist Studies* 33 (2000): 403-420.

Ross, Dennis B. "Yasir Arafat." *Foreign Policy* 131 (July/August 2002): 18-26.

Ross, Marc Howard. "The Relevance of Culture for the Study of Political Psychology and Ethnic Conflict." *Political Psychology* 18, no. 2 (1997): 299-326.

Rothbart, Myron. "Intergroup Perception and Social Conflict." In *Conflict between People and Groups: Causes, Processes, and Resolutions*, edited by Stephen Worchel and Jeffrey A. Simpson, 93-109. Chicago: Nelson-Hall, 1993.

Rothchild, Donald, and David A. Lake. "Containing Fear: The Management of Transnational Ethnic Conflict." In *The International Spread of Ethnic Conflict: Fear, Diffusion, and Escalation*, edited by David A. Lake and Donald Rothchild, 203-226. Princeton: Princeton University Press, 1998.

Rothman, Jay, and Marie L. Olson. "From Interests to Identities: Toward a New Emphasis in Interactive Conflict Resolution." *Journal of Peace Research* 38, no. 3 (2001): 289-305.

Roy, Sara. "The Palestinian-Israeli Conflict and Palestinian Socioeconomic Decline: A Place Denied." *International Journal of Politics, Culture and Society* 17, no. 3 (Spring 2004): 365-403.

Ruane, Joseph, and Jennifer Todd. *The Dynamics of Conflict in Northern Ireland: Power, Conflict, and Emancipation.* Cambridge: Cambridge University Press, 1996.

Rubin, Barry. "Israel's New Strategy." *Foreign Affairs* 85, no. 4 (July/August 2006): 111-25.

Rubin, Jeffrey Z., and I. William Zartman. "Asymmetric Bargaining." *Negotiation Journal* 11 (1995): 349-364.

Ruggie, John Gerard. "What Makes the World Hang Together? Neo-utilitarianism and the Social Constructivist Challenge." *International Organization* 52, no. 4 (Autumn 1998): 855-885.

"Ruined Remains of Rebel 'Capital.'" *BBC World News*, January 5, 2009. http://news.bbc.co.uk/2/hi/south_asia/7811360.stm.

Saad, Lydia. "Palestinians Have Little Faith in U.S. as Peace Broker." *Gallup News Service*, June 20, 2006. www.gallup.com/poll/23377/Palestinians-Little-Faith-US-Peace-Broker.aspx.

Saad, Lydia, and Steve Crabtree. "Israel/Palestine: Support for Potential Peace Brokers." *Gallup News Service,* January 26, 2007. www.gallup.com/poll/26290/IsraelPalestine-Support-Potential-Peace-Brokers.aspx.

Sabaratnam, Lakshmanan. "Sri Lanka: The Lion and the Tiger in the Ethnic Archipelago." In *State Violence and Ethnicity,* edited by Pierre L. van den Berghe, 187–220. Boulder: University Press of Colorado, 1990.

Saideman, Stephen M. "Discrimination in International Relations: Analyzing External Support for Ethnic Groups." *Journal of Peace Research* 39, no. 1 (2002): 27–50.

_____. "Explaining the International Relations of Secessionist Conflicts: Vulnerability versus Ethnic Ties." *International Organization* 51, no. 4 (Autumn 1997): 721–753.

_____. "Is Pandora's Box Half Empty or Half Full? The Limited Virulence of Secessionism and the Domestic Sources of Disintegration." In *The International Spread of Ethnic Conflict: Fear, Diffusion, and Escalation,* edited by David A. Lake and Donald Rothchild, 127–150. Princeton: Princeton University Press, 1998.

Salih, M. A. Mohamed. "Political Narratives and Identity Formation in Post-1989 Sudan." In *Ethnicity and the State in Eastern Africa,* edited by M. A. Mohamed Salih and John Markakis, 72–85. Uppsala: Nordiska Afrikainstitutet, 1998.

Schneckener, Ulrich. "Making Power-Sharing Work: Lessons from Successes and Failures in Ethnic Conflict Regulation." *Journal of Peace Research* 39, no. 2 (March 2002): 203–228.

Schopflin, George. "The Rise and Fall of Yugoslavia." In *The Politics of Ethnic Conflict Regulation,* edited by John McGarry and Brendan O'Leary, 172–203. London: Routledge, 1993.

Schwarz, Walter. *The Tamils of Sri Lanka.* London: Minority Rights Group, 1975.

Sekulic, Dusko, Garth Massey, and Randy Hodson. "Ethnic Intolerance and Ethnic Conflict in the Dissolution of Yugoslavia." *Ethnic and Racial Studies* 29, no. 5 (2006): 797–827.

Sells, Michael. "Crosses of Blood: Sacred Space, Religion, and Violence in Bosnia-Hercegovina." *Sociology of Religion* 64, no. 3 (2003): 309–331.

Seneviratne, H. L. "Buddhist Monks and Ethnic Politics: A War Zone in an Island Paradise." *Anthropology Today* 17 (2001): 15–21.

Seul, Jeffrey R. "'Ours Is the Way of God': Religion, Identity, and Intergroup Conflict." *Journal of Peace Research* 36, no. 5 (1999): 553–569.

"SF (Sinn Fein) Threatens to Collapse Assembly." *BBC News,* August 24, 2008. http://news.bbc.co.uk/2/hi/uk_news/northern_ireland/7580108.stm.

Shafer, Mark. "Images and Policy Preferences." *Political Psychology* 18, no. 4 (1997): 813–829.

Shain, Yossi, and Aharon Barth. "Diasporas and International Relations Theory." *International Organization* 57, no. 3 (Summer 2003): 449–479.

Sharkey, Heather J. "Arab Identity and Ideology in Sudan: The Politics of Language, Ethnicity, and Race." *African Affairs* 107, no. 426 (2008): 21–43.

Shikaki, Khalil. "The Future of Palestine." *Foreign Affairs* 83, no. 6 (November/December 2004): 45–60.

———. "Palestinians Divided." *Foreign Affairs* 81, no. 1 (January/February 2002): 89–105.

Shils, Edward. "Nation, Nationality, Nationalism and Civil Society." *Nations and Nationalism* 1, no. 1 (March 1995): 93–118.

Simmel, Georg. *Conflict and the Web of Group Affiliations*. New York: Free Press, 1955.

Simms, J. G. "The Restoration and the Jacobite War (1660–1691)." In *The Course of Irish History*, edited by T. W. Moody and F. X. Martin, 204–216. Cork: Mercier Press, 1967.

Singer, David J. "International Conflict: Three Levels of Analysis." *World Politics* 12, no. 3 (April 1960): 453–461.

———. "The Level-of-Analysis Problem in International Relations." *World Politics* 14, no. 1 (October 1961): 77–92.

Sinha, Ramashish Prasad. *Sri Lanka-United States Relations*. New Delhi: Commonwealth Publishers, 1992.

Sisk, Timothy. *Democratization in South Africa: The Elusive Social Contract*. Princeton: Princeton University Press, 1995.

Skjelsbaek, Inger. "Is Femininity Inherently Peaceful? The Construction of Femininity in War." In *Gender, Peace and Conflict*, edited by Inger Skjelsbaek and Dan Smith, 47–67. London: Sage Publications, 2001.

Skjelsbaek, Inger, and Dan Smith. "Introduction." In *Gender, Peace and Conflict*, edited by Inger Skjelsbaek and Dan Smith, 1–13. London: Sage Publications, 2001.

Slack, J. Andrew, and Roy R. Doyon. "Population Dynamics and Susceptibility for Ethnic Conflict: The Case of Bosnia and Herzegovina." *Journal of Peace Research* 38, no. 2 (2001): 139–161.

Slater, Jerome. "What Went Wrong? The Collapse of the Israeli-Palestinian Peace Process." *Political Science Quarterly* 116, no. 2 (2001): 171–199.

Slim, Hugo. "Dithering over Darfur? A Preliminary Review of the International Response." *International Affairs* 80, no. 5 (2004): 811–828.

Smith, Anthony D. "Culture, Community and Territory: The Politics of Ethnicity and Nationalism." *International Affairs* 72 (1996): 445–458.

———. *The Ethnic Revival*. Cambridge: Cambridge University Press, 1981.

———. *National Identity*. Reno: University of Nevada Press, 1991.

_____. *Nationalism: Theory, Ideology, History*. Cambridge: Polity, 2001.

Smith, David, and Gerald Chambers. *Inequality in Northern Ireland*. Oxford: Oxford University Press, 2001.

Smith, Graham. "Mapping the Federal Condition: Ideology, Political Practice and Social Justice." In *Federalism: The Multiethnic Challenge*, edited by Graham Smith, 1–28. London: Longman, 1995.

Smooha, Sammy, and Theodor Hanf. "The Diverse Modes of Conflict-Regulation in Deeply Divided Societies." *International Journal of Comparative Sociology* 33, nos. 1–2 (1992): 26–47.

Snyder, Jack. "Averting Anarchy in the New Europe." In *The Cold War and After*, edited by Sean M. Lynn-Jones, 104–140. Cambridge, Mass.: MIT Press, 1991.

_____. "The New Nationalism: Realist Interpretations and Beyond." In *The Domestic Bases of Grand Strategy*, edited by Richard Rosecrance and Arthur A. Stein, 179–200. Ithaca: Cornell University Press, 1993.

_____. "One World, Rival Theories." *Foreign Policy* 145 (November/December 2004): 52–62.

Snyder, Jack, and Karen Ballentine. "Nationalism and the Marketplace of Ideas." In *Nationalism and Ethnic Conflict*, rev. ed., edited by Michael E. Brown, Owen R. Cote Jr., Sean M. Lynn-Jones, and Steven E. Miller, 61–96. Cambridge, Mass.: MIT Press, 2001.

Sodarno, Michael J. *Comparative Politics: A Global Introduction*. Boston: McGraw-Hill, 2008.

Spencer, Jonathan. "A Nationalism without Politics? The Illiberal Consequences of Liberal Institutions in Sri Lanka." *Third World Quarterly* 29 (April 2008): 611–629.

Spiegel, Steven L., Elizabeth G. Matthews, Jennifer M. Taw, and Kristen P. Williams. *World Politics in a New Era*. 4th ed. New York: Oxford University Press, 2009.

Spinner-Halev, Jeff, and Elizabeth Theiss-Morse. "National Identity and Self-Esteem." *Perspectives on Politics* 1, no. 3 (September 2003): 515–532.

"Sri Lanka Army in Ghost Tiger Town." *BBC World News*, January 28, 2009. http://news.bbc.co.uk/2/hi/south_asia/7857247.stm.

Sriram, Chandra Lekha. *Peace as Governance: Power-Sharing, Armed Groups, and Contemporary Peace Negotiations*. New York: Palgrave, 2008.

Stedman, Stephen John. "Spoiler Problems in Peace Processes." In *Nationalism and Ethnic Conflict*, rev. ed., edited by Michael E. Brown, Owen R. Cote Jr., Sean M. Lynn-Jones, and Steven E. Miller, 366–414. Cambridge, Mass.: MIT Press, 2001.

Sterling-Folker, Jennifer. "Realism and the Constructivist Challenge: Rejecting, Reconstructing, or Rereading." *International Studies Review* 4, no. 1 (Spring 2002): 73–97.

Stern, Paul C. "Why Do People Sacrifice for Their Nations?" *Political Psychology* 16, no. 2 (1995): 217–235.

Stirrat, R. L. "The Riots and the Roman Catholic Church in Historical Perspective." In *Sri Lanka in Change and Crisis*, edited by James Manor, 196–213. New York: St. Martin's Press, 1984.

Stork, Joe. "Moving beyond the Goldstone Report." *Human Rights Watch*, November 9, 2009. www.hrw.org/en/news/2009/11/09/moving-beyond-goldstone-report.

Sutton, Malcolm. *Bear in Mind These Dead . . . : An Index of Deaths from the Conflict in Ireland, 1969–1993.* Belfast: Beyond the Pale Publications, 1994.

Sylvan, Donald A., Jonathan W. Keller, and Yoram Z. Haftel. "Forecasting Israeli-Palestinian Relations." *Journal of Peace Research* 41, no. 4 (2004): 445–463.

Tajfel, Henri. *Human Groups and Social Categories: Studies in Social Psychology.* Cambridge: Cambridge University Press, 1981.

Taliaferro, Jeffrey W. "Security Seeking under Anarchy: Defensive Realism Revisited." *International Security* 25, no. 3 (Winter 2000/2001): 128–161.

Tambiah, S. J. *Sri Lanka: Ethnic Fratricide and the Dismantling of Democracy.* Chicago: University of Chicago Press, 1986.

Tannam, Etian. *Cross-Border Cooperation in the Republic of Ireland and Northern Ireland.* New York: St. Martin's Press, 1999.

Tanner, Victor, and Jerome Tubiana. *Divided They Fall: The Fragmentation of Darfur's Rebel Groups.* Geneva: Small Arms Survey, 2007.

Tar, Usman. "Counter-Insurgents or Ethnic Vanguards? Civil Militia and State Violence in Darfur Region, Western Sudan." In *Civil Militia: Africa's Intractable Security Menace?* edited by David J. Francis, 131–160. Aldershot: Ashgate, 2005.

Thompson, Joseph E. *American Policy and Northern Ireland: A Saga of Peacebuilding.* Westport, Conn.: Praeger, 2001.

"Timeline: Northern Ireland's Road to Peace." *BBC News*, August 22, 2008. http://news.bbc.co.uk/2/hi/uk_news/northern_ireland/4072261.stm.

Tiruchelvam, Neelan. "Sri Lanka's Ethnic Conflict and Preventive Action: The Role of NGOs." In *Vigilance and Vengeance: NGOs Preventing Ethnic Conflict in Divided Societies*, edited by Robert I. Rotberg, 147–166. Washington D.C.: Brookings Institution, 1996.

Toft, Monica Duffy. "Getting Religion? The Puzzling Case of Islam and Civil War." *International Security* 31, no. 4 (2007): 97–131.

Tonge, Jonathan. *Northern Ireland.* Malden, Mass.: Polity Press, 2006.

Trew, Karen. "The Northern Irish Identity." In *A Question of Identity*, edited by Anne J. Kershen, 60–76. Aldershot: Ashgate, 1998.

Trew, Karen, and Denny E. Benson. "Dimensions of Social Identity in Northern Ireland." In *Changing European Identities: Social Psychological Analyses of Social Changes*, edited by Glynis M. Breakwell and Evanthia Lyons Speri, 123–143. Oxford: Butterworth-Heinemann, 1996.

Tsebelis, George. *Veto Players: How Political Institutions Work*. Princeton: Princeton University Press, 2002.

Tubiana, Jerome. "Darfur: A Conflict for Land?" In *War in Darfur and the Search for Peace*, edited by Alex de Waal, 68–91. Cambridge, Mass.: Harvard University, 2007.

Udombana, Nsongurua J. "When Neutrality Is a Sin: The Darfur Crisis and the Crisis of Humanitarian Intervention in Sudan." *Human Rights Quarterly* 27 (2005): 1149–1199.

United Nations. "Darfur—UNAMID—Background." www.un.org.depts/dpko/missions/unamid/background.html.

———. "Darfur—UNAMID—Mandate." UNAMID: African Union/United Nations Hybrid Operation in Darfur. www.un.org/depts/dpko/missions/unamid/mandate.html.

———. International Commission of Inquiry on Darfur. *Report to the Secretary-General*. Geneva, January 25, 2005.

———. Office of UN Deputy Special Representative of the UN Security-General for Sudan, UN Resident and Humanitarian Co-ordinator. *Darfur Humanitarian Profile No. 32,* July 1, 2008.

———. "Press Conference on Situation of Women in Occupied Palestinian Territory." United Nations Department of Public Information (March 4, 2009). www.un.org/News/briefings/docs/2009/090304_OPT.doc.htm.

———. "Sudan—UNMIS—Background." *United Nations Mission in the Sudan, 2008*, 9–10. www.un.org/depts/dpko/missions/unmis/background.html.

———. "United Nations Member States." http://un.org/members/list.shtml#y.

———. UNRWA. "Establishment of UNRWA." www.un.org/unrwa/overview/index.html.

———. UNRWA. "History and Establishment of UNRWA." www.un.org/unrwa/overview/qa.html#a.

———. UNRWA. "U.S. Government Contributes $55 million to UNRWA." www.un.org/unrwa/news/releases/pr-2009/jer_10jun09.html.

Unknown Author (Identity withheld for security reasons). "Sri Lanka's Week of Shame: An Eyewitness Account." Special issue, *Race and Class: A Journal for Black and Third World Liberation* 26 (1984): 39–50.

"UN Seeks $11m for Israeli Raids." *BBC News*, May 6, 2009. http://news.bbc.co.uk/go/pr/fr/-/2/hi/middle_east/8036054.stm.

U.S. Congress. House. *The Northern Ireland Peace Process: Policing Advances and Remaining Challenges*. Joint Hearing before the Subcommittee on Africa,

Global Human Rights, and International Operations and the Subcommittee on Europe and Emerging Threats of the Committee on International Relations. 109th Cong., 2nd sess., March 15, 2006. Serial No. 1509–152. Washington, D.C.: U.S. Government Printing Office, 2006.

U.S. Congress. House. *Political Crisis in South Asia: Pakistan, Bangladesh, Sri Lanka, and Nepal.* Hearing before the Subcommittee on the Middle East and South Asia of the Committee on Foreign Affairs. Serial No. 110–132. Washington, D.C.: U.S. Government Printing Office, August 1, 2007.

U.S. Government Accountability Office (GAO). *Darfur Crisis: Death Estimates Demonstrate Severity of Crisis, but Their Accuracy and Credibility Could Be Enhanced.* Washington, D.C.: GAO, November 2006.

Usher, Graham. "The Palestinians after Arafat." *Journal of Palestine Studies* 34, no. 3 (Spring 2005): 42–56.

_____. "Unmaking Palestine: On Israel, the Palestinians, and the Wall." *Journal of Palestine Studies* 35, no. 1 (Autumn 2005): 25–43.

"US Urges Quick Return to Mid-East Talks." *BBC News*, June 9, 2009. http://news.bbc.co.uk/go/pr/fr/-/2/hi/middle_east/8090761.stm.

Uyangoda, Jayadeva. *Ethnic Conflict in Sri Lanka: Changing Dynamics.* Washington D.C.: East-West Center, 2007.

_____. "Ethnic Conflict, the State, and the Tsunami Disaster in Sri Lanka." *Inter-Asia Cultural Studies* 6 (2005): 341–352.

Vaidik, V. P. *Ethnic Crisis in Sri Lanka: India's Options.* New Delhi: National Publishing, 1986.

Van Evera, Stephen. "Hypotheses on Nationalism and War." In *Nationalism and Ethnic Conflict*, rev. ed., edited by Michael E. Brown, Owen R. Cote Jr., Sean M. Lynn-Jones, and Steven E. Miller, 26–60. Cambridge, Mass.: MIT Press, 2001.

_____. "Primed for Peace: Europe after the Cold War." In *The Cold War and After*, edited by Sean M. Lynn-Jones, 193–243. Cambridge, Mass.: MIT Press, 1991.

_____. "Primordialism Lives!" *APSA-CP Newsletter* 12, no. 1 (Winter 2001): 20–22.

Varshney, Ashutosh. "Nationalism, Ethnic Conflict, and Rationality." *Perspectives on Politics* 1, no. 1 (March 2003): 85–99.

Velikonja, Mitja. "*In Hoc Signo Vinces*: Religious Symbolism in the Balkan Wars 1991–1995." *International Journal of Politics, Culture and Society* 17, no. 1 (2003): 25–39.

Verney, Peter. *Sudan: Conflict and Minorities.* London: Minority Rights Group, 1995.

Waage, Hilde Henrikson. "Norway's Role in the Middle East Peace Talks: Between a Strong State and a Weak Belligerent." *Journal of Palestine Studies* 34, no. 4 (Summer 2005): 6–24.

Walsh, Martha. "Profile: Bosnia and Herzegovina." In *Women and Civil War: Impact, Organizations, and Action*, edited by Krishna Kumar, 57-67. Boulder: Lynne Rienner, 2001.

Walt, Stephen M. "International Relations: One World, Many Theories." *Foreign Policy* 110 (Spring 1998): 29–46.

Walter, Barbara. "Designing Transitions from Civil War: Demobilization, Democratization, and Commitments to Peace." In *Nationalism and Ethnic Conflict*, rev. ed., edited by Michael E. Brown, Owen R. Cote Jr., Sean M. Lynn-Jones, and Steven E. Miller, 415–453. Cambridge, Mass.: MIT Press, 2001.

Waltz, Kenneth. *Man, the State, and War: A Theoretical Analysis*. New York: Columbia University Press, 1959.

Warburg, Gabriel. "Religious and Ethnic Conflict in Sudan: Can National Unity Survive?" In *Ethnic Conflict and International Politics in the Middle East*, edited by Leonard Binder, 110–128. Gainesville: University Press of Florida, 1999.

Wasara, Samson S. "Conflict and State Security in the Horn of Africa: Militarization of Civilian Groups." *African Journal of Political Science* 7, no. 2 (2002): 39–59.

Webb, Keith, with Vassiliki Koutrakou and Mike Waters. "The Yugoslav Conflict, European Mediation, and the Contingency Model: A Critical Perspective." In *Resolving International Conflict: The Theory and Practice of Mediation*, edited by Jacob Bercovitch, 171–189. Boulder: Lynne Rienner, 1996.

Weldon, Steven A. "The Institutional Context of Tolerance for Ethnic Minorities: A Comparative, Multilevel Analysis of Western Europe." *American Journal of Political Science* 50, no. 2 (April 2006): 331–349.

Weller, Marc. "Self-Governance in Interim Settlements: The Case of Sudan." In *Autonomy, Self-Governance, and Conflict Resolution: Innovative Approaches to Institutional Design in Divided Societies*, edited by Marc Weller and Stefan Wolff, 158–179. New York: Routledge, 2005.

"The Western Balkans: A Stuck Region." *The Economist*, February 12, 2009.

Wheare, K. C. *Federal Government*. 4th ed. London: Oxford University Press, 1963.

"Where Will It End?" *The Economist*, January 8, 2009. www.economist.com/world/mideast-africa/displaystory.cfm?story_id=12903402.

Whitson, Sarah Leah. "Israel's Settlements Are on Shaky Ground." *Human Rights Watch*, June 28, 2009. www.hrw.org/en/news/2009/06/28/israels-settlements-are-shaky-ground.

Wickramasinghe, Nira. *Sri Lanka in the Modern Age: A History of Contested Identities*. Honolulu: University of Hawai'i Press, 2006.

Williams, Kristen P. *Despite Nationalist Conflicts: Theory and Practice of Maintaining World Peace*. Westport, Conn.: Praeger, 2001.

_____. "Internationalization of Ethnic Conflict in the Balkans: The Breakup of Yugoslavia." In *Ethnic Conflict and International Politics: Explaining Diffusion and Escalation*, edited by Steven E. Lobell and Philip Mauceri, 75–94. New York: Palgrave, 2004.

Winter, Roger P. "Sudan and the National Congress Party." *Mediterranean Quarterly* 18, no. 2 (2007): 61–66.

Wittenberg, Sophie. "Security Council Resolution 1325 and CEDAW: Combating Gender-Based Discrimination and Violence in Bosnia and Herzegovina." *A PeaceWomen Project Analysis*, June 2006. www.peacewomen.org/un/ecosoc/ CEDAW/35th_Sesssion/SCR1325_CEDAW.html.

Wolff, Stefan. *Ethnic Conflict: A Global Perspective*. Oxford: Oxford University Press, 2006.

Woodward, Peter. *U.S. Foreign Policy and the Horn of Africa*. Aldershot: Ashgate, 2006.

Woodward, Susan L. *Balkan Tragedy: Chaos and Dissolution after the Cold War*. Washington, D.C.: Brookings Institution, 1995.

_____. "Redrawing Borders in a Period of Systemic Transition." In *International Organizations and Ethnic Conflict*, edited by Milton J. Esman and Shibley Telhami, 198–234. Ithaca: Cornell University Press, 1995.

Yiftachel, Oren. "Democracy or Ethnocracy? Territory and Settler Politics in Israel/Palestine." *Middle East Report* 207 (Summer 1998): 8–13.

_____. "'Ethnocracy' and Its Discontents: Minorities, Protests, and the Israeli Polity." *Critical Inquiry* 26 (Summer 2000): 725–756.

_____. "Israeli Society and Jewish-Palestinian Reconciliation: 'Ethnocracy' and Its Territorial Contradictions." *Middle East Journal* 51, no. 4 (Autumn 1997): 505–519.

_____. "The Shrinking Space of Citizenship: Ethnocratic Politics in Israel." *Middle East Report* 223 (Summer 2002): 38–45.

Zartman, I. William. "Putting Humpty-Dumpty Together Again." In *The International Spread of Ethnic Conflict: Fear, Diffusion, and Escalation*, edited by David A. Lake and Donald Rothchild, 317–336. Princeton: Princeton University Press, 1998.

Zunes, Stephen. "The Goldstone Report: Killing the Messenger." *Foreign Policy In Focus*, October 7, 2009. www.fpif.org/fpiftxt/6485.